C000291538

FINANCIAL MANAGEMENT

method and meaning

The Chapman & Hall Series in Accounting and Finance

Consulting editors
John Perrin, Emeritus Professor of the University of Warwick and Price Waterhouse Fellow in Public Sector Accounting at the University of Exeter; Richard Pike, Professor of Finance and Accounting at the University of Bradford Management School; and Richard M.S. Wilson, Professor of Management and Accounting at the University of Keele.

E. Clark, M. Levasseur and P. Rousseau
International Finance

H.M. Coombs and D.E. Jenkins
Public Sector Financial Management (2nd edn)

J.C. Drury
Management and Cost Accounting (3rd edn)
(Also available: *Students' Manual, Teachers' Manual, Spreadsheet Applications Manual, Guidance Notes and Disk, OHP Masters, Dutch Students' Manual*,* see also Gazely)

C.R. Emmanuel, D.T. Otley and K. Merchant
Accounting for Management Control (2nd edn)
(Also available: *Teachers Guide*)

C.R. Emmanuel, D.T. Otley and K. Merchant
(editors)
Readings in Accounting for Management Control

M. Ezzamel and D. Heathfield (editors)
Perspectives on Financial Control: Essays in memory of Kenneth Hilton

A.M. Gazely
Management and Cost Accounting Spreadsheet Applications Manual
(Also available: *Guidance Notes and Disk*)

P. Hancock
An Introduction to Taxation Policy and Practice

D. Henley, A. Likierman, J. Perrin,
M. Evans, I. Lapsley and J.E.H. Whiteoak
Public Sector Accounting and Financial Control (4th edn)

B.W. Koch
European Financial Reporting Practices

R.C. Laughlin and R.H. Gray
Financial Accounting: method and meaning
(Also available: *Teachers' Guide*)

T.A. Lee
Income Value Measurement (3rd edn)

T.A. Lee
Company Financial Reporting (2nd edn)

T.A. Lee
Cash Flow Accounting

T.A. Lee
Corporate Audit Theory

S.P. Lumby
Investment Appraisal and Financial Decisions (5th edn)
(Also available: *Teachers' Manual*)

R.W. Perks
Accounting and Society

A.G. Puxty and J.C. Dodds
Financial Management: method and meaning (2nd edn)
(Also available: *Teachers' Guide*)

J.M. Samuels, F.M. Wilkes and R.E. Brayshaw
Management of Company Finance (5th edn)
(Also available: *Students' Manual*)

J.M. Samuels, R.E. Brayshaw and J.M. Craner
European Financial Statement Analysis

C.M.S. Sutcliffe
Stock Index Futures

M. Tanaka, T. Yoshikawa, J. Innes and
F. Mitchell
Contemporary Cost Management

B.C. Williams and B.J. Spaul
IT and Accounting: The impact of information technology

R.M.S. Wilson and Wai Fong Chua
Managerial Accounting: method and meaning (2nd edn)
(Also available: *Teachers' Guide*)

*The *Dutch Students' Manual* to accompany the third edition of *Management and Cost Accounting* by Colin Drury, is not published by Chapman & Hall, but is available from Interfaas, Onderzoek en Advies, Postbus 76618, 1070HE, Amsterdam. Tel. (020) 6 76 27 06.

FINANCIAL MANAGEMENT

method and meaning

Second edition

Anthony G. PUXTY

Professor, Department of Accounting and Finance,
University of Strathclyde, Glasgow

J. Colin DODDS

Professor of Finance and Vice-President Academic and Research,
Saint Mary's University, Nova Scotia

Edited by Richard M.S. Wilson

Professor, School of Finance and Information,
The Queen's University of Belfast

CHAPMAN & HALL

London · Glasgow · Weinheim · New York · Tokyo · Melbourne · Madras

Published by Chapman & Hall, 2-6 Boundary Row, London SE1 8HN, UK

Chapman & Hall, 2-6 Boundary Row, London SE1 8HN, UK

Blackie Academic & Professional, Wester Cleddens Road, Bishopbriggs, Glasgow G64 2NZ, UK

Chapman & Hall GmbH, Pappelallee 3, 69469 Weinheim, Germany

Chapman & Hall USA., 115 Fifth Avenue, New York, NY 10003, USA

Chapman & Hall Japan, ITP-Japan, Kyowa Building, 3F, 2-2-1 Hirakawacho, Chiyoda-ku, Tokyo 102, Japan

Chapman & Hall Australia, 102 Dodds Street, South Melbourne, Victoria 3205, Australia

Chapman & Hall India, R. Seshadri, 32 Second Main Road, CIT East, Madras 600 035, India

First edition 1988
Reprinted 1990
Second edition 1991
Reprinted 1992, 1995, 1996

© 1988, 1991 Anthony G. Puxty and J. Colin Dodds

Typeset in 10/11pt Palatino by J & L Composition Ltd, Filey, North Yorkshire
Printed in Great Britain at the Alden Press, Oxford

ISBN 0 412 40970 4

Apart from any fair dealing for the purposes of research or private study, or criticism or review, as permitted under the UK Copyright Designs and Patents Act, 1988, this publication may not be reproduced, stored, or transmitted, in any form or by any means, without the prior permission in writing of the publishers, or in the case of reprographic reproduction only in accordance with the terms of the licences issued by the Copyright Licensing Agency in the UK, or in accordance with the terms of licences issued by the appropriate Reproduction Rights Organization outside the UK. Enquiries concerning reproduction outside the terms stated here should be sent to the publishers at the London address printed on this page.

The publisher makes no representation, express or implied, with regard to the accuracy of the information contained in this book and cannot accept any legal responsibility or liability for any errors or omissions that may be made.

A Catalogue record for this book is available from the British Library

Library of Congress Cataloging-in Publication Data
Puxty, Anthony G.
   Financial management: method and meaning / Anthony G.
Puxty, J. Colin Dodds: edited by Richard M.S. Wilson
-2nd ed.
   p.   cm.-(Chapman & Hall series in accounting and finance)
   Includes bibliographical references and index.
   ISBN 0-412-40970-4
   1. Corporations-Finance-Handbooks, manuals, etc.   I.
Dodds, J. Colin.   II. Wilson, R.M.S. (Richard Malcolm
Sano), III. Title.   IV. Series.
   HG4027.36.P.89   1991
   658.15-dc20
                                        91-13211
                                        CIP

∞ Printed on acid-free text paper, manufactured in accordance with ANSI/NISO Z39.48-1992 and ANSI/NISO Z39.48-1984 (Permanence of Paper).

*To Tony Lowe
and all our colleagues who,
over the years,
have helped in developing
the ethos embodied
in this book.*

Abbreviated Contents

Contents

Series Editor's Preface

The *Method and Meaning* series consists of a text-plus-workbook, along with a Teacher's Guide, for each of the main branches of the accounting and financial management domain:

- Financial Accounting;
- Managerial Accounting;
- Financial Management.

In broad terms this series offers an integrated set of introductory books to be used in courses from which students will emerge with an ability to approach — with a critical awareness — the design of accounting systems and the carrying out of financial analysis *within* an organizational setting, *within* a societal framework.

This approach aims to avoid the presentation of financial techniques in isolation, or as self-evident tools for decision-makers; and it seeks to discourage the uncritical acceptance of current financial practice as being the most appropriate (whether from the viewpoint of individuals, organizations, or society).

To be a little more specific, the series' objectives are:

1. to develop technical skills relating to procedural and computational aspects of accounting and financial management;
2. to develop analytical skills relating to the problem-structuring and systems design aspects of accounting and financial management;
3. to develop evaluative skills in relation to both the theory and practice of accounting and financial management;
4. to develop an understanding of the organizational and societal roles of accounting and financial management;
5. to pursue (1)–(4) in a way that highlights the linkages among financial accounting, managerial accounting and financial management.

From these aims you will see the logic underlying the series title: 'method' relates to the what, when, where and how aspects, whereas 'meaning' focuses on the why, for whom, how else and consequences aspects of the subject matter.

Within the *texts* there are clear educational objectives for each chapter, a structure that seeks to build a logical and ordered view of the subject matter, a concern with both exposition and evaluation, and annotated suggestions for further reading.

Each chapter in the texts is linked to a chapter in the integral *Workbooks* which contain discussion questions (with and without suggested answers), computational problems (with and without suggested answers), case studies, and reprinted items to illustrate key topics.

While the current institutional affiliations of the authors of the books in this series are diverse — England, Scotland, Northern Ireland, Australia and Canada — they have considerable experience of working together. Five of the six were colleagues at the same institution until 1982 when two left to take up overseas posts, but the first-named authors of each book continued to be based at that institution (the University of Sheffield) during the writing of the books, following which two have left to take up new positions elsewhere. From an editorial point of view it has been a privilege working with such talented colleagues, and I am grateful that they all responded so positively to my invitation to them to get involved with this project.

The writing process led to the production of trial editions of all volumes in 1986, and these were classroom-tested during 1986–7 in a variety of academic institutions (covering college, polytechnic, and university sectors). Substantial revisions have been made on the basis of feedback from students and teachers which should make the series more user-friendly and readable.

Apart from the benefits from testing, other major features of the series are:

1. introductory coverage is given across the whole domain of accounting and financial management;
2. all volumes are integrated via the careful initial planning of the contents of each against a common philosophy for the whole, and by means of subsequent cross-referencing at appropriate points;
3. the common philosophy takes a non-technical starting point (the societal role of accounting and finance) which is developed within an organizational setting (but which is *not* myopically restricted to one particular category of organization — such as the commercially oriented manufacturing company);
4. throughout each volume a major emphasis is placed on developing students' critical awareness and in demonstrating how to establish evaluative criteria for assessing alternative methods;
5. by following the books students should be able to construct *and* evaluate financial reports and so forth, but they will also have a broader perspective of the managerial processes that must be considered if accounting methods and financial analysis are to improve organizational — hence social — performance;
6. the inevitable jargon of the subject matter is explained, with terminology being consistent throughout the series;
7. risks of duplication are minimized, but necessary overlaps across the series are used to reinforce the coverage of major issues;
8. the approaches to the subject matter of individual volumes — as well as to the series as a whole — is innovative with a strong interdisciplinary flavour.

What is the role of accounting and financial management against this background? We can propose a role by identifying the main branches of the subject, as in the diagram on page xix. This shows that suppliers of finance (or investors) need to be persuaded to provide finance to enable an organization to get underway, or to grow or diversify once it has become established. Investors put their funds into organizations in exchange for either a share of ownership or a commitment from the owners/managers to repay the investors on specified terms. It is among the tasks of *financial management* to balance the sources of finance, and to ensure that the enterprise is able to 'service' its sources of finance (whether via the payment of dividends to shareholders, or of interest to those who have lent funds to the enterprise), and to repay loans on their due date. Appropriate financial analysis will clearly be necessary for these tasks.

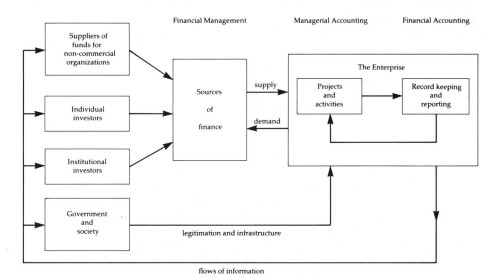

Financial Management   Managerial Accounting   Financial Accounting

Scope of accounting and financial management.

However, the above observations relate primarily to the *supply* of funds rather than to the demand for funds. Enterprises demand funds to facilitate their ongoing activities (e.g. paying suppliers, ensuring wages and salaries can be paid) and to facilitate new (or pending) projects of one kind and another. Determining these needs is another task for financial management — in association with *managerial accounting*. Once projects are under way, the routine handling of financial transactions and the production of annual financial statements is within the province of *financial accounting*, although the role of financial accounting in supplying information to interested parties is more significant than this diagram might suggest.

The three textbooks (and associated teaching material) covered by this series are seen as being usable singly, or in any combination of two, or in their entirety, as the basis for a number of categories of user. In every case the books are seen as being for compulsory student purchase rather than as optional sources of reference.

Intended markets consist of:

1. the primary market, made up of students pursuing degree courses in accounting and finance, commerce or business studies in British institutions of higher education (i.e. 'relevant degrees' in BAEC terms);
2. the secondary market, which partly consists of undergraduate students on the increasing range of degrees in, for example, engineering, pure science and economics that either require, or make available as an option, an introductory, self-contained course in accounting and financial management;
3. the secondary market also includes students on postgraduate programmes in the universities and polytechnics (e.g. for MBA degrees or for the Diploma in Management Studies) which involve an introduction to accounting and finance.

Richard M.S. Wilson
Professor, School of Finance and Information
The Queen's University of Belfast

Authors' Preface

There is some uncertainty — or at least disagreement — about what constitutes 'financial management' and how it differs — if at all — from 'finance'. The usual distinction is that finance is much more concerned with the financial markets external to the enterprise. Financial management is the task of the financial manager within the enterprise.

Broadly, that is what is intended by the title of this book. It is concerned with the problems that face the financial manager of the enterprise and how those problems might be solved. As such, it is intended for the first or second year undergraduate student in an institution of higher education. It may also be read with profit by many others, including students of the professional accountancy bodies and managers anxious to obtain an insight into the central role finance plays in the modern enterprise.

The book incorporates a quite heavy underpinning of theory. This is essential since, without theory, any subject reduces to a menu of half-digested anecdotes and unsubstantiated statements. At the same time, it cannot be said of financial management, any more than any other subject in the areas of management or social science, that we have 'all the answers' in our theory — or even, for certain, any of the answers. This may be dispiriting to the student who is hoping for a treatise on 'what you should know'. It is intended that the book should help in this regard, but nobody — and certainly not a textbook writer — has a monopoly of the truth on how to manage an enterprise's financial affairs.

It was said that financial management could be distinguished from finance, and this is probably true. Yet you will notice that the early part of the book includes a full, and fairly long, chapter on financial markets (see Chapter 2). This is not inconsistent with what we have just said, for the financial manager is constrained by the markets. He or she has to raise money in them, and the enterprise is accountable to them for its results. Understanding those markets and how they can be used by the financial manager is thus fundamental to the financial task.

We have written this book as part of the series which includes *Financial Accounting: Method and Meaning* and *Managerial Accounting: Method and Meaning*. Discussion of the way the three interlink is given in the series editor's preface. It may be helpful to the reader, however, to contribute a word or two about why we wished to write this book when so many others — frequently extremely good ones — are on the market.

One reason was the interlinkage, the belief that the subject could be understood better in the context of careful cross-referencing between accounting and financial management. Another was that no other text of which we are aware — and certainly no UK text — has fully incorporated the implications of the Big Bang, and of the global changes frequently known as internationalization, disintermediation, securitization, and so on. You will learn what these terms mean as you proceed and we shall not explain them here. Suffice to say that they affect the task of every financial manager, and recognition of the changes they entail is essential.

However, at least as important in leading us to write was the incorporation of modern financial theory in a *critical framework*. The major theoretical developments of the past few years have been inspired by economics, and particularly the economics of general equilibrium. The outcomes of the resulting theories have been remarkably successful in influencing the practice of financial management. Thus the theories must be given in a text, but they must also be subjected to serious criticism. We felt it important to write this book because such criticism in texts is not perhaps all that it might be. We strongly advise therefore that, even if the whole book is not covered, you should read Chapter 12. In that chapter we try to put into critical perspective the highly persuasive theories of the main body of the book.

Flicking through the pages will reveal a mixture of words and symbols. Two questions at least should form in your mind. What prerequisites are assumed in the book? And in particular, what is the level of mathematical sophistication expected?

As to the first, it is assumed that you have some knowledge of economics (the standard first-year course given by most institutions of higher education is quite adequate), that you have covered at least an introductory course in statistics, and that you have some knowledge of financial and managerial accounting (preferably from the associated texts in the *Method and Meaning* series). Lacking these will not mean the book is impossible to understand, but it will make the task of making the best use of the book so much more difficult.

As to the second, please do not worry. As mentioned above, some elementary knowledge of statistics is needed. Beyond that, calculus appears in a couple of places, but those without calculus can skim the relevant passages without irreparable loss. Other than this, the mathematics is really quite elementary.

Anthony G. Puxty
J. Colin Dodds

* Where the pronouns 'he' or 'she' have been used throughout the text in reference to an unspecified person, that person can be taken to be either male or female.

Acknowledgements

Writing was a mixture of pleasure and frustration. That is probably as it should be. However, we should like to take this opportunity to thank those who were helpful in putting the book and its ideas together. Most of all, perhaps, we should like to thank our co-authors on the project as a whole. Discussion of the common structure of the three books was never less than stimulating. Most thanks should go to Dick Wilson who took such care in reading the whole manuscript and making so many valuable suggestions.

This project has been a major task for our publishers, and we must thank Dominic Recaldin, Stephen Wellings, Alan Nelson and the Sub-editorial and Production departments who have lived through the vicissitudes of production with good humour and patience, as well as John Perrin for his pivotal role.

On a personal note we should like to thank our close families. Only those who have written texts involving the complex task of drafting and re-drafting, working through exercises and so on, will know the time and energy it takes away from those who deserve better. Our thanks therefore to Jenny, to Carol and to Alexander, Jonathon, James and Elizabeth.

Our final thanks to those who gave such sterling help on the secretarial side. In Canada, this means Susan Dauphinee for her patient typing of a major part of the original draft and Ursula Bohlmann for the second edition. In the UK, thanks to Lyn Daniel, Val Heap and Janet McLaughlin who spent such a long time over the copier. The final draft was word-processed, and we have to recognize the remarkable combination of an IBM-compatible micro-computer and the superb WordPerfect software.

Permission has been granted to use the following copyright material, for which we are grateful:

The editor of *The Accountant* for the article 'Chartists fly the flag' by Clara Furse, which appeared in *The Accountant*, 7 August 1985, pp. 14–15.

The Bank of England for an extract from 'New equity issues in the United Kingdom' in *Quarterly Bulletin*, May 1990, pp. 243–52.

Basil Blackwell for the articles 'Is the emphasis of capital budgeting theory misplaced?' by P. King, the reply by A.M. Tinker, and the response by P. King, from the *Journal of Business Finance and Accounting*, 1975 and 1977.

Professor E. Dimson and Professor P. Marsh for the case studies 'Bula Mines' taken from their book *Cases in Corporate Finance*, Wiley, London, 1988.

The editor of *The Economist* for the article 'Outside the law' from the *Economist*, 14 June 1986, pp. 76–7, and the article 'Waiting for the barbarians' from *The Economist*, 15 July 1989.

The editor of the *Financial Times* for the article 'Under the skin of an image problem', by John Plender from the *Financial Times*, 15 June 1987, and for extracts relating to Racal Electronics and GEC from the LEX column in the *Financial Times*, 7 December 1979.

The editor of *Futures*, for the article 'How corporations use off-exchange instruments' by L.R. Quinn from *Futures*, March 1989, pp. 44–7.

The Institute of Chartered Accountants in England and Wales for the Bowater–Scott case study reproduced from *A Casebook of British Management Accounting Vol. I*, ed. J. Sizer and N. Coulthurst, ICAEW, London, 1984.

Longman Group Ltd for the table showing cash proceeds from categories of seasonal equity issues by UK companies October 1983–September 1984 from the *Investment Analyst*, April 1986 (no. 80).

Professor Paul Marsh for the table showing UK rights issues from his PhD thesis *An Analysis of Equity Rights Issues on the London Stock Exchange*, University of London, 1977.

Moody's Investment Service for the description of bond-rating categories from Moody's Investor Service *Bond Record*.

The editor of *The Observer* for the articles 'BATS — the Defence' from *The Observer*, 20 August 1989, and 'BATS — talk about talks' from *The Observer*, 27 August 1989.

Professor B.O. Pettman of Barmarick Publications for extracts dealing with option pricing theory by D.B. Hemmings from *Managerial Finance*, vol. 8, no. 2, 1982.

Standard and Poor's for the bond-rating categories taken from *Standard and Poor's Bond Guide*.

The editor of the *Wall Street Journal* for the article 'Efficient-market, theorists are puzzled by recent gyrations in the stock market' from the *Wall Street Journal*, 23 October 1987.

Abbreviations

Financial management is littered with acronyms. Here are the most common, with their full names.

ACT	advanced corporation tax
ARIEL	Automated Real-Time Investments Exchange
ARR	accountant's rate of return
CAPM	capital asset pricing model
CML	capital market line
CP	commercial paper
CTD	certificate of tax deposit
DCF	discounted cash flow
EBIT	earnings before interest and taxes
EC	European Community
EMH	efficient markets hypothesis
EPS	earnings per share
FIMBRA	Financial Intermediaries, Managers and Brokers Regulatory Authority
FRN	floating rate note
FT-SE	*Financial Times* Stock Exchange (Index)
GPV	gross present value
IRR	internal rate of return
LIFFE	London International Financial Futures Exchange
LIBOR	London Inter-Bank Offered Rate
MCT	mainstream corporation tax
MFT	modern finance theory
MM	Modigliani and Miller
MPT	modern portfolio theory
NASDAQ	National Association of Securities Dealers Automated Quotation System
NIF	note issuance facility
NOI	net operating income
NPV	net present value
OTC	over-the-counter (securities market)
P/E	price/earnings ratio
PEP	personal equity plan
plc	public limited company
PV	present value
SEAQ	Stock Exchange Automated Quotations System
SML	security market line
TALISMAN	Transfer Accounting Lodgement for Investors, Stock Management for Jobbers
TOPIC	Teletext Output in Price Information by Computer
USM	Unlisted Securities Market
WACC	weighted average cost of capital

P A R T

1

Introduction and framework

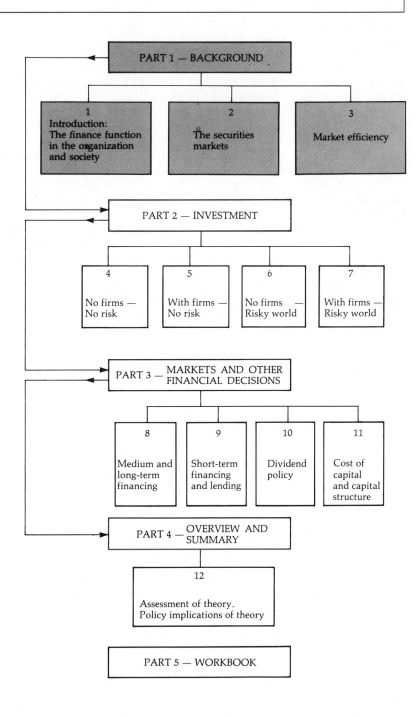

PART 1 — BACKGROUND

1
Introduction:
The finance function
in the organization
and society

2
The securities
markets

3
Market efficiency

PART 2 — INVESTMENT

4
No firms —
No risk

5
With firms —
No risk

6
No firms —
Risky world

7
With firms —
Risky world

PART 3 — MARKETS AND OTHER
FINANCIAL DECISIONS

8
Medium and
long-term
financing

9
Short-term
financing
and lending

10
Dividend
policy

11
Cost of
capital
and capital
structure

PART 4 — OVERVIEW AND
SUMMARY

12
Assessment of theory.
Policy implications of theory

PART 5 — WORKBOOK

Part 1   Introduction and overview

This book is structured into four parts. The way these fit together is shown in the accompanying diagram.

Part 1 has three chapters. In the first, we take a quite general look at the nature of financial management. We look at the functions of the financial manager within the enterprise and we look at the kinds of problems that confront him or her. In doing so, we develop a framework for the financial management function, enabling us to outline the constituents of the book as a whole and show how they fit together.

It is important that you read this chapter before going on to the more technical material of later chapters. It provides a *context* for understanding the techniques of financial management. It also shows how much of financial theory and practice integrates within itself.

In the second chapter we turn to look at the securities markets. The financial manager has to have a good knowledge of these for at least two reasons. First, because when an enterprise needs to raise external funds, it may well have to turn to the capital markets. Second, because a conventional view of financial management is that it should seek to maximize the value of the enterprise. Since, for all major business enterprises, the value is defined by the capital markets, it is necessary to understand how they carry out that valuation.

In the third chapter we look at a particular theory of financial markets, namely efficient markets theory. Having, in the previous chapter, described the nature of the markets, we are now turning to theories of how those markets operate.

With these three chapters understood we can then turn to specific matters concerning the financial management problem of the individual enterprise.

The finance function in the organization and society

Learning objectives

After studying this chapter you should be able to:

- define the subject of financial management;
- appreciate how the enterprise fits into the resource allocation process in society;
- understand the decision function within the enterprise, particularly to the extent that it affects the financial management function;
- understand how the various functions of the financial manager fit together;
- appreciate that a thorough knowledge in the foundations of finance theory will lead not only to policy prescriptions, but to practical applications;
- appreciate the key role that the finance function can now play within a firm.

1.1 Introduction

As you study this book you will no doubt have studied, or currently be studying, economics. Probably you will also have had a course in accounting. Now economics is concerned with the way resources are accumulated and distributed in society. You will therefore know something of factor (input) and product (output) markets, and the way a central feature of conventional microeconomics is the individual enterprise.

Stern (1986) argues strongly that certainly in the USA (and there is no reason to doubt that this is not the case in the UK and other countries with well-developed capital markets) boards of directors and financial managers subscribe to an 'accounting model' of the firm, following an objective of maximizing the reported earnings per share (EPS). This view of the world is challenged by Stern and others who argue for an 'economic model' of the firm which will give a better assessment of the *value* of the firm by focusing on expected after tax free cash flow in excess of that required to fund all projects that have positive net values when discounted at the relevant cost of capital. Such a model, he claims, gives a better performance and measurement guide and *ipso facto* better resource allocation in the economy as a whole.

To carry out its central function in our market society, the enterprise needs *funds*. Indeed, a feature of a market economy is the ability of individuals (and, through them, institutions) to accumulate wealth. This wealth is either consumed or reinvested. If it is consumed it is a matter for the product markets, and it is no concern of ours in finance. But if it is reinvested, it comes into our province, for the financial markets and the business (and other) enterprises we shall be concerned with in this book are focused around the way in which the best resource allocation might be obtained of those reinvestable funds. They are reinvested in *real projects*, and those real projects are undertaken by legally constituted enterprises. Investors, through the financial markets, place their funds with these enterprises so that they can be used profitably.

In this first chapter we take a look at how this is translated into practice. Hence the structure of this chapter is as follows:

1. *What is financial management?* In section 1.2 we begin by looking at the functions of financial management within the enterprise, and how these functions link with the needs of those investing funds in it. We look too at some of the newer challenges and opportunities facing the financial manager.
2. *How should we best understand the nature of the enterprise?* In section 1.3 we consider both the participant approach to the enterprise, and the ownership approach. Despite the popularity of the former in much organizational research, financial theory has tended to be based around the latter. We learn too from this that business enterprises are only a means whereby the funds of investors can be directed into real projects.
3. *How should we understand how the financial management function within the enterprise operates?* In section 1.4 we look at the financial function in two parts. First we look at the decision process more generally, then we see how it affects financial decision making.
4. *How do the various tasks of the financial manager hang together?* In section 1.5 we see what the financial management function consists of — an overview which also charts a course through the book itself — and then look at the way the various pieces of the jigsaw are linked. There are thus three parts here: the finance-raising function, the capital-budgeting function, and the linkage between the two.

1.2   What is financial management?

Accounting and financial management are frequently twinned, and yet they are essentially different subjects despite the links between them. Accounting is concerned with the processing and interpretation of information, whether to those within the enterprise (described in *Managerial Accounting: Method and Meaning*) or to those outside it (described in *Financial Accounting: Method and Meaning*). Financial management is not a service activity of this kind: it is concerned, in the main, with the management of the financial aspects of the enterprise. It is a *management function*, just as personnel management or production management are management functions. This is illustrated in Fig. 1.1 (which can also be found in *Financial Accounting: Method and Meaning* as Fig. 2.4).

The financial manager is part of the decision and control sub-system of the enterprise, which processes and outputs information from both within and outside the enterprise. In particular, he or she is concerned with managing the financial funds sub-system. Success in this role can be critical to the survival of the firm. For example, the management of exchange rate risk with volatility, both in the short and long term, is important. The figure shows inputs and outputs of financial funds. The information inputs reaching the financial manager will include:

'Substantial' environment to the enterprise

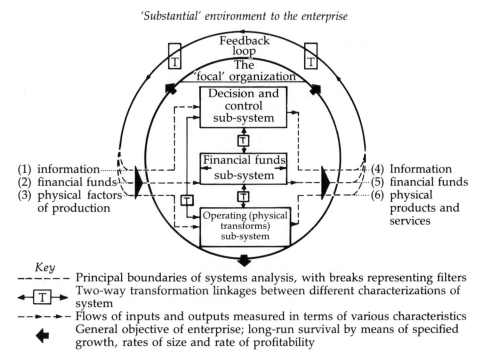

Key
----- Principal boundaries of systems analysis, with breaks representing filters
Two-way transformation linkages between different characterizations of system
----- Flows of inputs and outputs measured in terms of various characteristics
General objective of enterprise; long-run survival by means of specified growth, rates of size and rate of profitability

Figure 1.1 The organization as a financial–economic system portrayed in terms of (a) decision and control, (b) funds and (c) operations sub-systems.
Source: Adapted from Lowe, 1972.

1. *The cost of raising funds on the capital markets.* By capital markets we mean those markets to which the enterprise can turn to raise fresh capital through, for instance, an issue of equity (that is, ordinary shares) or debentures (also known as bonds — fixed interest obligations that are tradeable in the same way as equity). The chief capital market so far as the UK is concerned is the International Stock Exchange (ISE) based in London; but with the great integration of the world's financial markets — a trend now referred to as 'globalization' — it is no longer sufficient to rely on domestic capital markets. Short- and long-term interest rates are available on a continuous basis, and the financial manager can look up the current yield on a debenture issued by a similar company in the pages of the *Financial Times*. More detailed information before an issue would, of course, be collected from a specialist City institution known as an issuing house, of which we shall learn more later in this book.

2. *Current exchange rates.* Business is increasingly international, and the management of exchange rate risk is important as currencies reveal volatilities, sometimes very large in both the short and long term. Entry to the exchange rate mechanism (ERM) within the European Community (EC), which occurred in October 1990 should, of course, reduce this volatility for currencies within the EC. The importance of managing exchange rate exposure comes from the normal international trading activity of firms and the sourcing and utilization of funds, both short and

long term, by the firm. Techniques are, of course, available to reduce or hedge the exchange rate risk. The financial manager has to decide whether or not to engage in currency option trading, in currency swaps (see Chapter 8) or in buying/selling currencies forward (a forward currency transaction is one where a purchase or sale of currency is contracted for at a fixed price for delivery (supply) in the future).

With some of the shareholders and bond-holders of the firm being non-resident, they too will face currency risk from the dividends and interest payments being paid in sterling — unless the firm has issued a non-sterling financing instrument.

3. *The short-term interest rates on the money markets.* If a financial manager has spare funds available, which would otherwise be held as cash or on deposit with the enterprise's bank, he or she can lend them to borrowers who, for various reasons, are temporarily short of funds. The borrower will normally be of high quality (that is, a very safe investment) such as a local authority. A merchant bank or other specialist institution will bring the lender and borrower together. Short-term, in this context, can vary from overnight to a few weeks. Equally, the firm may engage in short-term borrowings.

4. *Information on new investment opportunities available to the enterprise.* The financial manager is concerned with these in at least three ways: first, in so far as they will entail a cash drain on liquid resources; second, because his or her expertise will be helpful to management more generally in deciding whether or not the new opportunities are desirable; and third, in how they impact on existing and planned projects.

5. *Financial innovation* and emergence of new financial instruments. Many of these have resulted from the structural changes that have occurred in the financial sectors of many economies with deregulation. Others are the result of the need for more efficient risk management instruments. Some are off-balance sheet with the consequent difficulty of assessing risk from the financial statements and by regulators. Developments in 'finance' theory have played a critical role here not only in providing the theoretical awareness for such innovation, but also in its practical application. For this we can cite the work of Markowitz (1952) on portfolio theory in the 1950s, Sharpe (1964), Lintner (1965), Mossin (1968) and Treynor (1965) for the Capital Asset Pricing Model (CAPM) in the 1960s, the arbitrage pricing theory of Ross (1976), and Black and Scholes (1973) for option pricing in the 1970s; other examples are the duration analysis of Macaulay (1938) and Hopewell and Kaufman (1973). There is less controversy between academics and practitioners in recognizing the contribution of theory in the area of 'investments' to practice.

In a similar way the outputs from the financial management decision sub-system would include:

1. information about the rates at which the enterprise will lend money;
2. information about the rates at which the enterprise will borrow money;
3. forecast information about the future cash needs of the enterprise;
4. advice on whether to raise new long-term debt, or equity, or a combination, short-term debt, or rely on internally generated funds;
5. the availability of risk management techniques.
6. forecasts of economic aggregates and the impact on existing and planned projects of the firm.

All of these are, of course, just examples. Turning next to the inputs to the financial funds sub-system, examples would include:

1. cash receipts from customers;
2. interest or dividends received on investments;
3. fresh inflows of debt or equity capital.

Examples of outflows would include:

1. cash payments to creditors;
2. dividends to equity shareholders;
3. interest payments to bankers or debt-holders.

Sub-system	
Decision and control	Financial funds
Information on interest rates	Cash from debtors
Information on capital availability	Interest received on invested funds
Information on exchange rates	Return of capital sum of invested funds
Information on new financial instruments	
Information on new investment opportunities for the enterprise	Dividends received on corporate investments
Decisions on the future debt/equity ratio of enterprise	Cash to creditors
Information on the interest rate at which the enterprise will be prepared to lend funds	Dividend payments to shareholders
	Interest payments to lenders

Figure 1.2 Examples of inflows and outflows for decision and control and financial funds sub-systems.

These functions are summarized with some examples in Fig. 1.2. All these functions are taking place in a world where the pace of change seems to be increasing constantly. Not so long ago, the task of the financial manager could have taken account of the UK environment only and, as we have intimated earlier, this is no longer true. Some reasons for this change include:

1. The internationalization of the capital markets. At one time the world's stock exchanges were fairly distinct from each other. With a few exceptions of really large international companies, you would find British companies quoted on the London Stock Exchange, US companies on the New York Stock Exchange, French companies on the Paris Bourse, and so on. With 24-hour trading and high-volume, large-value security trades, the markets are now inevitably tied together, particularly as there is now an increasing trend for the securities of multinational companies to be traded on the stock exchanges of more than one country. This multi-listing

raises interesting aspects of agency theory (see later in this chapter) and efficiency of markets (Chapter 3).

2. A second aspect of the internationalization of the capital markets is that invested funds can now move around the world more easily. Until 1979, for example, a UK investor could not easily invest outside the UK; permission was needed from the Bank of England before foreign exchange could be purchased. These *exchange controls* have now been abolished and there is no legal reason why capital should not move to any of a large number of countries' capital markets.

3. International financial instruments have become increasingly important. A particularly significant aspect of this is the *eurobond*. If a UK company wishes to raise debt (that is, raise long-term funds through the issuance of a bond, or debenture), it can do so through the 'normal' channel of a bond denominated in sterling and issued to UK investors. But if it wishes, it can instead issue a eurobond, which will be denominated in some other currency (for instance, US dollars or Swiss francs). In a typical such transaction, it will pay interest also in that currency, and hence the cost of servicing the debt interest and the cost of eventually repaying the bond will vary in sterling terms due to the fluctuating exchange rate between sterling and the currency in which the eurobond is denominated. (There are other similar, frequently used instruments such as *euro-commercial paper*. We shall see what commercial paper is in Chapter 2.)

4. Many of the largest UK companies are multinationals (for example, BP, ICI, Hanson Trust, BAT Industries, BTR, Grand Metropolitan). This means that they have production or service facilities in a number of countries. As a result, funds have to be moved around the world among the various parts of the company; goods may well be transferred within the enterprise across national boundaries giving rise to *transfer prices* (see *Managerial Accounting: Method and Meaning*, section 8.4); and funds may have to be raised in more than one country — for instance, a foreign subsidiary could itself make a share issue in its own country. It is now apparent that firms are seeking in structuring their new issues to appeal to foreign investors. This has even occurred in the privatization process in Britain as well as other countries in Europe. Another interesting development is the formation of strategic alliances by firms instead of the acquisition of outright ownership. In addition, exporting is still an increasingly important factor for UK companies, and since this will involve foreign exchange, the financial manager is again involved.

5. One of the problems of the internationalization of equity transactions has been the need to improve the efficiency of the settlement system, as well as to reduce the risks of an investment. To this end, the Group of 30, an informal group of exchange rate officials, regulators, brokers, dealers and large investors, particularly institutional, have made recommendations for implementation by 1992 to streamline the international settlement system. The need for this was made more apparent with the October 1987 stock market crash. The size of international trade is such that risks are large and the exchanges have to harmonize the settlement procedures. The Big Bang in 1986 led to London developing a computerized system for matching and handling trade in different currencies. Some countries are currently still using a manual system.

With the deregulation that is occurring in many domestic financial systems, coupled with the rapid innovation, investors and borrowers alike have to take account of this new financial world. All of these factors mean that the finance function is more important to the enterprise than it has ever been. This has been reflected, over the past few years, in an increasing tendency in the UK to create a separate post of *treasurer*, and indeed, for larger companies, a complete new department along with it, to deal with these issues. At one time it was felt that the accountant could deal with these problems — this is no longer the case.

In the opening paragraph of this chapter, we referred to Joel Stern's assertion that a knowledge of 'modern' finance is critical, and we quote him again:

> once management has the thorough grounding in the conceptual foundations of finance (which means, most important, a good understanding of how capital markets set corporate stock prices), they can use that foundation as the basis of establishing value-creating approaches. (Stern, 1986, p. 1)

It has to be stated that not all academics or practitioners, particularly accountants, share this view of the primacy of economic value determined in the market-place as opposed to accounting value, which focuses on earnings and their growth. Despite this fundamental difference of thinking over 'value', however, most if not all would accept the critical place that the finance function now plays within a firm (see Lessard, 1986). This is further illustrated by David Allen (a past president of the Chartered Institute of Management Accountants, and formerly financial director of Cadbury), who has remarked that

> The decision as to whether or not currency should be bought or sold forward tends, these days, to have a bigger impact on profits than the decision on whether or not to buy or sell the related materials or products. (Allen, 1986)

When all these factors are considered in relation to another factor, the *current instability of exchange rates and interest rates*, then the complexity and importance of the financial management sub-system (which we may consider to be the sum of the financial funds sub-system and that part of the decision and control sub-system that relates directly to it) is even further emphasized. We cannot go into the reasons for this instability here. Suffice it to say that when the international dimension becomes more important *and* the ability to predict the implications of internationalization decreases, financial management expertise and attention become still more significant. To those working in the finance area of enterprises, in the financial markets, and in developing our theoretical understanding of these developments, this has made for an exciting world.

In posing the question as to the characteristics of a chief financial officer in these new financial circumstances, we refer readers to an article in Chapter W1 (p. 320) which sets out a series of attributes which might appear simplistic, but which together can make for the success (or failure) of a firm.

At this stage, however, we can perhaps summarize the finance function within the enterprise by suggesting that it can be conveniently divided into two parts: that concerned with the *acquisition* of finance, and that concerned with its *allocation*. The first corresponds to the liabilities section of the balance sheet — both long-term and short-term decisions. It pertains to the raising of equity and debt, decisions on whether to lease equipment, decisions on paying dividends and decisions on the raising of short-term funds. This is usually known as the *financing problem*. The second corresponds to the assets part of the balance sheet: it concerns decisions over the use of the funds raised in financing projects, including acquisitions and divestitures (for divestitures, see Weston, 1989). This is known as the *capital-budgeting* problem.

Finance theory typically enforced the separation of these two decisions, with the investment decision receiving primacy. One of the thrusts of this book is to stress the relationships between the investment and financing decisions. Developments in the latter, some being off-balance sheet, are now commonplace and lead to financing decisions being ranked as at least equal in importance to investment decisions.

1.3   The enterprise and resource allocation

There are two basic approaches to the allocation of resources and rewards in the enterprise. One is the *participant* approach; the other is the *unitary* — ownership — approach. We shall look at both, although it must be empha-sized that the development of theory in financial management has tended to work very much along the lines of the latter.

(a) The participant approach

The basic assumption of the participant approach is that the enterprise is best understood as the coming together of various participant groups, all of whom are necessary to its existence and all of whom share in its rewards (examples include the workforce, customers, owners, lenders and those in the physical environment). There has already been some discussion of this in *Managerial Accounting: Method and Meaning*, Chapter 1. We shall continue the discussion in the context of financial management.

The focus of the participant approach is the bargaining that takes place among the various classes of participant. No one is given precedence as being more 'important' than any other: thus the rewards that go to each are related to various factors, in particular the alternative possibilities available to each participant group. The participants' joint efforts produce the output of the enterprise, and their relative strengths in bargaining determine the allocation of rewards that go to each group from the value added by their efforts. Although the privatization programme in the UK can be seen as strengthen-ing the ownership approach, the fact that share ownership has been encour-aged among the workforce of privatized companies and across UK society as a whole means that privatization can be interpreted as fitting the participant view.

In this approach, then, the fact that the shareholders are the legal owners of the business enterprise is not given any special precedence. Their dividend is just one reward among others, and not treated differently. (Contrast financial accounts here, in which all other participants' rewards are treated as *costs* whereas the amount payable to the shareholders is a *distribution* and hence of a different nature. Closer to a participant approach is the value-added statement — discussed in *Financial Accounting: Method and Meaning*, section 10.3.)

This is, moreover, acknowledged by management. They perceive their function as being to arbitrate among these groups and to allocate resources in such a way as to ensure the continued existence of the enterprise by sharing out rewards appropriately. Since the groups acknowledged as significant include relatively passive participants such as the 'general environment', or 'society', this implies that management must also acknowledge a social responsibility in carrying out their tasks.

One of the problems that arises here is that in many firms managers are also shareholders. This could be the result of active purchases on their part or the result of management incentive schemes, utilizing share purchase options. How then can shareholder-managers arbitrate? They also have information which is available only to managers — insider information, which they can use in their own shareholding role. In effect, such managers become inside as opposed to outside shareholders. With respect to organizational form, does a firm with superior management benefit the shareholders, or is there not a danger that these benefits are absorbed in additional managerial compensation? A study by Simpson and Ireland (1987) for the period 1961–80 utilized the same methodology of choosing 'excellent' companies as Peters and Waterman (1982). They found that over the whole time period, although shareholders were exposed to less risk, they did not also earn consistently higher returns.

Irrespective of the issues raised in the previous paragraph, the participant approach has not been the one that has formed the foundation of the great bulk of theory in financial management. Instead, most theory has started from the shareholders and lenders — the providers of capital — since financial management has concerned itself with the getting and use of funds.

(b) The unitary ownership approach

The second approach is to privilege the suppliers of loan and equity capital, and to conduct the whole analysis from their point of view. Financial managers in their evaluation of investment opportunities and selection of financing are hoping to increase the value of shareholders' investment. The creation of value for the owners of the enterprise is the very essence of corporate finance, although, as we have illustrated earlier, the brief of financial managers goes beyond the capital budgeting and capital structure decisions. Fig. 1.3 illustrates the mobilization of the capital of investors, using the firm as a vehicle and its investment in 'real', i.e. tangible, assets.

A developed economy must include some means whereby the private owners of financial capital can apply that capital to practical use. This practical use is concerned with some physical exploitation of resources, some service activity, extraction, and so on. The whole nature of economic development is tied to the efficiency with which this exploitation takes place. It is generally believed, therefore, that it is highly desirable that some institutional framework should exist that will direct the funds owned by those holding financial capital resources to their best use. In a Western developed economy the mechanism is, in the main, the market, and the vehicle through which the market makes use of those funds is the business enterprise.

In this discussion, then, and in Fig. 1.3, it must be emphasized that *the enterprise is only of secondary significance*. It is *only* a means whereby the owners of financial capital can be brought together with projects that use that capital to exploit investment opportunities.

In Fig. 1.3 we see a set of investment opportunities, described as 'projects'. Examples might be a proposal to build a hotel, to drill for oil, to resurface a road, or to extend a factory. These need capital. On the other hand, there are individuals with capital, or institutions (such as pension funds, unit trusts or life assurance companies) entrusted with capital. These need to use that

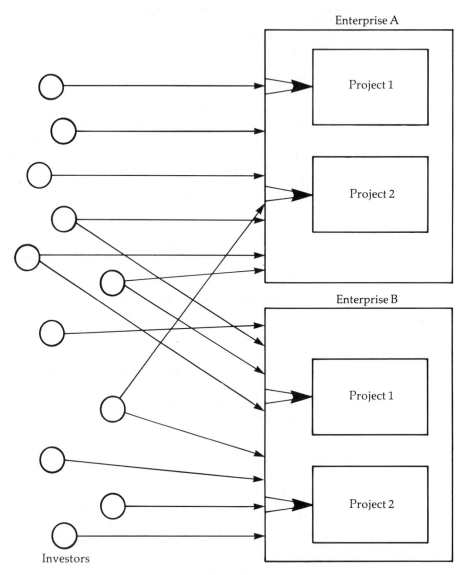

Figure 1.3   Investors, enterprises and projects.

capital to receive a future return on it. Although these funds could be placed
in financial institutions like building societies or banks, or in government
stocks, these uses would only be *intermediary*: fundamental uses of the funds
are real projects of the kind just described, and these financial intermediaries
would eventually have to redirect the funds into real assets in order to earn
the returns to pay their investors.

   Projects have to be found, there have to be applications of expertise in
exploiting the projects and there has to be information about the projects
going to potential investors. It is business and government enterprises that
carry out these functions. Such enterprises themselves are, again, just means

by which financial capital can be invested in real projects. As a result, it should be clear that, apart from one being more efficient than another for some technical reason (for example, its legal or organizational form), the nature of the enterprise itself cannot directly affect wealth, in terms of either the well-being of the whole economy or the wealth of individual investors. Only good, real projects can do that.

Hence, what you see in Fig. 1.3 is a set of investors who place their funds with enterprises, which in turn, and on their behalf, invest them in real projects.

Now of course this diagram could be elaborated. It omits, in particular, the financial markets themselves. Clearly, the investor does not 'just invest' in an enterprise. There are at least three complications:

1. The investor has to decide in which enterprise(s) to invest. There are many enterprises that would be pleased to receive investment funds. The investor must choose among them. There are various aspects of this, such as the transmission of information about different enterprises, the risk involved in each, the expected return the investor will get from each, and so on. The financial markets are the means whereby these problems can be resolved, in particular the twin problems of *information* and *ease of invest-ment*. Although it has been true that *by far* the greatest bulk of the investment funds used by UK enterprises have been generated by past profits (that is, profits withheld from distribution through dividend), the emergence of bank financing and capital issues illustrates the need for *intermediaries*, to lend and/or act on a fee-for-service basis. Intermediaries too are needed to inform investors either about new investment possi-bilities or about the status of existing enterprises where investments in them are being transferred from other investors. The market concerned with buying a security from another investor rather than from the enterprise itself is called a *secondary market*. Most securities are purchased from other investors rather than the original issuers.
2. The investor has to select that type of security which would be preferable. Enterprises themselves differ in their risks and the expected returns from investing in them. The securities they offer also differ — for instance, bonds (debentures, that is) are less risky than the equity of a given company. (Note, however, that with the emergence of new financial instruments the traditional distinction that applied to, say, debt and equity and between short- and long-term securities no longer applies (see Chapters 8 and 9).)
3. There may not be as much separation of ownership and control as the above two points imply. The usual picture that is drawn — and it is the picture that informs most of the theory in this book — is that the enterprise and the investors are entirely separate. Investors select among enterprises at arm's length. But in fact many small to medium (and even a few very large) companies have at least some element of management by the owners (inside shareholders). Trusthouse Forte is a good example. In these cases, factors other than simple economic calculation come into play — such as power and control, and the enjoyment that can come from them. Moreover, owner-managers know more about the internal workings of the enterprise than arm's-length investors who have to rely on public announce-ments. Thus their actions may be markedly different in a given set of circumstances from those of other shareholders. The Decca case in Chapter W1 considers owners involved in the day-to-day affairs of the company.

Institutions and individuals involved in the financial markets include stockbrokers, investment analysts, merchant banks and issuing houses. We shall look at their functions in Chapter 2.

The above, then, tells us about the functions of the market and the enterprise in directing investment funds to their best use. To see how the enterprise realizes this we need to focus on its operations. We now turn, therefore, to some internal factors affecting the enterprise. The following section is based on Bridge and Dodds (1975).

1.4   The finance function within the enterprise

(a) The decision process within the enterprise

In this section we shall focus directly on the financial management function within the enterprise. We shall begin by outlining the general systems understanding of all decision processes, and then apply this insight to the financial management function.

Our understanding of organizations and their behaviour has been promoted through general systems theory as described by Boulding (1956). A system is any entity which consists of interrelated, interacting or interdependent parts. In engineering we encounter mechanical systems; in the natural sciences we encounter physical and biological systems. In the social sciences we are concerned with more complex systems such as social organizations and national economies in which the relationships between the parts or sub-systems are often numerous and difficult to identify.

The most important contribution that general systems theory has to offer the subject of financial management is its emphasis on the *total* system. We stress this because, in a large organization, managers often become obsessed with the sub-systems for which they are responsible. The financial manager is concerned with the finance function of the enterprise, but decisions in production and marketing, for example, impinge on him or her. Likewise, the decisions the financial manager takes impinge on them. In large organizations there is a great danger of losing sight of the business as a total entity — how the decisions made in one part of the system interact with those made elsewhere, and how these influence the direction in which the whole enterprise will move. The finance function can assist in this process of focusing on the firm as a whole.

Systems are usually represented by flow charts in which the input, the process and the output are represented. For example, an enterprise can be described as a system in which inputs of financial, human and physical resources are converted via a process (in fact a complex of managerial and technical processes) into outputs of goods and services in order to achieve various objectives, e.g. profit, job satisfaction, consumer satisfaction, and so on.

In order to understand just how an enterprise achieves this conversion, systems analysis is necessary in which the components of the enterprise and their relationships are identified. However, quite a lot can be learned about a system by treating it as a 'black box', i.e. without probing into the process, or attempting to break the system down into its components. Instead of trying to discover how it works we can simply attempt to relate the input entering the black box to the output which leaves it. This type of approach, which relies on observation over time, helps one to make predictions about the probable behaviour of the system, even if we remain unsure of how it works. To a large extent this is what institutional shareholders and financial analysts do. They study the publicly available information released by the enterprise and attempt to understand it and relate it to the data they have on other enterprises, the domestic and world economy, and so on. The financial managers within the enterprise are, of course, concerned with examining the contents of the 'black box'. Unfortunately (or perhaps fortunately for finance as a discipline), the box is really like Pandora's. When it is opened up, we find a series of contentious issues.

It is reasonable to regard the management of an organization as a problem-solving apparatus, which produces decisions and subsequent action in response to the organization's needs. This is shown in Fig. 1.4. Systems analysis would reveal the management sub-systems within the complex whole, such as sales management, production management and financial management. Each of these is concerned with the solution of sales problems, production problems and financial problems by making appropriate decisions.

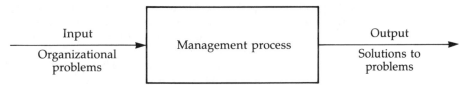

Figure 1.4 Input, output and management process of a system.
Source: Bridge and Dodds, 1975, p. 4.

How are organizational problems recognized? The prime source of information for management in recognizing problems is feedback data. These are the data which arise from the measurement of the organization's output in terms of profit, sales and other appropriate characteristics. Accounting statements, sales records and other documents are ways of communicating feedback data. The enterprise has a multitude of objectives expressed in terms of (for instance) profit, sales, production, market share, reputation; and comparison of actual performance as measured against the objectives or desired performance reveals organizational problems. It will be recognized that feedback is the critical aspect absent from Fig. 1.4.

For example, the target return from a particular capital investment might be set at 18% for the year 19X8. At the end of one year, perhaps only 12% had been achieved with a forecast of that return continuing for some time ahead. This gap between desired and actual (plus forecast) reveals a finance problem for management to tackle. Systems analysis might reveal that the manager is typically called upon to provide solutions to finance problems by making appropriate decisions. A systems analyst, however, would always look at the finance part of the organization in relation to the enterprise as a whole and recognize that solutions might be found in some related sub-system within the organization. Perhaps the shortfall in return was caused by production or marketing problems within the enterprise. Perhaps it was caused by factors outside the control of the enterprise (such as competitors' actions or government legislation).

When solutions to a problem have been found they are implemented by

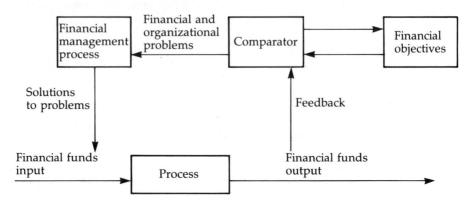

Figure 1.5   Control loop.
Source: Adapted from Bridge and Dodds, 1975, p. 5.

acting on the input of the enterprise. Here it must be borne in mind that management can only partially control the enterprise's output, not only because of the complexity of interrelationships within the system, but also on account of the multitude of external or environmental factors which influence the results that an enterprise produces. This means that when decisions are made, their outcomes are not known precisely.

We can show the sequence of organizational output, feedback, comparison, problem recognition, problem solving and acting on organizational input in a flow diagram drawn as a control loop (Fig. 1.5). We use the expression 'control loop' because the control or regulation of the organization within desired limits is achieved by the sequence of activities which form this loop.

As we have indicated earlier, to emphasize decision making as a function of management is not to deny the importance of the actions that decisions give rise to, but merely to acknowledge that conceptually decision and action can be separated.

Four main stages in the decision-making process can be identified.

(i) Recognizing and defining the need
Decisions are only necessary if there is a gap between what is desired or required, and what is actually going to be achieved. Reverting to Fig. 1.5 we observe that comparison between objectives and performance, as revealed by feedback, indicates where organizational problems exist and the need for remedial action, which in turn requires a decision. Feedback is not the only source of data for the decision process, but it is perhaps the most important one. Desired performance may be expressed as a target rate of return on capital employed (see *Managerial Accounting: Method and Meaning*, Chapter 10), although this is only one possible organizational objective as we shall see shortly. The need for a decision would be expressed in terms of the shortfall in performance. There may be some kind of trigger mechanism which warns management that the reality is different from the desired state of affairs, or managerial judgement may be involved.

Automatic devices like this form closed loops so that comparing actual with desired, if different, generates an 'error signal' which triggers off decision and action. The organization is often able to respond appropriately by using standard procedures for routine decisions, in response to the feedback or signal. Higher-level or strategic decisions, however, involve forecasting and managerial judgement before the need for a decision is recognized. Having recognized this need, a search is then instigated (for more detail, see *Managerial Accounting: Method and Meaning*, Chapter 9).

(ii) The search for alternative solutions

The complexity of search therefore depends upon the class of problem. For *operating* decisions, search is only initiated if standard procedures fail, whereas *strategic* decisions can rarely be reduced to set methods of solution. Generating the alternatives may require research, fact finding or discussion. In strategic decisions it may be necessary to consider alternatives outside the confines of the enterprise's existing activities. Finding courses of action which are feasible and likely to be successful will involve managerial judgement.

Ideally the enterprise should consider all solutions, but in practice it will normally base its decisions on relatively few alternatives for which it is possible to ascribe 'pay-offs'. It will not in practice seek complete or perfect information, but will consider alternatives which are feasible in that they can be subsequently implemented. These alternatives will consist of manipulations of factors which are within the control of management. Cyert and March (1963) point out that search tends to be localized initially, managers perceiving conspicuous alternatives, and that activity only becomes more widespread if a feasible alternative does not emerge in the early stages. Certainly the idea of search behaviour taking place as a consequence of a need or problem arising is very much a part of Cyert and March's 'behavioural theory', and something not immediately apparent to many of the financial models that are based on certainty. (There is further discussion of these approaches in *Managerial Accounting: Method and Meaning*, Chapter 2.)

(iii) Evaluation of alternatives

The decision-maker must then identify — and where possible quantify — the consequences of the alternatives. Somehow alternatives which are to be preferred must be isolated from the rest. Ideally, a strict ranking should be obtained before the decision is made. A systems analysis should encompass formal analytical studies designed to help a decision-maker identify preferred courses of action. Whatever the nature of the systems, sub-systems or alternative courses of action put forward, analysis is necessary in terms of both the resources used and the effectiveness of each alternative in attaining a specified objective.

For this purpose models are required, showing for each alternative what resources will be used and the extent to which objectives can be attained, the latter involving a 'pay-off' measure. Such models will be abstractions of the real world with or without empirical validity or mathematical equations, the important feature being their ability to relate cause and effect, input to output, usage and cost to effectiveness (see Fig. 1.6).

Criteria are then applied in order to rank the alternatives. Some measure of profitability will obviously be involved as it is a means of comparing outgoings of the enterprise with incoming revenues. Return on investment is the principal measure of cost-effectiveness of the business organization. Unequivocal criteria, however, are hard to come by, and rankings are moreover confounded by risk and uncertainty, which preclude any unique value being placed on an outcome. Vickers (1967) points to the role of judgement, in this instance 'value judgement', which may be exercised by the

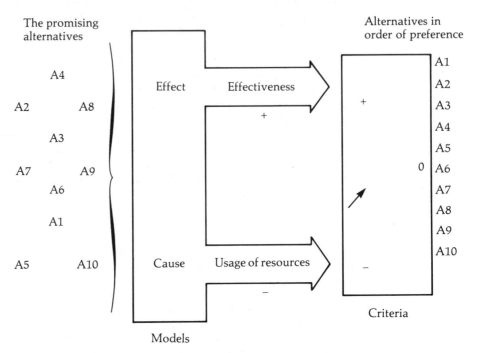

Figure 1.6 The structure of analysis.
Source: Bridge and Dodds, 1975, p. 15.

decision-maker in evaluating alternatives. There may be conflict situations with the biases and the aspirations of the various sub-units of the organization precluding an unequivocal choice. It is thus vital that criteria should be established wherever possible if the evaluation procedure is to be straightforward.

(iv) Decision — the act of choosing

A decision is a conscious choice from among alternatives. What has been emphasized so far is that decision making is directed towards definite objectives, that several alternatives may be possible and that each of these may consume different amounts of resources and result in varying degrees of effectiveness in meeting the objectives. If the criterion (or criteria) adopted gives a definite ranking, then the 'best' alternative should be chosen by the decision-maker. In Chapters 4 and 5, for example, in the case of capital investment decisions, we show how preferred investments can be identified using discounted cash flow techniques.

When uncertainty exists, the lack of a suitable criterion or managerial inability to judge precludes an optimal choice, and choosing an alternative which is satisfactory may prove a less demanding task. Indeed, it is argued by Simon (1976) that 'satisficing' behaviour is all we can strive for in organizations, and it is for this reason that the profit goal is most likely to be expressed as a target rate of return rather than the maximum possible.

Furthermore, once a satisfactory alternative has been discovered, Cyert and March (1963) have shown that a decision often follows immediately, so that the first satisfactory alternative is chosen and implemented. This implies that search and evaluation and even choice may take place more or less simultaneously. This is particularly true of repetitive operating decisions which often involve standard procedures (for instance, preparing a bill in a restaurant or hotel, or reminding a customer when an account is unpaid after 30 days). Such decisions may become programmed, i.e. a set response follows the recognition of a specific problem. So although decisions can be regarded as involving these four steps, in practice a simplified procedure may be possible.

Having decided on the course of action, managers must ensure that the decision is implemented. As stated earlier, this itself is an important function of management. After implementation comes measurement — the control function of management. The control mechanism provides a means of perceiving the need for decision in comparing actual with anticipated outcomes. A continuous cycle of decision–action–control–decision–action–control then results.

(b) Financial decisions within the enterprise

There is a debate and a lack of consensus over what does — or indeed should — constitute the finance function, and hence the subject matter of financial management. This illustrates the broadness of the subject, and the differences could be confirmed if one were to examine the diverse activities of finance officers in companies and other organizations.

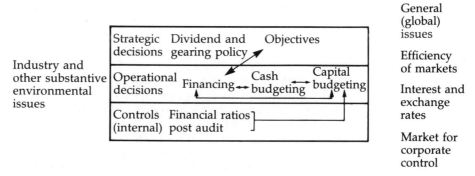

Figure 1.7 A typical finance function of an organization.

In Fig. 1.7 we present a typical finance function. We have divided the function into two decision types — *strategic* and *operating*. This implies, of course, that firms follow a hierarchical approach to decision making.

1. Strategic decisions are concerned with the relationship between the enterprise and its environment. Some of the strategic decisions will be determined simultaneously. For example, longer-term financing decisions such as dividends and debt (gearing) policy (see Fig. 1.7) are likely to be

determined simultaneously ahead of short-term financial flows (for an illustration of this, see the Chowdhury and Miles (1987) study and the coverage of the study in Chapter W9, where the model is illustrated).

Strategic decisions are bound up with both *time* and *knowledge*. So far as *time* is concerned, the enterprise's objective in pursuing profits is subservient to its ultimate goal of survival as a long-run entity. This raises interesting issues with respect to how managers and investors view the firm over the time. We have already made the point that, in terms of viewing the enterprise as permitting — through investment — the adding of value, the ultimate decision on that value rests with the market. What happens, we can ask, if the firm or investors, or both, are short-run orientated? There are many good reasons why they might be. In the UK, the enterprise reports its interim (six months) results, then its annual results. In North America, there is a quarterly reporting process. Presumably investors are waiting for the results and financial managers are aware of this and therefore mindful of being in a position to satisfy the market. There are echoes of this in terms of dividend payments that are discussed in Chapter 10. The short-run determinism can lead to a neglect of the long-run return (see Hayes and Garvin, 1982; Myers, 1987).

Knowledge leads us to the question of information flows and the uncertain world outside the enterprise, and to the fact that the enterprise is making crucial and often non-repetitive decisions on which little information is available. These decisions, which can have a profound effect on the enterprise's future position, given that they are committing the resources of the firm to projects which are generally non-reversible, are the concern of top management.

2. Operating decisions are concerned with internal resource allocation, and they translate the overall objective into effective action. They tend to be short-run decisions, concerned essentially with day-to-day operations. They are the bread-and-butter issues in the management function. Some of these decisions may be routine, in which case it is possible to have standardized procedures. Others will be unique and will require judgement with reference to the enterprise's particular environment.

Figure 1.7, then, illustrates the interrelationships of the elements within the finance function. For, although there is a natural division of the decision-making process into *financing* and *capital budgeting*, as we have argued earlier, they are not independent of each other. Both take place within the context of the interaction of financial decisions and other management functions. Financial management is thus an integral part of the management function. The finance function is inevitably more outward looking than some others (such as production) through its need to appraise various investment alternatives and to evaluate outside sources of finance. This brings it into direct contact with the environment of the enterprise, including financial and capital markets, not only of the domestic economy, but of the world. Figure 1.7 also illustrates that the planning and control elements inevitably imply mechanisms which can relate the changes in the environment to the policies of the enterprise via a series of feedback loops which bring about the internal corrective action.

Now when we consider the purpose of the finance function, we find that the conventionally accepted purpose is (surprise, surprise!) a financial one. For one of the underlying concepts in financial management is that of 'value' and the enterprise. If the enterprise has a stock exchange quotation, its finance function is inextricably involved with the capital markets because it is there that the value of the enterprise is determined by the buying and selling decisions of investors. But these decisions are themselves formed by a complex series of factors. Some of these factors are related to the performance of the enterprise itself: for instance, earnings (actual and potential) if investors follow the 'accounting model'. We referred earlier to the 'economic model' which focuses on economic value. We can be more specific, arguing that on this assessment performance is judged on cash and risk rather than earnings per share (EPS). This is true whether the firm is quoted or private. Shareholders, particularly institutional, will be concerned to earn the return equal to or greater than the alternative investments for equivalent risk (however measured). A critical factor here is the fact that the active investor in the market can determine a 'proper' pricing of shares. Empirical evidence is persuasive to suggest that investors are not confused by accounting adjustments and the like which have no effect on cash. Rather, they are more focused on the ability of a firm to generate cash and the risks associated with this. These risks are firm specific; others are market related, and may be the result of macroeconomic events and world economic prospects.

Yet, although this implies that 'value' is central to financial management, the enterprise can have an array of objectives. How does this relate to the notion of value maximization? For just as profit maximization is taken as all but axiomatic in the economic theory you will have learned, so wealth or value maximization is taken as a fundamental starting point by almost all financial theory.

Traditional economic theory, which underpins so much of modern finance theory, assumes profit maximization as the single objective of the enterprise. In a world of *certainty* this would pose no problems for managers. They would know which projects to choose so as to maximize the outcomes, and they would know what financing mix (for instance, how much equity and how much in bonds) to adopt. But the unitary objective of profit maximization for a business enterprise has been criticized on two main fronts:

1. *cognitive* — that even if they wished to, enterprises could not achieve this because of the problems of *complexity* and *uncertainty*: that is, lack of knowledge of all the alternatives and their outcomes;
2. *motivational* — that managers have other considerations to balance than purely those of the shareholders. This raises the issue of agency theory, to which we shall turn in sub-section (d) below.

We may, moreover, mention a further problem at this stage. If managers are to increase the value of the enterprise in the securities markets, then information is going to have to flow from the enterprise to the markets. 'Increasing the value' in a market means, quite simply, increasing the share or bond price that is quoted. Prices for the individual enterprise should be strongly influenced by its performance and expected future performance, and for the market to find out about that and respond with a higher price, information has to pass to it from the enterprise's management.

This is a problem of *information asymmetry*. We shall refer to information asymmetry frequently throughout the book. It means merely that some people have information that others do not. In the case of the market and the enterprise, the latter has the information. Management has internal, detailed reports about past financial performance, market surveys, technical detail, personnel and recruitment information, and so on. It is part of their job. The market does not have this amount of detail, and relies, among other things, on the enterprise to inform it. But the problem here is that the market may not believe what it is told. We live, unfortunately, in a world where it can pay to be economical with the truth. Equally, managers have asymmetry of information about investors and their wishes and how they will react, and this further confuses the whole process of information dissemination.

As a result, if management does pass information to the market, the market may not believe it because the market is suspicious. It knows there is an incentive for management to be flexible with the truth (for instance, management may be paid a bonus based on the share price at a point in time). So simply telling the market may not be enough. However, the market needs some channel it trusts, and an important channel is the *signal*. Once more we are back to the issue raised earlier as to the return on investment, the importance of cash and the risk associated with this. As the larger investors in particular are very footloose, we might expect management to understand the market pricing process and to use this in its operational decisions — e.g. in capital budgeting and in communicating with its shareholders. If they perceive this, they will know that actions speak louder than words. If management increase the dividend, for instance, this is an action. Something real happens (shareholders receive more cash, the enterprise has less cash in its coffers). So the market takes the increased dividend as a signal of something, when it would not have accepted a message. To put it another way, because it is suspicious about information, it looks to treat actions as information. Again, as we go through the theory, we shall come across the idea of *signalling* effects of managerial actions fairly regularly.

(c) Managerial behaviour

Originally the interests of shareholders were regarded as supreme so that, notwithstanding the divorce of ownership and control that now exists in so many enterprises, managers were supposed to accept their role as trustees or agents for the shareholders. However, some literature now informs us that they have the interests of their employees, of bond-holders and preferred shareholders, of social responsibility to the community and, more particularly perhaps, of the management group themselves in mind. This participant or pluralist model of the enterprise, taking account of the various interests of the coalition, has been described earlier in this chapter (section 1.3(a) — see also *Managerial Accounting: Method and Meaning*, Chapter 1). The attitude of modern finance theory is to take the view that, although it has a certain appeal, the interest of the community as a whole, the workers who may have profit-sharing plans and the other participant groups may well be best achieved by the enterprise's maximizing its profits, particularly its long-run profits, as the neo-classical textbook models would suggest. Whether it is right to do so is, of course, a legitimate matter for debate.

The interests of managers as the agents of the shareholders, however, may be less congruent with those of profit maximization. A range of models now exists which specify managerial discretionary behaviour in respect of objectives *either* following an alternative maximand of growth, sales, market share or some more complex utility function *or* specifying aspiration levels for a series of goals and following a satisficing approach. We shall meet some of these ideas in the course of this book.

Do managers maximize value for the owners? The empirical evidence, whilst it can point to cases where enterprises claim they are assuredly profit maximizers, recognizes that in a world of uncertainty the dynamics of the environment in which enterprises operate and the complexities of the enterprises themselves make profit maximization difficult to operationalize. One of the more recent studies, by Donaldson (1984) using US data for 12 of the large Fortune 500 companies, suggests that corporate managers were maximizing corporate wealth, which it defines as 'the aggregate purchasing power available to management for strategic purposes during any given planning period — this wealth consists of the stocks and flows of cash and cash equivalents (primarily credit) that management can use at its discretion to implement decisions involving the control of goods and services' (p. 3).

Managerial motives can detract from the achievement of a constrained maximand. Once uncertainty is taken into account, the return actually attained will fall still further. The presence of this managerial slack occurs in many areas, particularly when it comes to the acquisition decision, where it seems from empirical evidence that the shareholders of the acquiring enterprise gain little from the acquisition (at least in terms of share prices). The shareholders of the acquired company, on the other hand, may benefit considerably from the acquisition (for a survey for the USA, see Ott and Santoni, 1985). The Decca case in Chapter W1 illustrates how shareholders have the ultimate say in exercising their *de jure* control. So what we appear to have is asymmetry in respect of shareholder power and benefits.

If, however, it is recognized that the threat of an acquisition will be triggered by a low share valuation *vis-à-vis* the enterprise's asset base (and the potential value of assets), then managers have an incentive to seek to ensure a high share price as their own security may be threatened. Unlike shareholders who can diversify their holdings of shares to reduce the risk of loss, managers tend to be locked into the prospects of a particular enterprise. Their long-term prospects are congruent with those of the enterprise as a separate entity, and various performance measures and incentives, including stock options, can be used to ensure this.

But it is this *security* aspect which features in the managerial models in terms, say, of a maximum level of profit or a profit constraint. This has some parallels in the financial management literature in terms of a minimum acceptable rate of return, and more particularly in the management of the risk associated with projects to ensure survival. But the issues of growth and other objectives raised by Penrose (1959), Baumol (1958) and Marris (1964) in what are now regarded as classic works are largely ignored, although there is recent work by Murphy (1985). The agency literature covered in sub-section (d) encompasses, however, some of the issues raised in managerial motives *vis-à-vis* those of shareholders. Increasingly, the range of grants, allowances and other incentives available from the government and supra-national agencies such as the EC for enterprises engaging in investment are means to increase the social awareness and responsibility of business.

(d) Agency theory

We have said that the above models are largely ignored, even though many of them share the same disciplinary root as financial theory, namely economics. What then has displaced them? To a considerable extent, the answer is 'agency theory'. This is not a branch of economics that you are likely to have come across so far. Yet it is increasingly influential, and we shall refer to it at various points in this book (it is briefly referred to in Chapter 12 of *Managerial Accounting: Method and Meaning*). We shall now give a relatively non-technical run-down of the genesis, development and philosophy of agency theory. In doing so we are not necessarily espousing it.

Traditional microeconomic analysis this century has concentrated on the business enterprise in the market. The existence and nature of the enterprise as an entity has been taken for granted, and attention has focused on different market structures implicitly or explicitly for purposes of welfare analysis (in which we may include market efficiency). The starting point for the agency theorists' alternative approach was Coase's seminal 1937 paper which questioned the whole definition of the enterprise. Rather than take the enterprise for granted and the market as the analytic starting point, it took the transaction as its starting point. Transactions could take place either within or outside the enterprise: information and contract costs would possibly be greater in the market than internally, thus encouraging the enterprise to internalize transactions rather than go to the market.

This 'transaction costs' approach was taken up and developed in much more detail by Oliver Williamson (for example, 1975), who was able to reach policy implications from his analysis — in his case, the contention that anti-trust legislation might be misguided because of the cost (= welfare) advantages that can accrue from enlarging the enterprise to take decisions internally rather than having to use a costly market mechanism. In other words, whereas the thrust of neo-classical market theory was the problem that arose from the uncompetitive structure arising from imperfections in the market mechanism, including the power and distortion caused by the large enterprise, the transactions cost approach was making a case for the precise opposite.

The starting point for agency theorists is neither the market nor the transaction: it is the legal contract that naturally follows from the sanctity of property rights in a capitalist economy. Nevertheless, transaction cost theory can be seen as a starting point since, in agency theory too, the market as a fundamental aspect of analysis is abandoned. Indeed, in agency theory the enterprise can effectively disappear as a meaningful aspect of the analysis. Instead, the contractual relationships between parties takes it place, and the enterprise is reduced to the status of a phantom (for some of the earlier roots of agency theory, see Wilson, 1968; Ross and Wachter, 1973).

In applying agency theory to corporate finance issues, we are aware from earlier discussions in this chapter of the asymmetry of information. If the firm is attempting to maximize shareholder wealth, how can this be achieved and have investors know that it is being achieved? In subsequent chapters we utilize the assumption of full information as part of the trappings of finance theory. In Chapters 10 and 11, for example, in connection with the dividend and capital structure decision, finance theory would argue that a decision to pay a dividend or not is irrelevant and that capital structure is irrelevant. Yet in Chapter 10 we will illustrate that managers appear to follow a policy of dividend stabilization, and in Chapter 11 we find that firms do not take as much advantage of the tax shield as we might expect them to do. Some of these issues are the result of information asymmetries. In Chapter 10 in particular we refer to the signalling approach; signalling literature has a direct relationship with agency theory (see, for example, Spence, 1973).

The framework of agency theory

People act in self-interest to maximize their satisfaction from the contracts they undertake. In a capitalist economy they are free to make whatever contracts they wish concerning their rights in property. Especially important is the agency contract which pervades very many areas of economic life. In such a contract there are two parties, the agent and the principal. The principal has property that he or she wishes the agent to manage. This raises problems because acting in the principal's interest will not normally maximize the utility of the agent. Without safeguards, therefore, it will be expected that the agent will act in ways that the principal would not wish him or her to.

The principal solves the problem in two ways (Jensen and Meckling, 1976). First, the principal creates incentives for the agent to act in the way the former would like. An example might be the share option available to the enterprise's manager as an incentive to maximize the value of the enterprise, which is in the proprietor's interest, or perhaps a salary linked to profit. Second, the principal develops (costly) monitoring devices. For reasons that will become clear shortly, the agent may also wish to invest in some guarantee to act in the principal's interest: this is known as a bonding cost. Thus there are three types of cost, according to Jensen and Meckling:

1. the monitoring costs borne by the principal, which include not just the obvious costs for the owner of the enterprise such as financial reporting information, but also the costs of internal procedures such as budget restrictions and operating rules;
2. the bonding expenditures by the agent;
3. the residual loss, which is defined as the difference between what the agent actually does once (1) and (2) above have been developed optimally, and what would maximize the welfare of the principal.

Although the first principles have been developed in the context of the owner and manager of the enterprise, it is argued by agency theorists that their approach applies well beyond this. Agency-type problems exist wherever there is asymmetry between property rights and decisions, and between ownership and knowledge. Thus management has such a relationship not only to the owners, but also to other parties such as suppliers, customers and creditors.

For instance, Titman (1981) has suggested scenarios such as the following. An enterprise has an implicit contract with customers if it provides durable goods that may subsequently require servicing and/or repair. If the enterprise fails, the past customers lose out. Thus the enterprise will have to undertake certain agency costs such as changing its policies to appear less risky if it wants to attract customers. The alternative is to lower prices. So far as the labour force is concerned, insolvency means costs of finding new jobs (if there are any) and perhaps acquiring new skills. So it is argued that workers will accept lower wages, *ceteris paribus*, from enterprises that can show themselves less likely to fail. Each of these, then, has the characteristics of an agency relationship. The conclusion drawn by Fama (1980) is therefore that he can 'set aside the presumption that the firm has owners in any meaningful sense. The entrepreneur is also laid to rest, at least for the purpose of the large modern corporation.'

Instead, the enterprise dissolves into nothing more than a nexus of contractual relationships. The 'ownership' relationship is nothing special: it has common characteristics with other relationships of the agency type set out above. The ultimate implication follows: the whole economy is taken to be nothing but a very large number of contracts, and can be analysed as such. There is no need to mention the market or the enterprise at all.

Agency theory and corporate finance

As we have mentioned already, agency theory has been linked to attempts to provide theoretical explanations of dividend behaviour and capital structures (for an integration of signalling and agency approaches, see Edwards, 1987; John and Kalay, 1985). However, what are the practical use and implications of agency theory? Jensen and Smith (1985) explore applications of agency theory, in particular the market for corporate control (part of which is the inside–outside shareholder debate), the restriction of covenants in debt to reduce the transfer of wealth to shareholders and the use of alternative forms of debt and debt substitutes such as leasing contracts.

For the capital structure issue, the Bank of England (1988a) survey of the financial behaviour of industrial and commercial companies in the UK over the period 1970–86 found that

> [agency] costs vary according to the level of external funding . . . [and] are proportionately much higher when a company uses relatively large amounts of external funding, as in this instance much more strain is placed on the existing mechanism used to cope with the informational problems and conflicts of interest. (p. 77)

The survey goes on to argue that the data available on the sector in this period are amenable to interpretation in an agency theory format:

> Firms with more volatile rates of return tend to choose lower levels of gearing and lower ratios of dividends to capital employed and these financial policies reduce their need for external finance in periods when income is unexpectedly low. At the aggregate level, these considerations help to explain the fall in companies' gearing ratios in the middle and late 1970s, given the income uncertainties that they faced during that period. Furthermore, companies' continued reliance on retained profits after 1973, despite the fact that the imputation system offered a tax incentive in favour of external borrowing, may partly be attributed to the existence of agency costs. (p. 77)

The literature does not, however, find universal support for agency theory. The paper by Hackett (1985) is sympathetic to accepting the overall framework, but is critical of the applications in a real-world setting. One of his particular criticisms applies to how the financial world has evolved, claiming that it is very difficult now to think purely in terms of a separation between debt and equity financing. This is an issue that we will return to later in the book (see Chapters 8 and 9).

In respect of shareholders and other participants in the firm, clearly the larger institutional shareholders are in a position to enforce their agents to act on their behalf, both directly and in consort. Institutional shareholders have often formed protection committees in an effort to bring about changes. This can be seen in the Decca case (Chapter W1) and in the Coats Patons dividend case (Chapter W10). With the wider share ownership which has emerged largely as a result of the privatization programme, but also through tax incentives through the PEP schemes, the ability of these new investors to police the actions of managers is largely in doubt. (For coverage of both the theoretical and practical aspects of wider ownership, see Grout, 1987.) This is an important area because a recent Stock Exchange survey found that about 11 million people now own shares in the UK, and the stock market crash in 1987 and scandals such as Barlow Clowes, have led to scepticism among many of these new shareholders and also frightened off potential new shareholders.

(e) The finance function

Let us return to the finance function as outlined in Fig. 1.7. We have argued that the operating guide for the enterprise in its management of funds, whether sources or uses, will be the increase in 'value' of the equity. Thus the structure of the enterprise's assets will be the result of decisions taken on the uses of funds. Likewise the structure of liabilities will change as a result of financing decisions. What Fig. 1.7 shows is the interdependence of these structures.

Take the asset structure. It is here that we have a linkage to the productive processes of the enterprise. In its normal productive operations, the enterprise is transforming the factor inputs into product outputs, and choices have to be made as to what to produce, how to produce and in what quantities. The financial management function, while not involved as such in these decisions, nevertheless sees the consequences in terms of financial flows and cash requirements, and corporate policy on collection of debts and payment of creditors will feed into the budget of the enterprise. This budget process cannot be static, but will roll forward and will be continuously adjusted as sales patterns emerge, input price changes are taken account of, and so on.

These productive operations of the enterprise are largely the result of past investment decisions, and enterprises may have to continue to invest simply to replace worn-out or obsolete capital. Given that the life-cycle of the products will dictate changes in product strategy — sometimes drastic changes given the changing environment within which the enterprise operates — then the majority of enterprises, in order to survive, will need to do something more than simply replace capital, even if that replacement involves some technical change.

It is in this context that the capital investment or capital-budgeting decisions are taken. These decisions, on which the future of the enterprise rests, are conditioned by the opportunities offered by the environment of the enterprise and by the way these are perceived by management, as well as by the present structures of the enterprise. For while it is analytically convenient to examine capital projects on the basis of their marginal productivity compared to their marginal cost of money capital, this is in our view an error. The capital-budgeting decision is inextricably linked to the whole structure of the enterprise. Projects cannot be considered as if they exist in a vacuum. Their impact on other projects and the existing operations of the enterprise has to be considered. Added to this, the enterprise does not have infinite funds available. Its funds from internal sources are the result of its current operations, and its ability to borrow is a product not just of its future prospects, but also of its past performance. Faced with constraints on its capital availability, the choice of projects, as well as the whole make-up of the enterprise, will be influenced. In other words, all these kinds of decisions are *strategic*, and the strategic takes over from the merely tactical, and from any simplistic notion of straightforward value maximization, because (once again) of *uncertainty*.

Hence the capital investment decision is not just concerned with searching for and evaluating *new* projects, including the acquisition of other enterprises. Increasingly, companies have been forced into an evaluation of *past* decisions which has brought about a rationalization of their present productive capacity. This has led to an increased awareness of abandonment costs, as whole sectors or divisions of enterprises are scrutinized for cost savings, for spin-offs often by management buy-outs and even for complete closure.

Size, once the goal of so many firms, is no longer in vogue, although that is not to say that firms are merely trimming their operations to be smaller. With the increasing awareness of having to face global competition, firms in the 1990s will have to adopt a rather different strategy to that practised for many years. Previously firms have entered into markets by establishing subsidiaries and purchasing existing businesses. In the 1990s the concept of strategic alliances which was developed in the late 1980s will more than likely become the vogue, with firms working in consortiums to engage in a particular activity. There are many precedents for this: for example, in the 1970s large banks formed consortiums to deal with international banking activity. In a similar way it is likely that more and more firms will recognize that they cannot undertake all of the activity that they would like on their own and that it makes sense to pool their strengths with other firms. That is not to say that the firms work together in all sectors or divisions, but merely that they co-operate in those areas where they find a mutual advantage. This ability to form alliances in paralleled, as we have seen, by the ability of a firm to adjust its financial structure almost at will by the use of innovative financial instruments. The firm of the 1990s will therefore be more flexible and more competitive.

1.5   The financial management function and its linkages

In this section we look at the various tasks that financial managers have to perform, and that are described in the succeeding chapters of this book. In doing so, we shall not merely describe the contents of what is to follow: we shall show how they are linked together into a fairly coherent whole. It may be that this may not all be clear at this stage of your studies. No matter. It may well be helpful to return to this section in the future as you work your way through the rest of the book, so as to locate just where you are, and how the things you have learned up to any point interrelate to other aspects of financial theory.

The following discussion is based on Fig. 1.8. Before we begin one warning is necessary. No diagram can encompass the richness of the real world, and this one is no different. It does not mention, for example, lease financing or all the off-balance sheet financing that many firms now engage in. However, it is not the purpose of Fig. 1.8 to be comprehensive, merely to be a simple guide into the area of financial management.

Now a business enterprise (and to a lesser extent, other kinds of enterprise) will seek out, or be offered, desirable opportunities that require resources. These resources can be acquired by the raising or retention of funds by the enterprise. That is, the various factors of production, including managerial expertise, can be induced to contribute by offering their owners a share in those funds. Thus, as we have said earlier, there are two particularly fundamental aspects of financial management. One is the seeking and selection of projects in which the enterprise invests. The other is the provision of funds to resource those projects. We shall look at the raising of funds first.

(a) Raising capital

Funds can be raised in many ways, but we consider three here. First, there is *equity*; second, *long-term debt*; and third, *short-term debt* (though we have to caution the reader that the differences between these three methods are

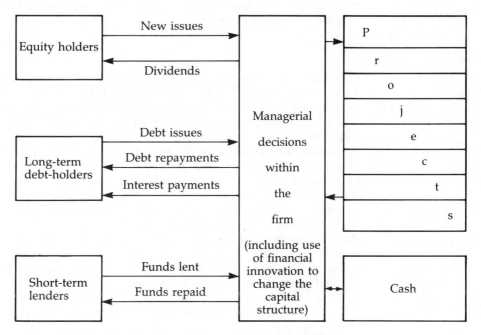

Figure 1.8 The managerial link between finance and investment.

blurred and at times it may be difficult even to think of these three as separate categories).

The financial decisions for the enterprise here include:

1. Should funds be raised at all?
2. If so, how can the firm structure its financing across these three broad categories?
3. Given that the enterprise has a continuous flow of funds in and out, to what extent should discretionary payments be made?

We may elaborate on these three issues. Given that there are good projects in which to invest, should new funds be raised, or should the enterprise rely on reinvested earnings? If new funds are to be raised, in what form should they be? There is a well-known measure of the relationship between long-term debt and equity: it is known as *gearing* (known in North America as *leverage*). The more debt in relation to equity, the more highly geared an enterprise is. Thus the financial manager must consider the desirable level of gearing. There is a considerable body of theory concerning the gearing level of the enterprise, how high it should be — and indeed, whether it matters at all. These matters will be taken up in Chapters 8 and 11.

Similarly, the enterprise may choose not to issue new long-term capital at all, but to rely on short-term funds. This will be discussed in Chapter 9.

Point (3) above refers to the fact that dividends are discretionary: the enterprise is not legally obliged, in any given year, to make a dividend payment. How should it decide on the proper level of dividend? This will be considered in Chapter 10.

These four chapters (8–11) between them discuss the problems the financial management function in the enterprise has in deciding on the various matters relating to the raising of funds.

(b) Project evaluation

The other side of the coin is the decision on whether to use funds to invest in a particular project. Will it be 'profitable'? In your study of accounting, profit was a result of the accountant's definition, and depended on various conventions under generally accepted accounting principles (as outlined in *Financial Accounting: Method and Meaning*). In financial management, this is not felt to be adequate. As we have argued earlier, we favour an economic value model rather than an accounting value model because the former offers objectivity by focusing on cash. After all, how can it be decided if something is desirable if 'desirable' is itself defined by an arbitrary set of rules developed by one particular set of functional advisers within the enterprise? As a result of this problem, financial management concentrates not on profits but on *cash flows*. These are not arbitrary. They can be observed, and are measurable with relative objectivity.

But we have argued earlier that projects have to be searched for; they do not just present themselves for appraisal. To this end, as we saw in section 1.4, the firm will develop a strategy for this. Myers (1988) argues strongly for an understanding between strategic planning and finance theory:

> Finance theory and strategy planning could be viewed as two cultures looking at the same problem. Perhaps only differences in language and approach make the two appear incompatible. If so, the gap between them might be bridged by better communication and a determined effort to reconcile them ... The gap between strategic and financial analysis may reflect misapplication of finance theory. Some firms do not try to use theory to analyze strategic investments. Some firms try but make mistakes. (p. 9)

We have already seen that the intention of financial management is generally taken to be value maximization. Now value is measured at a single point in time, usually right now. Profit, or indeed cash flow, is a measurement over a period of time; for a project, this means over its life. Thus future cash flows are converted into estimates of current values, in a way somewhat similar to economic value (see *Financial Accounting: Method and Meaning*, section 9.1). The expected future net receipts of cash are discounted back to the present time using the principles of compound interest. Value maximization, therefore, implies the optimization of these discounted values.

To develop this we need to understand compound interest, and how it is applied to project appraisal. This is discussed in Chapter 4. However, Chapter 4 does not itself suppose the existence of the business enterprise. The principles of Chapter 4 apply equally to the individual assessing that person's own investment decisions and the business enterprise deciding whether or not to invest in real assets. The latter, however, has its own special problems and so in Chapter 5 we look at investment specifically from the enterprise's point of view.

There is one key element omitted from these two chapters, namely risk. They necessarily simplify by assuming a risk-free world. In Chapter 6 we add risk as a fundamental factor in the real world, and see what happens to general investment criteria. In Chapter 7 we then move back to the specific enterprise and consider the investment decision for the (usually business) enterprise in a risky world.

Thus, in Chapters 4–7 we begin from a fairly abstracted model and move towards one that incorporates all the complicating factors of the real world, namely the existence of enterprises and risk.

(c) The central linkages

There are two ways in which the functions of the financial manager are linked together. The first is via the *cost of capital*. All funds are costly — even retained earnings, because of the opportunity cost involved in not distributing them to shareholders. Hence the projects in which the enterprise invests must be desirable *in terms of that cost of capital*. Put more simply, we can say that the projects should earn more than the cost of capital so as to make it worthwhile raising the capital. Only in this way can the value of the enterprise be increased.

But there is a background to all of the above, which acts as a kind of linkage throughout. Much of the book is, necessarily, concerned with theory. Theory is, after all, the only way we can make sense of a complex world. To get closer to 'good' answers to the problems of financial management we have to see what theory has to say about those answers. Now there is a large body of knowledge developed over the last few years known (hardly surprisingly) as *modern finance theory* (MFT). This links all of the matters we have just discussed in much the same way that general equilibrium theory purports to link the various aspects of economics. The central tenet of MFT is the notion of *market efficiency*. This means (to simplify somewhat) that markets are efficient at allocating resources, and at comprehending the nature of enterprises. It links investors, financing policies and capital project appraisal into an integrated whole. We look at the meaning of, and evidence for, market efficiency in Chapter 3.

It is necessary, however, having mentioned MFT, to note that, although it is persuasive and has many adherents, it is far from being definitive. There are many questions hanging over its assumptions and its evidence. Thus, although we shall use many of its ideas during the course of this book, we shall return in the last chapter to criticisms that have been made of it. It is unusually pervasive, in that (unlike many other theories in social science, including economics) some of its ideas are used in the practical world outside academe. Of course, this does not make it correct.

Summary

In this chapter we have looked at the nature of the financial management function. We have seen that it encompasses a wide variety of tasks, and that in carrying them out it must be integrated carefully with the rest of management's functions. We have seen, too, that the financial management function within the enterprise cannot be considered in isolation from the financial environment outside. We may summarize the chapter like this:

1. The financial manager performs a true management function, concerned with decisions and control over the financial affairs of the enterprise.
2. The environment of the financial manager is crucial, and yet constantly developing. New markets and new financial instruments, combined with

increasing volatility in the financial environment, make the task today more difficult and more complex than in the past.

3. Although there are good reasons for seeing the enterprise as a coalition of participant groups, financial theory has tended to take the alternative ownership view. As a result, the enterprise is seen as the vehicle whereby investors can focus their resources into real productive projects.

4. In carrying out their tasks on behalf of investors, the financial managers must see their task as fully integrated with the other managerial functions of the enterprise. Just like the management accountant, their expertise and knowledge should be part of all major decisions that have resource implications.

5. There are various ways the financial management function can be classified. One is into strategic and operational decisions. Another is a division between financing and capital-budgeting decisions. A third is between external and internal decisions. In any event, the linkages must be always taken into account. The problem is exacerbated because managers cannot necessarily be relied on to maximize the welfare of the owners.

6. We always assume, in our theorizing, that the management is attempting to maximize the value of the enterprise on behalf of the owners. This in turn is based on the assumption that the owners are utility-maximizers. We have shown that the two are essentially consistent.

7. This task is made difficult by the existence of uncertainty. Although many insights can be gained by assuming the uncertainty away, any prescription for managerial action must eventually be based on an uncertainty-based model.

8. A tool which will be used a great deal is modern finance theory. This integrates all the aspects which will be covered in this book through the framework of the efficient market.

9. The finance function is critical to the firm. Not only does it permit us to see the firm in a more holistic framework, but the success in the management of this function can lead to greater profitability of the firm. Profitability extends beyond that that arises from the making and selling of goods and services to the financing that it adopts, including the use of risk-reducing instruments such as swaps and the handling of foreign exchange rate risk.

Key terms and concepts

Here is a list of the key terms and concepts which have featured in this chapter. You should make sure that you understand and can define each one of them. Page references to definitions in the text appear in bold in the index.

- Eurobond
- Treasurer
- Secondary market
- Strategic decision
- Operating decision
- Wealth maximization
- Information asymmetry
- Signalling
- Agency theory
- Gearing
- Cost of capital
- Forward currency transaction
- Inside/outside shareholders

Further reading

Since we are at an early stage of understanding, it is best to look through the introductory chapters of other basic texts at this stage. They will have different perspectives, perhaps, or throw light on things we have not yet touched on. Useful reading of this type would include: Chapter 1 of Lumby (1984); Chapters 1 and 2 of Higson (1986); Chapter 1 of Samuels, Wilkes and Brayshaw (1990). These are all based on the UK. Good US introductions can be found in the first chapters of Brealey and Myers (1984) and Moyer, McGuigan and Kretlow (1987).

The Workbook material to accompany this chapter begins on p. 317.

2

The securities markets in financial management

Learning objectives

After studying this chapter you should be able to:

- understand the nature of the markets that face the financial manager;
- appreciate these markets' purposes;
- understand how they function, and how people trade in them;
- see recent developments in financial markets in focus, and realize how they affect the corporate financial manager;
- provide a linkage to Chapters 8 and 9.

2.1 Introduction

As we saw in the last chapter, we live in a world in which various institutional arrangements are necessary to ensure that the funds owned by individual and corporate investors get into real productive assets. Go back and look at Fig. 1.3 (p. 12). There are two major classes of decision-maker. One is the original investor. The other is the corporate executive who has been entrusted with the management of the investor's funds. It is the latter that is the subject of financial management.

However, when we come to look at financial markets we must never forget just how highly complex they are. Thus, it is not just individual investors who may buy shares on the stock exchange: companies may do so too (by investing in other companies, or even in themselves). So the corporate financial manager is interested in the financial markets for two reasons:

1. The first is that his or her own company will be reliant on those markets for raising funds and for the valuation of the enterprise in those markets (reflecting the liabilities side of the balance sheet).
2. The other is that the financial manager will have to use those financial markets to deploy the funds entrusted by the investors (the assets side of the balance sheet).

We just referred to 'the valuation of the enterprise in those markets'. This deserves a little more explanation. Let us start with equity shares. For simplicity we shall assume we are referring to a company quoted on the International Stock Exchange in London.

Each share is priced by the stock market — in other words, at any given time there will be a unique price (or a very small spread of prices) at which that share is bought and sold on the London market. If you multiply that quoted price by the number of shares currently issued, you arrive at the 'market value of the equity'. If the enterprise has no debt then this is also the *value of the firm*, as it is known. If, however, there is some debt (debentures, or bonds) then they too will be bought and sold in the securities markets. In this case, the value of the firm will be found by adding the value of the equity to the value of the debt (that is, the debentures, or bonds). A simple example of this is given in Fig. 2.1.

Flotsam plc is financed by 2,000,000 25p ordinary shares and £3,000,000 14% debentures. The share price at 21 April 19X8 is £1.20, and each £100 of bonds stand at 92. There are no other liabilities.

The value of the enterprise on that day is simply:

$$(2,000,000 \times £1.20) + (3,000,000 \times 92/100) = £5,160,000$$

Figure 2.1   Simple example of the value of an enterprise.

In Chapter 1 we referred to the maximization of wealth. Many people believe there is a corresponding criterion for corporate management. So the criterion for the enterprise becomes (if you believe in the notion of wealth maximization):

> The function of the enterprise's management is to maximize the value of the firm, which in turn means maximizing the combined value of the equity and debt in terms of their prices as quoted on the financial markets.

This is not at all straightforward, for at least three reasons:

1. The world is uncertain; hence, because it is hard to be sure what the future receipts of an enterprise will be, it is difficult to value it. This is supposedly solved by letting the market do the estimating, and the price that is freely arrived at by a large number of independent buyers and sellers of corporate securities is believed to reflect the best estimate of the firm's value (see Chapter 3 for further discussion of the efficiency of the market in achieving this).
2. It is not tenable to take only the long-term quoted securities as relevant. There may be many other ways by which the enterprise raises funds, for instance short- or medium-term bank loans, or commercial paper (we explain what this is in section 2.5(e), pp. 62–3. Probably the value of these in the market should be brought in too.
3. As we have seen already, a simple maximization objective for management is not necessarily tenable or desirable (see also *Managerial Accounting: Method and Meaning*, Chapter 1). Adoption of the coalition model of the enterprise implies that to take the investor's view only is unreasonable, and is taking a view that is both short-sighted and unfair. Others besides investors have rights in the enterprise. And yet . . . with the body of theory we have at present in financial management, we are effectively limited to investors in our discussions.

With these preliminary comments in mind we shall begin with a straight-forward account of the most fundamental markets: the markets for corporate securities (principally — until recently at any rate — shares and bonds). Later in the chapter we look at more recent instruments.

To begin with, then, how does the array of securities available appear to the investor?

2.2   The stock market

(a) The market and the individual investor

The investor is faced with a considerable choice in using his or her surplus funds. One possibility is to place them in one or more of a variety of 'safe' investments, e.g. Post Office savings accounts, building society accounts, bank deposit accounts. Then there are more risky investments, among which is of course an investment in the equity of a company quoted on the stock exchange. Finally, there are more exotic investments such as rare stamps, paintings, collectable coins or Victorian dolls.

The obvious common characteristic shared by the first set of investments listed is that they are comparatively *safe*. Little risk is involved, for banks, and building societies rarely cease trading. As for the third set of investments, they can be very risky indeed since there is no 'underlying' value. If collectors lose interest in Victorian dolls, for instance, their break-up value is negligible.

The second category is more interesting. There are many kinds of investment possible in this category. For although the stock exchange itself is the best-known market-place for such investments, other financial operations are possible — for instance, currency dealing, options, and financial futures. Indeed, there are many other markets available to some investors. These include commodities markets — in soya beans, for instance, or metals, or 'softs' (such as cotton). We shall not consider these further, however, since they are somewhat different, and tend only to be available to the specialist. Equally important are the money markets, which tend to deal with very large sums of money and where traders are limited to a small number of specialized financial institutions. Again, we shall ignore these for the moment, since we are considering the individual investor. Corporate investors find them more enticing, and we shall return to them later (see Chapter 9) for that reason.

The variety of investments available has already been reflected in a diversity in the markets within the stock exchange itself. This has more than one market, for in addition to the main market (which goes back long before this century) there is an Unlisted Securities Market (USM) for smaller companies.

(b) The Stock Exchange

The Stock Exchange is simply a market where securities can be bought and sold. These securities can be conveniently divided into two main groups:

1. equity shares, preference shares and debentures. These are all issued by public limited companies;
2. central and local government fixed-interest stocks (frequently known as *gilt-edged securities* or 'gilts').

However, no classification is perfect. This one makes sense in distinguishing between corporate and government securities (on the grounds that companies' securities are riskier because a company can go into liquidation whereas most Western governments — including that of the United Kingdom — can be taken to be effectively risk-free). But the classification is less rational in grouping fixed-interest corporate bonds (debentures) with equities, when they have so much in common with government bonds (which also offer fixed interest).

The stock exchange acts as both a *primary* and a *secondary* market. The difference is a crucial one.

(c) The Stock Exchange as primary market

As a primary market it offers companies the opportunity to raise large amounts of new capital. The company issues a security (for instance a share or a debenture), usually at a predetermined price, and through the stock exchange the investor can subscribe to this new issue.

In raising such funds, an enterprise may be coming to the market for the first time (good and well-publicized examples here are the privatizations by the government — British Telecom, British Airports Authority and so on), or it may be well established in the markets and need increased funds for new investments. In either case, a company would not approach the market directly. It would make use of an 'issuing house', which is a financial institution that specializes in advising on the pricing, timing and method of placing new stock issues, for a fee. Not only is advice of this kind highly valuable: the issuing house can also arrange for the issue to be *underwritten*. An underwriter agrees (again, for a fee) that if the market does not take up the full amount of the share issue, it will itself take up the remaining shares. This is most valuable to the company because it guarantees that the full amount of the issue (less the various costs) will indeed be made available. To the underwriter, of course, it is a business transaction in which a service is offered, and a risk taken, in exchange for payment. The risk is this. If the underwriting house does have to buy some of the shares because the market does not want them all, it will either be left with them for a while (which is not its business — it is in a fee-earning business, not share dealing) or it will unload them on the market at a lower price that attracts buyers where the offer price did not. Neither is a comforting prospect.

There is a way in which the underwriter can attempt to ensure that this does not happen. If the shares are a little underpriced compared to similar shares in the market, they will be snapped up by investors. The underwriter will get the fee. The loser is of course the company issuing the shares. It has not raised as much in capital as it would otherwise have done. Pricing an issue is a difficult task, and when an issue is underpriced, many more potential buyers will want the shares than there are shares to be had. This is called an *oversubscription*. A good example of this is the privatization programme undertaken by the UK government over the past few years. Most issues have been oversubscribed. Nevertheless merchant bankers have been hired each time to advise on the proper offer price for the shares, and the issues have all been underwritten (though it might be argued that the BP issue in October 1987 was a vindication of underwriting). We shall return to privatization in Chapter 8.

There are three main ways to issue shares (more detail in Chapter 8):

1. The most common method is the *offer for sale*. In this the company sells its shares to an issuing house which then offers them to the general public.

Keep watch in a recognized national newspaper, and you will see advertisements constituting such offers.

2. A second method is the *tender*. Here the public is invited to bid for the shares, with the allotment going to the highest bidder. Of course, this will usually mean that shares will eventually be sold to a set of bidders who have bid different prices. Under these circumstances the price will be the highest at which all the shares will be disposed of, and all buyers will (by stock exchange requirements) pay the same price.

3. Finally there is the *placing*. The public is not invited to subscribe. Instead, the issuing house sells them privately, usually to institutions known to it (such as pension funds and life assurance companies). Placing is not allowed for large issues, but is helpful to the small issue since it is relatively cheap. Placings are far more common on the USM than on the principal market.

You will also come across the *introduction*. This is not itself an issue of shares. It describes the admission to a recognized stock exchange of a company's shares that are already in issue. We shall look further at these different means of obtaining a quotation in section 2.4.

An instructive case showing the difficulties of pricing a share issue is that of Euro Disneyland, given in Fig. 2.2. To understand this example it is necessary first to mention three other matters briefly:

1. As noted above, the major problem in any share issue is the pricing of the share. If the issue is for shares already quoted, known as a 'seasoned' issue, then the problem is much smaller since there is a touchstone on which to base the price (which is not to say that the quoted price on any given day will be exactly the amount at which the new shares are issued). But if the issue is new to the market as a whole, an 'unseasoned' issue, the advisers to the issue (normally an issuing house) have to judge the market. Too high a price will lead to an insufficient number of the shares being bought (leaving them with the underwriter). Too low a price will lead to over-subscription (that is, more shares being demanded by investors than are available) and the company will have received less in new funds than it might have done.

2. A *stag* is an investor who expects the issue to be a popular one, so that some investors will be disappointed. He or she therefore subscribes to the initial issue so as to sell in the market immediately the share becomes quoted and the market finds an initial level based on supply and demand forces. If indeed the issue was oversubscribed then the market price will be higher than the issue price and the stag can take a profit. A stag is one particular type of *speculator*. We shall consider the activities of speculators (including those other members of the stock exchange menagerie, bulls and bears) in the next part of this chapter as we come to discuss trading in shares from day to day (see p. 39).

Given that the oversubscription might have been expected in a glamorous issue such as Euro Disney, we might suppose that at least some of the subscriptions might have been from stags. The discrimination against large applications by Disney may be evidence of attempting to head off stags.

It is interesting to note that, after the announcement described in Fig. 2.2, a 'grey' market opened in the shares. This term describes dealing in shares before the official date on which shares may trade on the market officially (in this case, before 6 November).

3. In general, a company can choose how it will allocate shares in the case of an oversubscription. It may favour large subscribers (which will have the advantage of keeping down the number of shareholders and hence the cost of running the share register) or it may favour the small investor, as is the case with Disney. A reason for the latter might simply be that, the higher the number of shareholders, the higher the number of people with an incentive to visit the Disney funpark! A ballot is not always used, but it was used in, for instance, the TSB issue.

Euro Disneyland allocations
Ray Bashford

A heavy oversubscription for the 10.7m shares offered in Euro Disneyland has forced a ballot to decide allocations which favour small shareholders.

SG Warburg Securities, lead-manager for the non-French portion of the £600m European issue, said 171,000 British investors applied for the shares and that the £67m UK offer for sale was 4.7 times subscribed.

The international offer, comprising 42.4m shares offered throughout the European Community excluding France, was 11 times subscribed.

The ballot covers applications for up to 1,500 shares under a scheme which is weighted in favour of those investors who made the smallest applications.

Those who applied for 100–300 shares will have a 50 per cent chance of receiving 100 shares, while applications for 500–750 shares will have a 45 per cent chance of receiving 200 shares and those seeking 1,000–1,500 shares will have a 45 per cent chance of receiving 300 shares.

Other allocation levels are: applications for 2,000–2,500 will receive 300 shares, 3,000–3,500 will receive 400 shares, 4,000 to 4,500 will receive 500 shares and 5,000–15,000 will receive 10 per cent of the number applied for.

Those potential investors who applied for 20,000 shares or more will receive no allocation.

It is expected that the shares will be listed on the Paris, London and Brussels stock exchanges on November 6.

Figure 2.2   The case of Euro Disney.
Source: Financial Times, *23 October 1989.*

(d) The Stock Exchange as secondary market

We turn now to the stock market as a secondary market. Once shares are issued, and they have been accepted by the Council of the Stock Exchange, they are said to be 'quoted' on the exchange, and the owners can sell them to others. Now the secondary market does not affect the company whose shares are being bought and sold. The transfer of shares from one investor to another is a simple change of a right to receive dividends and vote. The ownership goes from seller to buyer; payment goes from buyer to seller.

Directly, therefore, the company does not receive any of the sums paid for the shares. So on the face of it the company is indifferent to the price of its shares on the market. Its participation is limited to registering the change of ownership in the company's share register (as required by the Companies Act 1985).

Indirectly, however, there is a different story. Companies *do* care about their share prices, and there are a number of reasons for this.

1. It affects the sums that can be raised if the company needs fresh injections

of capital. The higher the price per share, the fewer shares the company has to sell so as to raise those funds. This dilutes the existing shareholders' equity less than if the price is lower. To put it another way, the lower the price in the market, the higher the number of shares that have to be issued. This is a larger proportion of the total number of shares after the issue than there would have been if the price per share had been higher.

2. It may affect the company's management directly if they hold shares in their own company. They may do so because they have bought them in the open market. Alternatively, they may have acquired them as a result of an executive incentive plan. Either way, their wealth goes down with the share price.

3. It may affect bonds with covenants attached. Frequently, on bank loans or bond issues, there are various stipulations about the powers lenders have in certain circumstances, in particular when the enterprise hits problems. One such covenant may well refer to the share price, perhaps giving bond-holders votes at meetings, or possibly giving the lender the right to cancel the loan contract and demand repayment. This can be most awkward if it is unexpected.

Now it need hardly be said that investors place their money in securities in order to make profits. There are two ways in which an investor can profit from holding securities:

1. capital appreciation, where the price of the security increases so that it can be disposed of at a profit;
2. dividends or interest payments received periodically.

You should note that although these are substantially the same to the investor, since either is an increase in wealth, the investor may not be indifferent between them for two reasons:

1. Capital appreciation is (normally) taxed as a capital gain, and capital gains tax is generally at a lower rate than the income tax that is charged on dividends or interest receipts. Moreover (under the tax regime current as this is written) there is a substantial first slice of capital gains that is tax-free.
2. If the shareholder wishes to spend the income generated, this can be done quickly and cheaply with distributions such as dividends. But to dispose of part of a shareholding to realize a capital gain will involve transaction costs (for instance, the commission charge by the stockbroker — and the psychological nuisance value!).

A crude distinction can be made (and it *is* crude) between those who 'genuinely' invest for a long period, and those who speculate for a quick profit. Speculators tend to be divided into two kinds:

1. *bulls*, who expect the market price of a security to increase, and thus buy now and hold it to realize a profit from selling once the market price has risen;
2. *bears*, who expect the market price to drop, and sell the security now hoping to buy it later at a lower price.

Note that a market operator need not pay for the securities if he or she is successful. This is because of the system of 'account periods'. Dealings are divided into two-week periods (occasionally three-week). Payment for shares bought is not required until *settlement day*, which is the Monday ten days after the Friday end of account. Thus if the shares have been sold then bought within the account period, only the difference (profit or loss, less broker's commission) will be paid or received. This allows all the paperwork to be completed. Note also that the speculator need not own the shares he or she is selling (indeed, this is by far the most frequent case). But when the time comes that delivery is due, the speculator must buy so as to be able to deliver.

As a result of these labels, a market in which prices are rising is frequently referred to as a 'bull market', and one characterized by falling prices as a 'bear market'.

Next, we turn to look at the way the market is structured and the way transactions take place. There are two aspects we must consider:

1. The market participants; in particular, stockbrokers and their relatonships to each other and to clients. How do they reach a price? And what are the procedures for buyers and sellers? This is dealt with in sub-section (e) below.
2. The three markets in which securities can be quoted (the principal market, the Unlisted Securities Market and the Third Market), which are currently being reduced to two. This is dealt with in section 2.4.

(e) Trading in the markets

There are stock markets in all the world's capitalist countries. Some are especially large and international; particularly significant here are New York, Tokyo, Frankfurt and, to a lesser extent, Zurich and the Paris Bourse. Others are quite small and localized, whether because they are in smaller countries, or because ownership patterns of industry and commerce have never been such that large companies are common and markets to trade in their securities necessary, or, indeed, because there is already a large exchange in the country concerned. As an example of the last, some provincial towns in the UK have stock exchanges — for instance Glasgow and Birmingham — but they are very small when compared to London. All of this is a necessary preliminary comment because the structures and dealing methods of stock exchanges are not universal. We cannot describe a 'typical' stock exchange — although there is some convergence among the very largest, as broking firms have formed international links.

We propose, then, to describe the London market. However, on 27 October 1986 the whole structure of the London Stock Exchange was radically changed, in a move that came to be known as the 'Big Bang'. Because this change was quite recent, we shall describe the nature of the change, including the trading system before the Big Bang.

2.3 The Big Bang

Until October 1986 the London Stock Exchange required its members to demarcate themselves rigidly between *brokers* and *jobbers*. It had done this since 1908. This was called a *single capacity system* because brokers and jobbers were only permitted to have one function (i.e. capacity) each. The exchange itself explained these functions like this:

Jobbers act as wholesalers in stocks and shares, which they buy and sell, making their living from the differences between their buying and selling prices. They compete with each other for the business available, but are not allowed to deal directly with the public, only with stockbrokers.

Brokers give investment advice, and take buying and selling orders for shares to the jobbers on the trading floor of the Stock Exchange. They make their living from commissions charged on the deals, acting purely as agents for the actual buyers and sellers.

This system has the advantage that it offers a large degree of built-in investor protection. A member of the public knows that brokers are offering impartial investment advice and have no financial interest in the shares they recommend. In their own interest, jobbers must pitch their prices as near as possible to the point where supply and demand for each particular share balances out in order to win the business.

Source: The Big Bang, *Public Affairs Department, The Stock Exchange, April 1986.*

The procedure facing an investor would have been as follows. The investor would approach a broker, asking to buy or sell a particular share. The broker would then go to the floor of the Stock Exchange, approach a jobber (jobbers specialized in particular industrial sectors, or gilts) and name the share. The broker would not say whether he or she wished to buy or sell. The jobber would quote two prices (one for buying, one for selling), and if these were satisfactory the broker would place an order for a sale or purchase. The various legal formalities would be carried out later, based on the account period.

Most of this has now changed. However, we do not propose to describe immediately the new system of trading on the International Stock Exchange (ISE). A good way to understand a situation is to study how it got to be what it is. In the case of the institutional arrangements in the ISE, this means going back to investigate the origins of the Big Bang. *Then* we can understand better why it occurred and what it entailed. And as a result of *this*, we can better understand the current operation of the securities markets.

Now the forces that acted together to lead to the Big Bang are quite complex, and to help you untangle them a large diagram is presented in Fig. 2.3. At first you may think that the diagram looks more complicated than the description could ever be! But, as we go through the factors involved, you should find it a help in getting your bearings. Two tips in reading Fig. 2.3. In general (though not always) it starts from the set of factors running down the left. And do not be put off by the necessarily cryptic descriptions in the boxes. All is revealed in the following text: the box titles are only *aides-mémoire*.

(a) What caused the Big Bang?

To investigate the cause of the Big Bang we have to turn to a little political and economic history. The early 1970s were a time of considerable upheaval. The system agreed by Bretton Woods in 1944 was under considerable strain. Among other things, the agreement had required that the major countries' currencies should be subject to fixed exchange rates. The reason led back to pre-war circumstances when countries hit by the depression had attempted to reduce the price of their exports and hence stimulate their economies by devaluation. Under the new system, countries would only devalue under exceptional circumstances.

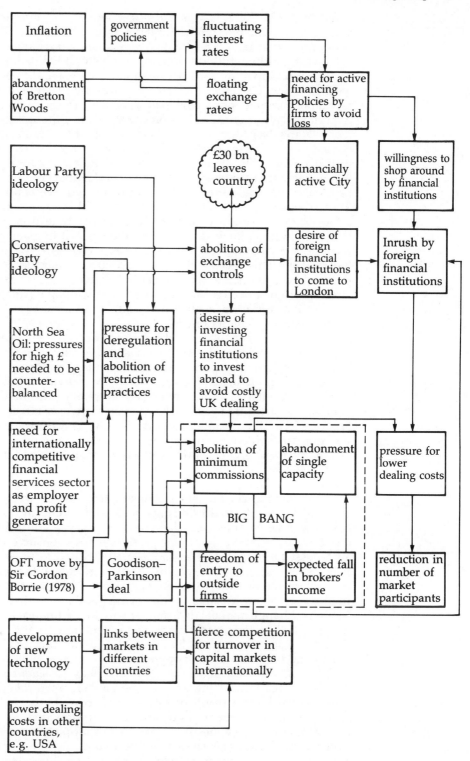

Figure 2.3 Factors surrounding the Big Bang.

But by the 1970s this was no longer workable. Differential productivity among countries, and different inflation rates, had led to the agreed parities becoming out of date. The solution was to allow exchange rates to float.

However, although this solved one problem, it led to another. If exchange rates drifted down, imports became more expensive. Moreover, there was a feeling in the UK that a falling exchange rate would damage the City's reputation among those who had deposited their funds in sterling — an important feature of the City's prosperity. For, although it might be argued that a falling exchange rate was good for industry because it could sell goods abroad more cheaply, it was also felt to be bad for the UK financial sector (as well as being politically unpopular — the rate of exchange against the dollar was widely regarded as a virility symbol of the time, and the government that had to devalue was a government that had failed). Thus the government had to keep sterling up, and an obvious way to do this was to adjust interest rates.

Government control of interest rates at the time was, if anything, even tighter than now. Bank rate as set by the Bank of England (based on a close relationship with the Treasury) would be moved up to encourage an inflow of 'hot money'. This became even more important after the 1973 oil crisis when petrodollars (that is, the hard currency earned by the oil exporting countries after the major price rise at that time) were seeking profitable use. A higher interest rate attracted such funds and, hence, increased the demand for sterling, thus raising its price.

To companies, the difficulty this caused was acute. Business was becoming increasingly international, both in terms of direct investment by multinationals and also by import/export trade. But as interest rates and exchange rates fluctuated, a more active financial policy for individual companies became a necessity. Until the 1970s, there had been little inclination in the UK to emulate the structure in the USA whereby there was a treasury function quite separate from the controllership function. In the USA the treasurer managed the company's finances. The controller ran the accounting systems. But in the UK the financial and accounting functions tended to be integrated into one, with few special skills in the financial markets. Hedging currencies, for instance, was quite rare.

But floating exchange rates changed this. When the prices charged or received for goods could fluctuate noticeably from day to day because the currency in which they were denominated was itself fluctuating, profits were substantially affected. Reported profit was also sensitive to exchange rates since losses under some translation methods had to be included if the rate had moved at the time of the balance sheet, however temporary the accountant might expect this change to be. So steps started to be taken to improve companies' skills in managing funds, whether by acting in the foreign exchange markets (in a similar way to the financial futures we discuss on pp. 61–2) or taking more care in the redemption and issue of corporate financial instruments such as bonds. Suddenly the cosy world of equity, bonds and bank loans was not enough.

This had two consequences. The first was to lead companies to shop around, instead of relying on just one banker, one broker, and so on. The other — partly as a result of this — was to wake the City up to consider whether the instruments and structures it provided to enterprises were adequate to their new needs. If they were shopping around, moreover, City profits could be at stake, so there was a double urgency. For as it became clear that companies would be prepared to abandon old-established ties, foreign firms began to see attractions in setting up business in the City.

But a separate set of developments was also afoot. A Conservative government had passed the Restrictive Practices Act 1973. A year later a Labour government came to office, and in 1976 it put through the Restrictive Trade Practices (Services) Order. Under the terms of the Order, the Stock Exchange registered certain of its practices with the Office of Fair Trading (OFT). These included its rules and regulations, Code of Dealing, and various pronouncements by its Council. As a result, the OFT, under its Director-General Sir Gordon Borrie, announced in 1978 that it had identified four principal types of restriction:

1. limits to brokers' freedom in serving their clients (which included the key factor of minimum commissions);
2. restrictions concerning the operation of the market system (which included the issue of single capacity);
3. restrictions relating to other activities of broking firms;
4. restrictions on the use of agents (Dundas Hamilton, 1986, p. 11).

In 1979 a new Conservative administration was elected. One of the planks of its beliefs was free market competition, and this necessarily entailed deregulation. One aspect of this was restrictive practices, and over the next few years much was heard about dismantling restrictions on trade so as to let markets operate more freely. Most associations concerned with restrictions fought successfully against the plans. Discussions of abandoning the special rights solicitors had to transfer property came to naught. So did talk of taking away restrictions on those people who were permitted to audit a company (for which professional accountants were duly grateful). Opticians were less successful, and so was the Stock Exchange. To be seen to be defending restrictions aiding a wealthy set of people such as stockbrokers was not felt to be politically desirable at the time, and over the next few years there were various political and legal manoeuvres.

But already the government's belief in opening markets to competition had had a quite separate outcome. Shortly after coming to office, Mrs Thatcher announced the abolition of exchange controls. For many years (in common with most countries of the world) the UK had operated a system whereby the permission of the Bank of England had to be obtained before capital could leave the country. Overnight this rule was completely abolished, and as a result, an estimated £30 billion left the country over the next few years.

There was more than just an ideological belief in free markets underlying this move. Two further factors could be identified:

1. There was the problem of North Sea Oil. Beneficial to the economy though it was, it had a side-effect that was seen as problematic: it strengthened the £. A strong pound means an exchange rate that makes industrial export more difficult, and permitting capital to leave the country was a good way of encouraging the sale of sterling and hence the easing of upward pressure on the £.
2. There was the more general need of the City. As we have already seen, a principal reason for the success of eurobonds was their unregulated market. International money required that funds should be easily moved across frontiers. The abolition of exchange controls would therefore be encouraging to overseas funds that would therefore (it was hoped) seek the services of the City. This in turn would be beneficial both in generating profits and in generating employment. The Stock Exchange did not

constitute the whole of the City: many other — arguably more successful — institutions had a worldwide reputation, and in two areas, insurance (through Lloyd's in particular) and international banking, the City was a world leader. In the capital market, it was falling badly behind.

A remarkable illustration of this is that in 1984 more shares in ICI were traded on the New York Stock Exchange than in London (Plender and Wallace, 1985, p. 23).

But the abolition of exchange controls did not only mean that funds could move more freely in and out of London. As we just said, the long-term movement over the past few years had been outwards. Once they had the go-ahead and could export funds, the institutional investors started to look to foreign dealing instead of London dealing. A particularly important reason was that dealing costs were lower in other countries, and this was blamed on the government's 2% stamp duty on securities transfers. In response to this the government cut the rate to 1%, and more recently still to $\frac{1}{2}$%.

(b) The changes

As a result of these pressures, Sir Nicholas Goodison, on behalf of the Council of the Stock Exchange, came to an agreement (after protracted negotiations) with Cecil Parkinson, then Secretary of State for Trade and Industry. There were to be four major changes in the rules of the Stock Exchange, and the implementation of these changes became known as the Big Bang. The changes were:

1. The dismantling of the minimum scales of commission by the end of 1986. It had been argued that these were in the interest of the small investor, because they meant brokers made disproportionate commissions from the small amount of work involved in trading large blocks of securities on the instructions of institutional investor clients. Hence, brokers could subsidize small investors. But far more important than this, in the eyes of the deregulators, was that these high commissions, coupled with the stamp duty just referred to, were the principal factors causing investors to deal in non-UK markets.
2. Permission for non-members (of the Stock Exchange) to act as directors of corporate member firms (as long as the majority of directors were members). As we shall see, this had massive repercussions as overseas institutions rushed in to buy up member firms at remarkable prices.
3. The setting up of an independent Appeals Tribunal, which would have the power to overrule the Council if it rejected an application for membership.
4. The introduction of 'lay members' to the institutions of the Exchange, in particular the Council and the Appeals Committee.

There was no mention of single capacity. Both parties (Goodison and Parkinson) were happy for it to continue. The pressure for the abolition of single capacity came, in fact, from the members of the Exchange themselves. With the abolition of scales of commission, they could expect their incomes to fall, perhaps drastically (this had happened when a similar move had taken place on Wall Street ten years earlier). Quite simply, this would be because of competition, and the largest brokers would get the best pickings, with dire consequences for smaller member firms. It was these smaller firms that pressed for dual capacity therefore, to give them the opportunity to make profits from both broking and dealing to compensate for the commission losses they expected.

In Fig. 2.3 these three features of the Big Bang are highlighted by a dotted line. It may not be immediately obvious to you why these changes should be considered so important as to warrant a sensational title such as Big Bang. In fact, the name does not exaggerate the impact of the change. Big Bang changed completely

1. who was dealing in the market;
2. how they dealt with each other;
3. how they competed;
4. what rewards they received.

In addition, complications such as confidentiality when dealing in two capacities (which have led to so-called Chinese Walls, which are attempts to ensure that different parts of the same institution are prevented from exchanging information) are entirely new to the City.

To take these four points in turn:

(i) The participants in the market

Before Big Bang these were firms of stockbrokers that were quite small in global terms. Full statistics are hard to get hold of, but we do have some numbers put together by Jacob Rothschild in a speech in 1983 (as quoted by Plender and Wallace, 1985, p. 54), which are quite remarkable.

As a result of the Big Bang, most members of the Exchange were taken over by, or sold large interests to, foreign securities houses. There is no exact correspondence between these institutions and the UK institutions because different combinations of functions are taken up in different countries. However, consider the market capitalizations shown in Table 2.1 (all figures in £ million).

Table 2.1

US financial services/brokerage firms		Japanese securities firms		UK merchant banks	
American Express	4,800	Nomura Securities	3,278	Kleinwort Benson	235
Merrill Lynch	2,648	Nikko Securities	1,356	Hill Samuel	184
Phibro-Salomon	1,392	Daiwa Securities	1,219	Charterhouse Group	171

It will be immediately noticeable that the largest US and Japanese securities houses are larger than the British by a factor of ten or more. Clearly this has both a domestic implication — in that far larger institutions will be dealing with each other post-Big Bang — and an international implication — for these massive international institutions already deal worldwide and hence will be linking in their UK operations to existing New York, Tokyo and other operations. One estimate is that, at the time of the Big Bang, the capital committed to the market increased by a factor of 15 (Neuberger and Schwarz, 1989).

Resulting from the opening up of ownership in market participants, the purchases were by a wide range of institutions. This is summarized in Table 2.2.

Table 2.2 Purchasers of ISE members

Outside entities	No. of outside entities	Jobbers	Brokers	Total participations
UK banks	14	9	17[a]	26[a]
Other UK institutions	16	1	30	31
Other UK entitities	6		9	9
US commercial banks	4	1	9	10
US investment banks	3	1	2	3
European banks	12	3	13[a]	16[a]
Other foreign banks	4		5	5
Other	6[b]		6	6
Total	65	15	90	105

Source: Bank of England Quarterly Bulletin, February 1987.
Notes:
[a] One broker is part owned by a UK bank and a European bank
[b] Includes, as a single entity, a group of British and foreign financial institutions holding small stakes in a single broker

Note also that some outside entities have interests in more than one Stock Exchange firm.

(ii) How they compete

Dealing before October 1986 was face to face. There had been some experimentation in the UK with computerized dealing — some major institutions had some years before set up a mutual trading system known as ARIEL — and in other countries such a system was already in place. Perhaps the most powerful of these foreign systems was NASDAQ in the USA. This is the dealing system of the OTC market in the USA, and OTC trade has grown substantially since the new technology has increased the efficiency of dealing.

The new system used by the International Stock Exchange is probably the most sophisticated in the world. Trading is based on a linked computer system known as SEAQ (the Stock Exchange Automated Quotation System). This puts together information from market-makers about current offered and bid prices. SEAQ is linked to TOPIC, which is a second computerized system which gives constant information on the prices of shares to subscribers. TOPIC is not new — it has been operating since 1972 and gives information on more than just Stock Exchange prices. There are some 5,000–6,000 terminals now receiving TOPIC information. On the SEAQ–TOPIC system, all the market-markers' prices for each share are listed, together with the volume at which the price holds. (This last point is important, because when a large block of securities is bought or sold this can affect the price: hence, if a market-maker is asked to take a larger block, the price offered for the shares will be lower.) The settlement of payment within the system for shares traded is also automated through the TALISMAN system (Transfer Accounting Lodgement for Investors, Stock Management for Jobbers, implemented in 1979).

It had been intended that the two systems — face-to-face dealing on the floor of the new Stock Exchange building, and computerized direct links among members — would continue in parallel. It quickly became obvious, however, that the floor of the Exchange was redundant, and effectively the London market is now completely computerized. This has had implications that are not fully worked out yet; reliability of the computer system (since it crashed on the first day) has since been very high. And the investment has been massive: each dealer's desk, with its multiple screens and miles of cable represents an investment of tens of thousands of pounds. What this means in terms of the efficiency of the market itself — and in a broader context of the efficiency of the UK commercial system — is difficult to judge.

(iii) The new system of competition

A major feature of the Big Bang has been the abolition of the separation of broker and jobber (jobbers were unique to London anyway: there was no parallel in New York, for instance). Now brokers trade directly with each other. This is called *dual capacity*. Brokers are now renamed 'broker-dealers' to signify they are now allowed to trade on their own behalf. Some brokers have been registered with the Stock Exchange as 'market-markers'. If they take this option, they are required to be prepared at all times to buy and sell particular shares in which they have chosen to specialize, and at the price they have quoted. This can be onerous because it implies high risk: only the largest securities houses can take this on. Hence the smaller broker-dealer will generally go to the market-maker to get a price of the security, and to act for the client as he or she would have done before. Finally, some brokers have chosen to continue with single capacity.

In New York, the results of abandoning minimum commissions in 1975 were a considerable shake-out of brokers and a far higher level of trading. Before 1975 the average share lasted 5 years in a portfolio (that is, around a fifth of shares were sold each year); ten years later it was less than two years. We shall discuss below the repercussions so far for the ISE.

There is no doubt that massive sums have been expended by international institutions to buy their way into the UK market, as we saw in Table 2.2. The sums involved are not known with certainty, but Plender and Wallace (1985) write that:

> ... on the authors' own crude calculations, taking the value of the shares at the time the deals were announced, the ultimate price agreed for the purchase of Stock Exchange firms alone would probably come to not much under £¾billion. By the time the new owners had pumped fresh capital into their new subsidiaries, the overall tally would comfortably pass the billion mark. (p. 123)

Yet, they go on, these figures need to be put into perspective:

> In fact the cream of the British stockbroking and stockjobbing had been knocked down for less than a third of the market capitalization of a single American broker, Merrill Lynch, at the time of the Parkinson deal.

(iv) The rewards they received

In the long term, the high salaries being paid to dealers in the City, which has resulted from the competition among the new participants to get a strong foothold, are far less important than the other three developments we have described. They have, however, had three implications, one internal to the City and two external:

1. Internally, they mean that pressure on dealers, always high, is probably far higher than before, and that when the weaker firms pull out, as some have already done, then salaries will fall back. One estimate for 1988, for instance (see p. 205), suggested that market-makers as a whole had lost £500 million — revenues being £350 million, costs £850 million. Clearly one aspect of those high costs — though by no means the only one — was the high salaries being paid.

2. Externally, one result has been to increase resentment around the country over the City. A number of studies have suggested that the City is not helpful to industry in raising capital (see, for example, Ingham, 1984). There are two reasons for this. First, because its interests are in many cases opposed to those of industry, for the City requires a strong exchange rate to increase the confidence of external users of its services, whereas industry needs a lower pound to make exports competitive. Similarly, when interest rates rise there is a transfer of wealth from the payers (industry) to the lenders (the City). Second, because studies doubt whether, net, any capital at all is raised by the City for industry (what we referred to earlier as the primary market). For evidence on this, see the article by Plender in Chapter W2 (p. 350) and his reference to the research of Mayer. High salaries have not helped the City's reputation in such conditions. However, it has to be said that these amounts are still small compared to Wall Street: it has been reported that the '$45 million annual income required to reach Wall Street's top ten was more than double the earnings of Mr Lee Iacocca, chairman of Chrysler and the highest paid industrial executive in the US last year', and that 'Mr Michel David-Weill, Lazard's chairman, came top of the list, with an estimated income of $125 million' (*Financial Times*, 15 June 1987).

3. A second external result, it has been suggested, is to entice some of the UK's brightest graduates away from activities that might have been more beneficial to the economy in the long term (such as scientific research) into the City for the quick rewards.

Further evidence of a gap between the City and industry came from a survey by Ernst and Whinney, a major firm of chartered accountants (now part of Ernst and Young), early in 1986. Interviewing 451 industrial and commercial companies about the Big Bang, it was found that those companies 'believed it will not lead to any increase in employment levels (85%), turnover (79%), profitability (68%), or volume of overseas trade (62%)'. And when it came to the cost of capital 'three-quarters of financial institutions believe the cost will be cheaper, but two-thirds of the major companies interviewed do not agree' (*Management News*, May 1986).

The feeling of resentment has also been exacerbated by the recent record of frauds and other scandals (such as those in Lloyd's and the Guinness affair in the UK; and that of Ivan Boersky in the USA). In the survey just referred to, 61% of non-financial companies thought the Big Bang gave increased opportunities for fraud and malpractice.

(c) The outcomes

As we have already seen, the Big Bang led to high overcapacity in the ISE. Quite simply, there was not enough business to go round, and to pay for the very considerable costs of running broker-dealer firms. Competition itself had obliged them to spend a great deal on capital equipment, to invest large amounts of capital so as to be able to keep extensive long positions in shares, to sustain extensive research departments and to pay high salaries. Moreover, in the chase for business, margins were cut drastically for large customers. Volume was needed to pay for this and, though volume in the first year after Big Bang was double levels before it, this was not enough to support the massive infrastructure that had been created. The result, as we have seen, was that massive losses were incurred.

Within a few months of Big Bang some traders pulled out of certain sectors (Robert Fleming stopped making markets in food manufacturers' shares; Barclays de Zoete Wedd in television companies); and as early as March 1987 Midland Bank, through its subsidiary Greenwell Montagu, pulled out of equity markets altogether. By the time the workings of the market were reassessed in what some called Big Bang Mark II (on 13 February 1989) seven market-makers had closed altogether. They included internationally known names Chase Manhattan, Morgan Grenfell and Wood Mackenzie. This was exacerbated by at least two events: the 1987 market crash and the price war that began in August 1988.

The market crashed just one year after Big Bang. On 19 October — Black Monday — the FT-SE had its largest fall ever, of nearly 11%. Between 12 October and 30 October the market lost 27% of its value. Markets all over the world suffered a crash at the same time, and by 27 January 1988 the *Financial Times* was able to report that 'in the 100 days after Black Monday, world share prices have dropped by almost as much as they did on the day of the crash itself'.

Because market-makers were long in shares (that is, they were holding them), they lost badly by the crash. Indeed, they had to buy more stock during the fall (£250 million in equities). There were some accusations that telephones were left unanswered at the height of the panic, although in fairness it must be acknowledged that turnover in the hectic days of 19–20 October was double the usual volume.

Faced with mounting losses and lack of volume, two firms set off a price war on 25 August 1988. Among other things this involved cutting spreads (the difference between quoted buying and selling prices). The efficiency of the market system was also being challenged because the screen was less reliable than it should have been in indicating firm prices:

> The philosophy behind SEAQ is that investors are best served by a central marketplace . . . 'The screen does not provide a central market; the largest trades are always negotiated on the telephone at prices different to those on the screen' argues James Capel.
>
> *Source:* The Economist, *26 November 1988*.

Large traders were increasingly upset by the transparency of the system. Its advantage, of course, was to stimulate competition, since broker-dealers could see all prices being quoted on any stock at any time, and indeed a yellow band on the screen helped further by indicating the best prices of all. But the downside, to dealers, was that the large market-makers lost at the expense of the small. They had to use capital to hold stocks extensively, and smaller firms could then use this as a backstop:

> Until now, a market maker has been able to call competitors to pass on the risk. 'They simply line up five guys on the phones and hit the five market makers in that stock' says Tony White, head of market-making at Nomura.
>
> *Source:* Observer, *29 January 1989*.

The large market-makers were central to the system. The ISE itself estimated that eight of them undertook 80% of the business.

Big Bang Mark II, as we may call it, changed two rules to respond to pressure from the large market-makers. First, it permitted market-makers to refuse to deal with each other. Second, it permitted market-makers to remain anonymous for the rest of that trading day. In addition, it required all trades to be reported to the Stock Exchange within three minutes, to ensure that volume was readily visible.

Market prices did recover from the 1987 crash; indeed a feature of the crash that was discussed by a large number of commentators was how little seemed to have changed as a result of the crash. The Wall Street crash of 1929 had triggered a worldwide recession. Even though the figures for 1987 were actually worse than 1929, there seemed to be a minimal effect on the economy outside the financial markets. And although the inquiry into the crash in New York was critical of a number of issues, in particular investigating whether certain complex computer-driven trading strategies had been responsible for the crash (the programs involved relationships between the NYSE itself and stock index futures), the ISE's report concluded that nothing was fundamentally wrong. Sir Nicholas Goodison, then chairman of the Exchange, was quick to point out that months later volumes were still high; investors had not been put off.

The market recovery came to a halt in October 1989. This, even more graphically than the 1987 crash, illustrated the interdependency of the world's stock markets, and in particular the golden triangle of New York, Tokyo and London. The FT-SE had bottomed on 2 December 1987, and since then had risen again. But on Friday 13 October, Wall Street suddenly plunged almost 7%. Because of the time differences among the three major markets, this meant that Tokyo first, then London, had to wait over the weekend before trading opened to see how their markets would react. Tokyo, it turned out, was steadier than New York, and lost only 2% that Monday. London started with heavy selling, lost 9% by 12.30, then rallied during the afternoon to finish down 3.16% for the day. The general agreement of market participants was that it was far milder than 1987.

What, then, do we conclude from this? Basically that overcapacity is still problematic in London, that the technology that accompanied the new market systems has borne up well, but that the increasing integration of the world's stock markets means that London can decreasingly be understood in isolation. We shall look at the globalization of markets presently; first, it is necessary to enhance our knowledge of the UK market. We now consider the three markets within the stock exchange.

2.4 The three markets within the Stock Exchange

(a) The principal market

The Stock Exchange has, for many years, imposed fairly onerous restrictions on companies that it allows to be quoted. As part of its attempt to ensure that problems are minimized, it has ensured a minimum size for companies seeking a quotation, and listed a considerable number of items that must be disclosed in the prospectus at the time of flotation. The main requirements are summarized in Table 2.3.

The cost of obtaining a listing on the main market is high because of the cost of advice, advertising and capital duties. In Table 2.4 we give an estimate from the Bank of England in 1986 as to the typical cost of a relatively small (£7 million) offer for sale. At 8% of the proceeds, some potential entrants to the markets may feel that this is too high.

Table 2.3 ISE requirements for entry.

	Main market	*USM*	*Third Market*
Minimum market capitalization	£700,000 for equities, but normally sponsors look for companies over £10 million for market liquidity and cost reasons	No minimum	No minimum
Minimum trading record	5 years	3 years	Usually 1 year
Annual turnover of company	No minimum, but sponsors normally look for over £10 million	No minimum	No minimum
Annual profit before taxation	No minimum, but sponsors normally look for over £1 million	No minimum, but normally over £500,000	No minimum
Minimum percentage of shares which must be held publicly	25%	10%	No minimum
Latest audited results in prospectus	Within six months	Within nine months	Usually within nine months unless a greenfield company
Publicity requirements:			
Introductions and placings	One formal notice in a national daily newspaper and circulation of listing particulars in the Extel Statistical Services	One formal notice in a national daily newspaper and circulation of prospectus in the Extel Statistical Services	One formal notice in a national daily newspaper and circulation of prospectus in the Extel Statistical Services
Offers for sale	Listing particulars to be published in two national daily newspapers and circulated in the Extel Statistical Services	One formal notice in a daily newspaper	One formal notice in a daily newspaper

Source: Quality of Markets (ISE, 1989).

Table 2.4 Conventional costs of an offer for sale of £7 million.

	£	% of sum raised
Capital duty	70,000	1.0
Stock Exchange listing fee	7,340	0.1
Accountants' fees	93,500	1.3
Legal fees	98,000	1.4
Advertising costs	98,000	1.4
Printing costs	30,000	0.4
Extel fees	1,500	0.0
Receiving banks' charges	10,000	0.1
Issuing house fee[a]	140,000	2.0
Additional advisers' fees	14,000	0.2
Total	562,340	8.0

Source: *Bank of England Quarterly Bulletin*, December 1986, p. 535.

Note: [a] Including sub-underwriting commission of 1.25% and the broker's fee of 0.25%.

Table 2.5 Country of origin of ISE-quoted companies.

	No.	%	Market capitalization (£m)	%	Average size (£m)
(a) Main market					
UK and Ireland	1,780	77.9	466,671.6	30.2	262.2
Australia	20	0.9	26,811.9	1.7	1,340.6
Bermuda	18	0.8	4,982.9	0.3	276.8
Canada	27	1.2	36,281.1	2.3	1,343.7
Cayman Islands	15	0.7	17,794.1	1.2	1,186.3
Japan	13	0.6	245,779.3	15.9	18,906.1
Luxembourg	15	0.7	4,729.7	0.3	315.3
Malaysia	14	0.6	2,627.4	0.2	187.7
Netherlands	13	0.6	42,902.3	2.8	3,300.2
South Africa	97	4.2	26,297.6	0.0	271.1
Sweden	14	0.6	10,689.9	0.7	763.6
USA	185	8.1	580,511.5	37.5	3,137.9
Other overseas (24 countries)	74	3.2	80,635.8	5.2	1,089.7
Total overseas	505	22.1	1,080,043.5	69.8	2,138.7
Total listed	2,285	100.0	1,546,715.1	100.0	676.9
(b) Unlisted Securities Market					
UK and Ireland	396	95.0	8,697.7	97.5	22.0
USA	15	3.6	160.2	1.8	10.7
Other	6	1.4	62.7	0.7	10.5
Total USM	417	100.0	8,920.6	100.0	21.4
(c) Third Market	60	100.0	560.8	100.0	9.3

Source: Adapted from *Quality of Markets* (ISE, 1989).

There are only around 2,300 companies quoted on the main market, out of about 1 million UK companies in total. They tend to include all the largest companies, of course. However, the first of these figures is deceptive. The ISE is well named: it is the most international of the major stock exchanges. In Table 2.5 we give the breakdown of countries of origin for the companies having shares traded on the London market. It will be seen that 505 companies (22.1%) are based outside the UK and Ireland; and that, because their average size is much larger than that for UK companies, they constitute a remarkable 69.8% of total market capitalization.

(b) The Unlisted Securities Market

Because of the restrictions and costliness of the principal market, there was in the late 1970s a tendency for companies seeking new capital that could not meet the criteria to have their shares traded on the over-the-counter (OTC) market. This is simply a network of brokers who deal outside the Stock Exchange itself. Details of the OTC market can be found in Chapter W2. It can be a minefield for investors since there is no guarantee that the shares peddled are going to yield much, or indeed any, return.

To combat this shift, and in response to critical comments in the report of the Wilson Committee (1980), the Stock Exchange set up a second market, the Unlisted Securities Market (USM) on 10 November 1980. Although it is under the auspices of the Stock Exchange Council, and although shares on the USM are quoted alongside those of the principal market in the pages of the *Financial Times*, they are nevertheless signalled as being more risky than others. The USM offers companies a chance to increase their capital at that tricky stage where they are too large for the local bank loan but too small for the expense of a full share issue (we described earlier the process of issue: the issuing house can charge heavily for its expertise and for the certainty yielded by underwriting, as shown by Table 2.4).

Thus the USM differs from the principal market in the following ways (Table 2.3):

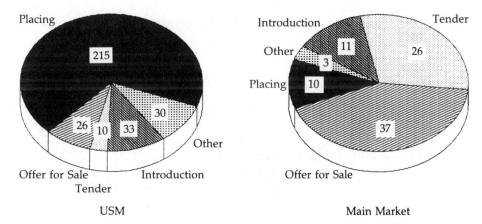

Figure 2.4   Methods of entry to markets 1980–85.

1. it is cheaper to obtain a listing (for instance, a public issue would require a smaller newspaper advertisement);
2. less disclosure at the time of issue is needed;
3. the company need not have reached as large a size as is necessary for a full listing.

It is interesting to note the preponderance of placings in the 347 companies listed by Buckland and Davis (1988) as entered or transferred to the USM between 1980 and 1985. You will see from Fig. 2.4 that more than two-thirds of the new entrants were by means of a placing (a placing, you will recall, is a cheap means of securing a listing, mainly because of the minimal publicity requirements). On the other hand, the offer for sale was the most popular means of obtaining a quotation for the 87 companies that entered the main market during that time.

A comparative summary of the average issue/quotation expenses for new entrants to each market is given in Fig. 2.5. This figure shows two things. First, you will see that average costs for entering the main market are higher whatever the method used. This is hardly surprising since the companies are larger. Second, you will see how much cheaper a placing is than either an offer by tender or an offer for sale (a comparison with the introduction is inappropriate since in an introduction no new shares are issued): for the USM, the placing is little more than a third of the cost of the other two. However, care should be taken in interpreting these figures: they do not control for the size of companies using each method, so it may be that those using a placing are on average smaller than the others, and that this accounts for part of the difference.

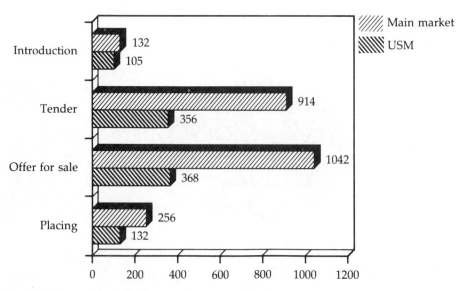

Figure 2.5   Average issue/quotation expenses (£000s).

(c) The Third Market

Despite the advent of the USM, the OTC market did not die. As a result, the ISE began the Third Market in January 1987. This had even less stringent requirements than the USM. It was, of course, correspondingly more risky for investors. However, it was not successful. As Table 2.5 shows, only 60 companies were quoted by the end of 1989. Events overtook the Third Market because two European Community directives loomed which required that listing and public offer requirements should be harmonized among the securities markets of Europe. London had the toughest requirements: the main market, for instance, looked for a five-year trading record, whereas other European exchanges tended to look for only a three-year record. The EC directive harmonizes this at three years (see Chapter W8).

As a result, the Third Market was abolished by the end of 1990. Many USM companies transferred to the main market; most Third Market companies qualified for the USM, which also had less stringent listing requirements.

2.5 Other securities

(a) Corporate bonds and gilts

So far we have looked at equities. Most of what has been discussed is equally true for corporate debt in the form of bonds. In the UK, the market value of equity is far larger than that of long-term debt. At the end of 1985 it was estimated that the market value of quoted equities was £250 billion. For debt the corresponding figure was just £8 billion. Moreover, the market in bonds is much thinner than it is in equities. In the great majority of cases bonds are bought by institutions rather than individuals, and they are held from issue to maturity. Life assurance companies and pension funds, for example, need to tie up their investments for perhaps 30 or 40 years until their obligations become due. Holding a long bond can achieve this at minimal cost, since if they buy and hold they do not incur brokers' commissions. For these reasons, you will find little mention of corporate bonds in the *Financial Times* daily share service.

However, although the domestic corporate bond market may be relatively small, the same is not true for either government bonds (known as gilt-edged securities, or gilts) or eurobonds. Since we are considering corporate financial management, gilts may not seem directly important to us. They are, in so far as they provide a benchmark. UK gilts are as near as we come to a default-free investment: the UK government has never defaulted on a loan.

Gilts constitute the bulk of the *national debt*. When the government needs to raise money it can do so in two main ways. One is to raise taxes. The other is to borrow. Gilts are one of the main borrowing instruments for the government. They may have lives up to 5 years ('shorts'), between 5 and 15 years (medium term) or over 15 years (long term). Some gilts are undated, which means that, although the government guarantees to continue paying interest on them, it need only redeem them if it wishes. Since they were issued at low yields (between 2.5% and 4%), governments do not find this prospect attractive: they would have to be replaced with loan stock at current market rates of nearer 12%.

Until recently there has been a tendency for government debt to increase.

Throughout the 1970s, for example, large budget deficits required that an increasing amount of gilts were issued. However in 1988/9 the Bank of England (on behalf of the government) bought back £4.7 billion of gilts — the result of the government's budget surplus that year. This was a sizeable reduction in the context of a £122 billion market. One result was that there was less business for those market-makers specializing in gilts, the number of whom shrunk from 27 at Big Bang to 19 three years later. The other result was to strengthen the corporate bond market because there were still investors wanting fixed-interest investments, and if fewer gilts were available, corporate bonds could perhaps fill the gap.

This has now been happening, with Bank of England encouragement. UK companies issued only £750 million bonds in 1980; ten years later they were raising closer to £20 billion this way. However, most of this was in eurosterling rather than the domestic sterling market. To understand what this means, we now turn to look briefly at the eurobond markets.

(b) Eurobonds

A eurodollar can be defined (roughly) as a dollar held in a bank deposit outside the USA. Similarly any eurocurrency — and there are euroyen, eurosterling, eurolire and so on — is a currency held outside the borders of the issuer nation. It does not have to be held in Europe, despite the 'euro-' tag.

A security can be issued in a eurocurrency instead of a domestic currency. For instance, a UK company, when raising money on a bond, can issue a bond denominated in eurodollars instead of sterling. If it does so, then normally it will pay interest in dollars, and repay the loan in dollars when it reaches maturity.

The eurobond market has grown at an explosive rate. Hamilton (1986) quotes the data in Table 2.6 from *Euromoney*. An even more extraordinary statistic is that turnover in the eurobond secondary market in 1984 was $1.5 trillion. This was, as Hamilton points out, four times the 1984 turnover of the stock exchanges of Tokyo, Paris, Toronto, the USA, West Germany, Zurich, London, and the US OTC market NASDAQ *all added together*. Why has the market grown so fast? In other words, what are the attractions of eurobonds when compared to domestic bonds?

Table 2.6 Issues in the eurobond market.

	1963	1970	1980	1983	1985
Number of issues	13	128	310	526	1,357
Value ($m)	147	2,762	26,423	46,376	135,676

Some advantages are to issuers, some to lenders. However, the two clearly interact, since an attraction to lenders will tend to move the cost of borrowing down, and hence increase the attraction to borrowers. The advantages are:

1. Eurobonds are bearer certificates. This means that the owner of the bonds does not register ownership with the issuing company. Instead, his or her identity is effectively secret, and when interest is due, a tear-off slip is taken from the bond and sent to the company. There are many lenders who like this anonymity — some for more respectable reasons than others.

2. No tax is deducted when interest is paid. Hence it is up to the lender to declare the income for tax purposes.
3. There is no regulatory authority governing the bonds' issuance, or the interest payable on the bonds.
4. Interest payable can be less costly to the borrower than a domestic loan. This is partly because of the factors above, and partly because there is no regulation setting minimum rates.

A recent development in the eurobond arena is the FRN (floating rate note). As the name suggests, the interest payable is not predetermined but varies according to some agreed baseline.

Interestingly, although London is the world's recognized centre for euro-bond issuance and trading, British merchant banks have little of the trade. For instance the largest trader, Credit Suisse First Boston, has 14% of the market, which is more than the total for all British banks put together.

(c) Options

We turn next to options. They are traded on the Stock Exchange, and have been since 1978. Futures contracts (see subsection (d) below), which have some similarities, are not traded on the Stock Exchange and have their own separate exchange. There are more details of options in Chapter W8.

We shall illustrate the nature of an option contract through an example. Suppose the shares of Erewhon plc rose in the market from £2 to £2.40 each between 1 January and 30 June in a given year. How might Mr Leech, a potential investor, have profited from this? Clearly one way is to buy in January and sell in June. However, this entails an expenditure of his funds, which are then locked into the purchase for six months.

An alternative is to buy an option contract on 1 January. Under this, Mr Leech pays for the right to buy a specified number of shares at a pre-determined future time (or within a specified period) at a specified price. In the case we just described he will pay a small sum, and later when the price goes up he will 'exercise' the option, buy at the specified price and (probably) simultaneously sell at the spot market price.

Suppose, for instance, that he bought the right to buy 1,000 shares after six months, paying 12p per share for the option. We shall ignore transaction costs. The 'exercise price' — that is, the price specified in the contract at which he can buy at the end of the period — is £2.10. Then he will choose to exercise the option, and the profit will be calculated like this:

	£
Cost of buying shares at exercise price (1,000 × 2.10)	2,100
Cost of option contract (1,000 × 0.12)	120
	2,220
Proceeds from selling at actual price (1,000 × £2.40)	2,400
Profit	£ 180

If the final price were less than the exercise price, he would not bother to exercise the option, and would lose on the transaction. The loss would, of course, be the amount paid at the beginning (i.e. £120).

If the actual price were in the range between the exercise price of £2.10 and £2.22, it would still pay Mr Leech to exercise the option. He would lose, but the loss would be less than the loss from not exercising (£120, the cost of buying the option contract). For instance, if the market price rose to £2.15, his loss would be:

	£
Cost of buying shares at exercise price (1,000 × 2.10)	2,100
Cost of option contract (1,000 × 0.12)	120
	2,220
Proceeds from selling at actual price (1,000 × £2.15)	2,150
Loss	£ 70

Mr Leech has lost £70, but this is less than the loss of £120 he would suffer otherwise.

Now options markets are far more complex than this. Briefly, some extra complications are the following:

1. We have just described a *call option*, which is an option to buy at a certain price. An alternative is a *put option*, which is an option to sell at a specified price. Clearly, the buyer purchasing a put option hopes the market will fall by the time of the expiry of the contract.
2. Also, we have described a contract where the option can be exercised only on the expiry date. This is the simplest type of option, and is called a *European option*. An alternative is an *American option*, which offers the opportunity to buy at any time up to the expiry date. These days, options traded on the London market are all of the American type.
3. A *traded option* is one that can be bought and sold. Thus between the contract date and the expiry date the purchaser of the option can sell it to a third party should he or she wish. Traded options (unlike traditional options, which can be created at any time) are set on a rota system. Traded options have nine-month lives and are created every three months. Here, for instance, is an extract from the *Financial Times* of Wednesday, 15 August 1990:

Option		Calls			Puts		
		Oct.	Jan.	Apr.	Oct.	Jan.	Apr.
GKN	330	32	45	52	7	11	16
(357)	360	13	27	35	21	25	28
	390	5	15	20	46	47	50

The 357 means the underlying share price is quoted at 357p. An investor could buy for 32p the right to buy GKN shares before some time in October at a price of 330p. Were he to do so now he would have paid 362p (i.e. 32p + 330p), would receive 357p, and would therefore lose 5p per share. He would, therefore, only gain if the price went above 362p before the expiry date (sometime during the next two months or so), and he chose then to exercise the option.

You will see that the option price for calls drops as the exercise price goes up. This is, of course, because there is a smaller chance that GKN will rise to a higher price, and hence a smaller chance that an investor could profit from the contract. As a result, the price is lower. Similarly, the price goes up as the period goes up (stretching into January and April 1991) because, the longer the period, the greater the chance that fluctuations will mean the price goes up beyond the exercise price quoted.

Having given some detail, it is as well to explain what options can be used for. Clearly, they may be nothing more than speculative transactions. Speculators can attempt to outguess the market (but see Chapter 3 on market efficiency) and to profit if they are right. Yet there are other, more 'respectable' uses. Far from being only risk-lovers' instruments, they can be ways of hedging against risk.

Suppose, for instance, that a pension fund holds a block of shares. Naturally there is a risk that they will go down in price. Now suppose the fund writes a call option on the same shares *as well*.

1. Suppose the shares do increase in price. Fine — the profit will be the price increase less the loss on the option, which will, of course, be exercised by the buyer. The profit will be reduced, in other words.
2. Now suppose the shares go down. Fine, too, because the loss incurred is reduced by the offsetting receipt of the option fee, which is now worthless to the buyer. The loss is reduced as well.

Thus by using offsetting options, risks of excessive price fluctuations can be reduced.

It can be seen, then, that options can be useful to the financial manager who wishes to reduce the risk on transactions in the future, or more generally the holding of financial assets that are likely to fluctuate in price. This is even more clear in the case of financial futures, which are broader in use than options, the latter being limited to corporate securities. We look at them next.

(d) Futures

Options can be traded not only on the Stock Exchange, but also on the London International Financial Futures Exchange (LIFFE), which opened for business in 1982. It has traded in options since 1985. However, as its name suggests, LIFFE was set up to deal in futures. Like options, they are contracts based on beliefs that prices will rise or fall. Unlike options, futures contracts *oblige* the contractor to buy or sell the security. They are defined by LIFFE itself like this:

> A financial futures contract is an agreement to buy or sell a standard quantity of a specific instrument at a future date and at a price agreed between the parties through open outcry on the floor of an organized exchange. (LIFFE, n.d.)

Let us take this apart, and see what the bits mean:

'a standard quantity' LIFFE deals in various different instruments. Each instrument has its own standard quantity — such as £1 million.

'a specific financial instrument' Examples of the instruments LIFFE trades in include time deposits, gilts and foreign currencies.

'open outcry' This is a system whereby deals are agreed by the members of the Exchange meeting together in a flurry of noisy activity, making individual deals at a rapid rate. The advantage of what has all the appearance of a well-attired riot is that all prices are instantly available to all involved.

Further, the obligations of the buyer and seller are not to each other but to the clearing house. Once the deal has been made the house intervenes, and the seller sells to the house, the buyer buys from it. This is intended to ensure that all transactions are honoured.

Like options, futures can be used as a means of speculating (by, for instance, buying a currency forward, hoping its spot price — that is, the price for immediate delivery at that time — will have increased by the end of the period; when the time comes to buy the currency, it can be simultaneously sold at the higher spot price, thus generating a profit). Like options too, they can also be used to hedge against risk.

As an example, suppose Mr Masterson were the risk-averse financial manager of an industrial company. In six months' time his company will need to borrow £5 million in the bonds market. If prices on the market fall (that is, interest rates for such bonds rise), by the time he comes to make the issue, his company will be worse off. He needs, therefore, a financial instrument that will enable him to *hedge* against the risk of such an adverse movement in interest rates. He can use a futures contract for this purpose. He sells financial futures short for the issue date. Now if his fears are realized, and rising interest rates have caused securities to fall, he can, on the maturity date, buy the securities cheaply so as to deliver them as promised in the short contract. The profit he makes will offset the loss when issuing the bonds at a lower price.

Take a second example. Mr Masterson is due to pay $500,000 for a consignment of goods ordered from the USA in three months' time. The payment is denominated in dollars, so that if the dollar rises against sterling in those three months he will need to find more sterling to pay the contract price fixed in dollars. To offset this risk he can buy a financial future contract for the $500,000. Then, whatever the dollar rate in three months' time, the cost to Mr Masterson's company is already assured.

You can get an idea of what is traded on LIFFE from the daily *Financial Times* listing of prices. The futures market is not for the faint-hearted, and deals are made in large sums. The standard contract size varies depending on the security traded: for three-month eurodollars it is $1 million, for 20-year gilts it is £50,000. There are now a variety of contracts available, from the easy-to-understand FT-SE index contract (where the trader is effectively betting on the future level of the 'Footsie' index) to the complex — such as the US Treasury Bond Futures Option, where an option is traded on the right to buy or sell a futures contract in US government stock. Since this last sentence is likely to make the reader's eyes glaze over, we shall pass on with relief to commercial paper.

(e) Commercial paper

We now turn to the last of the five instruments we set out to look at. To introduce commercial paper, let us remind ourselves of the nature of a bond. It is a long-term instrument, for which the issuing company receives cash in return for the promise to pay interest for a specified period, at the end of which it will repay the principal.

If the company wants long-term money this is fine. But until recently, if the company needed short-term money it borrowed it from its bank (or delayed paying creditors, or both). There was no equivalent to the bond for short-term money apart from the bill of exchange, which had other limitations. To issue such an instrument would have been illegal under UK banking legislation.

However, commercial paper — which is in essence a promissory note redeemable after a short period — has been popular in the USA and other countries for many years. Thus UK companies started to use the US market to issue commercial paper in the 1980s, and it was estimated that by the beginning of 1986 UK companies had $23 billion outstanding in the American market.

Similarly, UK companies started borrowing short term in the euromarkets. At first this was through a note issuance facility (NIF). Under this, paper was issued in eurocurrencies and underwritten by groups of banks under a revolving facility. If at any time during the agreement a note was not taken up by the market, the banks would pick it up so that the funds to the issuer were assured. However, increasingly companies began to issue the paper without the underwriting. This is generally known as eurocommercial paper, and whereas in 1985 two-thirds of such commercial paper was underwritten, the proportion dropped to a quarter in 1986.

As from March 1986, commercial paper (CP) may be issued in the UK. It is, however, a large company's instrument. Briefly, to be allowed to issue CP a company must be quoted on the International Stock Exchange, and must have net assets of at least $50 million. The paper must mature between 7 and 364 days from issue, and the minimum denomination is £500,000.

A final point must be made clear about CP. Unlike a bond, no interest is payable as such. The cost to the issuer is represented by the difference between the amount lent at issue and the amount repaid at maturity. In legal form, CP is an unsecured promissory note. Like a eurobond, it is in bearer form.

Why, we might ask, do companies' treasurers go to the trouble of issuing CP rather than relying on their bankers as before? The main reason is cost. If a company borrows from a bank, the bank in turn borrows from its depositors to fund the loan. By going directly to the market and bypassing the bank, the company 'cuts out the middleman' and can (usually) borrow more cheaply. In addition, the borrower can avoid the restrictive covenants that banks are prone to put on their loans. However, to the lender CP must be relatively free of risk, just as lending otherwise to a major joint stock bank would have been. Hence only the very largest companies issue commercial paper. Lenders on CP tend to be institutional investors such as insurance companies, corporations and pension funds (Topping, 1987).

This last paragraph raises some far larger issues than just a new debt instrument. The bypassing of banks in favour of direct market borrowing is not just a UK phenomenon, and it has been christened *disintermediation* because its effect is to cut out the intermediary in financial transactions. Another name for this is *securitization*, although this has other connotations too, of creating securities that can be traded which had never previously been traded. For instance, mortgage-backed securities are now traded in the UK. That is, institutions such as banks, building societies and insurance companies, whose assets are in the form of mortgages, sell the debts on financial instruments. Third World debt is also being sold (at a heavy discount). In other words, debts that were not tradeable as securities now are — hence, securitization.

And yet securitization is only one part of a massive set of changes to the world's securities and foreign exchange markets that are so profound that they cannot be ignored here. These changes are known as *globalization*.

2.6   Globalization

Not very many years ago, the financial markets of the world were fairly isolated from each other. It was true that a relatively small number of companies were quoted on the stock exchanges of more than one country, and there were investment institutions that spread their funds outside the boundaries of their own country. But these were relatively minor factors. The primary unit was the *country*. National barriers were major, whether because investors did not have experience outside their own countries, or because there were specific barriers (such as exchange controls) to international investment, or because those who might potentially be involved were not large enough to carry out global operations. There was, moreover, the problem of technology, for communications, though they have been good for many years now, could not have handled the large amount of transaction traffic implied by more general global integration of operations on the markets. Finally, it has to be said that national governments would have been most unhappy to have permitted very strong integration outside their borders. So long as the borders were in place, the authorities could control the activities of securities trading. The dangers of volatile markets were well known. And, moreover, there could be serious political implications if markets moved in a way inimical to the government's perception of what would be helpful (for instance, in terms of cooling down or stimulating an economy).

This has changed. It would not be too extreme to suggest that the nation has effectively disappeared as a control on the operations of financial markets internationally. The ability of financial institutions to move funds rapidly around the globe has meant that national policies must always be carried out with one eye towards the judgement of the international financial community. Nation states are no longer in control of their destinies so far as the currency and securities markets are concerned. Indeed, it would be very difficult for any country that has become involved in the new developments of international financial markets to pull out. Isolationism is not an option, since access to international capital is so important.

One result of this has been that, effectively, the global financial system is no longer under any control. Only market operations now affect the distribution of funds. A number of factors are involved in this.

(a) Stock market trading around the world is now a 24-hour activity. A

Table 2.7   Comparative size of major stock exchanges

	1989			1985		
	Tokyo	*New York*	*London*	*Tokyo*	*New York*	*London*
Market capitalization ($USbn) (A)	4,102	3,027	823	831	2,195	334
Annual turnover ($USbn) (B)	2,181	1,543	398	350	666	182
Domestic listed companies (C)	1,961	1,634	2,005	1,444	1,490	2,171
Foreign listed companies (D)	120	87	544	11	53	505
B/C	0.53	0.51	0.48	0.42	0.30	0.55
D/C+D	0.06	0.05	0.21	0.01	0.03	0.19

Sources: UK Stock Exchange Companion, 1985; Investors Chronicle, 23.3.1990.

large number of securities are traded on at least two markets. The three main markets have now settled themselves as New York, Tokyo and London. Table 2.7 gives some interesting comparisons among these three stock markets for the years 1985 and 1989. You should note, however, that the *comparative dollar figures* between the two years are not very meaningful both because of inflation and because of changes in the value of sterling and the yen against the dollar.

With this forewarning we note a number of things. First, so far as the international investor is concerned, we can say that Tokyo has now overtaken New York as the world's largest capital market. From little more than one-third of New York's size it has grown to one-third more than New York. London still trails well behind the other two. Second, whereas in 1985 London was relatively more active, as measured by the ratio of the turnover of shares to their total capital value, the three exchanges now display similar activity levels — and London is the least active of the three. Third, London is *far* more international than the other markets when the proportion of foreign companies quoted is taken as a criterion. The remarkable change to be observed here is in the absolute number of foreign companies quoted in Tokyo: it has risen from 11 to 120, much of this perhaps due to foreign government pressure on the Japanese government to open its markets to outsiders.

Although London is still recognized by most as the 'third leg' of the 24-hour trading network, Paris and Frankfurt are both increasing in activity relative to London: the Paris Bourse in particular has been undertaking heavy capital investment in its facilities, and in 1989 monthly turnover in Frankfurt on occasion overtook that in London. Although London has enjoyed a relatively unregulated time, and has gained up to now thereby, the advantage obtained from this and from its use of the English language cannot be relied on as a means of retaining its prime position in future.

We thus get the following list of factors that are internationalized:

1. Shares are bought and sold in foreign markets: for instance, Swiss investors turn to the New York market for equities.
2. There is inevitably an *arbitrage process* among these exchanges. If the prices in two markets for the same security are unequal, arbitrageurs will move in to buy and sell so as to equalize those prices.
3. There is the more general trading in the foreign exchange markets. This has now reached extraordinary proportions. It must be remembered that, without speculation of any kind, the only reason to buy and sell currency would be for real changes in ownership of real goods. In fact (although statistics differ) the former seems to be about 30 times the size of the latter — that is, for every £100 of 'genuine' foreign exchange transaction for the purposes of international trade there is £3,000 of dealing among participants in the currency markets.
4. There is the whole euromarket phenomenon, which we have looked at already. Companies raise funds in these offshore markets quite separately from domestic dealings.
5. There is international securitization. Securitization, you will recall from p. 63, is the dealing in various kinds of financial obligation as saleable securities. Very many different kinds of such securities have been developed, and the market shows no sign of flagging in its ingenuity in finding new ones.
6. There is the new phenomenon of *swaps*. We look at swaps in Chapter 8,

but mention their nature briefly now. Suppose two companies each have raised bonds, one in Swiss francs and one in US dollars. For various reasons they would like to change their obligations — the latter to have debts in francs, the former in dollars. They therefore agree to swap their obligations, and then pay the interest on each other's behalf to the investors. This is an example of a *currency swap*. There are also *interest rate swaps* where fixed rate debt is swapped for floating rate debt.

The market in swaps has reached massive proportions; the International Swaps Dealers' Association estimated swapped contracts outstanding at the end of 1988 at $300 billion (currency) and $1 trillion (interest rate).

7. Futures contracts in the foreign exchange markets. These have considerable effects, since if they are used speculatively they can affect exchange rates and hence (because of the links) interest rates in countries around the world.

8. Finally, we may mention forward rate agreements (FRAs). This market currently exists among bankers only, but this may change. When a bank issues an FRA it is guaranteeing a fixed rate of interest for a period in the future. Having done so, a secondary market in the FRA develops, and the agreement can be dealt in among finance houses. In 1985 the FRA market was estimated at $20 billion — small compared to swaps, but not negligible.

This, then, is a list of the factors involved in the international links among markets. But a further significant factor is the set of circumstances that led the markets into being increasingly volatile, a characteristic it displayed in a spectacular fashion on Monday, 19 October 1987 ('Black Monday') and again in 1989.

(c) Space does not permit a full analysis of the increasing volatility of international markets. This volatility is not, of course, just a volatility in the currency markets. It also affects interest rates, and the number and amount of new issues of government stock and (indirectly) new industrial equities and bonds. It is linked to the uncertainties of the international financial system such as government budget deficits, balance-of-payments surpluses and deficits, and domestic money supply announcements. And these, of course, are just the financial factors. Political factors such as wars, illness among statesmen and election results (or predicted election results) all affect these interlinked prices in the international markets. It is becoming increasingly difficult for central banks to stabilize and control the markets.

There are other changes that affect this volatility too. One is the problem of Third World debt to the developed countries' major banks. Uncertainty about its status, and about how that will affect the liquidity and viability of some of the world's largest financial institutions, leads to rumour and panic selling. Similarly, the recent development and demise of junk bonds in the USA has raised questions about the possibility of a domino effect in an institution that has bought junk bonds in bulk is endangered when trade hits a downturn and borrowers on the bonds are forced to default. (A *junk bond* is a bond issued by a relatively high-risk borrower. To reflect this increased risk, the coupon is much higher than that for 'first-class paper' issued by a highly secure company such as Exxon or Sears. The risk of the high interest payments combined with the already high risk of the industry concerned makes default the more likely. In general, junk bonds have been limited to the USA, but they have worldwide implications because of the central position of the major US financial institutions in the world markets.)

Summary

In this chapter we have looked at the operation of many of the securities markets that the financial manager can use.

1. The central market so far as we are concerned is the main stock market, because it is on this that the enterprise's own securities are traded. If we are concerned with the effects of our financial decisions on the enterprise, we can look to this to see how at least some experts (the traders in the markets) view our managerial decisions.

2. We have seen the two principal functions of the markets. One is to accommodate new issues by companies. This is a direct link. The other is to permit secondary trading. This, being buying and selling between parties other than the company itself, does not directly affect the enterprise, though it may do so indirectly.

3. The capital markets are layered, there now being a main market, an Unlisted Securities Market, and (though phased out) a Third Market. Some shares are also traded 'over the counter', having gone through no vetting process at all.

4. In addition we have considered some other instruments. Eurobonds and commercial paper are variations on fairly conventional securities. Eurobonds are just a special kind of bond which has extra features. Commercial paper is merely a mixture of a bank loan and a bond. Like a bank loan it is short-term debt. Like a bond it is paper that is tradeable on a secondary market.

5. Finally, we considered options and futures. Both of these are speculative, but both can be used either to increase risk or to decrease it. However, it must be remembered that both are investments just as much as equities or loans are, since they have all the characteristics of investments: they entail a current outlay in the expectation of a future gain.

6. Further coverage of some of these topics is to be found in Chapters 8–9.

Key terms and concepts

Here is a list of the key terms and concepts which have featured in this chapter. You should make sure that you understand and can define each one of them. Page references to definitions in the text appear in bold in the index.

- Value of the firm
- Gilt-edged security
- Underwriting
- Offer for sale
- Public issue
- Tender
- Placing
- Stag
- Seasoned issue
- Bull
- Bear
- Settlement day
- Account period
- Big Bang
- Broker
- Jobber
- SEAQ
- TOPIC
- TALISMAN
- Unlisted securities market
- Over-the-counter market
- Floating rate note
- Option
- Traded option
- Future
- LIFFE
- Commercial paper
- Disintermediation
- Securitization
- Globalization

Further reading

For securities more generally, look at Peasnell and Ward (1985) *British Financial Markets and Institutions,* and Rutterford (1983) *Introduction to Stock Exchange Investment.*

Lively discussions of the Big Bang can be found in Galletley and Ritchie (1986) *The Big Bang,* Kay (1986) *The Big Bang: An Investor's Guide to the Changing City,* and Plender and Wallace (1985) *The Square Mile: A Guide to the City Revolution.*

A more recent account covering the securities markets since the Big Bang is Thomas (1989) *The Securities Markets.*

For the globalization of financial markets, see Hamilton (1986) *The Financial Revolution.*

You may also find on the shelves of bookshops certain books about the securities markets that invite you to buy them so as to learn 'how to make money on the stock exchange' and similar. Courtesy (and the laws of defamation) preclude naming and commenting on these. Suffice it to say that they may well be useful to read about the nitty-gritty of share trading (for instance, they might illustrate a contract note, which texts like this one never do), but their comments on the more general ways in which the markets work are highly suspect, and ignore all the theoretical development of the past 25 years. One might say they bear the same relation to our work as astrology does to astronomy. Once you have finished this book you can return to them as comic relief.

The Workbook material to accompany this chapter begins on p. 349.

3

Market efficiency

Any board-room sitter with a taste for Wall Street lore has heard of the retort that J.P. Morgan the Elder is supposed to have made to a naive acquaintance who had ventured to ask the great man what the market was going to do. 'It will fluctuate,' replied Morgan dryly.

(John Brooks)

Learning objectives

After studying this chapter you should be able to:

- appreciate the nature of financial securities markets;
- understand the difference between chartism, fundamental analysis and efficient markets theory as ways of understanding share price valuation;
- appreciate the difference among the three forms of market efficiency (weak, semi-strong and strong);
- consider the evidence for and against market efficiency, and the problems of testing the efficient markets hypothesis.

3.1   Introduction

In Chapter 2 we made the point that a principal justification for a stock market is that it provides a way for companies to raise long-term capital and, in the case of the secondary market, it provides a meeting place for buyers and sellers of securities. Moreover, we said, it is the very existence of the secondary market that facilitates, or even makes possible, the primary market. In other words, if securities were not marketable, investors would hesitate to take up initial issues, and this in turn would kill off the primary issue of securities. Indeed, we see just this lack of liquidity in action in the case study 'The over-the-counter market in the UK' in Chapter W2.

Now let us look in more detail at the individual investor. We shall give most attention to the secondary market since that is the basis of the great bulk of market activity. Why does the individual or institution deal in that market? Pretty obviously, to make money. In general, there are two ways of making money on individual securities: first, from dividends or interest received, and second, from capital appreciation — that is, an increase in the price of security.

Of course, there are exceptions to this. If the security in question is the purchased put option, the investor gains from a reduction in price. But for securities in the market, this is a basic rule. In any case, we may see options (and for the index, futures) as just *derivative* securities. They 'ride on the back' of the shares themselves.

Now the market consists of nothing but prices for *traded goods* but unlike other traded goods, such as soya beans or tin, the securities are never 'consumed'. They have no intrinsic value (except in the case of a corporate liquidation, of course). So the benefit that is derived from them arises only from good prediction of what is going to happen to their prices next. If you guess the movement of prices well, you can make money. If you guess badly, you lose money. That is, if you reckon the price of a share you own is going to decrease, you sell it (remember, you can always buy it back again when the price has dropped). If you reckon it will increase, you buy. So, the way to gain from dealing in securities seems to lie in being able to estimate correctly the direction a price will move.

On the basis of this simple fact we have a large industry of people whose job it is to advise on the likely movement of securities. These include newspaper tipsters, analysts employed by broker-dealers, employees of financial institutions, independent chartists (we will see what chartism is below) and so on.

These advisers claim to be able to make estimates of future price movements better than the uninformed average investor, and in doing so they make a living. How do they do this? Mainly in one or both of two ways. The first is to undertake *fundamental analysis*, which means that they investigate the company involved intensively. This might mean reading the accounts and performing sophisticated analysis on them. It might mean studying industry trends. It might mean speaking to the company directly. As a result of such information they decide whether a share is 'underpriced' or 'overpriced'. If it is the former, you are advised to buy — and of course vice versa for the latter. The implication is that soon the market will realize that the security is under- or overpriced, and then it will catch up. If you, as an investor, realize this before the market as a whole, you can make a profit by buying (or selling) before everybody else catches on.

Let us put this more concretely. Suppose you do not hold ordinary shares in Bonanza Oil. They are currently quoted at £3.00. A news sheet from your broker advises that they have looked at Bonanza's financial statements and at industry prospects, and that they believe Bonanza's performance in the future is likely to be better than everybody else thinks. As a result they believe the shares are 'worth' £3.50. You are therefore advised to buy. There are two ways this might turn out to be profitable. First, others may soon undertake the same analysis (or something similar), come to the same conclusion and buy – and this will push up Bonanza's share price. You are then richer than you were. Second, Bonanza may, as predicted, perform better in the future. When those better results are announced, the price will increase and, as in the first example, you are again better off.

You should notice what is implicit in this claim. It is that there are *imperfections* in the markets. Some are better at understanding information than others. Your broker has noticed something that others have not. *The information is equally available to others.* They have just not realized as well as your adviser what the implications of the information are for Bonanza's future performance. Of course, you will be aware that there is also something called 'inside information'. This might be, for instance, information known by a company manager about a new product that will have a beneficial impact on earnings ('good news'); it might be information about 'bad news'. Indeed, newspaper tipsters may imply (though not say outright) that they have better information than others — and since information can be pretty neatly divided between publicly available information and inside information, then if they do indeed have the latter, they can give better advice than otherwise. The use of inside information for share dealing is illegal. Moreover, you might wonder why someone with such good information, and hence the ability to make a great deal of money, should reveal it to you as a reader of the newspaper.

There is a second possible method of predicting security prices, very different from fundamental analysis. This is *technical analysis* (as its practitioners like to call it) or *chartism* (as others sometimes do). This pays less attention to the intrinsic nature of the company or industry, and concentrates instead on the *previous pattern of price movements*. Analysts create charts of price changes and claim they can perceive a pattern in those changes. From these patterns, they believe the future price movements are predictable. The result is the same as that from fundamental analysis: because the information is publicly available, the chartist is gaining because of a skill greater than that of others in the market. Again there is an unspoken assumption that information in the market is not understood equally well by everybody — that the market is *not informationally efficient*. Indeed the chartist's claim is twofold. First, there are patterns in share prices. Second, some are able to understand and predict from those patterns better than others.

Like fundamental analysts, technical analysts do not claim to get their predictions right every time. They do acknowledge that there are surprises, and they can be shown to be wrong. But, from this point of view, these unexpected changes are only evidence of the fundamental irrationality of the market — an irrationality that they claim they can profit by, through their forecasting methods. Of course, faced with apparently inexplicable changes, some share-traders resort to other methods. Reuters, for example, noted the following observations by New York traders at Halloween, 1989:

> A lot of people believe that on full moons the market changes direction.

> After I've lost money I don't wear the same set of cufflinks until I find one that works. If I have a tie I lose money with, I throw it out.

> In the past five years every time Venus has formed a 120-degree angle to Uranus the stock market has risen two weeks into that date.

> I use green ink to record transactions — the colour of money. Red ink to a trader is like garlic to Dracula.

> Whenever I dine at the New York Stock Exchange Luncheon Club I always stop at a statue of a bull wrestling with a bear near the entrance and rub the bull.

Do not take this too seriously: we shall not be showing you how to read astrological charts or rub bulls. Rather, in the rest of this chapter, we propose to look at *evidence* as to how the market operates, rather than individual (and bizarre) *beliefs* about how it operates. This involves a key concept, which lies at the heart of the finance theory we shall be developing later in this book: the concept of the *efficient market*, through what is known generally as the *efficient markets hypothesis* (EMH). It is to this that we now turn.

3.2   The stock market

The stock market has one particular characteristic in common with games of chance: if you can tell what is going to happen, you can make a lot of money. Now generally, we do not believe the person who assures us that he or she has a 'system' that will break the bank at roulette. If it were true, after all, that person would not be telling us. He or she would be rich, and no doubt in a securely guarded beach-house in the Bahamas. Moreover, readers of this book will have studied probability theory to some extent, and will know what is meant by a random variable. Dice, coin tossing, well-shuffled cards, all exhibit randomness, and a characteristic of randomness is that it leaves no room for forecasting. It is perhaps curious that this person who has a system for roulette does not have one for a fair coin, or a fair die. Upon further thought, perhaps, it is understandable since the impossibility of prediction is so much more obvious with the coin or die than it is with the more complex roulette wheel.

Now those involved with the stock markets will frequently argue that market prices are not like that at all. Market prices are not random because they are the result of human actions. If good information arrives, after all (say that the balance of payments account is in surplus), then the market as a whole will move up. It will do so because of human action (those in the market presumably choose to increase the trading price because their expectations of future gains have changed). Moreover, market prices are the prices of real companies, and those companies' product markets, management action and hence profitability are clearly not random: they depend on the skill of the enterprise's directors and executives.

As we have seen, many of those who trade in the market believe that, given sufficient skill, its movement can be predicted. Some believe that there are trends, and that these trends can be forecast. Some believe that they can take an individual company and identify its future earnings better than others, thus discovering an *overvalued* or *undervalued* share. If they are right, of course, they can beat the market by, respectively, selling short or buying, because when the true earnings are revealed to the market it will adjust, and they can take their profits.

The idea of a trend is very important to the participant in the market. Look at Fig. 3.1, for instance. The market movement depicted for this share clearly shows an upward trend in the second half of the period shown, though it just fluctuated without any particularly strong movement either way in the first half. Moreover, even the untrained eye can see that it may well have hit a peak — it dropped from its highest point and, though it recovered at first, it may be on its way down now.

Now to claim that these movements can be forecast it is clear from the above discussion that one thing must not be true: market movements must not be random. If they were, then *by definition* price changes could not be forecast and hence abnormal profits could not be made. It would be exactly analogous to dice and coin tossing.

At this stage we can reveal our hand: the share price chart in Fig. 3.1 is nothing of the kind. It was generated by a wholly random process (we show how in Fig 3.2). It was not true that it mapped the movements of an actual share; *but it looks very like the chart of a share, or indeed of the market as a whole.* There are therefore some legitimate doubts as to whether or not share prices form any kind of pattern, or whether in fact they cannot be forecast in advance and are, indeed, random. If a chart such as Fig. 3.1 can be random

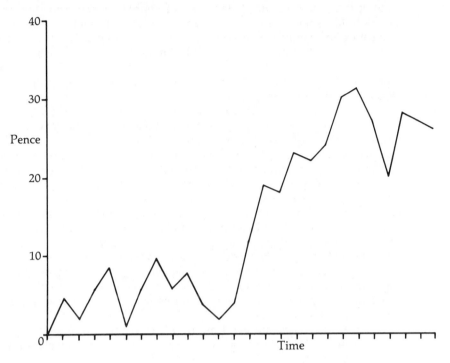

Figure 3.1   Share price fluctuation.

We mapped Fig. 3.1 by a simple combination of two random processes. To decide if the price was to go up or down, we tossed a coin — heads meant it went up, tails meant it went down. Second, we used a computer to generate random numbers between 1 and 9 (you could replicate this without a computer by using random number tables, of course). Then we put them together and plotted them. The basic data are given below, just to show how it is done. If you need to convince yourself, try the same experiment.

Coin toss	H	T	H	H	T	H	H	T	H	T	T	H	H	H	T	H	T	H	H	H	T	T	H	T	T
Movement	U	D	U	U	D	U	U	D	U	D	D	U	U	U	D	U	D	U	U	U	D	D	U	D	D
Random number	5	3	4	3	8	5	4	4	2	4	2	2	8	7	1	5	1	2	6	1	4	7	8	1	1
'Share price'	5	2	6	9	1	6	10	6	8	4	2	4	12	19	18	23	22	24	30	31	27	20	28	27	26

Figure 3.2   Formation of Figure 3.1.

yet look like the trace of a share's price movements, perhaps shares too are random in their movements.

3.3   Recap: what is a securities market?

Suppose that we imagined a world without business enterprises. What would we be left with? We should have *investors*, who had funds, and *projects* that needed funds. As we saw in Chapter 1, the business enterprise is a mechanism for bringing these two together, which it does through making use of the investors' funds (as well, of course, as the contributions of other stake-holders such as customers and employees). Each of the individuals or investing institutions is faced with a choice of an enterprise or enterprises in which to invest. Some are more risky than others. Some seem to offer better earnings prospects than others. Moreover, different investors may well harbour different *beliefs* about what those future earnings might be, and the likelihood of their being achieved.

As a result of these factors, the demand for and supply of securities give rise to the negotiation of a price for each security in the market. The market brings together the suppliers and users of funds and creates — so economic theory claims — an *equilibrium* price at any point in time that incorporates the beliefs and actions of the buyers and sellers of the securities quoted.

However, consider this price for a moment. How good a price is it? By this we mean: does it really reflect the best possible estimate of the risk and expected earnings of the enterprise it represents? In other words: is the market pricing mechanism *efficient*? Indeed, we can follow this question with a second question: does the price adjust *quickly* so as to reflect the best possible estimate of the underlying enterprise's future prospects? Given that there are many analysts looking for overpriced or underpriced shares, do they spot anomalies quickly so that mispricing is almost immediately corrected (because the person who spots the 'mispricing' then buys or sells until the price adjusts to its 'proper' level)?

Overall, these questions of the 'right' price and the quickly adjusting price are matters of the *efficiency* of the market. Let us look at the meaning of market efficiency more closely.

3.4   The notion of market efficiency

There are at least three meanings of efficiency that might be applied to an institutional structure such as a securities market. We shall dispose of two quite quickly.

(a) Input-output efficiency of the market structure

When we consider efficiency we do not mean the conventional idea of efficiency, which refers to the relationship between inputs and outputs (for further detail, see *Managerial Accounting: Method and Meaning*, section 1.4). This means that it does not refer to the efficiency of stockbrokers, for instance. They could be receiving monopoly rents (indeed, in the UK market they seem to have done so for many years) and still the market could be efficient in a different sense. As this discussion progresses, therefore, do not take any argument for efficiency to be a value judgement on the financial competitiveness of stockbrokers.

(b) Efficient allocation of resources

A second meeting, which we shall dwell on for a little longer, is the allocative efficiency of the economic market. Where a market is allocatively efficient, it is guiding economic resources to their best uses. There have been many arguments in the past that capital markets do this well. It can be argued, for instance, that the more efficient enterprises (efficient in their internal processes, that is) make higher profits *ceteris paribus*. Because those higher profits are communicated to the markets, their subsequent efforts to expand are supported by investors in the markets, since they will naturally invest in more profitable as opposed to less profitable enterprises. Hence, it is argued, markets allocate resources efficiently.

But this is by no means certain. The reasons why are summarized in Fig. 3.3. In the first place, it assumes that profits and efficiency go hand in hand. In highly competitive product and factor markets, they do. But most markets are not of this kind, and the profits may well just be the result of monopoly power.

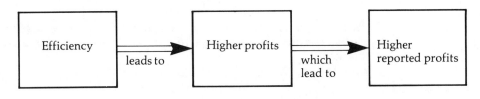

And the converse

Figure 3.3 Assumptions underlying the proposal that markets allocate societal resources efficiently.

Second, it assumes that those profits are not manipulated before they are communicated to the market. Evidence exists that they are (though, as we shall see later in this chapter, some aspects of 'manipulating' information do not so easily fool the market).

Third, it assumes that companies which used resources well in the past will continue to do so in the future. This is by no means certain (see, for example, the higgledy-piggledy growth in evidence put forward by Rayner and Little, 1966).

(c) Use of information

It is important to consider both kinds of efficiency discussed above, but the argument for market efficiency that we are now going to consider is of a third kind. It has implications for the above, especially the second, but is quite distinct from them. It operates within the normal constraints that govern capital markets, in particular the limitations of information they have. In fact, it is concerned with the way that securities markets *respond* to information.

3.5 The efficient markets hypothesis

We now turn to the central feature of this chapter: the efficient markets hypothesis (EMH). We begin by distinguishing a *perfect capital market* and an *efficient capital market*.

(a) Perfect capital markets

In a perfect capital market:

1. there are no transaction costs;
2. there are no taxes;
3. all assets are perfectly divisible and marketable;
4. there are no regulations governing the market's operation;
5. information is costless and received simultaneously by all market participants;
6. all participants are rational expected-utility-maximizers;
8. both product and security markets are perfectly competitive. In each there are many buyers and sellers, with the inability of any individual to influence price.

Source: Adapted from Copeland and Weston, 1983, p. 286.

In this kind of situation both product and securities will be fully efficient. These conditions are sufficient but not necessary for an efficient capital market.

(b) Efficient capital markets

In an efficient capital market we ask rather less: we ask only that the prices of securities in the market reflect all relevant available information. The idea that markets are efficient in this sense (which implies that no operator can consistently make abnormal profits as a result of his or her skill) has been encapsulated in the *efficient markets hypothesis*. To see how this works, we have to turn to a well-known distinction between three notions of capital market efficiency.

3.6   Three forms of market efficiency

As ideas of the efficiency of markets crystallized, it became necessary to define what information was believed to be incorporated in a share price. The three forms of the hypothesis, which suppose different *levels* of efficiency are now generally known as the *weak*, the *semi-strong* and the *strong* form of the theory. It has to be said, before we expand on these, that 'weak' does not imply criticism in any sense. It is solely a technical term.

(a) Weak-form efficiency

Go back to Fig 3.1. In this, the change from one 'price' of a share to the next was the result of a wholly random process. The implication of this is that there are no trends. Each toss of the coin, or access to a random number, is independent of the previous ones: each time it starts afresh. It could be said, therefore, that the process has no memory. This is a way in which weak-form efficiency is usually discussed: it is proposed that *the market has no memory*. The path that a security price follows is thus known as a *random walk*.

At first, this proposal caused some surprise: it was felt that randomness was at odds with the idea that the stock market is rational. There is nothing in randomness, it was said, that is consistent with rationality. On the contrary, rationality implied purposefulness.

It has now been realized that, on the contrary, full rationality on the part of the market *requires* that changes must exhibit such a random quality. To see why, we must investigate a little more closely the way the market operates and, in particular, the way it uses information to set and adjust a price.

Let us consider the price of a single security at a point in time. The price will, of course, reflect the forces of supply and demand for the security, and these in turn will be predicated on the information available to the market participants. One particular aspect of that information is information about the past history of the share prices. It may be supposed that this history is known: operators in the market have access to it. Other information too is known — about the national inflation rate, the weather, the technological development of the industry, forecasts of future profits by the chairs of this and other companies, and so on. At a point in time, the, we may suppose that *this information is impounded in the price of the share.*

Potential buyers and sellers of the share have this information available, and clearly being rational they will act on it. This means that *in the absence of any further relevant information, the price will not move.* Unless there is a change among the participants themselves (such as a change in their liquidity preference) there is nothing to change the price of the share: it will be in equilibrium given the information available.

It follows from this that the only factor which can change the pricing of the security is a change in the information available. But the very fact that this information is new means, by definition, that it was unpredictable. If you could have predicted it, then it was not new. Hence, the share price will change only with unpredictable events (new messages) and thus the price movements themselves will be unpredictable — that is, random. Thus the reason why the price has 'no memory' is that the changes are not a function of past changes, only a function of new information.

Moreover, this is wholly rational. It is rationality that leads the market to impound information about past prices into the price at a point in time. It is rationality which thus leads to equilibrium. And it is rationality which causes the price to change when new information, which could affect the earnings prospects of the share, is received. Hence *the very unpredictability of the share is evidence of market rationality.*

Now the weak form of the EMH says nothing about the way the share reacts to new information. This is not stated or tested. It is concerned solely with the pattern of share price movements, and the testing of those movements to find any possible trends. In a market that is weak-form efficient, there are no predictable trends.

(b) Semi-strong-form efficiency

The semi-strong form of the EMH incorporates the weak form. It requires, that is, that there should be no discernible trends in price changes. But it adds a further claim: *that the market quickly and without bias impounds all newly published relevant information into the share price.*

The implication of this is significant for the investor who believes it is possible to identify undervalued or overvalued shares. That such experts exist is the stuff of legend. It has been said of, for instance, J.M. Keynes and Jim Slater, that they had an ability to identify, from published information, shares whose potential had been missed by the market (though in the case of Keynes doubts have recently been voiced). Anyone who wishes to 'dabble' in the exchange and profit in it supposes that, if they are going to beat the market index, they are going to have to have these kinds of skills, and there is a general belief that, since the market index is an average, and some investors perform better than others, it follows that expertise in analysing information will result in beating the market, while the less efficient are the losers.

The semi-strong form, if true, means that this is impossible. The market receives new information and almost instantaneously incorporates it. The price adjusts quickly if it is necessary that it should adjust at all, and from that point onwards, since the change was unbiased, nobody can, on average, consistently beat the market.

It is important to note that we say 'consistently' here. Clearly, some will be lucky — in one or a few dealings they will do well. The theory states, however, that by definition this cannot continue systematically because the very process which, it is claimed, leads to high performance (namely processing information more effectively than the market to value a share) is impossible because all relevant information has already been taken into account unbiasedly by the market in settling the share price.

(c) Strong-form efficiency

This form of the EMH is much the same as the semi-strong form except that it adds a further requirement, that the market impounds not only published information into the price, but *all* information. If this form is true, then even 'insiders' — for instance, managers of a company who know of a new scientific discovery not yet officially disclosed — cannot trade in the company's shares at a profit. Recent evidence in the UK (Mr Collier) and in the USA (Mr Boersky) would — through 'casual empiricism' — tend to suggest the opposite, of course.

3.7   The evidence

These, then, are the three forms in which EMH exists. Each is testable (although, as we shall see subsequently, there are serious problems with many tests). We turn next, therefore, to the evidence for the correctness of the three forms. One matter has to be mentioned before we begin, since it pervades the tests.

We have pointed out that a perfectly efficient market would have certain characteristics, including especially a large size (so that buyers are price-takers). We have also said that the rigorous requirements of a perfect market are not essential for an efficient market. However, this matter of size is important to testers, and most tests that have been carried out have been on large markets such as the New York Stock Exchange, the American Exchange, and the London Exchange. Selecting them for tests is reasonable — their size means they are the world's most important securities markets. But some markets are not this large, and it would be wrong to suppose that all securities markets exhibit some form of efficiency just because large markets do. Tests have been carried out on smaller markets (for instance, Greece, Kuwait, Singapore) and their results are more equivocal. Moreover, even within large markets there are 'pockets' of thin trading — that is, groups of shares that do not get bought and sold so often — and these cause severe testing problems.

To begin with we shall ignore these problems as we consider the more general evidence of market efficiency.

(a) Tests for weak-form efficiency

Since weak-form efficiency is concerned only with the pattern of share prices, the statistical tests that have been used to examine its validity have naturally been tests concerned with patterns of data. After some quite straightforward tests in the early days, tests have become quite sophisticated in recent years. We shall look briefly at some simple ideas of tests that will give a flavour of the way a random walk can be identified.

Two types of test in particular are relevant and have been used. The first type is an examination of the extent of randomness of price movements directly, using either serial correlation tests or runs tests. The second type applies 'filter rules' to discover whether profits could be made through buy/sell techniques.

1. *Serial correlation.* If there are true patterns, or trends, then movements of price in one direction will tend to be followed by other movements in that same direction. If we then test to see whether there are correlations among successive changes, the presence of such correlations will indicate non-randomness: that is, be inconsistent with market efficiency. Thus if we define $x(t)$ as a movement in price, we can test its correlation with the previous movement $x(t-1)$ by regressing the equation:

$$x(t) = Rx(t-1) + e(t)$$

where $e(t)$ is the error term. If the coefficient R (representing the correlation) is significantly different from zero, then the changes do not follow a random walk.

2. *Runs test.* This is an even simpler test: it plots each change in terms of its direction, up or down. This leads to a run of changes such as U D U U U D D U D D U U U D D D U D U D D. If the random walk hypothesis is true, there will be no pattern in these changes: they themselves will be random. A standard statistical test is in fact available to test for randomness in a series of this kind.

3. In a rather different category there is the *filter test.* This checks to see whether a filter trading rule leads to profits after transaction costs. A filter rule might, for instance, be: 'If the share goes up 5% then buy; if it goes down 5% then sell.' If this rule is applied consistently to all changes in the security price and it turns out that a profit could have been made, then the market is not efficient.

The many tests that have been applied to large markets using the first two kinds of rule have led to a remarkable unanimity: the market does indeed follow a random walk. There are no trends such that profits could be made by assuming their existence. Many tests have been attempted using trading rules such as filter techniques. The potential number of such tests is, of course, infinite because so many trading rules could be dreamed up. Thus if the filter described in (3) above were tested, the tests could be applied for 5%, 6%, 7% and so on. The evidence that has been collected (see, for instance, Alexander, 1961; Dryden 1970; Jensen and Bennington, 1970) suggests that such rules may lead to small profits, but those profits are wiped out by transaction costs.

(b) Tests for semi-strong efficiency

Senator Thomas J. McIntyre, Democrat of New Hampshire and a member of the powerful Senate Banking Committee, brought his dart board in one day. Senator McIntyre had tacked the stock market page on his dart board and thrown darts at it, and the portfolio picked by his darts outperformed almost all the mutual funds. (Smith, 1986, p. 137).

If the market is semi-strong efficient, then it will react quickly and in the 'right' direction to any new information that arrives. It has already incorporated all existing information, so once new information arrives, a semi-strong efficient market will incorporate that too. If the information were not impounded quickly, abnormal profits could be made during the settling-down period and it would not be efficient. Likewise, if the reaction to the information were not accurate, an observer could react to the information more effectively and, again, beat the market by using that information.

Simon Keane (1983) makes a useful distinction between tests of the semi-strong form that are *direct* and those that are *indirect*. The former, direct tests, identify information that has the following qualities:

1. it is new — that is, it is information that the market did not have before;
2. the time of its arrival at the market can be ascertained exactly;
3. the implications of the information are relatively unambiguous. For instance, it should be clear to everybody, both those in the market and the researcher, whether it is 'good news' or 'bad news'.

The latter, indirect tests, look for other situations in which those with a better ability to understand information might outperform the market using that interpretive expertise.

(i) Direct tests
We need not consider here the very many tests that have been carried out. We look at two tests in detail, and summarize the broad conclusions that have resulted from the tests more generally.

A classic study was that by Fama *et al.* (1969). They looked at market reaction to news of 'stock splits' (known in the UK as 'bonus' or 'scrip' issues). Now in themselves stock splits have virtually no economic effect. They are a bookkeeping exercise that can make shares easier to trade by making their market value per share lower (while at the same time, of course, increasing the number of shares in exact proportion). But they are generally taken to be a *signal* that management is confident of a good performance in the future. They are, that is, 'good news'. The finding was that the market did indeed react quickly and completely to the announcement of the split so that no abnormal profits could be made by trading on the information.

A second important set of tests has considered the changes in reporting method that are used in companies' financial statements. It is generally believed that companies will try to put a gloss on their results — to change accounting policies if that makes earnings look better. Clearly this is only worthwhile if the readers of financial statements are indeed fooled. However, the change of policy will generally be noted in the accounts, albeit buried in the small print of the 'notes to the accounts'. If the market is efficient in using information, it will adjust for these cosmetic changes. Researchers who have investigated such changes have almost unanimously come to the conclusion that the market does indeed 'see through' such manipulations of earnings. Casual empiricism can sometimes lead one to doubt this. Consider, for instance, the following extract from the *Financial Times* of 26 June 1987:

Shares across the stores sector tumbled yesterday on fears of an onset of conservative accounting. The widespread decline was triggered by the Argyll Group's decision to treat the £90 million cost of reorganizing its Presto stores as an 'exceptional' item rather than an 'extraordinary' one.

The move, following the company's £681m acquisition of Safeway in January, will reduce the company's pre-tax profits and earnings per share over the next four years.

One analyst said: 'It was an immediate emotional reaction.'

(ii) Indirect tests

A classic study here is of unit trust performance. The common claim of unit trust managers has for many years been that they have an expertise in the market so that it is wise for investors to place their money with them rather than take the risk of making their own investment decisions. Now for this to be true it is necessary that they should at least be able to beat a 'buy and hold', i.e. passive, strategy. Of course, in their analysis of the markets unit trust managers buy and sell quite frequently, and this incurs transaction costs. Moreover, there are fund expenses to be met, including the managers' not inconsiderable salaries. These twin expense factors mean that the managers have to be very good to beat the market, and the evidence all points to the fact that a passive strategy will, in the long run, outperform any unit trust (the classic study here was by Jensen (1968) who tested 115 unit trusts over the period 1945–64). This academic conclusion is not, of course, one that endears research and researchers to the market. It has, however, been taken on board by some US unit trusts (called mutual funds there) which advertise their services in terms of keeping costs to a minimum and minimizing trading, rather than claiming to be able to beat the market. Clearly they are assuming a sophistication on the part of their clients, supposing that they accept the evidence for market efficiency.

(c) Tests for strong-form efficiency

It would be asking a great deal of a market for it to be strong-form efficient. The strong form it will be recalled, requires that *all* information, whether publicly available or not, should be incorporated in the share price. Hence 'insiders' who are privy to as yet undisclosed corporate information can nevertheless not profit from their knowledge. This is very hard to swallow. After all, suppose that a chairman and managing director receive information from a geologist that their mining operations have uncovered unexpected reserves of a precious metal. The only people who know are the mining engineer, and these two top managers. According to the strong form of the EMH, they could not use the information to make profits before the official announcement: the market would have incorporated the information already. Since nobody knew about it, this is a remarkable requirement, and not surprisingly the sparse evidence suggests that insiders can trade profitably. The market is not strong-form efficient.

3.8 Counter-evidence and testing problems

Not all evidence now supports the EMH. A mass of early evidence all tended to corroborate it: it became what Galbraith has called 'the conventional wisdom'. It was argued to be the most confirmed building block of modern finance theory. To change the metaphor, it became the keystone upon which much of the rest of the theorizing we meet later in this book depends. For some years, there were a small number of dissenting voices, and a small number of studies that seemed to present evidence against aspects of market efficiency. Few were published, on the grounds perhaps that, since we knew EMH was true, there must be something wrong with the empirical method used in the studies. The voices continued with their disquiet; and their evidence became accepted and labelled as 'anomalies'. The theory was basically sound, it was said; there were just these oddities of evidence that currently could not be explained. The highly respected *Journal of Financial Economics* eventually, in 1978, devoted a whole issue to these 'anomalies'. From then, interest grew.

The evidence against market efficiency includes the following.

(a) The low p/e–small-firm-effect

This was begun with an article by Basu (1977). After adjusting for beta (we shall explain the meaning of 'beta' in Chapter 7), he gathered shares into high P/E to low P/E groups, using the calendar year, the end-of-year share price and the year's earnings. He then assumed that investors had that information by the following 1 April and calculated the annual returns on the portfolios he had constructed, getting the following results:

Portfolio	Excess return	
1	−3.3%	High P/E
2	−2.8%	
3	+0.2%	
4	+2.3%	
5	+4.7%	Low P/E

Now of course a low P/E ratio is a sign that the market has high expectations of the share's subsequent growth in earnings. The evidence seemed to suggest that investors could consistently receive excess returns by investing in low P/E shares. Subsequent work by Reinganum (1981) and by Banz (1981) have suggested that such results do exist, but that they result not from particular P/E ratios but, rather, from size. Small organizations peformed better than could be explained by their beta.

(b) The January/Monday effect

We looked earlier at the notion of a 'filter rule'. More generally, you can consider *any* rule, if it turns out to be valid, to be counter to the EMH. A consistent rule means that profits that are consistently greater than average can be made by following that rule. Market theorists refer to greater-than-expected profits as 'abnormal returns'. A return is the profit from holding a security during a period: that is,

$$r_t = \frac{D_t + (P_t - P_{t-1})}{P_{t-1}}$$

where r_t is the return on holding a security between time $t-1$ and time t; D_t is any dividend that might be paid during that period; and P_t is the price of the security at time t. Abnormal returns should not happen consistently, according

Efficient-Market Theorists are Puzzled by recent Gyrations in the Stock Market
Barbara Donnelly

What does efficient-market theory have to say about the stock market's recent gyrations, especially Monday's crash?

'We're all totally perplexed,' concedes William Sharpe, Timken professor of finance at Stanford University.

In simple terms, efficient-market theory holds that investors act rationally and that prices react only to unanticipated events; thus, all publicly available information is worthless because it already has been discounted in current prices.

But so far, efficient-market theorists haven't been able to identify anything that would account for the market's convulsion — other than the convulsion itself.

'It's conceivable that a change in the well-informed forecast of future economic events moved the market as it did; you can't prove it one way or the other,' ventures Prof. Sharpe. 'On the other hand, its pretty weird.'

Costly Volatility

One factor might have been the increased volatility of the market in the days leading up to Monday's collapse, says Fischer Black, a partner at Goldman, Sachs and Co. and co-author of the standard option-pricing model that is a foundation of the widely used hedging strategy known as portfolio insurance.

In this view, rising expectations about volatility would depress prices as investors found it worthwhile to take on that added uncertainty only if prices were discounted to compensate for the added risk.

Estimates of the volatility — measured in terms of the standard deviation of prices observed in the market — have risen from 16% a few months ago to an average of 20% last week. 'On Mondays, of course, it was much higher — exceeding 100% with no trouble at all,' adds Mr Black. His prediction for the next three months is 38%.

Indeed, Mr Black says, 'the only insight that market theory offers at this point is that stock prices are going to be more volatile than they have been.' But, he adds, 'we don't know in what direction.'

The theorists are also puzzled that they can't find anything to explain why the market had remained so out of line with other assets, such as bonds, for so long before the crash. 'There was no rational case for things being so far up there, only romantic reasons — things like new buyers such as the Japanese coming in because they saw value there,' says Peter Bernstein, an efficient-market theorist and president of a pension-consulting firm bearing his name.

Moreover, when things began to fall apart, there was a persistent pricing discrepancy of 10% to 20% between stock index futures contracts and the underlying stocks that started Monday and has persisted on and off since. 'That shouldn't have existed,' says Mr Black.

At least some efficient-market proponents insist that the discrepancy can be explained partly by chaotic trading conditions and the restrictions imposed starting Tuesday on futures trading and program trading — a strategy of trading on price differences between futures and stocks. 'Efficiency is affected by the cost of transactions, and the big overload in the system meant those costs became very high — not just the real cost of execution but in terms of uncertainty,' says Merton Miller, a professor of finance at the University of Chicago School of Business. This hasn't provided 'a fair test', he says.

Clear Gap

Maybe, but for efficient-market critics such as Lawrence Summers, a professor of economics at Harvard University, that's a little like saying the efficient-market theory didn't hold because the market in reality wasn't efficient. The fact that the discrepancy existed for days 'is a clear gap with the theory', he says. For years, 'every finance professor in America has taught that can't happen.'

All the puzzlement in the ranks of the efficient-market theorists is being watched with glee by Prof. Summers and other 'investment behaviourists', who maintain that things such as greed, fear and panic play a much bigger role in determining stock prices than accepted market theory admits. Robert Shiller, an investment behaviorist and a professor of economics at Yale University, says: 'The efficient-market hypothesis is the most remarkable error in the history of economic theory. This is just another nail in its coffin.'

Prof. Summers adds, 'If anyone did seriously believe that price movements are determined by changes in information about economic fundamentals, they've got to be disabused of that notion by Monday's 500-point movement.'

Figure 3.4
Source: The Wall Street Journal *23 October 1987.* Reprinted by permission of the *Wall Street Journal,* © 1987 Dow Jones & Company, Inc. All rights reserved worldwide.

to the theory. That is, there should be no trading rule that gives consistent abnormal returns.

Yet one apparently consistent pattern that would enable abnormal profits to be made is the January effect. Research on past monthly prices suggests that returns in January are greater than in other months. This would enable traders to profit by knowing the rule, of course — and should be arbitraged out, through buying in anticipation of the rule operating, *which stops the rule operating.* The evidence is not wholly accepted: compare Rozeff and Kinney (1976) with Ritter and Chopra (1989).

There also seems to be a day-of-the week effect. Suppose you looked at the daily returns of a security. You should find no pattern: the average return on Monday should be the same as that for Tuesday, Wednesday and so on. This does not seem to be true for Monday. The average return on Monday appears to be significantly lower than for other days. This has led to what is known as the 'weekend' or 'Monday' effect (see French, 1980).

Other evidence against EMH includes that concerning earnings forecasts issued by US brokers. This suggests that they have information content, and that the effect on market prices is sufficiently slow for investors to profit from trading early on their content (Givoly and Lakonishok, 1979).

Finally, we refer you to Fig. 3.4. This reading concerns the stock market crash in October 1987, discussed in Chapter 2. Was that crash consistent with market efficiency? In particular, if prices move only in response to new information, what was the new information that caused such a major price upheaval throughout the markets throughout the world? There appears to be no easy answer, though you will notice that some theorists are more concerned than others.

However, all the above evidence has to be taken with as much caution as evidence supporting the EMH. This is because of the severe testing problems concerned. In the particular case of (a) above, it has been suggested that the shares of small enterprises are less marketable than large ones (that is, their market price is more likely to be affected by block trading because there are fewer securities in the market). This lack of marketability would depress the price of small companies' shares more than large ones, and hence account for the anomaly.

More generally, there is the problem arising from the Roll critique that we shall discuss in our look at testing the CAPM in Chapter 7. Tests for market efficiency adjust for risk. The accepted risk measure is beta, and this relies upon a true measurement of the market portfolio (since beta is defined as the relationship of a share to the market portfolio). But the market portfolio cannot be measured since it must consist of all possible risky securities (including Krugerrands, paintings, stamps, real property and so on). Thus if the adjustment is ungrounded, so are all tests that use it.

However, the critique itself has been subjected to criticism, and not only is it now generally accepted that it does not apply to the 'direct tests' we looked at, but moreover it may not be really significant for indirect tests either, since such tests seem to be insensitive to different proxy market portfolios (Peterson and Rice, 1980).

3.9   The EMH and accounting

Whether the stock market really is efficient also has other implications. One area affected by this question is the area of accounting. There seem to be three implications:

1. You can find the value of any accounting information by measuring its impact on share prices. If the impact is significant, this suggests that the market is receiving information that it judges to have real economic value.
2. The EMH gives a benchmark against which you can judge different accounting alternatives. If method A has more impact than method B, it should be chosen because it has more information content.
3. Possibly this means that the accounting methods to be used are those that keep long-run variability to a minimum — because that is the nearest to some kind of 'intrinsic value' (if such a thing exists).

3.10   Conclusions

Some simple conclusions from the above seem to be as follows:

1. Large markets are weak-form efficient. So are many smaller markets.
2. Large markets are probably, in general terms, semi-strong efficient. This means that there are doubts as to unit trust managers' normal policy in the UK. It also means that accountants cannot fool the market by changing accounting policies. Smaller markets do not seem efficient in this way.
3. Markets are not strong-form efficient.

The implication for the financial manager is that the market can, in general terms, be relied upon to recognize good financial decisions (for instance, the development of projects with positive NPVs).

Summary

1. There is a folk-belief that abnormal profits can be made on the stock exchange. This requires that the exchange be inefficient, because if it were efficient, all such opportunities would have evaporated through the market pricing mechanism.

2. There are various people employed to try to beat the market, in particular chartists and fundamental analysts. If markets are indeed efficient, they cannot achieve what they claim; indeed, it is they who make the market efficient through constant watchfulness.

3. Market efficiency does not mean the market is efficient at allocating resources through the economy, or good at forecasting what will happen in the future.

4. Market efficiency exists in three forms. The weak form, which just says that price movements are random, seems almost certainly true for all large markets. In the main there is also strong evidence for the validity of the semi-strong form — although it is concerned with speed of reaction rather than with 'appropriate' reaction. The latter cannot be tested because there is no exogenous concept of what might constitute 'appropriate'. Strong-form efficiency does not exist.

5. The EMH has marked implications for financial reporting and accounting standard setting, so long as market pricing is seen as the most important criterion for financial reports. This does not seem to be acknowledged by the Accounting Standards Committee.

Key terms and concepts

Here is a list of the key terms and concepts which have featured in this chapter. You should make sure that you understand and can define each one of them. Page references to definitions in the text appear in bold in the index.

- Overvalued share
- Undervalued share
- Chartist
- Efficient markets hypothesis
- Weak form
- Semi-strong form
- Strong form
- Random walk
- Filter test
- Abnormal returns

Further reading

A short, excellent and most readable book is Keane (1983). You may also wish to take a sceptical look at some popular work such as Stewart (1987). The classic by Ball and Brown (1968) still makes interesting reading.

The Workbook material to accompany this chapter begins on p. 371.

2

Investment

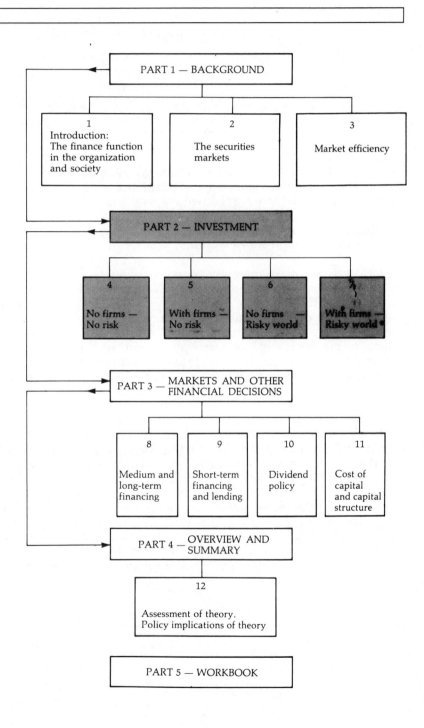

Part 2 has four chapters. These are structured around two central notions in financial management. The first is the firm; the second is risk.

You can see how these relate to the book as a whole in the diagram on p. 87. However, there is a clearer way to depict the way the four chapters are linked. Look at the diagram below.

	Without business firms	With business firms
Without risk	Chapter 4: A risk-free model for investment	Chapter 5: Enter the enterprise: the risk-free model
With risk	Chapter 6: Portfolio theory	Chapter 7: The capital asset pricing model

In Chapter 4 we make two unrealistic assumptions. (Perhaps you are unhappy at assuming unrealistic worlds. We sympathize. However, as long as we end up with the more realistic world of Chapter 7, we hope this does not trouble you too much.) The two assumptions are:

1. that there are no business enterprises in society;
2. that we live in a risk-free world.

Of course we make these assumptions merely to ease the exposition. By Chapter 7 the theory will be getting a bit complex. It is easier to omit the complexities to start with. Now to say 'we assume no firms' would be unnecessarily drastic, so although nothing that is dealt with in Chapter 4 *requires* the existence of business firms, it would be foolish to omit reference to them where necessary (for instance, to add authenticity to examples or illustrations). So we are not slavish to the assumption.

In Chapter 5 we stay with the risk-free world and consider the realities of business enterprise. Much of what is said in that chapter may be true of public enterprise too; however, the principles can be seen at their clearest in the profit-making business.

In Chapter 6 we relax the assumption that there is no risk. This means that the model we develop in Chapter 6 (the Markowitz portfolio model) should hold true of any institution, whether individual investor or enterprise. This is not to say, in reality, that there might be good reasons outside the model for pulling back from this a bit later. Nevertheless, the essential point is the *universality* of the model (given the assumptions we set out, of course).

Finally, in Chapter 7, we get the closest we can to reality, where investors invest in risky companies, in the expectation that they will — in the long run and on average — achieve a better return on their invested funds than placing them in safe assets such as government bonds or bank deposits.

4 A risk-free model for investment

Learning objectives

After studying this chapter you should be able to:

- discuss the notion of time preference and why future benefits should be discounted for assessment at the present time;
- understand various compound interest expressions, including the present value and amount of individual sums and series of sums, both even and uneven, and know how these relate to an underlying exponential growth pattern;
- appreciate how one can find the net present value (NPV) and internal rate of return (IRR) of future series of receipts and payments;
- define the relationship between NPV and IRR.

4.1 Introduction

As explained in the overview to Part 2, this chapter is based on an unreal world in which there is no risk. We shall introduce risk in Chapter 6.

Now although it is traditional, for the sake of exposition, to suppose there is no risk (it makes understanding the ideas involved much easier for you), there is a problem that must be faced. By claiming that there is no risk, we mean that where we invest a single sum (for instance £100 today), in order to receive a stream of benefits in the future, all those future benefits are certain to arrive. This is problematic because the purpose of the analysis is basically to enable us to distinguish among projects (some offering preferable future cash flows to others). If the world were to entail no risk, this must mean that all future cash flows would be known with certainty. Were this to be so, then so far as solely financial criteria are concerned, no investment opportunity could be any better or worse than any other.

Suppose, for instance, that the prevailing rate of interest were 12%. Now suppose an investor wished to invest in a new machine. The price of the machine would be fixed in the market. Since the future cash flows that the machine could generate would be certain, both buyers and sellers of such machines would be aware of these returns. Buyers would be prepared to pay a price up to that which would bring the returns down to 12%. At any higher price they would not buy, since other opportunities would be available to them giving this return. Sellers similarly would not price the machines any lower, since buyers would be willing to pay that price which led to a 12% return.

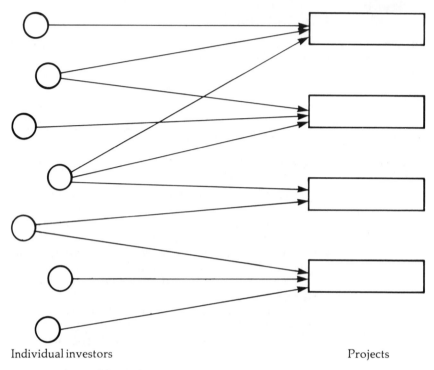

Figure 4.1   Flows of funds from investors and projects.

Thus any asset in a world of risk-free markets would, as a result of the market forces acting on the asset price, generate neither more nor less than the prevailing interest rate. Hence there would be no investment decision problems whatever because all assets would be equally desirable as uses of the investor's funds.

There is no 'correct' solution to this problem. Since a risk-free world is unreal in any case, and involves a suspension of belief for a while, a similar suspension of belief must be asked for concerning the problem we have just discussed.

There is one more element in the exposition here that is unreal, and again helps our understanding of what is taking place. We shall assume that there are no companies in the world we are concerned with. There are, instead, a large number of individuals, each of whom would like to invest in one or more of a large number of investment opportunities. These opportunities could be of various kinds: extraction, manufacturing, service, for instance. They are projected courses of action that will result in productive activity, and hence positive cash flows will arise in the future. It is being assumed that there are no companies so as not to obscure the fact that, in the economy, there are *investors* and *projects* (see Fig. 4.1) and, whatever the complications that arise later as a result of the institutional structures that inevitably constitute the real world (because they are more efficient for wealth creation), they only exist to enhance the relationship between providers of funds and the projects that use those funds. Of course, we have already seen how firms fit into Fig. 4.1 — this was shown in Fig. 1.3.

Having defined our problem as one of selecting projects that are desirable, we must now consider what we mean by 'desirable'. We assess utility in terms of wealth, and hence we suppose that a project is desirable if it leads to an increase in a person's wealth. Now wealth is best measured at a single point in time. This enables comparisons to be made. We can say that A is wealthier than B as at today's date, for instance. More importantly, we can say that if A receives £X rather than £(X — Y) today (where X and Y are positive sums of money), then A would prefer it. It is not easy to compare cash flows that arise at different times. So, for instance, we could not, in the absence of further information, be sure whether A would prefer £(X — Y) now or £X next year.

Thus the problem is one of selecting projects in which to invest now that yield inflows of cash in the future; and to measure how much they enhance current wealth we have to restate those future cash flows in terms of a single sum today. This is done by *discounting* them, so that a series of net inflows of cash in the future (by net inflows we mean the difference between cash inflows and cash outflows) is restated to be exactly equivalent to a single inflow at the present time. This can then be compared with the outlay that has to be invested in the project to see if the present value of the future cash flows is greater than the outlay.

4.2   Time preference

In general it can be said that a sum of money received now is preferred to that same sum receivable at a future time. The reason for this is neither inflation nor risk. *Time preference* must not be confused with inflation for, although it is true that in most Western countries the value of money has consistently declined over time, this is a separate issue. Even if there were no inflation, present consumption would be preferred to future consumption. The same is true of risk: present consumption is preferable to that in the future, even if the future consumption is absolutely certain.

This can be explained through the concept of *opportunity cost*. If a sum is received immediately, it can be invested in one or more projects (or lent to somebody else who will invest in a project) and yield a return. A loan, for instance, will yield interest. The deferral of the receipt to a future time means that the opportunity to invest is now lost, and the difference between present and future receipt can thus be understood as the opportunity cost of the investment opportunity forgone. (A simple example to illustrate this is given in Figure 4.2). It can also be understood in a non-market context. Waiting for

---

Pam Gaunt is going to receive £100 promised to her in her uncle's will. Today is her seventeenth birthday; the sum will be paid to her when she is eighteen. Had she received the £100 now, she would be able to invest it in a building society account at 8%.

Had she received the bequest now, she would have £108 by the end of the year. Thus the opportunity cost of having to wait a year is the interest she would have otherwise had — in this case £8. This is true even when there is no inflation.

Figure 4.2   Simple example of opportunity cost.

something before you can consume it involves a sacrifice — just consider, for instance, the child who 'cannot wait' to receive a Christmas present. (There is further discussion of opportunity cost in *Managerial Accounting: Method and Meaning*, Chapter 4.)

Because future inflows of cash are less desirable than present ones, they must be *discounted* at some rate of interest so as to become equal to similarly desirable sums receivable immediately. In the case of the individual, that rate of interest will depend on his or her own particular time preference. For instance (to take the example of the child just given), some people are more able to wait for their Christmas presents with equanimity than others. For them, the rate of interest, representing their sacrifice in waiting, will be lower.

(a) The calculation of present value

We calculate the present value of future receipts using the mechanisms of compound interest. To begin with, suppose Mr Smith had £100 now (which we can call t_0) and wishes to know its worth at 10% after one year (that is, at time t_1). Clearly, it will be £110. Symbolically, this can be expressed as £100 (1.10), or more generally for a sum of money P (the principal) and an interest rate i, as $£P(1 + i)$. Notice that i is expressed as a decimal, so that 10% becomes 0.1.

Thus P grows to $P(1 + i)$ after one year. This can be expressed another way, namely that P is the present value of $P(1 + i)$. To find the present value of a sum receivable in the future, all we have to do is to divide each of the two expressions (the present and future amounts) by $(1 + i)$. Then we find that the present value of a sum of money P receivable or payable in one year's time is:

$$\frac{P}{(1 + i)}$$

This is also illustrated diagrammatically in Fig. 4.3. Taking a further simple example, the present value equivalent of £100 receivable in one year's time at a rate of interest of 10% is $100/1.1 = £90.91$ (to the nearer penny).

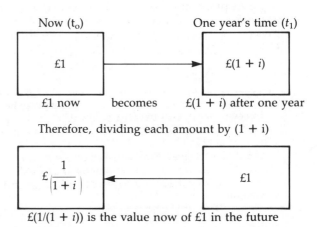

Figure 4.3 How present value works.

Now discounting generally involves the use of $1/(1 + i)$ and its derivatives a great deal, so symbols have been developed to simplify these expressions. In this case we *define*:

$$v = \frac{1}{(1 + i)}$$

so that, for instance, we would write $£100v = £90.91$.

It is quite straightforward to extend this principle beyond one year. Since an amount of 1 will grow to an amount of $(1 + i)$ after one year, then after the second year the amount of $(1 + i)$ will similarly have accumulated interest, and hence it will have grown to $(1 + i)(1 + i)$: that is, $(1 + i)^2$. For example, a principle of £100 will have grown to $£100(1.1)^2 = £121$ if the ruling interest rate is 10%. Eventually, therefore, we have increasing values of an invested sum as it remains in a position of accumulating interest:

After 1 year £100 grows to $£100(1.10)^1 = £110.00$
After 2 years £100 grows to $£100(1.10)^2 = £121.00$
After 3 years £100 grows to $£100(1.10)^3 = £133.10$
After 4 years £100 grows to $£100(1.10)^4 = £146.41$
After 5 years £100 grows to $£100(1.10)^5 = £161.05$

and so on.

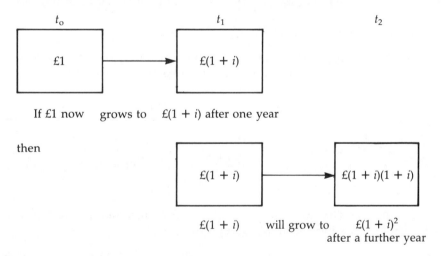

Figure 4.4   Accumulating beyond one year.

By the same principle, the present value of £100 receivable in two years' time, assuming the same rate of interest prevails will be $£100v^2_{10\%} = £82.64$. This is illustrated diagrammatically in Fig. 4.4. So, we can write that:

The value now of £100 due in 1 year's time is $100/((1.10))^1 = £90.91$
The value now of £100 due in 2 years' time is $100/((1.10))^2 = £82.64$
The value now of £100 due in 3 years' time is $100/((1.10))^3 = £75.13$

The value now of £100 due in 4 years' time is $100/((1.10))^4 = $ £68.30
The value now of £100 due in 5 years' time is $100/((1.10))^5 = $ £62.09

The general principle, therefore, is that the present value of an amount P receivable in n years' time, where the prevailing interest rate is i, is:

$$PV^n{}_{i\%}$$

(b) The present value of a series of receipts

If an investor places his or her funds in a fixed-interest-bearing security such as a government bond or a company's debenture, a regular flow of equal amounts will be received. To find the present value of these we could, of course, apply the factor v^n to each, but for a 20-year bond this would mean 20 separate calculations plus the addition of them all together to find their total value. This would be very time consuming, but it is unnecessary, since an expression can easily be produced that gives the present value of a series of equal receipts. The method is the well-known one for finding the total of an arithmetic series. This is how we do it.

Suppose we wish to find the present value of a series of amounts of £1, receivable annually in arrears (that is, at the end of each period), where the interest rate is i and the series is n periods long. This series is called an *annuity*, and there is another special symbol available to describe this series: $a_{\overline{n}|}$, where the a denotes 'annuity' and the symbol $\overline{}|$ indicates 'years'. (Strictly, in actuarial terms, this symbol refers to 'periods' more generally rather than years specifically. Since, however, we shall in general avoid compounding periods other than one year, it may be taken as the equivalent of one year. The symbol is only used in expressions denoting a series of payments.)

This means that:

$$a_{\overline{n}|} = v + v^2 + v^3 + \ldots + v^n$$

We can evaluate this expression simply by multiplying throughout by $(1 + i)$, and deducting the original expression, like this:

$$
\begin{aligned}
(a_{\overline{n}|})\,(1 + i) \quad &= 1 + v + v^2 + v^3 + \ldots + v^{n-1} \\
\text{less} \quad a_{\overline{n}|} \quad &= v + v^2 + v^3 + \ldots + v^{n-1} + v^n \\
\hline
a_{\overline{n}|}\,(1 + i - 1) = 1 \quad & \phantom{= 1 + v + v^2 + v^3 + \ldots + v^{n-1}} - v^n
\end{aligned}
$$

so that:

$$a_{\overline{n}|} = \frac{1 - v^n}{i}$$

The implications of this simple formula are best understood through the simple example given in Fig. 4.5

Suppose that Mr Smith were to purchase the right to receive interest payments of £500 at the end of each year for the next twenty years. At an interest rate of 15%, what is the present value of this stream of future receipts?

Now in this case v^n is $1/(1.15^{20})$, that is 0.0611. So $a_{\overline{n}|}$ will be $(1 - 0.0611)/0.15 = 6.259$. Thus the present value of a stream of £500 per annum will be $[500 \times 6.259] = $ £3,130.

Figure 4.5 Simple example of present value.

A simpler explanation of the derivation of $a_{\overline{n}|}$ is given in the Workbook (in sub-section W4.2(b)). We give this method here because it can be developed for different patterns of cash flows (also illustrated below and extended in the Workbook in the worked examples to sub-section W4.2(b)).

In fact there is usually no need to turn to this formula, since discount tables are available that have such values computed for a range of interest rates and terms. A number of tables are given at the end of this book (see pp. 614–21). We have supplied tables for $(1 + i)^n$, v^n, $a_{\overline{n}|}$ and $S_{\overline{n}|}$ (we explain the last of these later in this chapter).

Let us see how to use the tables. Turn to Table III($a_{\overline{n}|}$) on p. 618. You will see that interest rates are listed along the tops of the columns, number of years down the rows. Let us think about the example of Mr Smith that we just worked out in Fig. 4.5. The rate of interest was 15%, and the term of his right to receive interest was 20 years. Run your finger down the 15% column until you meet the 20 years row. You will find the value of 6.2593, which is the factor for $a_{\overline{n}|}$ that we calculated in the example. As long as the value you want is within the range of the table, using the table is quicker and easier than calculating the value. Occasionally you may want a value outside the table's range. Then you will have to use the expression we derived, or go to a specialist set of tables published for the purpose (such as Lawson and Windle, 1965).

If the tables can be used so easily, why have we troubled to explain the formula and derivation in such detail? Because the method can be used to complete more complex expressions where necessary. Let us see how.

Remember, we are concerned with the present value of receipts from an investment. Now if the stream of these receipts is very uneven, individual present value calculations need to be made. For instance, if the receipts expected over the next five years were to be £5,000, £8,000, £10,000, £2,000 £1,000, then five present value calculations would be necessary. If it is even, we can use the expression for an annuity that we have just developed. But two other possibilities sometimes turn up and we should look at them for the sake of completeness. One is an annuity that is delayed for some reason. The other is a regularly increasing or decreasing series of amounts.

The latter would be pretty unusual in practice. Yet the problem might well arise as a result of an *assumption* that the accountant has to make. Future flows are only estimates, and if the best guess is that receipts will 'roughly' increase or decrease, the method is helpful.

(c) An annuity deferred

The first case is known as a *deferred annuity*. Suppose the right is purchased to a series of cash flows like this: for the first ten years, £500 per annum in arrears. For the next ten years, (that is, commencing in eleven years' time), £700 per annum. The discount rate is expected to be 12%.

There are two ways this can be calculated.

Method 1
The value of the first stream will be:

$$£500[a_{\overline{10}|}] = £500 \times 5.650 = £2.825$$

The value of the second stream *at time* t_{10} will be:

$$£700[a_{\overline{10}|}] = £700 \times 5.650 = £3,955$$

The value of the second stream at present is clearly:

$£3,955v^{10} = £1,273$

Therefore the value of the total will be:

$£2,825 + £1,273 = £4,098$

A *warning*: because the second stream begins in the eleventh year it is an easy error to discount it back by v^{11}. Be sure you understand why this is wrong. It is for this reason that method 2 below, although less obvious, is perhaps better.

Method 2

The amount can be considered as two streams: £700 for twenty years, less £200 for the first ten years. Thus the present value of the stream is:

$$£700[a_{\overline{20}|}] - £200[a_{\overline{10}|}] \;=\; (£700 \times 7.469) - (£200 \times 5.650)$$
$$= £5,228 - £1,130$$
$$= £4,098$$

(d) An increasing or decreasing annuity

Our second case is an annuity that increases or decreases smoothly. Suppose we are presented with the following problem:

Mr Smith is invited to participate in a manufacturing project. It is expected that net cash flows will be £10,000 at the end of the first year, and increase by 20% per annum for the following five years (as the product becomes better known). At the end of that time (that is, after the sixth year), the equipment will be exhausted and operations will cease. The discount rate for Mr Smith is 14% per annum. What is the present value of the project to him?

The problem is solved simply be adapting the method for the calculation of an arithmetic series that we saw for calculating $a_{\overline{n}|}$. If we denote the present value of the project as PV and the growth rate of the receipts (in this case 20%) as g then we know that:

$$PV = \frac{10,000}{1+i} + \frac{10,000(1+g)}{(1+i)^2} + \ldots + \frac{10,000(1+g)^5}{(1+i)^6}$$

Clearly we can multiply throughout by $(1+i)/(1+g)$ and deduct the result from the original equation. After rearranging, the result will be:

$$PV = \frac{10,000}{g-i}\left\{\left[\frac{1+g}{1+i}\right]^6 - 1\right\} = \frac{10,000}{0.2-0.14}\left\{\left[\frac{1.20}{1.14}\right]^6 - 1\right\}$$

$$= £60,062$$

If the growth pattern is different from this one (a decay in the cash inflow pattern, or growth beginning after the second year, for instance) then the idea can be adapted quite simply (more complex examples are given in the Workbook).

(e) The terminal value of an annuity

So far we have been concerned with the present value of a series of receipts because that is normally of importance to good decision-making. It must be noted that a similar sum-of-series method can be used to find how much the series of receipts would be worth at the end of the period (i.e. its terminal value). This is denoted by $S_{\overline{n}|}$ and is, of course, the sum of the series.

$$S_{\overline{n}|} = 1 + (1 + i) + (1 + i)^2 + \ldots + (1 + i)^{n-1}$$

which can be condensed into the expression:

$$S_{\overline{n}|} = \frac{(1 + i)^n - 1}{i}$$

using the same method we employed to derive $a_{\overline{n}|}$.

It should be clear to you that, since the same series can yield $a_{\overline{n}|}$ as its value at t_0 and $S_{\overline{n}|}$ as its value at t_n, then $S_{\overline{n}|}$ must also be the product $(a_{\overline{n}|})(1 + i)^n$ (see Fig. 4.6).

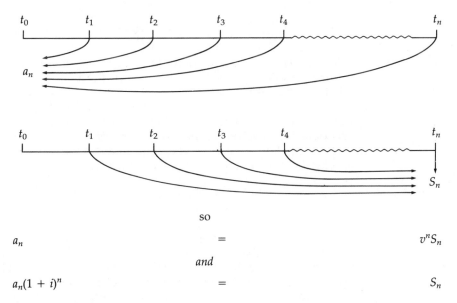

so

$$a_n \qquad = \qquad v^n S_n$$

and

$$a_n(1 + i)^n \qquad = \qquad S_n$$

Figure 4.6   The relationship between $a_{\overline{n}|}$ and $S_{\overline{n}|}$

(f) Continuous compounding

The final aspect of discounting we shall consider is the special case where funds come in continuously rather than at the end of each year. This happens quite frequently in the financial world: for instance, insurance companies receive premiums and dividends every day. As we shall see in this sub-section, receipts every day are in practice indistinguishable from the theoretical possibility that they arrive continuously (that is, in a steady stream rather than at discrete intervals, however short those intervals might be). In what follows we shall for the first and last time break the promise made earlier that 'periods' would always mean 'years'.

Let us begin with government stocks, and suppose they pay interest quarterly and not yearly. Say we had a stock nominally yielding 4%. This would mean that for each £100 of face (that is, nominal) value of the stock that was purchased, the government would pay the holder £4 per annum. This would be paid not as £4 at the end of the year, but as £1 at the end of each quarter. Now in this case the recipient will clearly be better off than with a stock that yielded only £4 at the end of the year, because he or she will be able to reinvest the £1 received at the end of the first three quarters.

At the end of the first year, the £1 received at the end of the first quarter would have been reinvested to yield nine month's extra interest; the payment received at the end of the second quarter would have earned a further six months' interest; and so on. As a result, the amount our investor would have at the end of the first year would be roughly as follows (we assume the reinvestment rate is the same as the basic rate):

$$
\begin{array}{ll}
£1 + (1 \times 4\% \times 0.75\text{yr}) & = £\ \ 1.03 \\
£1 + (1 \times 4\% \times 0.50\text{yr}) & = £\ \ 1.02 \\
£1 + (1 \times 4\% \times 0.25\text{yr}) & = £\ \ 1.01 \\
£1 & = £\ \ 1.00 \\
\text{Principal} & = £100.00 \\
\hline
& £104.06
\end{array}
$$

Now this is an approximation, because just as compound growth is curvilinear in product, so is the behaviour of the interest receipts here. In fact, what has happened is that the 'year' has now become a quarter. In other words, the principles of compound interest apply to *periods*, not years, and those periods are to be counted as the dates on which the *receipt of interest*, and hence the compounding itself, *takes place*.

With this knowledge we can recalculate the growth of the sum as being exactly the same as a growth of a principal at 1% per annum for 4 years, that is $(1.01)^4$, or 1.0406. More generally, for compounding n times per year, the expression will be $(1 + i/n)^n$ for one year, and $(1 + i/n)^{nt}$ for t years.

When receipts arrive more frequently than yearly, we could express the interest rate at $x\%$ per quarter, half-year or whatever. This does not usually happen; rather we refer to the *apparent* annual rate as a *nominal* rate. We may now observe what happens when the period of compounding increases. As we have seen, the actual rate for calculation purposes is the nominal rate divided by the number of periods of compounding. It might be guessed that, as the compounding became very frequent, the resulting sum would become very large indeed, but it does not. You can see this in Table 4.1.

Table 4.1   The result of increasingly frequent compounding

Frequency of compounding p.a.	Periodic rate	Sum	Difference
1	(1.0400)	1.040000	
2	$(1.0200)^2$	1.040400	0.000400
4	$(1.0100)^4$	1.040604	0.000204
8	$(1.0050)^8$	1.040707	0.000103
16	$(1.0025)^{16}$	1.040759	0.000052
32	$(1.00125)^{32}$	1.040785	0.000026

It will be seen that the differences are declining. In fact they reach a limit where the frequency of compounding is continuous. This can be found by using the exponential function, and in this case it will be $e^{0.04 \times 1} = 1.040811$. Conventionally, the Greek symbol δ (delta) is used rather than i to denote interest, and actuarially it is known as the *force* of interest rather than the *rate* of interest. The general expression for continuous compounding is then:

$$e^{\delta t}$$

where t is, of course, the period over which the principle is to accumulate. This is illustrated in the simple example given in Fig. 4.7.

Ms Smith has £500 to invest. What will it grow to over a period of five years if the interest is at 12%, and the compounding is (i) annual, (ii) monthly, (iii) continuous?

Solution:
  (i) £500 $\times$ $(1.12)^5$ = £881
  (ii) £500 $\times$ $(1.01)^{60}$ = £908.35
  (iii) £500 $\times$ $e^{0.12 \times 5}$ = £911

Figure 4.7 Simple example of continuous compounding.

Similarly, present values may be found by:

$$e^{-\delta t}$$

and the present values and terminal values of series of flows can be found by integrating these. This is developed further in the Workbook (sub-section W4.2(c)).

It is not commonly appreciated that an 'equivalent' rate of interest to a force of interest can be found and thereafter substituted for it, which may make calculation more straightforward. This is possible because both $(1 + i)$ and e are exponential functions and hence behave in just the same way.

For example, to find the rate of interest equivalent to the force of interest of 15%, solve the equation.

$$(1 + i) = e^{0.15}$$

for i. In this case $i = 0.1618$ or 16.18%. If you wish, this rate can then be used for numbers of years or fractions of years in place of the force 15%, since in each case the resulting sum is found by raising the expression to the appropriate power.

4.3 Bond valuation

We shall now apply the ideas we have learned to a particular type of problem that occurs in the financial world: the valuation of a bond.

(a) Bond valuation at the time of issue

As we already know, bonds are issued both by the government (gilts) and by companies. Let us begin by imagining the issue of a corporate bond at a time when the reigning interest rate is 14%. The bond is issued in denominations of £100 (this is normal for bond issues). In this first example, the face value of £100 is also the issue price of the bond. The bond is redeemed 15 years later. Interest is payable yearly.

This means that we have the following straightforward situation. Mrs Isolde buys a £100 bond, paying cash of £100. She then receives £14 each year for 15 years in arrears. At the end of the 15 years she is repaid the £100 by the issuer. Clearly the cost to the issuer has been 14%. You can check this for yourself by calculating the present value of the cash flows:

$$\begin{aligned} PV &= £14/(1.14) + £14/(1.14)^2 + \ldots + £114/(1.14)^{15} \\ &= £14a_{\overline{15}|} + £100v^{15} \\ &= £14 \times 6.142 + 100 \times 0.1401 \\ &= £99.998 \end{aligned}$$

that is, £100 subject to a small rounding error.

Now, in reality, bonds usually pay interest half-yearly in arrears. If the nominal rate on the bond is 14%, then Mrs Isolde receives £7 each half-year from the company, and the effective rate she earns is $(1.07)^2 = 1.1449$ or about 14.5%.

But now suppose that the ruling rate of interest in the markets is a little higher or lower than 14% — say, 14.8% for bonds of this kind. It is very messy to issue a bond with a rate stated on its face of 14.8% and to call the bond a 14.8% bond throughout its life. So instead, the issue price is adjusted, the bond is still nominally a 14% bond, and each £100 bond is sold for some price other than £100. In this case, since we wish the effective rate to the borrower and lender to be higher than 14%, we shall issue the bond at a discount — that is, at a price lower than £100.

If we are due to pay the interest half-yearly, then of course there is already an effective rate of about 14.5% in any case. So how do we decide what the issue price should be so as to lead to an effective rate of return of 14.8%?

The problem is a straightforward one of discounting. We know the future cash flows. They are as in Fig. 4.8. We are looking for the present value of the stream as follows:

$$\begin{aligned} \text{Bond price} &= £7/(1.074) + £7/(1.074)^2 + £7/(1.074)^3 + \\ &\quad \ldots + £7/(1.074)^{29} + £107/(1.074)^{30} \\ &= £7a_{\overline{30}|}^{7.4\%} + £100v^{30}{}_{7.4\%} \end{aligned}$$

Of course, we do not have tables for a rate of 7.4%, so we can either work the problem out exactly using a financial calculator or spreadsheet, or we can approximate by interpolating in the discount tables.

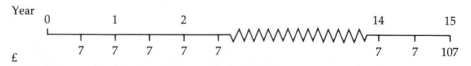

Figure 4.8

The correct answer is £95.23. However, let us attempt a solution interpolating on the basis of the discount tables at the end of this book. From Table III we find than $a_{\overline{30}|}$ at 7% is 12.41, and $a_{\overline{30}|}$ at 8% is 11.26. A linear interpolation for 7.4% therefore gives 11.95. Similarly, v^{30} at 7% is 0.1314 and at 8% is 0.0994. Thus the interpolated value is 0.1186. Hence we have an approximate solution of

$$£7 \times 11.95 + £100 \times 0.1186 = £95.51.$$

This is very close: in fact, an error of only 0.29%

Thus if the company wished to issue bonds to yield 14.8% to purchasers such as Mrs Isolde, it would ask a price of £95.23 for each £100 of bonds. If, for instance, she bought £1,000 of the bonds, she would pay the company £952.30 now, would receive £70 interest each half-year for 15 years, and then receive £1,000 from the company upon redeeming the bonds. The *effective yield* of these cash amounts would be 14.8%

Well, actually it would not be. The above calculation makes one simplifying assumption. To understand this, we have to remember how those in the financial markets talk about bonds. If this bond had paid half-yearly interest of £7 on each £100 of the bond, we have already seen that the *effective* interest rate is a little higher than 14%. Nevertheless, it will always be described in the markets as a 14% bond: we say that the *nominal* interest or coupon rate is 14%. This nominal rate is distinguished from the *real* or *effective* yield of about 14.5%.

The calculation above would be correct *if* the 14.8% mentioned at the beginning of the calculation above were a nominal rate because all we did in our calculations was to halve the 14.8% to 7.4% half-yearly and use this. But this would not give a real rate of 14.8%, but of $((1.074)^2 - 1) \times 100\%$: that is, 15.348%. So, if the *real* market rate were 14.8%, we would use the same calculation procedure as above *except* that the interest rate embedded in the calculations would be $(\sqrt{(1.148)} - 1) \times 100\% = 7.1448\%$, say 7.15%. This would give a bond price of £98.166 or £98.17. This is, of course, higher than the previously calculated price of £95.23 because we wish the rate of return earned to be lower (a real rate of 14.8% instead of 15.35%).

We can summarize this little complication then by saying that

1. if the rate of return in the markets is a nominal rate, we can just halve it to perform our calculations;
2. if the rate of return in the markets is an effective rate, we have to find the corresponding (lower) half-yearly rate that, when compounded, leads to that annual effective rate.

(b) Bond valuation part-way through its life

Now let us consider what happens part-way through the life of the bond. Throughout this example we shall assume the annual rates are nominal rates, as in the first approach above. But do remember that the same complication applies in valuations for the secondary market as applies on original issue.

Taking the same bond as above, suppose that after 3 years the ruling interest rate is only 9%. What would you expect the market price for each of Mrs Isolde's £100 to be?

The answer is found in the same way as the example we have just seen. The buyer of the bond is buying the right to receive £7 each half-year for 12 years, plus the £100 redemption amount. Thus the price is simply:

$$£7a_{\overline{24}|}{}^{4.5\%} + £100v^{24}{}_{4.5\%}$$

which turns out to be £136.24.

Note: once the bond has been issued, there is very little meaning in the par value (that is, the face value of the bond). Nor is there any meaning in the coupon rate (that is, the rate stated on the face of the bond). It is important to realize this because otherwise a question can look very complex. For instance, suppose you were asked the following question:

A 17-year 6% bond was issued four years ago at 97, redeemable at par. What should the price be if the coupon is payable yearly in arrears and the current interest rate for bonds of this type is 11%?

In answering this question, note that the issue price of 97 is now entirely irrelevant. The 6% is relevant only in that it tells us that the amount paid each year is £6. *The valuation is concerned only with future receipts.* Thus it is simply:

$$£6a_{\overline{13}|}{}^{11\%} + £100v^{13}{}_{11\%} = £66.25$$

You will see that, from the first example, if the ruling interest rate rises, the price of the bond drops and vice versa. This is because the buyer wishes to receive a return of that rate on her purchase of the bond. She is buying the right to receive the interest payments, and (in the last example) if the receipts are £6 then a lower price will have to be paid so that these receipts correspond to a return of 11%.

Finally, in this section, let us recap on — and extend — the nomenclature.

The *coupon rate of interest* is the rate stated on the face of the bond. In the case above it was 6%.

The *interest-only yield* (or simply *interest yield*) is the effective rate of the interest given the current price. In the cases above it was $(6/66.25 \times 100)\% = 9.06\%$. This will commonly ignore the fact that interest may be payable other than yearly. Thus, if in this example the interest had been 6% nominal — that is, £3 payable every half-year — it would still usually have been referred to as 9.06%.

The *redemption yield* is the yield to maturity of the bond, taking into account the sum payable on redemption. In the example above it was 11%. There are certain fixed interest securities (such as Consols 4%, which are government stocks) that are undated — that is, they have no binding maturity date and the government is not obliged to repay them. In this case the interest yield is the *only* yield, and is referred to as the *flat yield*.

(c) Deep-discount and zero-coupon bonds

So far we have referred only to bonds that have coupons — that is, bonds that pay interest during the bond's life. In the last few years a variant has become particularly popular: the deep-discount bond (DDB) and its extreme form, the zero-coupon bond (ZCB).

Before giving detail of DDBs and ZCBs, it is worthwhile going over the nature of gains from holding bonds because this will be substantially affected by these securities. There are three ways to gain from holding a conventional bond:

1. There is the periodic interest paid from the company to the investor.
2. There is the *reinvestment* yield. As the bond-holder receives the coupon payments, they are assumed to be reinvested. Since market interest rates are continually changing, the interest received from this reinvestment may

be more or less than the coupon rate. However, because estimates of these changes cannot be accommodated in our calculations, we find that the methods used in this chapter *imply* that the reinvestment rate is equal to the redemption yield.
3. There is a capital gain if the issue price is less than the face value (because, as we saw in sub-section (a) above, any bond can be issued at a price different from par so as to adjust for the 'fine tuning' of interest rates).

A *deep-discount bond* is a bond that is issued with a very low coupon — it may be just 3%, for instance, when the market redemption rate is at 14%. To make up the difference, the bond is issued at a very low price, so that a large proportion of the redemption yield consists of its capital growth.

Example

Joyo plc, manufacturers of the new toy sensation Senile Mutant Sumo Hippos, issues a seven-year deep discount bond with a 2% coupon payable annually in arrear. If it wishes the resultant redemption yield to be 15%, what should the price of the issue be?

Answer

We have:

$$\text{Issue price} = £2a_{\overline{7}|}^{15\%} + £100v^7_{15\%}$$
$$= £2 \times 4.160 + £100 \times 0.3759$$
$$= £45.91$$

The *zero-coupon bond* extends the deep-discount bond to its logical conclusion: there is no coupon at all, and all the gain from holding the bond results from capital growth. The calculation of the yield is therefore very straightforward.

Example

Joyo thinks instead of issuing a seven-year zero-coupon bond to yield 15%. What should the issue price be?

Answer

$$\text{It must be } £100v^7_{15\%} = £100 \times 0.3759 = £37.59$$

Thus whereas at the beginning of this section we pointed out the three gains from holding a bond (coupon, reinvestment of coupon, and capital gain), the first two of these vanish with the ZCB.

The advantages to the *investor* of a zero-coupon bond include the following:

1. *Reinvestment risk reduction.* Since there are no interest payments, there is no uncertainty about reinvesting the coupon interest receivable. All the yield is locked up in the capital appreciation.
2. *There is a higher volatility.* For a given change in market interest rates, a DDB or ZCB will fluctuate more in price than a conventional bond. For speculators, this is desirable.
3. *Call protection.* Some conventional bond contracts include a provision that after a certain period the issuer can force redemption of the bond. Issuers will do this at a time when interest rates have fallen. They can then redeem and issue a new bond with a lower coupon. With a DDB early redemption is less likely because rates are so unlikely to fall to the very low coupon yields paid on the bonds.
4. *Immunization.* We mention this only for completeness: it involves complex issues that are outside the scope of this book.

The advantages to the *issuer* of a zero-coupon bond include the following:

1. Since no interest need be paid for a long period, there are major improvements to cash flow (although the company might wish to set aside a *sinking fund*: that is, an internal fund, to be ready to redeem the bond when it expires). This is not, of course, necessary should it intend to *roll over* the bond: that is, issue a new bond, the proceeds of which repay the old bond.
2. The yield of DDB/ZCB will be lower than that for a conventional bond because of the attractions listed above for investors.
3. The tax position for an issuer is that the interest difference between a market rate for a conventional bond and the actual interest of the DDB is deemed to accrue using a compound interest basis (that is, the company can charge interest to tax that is not being paid on cash). For an investor, on the other hand, no tax on this is payable until the bond is either sold or matures. This is *asymmetrical* (that is, the interest to the investor is not charged on an accruals basis as it is allowed for the issuer). The asymmetry leads to a general joint tax advantage for the DDB. This also can lead to lower effective redemption yields for the company, since holding DDBs/ZCBs is so advantageous to buyers.

4.4 Investment appraisal methods

Having discussed the techniques we shall use, we can now move to the central issue of this chapter: the means by which the desirability of investing funds can be decided upon. We suppose that an investor is presented with a project or series of projects and must decide whether or not to invest in one or more of them. For the present we assume that each project is independent of the others: that is, none of them requires that any other must be undertaken at the same time (i.e. none is *joint*) and none of them are alternatives to the same end (i.e. are mutually exclusive).

We discuss the two principal methods here. They are usually known as the *net present value* (NPV) method and the *internal rate of return* (IRR) method (sometimes known as the *yield* method). As we shall see, the former is superior for a number of reasons, but because both are used in practice we shall describe both.

(a) Net present value

Happily, this theoretically preferable method is also the easier to calculate. It consists of the following simple steps:

1. Find the present value of the project's cash inflows.
2. Find the present value of the project's cash outflows.
3. Invest in the project if (1) exceeds (2).

The future cash flows will, of course, be discounted. For the present we shall put to one side the problem of finding the appropriate discount rate. We shall give this considerable attention later in the book, particularly in Chapter 11.

Formally the method consists of finding the NPV where:

$$NPV = \sum_{t=0}^{n} K_t v^t$$

where K represents the amount of each of a series of n receipts. We can illustrate this with the simple example given in Fig. 4.9.

Ms Jones is offered an investment which requires her to lay out £5,000 immediately. In return she will receive £2,000 at the end of a year, £2,000 after two years and £3,000 after three years. If her personal discount rate is 17%, should she invest in the project?

Solution:

The present value of the cash inflows is:

$[2,000 \times (1.17)^{-1}] + [2,000 \times (1.17)^{-2}] + [3,000 \times (1.17)^{-3}] = £5,043.54$

The present value of the outflows is, of course, £5,000. Since £5,043.54 is greater than £5,000, she should go ahead and invest in the project.

Figure 4.9 Simple example of NPV investment appraisal

This example raises an important issue. We have said that the proposal should be accepted because the NPV shows a surplus of £43.54. But what does this sum actually represent? It is the extra wealth (measured now) gained by Ms Jones through undertaking the project. She is better off through the future receipts due to her, and the present value of the surplus of those future receipts (over and above the amount of the future receipts necessary to recoup the investment of £5,000) is £43.54. Of course, she does not receive that sum immediately. Yet, given high-quality information, she could sell to somebody else, in a perfect market, her right to receive the future cash flows and that right, after taking account of the £5,000 cost to her, will have a market value of £43.54. In effect, if the company were quoted, the share price should increase by the amount of the NPV (divided by the number of shares).

(b) Internal rate of return

Although the concept of the internal rate of return method is no more difficult to understand, and though the mathematics are just as easy, it is trickier because in normal circumstances the solution can only be found by trial and error. The steps in this case are:

1. Select an apparently reasonable interest rate.
2. Discount the present and future net cash inflows and outflows at this rate.
3. If the result of the previous step is not zero, return to step (1) and select a different interest rate.
4. Continue until the result is zero. The interest rate at which this is true is called the *internal rate of return (IRR) of the project* – the gross redemption yield from the bond valuation model on p. 102.
5. If the IRR exceeds the personal discount rate, invest in the project.

Thus the goal in this method is to find an interest rate at which inflows exactly equal outflows (in practice they will usually be close but not equal). If the investment project is for a period longer than two years, trial and error methods are essential.

(*Curiosity Corner:* You may wonder why this should be so. If you have already understood without the explanation, well done. What we have here is the solution of a polynomial, and no formula to solve an equation of degree greater than two exists. Put another way, we can solve quadratics, but not cubics, quartics or other polynomials.)

Formally the method consists of finding a rate r such that:

$$\sum_{t=0}^{n} K_t v^t = 0$$

Again, we shall illustrate this by means of simple example, given in Fig. 4.10.

Ms Green is offered an investment which requires her to invest £7,000 immediately, offering in return £4,000 after one year, £3,000 after two years and £2,000 after three years. Her personal discount rate is 13%.

Solution:

We need to solve the equation:

$$-7{,}000 + 4{,}000/(1 + i) + 3{,}000/(1 + i)^2 + 2{,}000/(1 + i)^3 = 0$$

for i. Trying $i = 0.15$ we find the right-hand side is 61.7; trying $i = 0.16$ gives a value of -40.9. Clearly the correct rate such that the present value of the cash flows is zero lies between these points. For $i = 0.155$ the value is 10, and in the circumstances this is near enough to zero. We can say therefore that the internal rate of return is 15.5%, and since this is greater than her personal discount rate of 13%, Ms Green should invest in the project.

Figure 4.10   Simple example of IRR investment appraisal.

Let us take the case of Ms Green given in Fig 4.10. Suppose we had taken 10% and 20% as our first two guesses. These give NPVs of £562.12 and −£354.94 respectively. Making the assumption that the relationship is linear we can find the proportion:

$$562.12/(562.12 + 354.94) = 0.61$$

This can then be applied to the difference between 10% and 20%, as:

$$0.61 \times (20 - 10)\% = 6.1\%$$

Adding this to the baseline 10% gives 16.1%. As it happens we have already calculated the correct value as 15.5%, so the error of 0.6% is quite reasonable.

Let us reinforce this with a further example. Say we had guessed at 12% and 25%, again for the case of Ms Green. Then we would have had NPVs of £345.15 and −£684.80 respectively. Interpolating would lead to a value of:

$$12\% + (13\% \times 345.15/(345.15 + 684.80))$$
$$= 12\% + 13\% \times 0.34$$
$$= 12\% + 4.42\% \quad \text{say } 16.4\%$$

This is not quite so good as the previous guess, but it is still within 1% of the correct value, and cuts down the calculation time.

Figure 4.11   Approximating the IRR.

There is a way of quickly approximating to the IRR. Take a rate you expect to be higher than the actual IRR and a rate expected to be lower. Then *interpolate* between the two. The result will not be exact, but it will quickly tell you the region to look for the correct IRR. Figure 4.11 gives some illustrations of this method.

(c) NPV and IRR compared

It should be clear that when just one project is being considered, both methods must always give the same accept/reject signal. If the NPV is positive, the IRR will be greater than the personal discount rate and vice versa. However, IRR has a number of important deficiencies. We mention two here:

(i) Internal rates of return are non-additive
Additivity is an important quality in functions such as these, since we may wish to combine projects. Not only is this impossible with IRR, but some very odd results can occur when projects are looked at together. Figure 4.12 is an example modified from Treynor and Black (1976).

Project	t(0) £	t(1) £	t(2) £	IRR(%)
A	−1,000	0	1,250	11.8
B	−1,000	1,100	0	10.0
C	−1,000	1,300	0	30.0
A + C	−2,000	1,300	1,250	18.0
B + C	−2,000	2,400	0	20.0

Figure 4.12   Example of non-additivity of IRR.

Suppose that the choice is between the mutually exclusive projects A and B. The IRR of A is higher, and hence this is a preferable investment. But now suppose C becomes available, and there are sufficient funds to combine A with C or B with C. Now we see that A combined with C does not offer such a good IRR as B combined with C. In other words, once C is added as a possibility, B becomes preferable. This is disturbing: why should the existence of C affect the choice between A and B?

(ii) There may be more than one IRR for a given project
To understand this intuitively, think back to our description of IRR as a polynomial. The most familiar polynomial is, of course, the quadratic equation, and we are aware from elementary mathematics that such equations always have two roots (although on occasion the two roots may be identical). Now on many occasions one root will be positive, one negative. In such cases we are able in practice to ignore the negative root in investment analysis, since we do not concern ourselves with negative rates of interest. But, for instance, the equation $x^2 - 5x + 6 = 0$ has the two positive roots 2 and 3. Similarly, the IRR problem that reduces to the equation $15,200 - 35,000/(1 + i) + 20,000/(1 + i)^2 = 0$ has the two solutions such that i is both 5.25% and 25%.

If the personal discount rate is 10% this makes an acceptance decision somewhat awkward? Should the IRR be taken as 5.25% (reject) or 25% (accept)?

(*Curiosity Corner:* It will be seen that in this equation there are two changes of sign: positive to negative, and back again. In general, it can be shown that for *n* changes of sign there will be a maximum of *n* real, positive roots.)

This example is not just an armchair invention. It can in fact be argued that this kind of pattern of cash flows is the normal one. After all, people will normally pay income tax on the profits from their investment, and the net cash flows should be considered *after deduction of that tax*. Now income tax is payable some time after the end of the year to which it relates (the rules governing the exact date at which payment is due are somewhat complicated). This means that a typical pattern of after-tax cash flows will be:

1. initially negative, as the investment is made;
2. subsequently positive as the returns on the investment flow in;
3. negative again in the final year *which succeeds the final operating year of the project* as the negative cash flow of tax payable to the government takes place.

There are other occasions when this can happen too:

1. There may be abandonment costs. When a quarry is exhausted cash flows turn negative as the local government may require that relandscaping takes place.
2. When a factory is closed there are costs of making the workforce redundant.
3. When a North Sea drilling platform has exhausted economic reserves there is the cost of removing it.
4. There may be examples part-way through a project too, as when a product needs a relaunch to extend its product life-cycle (that is, to counteract the falling off of consumer interest), and this temporarily causes cash flows to become negative as publicity costs are expended.

(d) Mapping NPV and IRR graphically

So far NPV and IRR have been treated as if they were two separate methods that gave the same signal under many circumstances. It should be clear that they are closely related to each other, and in fact it can be shown that the relationship is even closer than we have so far suggested.

A helpful way of seeing the relationship between NPV and IRR is to plot the returns from a project on a graph at various rates of discount. Consider Fig. 4.13. The curve plotted here is for the investment opportunity offered to Ms Green in Fig. 4.10. If the discount rate is zero, then clearly the NPV will be the undiscounted net sum of the inflows and outflows, that is:

$$-£7,000 + £4,000 + £3,000 + £2,000 = £2,000$$

If the NPV is zero, then the relevant rate of discount is, of course, the internal rate of return of the project — in this case, 15.5%. Now any rate of discount could be applied to this project, and the resulting curve would show the NPV of the project at each different discount rate — the curve being smooth because the discount rate can change continuously. It will be seen too

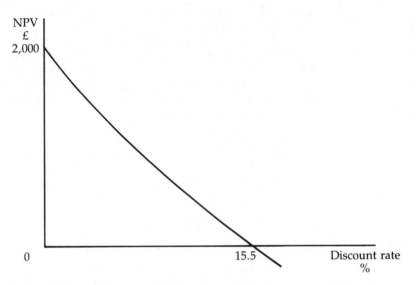

Figure 4.13 The relationship between NPV and IRR.

that the curve is *concave to the origin*. This wll always be the case. Finally, it will be seen that the curve can continue below the axis where NPV = 0. After all, negative NPVs are found if a discount rate is chosen that is higher than the IRR.

Something else is made clear by using a graph of this kind. We have already seen that there can be two or more solutions when seeking the IRR of a project. This can be explained further by the use of a similar graph. Consider the project:

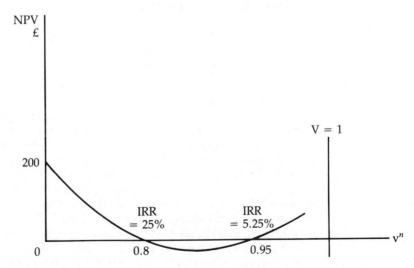

Figure 4.14 Illustration of multiple rates of return.

$$£15,200 - £35,000/(1 + i) + £20,000/(1 + i)^2$$

This is the equation used in the earlier example on p. 107. Its graph looks roughly as in Fig. 4.14.

It will be seen that the graph cuts the horizontal axis at two points, reaching a minimum value between those two points. This minimum value can be found easily if required; it is just a matter of differentiating the equation of the curve and finding the minimum value in the usual way (that is, where the slope of the curve is zero). In this case, for example, we can set $NPV = f(v)$ from which we may write:

$$f(v) = 15,200 - 35,000v + 20,000v^2$$

and hence:

$$f'(v) = -35,000 + 40,000v$$

Thus, setting $f'(v) = 0$ we have:

$$40,000v - 35,000 = 0$$

and hence:

$$v = 0.875$$

from which we deduce that the NPV reaches its minimum value where:

$$i = 14.3\%$$

(e) Comparing two projects

We have seen that NPV and IRR will always give the same signal (accept or reject) when they are used to assess a single project. Frequently, however, it may be necessary to compare two or more projects. It is then that problems can arise. Consider the following pair of possible projects, which we shall assume to be mutually exlusive:

		Project A £	Project B £
Outlay period	0	(15,000)	(15,000)
Inflow period	1	7,000	2,000
	2	5,000	3,000
	3	4,000	7,000
	4	4,000	10,000

It is necessary to decide which is the more desirable project. Now suppose that the appropriate discount rate is 10%. In this case the present values are: $NPV(A) = £1,233$; $NPV(B) = £1,387$. The better project appears to be B. However, suppose instead that the 'hurdle' rate (that is, the rate over which an investment must give a return in order to be desirable) were 12%. Then the present values would be $NPV(A) = £625$; $NPV(B) = £515$. Thus the project with the higher present value in these circumstances is project A.

To understand why these results differ, it is necessary to graph the two projects as we have done above. To do this the IRR of each project is required: it turns out that IRR(A) is about 14% and IRR(B) is about 13.25%. Thus mapping them both on to a graph gives the result in Fig. 4.15.

The two curves cross (at a discount rate of about 11.25%). Above this rate, A is a superior investment. Below this rate, B is superior. A little thought will make the reason clear: the bulk of the cash inflows from B arrive in the

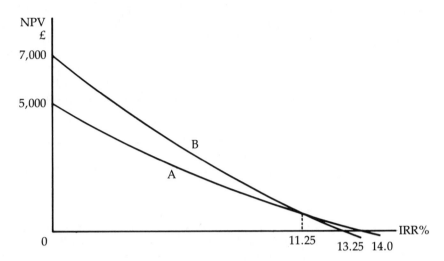

Figure 4.15   Mapping the returns on two projects.

later years, and hence at higher rates of interest they are discounted more heavily.

4.5   Discussion

In this chapter we have made a number of unrealistic, simplifying assumptions. We have supposed that there is no risk and that there are no companies in the economy so that investors are faced with projects themselves. This has been done for a purpose: to emphasize that these are the *basic building blocks* and that the corporate form, which is so pervasive, is just a way (so far as finance theory is concerned at any rate) of bundling projects together in a more efficient form (because, for instance, there are managers who can organize the projects more capably than individual investors could, though agency issues then arise).

The principles of compound interest that we have considered are extremely general. Time preference is common to all factors in the economy, and hence all decisions made will, in so far as they are concerned with future costs and/ or benefits, be made subject to discounting. We have seen that there are two principal mechanisms of discounting, NPV and IRR, though we have also seen that they are closely linked. It has been emphasized that NPV is the better method of the two, for at least three reasons:

1. because it is simpler to calculate;
2. because IRRs are non-additive (important when there are multiple projects to consider);
3. because projects can have multiple internal rates of return.

There are deeper reasons still for preferring NPV. We shall examine these later, in Chapter 6.

Before turning to the summary, let us make one or two cautionary points about the ideas we have developed.

First, we have discussed fairly glibly the 'net cash flows' that are to be discounted. There is a danger that you will assume that the collation of this information is a straightforward affair, and the mathematics and financial problems we have considered are the difficult part. Not so. Indeed the reverse is true, for the uncertainty of the real world is such that the experts in the marketing and production departments, who provide most of the figures for incorporating into these methods, have the difficult problem. Plugging their numbers into discounting methods is comparatively straightforward. We have said nothing about this problem because:

1. the skills involved in estimating future cash flows are outside the scope of financial management;
2. it is difficult to tie down methods of working. These methods will depend on the particular problem concerned.

Second, there is a likelihood that our method of exposition has implied that investment *in itself* will lead to a series of positive cash flows. Wrong again. The positive future cash flows may be attributable to the buying decision concerning, say, a new machine, but they will only result from the purchase of that machine if the rest of the organization is in good order — in particular in marketing the product of the machine.

Summary

Now we may summarize the chapter. We have developed the following points:

1. People have a time preference: that is, they prefer a benefit sooner rather than later (and, of course, a cost later rather than sooner). This is quite independent of inflation. It can be taken as a general characteristic of all people, and it arises because of the opportunity cost of deferring the benefit.
2. Hence receipts and payments at different times in the future will have different discount rates depending on how far into the future they occur. As they stand, they are not comparable with each other. They can be made comparable by discounting them back to the present time.
3. This is achieved by the use of compound interest. In the chapter we saw how a single sum is compounded; how a single sum is discounted back to the present; how a series of equal sums is discounted back to the present; and how that series can be accumulated to a terminal value. We also discovered how to treat constantly changing series of sums.
4. These principles are based on the (unrealistic) assumption that all sums are received or paid at the end of the period (usually the year). This can be corrected by the use of continuous compounding. Usually there is no need to use this because the discrete case gives a sufficiently good approximation.
5. These principles can be used to assess an investment, whether the investment of an individual in a business firm or the investment of an enterprise in a project. There are two ways this can be done: the net present value method and the internal rate of return method. Analysis shows that they are closely intertwined, and this can be demonstrated graphically.
6. When we compare two projects we may find that the decision as to which is preferable will depend on the discount rate chosen.

Key terms and concepts

Here is a list of the key terms and concepts which have featured in this chapter. You should make sure that you understand and can define each one of them. Page references to definitions in the text appear in bold in the index.

- Time preference
- Opportunity cost
- Annuity
- Deferred annuity
- Coupon rate
- Interest yield
- Flat yield
- Redemption yield

- Nominal interest rate
- Force of interest
- Net present value
- Internal rate of return
- Roll over
- Deep-discount bond
- Zero-coupon bond

Further reading

A good introduction to financial mathematics (as it is sometimes known) is Cissell and Cissell (1973). A rather more advanced treatment will be found in Donald (1970). The classic — but a very complex — work is Todhunter (1947). No reading is suggested for NPV and IRR at this stage, since most authors treat it alongside many of the ideas we shall meet in Chapter 6.

The Workbook material to accompany this chapter begins on p. 383.

5

Enter the enterprise: the risk-free model

Learning objectives

After studying this chapter you should be able to:

- see how some of the realities of the world, including business enterprises, can be brought into theoretical models so far developed (but ignoring risk);
- understand both the problems of dividend valuation models for the pricing of shares and issues of capital expenditure decisions within the enterprise;
- describe and evaluate the non-DCF methods of investment appraisal that are found within enterprises in practice;
- understand simple capital-rationing models;
- appreciate the implications of inflation and tax issues for the investment appraisal model.

5.1 Introduction

In Chapter 4 we tried as much as possible to ignore the existence of organizations, and assumed there was no risk. We shall drop the second assumption in Chapter 6, and we shall drop the first assumption in this chapter. In Chapter 7 we shall drop both assumptions together and develop what has now been generally accepted to be the best approach we yet have for understanding the investor and the enterprise in a risky world.

It will be recalled from Fig. 1.3 that in financial theory organizations interpose themselves between investors and projects. What becomes clear straight away from the approach we have taken, and must be borne in mind when seeking to understand Fig. 1.3, is this: *the enterprise only exists as a convenience for investors. It does not alter the basic relationship between investors and projects.* This is especially important, when, in Chapter 8, we come to consider the effects of different ways of financing projects (through equity, debt, retained earnings and so on).

But there is a further crucial implication of Fig. 1.3. We have said so far that the proper criterion for investment appraisal is net present value rather than internal rate of return. This is true both for the individual investor and for the enterprise. Figure 1.3 shows why: it is because the relationship between them is *recursive*. Since the appropriate way to judge investment decisions in projects is NPV, then it follows that *both* the investor's decision on investing in the enterprise *and* the enterprise's decision on investing in the project should be based on NPV. In that way, there is uniformity as the decision is moved back from the project to the investor.

The reasons why investors choose to use the vehicle of the business enterprise rather than invest directly in projects themselves may be summarized as follows:

1. Business enterprises are identifiable units. They can become sufficiently large, and at the same time take on a sufficient identity, for investors to buy and sell the rights to the enterprises' incomes (these are, of course, *shares*, possibly quoted on a recognized securities market such as the International Stock Exchange). Hence they offer potential liquidity.
2. The existence of business enterprises means that a multiplicity of different types of security can be developed for different purposes. Chief among these are equity shares and debentures (loan capital).
3. Business enterprises can attract skilled and specialized managements who can deal with the projects of the organization better than the individual investor.
4. Business enterprises can deal in projects more directly, moving resources (people, materials, plant) to more effective uses if they have a multiplicity of projects.
5. Business organizations can offer the advantage of limited liability. Thus individuals limit their downside risk through ensuring that control and responsibility is restricted to the corporate entity.

A theory that purports to explain the relationship between the owner and the organization, and the various characteristics of organizations, is the *agency model*, which was discussed in Chapter 1. In effect an implication of the agency model is that the relationship between the investor (principal) and the management (agent) is one in which various monitoring and bonding devices are necessary to try to ensure that the agent does as the principal would wish. In this case the business enterprise has many advantages to the individual shareholder, but one problem is inevitably the costliness of the agency relationship.

In common with the agency model, the approach of Fig. 1.3 is narrow in that it deals only with investors: in other words, with the property relation. Because the holders of the equity and loan securities have rights that can be traded in secondary capital markets, and because the investment of capital is seen as pivotal to the nature of the enterprise, this is believed by most finance theorists to be a satisfactory picture.

It is not without its flaws, however. One that is pertinent at this stage is the following: *that claims on the enterprise other than those of capital are taken as given in all the theory that follows.* That is, the project's net cash flows are considered as a first step, estimating the likely revenues from the asset under consideration and the likely cost of generating those revenues. Once these are estimated the resulting net cash flows can be plugged into a DCF calculation and the benefit to the enterprise — by which we mean the *enterprise's equity owners* — is ascertained and communicated to the market-place. This ignores one factor and distorts a second.

It ignores the fact that return to equity holders does not take place in a vacuum. There is, over the period of the project, a feedback (real or potential) of information concerning the returns accruing to the shareholders (go back to Fig. 1.1: the feedback of information cannot be overemphasized). If these are high then there is a possibility that their magnitude will itself have a feedback effect on, say, wages. The existence of large returns to capital may embolden increased wage demands. These will, if successful, affect the net cash flows.

But the nature of the calculation method means that this iteration will be ignored.

The second factor is a distortion of the nature of the enterprise in society. As we saw in Chapter 1 (and as the *Financial Accounting* and *Management Accounting* texts in this series emphasize), the enterprise is a coalition of participants whose influence — in terms of bargaining power over a share of the value added by the enterprise — waxes and wanes relative to each other over a period of time. In this societal sense no one party takes precedence over another. But the standard financial model that we are considering here does take the property relation as paramount and all other rewards as 'costs' (for instance, wages, raw materials, taxes) in arriving at the final result.

For the moment we shall leave these objections to the standard model in abeyance while we consider the nature of the shareholder decision in the private-sector business enterprise. We shall return to them briefly at the end of this chapter when we turn to a consideration of public-sector enterprise and its financial decisions.

5.2 Valuing shares

We have seen in Chapter 4 that any asset, such as an investment in a project, is valued by considering the rights to net cash inflows in future periods and applying a discount rate to bring them to present-time equivalents. For projects these cash inflows were the net operating revenues generated by the assets. For the securities that investors own, the cash inflows are clearly the *dividends* that the enterprise pays to the shareholders. It follows, therefore, that to value shares we must look at the expected future stream of dividends.

Before we turn to this in detail two matters must be cleared up:

1. You may be concerned that, if this statement is true, then the company that does not pay out dividends will have a market value of zero. Yet an examination of the dividend records of a number of companies will show that a few have not paid any dividends for a very long time, and their market values are far from being zero. We shall return to this matter at the end of this section, but we shall give a pointer to the answer now.

    All profits are generated in the name of the shareholders: the dividend is the amount the directors choose to distribute instead of retaining within the enterprise. If no dividends are paid — perhaps because the enterprise is undergoing rapid expansion — the underlying growth of assets will represent an underlying increase in the value of the enterprise to the shareholders. If dividends are passed up now, the potential for future dividends is thereby enhanced (though as the Coats Paton case in Chapter 10 illustrates, this may not be accepted). The growth of assets will be reflected in a growth in the market share price, and the shareholders can 'manufacture' their own dividends (they could be called *home-made dividends*) by selling a portion of their shareholdings. Since the price has gone up — in a perfect world without taxes it would have gone up by exactly as much as the dividends forgone — the shareholders are no worse off.
2. The attentive reader may well have objected to the statement at the end of the opening paragraph of this section (that to value shares we look to future dividends) as follows: 'Since the shares must exist in a market, then surely the share price will be the result of supply and demand forces in that market?' And this is, of course, true.

But it is not at variance with our proposal to value the shares-based on future dividend receipts. Consider the buyer and the seller. Each will have a notion of a price at which he or she is prepared to trade in the market for the shares. That notion must come from somewhere. Now since there are other opportunities around so far as the buyer is concerned, he or she will consider each possible investment opportunity in terms of the opportunities offered by the others. Each will be evaluated in terms of the benefits it can bring. The price the buyer will be prepared to pay will reflect his or her expectations regarding future benefits. Likewise the price the seller will accept will result from the alternatives available to him. If the price is insufficiently high compared to other uses (whether reinvestment in other securities or consumption), he will not sell. Thus the equilibrium price at which an exchange takes place will reflect the future benefits from the security in the light of the future benefits from other securities in the market for both the buyer and the seller.

Now consider the estimate of the future benefits from the security. We have looked already at the benefits from projects, and the calculation of the NPV of these in Chapter 4. *The principle is the same* for the shareholder in the enterprise, but with one practical difference. Whereas the life of most projects is finite (because, for example, products will only sell for a period before they are superseded, and plant or other investment goods will wear out in time), the life of a company is not. This is not to say that it *will* go on for ever. But since the joint stock company has a legal form that envisages continuity beyond any individual shareholder's lifetime, any estimate of future dividends to be received from the company may assume that dividends will continue into the future without end. It may not turn out to be so, but it is the most realistic assumption we can make (just as it is the most realistic assumption for the financial accountant who assumes a 'going concern' — see *Financial Accounting: Method and Meaning,* section 7.2).

If therefore the dividends are expected to remain static as far as can be ascertained, and the shareholder is assumed never to sell the shares, then the price of the individual share P_0 at time zero will be a perpetuity as described on p. 384 of Chapter W4.

$$P_0 = \text{Dividend}/r$$

where r is the market rate of interest for a share of this kind (see Fig. 5.1). We cannot be more specific about the nature of this discount rate at this stage because it is an uninteresting concept so long as the unrealistic assumption of a risk-free world is maintained. Once risk is brought into the picture then r will vary depending on the *risk class* of the security concerned. It should be clear by now that the ruling discount rate is one of the most central concepts in financial management.

If the current dividend of ABC plc is 80p per share, which is expected to remain unchanged into the foreseeable future, and the current discount rate is 13%, then the price of the share will be 80p/0.13 = £6.15.

Figure 5.1 Calculation of share price.

(a) Earnings or profits?

Although in the previous paragraph we suggested that the shareholder will value securities depending on the cash flows that he or she expects to receive, in the case of shares matters are not quite that simple. The cash flows are, in general, dividends. But dividends arise from profits, and the dividend rate is set (in theory) at the behest of the directors, not only as a result of the company's cash flow generation, but depending on other factors too.

This means that earnings (or profits, or income) may be said to underlie dividends. Perhaps they might be considered by the analyst to be a better basis for valuing the share precisely because they are not as subjectively decided as dividends. Hence we have a general model of future flows like this:

$$P_0 = CF_1 v + CF_2 v^2 + CF_3 v^3 + \dots$$

where CF equals cash flow and may be defined *either* as dividends *or* as earnings. If, of course, the company were always to pay out all of its available earnings as dividends, then the two sets of figures would be much the same (once tax has been paid).

There are signs that the markets do indeed consider earnings to be highly significant. The *Financial Times*, for example, gives P/E ratios as a matter of course in its daily listings — it would not bother were market participants uninterested in them. Nevertheless, although in this book we could build models based on earnings, we shall not do so in line with our discussions in Chapter 1 of the importance of cash: we shall stick to dividends since these are so readily identifiable as 'true' cash flows in the pocket of the investor.

(b) The significance of capital growth for share valuation

This brings us to the next point that can easily confuse. Think of each individual share, and how it can generate earnings for its owner. There are two kinds of gain from owning shares. One is the dividend received (usually half-yearly, but we shall for simplicity's sake assume it is annually). The other is the capital given when the owner sells the share. If, for instance, the shareholder held the share for just one year, receiving the dividend at the end of the period and immediately selling the share, the return would be as follows:

$$r = \frac{D_1 + (P_1 - P_0)}{P_0}$$

where r is the rate of return earned
D_1 is the dividend received after a year
P_1 is the price at the end of the year (ex-dividend)
P_0 is the price at the beginning of the year.

We have, of course, ignored here the complications that surround the time at which a share is declared ex-dividend.

If a share costs £2 at the beginning of the year, and after a dividend of 30p has been received can be sold for £2.40, then the return is (30 + (240 − 200))/200, or 0.35: that is, 35%.

Figure 5.2   Example of gains from holding a share for one year

Now in fact, when considering models like this, we can generally ignore price appreciation by taking dividends for a long period. To see why, let us take the simplest possible model, where the market assumes the dividend rate will stay unchanged for ever, as in Fig. 5.1. As we have already seen, the price is D/r, that is:

$$P_0 = Dv + Dv^2 + Dv^3 + \ldots \tag{5.1}$$

Now if we were to try to value the share based on selling it after t years, the price would be:

$$P_0 = Dv + Dv^2 + Dv^3 + \ldots + Dv^t + P_t v^t \tag{5.2}$$

that is, the present value of the dividends receivable plus the present value of the price when the share is eventually sold.

However, let us look in more detail at this latter price P_t in equation 5.2. Clearly, that price too will be the present value of the future stream of dividends. In this case:

$$P_t = Dv + Dv^2 + Dv^3 + \ldots \tag{5.3}$$

so that we can multiply this throughout by v^t to find the final term in the valuation of P_0:

$$P_t v^t = Dv^{t+1} + Dv^{t+2} + Dv^{t+3} + \ldots$$

and substituting this for $P_t v^t$ in equation 5.2 leaves us with

$$P_0 = Dv + Dv^2 + Dv^3 + \ldots + Dv^t + Dv^{t+1} + Dv^{t+2} + Dv^{t+3} + \ldots$$

which is, of course, the same as equation 5.1. This is illustrated in Fig. 5.3.

Case

A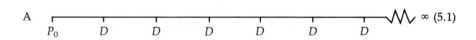

B

C

And Case B + Case C = Case A

Figure 5.3

What all this means, then, is that our calculations will be the same whether or not the share is sold; and this also means that, if the share is sold, they will be the same whatever the time the share is sold (you may wish to prove this for yourself).

Having established that

1. we may take dividends rather than earnings to value a share;
2. we may take dividends throughout the period of the company's life ignoring any sale of the shares in the meantime;

we may now go on to develop a model for share valuation.

(c) The Gordon growth model

In the simplified model just given for illustrative purposes, we assumed that dividends would be constant. However, it would be unusual if the expectation were for an unchanged dividend. Over the course of this century there has been a general pattern of growth in the economy, and companies generally hold themselves out as proposing not just to grow with the economy, but to grow faster. Although in some industries a decay in dividends may be foreseen, it is more normal to expect growth. (Dividend policy is discussed at length in Chapter 10.)

In Chapter 4 a model was developed for valuing a project with a finite life of n years where the net cash inflows were expected to grow at a rate g (see page 96). The expression was:

$$\text{NPV} = \frac{NCF_1}{(1+r)} + \frac{NCF_1(1+g)}{(1+r)^2} + \frac{NCF_1(1+g)^2}{(1+r)^3} + \ldots +$$
$$\frac{NCF_1(1+g)^{n-1}}{(1+r)^n}$$

where NCF_1 represents the net cash flow of the project at t_1.

A similar model can be developed for valuing a stream of dividends from an enterprise, with just two differences. One, of course, is that there is no horizon n. The flows are assumed to continue indefinitely. The second is that, rather than begin with cash flow at the end of year 1, the starting point is a dividend *that is known*, namely the last annual dividend declared, which we assume to have been declared at t_0. On this basis we can develop what has come to be known as the *Gordon growth model* after the person who first proposed it, Myron Gordon.

The share price under these conditions will be:

$$P_0 = \frac{D_0(1+g)}{(1+r)} + \frac{D_0(1+g)^2}{(1+r)^2} + \ldots + \frac{D_0(1+g)^\infty}{(1+r)^\infty}$$

where D_0 is the immediate past dividend. Under these conditions the price P_0 can be found by multiplying each side by $(1+r)/(1+g)$ and deducting the resulting expression from the expression above. For the price on the left of the expression, this causes no problem, of course, nor does it for the early terms of the series. However, this is an *infinite* series, and hence we cannot treat the last term as if it were the final term of a finite series. Instead we have to look more closely at what is happening as the series progresses to very high powers of $(1+g)/(1+r)$.

Now if g is greater than r, clearly the expression $(1+g)/(1+r)$ will become very large as the series progresses to higher powers. Since the series is of infinite length, and each term is added to the previous one, the series will grow to infinite magnitude – in other words, it will imply an infinite share price. This is clearly unrealistic and, indeed, it is hard to envisage that any growth rate can continue at a high rate. The alternative is to accept that g will be less than r. If this is so, then the terms of the series will become gradually smaller until they tend to zero as the series tends to infinity.

If the terms of the series are tending to disappear, then we can simply ignore them as they become progressively smaller, and thus the result of the difference between series given above will be:

$$P_0[1-(1 + r)/(1 + g)] = - D_0$$

And since:

$$[1 - (1 + r)/(1 + g)] = [(g - r)/(1 + g)]$$

we may say that:

$$P_0 = \frac{- D_0}{(g - r)/(1 + g)}$$

$$= \frac{D_0(1 + g)}{r - g}$$

$$= \frac{D_1}{r - g}$$

This is a very simple model for valuing the price of a share and is illustrated in Fig. 5.4.

What is the price of a share whose last dividend was 65p, given that a growth rate of 4% is expected, and the current discount rate is 12%?

Solution:

$(65 \times 1.04)/(0.12 - 0.04)\text{p} = 845\text{p}$
$= \text{£}8.45$

Figure 5.4 Calculation of share price using the Gordon growth model.

A simple method is needed to estimate the growth rate of the dividends, and this is available. In the absence of any other information (and, clearly, this is a crucial assumption), all we have to go on is the past dividend behaviour. The pattern this shows may be taken as an indicator of future dividend growth (or negative growth, of course) and the past growth rate used as the estimated future growth rate in the expression we obtained. This is illustrated in Fig. 5.5.

The dividends on a share have for the past 5 years been 45p, 47p, 51p, 49p, 53p. If the current discount rate for such a share is 14%, what should the share price be according to the Gordon growth model?

Although the growth has not been smoothly continuous (this would hardly be realistic), we can take the growth from 45p to 53p to represent four years' growth rate that will probably continue, since we have no reason to suppose it will not. Thus $45p(1+g)^4 = 53p$ and hence the growth rate g is:

$$\sqrt[4]{\frac{53}{45}} - 1 = 0.0418 = 4.2\%$$

and substituting this as the growth rate for the model gives:

$$P_0 = 53(1.042)/(0.14 - 0.042)p = £5.64$$

Figure 5.5. Calculation of dividend growth using the Gordon growth model.

Having suggested this procedure, its practicality must be assured. It could be argued that:

1. dividends do not grow smoothly;
2. nobody would expect them to grow smoothly;
3. hence it cannot be assumed that any given growth rate is appropriate to the model.

Indeed it could also be argued that this implies that:

4. a company that has not paid a dividend in recent years will have a zero value (cf. the Crown Cork case given in Chapter W1).

In fact this is not an insuperable objection. It must be borne in mind that this is a *heuristic*: a guide to the pricing of securities. Both (1) and (2) above are perfectly true, but they do not imply (3). We are concerned merely with the best possible guess in an uncertain world as to what the pattern of dividends is likely to be. For the same reason, it is no objection to the model that nobody expects a growth of dividends for ever. There are two reasons for this:

1. if there is no reason to suppose that dividends will cease or change their pattern on a particular date, then to assume they will continue unchanged is the best we can do;
2. in any case, as the dividends become distant (especially over ten years at reasonably high rates of discount), the more distant dividends are discounted so heavily that any error in estimating them is of minor importance.

As to the company that has recently paid zero dividends, the heuristic again has to be noted. It is a means of *estimating the future* and will generally be considered in the context of other factors. The company that has not recently paid a dividend may be in difficulties (so there is little cash flow available) or it may be highly successful and using the available funds for expansion. Only other information can help here – over-reliance on mechanical models such as this one can be very risky. Once again, you are referred to Chapter 10 where dividend policy is discussed in detail.

Now we can return to the problem we raised at the beginning of this section. How do we value the enterprise that ploughs back all its earnings and pays zero dividend? The lack of a dividend next year means we cannot easily just plug values into the Gordon model.

The answer is, of course, that the Gordon model cannot handle such an (unusual) eventuality. It was derived on the basis of a continuingly increasing stream of dividends. If dividends are being held back for a few years, this growth that is so central to the Gordon model is invisible. The mechanical methods fail us and we are back to considering in reality how we might value the securities of such an enterprise.

5.3   Project valuation within the enterprise: the alternatives to DCF

In section 5.2 we looked at the valuation of the equity of the enterprise. We can now turn to the second step of Fig. 1.3: valuing the project within the enterprise.

It was emphasized in Chapter 4 (pp. 104–11) that NPV is superior to IRR as a means of evaluating possible investment projects (though it suffers itself from a scaling problem, favouring large projects over small ones – we shall look at the solution to this later, in section 5.4). In this chapter so far we have seen a further reason why NPV is preferable: because of the recursion between the project–enterprise evaluation and the enterprise–shareholder evaluation. Both must be based on NPV so as to ensure consistency and that the model of Chapter 4 is conserved: that is, that the optimal risk-free criterion is used for projects so far as the eventual beneficiaries are concerned.

However, although it has been argued that, given the assumptions we have made concerning the goals of the enterprise, the NPV criterion should be used, business enterprises do not all use DCF methods. One of the principal criticisms of discounting methods has been that the methods themselves are very precise, and yet the data that are fed into them are highly *imprecise*. Consider a ten-year project in a new product line. It is difficult to be sure of the first year's sales with any certainty. It is next to impossible to estimate sales and costs ten years later. To some extent this problem is ameliorated by the very nature of discounting, as we saw in the case of the Gordon growth model, because the discounted value after ten years is quite considerably reduced by the discount factor – for instance, at a discount rate of 15%, £100 due in ten years' time is worth less than £25 today. This means that the present value of any error in estimating has only a quarter of its apparent significance.

There are two other methods of investment appraisal that are commonly used (although not so commonly as they once were: evidence on the use in UK industry of the various techniques is given later in this section). These are known as the *payback method* and the *accounting rate of return* (ARR). These are simpler to calculate and understand than DCF methods, and given the uncertainty of estimates of future cash flows it is far from surprising that they have survived.

Yet, though the criticism of discounting techniques is a valid one, the methods looked at in this section are not in themselves any better as a solution to the problem. If anything they only add further errors. Interestingly, recent research has claimed to show that ARR can, under certain conditions, be a good approximation to IRR (see, for example, Kay, 1976; Steele, 1986). It has also been argued that there can be a good correlation between payback and DCF under certain conditions (since the inverse of payback is an approximation to IRR: see Gordon, 1955, and critical comments by Sarnat and Levy, 1969. For all these reasons we now turn to describing these methods.

(a) The payback method

The first method is known as the payback method. It asks the question: how soon will the initial outlay be recouped by the expected cash flows? There are in fact two ways of calculating it, and for variable cash flows they normally give different results. Method 1 is described in Fig. 5.6, and method 2 in Fig. 5.7.

Payback is of very limited use in judging one project. If, for instance, the

Suppose the following projects are available:

	Project A £	Project B £
Outlay period 0	(10,000)	(10,000)
Inflow period 1	4,000	1,000
2	4,000	2,000
3	4,000	5,000
4	4,000	9,000

It will be seen that each project has to be judged by how quickly its inflows reach £10,000. Project A has returned £8,000 after two years, and interpolation during the third year (to find how soon the remaining £2,000 is recovered during the third year) suggests that the £10,000 is recouped after two and a half years. Project B, on the other hand, has only recovered £8,000 after three years, and a further two-ninths of the fourth year is needed before the full amount of the £10,000 is recovered. Thus the payback method suggests that project A is to be preferred.

Figure 5.6 Payback method of investment appraisal(1).

We use the same cash flow patterns as in Fig. 5.6. However, this time we take all the cash flows into account, and ask ourselves about the *equivalent period* on average that would equal the outlay. This is calculated as the outlay divided by the average annual cash inflow.

In the case of project A this is £10,000/£4,000 = 2.5 years, as before. For project B, the average cash inflows are:

(1,000 + 2,000 + 5,000 + 9,000)/4 = £4,250.

Thus the payback period is £10,000/£4,250 = 2.35 years.

This is not, of course, a 'strictly correct' payback period as the idea is defined. Method 1 does give such a solution. This method does, however, avoid one of the disadvantages given in the body of the text: it does not ignore cash flows after the payback period.

Figure 5.7 Payback method of investment appraisal (2).

payback period is four years, is this good or not? This is difficult to judge. However, it is of a little more use when comparing two projects and favouring the one with the shorter payback period (on the grounds that the risk is lower because the outlay is recouped sooner).

There are two major criticisms that can be made of the payback method:

1. It ignores the time value of money, treating all cash inflows and outflows equally. This can be accommodated using *discounted payback* — we shall return to this in a moment.
2. It ignores all inflows after the payback period (under method 1, which is the more common method). This means that if, for instance, there had been a fifth year of each project's life in which project B generated an inflow of £10,000, and project A generated nothing at all, then project B would become preferable, yet the method would still signal a preference for project A.

There are two justifications for using payback that have at least some validity:

1. It recognizes that decisions are made in a risky world (remember, in this chapter we are assuming that there is no risk attaching to projects). If there is risk, then there are various ways of handling it which are looked at elsewhere, particularly in Chapters 6 and 7. For the present it is sufficient to note that, where the future is especially risky, the sooner that the initial investment is recouped, the safer the investor will feel. Even if things go wrong beyond that period, the investor has at least got his or her money back. (There is in fact an answer to the objection that it is not *really* a return of the original money because of the opportunity cost of investing it for the payback period, though the *discounted payback* method removes this objection.)

   This risk can be of various kinds, and some are more akin to *uncertainty* than risk. There is a risk that technology will move on, leaving the project obsolescent; there is political risk; there is (for the multinational and the enterprise that deals substantially with imports or exports) foreign exchange risk — both the risk that the exchange rate will move adversely and the risk that a currency will be blocked; and there are risks that the customers will not materialize, that the cost of production will be higher than expected, and so on. In fact some managers (as we shall see in a moment) use payback more as a *screening device* in conjunction with DCF. It has also been suggested by researchers that payback is used by those unable to understand DCF, so that it is used at the lower levels of the organization to filter out ideas before reaching the middle management who will apply DCF techniques, and by the latter when presenting the project to directors who are similarly unsophisticated.
2. It provides a quick measure of likely short-term future liquidity. The quicker the payback period, the quicker the cash flows coming in are available.

(b) Discounted payback

The discounted payback method is a straightforward adaptation of the payback method. Future expected cash flows are discounted and *then* the payback period is found. The method is illustrated by a numerical example in Fig. 5.8.

We take the cash flows of Fig. 5.6 as an example, and discount them at 9%. This gives the following results:

Period	Project A £	Project B £	Discount factor 9%	Project A discounted £	Project B discounted £
0	−10,000	−10,000	1.0000	−10,000	−10,000
1	4,000	1,000	0.9174	3,670	3,367
2	4,000	2,000	0.8417	3,367	2,834
3	4,000	5,000	0.7722	3,089	2,385
4	4,000	9,000	0.7084	2,834	2,007
Total				12,959	10,593

Thus the discounted payback periods are 2.96 years for project A and 3.71 years for project B.

Figure 5.8   Discounted payback method.

Discounted payback attempts to combine the advantages of payback (as a surrogate for risk and a guide to liquidity availability) with the advantages of discounting future cash flows. Although it is not strictly justified theoretically, it might be argued that, in a world of uncertainty, it is justified by the limits of human ability to adjudge cash flows well into the future: that, in other words, the NPV method is claiming spurious accuracy in discounting cash flows often ten years and beyond when product prices, production costs and financing costs are all very difficult to forecast (as a check on this, try guessing your own income in ten years' time). Moreover, political effects on markets make this many times worse. Just imagine a multinational assessing future markets in early 1989; then think of the massive changes in Eastern Europe, the seeming beginnings of rehabilitation of South Africa in the world community, and (at the time of writing) the crisis in the Persian Gulf.

(c) The accounting rate of return

This method works by:

1. taking the *average* inflows to be received over a project's life;
2. deducting from this the depreciation on the initial outlay; then
3. dividing the result by the average amount of investment over the period of the project.

The method is illustrated in Fig. 5.9. (Note that some descriptions of the ARR method suggest merely that the numerator is divided by the outlay rather than the average outlay. Since the ARR method is normally used for comparing two or more projects, the difference is unimportant in practice, since it simply has the effect of halving all the rates of return shown.)

This method answers one criticism of the payback method (that it ignored cash flows after the payback period), but itself is subject still to the criticism that it ignores the time value of money. A further criticism is possible too, for its theoretical roots are somewhat dubious (although as we pointed out there is a body of academic literature investigating the conditions under which it is

Consider the projects being evaluated in Fig. 5.6 above. The ARR for project A will be:

$$\frac{\dfrac{4,000 \times 4}{4} - \dfrac{10,000}{4}}{\dfrac{10,000}{2}} = 30\%$$

For project B the ARR is 35% (try to confirm this for yourself). Hence the method suggests that project B is better, in contrast to the payback and discounted payback methods which favoured A.

Figure 5.9 The accounting rate of return (or average rate of return) method of investment appraisal.

a reasonable approximation to, and substitute for, the IRR). We said above that more than one interpretation of the method exists, and this itself should ring warning bells.

Since it has already been suggested that discounting methods are better, it is instructive to apply them to the data used in the examples of payback and ARR given in Figs 5.6 to 5.9. The NPVs of the projects depend, of course, on the discount rate used. If we assume a discount rate of 15%, then the NPV and IRR of the two projects are as follows:

	Project A	Project B
NPV	£1,420	£815
IRR	22%	18%

Thus the NPV method suggests that project A is to be preferred where the hurdle rate is 15%, and the IRR method gives a similar signal. In this case they agree with the payback method. But this need not necessarily be so. Were the hurdle rate only 7%, the NPV of project A would be £3,549 and that of project B £3,629, which reverses the preference ordering.

5.4 The problem of unequal lives

Having looked briefly at alternatives to DCF, we now return to an extension of net present value (it also affects internal rate of return, but we need not go into the detail of that here: having discredited it, we need add no further sophistiation). It concerns comparable projects that have unequal lives.

The problem is best understood through a specific example. Table 5.1

Table 5.1

	Project A £	Project B £
t_0	(10,000)	(6,000)
t_1	4,000	4,000
t_2	4,000	5,000
t_3	4,000	
t_4	4,000	
NPV ($i = 12\%$)	2,149	1,557

shows two possible investment opportunities, both of which achieve the same thing: in other words, they are mutually exclusive. We have to choose between them.

Let us suppose the discount rate to be 12%. Then the net present values of projects A and B are £2,149 and £1,557 respectively. On this basis, A seems to be better.

However, this ignores a crucial factor. The capital is tied up in project A for four years. But project B is completed in two years, and the capital could then be reinvested — for instance, in a bank account earning interest, or in another investment project, similar to the first. This has to be taken into account. The usual way to do so is to assume that a project with a similar set of cash flows to the first 'fills the gap'.

We do this as follows. The NPV of the first two years' cash flows is £1,557. If this were replicated, we would have a NPV of £1,557 two years later too. But since this second, assumed, project brings in the cash flows two years after the first, we need to discount the second amount of £1,557 by v^2. Then the *total* amount for project B is the sum of the first set and the second set, like this:

DCF of current project	£1,557	
DCF of replicated project		
£1,557 × v^2	£1,242	
	£2,799	

and since £2,799 is greater than £2,149, we now see that B is better than A because of the reinvestment opportunities.

Now this problem has been simplified, through taking project A as an exact multiple of project B (that is, exactly twice as long). Often this will not be the

	Project X £	Project Y £
t_0	(60,000)	(50,000)
t_1	10,000	11,000
t_2	12,000	26,000
t_3	12,000	28,000
t_4	14,000	
t_5	14,000	
t_6	15,000	
t_7	20,500	
NPV (i = 12%)	750	478

The unequal lives problem is solved in this case by creating an *equivalent annuity*. That is, the net present value is spread back over the life of the project. This is done by dividing it by $a_{\overline{n}|}$. The results for projects X and Y are:

Project X: £750/$a_{\overline{7}|}$ = £750/4.564 = £164
Project Y: £478/$a_{\overline{3}|}$ = £478/2.402 = £199

Since £199 is greater than £164, we can say that project Y is the better.

Figure 5.10   NPV of projects with unequal lives.

case. For instance, one project may be for five years, the other for six. To use the same method as above would mean looking for the lowest common multiple, and replicating each through to that. In this case it would be 30 years — so one project would be replicated five times, the other six times. This would clearly be messy and time consuming, so a simpler method is used. It is illustrated in Fig. 5.10.

The method works through the notion of the *equivalent annuity*. We ask: given that we know the net present value, what annuity over the life of the project would generate this net present value? We can then compare annuities, and the greater equivalent annuity gives us the better project.

5.5   How much are DCF methods used in practice?

Until quite recently it would have been true to say that DCF methods of investment appraisal were confined to a few companies in the UK. This is no longer true, and surveys generally seem to suggest that their use is becoming widespread.

In the UK, as in other countries, there is a pronounced size effect in the use of discounted cash flow techniques. Although they are now heavily used in large companies, their use decreases, perhaps substantially, for medium and small enterprises.

Partial results of a major study by Pike (1988) into the very largest companies (all within the top 200 or so) are given in Table 5.2. The growth in use of DCF is quite dramatic. It is far less so in the McIntyre and Coulthurst

Table 5.2   Investment appraisal techniques in large UK companies.

	1986 %	1981 %	1975 %
Payback	92	81	73
ARR	56	49	51
IRR/NPV	84	68	58
IRR	75	57	44
NPV	68	39	32

Note: Percentages do not sum to 100 because many companies use more than one technique.
Source: Pike, 1988.

Table 5.3   UK methods of project evaluation.

Single evaluation criteria	%	Multiple criteria	%
Discounted cash flow	13.2	Solely DCF methods	2.7
Payback	73.5	Payback or ARR plus DCF	41.1
Accounting rate of return	8.8	Payback and ARR plus DCF	30.1
Other	4.4	Other	26.1
Sample size	68	Sample size	73

Source: Adapted from McIntyre and Coulthurst, 1985.

Fig. 5.8.

(1985) survey, which considered medium-sized enterprises (the criterial for 'medium-sized were a little involved, but the companies had turnover and assets in the low £ millions). Their results are adapted in Table 5.3.

To some extent, these figures can be compared with those in other countries. Klammer and Walker's (1984) paper reports results for large US companies that are therefore comparable to Pike in the UK, although they report only the major technique employed, so comparison is limited. This study is different in its orientation, since it distinguishes among different types of investment (for example, expansion of existing operations, foreign operations, abandonment and social expenditures). For the expansion into new operations. The percentages for the expansion into new operations are reproduced in Table 5.4. It will be seen that ARR and payback are disappearing fast.

Table 5.4 Principal technique used in large US companies.

	1980 %	1975 %	1970 %
DCF methods	71	58	41
ARR	10	17	28
Payback	5	12	15
Other/no response	14	13	16
	100	100	100

Source: Klammer and Walker, 1984.

Finally, a recent study by Yoshikawa (1988) has compared UK and Japanese methods. Corporate size is not reported in the survey, but comparing the UK figures with those of Pike we may suppose that many of the respondent companies were not large. We give the UK as well as Japanese results, since we may suppose that the populations in each are comparable. It is interesting that Japanese companies seem indifferent to 'sophisticated' methods. Perhaps this is a reflection of the absence of Western-style business schools in Japan, which are frequently credited with influencing business practice. The results are shown in Table 5.5.

Table 5.5 UK vs Japanese investment appraisal techniques.

	UK %	Japan %
ARR	14	33
Payback	42	29
NPV	19	7
NPV Index	2	1
IRR	21	3
Other	2	1
No model used	0	26
	100	100

Source: Yoshikawa, 1988.

5.6   Project valuation within the enterprise: capital rationing

In Chapter 4 the model we developed suggested that the investor should accept any project offered if its NPV was positive. The same is true for the organization. However, to do this it needs to obtain the funds from the market (or from reinvested funds) so as to invest them. Now according to the pure model this should cause no problems because so long as it has opportunities to make investments with positive NPVs, the enterprise should invest in them; and so long as it has these opportunities, the market will be happy to provide the funds for it to do so.

Reality is not like this, of course. One reason for this may simply be that, even in the economy as a whole, there are not sufficient holders of funds who wish to invest – maybe there has been a boom in good investment opportunities and the enterprise concerned has to take a back seat. Or maybe the government is borrowing heavily and crowding out finance that otherwise would be available to the individual company. But there are two more common reasons why the business enterprise may not go to the market for funds, or may not get them if it does so.

1. The directors may be reluctant to approach the market, where reinvested funds have proved insufficient to finance the opportunities available. There may be a number of reasons for this. They may feel that the transaction costs do not justify the marginality of a particular investment. They may feel that they intend to go to the market in the near future (or have done so in the recent past) and guess that the market will be reluctant to fund a company so frequently (for reasons why, see (2) below). It may be that there *are* reinvestable funds available, but that dividend policy demands that they be distributed to shareholders (see Chapter 10 below for some discussion of the logic of this attitude).
2. The market may not be prepared to provide the funds even though the enterprise has good opportunities. The principal reason for this is *information asymmetry* (discussed in Chapter 1). The enterprise has information about the investment and its quality, but the market does not. Communication of the information will be no certain remedy because the market may not believe it. (For reasons why directors' statements may be treated warily you are referred to the discussion of agency theory in section 1.4(d), pp. 23–6). Certainly, even though the enterprise might be prepared to give some information about the potential investment project, that information would not extend to the kind of detail available to the enterprise. Indeed, there will inevitably be some doubt within the enterprise too, since all such information is based on estimates of an uncertain future.

The result of this shortage of required funds is known as *capital rationing*. Note that capital rationing can be *external* where the market does not provide sufficient funds for the enterprise as a whole, or *internal* where the company restricts the amount available to particular divisions or departments. Of course, the former is a powerful reason for the existence of the latter. Under these circumstances the enterprise cannot accept all the projects it would like to. Thus it needs a method of choosing among projects to find the best projects available.

On the twin assumptions that:

1. each project consists of just one initial cash outflow followed by a series of cash inflows;

2. each project is infinitely divisible;

the method to be used is the *profitablity index*. The method is essentially simple:

1. find the NPV of each project;
2. divide each project's NPV by the outlay for that project — the resulting figure is the profitability index;
3. rank the projects in order of profitability index;
4. accept all projects in their rank order up to the limit of the amount of the funds available.

It should be clear that all the method is doing is taking each project's NPV and reducing it to common terms by dividing its project outlay. Fig. 5.11 illustrates the method.

A company is faced with four investment projects with cash flows as follows:

Year	Project A £	Project B £	Project C £	Project D £
0	(28,000)	(68,000)	(132,000)	(19,000)
1	10,000	20,000	15,000	2,000
2	10,000	20,000	35,000	4,000
3	10,000	30,000	50,000	20,000
4	10,000	30,000	60,000	
5	—	—	35,000	—

The company only has £190,000 available. If the cost of capital is 10%, in which projects should it invest?

Solution:

Although we have calculated each discounted flow in full, this is not, of course, necessary for all these — for instance, Project A can be evaluated using $a_{\overline{n}|}$.

Year	Discount factor	Project A Cash flow £	Project A DCF £	Project B Cash flow £	Project B DCF £	Project C Cash flow £	Project C DCF £	Project D Cash flow £	Project D DCF £
0	1.0000	−28,000	−28,000	−68,000	−68,000	−132,000	−132,000	−19,000	−19,000
1	1.1000	10,000	9,091	20,000	18,182	15,000	13,636	2,000	1,818
2	1.2100	10,000	8,264	20,000	16,529	35,000	28,926	4,000	3,306
3	1.3310	10,000	7,513	30,000	22,539	50,000	37,566	20,000	15,026
4	1.4641	10,000	6,830	30,000	20,490	60,000	40,981		
5	1.6105					35,000	21,732		
NPV			3,698		9,740		10,841		1,150
PI			0.132		0.143		0.082		0.061

Figure 5.11   Calculating the profitability index of four projects.

You are advised to follow each step through in Fig. 5.11 so that each operation is understood. For each cash flow a discount factor has been applied so that the NPV can be calculated, and this NPV is then divided by the outlay to find the profitability index (PI). Having found the PI for each project, it is now possible to decide how to apply the £190,000 funds as shown in Table 5.6.

Table 5.6

Project	PI	Outlay £	Accumulated outlay £
B	0.143	68,000	68,000
A	0.132	28,000	96,000
C	0.082	94,000	190,000

It will thus be seen that, in the example given, only part of project C could be accepted, and none of project D.

In the example given in Fig. 5.11 it was assumed that projects are infinitely divisible. For some types of project this is clearly not true: the purchase of a lathe, for instance, or the 100% takeover of another company. (We do not give takeovers a prominence in this text. Note, however, that, although there are many factors involved in a takeover, in the simplest terms it is just another way in which a company uses funds it has raised in what it judges to be a profitable way. In this sense payment for another company is no different from payment for the bundle of projects that the company represents. Go to the Decca case in the Chapter W1 and consider the ability of the bidders to take a less than 100% stake in Decca.) For other projects divisibility is approximately true — a new greenfield site factory can be designed for different possible sizes at the planning stage. For yet other uses of funds it is perfectly true: for instance, deciding on the proportionate holding in a new consortium where there are a number of other contractors eager to participate.

Hence the example is far from unrealistic.

5.7 Project valuation within the enterprise: dealing with inflation

It is essential to bear in mind, in understanding the idea of discounting, that it is an entirely different matter from inflation. Future receipts need to be discounted even in an inflation-free world, and so far we have ignored inflation because the principles have not required it. However, inflation has characterized the UK economy on and off for centuries, and since World War II it has ranged from 4% or so per annum to nearly 30% in the mid 1970s. It would be unwise, therefore, not to distinguish between real returns and monetary returns. So we now take a look at the way we can incorporate expected inflation rates into capital-budgeting decisions.

The problem can be stated simply: since there is likely to be a general inflation over the period of investment, should the assessment of the investment take the inflation into account?

This statement is somewhat woolly. To be more precise, there are two factors that are affected — or potentially affected — by inflation that are important in investment evaluation. One is the amount of the cash flows. The other is the discount rate applied. We shall investigate how to proceed with an example, given in Fig. 5.12.

> Foliage Ltd is considering buying a new grinding machine. It will cost £18,000, is expected to have a useful working life of 8 years, and will have an expected scrap value of £1,800 at the end of its working life. It is expected that the machine will increase net cash flows to the enterprise by £3,500 each year until that time. If the current market interest rate is 13%, and the inflation rate is 6%, what is the NPV of the machine?

Figure 5.12   The problem of NPV and inflation.

Let us begin by reminding ourselves of the nature of inflation. In a general inflation, prices in general rise, hence the 'money labels' attached to real goods change because money itself has changed in value, not because of any intrinsic property of the goods themselves. It is the real goods that matter, of course, since it is they that provide benefits. However, in the problem in Fig. 5.12 the *cash sums* coming in over the period of the investment do not change. A constant stream of similar amounts of cash therefore represents a declining real value of income in terms of its purchasing power over real goods.

Now let us turn to interest rates. We showed in Chapter 4 that the rate of discount reflects opportunity cost: that is, the sacrifice the consumer makes in deferring consumption. Now that sacrifice will be made in terms of *real* future benefits. This means that the discount rate before any account is taken of inflation will also reflect real sacrifice.

We can now distinguish between two things:

1. a set of *real* future benefits that will be discounted by a *real* discount rate unadjusted for any inflationary element;
2. a set of *monetary* future benefits that will be discounted by a *monetary* discount rate which takes inflation into account.

| | | CASH FLOWS | |
		Real	Monetary
	Real	OK	x
DISCOUNT RATE			
	Market	x	OK

Figure 5.13   Inflation, cash flows and interest rates.

The market as a whole will take the changing value of future benefits that accompanies inflation into account when it sets discount rates: thus we can say that the market rate of interest is the monetary rate of interest. And thus, *either* of the two alternatives in (1) and (2) above, used consistently, will give the same correct answer. That is, you can either discount real cash flows at a real discount rate, or monetary cash flows at a market interest rate. This is illustrated in Fig. 5.13.

In practical terms, method (1) above will tend not to be used because the real benefits (monetary benefits adjusted by an inflationary term) are not known. The monetary benefits and the market rate of interest, on the other hand, are known. Care should be taken here, however. In an examination or textbook calculation the future cash flow will tend to be given to you. In the real world where cash flows have to be estimated, the management that makes those estimates will have to do so by incorporating expected inflation rates into their calculations. Aware or not, what they are doing is beginning with a *real* future benefit, then adjusting it for inflation. If (as in the case of Foliage Ltd), the future flows are stated to be constant, management must have decided that they cannot raise prices in line with inflation and hence are resigned to a decline in real benefits over the years.

Thus in general no special notice need be taken of inflation and the solution to Foliage Ltd will be as in Fig. 5.14.

The net present value will be:

$$-18,000 + 3,500a_{\overline{8}|} + 1,800v^8$$

discounted at 13%. This gives:

$$-18,000 + 16,796 + 677 = £(527).$$

Figure 5.14 Solution of Fig. 5.12.

To understand the example more fully it is necessary to ask: what is the *real* rate of interest underlying the nominal market rate of 13%? Let us begin with a one-period model and call the real rate r. Then any investor who accepts the rate r as representing his or her sacrifice and invests £1 now will require £$(1 + r)$ at the end of a year. But if there has been inflation, so that a money amount received will be less than it would have been if real values had been maintained, then the investor will require that money amount to be higher by the amount of inflation (this is called the Fisher effect). If, for instance, the inflation rate were f, then the investor would require £$(1 + r)(1 + f)$ in money terms at the end of the period. Thus if we represent the market discount rate by m we can state that:

$$(1 + m) = (1 + r)(1 + f)$$

and thus the real interest rate r will be:

$$\frac{1 + m}{1 + f} - 1$$

In the example given in Figs. 5.12 and 5.14 then, the real rate will be:

$$(1.13)/(1.06) - 1 = 0.066 \text{ or } 6.6\%$$

5.8 Project valuation within the enterprise: tax considerations

Taxation has for the greater part of this century been a major consideration for companies. Sometimes corporate taxation has been high (it has reached 52% before now), sometimes it has scarcely been of any practical importance. (Through much of the 1970s the government introduced measures to aid corporate cash flows under inflation that effectively made the payment of tax optional.) To add a further complication, the corporate tax *system* has changed. Before 1965 there was a system based on income tax; from 1965 there was the 'classical system' of taxation (which is still used in the USA, among many other countries); and currently the system in operation is the 'imputation system'. For the sake of continuity we shall not give details of the UK tax system in this chapter. Brief, but hopefully adequate, detail is given in the Workbook (see p. 426–7). We shall for the present assume that the imputation system is in operation at the current (1990/91) rate of 35%.

Bringing tax into account in investment appraisal decisions involves no new principles. The corporation tax is charged on the company's profits (after various adjustments), and so far as any investment project is concerned, tax is just another cash outlay. However, the *magnitude* of corporation tax is sufficiently high to render it very significant for corporate decisions. In particular, issues such as the timing of tax payments become significant. We shall in our examples assume that tax is paid one year after the period to which it refers, but in fact this is dependent on a number of factors.

In what follows we shall use the NPV method. Consider the example given in Fig. 5.15. For the sake of simplicity, we shall assume for the present that the taxable profit (before capital allowances) is the same as the net cash flows. We also ignore advanced corporation tax. On this basis the solution is as in Fig. 5.16.

Each cash flow (profit before deduction of depreciation) is reduced by a capital allowance before tax is calculated. The capital allowance itself is 25% of the outstanding balance of the unused capital allowances. Thus, the first year's capital allowance is 25% of the capital sum. The second year's capital allowance is 25% of the capital sum less the first year's capital allowance — and so on. Readers familiar with the reducing balance method for depreciation in financial accounting (see *Financial Accounting: Method and Meaning* Chapter 5, p. 121) will observe the similarity immediately.

Hummel Ltd has developed a project that will entail the outlay of £25,000 immediately, and net cash inflows of £8,000 for the next five years. It is estimated that the asset can then be sold for £3,000. If the corporation tax rate is 35%, capital allowances are 25% and tax is paid one year in arrears, what is the NPV of the project? Assume a discount rate of 12%.

Figure 5.15 The problems of NPV and tax.

The use of the reducing balance method means that increasingly smaller capital allowances will be deducted; and they will continue indefinitely. However, when the asset is sold, a balancing allowance is made which takes into account the total net cost of the asset (original cost less any receipt on its sale) and the capital allowances already made, and permits the first less the second to be charged against profits in the year of sale.

It will be seen that the resulting corporation tax (column E) is lagged one year (column F) to allow for delay permitted before payment to the Inland Revenue need be made. Thus the discounted amount in the DCF calculation is the pre-tax cash flows less this lagged amount. It will be seen that, in the example given, the NPV is positive (£1,085).

Yr	Net cash flow	Capital all'ce	Taxable surplus B − C	Corp'n tax (CT) 35% × D	CT lagged 1 year	Cash flow after tax B − F	Discount factor	Discounted cash flow G × H
A	B £	C £	D £	E £	F £	G £	H £	I £
0	−25,000					−25,000	1.0000	−25,000
1	8,000	6,250	1,750	613		8,000	0.8929	7,143
2	8,000	4,688	3,312	1,159	613	7,387	0.7972	5,889
3	8,000	3,516	4,484	1,570	1,159	6,841	0.7118	4,869
4	8,000	2,637	5,363	1,877	1,570	6,430	0.6355	4,087
5	11,000	4,910	6,090	2,131	1,877	9,123	0.5674	5,177
6					2,131	−2,131	0.5066	−1,080
								1,085

Column B for year 5 is the sum of the investment inflow and the asset sale. Column C is 25% applied to the remaining balance: for example, in year 3, the capital allowance is 25% of (£25,000 − £6,250 − £4,688) = £3,516. The final item in column C is (£25,000 − £3,000) − (£6,250 + £4,688 + £3,516 + £2,637) as a balancing allowance.

Figure 5.16   Solution to Fig. 5.15.

5.9   General considerations

In this chapter we began by taking into account some general consequences of introducing the enterprise into our model, and this has enabled us to bring into play some practical considerations. In particular, we have seen how the fundamental NPV model works when applied to shareholders of business enterprises on the one hand, and within those enterprises on the other hand. However, the context of these matters must be kept in mind.

The development of the model has *assumed* that it is concerned only with the private business enterprise, and moreover has assumed that the enterprise is wealth maximizing. Now the issue of whether the business enterprise is indeed wealth maximizing is a contentious one which has exercised economists and others for decades. Models such as those of Herbert Simon (discussed in Chapter 1 of *Managerial Accounting: Method and Meaning*) have challenged this. So have many others (for example, Marris, Baumol, Williamson), and they were considered in Chapter 1 of this book. This raises two issues that we shall now discuss briefly:

1. If the private enterprise is not wealth maximizing, what are the implications for the theory we have just developed? So far as the model of the individual investor is concerned, this issue is unimportant. For models of organizations, we may suppose that either:

   - the search procedure is not exhaustive so that, of the projects available to the enterprise, it does not necessarily select the best ones for analysis (Simon's satisficing approach); or
   - the criterion that is applied to the project is some criterion other than wealth maximization (for instance, sales maximization).

   In the first case the NPV model is relevant once the projects have been selected. In the second case it will not be applied. The evidence as to whether or not managerialist economic theories are correct is inconclusive. If they are, then this might well explain why many enterprises do not use discounted cash flow methods exclusively in investment appraisal. On the other hand, there are many equally persuasive explanations for this.

2. Given that many other organizations have to access new projects (for example, governmental bodies for new transport schemes, local authorities for new schools, leisure facilities or police stations, nationalized industries for new projects), what are the implications for them? Taking the NPV criterion as a *normative* model, the general solution in the absence of a wealth-maximizing criterion is to be found in the area of *cost–benefit analysis*, where the financial considerations are taken as a first step and then modified as appropriate by broader social factors (such as externalities). In Chapter W5 we consider not just the social factors for the non-business enterprise but also, in the Ford Pinto case, the arguments for such factors to be raised in the case of private enterprise.

Summary

In this chapter we have proposed the following:

1. The enterprise is inserted between the investor and the project for convenience. On balance, the individual and the economy are better off with it than without it. Nevertheless, it does cause agency problems (though these have solutions).
2. Because it is only secondary, the existence of the enterprise just highlights the importance of NPV, because it acts as a recursive criterion, both between investor and enterprise and between enterprise and project.
3. Turning to the investor–enterprise relation, we need a model for valuing the enterprise and, in particular, the shares that constitute its ownership. It was argued that the Gordon growth model is a helpful way of managing this.
4. Turning next to the enterprise–project relation, we noted project evaluation methods other than discounting ones, specifically payback and the accountant's rate of return. Neither was really satisfactory.
5. Then we acknowledged that capital rationing might exist, either as far as the whole enterprise was concerned, or some part of it. Taking the simple case where one outflow was followed by a series of inflows, the profitability index was shown to be a helpful means of allocating funds to their best uses.

6. Next we considered a particular problem — that of inflation — and how it might be dealt with in the framework of the DCF methods so far discussed.
7. Finally, we saw the way we might deal with tax in capital-budgeting decisions.

Key terms and concepts

Here is a list of the key terms and concepts which have featured in this chapter. You should make sure that you understand and can define each one of them. Page references to definitions in the text appear in bold in the index.

- Home-made dividend
- Gordon growth model
- Payback
- Discounted payback
- Accountant's rate of return
- Capital rationing
- Profitability index
- Monetary discount rate
- Real discount rate
- Imputation tax system

Further reading

The mechanics of this chapter are really pretty straightforward — they just extend the ideas already consolidated in Chapter 4. More important is the context of the techniques. The readings given in the Workbook (King, Tinker and the reply by King) are helpful here. So is Cooper (1975). A fascinating use of project appraisal is to be found in the analysis of the Lockheed Tri-Star project, which virtually bankrupted the company (Reinhart, 1973).

The Workbook material to accompany this chapter begins on p. 405.

6

Portfolio theory

Learning objectives

After studying this chapter you should be able to:

- list the advantages to be gained from diversifying a portfolio;
- appreciate how to construct portfolios of two or more projects, and how to calculate their risk and expected return;
- illustrate graphically such portfolios;
- understand the significance of the envelope curve, the efficiency frontier and the market portfolio;
- appreciate why it is preferable for the rational risk-averse investor to position himself or herself on the capital market line.

6.1 Introduction

To recap: in this chapter we continue the unrealistic assumption of Chapter 4, in that we do not take any particular notice of the existence of the business enterprise. However, we now turn to look at the way the principles of Chapter 4 may be changed once we recognize that the world is a risky place.

In Chapter 4 we took a straightforward purpose: wealth maximization. We had already seen in Chapter 1 that this might not indeed be wholly realistic. However, it is a simplifying assumption without which, it is argued by most commentators, we cannot proceed to suggest policies for investment decision-making. To put it another way: if you start with the wealth maximization assumption and see where it leads, you can afterwards weigh the prescription you have in front of you against any other objectives you may have. This is, of course, particularly true for the non-commercial organization. It may be true for the unit trust (a trust in which investors pool together their funds that are then diversified among a large number of securities) that explicitly follows a social objective. It may, for instance, refuse to invest in tobacco companies, or those that pollute the environment, or those dealing with South Africa. All these can be compared against the touchstone we are developing now. Once you know the implications of wealth maximization, you can make an informed judgement about the result of deciding *not* to wealth-maximize.

Now in Chapter 4 we only recognized *returns*. These returns were the net cash flows that resulted from investment. Once we begin to acknowledge risk, we have to ask: how sure are we that these returns are actually going to be received? In other words, the operationalization of the idea of risk is one in which *we look at the chances of getting or not getting the returns we expect*.

Of course, we have said something about risk already. In Chapter 2, much of the discussion was concerned with risky securities markets. We showed how options and futures could be used either to increase or reduce risk. But all this was fairly intuitive. To go any further we need to consider more rigorously what risk *means*, how we can *measure it* and how we can *reduce it*.

What results in the *two-parameter* model. The two parameters referred to are return and risk. So when we consider any investment we ask not just — as in Chapter 4 — what the return is, measured through NPV or IRR, but also the probability of receiving that return. Yet this is not quite adequate either. We are concerned not just with the probability of the single return that we think is most likely, but the probabilities of a whole set of possible returns.

In this chapter, then, we look at how to handle these problems through two-parameter theory. We see that return and risk are measured as mean and standard deviation respectively (which you will be familiar with through your studies of statistics) and see how to understand the way in which they relate to people's preferences for different amounts of risk and return. Finally — and intuitively this is not at all obvious — we see that in most cases it is worthwhile holding (or owning) risk-free assets as well as risky ones, even though we are content to take some risk so as to get a better return.

6.2   The two-parameter model: the two-investment case

Let us begin by being a little more explicit about the nature of return. It can come about through two basic mechanisms:

1. The first is a cash return from the investment: for the share this is the dividend, for the project this is the net cash flow generated.
2. The second mechanism is *capital growth*. This can exist for the project — for instance, if we build up a business based on a good idea, the whole can then be sold and we have made a capital profit as a result of the goodwill. This goodwill in turn means that, because we have built up a customer base, expertise, market share and so on, the future returns will be higher. Thus capital growth arises from the expectation of higher future cash returns — nothing more nor less. For the share, capital growth is the proportionate increase in the share price from one period to the next.

In the exposition that follows, we shall normally assume that we are considering the investor who holds shares, because that is the easiest way to explain what is happening. You should remember, however, that these are *general principles* that are true of any investment that has the two characteristics of return and risk. (There is a somewhat different discussion of risk in *Managerial Accounting: Method and Meaning*, Chapter 4. We shall restrict ourselves to the conventional views of financial theory here.)

Because both cash return and capital growth are ways of receiving a return, we can add the two together. This means that the return the investor gets can be measured as:

$$\text{Return} = \frac{\text{Dividends} + (\text{Market price}_t - \text{Market price}_{t-1})}{\text{Market price}_{t-1}}$$

UK public companies will usually pay an *interim* and a *final* dividend. The former is declared after six months of the financial year, the latter after it has ended. Interim dividends tend to be conservative: that is, less than half what the company expects to be able to pay at the year-end. This means that, if the period concerned is a year, the 'dividend' portion will probably consist of an interim and a final dividend, and the price difference in the brackets will be the growth (or fall) in the price over that year. The period may, of course, be only a month or a week. In that case there may or may not have been a dividend declared. It could also be true for a period of many years. This is less common because we tend to think in terms of a 'return per annum' and not, say, a return per five-year period.

Now this is all very well on its own if it is *ex post*. Once the period is over, we know what the return was. Usually this is not the problem we are faced with, though. If we are trying to decide what to do in advance, so as to make a decision, then we do not know for certain what the return will be. We know neither the dividend nor the change in market price. So each of these has to be measured as an *expectation*. We measure the expected dividend and the expected capital growth or loss: in other words, we are concerned with *expected return*. And since this is uncertain, there is a risk that the expected return will be one of a number of different sums.

(*Note:* We take the term 'risk' to refer to good things as well as bad ones. This is not usual in everyday speech: we do not speak of the risk of winning a football pool. But so far as measurement is concerned, there is no difference between 'upside' and 'downside' risk. Roughly we can say that upside risk is the chance that a return will be better than expected, downside risk the chance that it will be worse than expected. Both are referred to as risk. As you will see shortly, we tend to measure risk through the normal distribution, which is symmetrical. Hence more upside and downside risk must go exactly together, since they are either side of the mean.)

We begin with the simplest case: where there are two possible investment projects.

Table 6.1 Probabilities and returns of two investments

Advertising (A)		Boots (B)	
P_A	R_A %	P_B	R_B %
0.05	10	0.05	2
0.20	15	0.25	12
0.50	20	0.40	20
0.20	25	0.25	28
0.05	30	0.05	38
1.00		1.00	

Note:
P_A = probability of return on A
R_A = the corresponding return on A
P_B = probability of return on B
R_B = the corresponding return on B

(a) A two-project example

Suppose Ms Connors is considering two investments. The first is in an advertising agency (A), the second is in a boot-manufacturing company (B). She is concerned with the return and risk after one year, and has already taken into account both expected dividend and capital growth when calculating the expected return (we shall look at the mechanics of this calculation later in this sub-section). She estimates that the likely returns, and the chances of receiving them, are as in Table 6.1.

In other words, in the advertising investment, she thinks there is a 5% chance that the return on her investment after a year will be 10%, a 20% chance that it will be a 15% return, and so on. Since she has taken all possibilities into account, the probabilities must sum to 1.00.

If we then calculate the mean and dispersion of these two investments we find the following results:

Mean or expected return of A = 20   of B = 20
Variance of A   = 20   of B = 64.4
Standard deviation of A   =   4.47 of B =   8.02

If we then plot these probabilities against the returns, we find something that, if extended to a continuous set of possibilities, looks something like Fig. 6.1. The returns for the two investments are the same, but the riskiness is different. B gives more chance of upside gain, but also more downside danger.

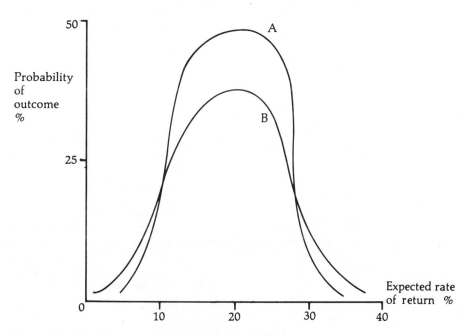

Figure 6.1 Possible outcomes of two independent investments.

Let us turn to a second example. In this case we are not going to measure the risk in terms of expected probabilities of different returns. The reason is straightforward: it is pretty difficult to attach prior probabilities to expected outcomes. Instead we shall use the *history* of returns in the past to give us a good estimate of the likely riskiness in the future. The greater the dispersion of returns in the past, the more risky we shall assume the future is going to be.

Thus expected return is measured as the expected mean of the returns that might accrue from the investment. Expected risk is the chance that various outcomes might be forthcoming, and is measured as the standard deviation of the past returns. However, one matter should be clarified here, since it can give rise to misunderstanding.

The returns from a security in the future are not known. If they were, it would be risk-free. What is (probably) known is the record of past returns from the security. It is conventional to use these past (or *ex post*) returns as an indicator — in the absence of any better information — of the future risk. *But they are not the same thing.* The past is known, the future is not. Hence the variation in past returns that is plugged into the two-parameter model is an *estimate* of the future (or *ex ante*) risk of the investment. It does not itself constitute that risk, because it cannot: all those past returns are already known.

Let us suppose that Ms Ferguson is being offered the opportunity to invest in a project. This project is marketable (if it were not she would not be able to buy into it). She asks what the market price of the project has been for the last few years, and is given the information in Table 6.2. From this she needs to find the mean return she would have received from the security, and the variation in the returns that have been received. These she will take as the best surrogates she has for the security's future return and risk.

Table 6.2   The market prices of security S for the past six years

Year	Market price £
1	100,000
2	122,000
3	112,240
4	85,300
5	93,830
6	112,600

The return may be taken from period to period. That is, since she may be obliged (for reasons of liquidity, for instance) to sell the security at any time, she will consider each year's return on the security to be the profit or loss arising from the difference in price between one year and the next. For example, between t_1 and t_2 her £100,000 investment would have grown to £122,000. Clearly this is a gain of 22%, measured as:

$$\text{Return } (r) = \frac{£122,000 - £100,000}{£100,000}$$

Similarly, the return for the next period can be found as (£112,240 − £122,000)/£122,000 = −8%. This means that for each of the five periods between the six successive market prices a return can be calculated, which is shown in Table 6.3. (You are advised to verify all the figures in Table 6.3.) From this information the mean and standard deviation can be calculated: they turn out to be respectively, 4% and 17.57%. (More detail of this calculation will be found in the Workbook.)

Table 6.3 The returns from holding security S for the past five years

Year (t)	Market price £	Return
1	100,000	
2	122,000	22%
3	112,240	−8%
4	85,300	−24%
5	93,830	10%
6	112,600	20%

We now suppose that Ms Ferguson has a second possibility open to her: an investment in a second project. We shall call the previous project S, and this second project T. We can perform a similar calculation to get the returns from the successive past year's record of the market prices of investment T, and the result is given in Table 6.4.

Table 6.4 The pricing and returns from project T

Year (t)	Market price £	Return
1	100,000	
2	90,000	−10%
3	87,300	−3%
4	87,300	0%
5	99,520	14%
6	118,430	19%

In fact, this share has the same mean return as share S (4%) but the standard deviation of past price changes has been only 10.83. Now clearly if Ms Ferguson chose to invest in equal proportions of S and T, the return she would receive would be 4%: the mean of the return of 4% on each investment. The risk would not, however, be the mean of the two risks 17.57 and 10.83 but something rather less than that mean, for whereas that mean would be 14.20%, in this it is only 11.44%.

There are two ways we can arrive at this figure. One is to create a set of *portfolio returns* by simply combining the two investments in each period, finding the mean return each year, and then calculating the standard deviation of the resulting price movements. This is illustrated in Table 6.5.

The other way is to use the following expression, which gives a variance for two shares (here given as x and y):

$$\text{Var}(x,y) = w_x^2.\sigma_x^2 + w_y^2.\sigma_y^2 + 2w_x w_y \sigma_{xy} \tag{6.1}$$

where w_i are the weights of x and y ($\Sigma w_i = 1$)

$\quad$ σ_i are the standard deviations of x and y

$\quad$ σ_{xy} is the covariance (which is the same as $\rho_{xy}\sigma_x\sigma_y$).

Table 6.5 Combining the two sets of returns

	Return (S)	Return (T)	Return (S and T)
	22%	−10%	6%
	−8%	−3%	−5.5%
	−24%	0%	−12%
	10%	14%	12%
	20%	19%	19.5%
Mean	4%	4%	4%
SD	17.57%	10.83%	11.44%

We can show that this gives the same result. The correlation co-efficient between the two investments S and T turns out to be 0.2565, so the covariance is (0.2565) (17.57) (10.83) = 48.81. Thus, using equation 6.1 we have a portfolio variance of:

$$(0.5)^2(17.57)^2 + (0.5)^2(10.83)^2 + 2(0.5)(0.5)(48.81) = 130.90$$

Hence the standard deviation is $(130.90)^{0.5}$ = 11.44% as before.

It can be seen even more clearly how diversification is helpful if we take two projects each of which has the same risk and return. Suppose we have risk and return of each project of 14% and 12% respectively, with correlation between their movements of 0.25. Even though this is not a zero or negative correlation, it pays to diversify because the mean of the two (that is, sharing available funds equally between them) is also 12%, but the risk (variance) is only:

$$2(0.5)^2(14)^2 + 2(0.5)(0.5)(14)(14)(0.25) = 122.5\%$$

and hence the standard deviation is 11.07% (which is, of course, reduced from 14% by the simple expedient of diversification).

(b) A more realistic case

Usually you will not find that the parameters of two investments are the same. The benefit of diversification then comes about because the mean expected return from the investments is the mean of the individual investments, but the risk is *less* than this (and, of course, this is true of any other weighting system between the two investments). This means that it pays the investor to diversify.

Suppose, for example, that we have investments with year-on-year returns as in Table 6.6. We can then weight combinations of them in various ways. In Table 6.7 we see weights of two-thirds/one-third, half/half and five-sixths/one-sixth. It must be emphasized that these are just *examples*. The curve that

Table 6.6 Year-on-year returns from investments X and Y

Year	X	Y
1	27%	8%
2	15%	14%
3	−10%	−6%
4	−30%	4%
5	38%	−10%

joins the investments X and Y is a curve that encompasses *all possible combinations* of X and Y and is, of course, a continuous function. For the data in Table 6.7 a graph can be drawn, as in Fig. 6.2. In drawing the latter figure, it should be noted that rather more points than in Table 6.7 were plotted to ensure the true curve was developed.

Table 6.7   Various combinations of investments X and Y

	All Y	(a)	(b)	(c)	(d)	All X
	8.00	11.17	14.33	17.50	20.67	27.00
	14.00	14.17	14.33	14.50	14.67	15.00
	−6.00	−6.67	−7.33	−8.00	−8.67	−10.00
	4.00	−1.67	−7.33	−13.00	−18.67	−30.00
	−10.00	−2.00	6.00	14.00	22.00	38.00
Mean	2.00	3.00	4.00	5.00	6.00	8.00
Variance	78.40	66.32	94.89	164.10	273.96	615.60
SD	8.85	8.14	9.74	12.81	16.55	24.81

Note: (a) 0.833Y + 0.167X
      (b) 0.667Y + 0.333X
      (c) 0.5Y + 0.5X
      (d) 0.167Y + 0.833X

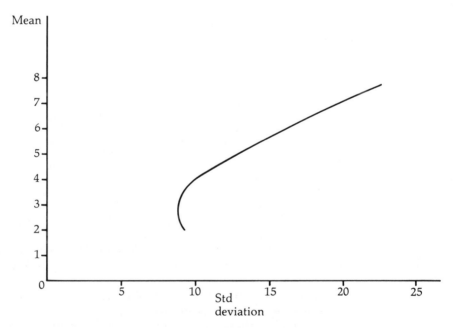

Figure 6.2   A graphical representation of Table 6.7.

6.3   Portfolios of more than two projects

(a) Diversification

We have devoted some space to the case of two investments because the general principles of portfolio diversification can be seen more clearly this way. However, it will generally be the case that an investor is presented with more than just two investment opportunities. Is it worthwhile diversifying beyond two investments?

To understand the answer to this, let us suppose that our investor is being offered three investments as in Table 6.8. Then the choice available is to invest in any one of the three A, B and C, in any combination of two investments (A and B, A and C, or B and C), or in all three at once. To take the simple case, we suppose that the choice is among just the following: all funds placed in one investment; equal (50%) investment in any of the three available combinations of two investments; or equal funds (one-third each) in the three-investment portfolio. The results are as in Table 6.9.

Table 6.8   Risk and return of three investments

Investment	A	B	C
Mean	12	15	22
SD	14	19	24
	A–B	A–C	B–C
Correlation	0.30	0.40	−0.35

Table 6.9   Parameters of various portfolios

	Mean	SD
Portfolio A + B	13.50	13.38
Portfolio A + C	17.00	16.13
Portfolio B + C	18.50	12.43
Portfolio A + B + C	16.33	11.75

It will be seen that *in this particular case* it has been possible to reduce the risk below that which applies for any individual investment or any pair of investments by diversifying across all three. However, it must be emphasized that:

1. it need not be true that an equal share among the investments will itself necessarily reduce risk in this way;
2. nevertheless there will be some combination among the three investments that will prove to have a lower risk than any point on the loci joining the individual investments;
3. in every case the whole picture of diversification must be looked at, rather than just a few points as we have done here.

We can now explain more precisely how the above figures were arrived at, looking at the more general case of diversification among n investments. So far as the expected mean return is concerned, the calculation is straightforward, being:

$$E(R_p) = \sum_{i=1}^{n} w_i E(R_i)$$

where $E(R_p)$ is the expected return on a portfolio
  w_i are the weights of the n investments
  $E(R_i)$ are the mean expected returns of the n investments.

The expected risk is more complex. It can be shown (see Copeland and Weston, 1983, pp. 169 *et seq.*) that the variance of a portfolio is found to be:

$$\text{Var}(R_p) = \sum_{i=1}^{n}\sum_{j=1}^{n} w_i w_j \text{Cov}(i, j) \tag{6.2}$$

This can be explained in more detail as follows. Let us begin with the two-share example with which we are now familiar. It will be seen from equation 6.2 that the relevant terms are the weights of the investments and the covariance between the investments. The apparent absence of the variance that will be observed in equation 6.1 is explained by the fact that variance is simply a special case of covariance: it is, in fact, the covariance of a random variable with itself. The portfolio variance for two investments A and B is then found by:

$$w_A w_A \sigma_{AA} + w_B w_B \sigma_{BB} + w_A w_B \sigma_{AB} + w_B w_A \sigma_{BA}$$

which of course is the same as:

$$w_A^2 \sigma_A^2 + w_B^2 \sigma_B^2 + 2 w_A w_B \sigma_{AB}$$

as in equation 6.1.

Thus for the two-investment example there are four terms. Beyond this the number of terms increases substantially: in the three-investment case, for example, there are basically nine terms. In general, for the n-investment case there are n^2 cases, being represented in a $n \times n$ matrix. In matrix terms, equation 6.2 expands to:

$$[w_A w_B \ldots w_n] \begin{bmatrix} \sigma_{AA} & \sigma_{AB} & \cdot & \cdot & \cdot & \sigma_{An} \\ \sigma_{BA} & \sigma_{BB} & \cdot & \cdot & \cdot & \sigma_{Bn} \\ \cdot & \cdot & \cdot & \cdot & \cdot & \cdot \\ \cdot & \cdot & \cdot & \cdot & \cdot & \cdot \\ \sigma_{nA} & \sigma_{nB} & \cdot & \cdot & \cdot & \sigma_{nn} \end{bmatrix} \begin{bmatrix} w_A \\ w_B \\ \cdot \\ \cdot \\ w_n \end{bmatrix} \tag{6.3}$$

which can be solved by the normal methods of matrix algebra.

Look more carefully at the matrix. The diagonal consists of the variances of the investments, so that for n investments there are n variances. The other elements are covariances, and there are $(n^2 - n)$ covariances. It would be a useful exercise at this point to solve this matrix for two investments. You will find that the result is equation 6.1.

Let us illustrate this further by means of the problem given in Fig. 6.3. The amount of calculation required to solve this problem, as you might expect from the explanation above, is considerable. First it is necessary to find the parameters of these investments. They may be calculated as shown in Table 6.10.

The table was calculated using a spreadsheet, and if you have access to one you are encouraged to replicate it. The first six columns show the past movements of the three investments together with their squares. This enables

Ms Newis has the opportunity to invest in three projects, which have had a history of returns as follows:

A	B	C
10.00	15.00	25.00
5.00	20.00	20.00
−5.00	40.00	20.00
−10.00	15.00	15.00
10.00	−20.00	−5.00
15.00	20.00	−5.00

She would like to know how much she should invest in each.

Figure 6.3 The three-investment problem.

Table 6.10

	A	A^2	B	B^2	C	C^2	D	E	F
	10.00	100.00	15.00	225.00	25.00	625.00	0.00	77.78	0.00
	5.00	25.00	20.00	400.00	20.00	400.00	4.17	6.94	41.67
	−5.00	25.00	40.00	1600.00	20.00	400.00	−229.17	−76.39	208.33
	−10.00	100.00	15.00	225.00	15.00	225.00	0.00	−47.22	0.00
	10.00	100.00	−20.00	400.00	−5.00	25.00	−204.17	−97.22	583.33
	15.00	225.00	20.00	400.00	−5.00	25.00	54.17	−180.56	−83.33
Mean	4.17		15.00		11.67				
Var		78.47		316.67		147.22			
SD		8.86		17.80		12.13			
Cov							−62.50	−52.78	125.00
Corr							−0.40	−0.49	0.58

Note: D = [A−E(A)][B−E(B)]
E = [A−E(A)][C−E(C)]
F = [B−E(B)][C−E(C)]

us to calculate the variance and standard deviation of each (as SD = $(E(A^2) −$ $(E(A))^2$, etc.). The final three columns, as explained in the note, are the deviations of each pair of investments from their mean multiplied together, and the covariance is the expected value of these. Finally, the correlation coefficient is found as the covariance divided by the multiple of the stardard deviations of each pair of investments.

For the risk of the three-share portfolio these now have to be plugged into equation 6.3. For this we need some weights, and the matrix has to be solved for each set of weights. This is clearly a major task — even for one set of weights the hand calculation takes some time. Once again the spreadsheet comes to our aid.

First, we expand equation 6.3. This gives:

$$\text{Var}_p = (w_A\sigma_A)^2 + (w_B\sigma_B)^2 + (w_C\sigma_C)^2 + 2w_Aw_B\sigma_{AB} + 2w_Aw_C\sigma_{AC} + 2w_Bw_C\sigma_{BC}$$

Next, we calculate Var_p for sample weights. It is here that the first difficulty becomes apparent. For the two-portfolio case we could take various weights of one investment, (w_i), with the weight of the other automatically being

$(1 - w_i)$ for each value of i. With three weights this is no longer possible. We shall begin, therefore, by creating three two-share portfolios (A + B, A + C and B + C) by holding each weight constant at zero in turn, while considering the weights of the others. This has been done in Table 6.11.

Table 6.11   Three-share portfolio risks in various combinations

A	B	C	D	E	F	G
0.00	12.13	12.13	17.80	11.67	11.67	15.00
0.10	12.04	10.51	15.69	12.00	10.92	13.92
0.20	12.12	8.97	13.64	12.34	10.17	12.83
0.30	12.37	7.56	11.66	12.67	9.42	11.75
0.40	12.79	6.35	9.83	13.00	8.67	10.67
0.50	13.36	5.49	8.22	13.34	7.92	9.59
0.60	14.06	5.15	7.00	13.67	7.17	8.50
0.70	14.87	5.44	6.38	14.00	6.42	7.42
0.80	15.77	6.27	6.55	14.33	5.67	6.34
0.90	16.75	7.46	7.45	14.67	4.92	5.25
1.00	17.80	8.86	8.86	15.00	4.17	4.17

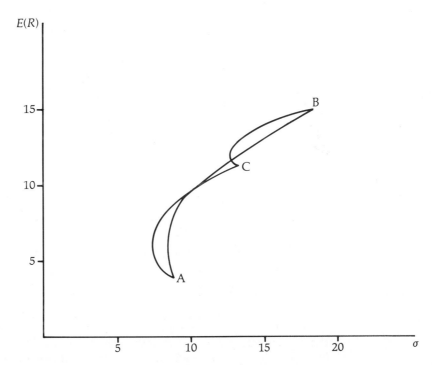

Figure 6.4   Sample values of the three-share portfolio of Table 6.11.

Columns B, C and D are the standard deviations of the two-investment portfolios; columns E, F and G are the corresponding expected returns. Columns B and E hold w_A constant at zero, the weights in column A being applied to w_B. Columns C and F hold $w_B = 0$, and columns D and G hold $w_C = 0$. In this way the three two-share portfolios plotted in Fig. 6.4 develop.

Now consider the first case again, where w_A is being held at zero while the other two are varied. For *each of the eleven calculations* which went towards forming the continuous line joining B and C we could apply $w_A = 0.1$, 0.2, 0.3, etc. Moreover, these are only individual possibilities: the possible weights of w_A are also continuous. It should be evident then that if we combine three investments we get a *continuous surface* rather than a line. This is illustrated in Fig. 6.5. This surface *goes to the left beyond* the curves AC and CB because the addition of the third share improves the risk–return profile further. Any point on this surface can be achieved by some weighted mixture of the investments A, B and C.

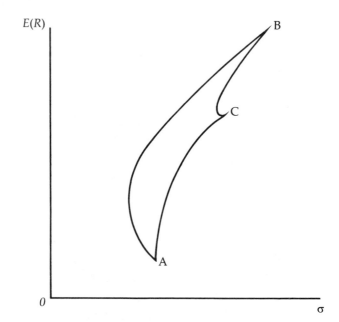

Figure 6.5   The set of available possibilities.

(b) A digression: the indifference map

Before we can continue our analysis of the envelope curve and its implications for investor choice, we need to digress a little. We need to remind ourselves of the economist's notion of an indifference curve.

Look at Fig. 6.6. The axes are the same as those we have been considering in all the diagrams so far. In this figure we have illustrated two indifference curves, labelled $I'I''$ and $J'J''$. As with any indifference curve, each of these traces the locus of points along which an individual is indifferent as between a series of possibilities.

To clarify this, let us take curve $I'I''$, beginning with points K and L. Point K shows that point at which the investor can expect a return of $E(R_K)$ subject to a risk of σ_k. Similarly, point L shows that point at which the investor can expect a return of $E(R_L)$ subject to a risk of σ_L. We have discovered that the

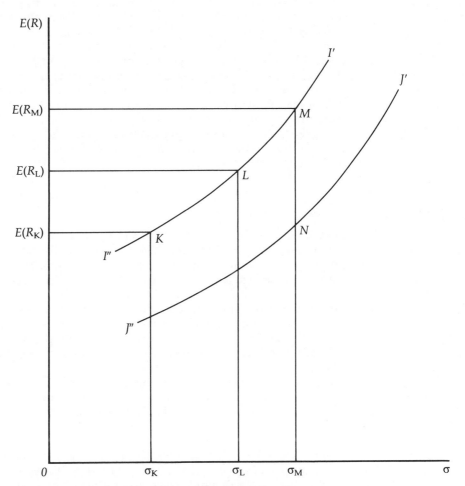

Figure 6.6 Part of an investor's indifference map.

investor would be equally happy at each point — that is, she would happily trade in the extra risk ($\sigma_L - \sigma_K$) in order to receive the expectation of increased income $E(R_L) - E(R_K)$. The points between K and L, of course, are all equally acceptable.

If, however, we asked our investor how much extra risk she would accept in order to get the expectation of a return $E(R_M)$ — that is, how much extra risk for the extra expected income $E(R_M) - E(R_L)$ — the answer would be only $\sigma_M - \sigma_L$. *Notice that $\sigma_M - \sigma_L$ is less than $\sigma_L - \sigma_K$*. That is, for increasing returns she is decreasingly willing to accept extra risk. This could be put another way: she would want increasingly higher returns to compensate for given increases in risk.

This tells us the shape of the curve: as we see from the diagram, each indifference curve slopes upwards with an increasing slope. It will be obvious from visual inspection of Fig. 6.6 that it is the increasing unwillingness to take on extra risk that accounts for the increasing slope.

Thus any point on the indifference curve $I'I''$ is equally acceptable to our hypothetical investor. Other points on the diagram also lie on indifference curves. Some are higher than $I'I''$, some lower. If they are higher they are more desirable. If they are lower they are less desirable. This is illustrated by drawing the second curve, labelled $J'J''$. Every point on this curve gives less satisfaction to this investor than any point on $I'I''$. We can see this by comparing point M on $I'I''$ with point N on curve $J'J''$. Both entail the same risk σ_M; but the expected return from M is higher than that from N.

Different investors will have different-shaped indifference curves — some will be flatter than others. This shows different attitudes to risk. We shall meet this matter later in Fig. 6.10.

We see the importance of the analysis we have just given when we come to combine the surface of investment possibilities shown in Fig. 6.5 with the indifference curves of Fig. 6.6.

(c) The envelope curve

First, let us be quite clear about the difference between our set of indifference curves and the shaded area. Indifference curves show what investors' attitudes are to different possibilities. Some points on the indifference map are possible to achieve, some are not. The shaded area is *that set of investments which is available* to investors. Any point within the shaded area can be achieved with the right mix of shares A, B and C. The rest of the (white) space cannot be achieved. Given that any point in the shaded area is available, therefore, we now come to the crucial question: which of the infinite number of possibilities that an individual investor might choose is the best one?

Now look at Fig. 6.7. This combines the shaded opportunity set of Fig. 6.5 with indifference curves such as in Fig. 6.6. In this figure, consider an amount of risk σ_X. Any point on the line joining points X and Z is available to the investor, with resulting expected returns between $E(R_X)$ and $E(R_Z)$. When given the choice between a lower and a higher return for the same risk, the investor will obviously prefer the higher to the lower. This means that for risk σ_X, point X will be preferred to any of the points below it, such as point Z.

This clearly links to our discussion of indifference curves. Fig. 6.7 illustrates just three indifference curves out of an infinite number for a given investor. We have already seen that the investor will prefer an indifference curve as far outwards as possible. This means that, in the case shown in Fig. 6.7, the investor illustrated will select a point on the highest possible indifference curve which is at the same time on the feasible set of opportunities. Clearly this will be on the highest point.

We may generalize from this observation. Whatever the slope of the indifference curve, the most preferred point will always be the highest from a given quantity of risk, and hence the only important points on the shaded space are those that lie along the top of that space. Because of the importance of these points, the line that consists of these points is given a special name. The line that runs around the space is called the *envelope curve*, and the particular set of points that dominates the others (that is, is always chosen in preference to the others) is called the *efficiency frontier*. This is shown in Fig. 6.8. Hence, in Fig. 6.7, both points X and Z lie on the envelope curve, but only point X lies on the efficiency frontier and is thus a member of the set of most efficient points from which to select a portfolio of investments.

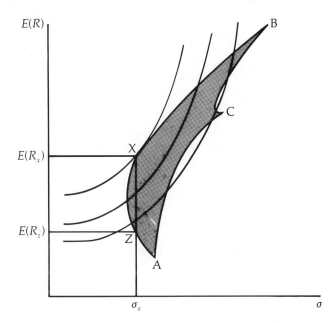

Figure 6.7   The optimal choice available from a set of possibilities with risk

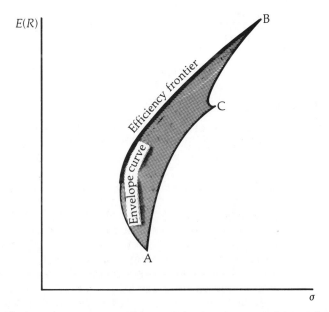

Figure 6.8   The envelope curve and the set of risk–return possibilities showing the efficiency frontier

We may now return to the question we posed in Fig. 6.3 at the beginning of this section. We asked about Ms Newis's choice of investments, and how she should share her funds among the three opportunities available to her. The conclusion we are obliged to draw from the foregoing discussion is that *we cannot advise her*, without further information. We do not know her attitude to risk, and the risk–return trade-off that she would wish in given circumstances.

Since the imaginary Ms Newis represents any intending investor, it seems we have reached a conclusion that information from past security performance alone is insufficient for us to recommend a portfolio. Investors differ in their attitude to risk. So long as there are only risky securities available, this is indeed true. However, once risk-free securities are also made available to the investor, the theory of finance suggests that we can in fact advise her on her selection of risky investments — and that we shall advise her to buy exactly the same set of investments as everybody else, regardless of her, and their, risk preferences.

To see how we arrive at this startling conclusion, we need first to investigate what happens as the number of investments increases beyond just two or three. We can then turn to the *Tobin separation theorem* in section 6.5 to see how we arrive at this remarkable — and, given what we have just argued, counter-intuitive — result.

6.4   More than three projects

We have now seen that a better risk–return profile can be obtained by diversifying beyond two projects to three projects, if this is feasible (that is, if such projects are on offer). This raises two connected points:

1. is it desirable to diversify beyond three investments to as many as possible?
2. if a very wide diversification is achieved, does there come a stage at which all risk has been diversified away?

Let us consider each of these points in some detail.

(a) Fuller diversification

In the case of a two-investment portfolio, it is possible that diversification might not help the risk–return relationship, but this is only true in the exceptional case where the two investments' returns are perfectly correlated. The general rule is that diversification from one investment to two is helpful, and above we have seen that extending this from two to three investments is also helpful. Now if two or more projects are not perfectly correlated among themselves (and this is so unlikely that it can be dismissed as a possibility for all practical purposes), then clearly any additional project taken on will also be helpful because it cannot be perfectly correlated with both or all of the existing projects. In other words, if the portfolio consists of the n projects P_1, P_2, ... P_n then any further project P_{n+1} can at the most be fully correlated with one of the existing projects — say P_i — but since P_i is less than perfectly correlated with all other projects, so P_{n+1} must also be less than perfectly correlated with them. Hence we can conclude that further diversification is worthwhile.

To illustrate this would in most cases be complex in view of the large number of calculations that would have to be made. However, in the special case where the investments are uncorrelated we can show easily how increasing the spread reduces the risk. This is because, for a correlation coefficient of zero, the last term in equation 6.1 will vanish in the two-investment case and, indeed, all but the diagonals of the n-case matrix solution of equation 6.3 will vanish also, leaving the variances along the diagonal.

For the two-investment case, therefore, the expression for the portfolio variance is:

$$w_A^2 \sigma_A^2 + w_B^2 \sigma_B^2$$

and for the n-investment portfolio case it is:

$$w_A^2 \sigma_A^2 + w_B^2 \sigma_B^2 + \ldots + w_n^2 \sigma_n^2$$

Sharpe (1985, p. 133) points out that this can be simply illustrated by assuming weights divided equally among the investments with all the investments having the same risk σ_i. In such a case, for n investments, the portfolio variance where all investments are uncorrelated will be:

$$
\begin{aligned}
\text{Var}_p &= \left[\frac{1}{n}\right]^2 \sigma_i^2 + \left[\frac{1}{n}\right]^2 \sigma_i^2 + \left[\frac{1}{n}\right]^2 \sigma_i^2 + \ldots \\
&= n \left[\frac{1}{n}\right]^2 \sigma_i^2 \\
&= \frac{\sigma_i^2}{n}
\end{aligned}
$$

so that:

$$\sigma_p = \frac{\sigma_i}{\sqrt{n}}$$

In Table 6.12 the values of σ_p are given for a value of $\sigma_i = 15\%$; they are shown on a graph in Fig. 6.9. It will be seen that, as the portfolio widened, risk does indeed reduce virtually to zero.

Table 6.12   The effect of increasing the size of a portfolio on its risk.

No. of investments	Risk (SD)
1	15.00
2	10.61
3	8.66
5	6.71
10	4.74
50	2.12
100	1.50
200	1.06
500	0.67
1,000	0.47
10,000	0.15

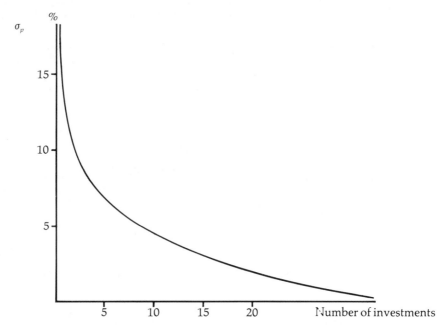

Figure 6.9 The pattern of decreasing risk with various sizes of portfolio.

(b) Can all risk be avoided through diversification?

If two investments are perfectly negatively correlated, then there has to be some proportion between the two that would result in zero risk. Can this be reached in the real world with a large number of assets? Indeed, are there any limits to the reduction in risk possible through diversification?

We can gain an intuitive answer to this by imagining what a very high diversification means. We have to suppose, of course, that some mechanism exists whereby we might be able to invest in many projects. Of course, such a situation does occur in reality: since it is possible to invest in the stock market, and many shares are on offer, then the individual investor can diversify widely. Indeed, there is no reason why he or she should not diversify right across all the projects currently being undertaken in the UK economy, perhaps through the medium of a unit trust. If this does happen, then (particularly in the special case where these holdings are in exact proportion to the size of the total projects) the risk to that individual is the risk of the whole economy.

Of course, the risk of the whole economy is not zero. Taking all risky assets together, there will still be some risk involved in holding them. Risk is concerned with the likelihood of increase and decrease in the market price and the stream of income arising from holding assets, and just as the fortunes of the individual investment change, so do the fortunes of whole economies. Factors that affect economies include:

1. world trade prospects generally;
2. the trade cycle;
3. the changing competitiveness of other nations;

4. innovation in whole industries or particular products;
5. changing patterns of protectionism;
6. natural factors (such as droughts and famines);
7. wars; and so on.

Thus even diversification as wide as this cannot avoid risk completely. Indeed, it is possible to diversify worldwide and still many of the factors listed above would mean that there was a 'world risk' that was not zero.

In fact the pattern that is found is similar to the curve of Fig. 6.9, with the risk reducing steeply as the number of investments increases to around 20 to 50 and much more slowly thereafter. However, unlike Fig. 6.9, the risk does not go below about 30% (the exact figure depends on which 'total' set of investments is being considered — the usual proxy is one of the indices that represents a major stock market such as the International Stock Exchange in London or the New York Stock Exchange). This is illustrated in Fig. 6.10.

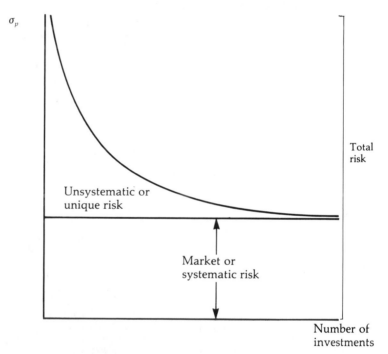

Figure 6.10 The limit to the benefits of diversification.

Figure 6.10 is most important because it gives a clue to the extension of the risk–return analysis that we shall take up again in Chapter 7. It tells us that, by diversifying, risk can be reduced, but that there comes a point at which risk cannot, for practical purposes, be reduced any further. This is the risk of the market, and is sometimes called *market risk*. Alternatively it is referred to as *systematic risk* because it is the risk of the total economic system.

Now think of any individual investment. It has its own risk, but much of this (we have implied that on average it is about 70%) can be diversified away. This means that, *for all practical purposes*, this part of the investment's risk is irrelevant. The difference between the total risk of the investment (or any set of investments) and the systematic risk is called the *unique risk* or *unsystematic risk*. The profound consequence of this is that, whereas up to now we have implied that the important two parameters for the investor are the project's return and risk, we must now modify this to the return and its *systematic risk*. There is, however, a great deal more to be said about the nature of systematic risk, and we shall return to that in Chapter 7.

6.5 Combining risky and riskless investments

Up to now we have also implied that the investor will select a position on the efficiency frontier of the envelope curve that reflects his or her own personal preference for risk and return, expressed through the indifference curve. This can be seen in Fig. 6.11 which illustrates the envelope curve enclosing the universe of possible investment opportunities, together with indifference curves for two investors A and B. Investor A is willing to take a greater risk, and thus his highest feasible indifference curve $A'A''$ is tangential to the envelope curve at A^*. Investor B, on the other hand, has an indifference curve $B'B''$ which leads to a risk–return tangent to the efficiency frontier at B^*. It is evident that both the risk and return of A are higher than those of B.

However, this is only true if the only investments available to A and B are risky investments. In these circumstances it is true that these are the highest

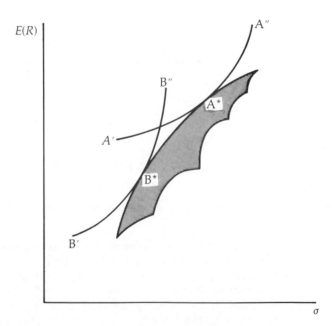

Figure 6.11 The envelope curve with two investors' indifference curves.

feasible curves within the indifference maps of A and B. But this assumption of solely risky investments does not reflect the securities available to the investor in the real world: there are also many *risk-free* securities available, such as government bonds. The investor is thus free to combine risky with risk-free securities.

Once this is done, it becomes clear that it is possible for the investor to reach a higher point on his or her indifference map. This is illustrated in Fig. 6.12.

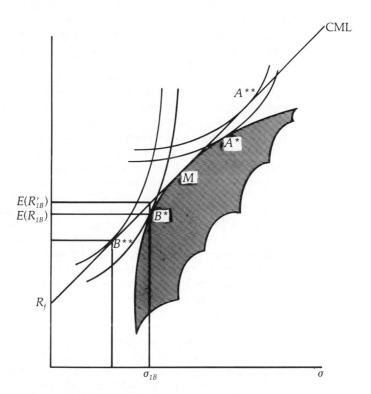

Figure 6.12   The capital market line.

The risk-free rate offered on, say, short-dated government stocks is shown as R_f. Any investor is free to divide his or her funds between an investment in the set of risky assets represented by point M on the efficiency frontier, and the risk-free stock R_f. This gives a linear combination of the form:

$$w_m M + (1 - w_m)B$$

where M represents a parameter of the risky investments, B a parameter of the risk-free investment, and w_m the proportion placed in the risky investments. Thus, for instance, if the expected return on risky investments is 20%, the return on risk-free investment is 12% and the proportion invested in the former is 60%, then the expected return of the portfolio is the linear combination:

$$0.6 \times 20\% + (1 - 0.6) \times 12\% = 16.8\%$$

All points that represent such combinations of risky and risk-free securities must, since we have a linear combination, lie on the straight line that joins R_f to M. If the investor prefers less risk, the position will be nearer to R_f; if he or she prefers more risk, the position will be nearer M (or, as we shall see shortly, beyond M).

Let us return to investor B to illustrate what this means for his selected portfolio. Without the opportunity to invest in risk-free assets he is at position B^* with risk σ_{1B} and expected return $E(R_{1B})$. Once risk-free assets are available he can combine his holdings between M and B in such a way as to get a higher return $E(R'_{1B})$ for the same risk. In fact, given the nature of the indifference map, he prefers to move to point B^{**} where the return is slightly lower but the risk is substantially lower. We know that investor B prefers this position (slightly lower return but substantially lower risk) because the indifference curve cutting R_fM at B^{**} is a higher indifference curve than that which goes through the point B^*.

Now let us turn to investor A. He prefers more risk, as we have seen. However, his indifference map takes him beyond that applicable to portfolio M. He does not divide his money between M and B; instead he *borrows* at the risk-free rate R_f and uses the borrowed funds, plus those funds he already has, to invest so as to reach point A^{**}.

The straight line we have referred to is generally referred to as the *capital market line* (CML). The clear separation between risky and risk-free assets has led the solution above to be known as *Tobin's separation theorem*.

Now consider portfolio M. Investor A employed this combination of risky assets. So did investor B. Clearly, given the advantages that accrue to it, any investor will invest in this combination — that is, *all* investors will select this combination. In equilibrium, therefore, this is the only portfolio that will be held by every rational risk-averse investor (by risk-averse we do not mean that the investor dislikes risk altogether; we merely mean that, given two investments with equal returns and different risks, the lower risk will be preferred). It therefore becomes the *market portfolio*, and, in equilibrium, it must represent the total number of risky investments available, in the proportions that their values represent compared to the whole.

This statement can be justified using the familiar equilibrium argument. Suppose that we begin from a position of equilibrium in the conditions just stated. Then suppose that one investor attempts to sell his holding of an investment i and buy instead an investment j. Since all investment j is already taken up by other investors, the only way to acquire it is to pay more than the prevailing market price for an investment with its expected return and risk. However, the rational investor will not do this if he holds the same expectations of the likely returns from j as the rest of the market. To make it worth his while to pay more than the market price, therefore, he must have good grounds for believing that he can predict future earnings from the investment better than the other investors in the market. But, as we saw in Chapter 3, this is not possible since the great bulk of the evidence suggests that the market has incorporated all information into the price of the investment in the case of a large efficient securities market, and hence by paying more than the equilibrium price for j a lower yield, given the expected risk, will be accepted by the investor. But this is irrational behaviour, and we have stated that the investor is assumed to be rational. We must conclude, therefore, that the equilibrium will stand.

Summary

This chapter has been more advanced than others mathematically. However, it is easy to be blinded by the mathematics, to pore over them, and to miss the message underneath. They are only a means to an end, and that end is an understanding of how a rational investor should behave *if* the only things that matter to him or her are the risk and the return of a possible investment.

Usually we can make that assumption. Based on this, we can say that portfolio theory gives a mechanism to help in the selection of investments by considering not just their return, not just their risk, but the way the risks of the different investments relate to each other. Having seen this mechanism, the investor who wants to take social factors into account can do so with a better knowledge of the costs and benefits involved.

Hence we can sum up this chapter as follows:

1. Returns are not certain for most investments. Therefore some way of dealing with the risk is needed.
2. Although stochastic dominance has some clear advantages (it is explained in the Workbook, pp. 439–42) it is difficult to operationalize. It is therefore assumed that all investors can make their decisions based on two parameters: the returns they expect and the chances of receiving those returns — that is, risk.
3. Return and risk can be measured through the statistical moments of mean and standard deviation (or variance) respectively. Thus these two statistical measures become the basis for financial decisions.
4. The relationship between risk and return can be improved by diversifying among a number of investments rather than restricting choice to one or a few. This is because investments are rarely perfectly positively correlated. Hence, though the return to be received will be the arithmetic average of the returns of the individual investments, the risk will be less than that average.
5. For a set of risky investments there will be an efficiency frontier that represents the most efficient combinations in terms of the maximum return for the minimum risk.
6. Any investor faced with a choice among only risky securities will therefore choose a selection that is on that efficiency frontier.
7. However, default risk-free investments such as government bonds are usually available. In this case a better solution can be found by mixing risky and risk-free investments. The resulting set of optimal investments is known as the *capital market line*. This mixes those risk-free investments with the market portfolio. Hence the prescription of portfolio theory is that all investors should hold the same mixture of risky securities, and that mixture should be all the shares in the market (though a substitute of a substantially smaller set of securities will usually be sufficiently diversified for this purpose).

Key terms and concepts

Here is a list of the key terms and concepts which have featured in this chapter. You should make sure that you understand and can define each one of them. Page references to definitions in the text appear in bold in the index.

- Unit trust
- Two-parameter model
- Portfolio
- Envelope curve
- Efficiency frontier
- Diversification
- Market risk
- Systematic risk
- Unique risk
- Unsystematic risk
- Capital market line
- Separation theorem
- Market portfolio

Further reading

The classic work on the principles of portfolio theory was set out by Harry Markowitz, first in a paper and later in a book (Markowitz, 1952, 1959). A further classic was Sharpe's model, which gave the principles for calculating the parameters for n-security models for substantially less calculation (Sharpe, 1963). A more recent, and fairly exhaustive, treatment of the subject can be found in Francis and Archer (1979).

The Workbook material to accompany this chapter begins on p. 439.

7

The capital asset pricing model

Learning objectives

After studying this chapter you should be able to:

- appreciate the nature of an n-investment portfolio and the gains from widespread diversification;
- understand how to construct the capital market line;
- see why the capital market line is preferable to the efficiency frontier for the rational investor;
- understand how to derive the capital asset pricing model from Markowitz diversification theory and know the assumptions required for its construction;
- draw the security market line;
- appreciate the meaning of beta, R^2, systematic and unsystematic risk;
- outline the results of empirical testing of CAPM.

7.1 Introduction

In this chapter we develop the risk model of Chapter 6 in the context of enterprise as discussed in Chapter 5. There are two major strands to this.

First, we look at the market model. This is an *ex post* analysis of the way shares are related to the market. It is shown that using this kind of model can speed and simplify the calculations required by Markowitz diversification.

Second, we build the capital asset pricing model (CAPM), discuss its use and outline some tests of its validity. CAPM can provide, based on certain assumptions, an answer to the problem of share valuation.

7.2 The market model

In Chapter 6 we learned a lot about the prescriptive model for what an investor should do. According to that, the investor should mix risky assets (in the form of the market portfolio) with risk-free assets (like government securities). This would give a position on the capital market line, and that would be efficient, since it gave the best risk–return relationship for that investor's own particular risk preference.

Now one aspect of the model that turns out to be very messy in practice is the covariance matrix of section 6.3 (p. 149). Say you are building a portfolio of 20 shares. You need to know the covariance between all pairs of shares, as well as the variances of the 20 shares. This involves calculating $(n^2 - n)/2$

covariances and n variances, which you can do through linear regression. For 20 shares this means 190 calculations of covariances, plus 20 variances. This gets quickly worse as the number of shares increases, of course. For 100 shares you have 4,950 covariances and 100 variances. For the 2,500 or so shares in the market you have 3,123,750 covariances and 2,500 variances. That is a lot of regression – impossible with a hand-held calculator and very time consuming even for a mainframe computer.

However, there is a way out of this problem. It involves relating the individual shares to the market as a whole instead of to each other. It involves one assumption: that the relationship between each share and the market is linear. Once that assumption has been made, each share can be regressed on to the market intead of to each other. For 20 shares this means 20 regressions, and so on.

Now any linear regression is of the form:

$$y = a + bx + e$$

where y is the dependent variable
       x is the independent variable
       a is a constant term that is independent of x
       b is the coefficient of x representing the slope of the curve
       e is a residual error term.

When mapped on to a Cartesian plane it gives a straight line with a as the intercept with the vertical (y) axis and b as the slope of the line.

In the case we shall look at, the independent variable will be the return obtained by investing in the market for a given period – in the case of this model, a single period. The dependent variable is the return on any share: we shall call it share j. We can then create a graph with the market return on the horizontal axis, and the share's return on the vertical axis.

If we then suppose that the share's return is just a function of the market's return, we get a straight line with α as the intercept and β as the slope of the line. The equation then becomes

$$R_j = \alpha_j + \beta_j R_m + e_j \tag{7.1}$$

If this ideal model works, we then find this line, known as the *characteristic line*, as in Fig. 7.1.

The part of this equation that is especially interesting is the coefficient of R_m. We have expressed it as β_j (this is, of course, the Greek letter beta), and beta has become a part of the natural language of finance. (*Cautionary note:* There are alpha stocks, beta stocks and gamma stocks on the International Stock Exchange. These terms refer to the frequency of trading of the shares. This is an entirely different use of the term, so do not get confused.) So beta refers to the relationship between returns on the individual share and returns on the market. It tells us how much the one moves (on average) when the other moves. Thus it is a measure of covariance – as we would expect from the earlier discussion.

Now we have to distinguish between two models. One of them is the theoretical supposition we have just given. We have said that *if* the return on any share j is a function only of the market's return, *then* we will get the characteristic line described. If it is not, but the relationship turns out to be something fairly similar, then we shall find that we can map a series of points on to this space and get a scatter which, although not lying exactly on the line, approximates to it, and which can generate the characteristic line if we apply the familiar least-squares regression technique to them.

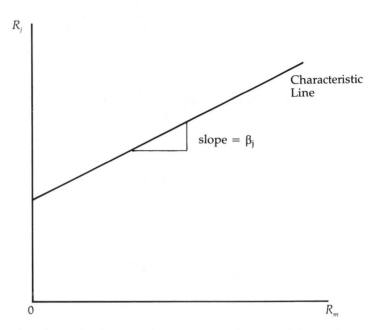

Figure 7.1 The relationship between the return on a share *j* and the market *m*.

To see this in operation, let us take an actual example. The share prices we shall use are actual prices. The market index numbers are not, but they are a realistic simulation. The example has been put together in the way it has to simplify the exposition, and nothing more should be read into it.

In Table 7.1 you will see the series of share prices and the level of the market index on the same day.

Each of these will give rise to a return which can, of course, be found by:

$$\frac{\text{price } (t_1) - \text{price } (t_0)}{\text{price } (t_0)}$$

or for the market index:

$$\frac{\text{index}(t_1) - \text{index}(t_0)}{\text{index}(t_0)}$$

Each is multiplied by 100 to get a percentage return. For example, the return on the index for period 10 must be:

$$\frac{1{,}848 - 1{,}915}{1{,}915} \times 100 = -3.50\%$$

Having obtained the returns for 29 periods, we may then chart the returns. As we have said, they are mapped into a space with axes R_m and R_j. A least-squares regression can then be calculated. This turns out to indicate an intercept α of 0.237 and a slope β of 0.534. The fit between the independent and dependent variables is quite good: the R^2 is 0.293, which indicates a correlation of 0.541. You will recall from your statistics that the R^2 can be interpreted as suggesting that 29.3% of the variation in the share price can be

Table 7.1   A set of share prices, market indices and returns

Period	Share price	Index	Change in SP (%)	Change in index (%)
0	134.5	2,008		
1	131.0	2,008	−2.60	0.00
2	131.0	2,064	0.00	2.79
3	132.5	2,049	1.15	−0.73
4	129.0	1,990	−2.64	−2.88
5	128.5	1,975	−0.39	−0.75
6	127.5	1,908	−0.78	−3.39
7	126.5	1,901	−0.78	−0.37
8	126.0	1,908	−0.40	0.37
9	125.5	1,915	−0.40	0.37
10	123.5	1,848	−1.59	−3.50
11	124.0	1,890	0.40	2.27
12	126.5	1,905	2.02	0.79
13	125.5	1,890	−0.79	−0.79
14	129.5	1,897	3.19	0.37
15	130.0	1,912	0.39	0.79
16	127.5	1,897	−1.92	−0.78
17	127.5	1,838	0.00	−3.11
18	129.5	1,887	1.57	2.67
19	127.5	1,827	−1.54	−3.18
20	128.0	1,835	0.39	0.44
21	126.5	1,798	−1.17	−2.02
22	127.5	1,798	0.79	0.00
23	131.5	1,784	3.14	−0.78
24	136.0	1,805	3.42	1.18
25	136.0	1,833	0.00	1.55
26	131.0	1,781	−3.68	−2.84
27	132.5	1,774	1.15	−0.39
28	131.0	1,745	−1.13	−1.63
29	134.0	1,759	2.29	0.80

explained by reference to the market price. The scatter of R_j, R_m points is mapped together with the regression line in Fig. 7.2.

Let us be quite clear about the distinction between our first characteristic line in Fig. 7.1 and the characteristic line in Fig. 7.3 that results from a regression of observations. The first is a purely theoretical construct, to which we hope to find a model. The second is a wholly empirical construct that results from inferring a possible relationship from actual observations in the real world. If we develop a model to predict where the line in Fig. 7.1 should lie (as we shall proceed to do in this chapter), then it may or may not coincide with the regression from actual observations; and, of course, the regression itself will vary from sample to sample.

Naturally, estimating it means making some further assumptions. Does it stay the same over a period of time? Not necessarily. So if you take a very long time period for the regression, you may be averaging different things. On the other hand, too short a time period is not significant enough to be meaningful. In practice, something like five years (based on monthly data, making 60 measures) to get the estimate is reasonable.

This is known as the *market model*. By regressing returns the way we just suggested, we get an estimate of the risk of any share *j* like this:

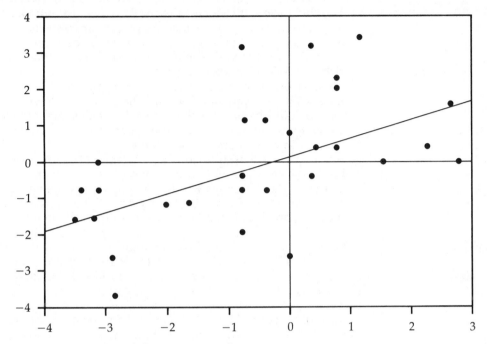

Figure 7.2   Scatter of share against index.

$$\mathrm{Var_j} = \beta_j^2 \mathrm{Var_m} + \mathrm{Var}(e_j) \tag{7.2}$$

You will see that the risk (which we measure as variance, remember) of the share is the result of adding two other risks together. One ($\beta_j^2 \mathrm{Var_m}$) is a measure of the way the risk of the share is related to the risk of the market. It is called the *market risk* or *systematic risk*. (There are alternative names for the same thing; people use them interchangeably — so shall we.) The second part ($\mathrm{Var}(e_j)$) is the risk left over after the market risk has been allowed for. This is called the *unique risk* or *unsystematic risk*.

Does this seem complicated? Maybe so at first, but it soon falls into place. Let's look at it another way. We are saying that when the market goes up, many of the shares in the market tend to go up. This is pretty reasonable: after all, the market just consists of the sum of individual shares! So if there is a partial tendency for the share to go up with the market and down with the market, we have a relationship between them. Covariance measures that relationship statistically.

But the change in the market does not explain everything about price changes of shares. Sometimes it changes for unique reasons. If BP strikes a new oil field, its share price will probably go up. But that has nothing to do with share prices more generally: it is unique to BP.

So we have seen how to work this out. But what use is it? We shall build on the ideas as we go along, but we can suggest two things now:

1. A shareholder will get richer when the market goes up and poorer when it goes down. If the shareholder is holding a mix of shares that is roughly as risky as the market itself (which means the beta is about 1.0 — it goes up and down with the market in equal amounts) then we have a market risk.

If we select a set of shares in our portfolio that all have betas bigger than 1.0, this means that when the market goes up, our portfolio will go up even faster. On the other hand, when the market goes down it will drop even faster. This is a *gearing* relationship: beta can be used to gear a portfolio. It gives you a chance to be aggressive (that is, happier to take risks) or defensive (disliking risk).

2. The fact that risk of portfolios can be related to the market through beta means that we can put flesh on the bones of diversification that were looked at in Chapter 6. There we said that all shareholders would tend, in equilibrium, to hold the market portfolio. The market model is not necessarily an equilibrium one, but its division of risk between market and unique risk is helpful in further understanding diversification. If everybody holds the market portfolio, they do not suffer any risk other than that of the market. In other words, there is no unique risk at all: it has been diversified away. So that part of equation 7.2 drops out, leaving the return on the individual share to be related only to the market as a whole.

Now the market model tells us something about how the risk and return on a share are related to the return on the market over a certain period. It does not help with a crucial problem: the valuation of the share. So far we have only the Gordon model to help us in valuing a share, but that is limited because it still leaves questions unanswered about, in particular, the appropriate rate of return demanded on the share, which is an essential part of the model. However, with some assumptions added, we can develop what we have said so far into a model that gives a share valuation. This is the *capital asset pricing model*.

7.3   The capital asset pricing model

In Chapter 6 we discovered that a key advance for the individual investor was to invest in a mixture of risky and risk-free projects. Since we have now moved on to consider the situation in a with-firm world, this can be slightly restated. The portfolio that is usually assumed is the market portfolio, and this in turn consists of all the risky securities quoted on the International Stock Exchange.

In fact this is unduly restrictive. Many investments other than equity shares exist, and are held, such as Krugerrands, rare stamps and real estate (many people own their own home subject to borrowing). The assumption that the only market to consider is that for quoted shares is made to simplify the analysis, since changes in that market are easily observed. It is worth adding a warning, however, that market indices themselves are somewhat different, and this makes the use of the models we are developing somewhat problematic. Beta, you will remember, links a share's return to the market return. But how do you measure 'the market' with some sort of proxy? The FT–SE 100-share index? The 500-share index? The all-share index (714 shares)? They will lead to different betas We shall, however, continue, though bearing this in mind.

(a) The equation of the capital market line

To develop the model we need to go back to the CML, and derive its equation. We do this only so that we can plug it into our equations later on.

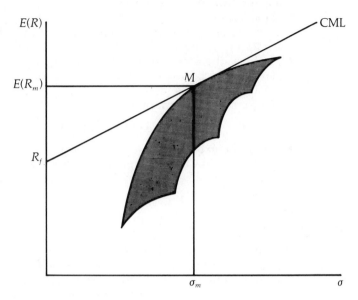

Figure 7.3 The capital market line.

Given that in equilibrium shareholders should be concerned to invest on the CML, we begin our analysis by considering the equation of that line. It is illustrated in Fig. 7.3.

The CML runs from a point R_f (i.e. the risk-free rate, which we may approximate by short-term bonds) on the vertical axis to the point M (the market portfolio) where the CML touches the efficiency frontier. At this point the expected return is $E(R_m)$ and the risk is σ_m. Now at any point on the line the expected return will be some weighted combination of R_f and $E(R_m)$. If, therefore, we take the weight of R_f to be w, the expected return on the resulting portfolio $E(R_p)$ will be:

$$E(R_p) = wR_f + (1 - w)E(R_m) \tag{7.3}$$

and since we may take government Treasury bills to be risk-free, then the expected risk for the portfolio will be:

$$\sigma_p = (1 - w)\sigma_m \tag{7.4}$$

From equation 7.4 we see that $(1 - w) = \sigma_p/\sigma_m$. This can be substituted into equation 7.3. Also further minor manipulation of equation 7.4 shows that $w = (\sigma_m - \sigma_p)/\sigma_m$ which can also be substituted into equation 7.3. Then equation 7.3 becomes:

$$
\begin{aligned}
E(R_p) &= wR_f + \sigma_p/\sigma_m(E(R_m)) \\
&= [(\sigma_m - \sigma_p)/\sigma_m]R_f + (\sigma_p/\sigma_m)\,(E(R_m)) \\
&= (1 - \sigma_p/\sigma_m)R_f + (\sigma_p/\sigma_m)(E(R_m)) \\
&= R_f - \sigma_p/\sigma_m(R_f - E(R_m))
\end{aligned}
$$

which can be written more clearly as:

$$E(R_p) = R_f + \frac{E(R_m) - R_f}{\sigma_m}\,\sigma_p$$

This equation provides the usual parameters for a linear function: there is an intercept (R_f) and a slope $((E(R_m) - R_f)/\sigma_m)$ applied to the independent variable (σ_p).

It can be easily shown that this is indeed the CML. We shall show this by considering the equation for the point M and the point R_f. First, the market M. If this is the portfolio we select (i.e. one without any risk-free assets at all, either lent or borrowed), then the risk of our holding will be the risky portfolio risk: that is, $\sigma_p = \sigma_m$. In equation 7.5, therefore, these cancel out to leave a portfolio return of:

$$E(R_p) = R_f + (E(R_m) - R_f) = E(R_m)$$

as would be expected.

In the second case we apply equation 7.5 to a portfolio consisting solely of risk-free assets. Then, since risk is zero, the second part of the right-hand side disappears $(\sigma_m = \sigma_p = 0)$ leaving $E(R_p) = R_f$.

(b) Finding the expected return on a single security

We saw in Chapter 5 that a single security can be valued by discounting the expected future benefits that should accrue from it. Frequently, however, this is of very limited use. In a risky world those future benefits are uncertain, and one person's view may differ from another's. In the market these differing expectations come together to form an equilibrium price at any point in time. If we wish to estimate the price in the market (say, for a new issue, or when we suspect the market is not efficient for some reason), then we must return to the highly subjective dividend growth model or something very similar.

Over the past 25 years considerable research has taken place to resolve this problem, and a number of models have been proposed to price a security in a risky world, or indeed, any project that has the characteristics of risk and return. The most important of these models is known as the capital asset pricing model (CAPM). It is strictly only a one-period model and can be derived by making certain assumptions as follows:

1. investors have the same information and all agree on its implications for future profits and dividends;
2. investors are only interested in risk and return;
3. there are no transaction costs;
4. every investor can invest or borrow at the standard risk-free rate;
5. taxes are irrelevant to investors' decisions.

The usual warning must be given about these utterly unrealistic assumptions: some of them are not very important (that is, the model turns out to be fairly robust — but the assumptions have to be made otherwise the mathematics would be very messy) and, many would argue, if tests show that the model seems to work — by which they mean that people seem to invest as if they were using the model — then the unreality of the assumptions is unimportant. Although the second of these underlying assumptions is questionable and, as we shall see later, there are severe testing problems of the model, nevertheless it does seem roughly to work, and it is the best model we have so far.

Two further matters must be touched on before we go any further. First, the market model we looked at earlier was an *ex post* model. It took observations of what had happened and sought relationships between variables by the use of statistical techniques. Already, with the equation of the CML (equation 7.5) we have used expressions for *expected* return and similar ($E(R_m)$ instead of R_m, for instance). These are, therefore, *ex ante* models. They are based on proposals about what would be the case under defined circumstances. When we come to look at the adequacy of the models we shall go back to *ex post* data to check if the model we derive is a good one.

Second, the next sub-section has some slightly fierce mathematics. Do not panic, but do try to understand the argument. We have not given the derivation of the model for nothing. Understanding the arbitrage nature of the proof is, we believe, essential to an understanding of the model. So look at the processes that surround the mathematics, even if your calculus is a bit rusty.

(c) Deriving the capital asset pricing model

Imagine an investor who has a portfolio of two items: first a risky asset i, and second the market portfolio (this, of course includes asset i, but we ignore this matter for the present). We can apply the usual equation (as given in Chapter 6) to find the expected return and risk of this 'two-security' portfolio in the usual way (notice here that we are treating the market portfolio as itself a 'security'. This is perfectly reasonable since it has all the attributes we require of a security, namely risk and return). We take the proportion of security i as being w and that of the portfolio as $(1 - w)$. The risk is measured as the standard deviation as usual, with σ_p, σ_i and σ_m being the risks of the portfolio, security i and market respectively, and σ_{im} being the covariance between the security i and the market m. This gives:

$$E(R_p) = wE(R_i) + (1 - w)E(R_m)$$

and:

$$\sigma_p = [w^2\sigma_i^2 + (1 - w)^2\sigma_m^2 + 2w(1 - w)\sigma_{im}]^{0.5}$$

Now consider the expected return and risk from the *marginal investment*. This can be found by partially differentiating each expression with respect to w:

$$\frac{\partial E(R_p)}{\partial w} = E(R_i) - E(R_m) \tag{7.6}$$

and:

$$\frac{\partial \sigma_p}{\partial w} = 0.5[w^2\sigma_i^2 + (1 - w)^2\sigma_m^2 + 2w(1 - w)\sigma_{im}]^{-0.5} \times [2w\sigma_i^2 - 2\sigma_m^2 + 2w\sigma_m^2 + 2\sigma_{im} - 4w\sigma_{im}] \tag{7.7}$$

Let us now return to the nature of the problem so as to proceed further. We described a portfolio in which the investor held a security i in addition to a market portfolio that included that security. This implies, of course, that the investor is holding a *surplus* of security i, since as we saw at the end of Chapter 6, no rational investor would hold more than the appropriate proportion of the market portfolio. Since equilibrial forces would tend to work to urge the investor to cease holding this surplus, we can take this proportion w to vanish to zero for the marginal investment. Restating equations 7.6 and 7.7 with $w = 0$ gives:

$$\frac{\partial E(R_p)}{\partial w} = E(R_i) - E(R_m) \tag{7.8}$$

and:

$$\frac{\partial \sigma_P}{\partial w} = 0.5[\sigma_m^2]^{-0.5}[-2\sigma_m^2 + 2\sigma_{im}]$$

the latter being restated as:

$$\frac{\sigma_{im} - \sigma_m^2}{\sigma_m} \tag{7.9}$$

Let us stop and consider the meaning of these expressions. Each is concerned with the risky market portfolio: that is, the area bounded by the envelope curve. However, by specifying that $w = 0$ we have specified that they relate to the market portfolio in equilibrium, that is to the point M on Fig 7.3. Each of equations 7.8 and 7.9 gives the return and risk respectively at the margin. Hence the slope of the envelope curve at point M must be the one divided by the other, that is:

$$\frac{E(R_i) - E(R_m)}{[\sigma_{im} - \sigma_m^2]/\sigma_m} \tag{7.10}$$

Now we have already seen that the envelope curve meets the CML at point M. Since the one is tangential to the other, it follows that they have the same slope. But we know the slope of the CML from equation 7.5. Thus we can set this slope equal to the slope of the envelope curve given in equation 7.10:

$$\frac{E(R_m) - R_f}{\sigma_m} = \frac{E(R_i) - E(R_m))}{[\sigma_{im} - \sigma_m^2]/\sigma_m}$$

This can be rearranged to solve for $E(R_i)$, and by simple manipulation leads to the expression:

$$E(R_i) = R_f + [E(R_m) - R_f]\frac{\sigma_{im}}{\sigma_m^2}$$

This is the capital asset pricing model (CAPM). It gives the expected return for any investment or security i in equilibrium as a function of a small number of readily ascertainable variables:

1. the risk-free rate — a usual approximation is to take the short-term rate on government bonds, usually a Treasury bill, which is easily found from any good newspaper (see Table W9.7 for some data). An issue to be resolved is whether we simply take a quote at a single point in time or an average. Readers will note that it is R_f not $E(R_f)$: that is, it is not presumed to have a distribution. A quick analysis of the data in Table W9.7 would suggest that it does!
2. the expected rate for the market as a whole — this cannot be ascertained directly, since we do not know what the market is expecting, but a quite simple approximation would be, for instance, the current rate of return on the market, which is ascertainable by calculation of the current market prices and yields;
3. the *relationship* between the market and the security i. This is given as the covariance between them divided by the variance of the market portfolio. Once again, an approximation to this for practical purposes can be found by looking at the past record of the relationship between market movements and the movements of security i.

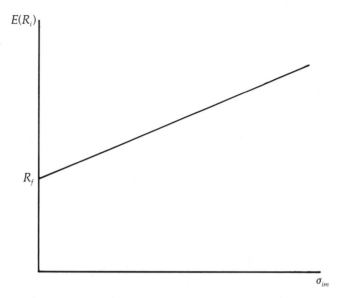

$E(R_i)$

R_f

σ_{im}

Figure 7.4 The security market line.

The CAPM is a linear function relating the expected return $E(R_i)$ to the covariance σ_{im}, with intercept R_f and slope $[E(R_m) - R_f]/\sigma_m^2$. It is graphed in Fig. 7.4.

There is, however, a more common way of expressing this. In the above the slope was $[E(R_m) - R_f]/\sigma_m^2$. We can instead treat $[E(R_m) - R_f]$ as the slope, and the horizontal axis as σ_{im}/σ_m^2. In this case we rename σ_{im}/σ_m^2 as beta (β), that is:

$$\beta = \frac{\sigma_{im}}{\sigma_m^2} \qquad (7.11)$$

This is indeed the very same beta we saw earlier when considering the market model. We now have a function called the *security market line* (hereafter SML), which can be seen in Fig. 7.5.

It is well to be clear now about the distinction between the SML and the CML. Superficially when graphed they look similar. However, the CML is concerned with the expected return and total risk of a portfolio of risky and risk-free investments related to each other. The SML is concerned with *any one security*, relating it to the market by means of its covariance with the market. It states that, as the covariance between the investment and the total market increases, the return expected by the investor from that investment also increases.

Thus the final form of the capital asset pricing model is:

$$E(R_i) = R_f + \beta_i(E(R_m) - R_f) \qquad (7.12)$$

This must be memorized. Beta is a central concept in finance theory; presently we shall turn to some of its properties. First, it is worthwhile discussing further its use and meaning.

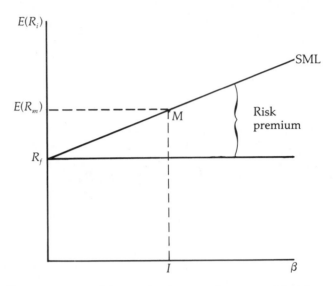

Figure 7.5   The parameters of the market (expected return and beta).

7.4   The use and meaning of beta

Because it measures the sensitivity of a security to the change in the market as a whole, beta is a highly significant measure of the relevant risk of a project *in terms of the economy more generally*. After all, the general market index, as we saw in Chapter 6, reflects general economic prospects. Thus the beta tells us how the individual security relates to this. If beta is more than one, the security is more volatile than the market. This means that, on average, if the market goes up, the security will go up more (how much more, of course, depends on the value of beta). If the market goes down, the security will go down more. Hence it can be thought of as a kind of leverage. Generally it would be expected that risky industries that were sensitive to economic prospects more generally — perhaps capital goods manufacturers — would have high betas. Low betas, on the other hand (less than 1), go with comparative safety and lack of risk in the industry concerned. In principle it is quite possible for a share to have a negative beta. In practice this is rare.

Now there is no reason why beta as a concept should be limited exclusively to individual securities. On the contrary, the idea holds for portfolios, and portfolios can be created with high or low betas. Indeed, it may well be that the unit trust or investment trust that is highly successful compared to the market has this property not because of the skill of its management in 'beating the market' (we saw in Chapter 3 that this notion is very questionable), but because the fund involved has chosen high beta shares, and there is a general bull market. When the market falls, the fund will fall even more sharply than the market.

One interesting sidelight on beta should be mentioned now. It is generally accepted — and indeed we have stressed throughout the book so far — that a riskier security will have to offer a higher return, and if it is quoted in the market the price will adapt to reflect this relative risk. The higher the risk, the higher the expected return. We have now suggested that beta is the appropriate measure of risk where diversification is possible, so the rule becomes: the higher the beta, the higher the expected return (which is the same as saying that the SML always slopes upwards).

Now consider securities in two organizations: a large chain store, such as Marks and Spencer plc, and a gold prospecting company. Until now we would have taken it for granted that the latter would offer a higher return to the investor than the former. However, consider their comparative betas. That for a chain store will approximate to the market: Marks and Spencer in early 1988, for example, was around 0.8. This is because the fortunes of the retailing trade tend to depend on the fortunes of the economy more generally. But the success of the gold prospecting company are virtually unaffected by the market, or the economy. It relies on the chance of finding the right geological strata. Hence, the fortunes of the latter are independent of the market and beta will be virtually zero. Hence, according to CAPM, the expected return will be *lower* than that of the retail chain.

This appears to be a curious paradox, since it flies in the face of all expectations. In practice, however, it would only happen if the beta were completely unrelated to the total risk (which, all would agree, is high). Research tends to show, however, that companies with high total risk tend to have high beta, and vice versa. In other words, high systematic risk seems to be correlated with high unsystematic risk. Thus, although in principle feasible, this artificial example is unlikely to correspond to real-world beta values.

7.5 Properties of beta

(a) The beta of the market

We have already seen that beta acts in the same way as covariance. It is, in fact, just covariance 'normalized' by dividing by the market variance. Beta tells us about the way the risk of a share is related to the risk of the market as a whole. Consider, to start with, the beta of the market itself. Now if the 'security' we are considering is the whole market, then the numerator of equation 7.11, σ_{im}, becomes σ_{mm}: that is, σ_m^2. Hence beta is 1. We can say, therefore, that *the beta of the market as a whole is unity*. This is illustrated in Fig. 7.5.

(b) Beta, systematic risk and R^2

Next, let us think back to the end of Chapter 6. There we concluded by pointing out that the total risk of a security consisted of two parts: systematic risk and unsystematic risk. We can now be more precise about the meanings of these terms.

As with any other measure of risk, systematic and unsystematic risk can be measured in terms of either standard deviation or variance. The variance form is possibly a more useful way of approaching them since we can derive the unsystematic risk more directly from the systematic risk. They can be expressed in more than one way.

We take the systematic risk first, giving two ways of expressing it, but we must emphasize that *they are exactly equivalent* and one can be derived easily from the other. We give the two different expressions because choosing which is more helpful will depend on what information is available to calculate the systematic risk. The two measures are:

$$\text{Systematic risk} = \sigma_m^2 \beta_i^2$$
$$\text{and} \qquad = \sigma_i^2 \rho_{im}^2$$

Once this has been calculated, the unsystematic risk is simple to work out. It is just the total risk less the market risk, that is:

$$\text{Unsystematic risk} = \sigma_i^2 - \sigma_m^2 \beta_i^2$$

. One more related measure will be mentioned at this juncture. This is the R^2 of the investment or security. Those familiar with multiple regression will recognize this as a measure of goodness of fit. This is indeed where it is derived, and it tells us *the proportion of the investment's variance that is related to the market variance*. It is found by dividing the systematic risk by the variance of the investment, that is:

$$R_i^2 = \frac{\sigma_m^2 \beta_i^2}{\sigma_i^2}$$

It is best to illustrate these relationships by means of a wholly unrealistic example, Table 7.2. Because it is so artificially simple, the relationships and meanings of the expressions are far more easily understood. In Table 7.2 there are the prices of two securities, i and j, and the market index. These may be converted into periodic returns for all three, as illustrated in Table 7.3. Following from this, Table 7.3 also gives the standard deviations of all three, plus the correlations of each share with the market.

Table 7.2 Relationship between beta, systematic risk and R^2

i £	j £	m £
100.0	100.0	100.0
110.0	95.0	105.0
66.0	114.0	84.0
99.0	85.5	105.0
99.0	85.5	105.0
138.6	68.4	126.0
124.7	71.8	119.7

Table 7.3 Returns on securities i and j and on the market index

	i	j	m
	10.0	−5.0	5.0
	−40.0	20.0	−20.0
	50.0	−25.0	25.0
	0.0	0.0	0.0
	40.0	−20.0	20.0
	−10.0	5.0	−5.0
SD	30.24	15.12	15.12
Corr. coeff. with m	1.00	−1.00	

Now consider carefully the meanings of these statistics. You will see that the two securities are fully correlated with the market, one positively, one negatively. Security i moves twice as much as the market (for instance, in the second period it has gone down 40 points where the market has decreased by 20). Security j moves just as much as the market but in the opposite direction. A short cut to the calculation of beta is to note that:

$$\beta_i = \frac{\text{Cov}(i,m)}{\sigma_m^2} = \frac{\sigma_i \sigma_m \rho_{im}}{\sigma_m^2} = \frac{\sigma_i \rho_{im}}{\sigma_m}$$

Hence:

$$\beta_i = \frac{1 \times 30.24}{15.12} = 2 \qquad R_i^2 = \frac{(15.12)^2(2)^2}{(30.24)^2} = 1.0$$

$$\beta_j = \frac{-1 \times 15.12}{15.12} = -1 \qquad R_j^2 + \frac{(15.12)^2(-1)^2}{(15.12)^2} = 1.0$$

Thus we see that, where a security moves exactly twice as much as the market, it has a beta of 2. Where it moves the same amount but in the opposite direction, the beta is -1. In both cases the R^2 is 1.0 because the market accounts for all the change (risk) in both i and j.

Note the relationship between beta and systematic risk. Since the market risk is given, systematic risk and beta will differ in just the same way from one security to another. We sometimes even loosely refer to beta as systematic risk. This is wholly reasonable: each of them is concerned with the relation-ship of the risk of the individual security to the risk of the market. Just as we said in Chapter 6 that *systematic risk* is the only kind of risk that matters to the investor (since the unique risk can be diversified away by judicious selection of a portfolio), so we can now say that CAPM tells us that *the only risk that is important to the investor is beta.*

(c) Beta additivity

We turn next to the result of combining investments: how do we combine their betas? We have already seen that expected returns are additive (that is, we can just average the returns to get the return of the combination). Risk as measured by total risk (standard deviation or variance), on the other hand, was not linearly additive. It turns out that betas *are* linearly additive. This means that, for instance, if we have two investments A and B, and invest a proportion w in A and $(1 - w)$ in B, then:

$$\beta_p = w\beta_A + (1 - w)\beta_B \qquad\qquad (7.13)$$

We illustrate this in Fig. 7.6.

Mr Deeds invests 70% of his wealth in Amalgamated plc and 30% in Consoli-dated plc. If the beta of Amalgamated is 1.6 and the beta of Consolidated is 0.9, what is the beta of the combination?

Solution:

The answer is simply:

$$(0.7 \times 1.6) + (0.3 \times 0.9) = 1.39$$

Figure 7.6   Beta additivity.

With this understanding of beta additivity we can move to more central concerns: the way beta is fundamental to the enterprise's operations, its relationship to gearing, and its implication for capital budgeting.

7.6 Using asset betas

(a) The gearing effect

We have discussed the betas of particular investments and the betas of companies as if they were interchangeable. In one sense they are, but there may well be some significant differences. To understand this, we return to an important distinction that we saw early in this book.

The risk of a company can be of two kinds: financial risk and business risk. The former results from the financial policy (in particular, whether capital is

---

We have said that an enterprise is nothing more nor less than a collection of projects. Let us imagine a company, Prosciutto plc, which consists of four projects. We can illustrate it like this:

Project A Parameters: $E(R_A)$ β_A Size S_a	Project B Parameters: $E(R_B)$ β_B Size S_B
Project C Parameters: $E(R_C)$ β_C Size S_C	Project D Parameters: $E(R_D)$ β_D Size S_D

Each project has risk and return, where the relevant risk measure is beta. The projects are, of course, of different sizes, which are also given. Thus the size of project C is S_C, measured as NPV. The beta of C is β_C and its expected return is $E(R_C)$. So we find the expected return and risk by taking a weighted average of the individual project returns and risks. Thus, where the size of Prosciutto as a whole is S_P (that is, $S_A + S_B + S_C + S_D = S_P$), the expected return of Prosciutto *as a whole* is:

$$\frac{E(R_A).S_A + E(R_B).S_B + E(R_C).S_C + E(R_D).S_D}{S_P}$$

and the beta of Prosciutto *as a whole* is:

$$\frac{\beta_A.S_A + \beta_B.S_B + \beta_C.S_C + \beta_D.S_D}{S_P}$$

Figure 7.7 Weighting asset returns and betas.

raised through equity or debt); the latter results from the nature of business operations. When we consider an investment, or project, then the risk is solely business risk. Some projects are more risky than others, and naturally a higher return is expected from the more risky ones. Now we have seen that, because of linear beta additivity, we can just average the betas of assets to get to the betas of a portfolio of assets. *But this is precisely what a company consists of* — it is a set of projects, or assets, some of which will be riskier than others. Now since we have argued that only beta matters (and not the unsystematic risk), then for each individual project within a company there will be a beta and an expected return, and the beta and expected return of the company as a whole will be just the weighted average of the individual project betas and returns. This is illustrated in Fig. 7.7.

This is an important insight, and results from the insistence in the first part of this book that the existence of the enterprise is secondary — it is just a vehicle for investors to invest more easily in portfolios and projects. When we bundle the projects into enterprises, their risk (= beta) and return are just combinations of the projects.

However, there is frequently one important difference between the enterprise's beta in the stock market and the betas of the underlying assets. This arises from the second type of risk, *financial risk*. Although it is true that the *business risk* of the enterprise is the combination of individual business risks, this is then adjusted because gearing up the company by introducing debt changes the return expected by the shareholders. They are faced with increased risk as a result of gearing — they correspondingly expect a higher return.

Fortunately, because of linear beta additivity, this can be handled very simply. If we denote the beta of the underlying projects (assets) as β_A, the beta of the equity as β_E and the beta of the debt by β_D, then the beta of the enterprise as a whole is simply the weighted average of the betas of the equity and debt, like this:

$$\beta_A = \beta_E\left(\frac{\text{Equity}}{\text{Equity} + \text{Debt}}\right) + \beta_D\left(\frac{\text{Debt}}{\text{Equity} + \text{Debt}}\right) \qquad (7.14)$$

This is illustrated by the example in Fig. 7.8.

Now this may not be realistic beta for debt, but perhaps it is no less realistic than the frequent assumption that the debt's beta is zero — which of course assumes that corporate debt can be as safe as government securities. This is not so, but nevertheless it is frequently acceptable for the purpose of calculations such as that in Fig. 7.8 to assume a debt of zero, which of course simplifies equation 7.14 to:

$$\beta_A = \beta_E\left(\frac{\text{Equity}}{\text{Equity} + \text{Debt}}\right)$$

The fact that we are always working with approximations and estimates in the real world must not be forgotten.

(b) A return to capital budgeting

We now return to capital budgeting, to consider the implications of asset betas for the accept/reject decision on capital projects. So far we have not considered the hurdle rate in great detail; we have, in effect, assumed that it is the cost of capital of the enterprise. By this may be assumed the *historical cost*

Hadlee plc has three divisions, with betas and proportions of the company's total assets as follows:

| | Division | | |
	Willow	Pine	Elm
Beta	2.1	1.6	1.2
Proportion	60%	15%	25%

The beta and market value of its equity shares on the stock market are respectively 2.20 and £20m, and the enterprise's total market value is £25m. What is the beta of the debt?

Solution:

The beta of the assets as a whole is:

$$(0.6 \times 2.1) + (0.15 \times 1.6) + (0.25 \times 1.2) = 1.80$$

Rearranging equation 7.14 for the beta of the debt gives:

$$\beta_D = \frac{\beta_A - \beta_E\left(\dfrac{E}{D+E}\right)}{\left(\dfrac{D}{D+E}\right)}$$

$$= \frac{1.80 - 2.20(20/25)}{(5/25)}$$

$$= 0.2$$

Figure 7.8   Beta of an enterprise as a whole.

of capital for the enterprise as a whole, and the criterion that was taken in Chapter 5 was that a project was acceptable if its expected return was greater than the cost of capital. This was, however, in a risk-free world. We may now consider the implications of bringing risk into the picture.

It is obvious from Chapters 2 and 6 and from the present chapter so far, that higher rates of return are required for riskier projects. Now, so far as the historical cost of capital is concerned, it is clear that some industries are riskier than others. This means that organizations in some industries will be expected to have higher costs of capital than others as a result of their business risk (financial risk, as we have seen, is another matter again). But it would not necessarily be safe to assume that the risk of a new project was the same as the historical average risk of existing projects, even if the new project is broadly in the same industry. Moreover, this kind of approach will not work where the enterprise operates in more than one industry. Then the historical beta of the underlying assets of the business enterprise as a whole will be the average of the various industries it is concerned with. This will perhaps bear little relevance to a new project which is being evaluated.

This means that, when a new project is being considered, the historical cost of capital for the enterprise as a whole is probably not the relevant rate to use, both because it *is* historical and because it is an average of a number of project returns. The beta for the new project may well be very different.

The conclusion that much be reached, therefore, is that the hurdle rate for any new project must be the result of taking into account *the expected beta of that project*. Let us turn to the mechanics of this to see how it might work in practice. (You are invited to pay particular attention to the Bowater-Scott case in the Workbook, pp. 468–79.)

When we considered the idea of the net present value in Chapter 4, we took the rule to be as follows: that future cash flows were discounted at some rate of opportunity cost (which we later learned was effectively the cost of capital), and that if after deducting the initial outflow the result was positive, the project should be accepted. Formally:

$$\text{Accept if: } \sum_{t=0}^{n} K_t v^t > 0$$

or, expanding v^t.

$$\text{Accept if: } \sum_{t=0}^{n} \frac{k_t}{(1 + r)^t} > 0$$

Now according to the model we have discussed in this chapter, r for any project must be based on the expected beta of the project applied to the capital asset pricing model in equation 7.12. Hence for project j the acceptance rule will be:

$$\text{Accept project } j \text{ if: } \sum_{t=0}^{n} \frac{K_{jt}}{(1 + R_f + \beta_j(E(R_m) - R_f))^t} > 0$$

Now of course it may well turn out that, if the project is one with a low beta, it could be accepted under conditions where the previous approach —, which implicitly assumed that the rate of discount was the historical cost of capital — would have signalled reject. This is perfectly reasonable *because once the new project comes on-stream it will itself reduce the beta of the enterprise as a whole*. In saying this we are assuming that, to the extent that the criterion for beta is the securities market, we can assume that news of the lower beta filters through. Inevitably this is a big assumption, and one that may well, in the short term at least, not be fulfilled. The problem of information asymmetry (recall our discussion of information in the context of agency theory) may well mean that either there is no channel through which the information can reach the market in the short term, or the information will be signalled to the market but the market will discount it in some way.

As we have already said, so far as the total enterprise's beta is concerned, the market has only past prices to go on and its experience of similar organizations, news that arrives about the extent to which past trends are likely to be followed in the future, and so on. *Ceteris paribus* the market has to assume that business enterprises will continue the way they have been in the past. Unless there is information to say an enterprise will not carry on in the same industry, with the same kinds of project and the same risk, it has to be assumed that it will. But even when projects are taken on with betas that will over time affect the *actual* enterprise's beta, this is no guarantee that the market will immediately and automatically change its estimate of the enterprise's beta. Hence in the short term it could be argued that using CAPM rather than historical cost of capital is mistaken. On the other hand, if we assume some efficiency in the market in encompassing information of this kind — and such information impounding was discussed in Chapter 3 — then in so far as the enterprise is trying to increase its value in the long run, projects should be assessed on a basis that takes account of their own risk rather than that of other projects that have been accepted in the past (where, of course, by risk we mean beta).

This raises a further problem. How in fact does the management estimate the future beta of the project? If the project is roughly of the same kind as existing projects, then its beta is likely to be much the same as the historical asset beta. If it is reckoned to be different, some other method must be found. One method that has found some favour is for the enterprise to look at other companies that have activities that are much the same as the new project. This may work, but for many projects there are no single-product enterprises that can be used as guides in this way. And in any case, there are many reasons why a new project in the company concerned may have a different risk. The management may be less experienced in handling it, or it may be able to provide ready-made distribution channels from its other activities that similar enterprises do not have — and so on. In the end such a decision can only be wholly pragmatic, but it can be argued that it is better to make the decision on this basis and make some minor errors than to use less sophisticated methods that lead to larger errors.

We must turn next to the matter of *beta stability*. We shall look at this together with the empirical evidence that surrounds CAPM.

7.7   Beta stability

Beta stability is a subject which is difficult to study for the individual project within the enterprise. It is, however, much more straightforward for business enterprises as a whole in the market. The problem comes about because investors need to estimate the beta of a share. In doing so they are interested in the extent to which the share will covary with the market *in the future*. We have seen that betas can vary, and the meaning of this variation — that enterprises with high betas are riskier than the market even given the diversification away of unique risk. But of course it is very difficult to estimate a future beta. It is difficult enough to make any kind of forecast of the future concerning an enterprise and its securities — which is why there are so many highly paid analysts employed by stockbroking firms, investment and unit trusts, pension schemes and life assurance companies who attempt to estimate enterprises' future prospects. They would do well if they could estimate mean earnings over a short period such as five years. To estimate beta at all accurately, then, would clearly be fanciful.

In these circumstances, investors turn to what is available, and this is past evidence of a company's beta. As we said earlier, this forms a starting point for estimating future risk — it must be assumed that the companies that have in the past had higher betas will continue to do so in the future. This assumption has been tested in the USA. A method of testing is, for example, to select a set of shares and rank them in order of beta, then divide into n sets (say, ten). Thus there will be the decile with the lowest betas, the decile with the next lowest, and so on. The researcher then sees what proportion of shares moves from one decile to the next, or two deciles distant, and so on, over one, two or more years. Although the results do not suggest very high stability, there is sufficient stability for historical values to be useful as predictors for the future (which is comforting for commercial producers of data on beta values).

7.8   Testing the capital asset pricing model

(a) How to test

A good approach to understanding tests of CAPM is to look at beta from a different point of view. It has been said that beta is concerned with a relationship between the risk of the returns of the individual share and that of the market. This is evident if we remind ourselves of the nature of the information in Table 7.2 from which we derived some data to develop beta values for two securities. The basic data are the price movements of the share compared to the price movement of the market as a whole. Since we are comparing one with the other, their returns can be graphed against each other as in Fig. 7.9 (which considers security i only).

Recalling Fig. 7.1, this is called the *characteristic line*. Its slope is beta (in this case, $\beta = 2$). It should be obvious that this is an artificial example because we deliberately designed the information in Table 7.2 in such a way that there was perfect correlation between the security i and the market. It is for this reason that all the plotted points fall on the characteristic line. Normally they do not, and the line is derived by regression from the relationship between R_i

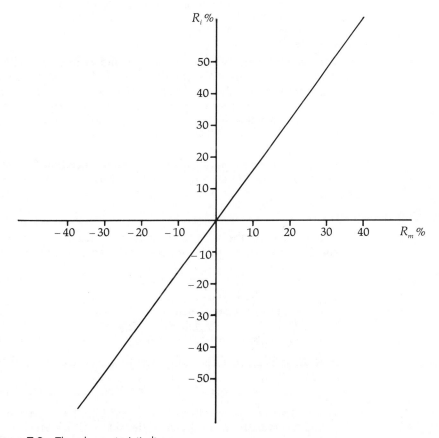

Figure 7.9   The characteristic line.

and R_m. We have already seen this line. It is the same line that we developed in our discussion of the market model, and it is the same graph that we developed in Fig. 7.1.

It is from an understanding of this line that we can obtain an understanding of testing CAPM. (The following description is inevitably simplified from the sophisticated statistical procedures undertaken in recent years to assist the reader. The principle, however, remains.) A procedure for testing CAPM would have two stages.

Stage 1

The first stage is to take each security to be tested, and graph its returns against the returns on the market for a number of periods. For example, the tester may decide upon weekly data and plot 52 relationships over the period of one year. Alternatively, it may be felt that there is less bias in monthly data, and, say, 60 monthly returns for five years would be regressed. The result will be an estimate of the *actual beta* observed over those five years. (Not the result of using expected returns, as is specified in the model. Those are unobservable. The tester therefore takes the only data available, namely the actual returns. This, of course, raises doubts about the tests because expectations are not generally fulfilled. We shall return to this point later.)

Thus from a period of weeks or months, the tester obtains the observed beta of each security. This procedure is undertaken for each of a large number of securities. The return of each is plotted against the market, and a beta for each is calculated.

Stage 2

The second stage is to perform a second regression. This time the independent variables are the betas of the individual securities — that is, the coefficients from the first regression — and the dependent variables are the returns of the securities. The resulting linear function should, if CAPM is correct, equal the SML (which can, of course, be calculated using the same, actual (rather than expected) data). If it is, then the intercept with the vertical axis should be the risk-free Treasury bill rate, R_f, and the slope will be $[E(R_m) - R_f]$. If it is, then there is prima facie evidence that CAPM correctly describes actual investor behaviour. If it is not, then CAPM is incorrect.

(b) Empirical tests: results

The normal method for testing in fact modifies the previous formulation slightly. R_f is deducted from each side, so that the model tested is:

$$R'_j = \gamma_0 + \gamma_1\beta_j + SE_i$$

where R'_j is the excess return $R_j - R_f$
  γ_0 is a constant term
  γ_1 is the excess risk $R_m - R_f$
  SE_i is the error term.

In testing, j can be either an individual security or a portfolio constructed by the investigator.

If the CAPM is correct, then empirical tests would show the following:

1. On the average, and over long periods of time, there should be a linear relationship between systematic risk and return. That is, securities with high systematic risk should have high rates of return, and vice versa.

2. The slope of the relationship (γ_1) should be equal to the mean market risk premium ($\bar{R}_m - \bar{R}_f$) during the period used.
3. The constant term (γ_0) should be equal to the mean risk-free rate (R_f).
4. Unsystematic risk, as measured by SE_i, should play no significant role in explaining differences in security returns.

There have been many studies of the validity of CAPM. It could be argued that, in the light of Richard Roll's critique (1977), they are all meaningless. However, they do shed an interesting light on the extent to which CAPM is a fair approximation.

We shall give the results of just two studies in some little detail so as to offer a flavour of what was found.

(i) The Jacob study (1971)

The study deals with the 593 New York Stock Exchange shares for which there are complete data from 1946 to 1965. Regression analyses were performed for the 1946–1955 and 1956–1965 periods, using both monthly and annual security returns. The relationship of mean security returns and beta values is shown in Table 7.4.

Table 7.4 Result of the Jacob study (1971)

		$r_j = \gamma_0 + \gamma_1\beta_j + u_j$				
Period	Return interval	Regression results			Theoretical values	
		γ_0	γ_1	R^2	$\gamma_0 = 0$	$\gamma_1 = R_m - R_f$
1945–55	Monthly	0.80	0.30 (0.07)	0.02	0	1.10
	Yearly	8.9	5.10 (0.53)	0.14	0	14.4
1956–65	Monthly	0.70	0.30 (0.05)	0.03	0	0.8
	Yearly	6.7	6.7	0.21	0	10.8

Note: The figures in brackets are standard errors.

The results indicate that over the complete 35-year period, average return increased by about 1.08% per month (13% per year), for a one-unit increase in beta. This is about three-quarters of the amount predicted by CAPM. There appears to be little reason to question the linearity of the relationship over the 35-year period.

Black, Jensen and Scholes also estimated the risk–return trade-off for a number of sub-periods. The slopes of their regression lines tended in most periods to understate the theoretical values, but were generally of the correct sign. Also, the sub-period relationships appeared to be linear.

Thus there is substantial support for the hypothesis that realized returns are a linear function of systematic risk values. Moreover, it appears that the relationship is significantly positive over long periods of time.

(ii) The Fama and Macbeth study (1973)

Fama and Macbeth extended the Black, Jensen and Scholes tests to include two additional factors. The first was an average of the β_i^2 for all individual securities in portfolio p, designated $\bar{\beta}_p^2$. The second was a similar average of the residual standard deviations ($\hat{SE}_i$) for all shares in portfolio p, designated

$\hat{S}E_p$. The first term tests for non-linearities in the risk–return relationship; the second for the impact of residual variation.

The equation of the fitted line for this study is given by:

$$\bar{R}_p = \gamma_0 + \gamma_1\beta_p + \gamma_2\beta_p^2 + \gamma_3\hat{S}E_p + u_p$$

where, according to CAPM, we should expect γ_2 and γ_3 to have zero values.

The results of the tests suggested that, while estimated values of γ_2 and γ_3 were not equal to zero for each interval examined, their average values tended to be insignificantly different from zero. Fama and Macbeth also confirmed the Black, Jensen and Scholes result, that the realized values of γ_0 are not equal to $\bar{R}_f$, as predicted by CAPM. For example, a substantial positive correlation exists between beta and $(SE_i)^2$. Thus unsystematic risk will appear to be significant in tests from which beta has been omitted, even though it may be unimportant to the pricing of securities. This sort of statistical correlation need not imply a causal link between the variables.

The third test included both beta and $(\hat{S}E_i)^2$ in the regression equation. Both were found to be significantly positively related to mean return. However, the inclusion of $(\hat{S}E_i)^2$ somewhat weakened the relationship of return and beta.

The interpretation of these results was again complicated by the strong positive correlation between beta and $(\hat{S}E_i)^2$, and by other sampling problems. For example, skewness in the distribution of returns can lead to spurious correlations between mean return and SE_i. In any case, the results do show that shares with high systematic risk tend to have higher rates of return.

(c) Discussion of tests

The general conclusion from the tests that have been carried out is that the CAPM is not verified. The intercept a_0 is greater than zero (which it should be since it should correspond to $R_f - R_f = 0$). The slope of the regression on β, on the other hand, is less than CAPM predicts. However, although beta is not the perfect predictor, it is shown by the tests to be far better than unsystematic risk.

The conclusion to be drawn from this would seem to be that CAPM is not correct. However, this cannot in fact easily be concluded. The reason lies in the problems of testing the theory. There are two principal problems:

1. expected returns, which constitute CAPM, cannot be observed, and actual surrogates need to be used;
2. the 'true' market portfolio would consist of all risky assets that might be held (including international assets) — tests are obliged to use the one-country stock market as a surrogate.

Moreover, the methods used test the efficient markets hypothesis and CAPM jointly (Roll, 1977). This leads to a logical problem in specifying what is being tested. Hence, it is perfectly possible that CAPM is correct and the tests are flawed, or it is possible that CAPM is not correct, but not for the reasons stated in the tests. We cannot tell.

It is true, however, that CAPM is probably the best tool we have at this stage for valuing securities, and hence for practical use in capital budgeting and similar decisions. We continue to use it because there is nothing better. Indeed, there are commercial beta services which are subscribed to by investors (such as Datastream and the London Business School service). They presumably find the information useful (although acceptance of CAPM by the investment community is far from widespread). Other candidates are being put forward to supplant CAPM (such as Ross's arbitrage pricing model, which takes return to be a linear combination of a number of (undefined) factors rather than just the market return). These are as yet in the early stages of development, however, and are not available for practical use.

Summary

1. We first looked at the market model and saw how it could be used to bypass the considerable computational detail required by Markowitz's original formulation. This was, however, at the price of making the assumption of linear relationships.
2. We then turned to the capital asset pricing model which, through showing expected return, gives a basis for pricing a share.
3. This was developed first by deriving the equation of the capital market line, and later by using arbitrage arguments to show how, under certain conditions, the simple linear model of CAPM could be derived.
4. We then showed how beta essentially applies to any asset, and hence how enterprises are just bundles of projects. Thus the fundamental building block was the asset beta. Complications such as gearing could be handled simply by using a linear combination.
5. A further implication was that, using return and beta to assess new projects, these might be accepted even though they gave a negative NPV when based on historical cost of capital, since they needed only to justify their own beta, not the historical beta of the other assets of the enterprise.
6. Finally, tests have seemed to show that the model is a fair approximation, but not as 'correct' as some would like.

Key terms and concepts

Here is a list of the key terms and concepts which have featured in this chapter. You should make sure that you understand and can define each of them. Page references to definitions in the text appear in bold in the index.

• Market model	• R^2
• Beta	• Business risk
• Capital asset pricing model	• Financial risk
• Security market line	• Characteristic line

Further reading

There is a wealth of literature on CAPM. A fair summary — albeit a technical one — can be found in Copeland and Weston (1983, Chapter 7). Sharpe was one of the pioneers of the theory, and two of his papers (Sharpe, 1963, 1964) are classics. A very readable (and brief) discussion that puts the theory in the perspective of its usefulness can be found in the readings by MacQueen (1986) and Rosenberg and Rudd (1986).

The Workbook material to accompany this chapter begins on p. 457.

P A R T
3
Markets and other financial decisions

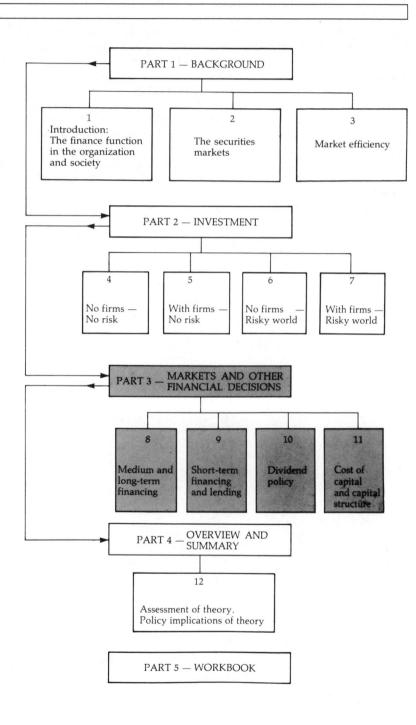

PART 1 — BACKGROUND

| 1 Introduction: The finance function in the organization and society | 2 The securities markets | 3 Market efficiency |

PART 2 — INVESTMENT

| 4 No firms — No risk | 5 With firms — No risk | 6 No firms — Risky world | 7 With firms — Risky world |

PART 3 — MARKETS AND OTHER FINANCIAL DECISIONS

| 8 Medium and long-term financing | 9 Short-term financing and lending | 10 Dividend policy | 11 Cost of capital and capital structure |

PART 4 — OVERVIEW AND SUMMARY

12 Assessment of theory. Policy implications of theory

PART 5 — WORKBOOK

Part 3   Introduction and overview

In Part 3 we move on to broader matters. So far we have seen the way that investment decisions relate throughout the economy, and in particular the implications this has for the individual enterprise.

Chapters 8 and 9 are concerned with the raising of funds. In Part 2 this was taken as unproblematic. Though we acknowledged that funds had to be forthcoming for the enterprise to be able to carry out its investment plans, we did not look at the various mechanisms available to raise funds. In Chapter 8 we look at medium- and long-term financing. In Chapter 9, we turn to short-term financing. However, as we see in Chapter 10, these are closely linked to the *dividend decision*, because the payment of a dividend to shareholders is exactly the opposite of raising funds from shareholders.

Finally, these come together in Chapter 11, when we go to the pivotal concern for the financial manager: the cost of capital. We have seen already how this relates the raising of finance to the enterprise's disposition of it — sometimes under the name of the 'hurdle rate'. Now we look at the different theories surrounding capital structure (that is, the relative use of different types of finance) and the implications this has for the cost of funds to the enterprise as a whole.

CHAPTER

8

Medium- and long-term financing

Learning objectives

After studying this chapter you should be able to:

- understand the rather artificial distinction that exists between short- and long-term financing;
- appreciate how medium- and long-term funds can be raised from both *internal* and *external* sources, and recognize that differences exist in the financing decision between 'small' and 'large' firms;
- outline the sources of medium- and long-term finance;
- list the characteristics of company securities — corporate debt (including convertibles), preferred shares and ordinary shares;
- outline the methods of raising ordinary share finance and the difficulty of pricing new share issues;
- appreciate the mechanics of the pricing of pre-emptive rights;
- understand the problems that may arise in the provision of finance for new businesses;
- understand the nature of interest rate and currency swaps.

8.1 Introduction

(a) Design of chapter

In this chapter we are concerned with the medium- and long-term financing of the enterprise. We shall discuss the other class of financing — short-term financing — in Chapter 9. Enterprises do, of course, have considerable freedom in the way they seek finance — though there are many constraints, not the least of which are the availability and cost of raising funds.

Thus the structure of this chapter is as follows:

1. In sections 8.2 and 8.3 we examine the sources of medium- and long-term financing respectively.
2. In section 8.4 we turn to the characteristics of corporate securities.
3. The methods of raising ordinary shares are discussed in section 8.5.
4. In section 8.6 we cover the pricing of pre-emptive rights.
5. Finance for new businesses is discussed in section 8.7.
6. The rapidly growing swaps market is examined in section 8.8.

(b) The context of this chapter

Although there are four chapters in Part 3 of this book, this chapter and the next may be seen as forming a special sub-part. In Part 2 we looked at how the enterprise decides on using its funds; here we consider the raising of those funds. The market efficiency we looked at in Chapter 3 should mean that the cost of funds in any particular form — for instance, equity versus short-term bank loan — can be taken to result from a kind of equilibrium, in the sense that there are many lenders and borrowers in the capital markets. We use the plural here to stress the opportunities that exist outside of the UK as a source of funds. With the increased integration of financial markets, however, differences in nominal rates may decrease. With market efficiency, any discrepancies that remain particularly in short-term rates will be removed by exchange rate movements. Likewise if short-term funds are cheaper than long-term, one possible reason is that the market more generally expects interest rates to rise in the near future. Market efficiency suggests that no individual borrower can 'beat the market' consistently by choosing the better option given the future direction of interest rates (though that will probably not stop many corporate treasurers trying).

One further preliminary may be helpful to put this chapter in context. We gave some emphasis to the notion of the cost of capital when we were looking at corporate investment decisions — particularly in Chapter 5. Still, we have not discovered quite where the rate comes from. Clearly equity, bank loans, debentures, commercial paper and so on will all tend to have different costs. We shall see how to pull all this together — including the material of this chapter and the next — in Chapter 11.

(c) Some preliminaries

We are concerned in this chapter with the medium- and long-term financing of the enterprise. Yet the distinction between short term and long term has become blurred. With financial innovations, enterprises have a greater freedom to move around between financing over different time periods.

As a starting point, we can define:

1. 'short' to be less than three years, but generally less than one year;
2. 'medium' to be three to ten years;
3. 'long' to be over ten years.

The two primary sources of funds — *internal* (from the operations of the enterprise comprising of profits after tax and dividends, but plus depreciation provisions) and *external* (creditors and investors) — are available across all time periods. As Table 8.1 shows, internal funds were the dominant form (around 70%) of finance for business enterprises in the United Kingdom in 1985. Although these data are in the aggregate, variations exist across all size groupings of companies, particularly small ones. Indeed the Macmillan Gap — the lack of provision of equity and loan capital to *small* companies of the 1930s — is still raised as an issue today (for instance by the Wilson Committee, 1980). However, two junior markets were created that, as Chapter 2 illustrated, have made it easier for smaller and growing firms to gain access to equity finance. The changes proposed by the Russell Committee (see Bank of England, 1990b) should enhance this.

In some dated, but still important studies Meeks and Whittington (1975, 1976) found some interesting divergences in that external sources were more

Table 8.1   Sources and uses of capital funds of industrial and commercial companies: (a) £m, (b) %

	1985 £m	1986 £m	1987 £m	1988 £m	1989 £m	Average £m
(a)						
Sources of funds:						
Internal	32,250	27,903	36,642	36,959	30,810	32,913
Capital transfer (receipts)	591	720	511	1,020	540	676
Import and other credit received	104	−157	95	127	292	92
Other external borrowing:						
Bank	7,454	9,096	12,141	31,064	33,935	18,738
Other loans and mortgages	876	1,450	2,720	3,771	7,964	3,302
UK capital issues:						
Ordinary shares	3,522	5,608	13,338	4,817	2,594	5,976
Debentures and preference shares	816	490	534	1,207	3,092	1,228
Capital issues overseas	770	1,492	3,969	3,092	5,026	2,870
Overseas investment	−198	2,135	1,465	2,383	5,327	2,222
Total (identified)	46,185	48,737	71,415	84,440	89,468	68,049
Use of funds:						
Capital transfers (payments)	479	668	882	1,232	1,835	1,019
Gross domestic fixed capital formation	24,876	26,682	32,254	40,071	46,564	34,090
Increase in book value of stocks	2,374	2,574	5,946	9,781	9,929	6,121
Investment in UK company securities	3,664	2,602	2,817	10,167	15,531	6,956
Direct investment in overseas securities	3,436	5,166	10,145	8,392	13,770	8,182
Other investment overseas	1,484	780	6,310	6,133	3,451	3,632
Exports and other credit given	374	395	528	1,468	−450	463
Liquid assets	4,835	10,599	8,744	5,532	14,279	8,798
Other financial assets	548	−1,731	2,675	−1,241	−2,198	−389
Unidentified (balancing items)	4,115	1,002	1,114	2,905	−13,243	−823
Total	46,185	48,737	71,415	84,440	89,468	68,049

	1985 %	1986 %	1987 %	1988 %	1989 %	Average %
(b)						
Sources of funds:						
Internal	70	57	51	44	34	48
Capital transfer (receipts)	1	1	0	1	0	0
Import and other credit received	0	0	0	0	0	0
Other external borrowing:						
Bank	16	19	17	37	38	28
Other loans and mortgages	2	3	4	4	9	5
UK capital issues:						
Ordinary shares	8	12	19	6	3	9
Debentures and preference	2	1	0	1	3	2
Capital issues overseas	1	3	6	4	6	4
Overseas investment	0	4	2	3	6	3
Total	100	100	100	100	100	100

Table 8.1   Continued

	1985 £m	1986 £m	1987 £m	1988 £m	1989 £m	Average £m
Use of funds:						
Capital transfers (payments)	1	1	1	1	2	1
Gross domestic fixed capital formation	54	55	45	47	52	50

	1985 %	1986 %	1987 %	1988 %	1989 %	Average %
Increase in book value of stocks	5	5	8	12	11	9
Investment in UK company securities	8	5	4	12	17	10
Direct investment in overseas securities	7	11	14	10	15	12
Other investment overseas	3	2	9	7	4	5
Exports and other credit given	1	1	1	2	−1	1
Liquid assets	11	22	12	7	16	13
Other finance assets	1	−4	4	−1	−2	0
Unidentified (balancing items)	9	2	2	3	−15	−1
Total	100	100	100	100	100	100

*Note:*All data are rounded.
Source: Financial Statistics, table 8.2 (CSO)

important to the fast-growing 'small' quoted companies and the larger companies, particularly the very large or giant enterprise. A recent study by Chowdhury and Miles (1987) which examines long-term financing decisions for dividends and debt, following up on an earlier study for short-term financing, does find a diversity in company financing by size. Utilizing published balance sheet data for 650 UK companies, they found that

> smaller companies in the sample appeared more risk-averse, reducing dividends and strategic debt finance by more than larger firms when measures of risk rose. In general, larger companies seemed happier with higher levels of strategic debt, financing rather more of their investment expenditure in this way and paying out somewhat more of their income as dividends. Responses to tax and interest rate changes also appeared to differ between companies with larger companies responding to a greater extent. (p 264)

Yet despite these differences with the size structure of organizations, internal finance is still an important element, though the proportion has fallen quite dramatically to under 50%. Its relative importance fluctuates over the cycle of economic activity, with external funds appearing to reach their peak in relation to internal funds in the year following the profits cycle (see Bridge and Dodds, 1978). What Table 8.1 reveals is the importance of bank and other lending to business enterprises.

8.2   Medium-term financing

We have defined medium finance as that raised with a three- to ten-year repayment horizon. Typically it is raised from banks as a *term* loan, although other institutions will also provide funds, in the form of instalment credit and lease agreements. The enterprise will frequently use this form of finance either for assets of corresponding lives — certain kinds of plant and machinery, for example — or to provide a baseline tranche of working capital. If it is a *bank* term loan, it can have a variable or fixed rate of interest. If it is a fixed rate, the bank takes out the downside elements of the interest rate risk, but the enterprise loses the chance to benefit if interest rates fall. With variable rates, the enterprise has to meet both the upside and downside risks.

Although these term loans are generally more expensive in both interest cost and set-up costs than short term loans (see Chapter 9), they give the borrower some stability. This is especially important if there is a particular asset involved for which the funds were borrowed. Presumably this asset is producing earnings (see Chapters 4 and 5) which will meet the regular repayments of principal and interest. Thus by matching a loan to its economic life the enterprise faces fewer problems in the financing decision. If the medium-term financing is to provide a tranche of permanent working capital then, although this may be a risk-averse form of borrowing, it can have its costs and it will involve the enterprise in the scheduled reduction and repayment of the loan.

An alternative to bank finance for medium-term financing is that of credit either by *hire-purchase* or *leasing*.

1. *Hire-purchase* is a means of buying an asset whereby the purchaser has the use of the asset while it is being paid for, but the financier has the legal ownership. For instance, a salesperson's car can be bought on a two-year hire-purchase deal. The salesperson can use the car just as if it were his or her own, and will be expected to maintain it in good order. But ownership is vested in the finance company that paid for the vehicle, so that if the enterprise goes into liquidation, the finance company has a prior charge and can repossess their property. It is thus less risky for the financier. Contrast this with arranging bank finance: the car would then belong to the borrower.
2. A *lease* is a contract under which an enterprise wishing to have use of an asset (known as the lessee) arranges for the asset to be purchased by the finance company (the lessor), and then pays rent for the right to use it. The terms of a lease can vary greatly. Often, for instance, the lessee will have the right at the end of the (fixed term of the) lease to purchase the asset for a nominal sum. Leases can be used for both real assets (land and buildings) and movable assets (like plant or motor vehicles) — more detail is given in section 8.3. A common means for an enterprise to gain liquidity is to sell an asset to a finance company and lease it back (known as a sale and leaseback deal). It loses ownership, retains use, gains cash and has a charge against profit of the rent (instead of the previous depreciation charge).

Hire-purchase is usually not available beyond five years and is used more frequently for assets with lives of less than three years (see Chapter 9). Leasing too can be short-term, but it can extend up to ten years for equipment and be a source of long-term finance for land, buildings, etc. There are two forms of lease we shall consider — *financial leases* and *operating leases*.

1. A *financial lease* is often referred to as a full pay-out lease, and the time period of the lease extends over a period sufficient to return the leasing company a profit after it has met the capital and interest costs.
2. The *operating lease* is a short-term lease, so typically the lease would run for any period up to the economic life of the equipment. For the leasing

company to make a profit, it has to lease the equipment to others over its lifetime. This type of lease is particularly attractive to an enterprise in an industry which has cycles, since the lease can often be cancelled at the lessee's option. Also, with equipment that is particularly susceptible to technological change, the risk is borne by the lessor rather than the lessee. Operating leases are thus particularly attractive in the case of complete systems and specialized equipment such as copying machines, cash registers, cars, etc.

Types of lease do vary and the responsibilities of the lessee under them for maintenance, for instance, also vary. The financial lease, being for a longer term, involves the enterprise in committing its resources for that period — similar to a term loan or a bond. These leases are generally non-cancellable and are used particularly for land and buildings, and sometimes for large fixed equipment. This has important effects on the operating leverage of the enterprise, and disclosure of the lease in the financial statements enables the enterprise's supplier of funds to have a more accurate idea of the fixed charges of the enterprise (for further coverage, see Taylor, 1982). The Bank of England publishes annually (in November) data on financial leases. For the year 1988 the total assets acquired were £6.9 billion, of which £3.8 billion were for manufacturing industry.

8.3   Long-term financing

For long-term financing (over ten years), an enterprise may use banks and other financial institutions or it may issue company securities such as equity shares, preference shares and debentures. Long-term financing is generally used for major fixed assets such as buildings, plant and machinery, and to support the acquisition of whole companies. The acquisition and merger decision is often related to the underlying strength of the economy and helps to fuel the upward pressure of the stock market. Although in the recent past the issue of shares — both ordinary and preference — was the major financing tool, in 1988 and 1989 the use of cash far outweighed shares. The figures for 1989 were that for 1,039 acquisitions for a total consideration of £26 billion, £21.5 billion was paid by cash (including bank borrowing) and the balance in shares, of which £3.3 billion was in ordinary shares and £1.3 billion in preference shares and loan stock.

Finance in the form of long-term loans can be arranged with the banks at fixed or floating rates of interest secured against the assets of the enterprise. An increasing trend internationally is for more lending to be securitized, with banks operating on a fee-for-income basis. Loans are more difficult to obtain for newer companies, particularly small ones, because they do not have a long-term track record. In addition extra security is usually required in the form of loan guarantees (for instance, from a parent company). Banks are nevertheless the major supplier of finance to small business (see section 8.7).

Pension funds and life assurance companies can often provide long-term financing in the form of mortgage loans tied to land and buildings, or they can arrange a sale and leaseback. This simply means that the enterprise sells an asset to the financing company which then leases it back to the enterprise. Leases of this kind can extend for very long periods, and they have been used extensively by enterprises wishing to release cash yet not lose the use of an asset. Typically what could be involved here is the sale of the freehold of a property, the simultaneous leaseback of the property and the use of the cash freed to develop the property and/or elsewhere in the operations of the enterprise.

For the issue of securities, there are various alternatives, including the sale of additional share capital:

1. the *ordinary shares* of the company, which give their holders a right to any dividends and the net worth of the company on liquidation;
2. *preference shares*, which give the holders a right to a fixed interest payment before the ordinary shareholders receive anything;
3. *debentures* (either secured or unsecured), which yield fixed income and have a prior claim on earnings ahead of either preference or ordinary shares.

There are variants of all three of these forms of security, but together they are regarded as the permanent capital of the enterprise. (The debentures will, however, generally have a maturity date. Frequently this does not matter so far as liquidity is concerned because the debt can be rolled over: that is, the enterprise can issue a new bond to pay off the old one. The new bond may be more expensive if interest rates have risen in the meantime. We discuss some of these issues later in this chapter.) Shares and debentures together account for over 50% of the total liabilities of the corporate sector in the United Kingdom. In section 8.4 we shall examine them in more detail. You should note that the changes in financial markets are such that differences are being narrowed as financial instruments are being introduced which embody features of debt and equity, preferred and equity, etc.

The final sources of long-term finance are the government and specialist financial institutions or supra-national agencies. The former would be found where, say, at a time of financial collapse new funds have to be injected. For a long time the National Enterprise Board (under the terms of the Industry Act 1975) provided equity and loan finance in this capacity, and the Department of Trade and Industry had the power to lend too. Assistance of this sort is only one of the policies of government, and in recent years we have seen a shift away from this kind of collectivism to privatization (for the privatization that has occurred, see Chapter W8) and more selective use of the tax system to provide assistance (see Midland Bank, 1986).

Where a major investment is being undertaken which would not proceed without government funding (for instance, the development of Concorde), successive governments have often provided funding. The Channel Tunnel is, however, an example of a major capital project without direct government finance. Generally local authorities provide a whole battery of financial assistance to enterprise investment, especially in areas of heavy unemployment. Apart from the national government, various other supra-national agencies lend funds, particularly in the EC, such as the European Investment Bank, European Regional Development Funds, and the European Social Fund. The European Investment Bank (EIB), for example, will give loans to finance industrial or infrastructure projects which are seen as being in the common interest of the EC and/or useful in regional development. They are available for up to ten years. There are also a lot of specialist financial institutions that provide finance, often in equity form, and here we can cite Investors in Industry (3i's), an institution owned jointly by the Bank of England and the major clearing banks, as an example.

Returning to the securities issued by the enterprise, reference back to Fig.

8.1 reveals that capital issues are generally swamped by other methods of raising finance. Nevertheless, it is instructive to examine the former in more detail. Table 8.2 offers data on the new issues of corporate securities in the United Kingdom from 1985 to 1989. It is not perhaps surprising to see the importance of debt finance as this can only be raised *externally*, whereas equity financing can be obtained internally by retention of earnings: that is, by withholding part of a potential dividend (for more detail on dividends, see Chapter 10).

It will be seen from these data that the usual method for external equity finance is still by means of a *rights issue*, where the company gives its existing shareholders the right to buy new shares at a discount, and allocates the new shares pro rata to shareholders' existing holdings. The logic behind a pre-emptive rights issue is that it can permit shareholders to preserve their proportionate holding in the enterprise by taking up the rights (see section 8.6, pp. 210–13).

Table 8.2   Capital issues and redemptions in the UK 1985–1989

	1985	1986	1987	1988	1989
Gross issues:					
Rights	3,952	5,790	10,465	4,906	4,285
Total	6,238	10,053	17,133	8,090	11,013
Redemptions	1,063	998	1,747	1,028	3,150
Net issues:					
Ordinary shares	4,234	7,804	14,907	5,153	3,634
Preference shares	414	66	658	964	898
Loan capital	527	1,185	−179	945	3,331
Total UK borrowers:	4,500	8,519	15,201	6,659	6,816
Listed public	5,066	8,721	15,376	6,693	6,827
Local authorities and public corporations	−566	−202	−175	−34	−11
Total overseas borrowers	675	535	185	403	1,047

Source: Financial Statistics, table 12.1 (CSO).

8.4   Characteristics of company securities

In section 8.3 we divided company securities into corporate bonds, preference shares and ordinary shares, though we mentioned that there were various types of each. By law the company has to have ordinary share capital, so its decision to issue debt is a discretionary one. The effect of this on the company will be examined in Chapter 11. To obtain a listing within the current three tiers of the International Stock Exchange, additional *initial* and *continuing* obligations are required. The ISE has a 'Yellow Book' which details the rules, but we can quote from the Bank of England (1990b) the two principal requirements:

> that the company must observe specified and reasonably strict standards in disclosing financial and business information to the market. This is to ensure that the shareholders and the market are properly informed and that particular groups of shareholders do not have preferential access to information. The second requirement is that a minimum proportion of a company's shares should be available to investors who are not otherwise directly associated with the company and who do not have a large stake. This is to ensure that there is a

sufficiently active market and the company shares for them to be reasonably liquid. If a company is too closely held, it could be difficult to buy or sell a holding of reasonable size without having an undue influence on the price. Thus the rules imposed by the Exchange are intended to provide a form of quality control over the securities being traded on the exchange. (p. 243)

For convenience, we shall take the types of security in order. The following section is taken from Dodds (1979).

(a) Corporate debt

Corporate debt is typically in the form of fixed interest securities issued by companies in denominations of £100. They are loans carrying no claim to ownership. They have many similarities to the bonds issued by governments; indeed, companies issuing debt take the yields that are ruling in that market as the starting point for pricing debt issues. The price at which the government bond sells on the market is a function of the coupon rate, the date of maturity and any special features it may have. With corporate bonds the problem of default risk arises and we discuss this later in this section. Corporate bonds are generally redeemable, often with a shorter life than government bonds, and sometimes with a range of maturity dates (say 2001–2004). Most have a fixed-interest coupon, though there are some that are issued with a floating rate tied to the six-month inter-bank rate. Most have a trust deed (see the Workbook, p. 485).

The corporate sector, unlike the government, does not have the power to tax, and therefore its borrowing is subject to default risk — and there are many classic defaults in history, even recent history, to urge caution. To give the holders a strong element of safeguarding their capital, corporate bonds have an *a priori* claim on the assets of the company. So the bond-holder in effect owns the assets, but in terms of option pricing (see Chapter 2 for a preliminary discussion) gives a call option on those assets to the share-holders. This aspect will be raised in Chapter 10, where cash dividends 'represent dispersal of debtholders collateral' (Riding, 1984, p. 164), and will be more fully explained in Chapter 11. Bonds stand before the preference and ordinary shareholders. But to make that claim more explicit and/or to distinguish among the various debt issues as to its seniority, we can observe that corporate debt is often secured (and referred to as debentures) on the assets of the enterprise, either as a floating charge on, say, the accounts receivable or as a mortgage on the land, buildings and other fixed assets. But the debentures themselves may have a ranking, so we can have a series of subordinated debt. If the debt is not secured then it is a straight loan stock.

What corporate bonds do not have in the United Kingdom (in contrast to the United States and some other countries) is the existence of an established bond-rating service to establish credit standing. By this we mean a system that looks at all bonds and places them in classes of risk depending on an exhaustive analysis by the rating firm. Where there is such a system the yields of bonds will correspond closely to the risk the raters estimate is inherent. Despite exposure drafts written in the early 1970s (see, for example, *British Bond Ratings*, 1974; an exposure draft produced by a joint study group of the Institute of Actuaries and the Society of Investment Analysts; and also *British Bond Ratings — A Reply* (1976), a document prepared for the Accepting House Committee and the Executive of the Issuing Houses Association), nothing formal has emerged, whereas in the United States, Standard and Poors,

Moodys, etc. have graded corporate and other debt for the last 50 years. So although the yields of the bonds will refect their default risk, estimates of the latter are formed by individual investors, brokers and so on. This may be a factor militating against a more active secondary bond market.

In assessing default two considerations are important:

1. the chance of the default;
2. if it occurs, the security of the principal *vis-à-vis* other creditors.

Two variants of accounting ratios are often used to assess these, and although they are crude, they at least give some insight. The first one is the *times interest earned* (TIE), which has in turn at least two variants, and focuses on the ability of the enterprise to service the interest payments on the debt out of earnings before interest and taxes (EBIT). Therefore we have:

$$1. \ \text{TIE} = \frac{\text{EBIT}}{\text{Debt interest (annual)}}$$

and:

$$2. \ \text{TIE} = \frac{\text{EBIT} + \text{Non-cash charges}}{\text{Debt interest (annual)}}$$

The reasoning behind (2) is that there are major non-cash flows involved in the enterprise, such as depreciation. Whilst the whole purpose of the depreciation provision is to maintain the capital stock, an enterprise if pushed could use this to meet interest payments. Generally, however, (1) is more widely used.

The second ratio is *burden coverage* (BC). This recognizes that, in addition to debt interest, the enterprise may have to meet lease payments and sinking fund payments (that is, sums set aside to extinguish a debt over a given period).

$$\text{BC} = \frac{\text{EBIT} + \text{Non-cash charges} + \text{Lease payments}}{\text{Interest} + \left(\dfrac{\text{Sinking fund}}{1 - \text{Tax rate}} \right) + \text{Lease payments}}$$

The interest and lease payments are on a before-tax basis as they are tax deductible. As sinking fund payments (if any) are made from after-tax earnings, they are adjusted to a before-tax basis.

Although both these ratios are utilized in practice, again judgement is necessary to compare them with industry norms, etc. An alternative model to value the default risk is to employ option pricing and to view the value of the bond as the bond value without default (e.g. a comparable government security) minus the value of a put option. The latter is the value of the limited liability. This aspect of option pricing and bonds was raised earlier in this chapter, and the Workbook contains a short primer on option pricing (see pp. 500–12).

Most corporate bonds are not perpetuities — they have to be repaid (unless they have convertibility options which are exercised). The enterprise therefore has to be in a position to fund the principal and plan for this contingency. Assuming that the loan has been sought to finance a capital project with a positive NPV, the enterprise has the flow of earnings from which to make regular payments of principal. To effect this the enterprise can have a *sinking fund* provision built into the bond so that either the cash flows accumulate to repay the principal on maturity, or bonds are retired so that the whole issue is redeemed by the maturity date. Sinking funds can give a bond a greater security feature to an investor. From the point of view of the enterprise, though, the provision of a sinking fund can be costly and forces the enterprise to be continually aware of the need for repayment. The offsetting argument to that, of course, is that if the debt is retired the enterprise can then issue new debt to match that retired. It will have to face market scrutiny for this.

The enterprise has a strong incentive to issue bonds in that the interest is classed as an operating expense and therefore is tax deductible (though some recent issues have been zero-coupon). Whilst they are a cheaper form of finance, both with and without the tax shield (explained in Chapter 11), they involve the enterprise in *financial gearing* — the fixed payment of interest. This is precisely the feature that investors look for in their decision to purchase. Indeed, since the market for them is so thin that active buying and selling is not possible (though for the trading that does occur gains are tax-free if the security has been held for at least one year), generally speaking investors purchase them for their income as new issues.

One of the biggest drawbacks to investing in corporate bonds is their scarcity. The extent to which demand can be satisfied given the propensity to acquire new issues is limited by the overall supply, and this itself will be a reflection of the environment within which business operates as well as the competing demands for finance from other borrowers, particularly central government and local authorities. Business profits reflecting the ability to service the fixed charge that corporate debt brings do fluctuate quite markedly, so that at times there is a dearth of issues and other times a flood of them, although these new issues, as with ordinary shares, are controlled (when over £3 million) by the Bank of England. There is then often a bunching of bonds with similar coupons (with no lower or zero coupons for net funds investors such as some of the financial institutions) and maturity dates; and as time passes, and given that the length of life at issue is generally shorter than similar government issues, holders can find themselves cluttered with a mass of short-dated stock which they may have difficulty selling to switch into longer-dated stock.

Corporate bonds may contain other features such as *callability* and *convertibility*. If the bond is callable, then the company has the right to repay the issue and reissue it (if it so chooses) with another bond on more favourable terms to the enterprise, e.g. a lower coupon. So if the structure of interest rates has declined, this could signal a call which permits the enterprise to refinance at a saving, a method often referred to as a *bond refunding*. Investors lose out, of course, so many expect a callable bond to trade at a higher yield to compensate for this feature. However, there may be a call premium paying the investor more than the face value to compensate for the loss involved in the call. The refunding of a bond to take advantage of a reduced level of cash outflows is essentially the same as the replacement capital-budgeting decision. In other words, it is an NPV decision involving calculating the incremental initial investment associated with refunding and the incremental cash savings resulting from the refunding. Once these have been arrived at, the NPV is calculated using the after-tax interest rate on the new bond or the disount rate.

Convertibility is a more fundamental and interesting feature of a bond. A convertible bond is really a hybrid between a fixed income bond with its security and a long-term option on the share which investors will exercise if it is to their advantage. A valuation method is given in the Workbook (see pp. 486–9). The reason for issuing convertible bonds is that they can be considered to be delayed equity financing.

Companies benefit from the lower debt costs (they are generally cheaper for an enterprise than a straight bond), and by setting the conversion price above the current market price they benefit ultimately from selling shares at higher prices than they could have obtained when the bond was first issued. They are also freed from the need to repay the bond *and* can permit further gearing to occur. The enterprise saves on the interest payments, but loses the tax shield and now has to meet dividends on a wider number of shares at amounts in excess of the savings; shareholders can face both a dilution of ownership and a dilution of dividends unless the enterprise operates a dividend stabilization policy (see Chapter 10).

The discussion so far on bonds has been on a domestic front. In fact, as we saw in Chapter 2, there is a large international bond market which is made up of *eurobond* issues (bonds denominated in the currency of one country and issued in another country or countries) and *foreign* bond issues (bonds denominated and issued in the country of the currency). The borrowers in these markets have typically possessed a high credit rating, e.g. international organizations such as the World Bank, and public- and private-sector institutions of developed countries. Syndicated banks will generally manage and underwrite the issue, often by public offering, sometimes with a tender system, but the secondary market is usually OTC, although some eurobonds issued by the UK and other borrowers are quoted on the ISE. The attraction they have to a holder is that they are generally anonymous: for instance, with certificates in bearer form. Interest is paid gross without withholding taxes.

The most popular currency used is the US dollar, followed in 1989 by the Swiss franc. For equity-related issues, the Japanese yen for straight fixed issues and sterling for floating rate notes are the most popular (the data are given in the Workbook, Table W8.5, p. 489). The same characteristics of sinking funds and call features are often present in the bonds, but the international market has seen more financial innovation than the domestic bond market of the United Kingdom. An example of this is a 'drop rock' bond. This is a floating rate note which, when the short-term rates fall to a given level, triggers conversion to fixed rate bonds. Moreover, since 1979, with rising interest rates, there has been a significant increase in floating rate notes as well as syndicated eurocurrency bank credit.

(b) Preference shares

The other fixed interest corporate security available is that of *preference* shares. There are many different types but they have declined in importance, as taxation changes have rendered their issue an expensive method of raising capital when compared with debentures. They cannot compete on cost due to absence of a tax shield and their increased riskiness. Their limited supply and small secondary market in which prices are very volatile are disadvantages to investors. They are normally irredeemable, but some have call provisions and some even have convertibility features. Although there is no absolute security of income, cumulative preference shares require the payment of any dividend passed and some shares have a participating feature (participating preference) in the profits of the enterprise over and above the fixed income, which can offer a hedge against inflation.

Despite the seemingly negative comments on preference shares, they are cheaper to service than ordinary shares and their issue in place of debt does not produce the same degree of gearing. So an enterprise with an existing high level of gearing may find it possible to make an issue of preference shares to increase its equity base, yet not dilute ownership. This issue of ownership has also been an important consideration in the issue of preference shares in many management buy-outs and reference has already been made to the size of expenditures of preference shares in the acquisition of companies in the UK. The managers hold the ordinary shares and the institutions and others who have funded the buy-out hold the preference shares. The latter will have a convertibility feature, making it possible to change them into ordinary shares so that the investors have a greater measure of security and control as a last resort.

(c) Equity capital

The equity capital of a company is the owners' interest in it, and this comprises the capital 'permanently' invested by them (excluding loans) and any retained profit. This is the risk capital of business, though with the existence of limited liability, the downside of the risk is limited to what the investors have put in or promised to put in. (*Note:* If a share is not fully paid-up then shareholders, if the need arose, could be required to pay the share up. For instance, in the privatization of the British Airports Authority, with a share price of £2.45, £1.00 had to be paid immediately, the remainder at a later date.) They carry no prior claims on the assets of the enterprise, though they own its 'net worth' and when a company does retain profits (see Chapter 11) these are the undistributed dividends of the shareholders.

Ordinary shares are the true permanent capital of the enterprise as they are perpetuities and under normal circumstances are not redeemable. However, if the enterprise goes into liquidation or is acquired by another enterprise, then the share will effectively disappear. But if the enterprise or the investors wish to modify their preferences as to the issue and holding of shares, this is of course possible. Companies can make new issues of shares as we shall see in section 8.5, but the timing of these may be dictated, not by the company's needs, but rather by the willingness of the market to subscribe. Generally investors are more willing in bull markets. Companies under the 1985 Companies Act can, under certain circumstances, also buy back their own shares and cancel them (see Bank of England, 1988). Investors can, provided the shares are listed, use a stock market (for example, the ISE) to liquidate their holdings at a price determined by that market based on the investors' evaluation of the current and expected (therefore risky) prospects of the enterprise. Recall, too, from Chapter 3 that the empirical evidence found these markets to be efficient in both weak and semi-strong form. Turnover on the ISE domestic market in listed equities was over £300 billion.

However, the market for shares is really a series of markets for listed and unlisted shares, including listings on overseas markets. In addition there is ARIEL (Automated Real-Time Investments Exchange Limited), a computer-based OTC market which bypasses the Stock Exchange.

As market values can fluctuate, the investor is exposed to capital market risk. For the downside risk we can cite the very dramatic falls in United Kingdom stock market prices in 1974–75 and the worldwide October crash in 1987. Since then losses simply of member firms of the ISE, as brokers, dealers and market-makers in UK equities, have been estimated at £500 million in

1988, with a similar figure in 1989 (see Scott-Quinn, 1990). There is also the inherent default risk, and income risk, as dividends can fluctuate (see Chapter 10). Equity can be an attractive investment, particularly to the longer-term investor, as it can give some protection against inflation and provides a hedge against rising interest rates.

We mentioned earlier that, just as with bonds and preference shares, there are several kinds of ordinary share. We can recognize two main distinctions: the distinction between preference and deferred shares, and that between voting and non-voting shares.

Taking these in order, *preference* and *deferred* are quite rare apart from in private companies, but as the name suggests, the preference rank before the deferred in the payment of dividends. Where they do exist, the deferred will only receive dividend entitlement after a specified period or when profits have reached a particular stated level. Some preference shares have a specified rate of dividend, too. Turning to the issue of *voting* shares, given that they are the risk capital of the enterprise, they should, one would imagine, allow investors (preference and deferred) the ability to articulate their preferences on managers, otherwise the issue of agency theory raised earlier (pp. 23–8) will very much come to the fore. However, in the UK, both voting and *non-voting* shares (these latter often referred to as 'A' shares) can exist side by side. Apart from specific justifications where the non-voting shares have been used to preserve control in the hands of the UK investors, their existence is largely a carry over from the past where family companies have raised equity finance but did not wish to give up control. Whilst generally they are frowned upon on the basic issue of shareholder democracy, one argument raised for their continuation is that, since they sell at a discount, yet rank *pari passu* for dividends, they can therefore be attractive to those investors who are willing to 'sell' their votes. Thus the discount reflects the market's assessment of the value of the votes.

Apart from the use of employee share purchase plans and scrip dividends, which will raise the amount of issue share capital, an enterprise will often wish to raise further share financing. This may be to promote fixed capital investment, repay some short- or long-term borrowing (capital structure issues) or be used in a merger by means of a share exchange. There are various methods to achieve this and they are examined in the next section.

8.5   Methods of raising funds via ordinary shares

In discussing the raising of share finance we have to distinguish between *private* and *public* (plc) companies. For *private* companies the raising of new share capital and the maintenance of the permanent existing capital of the enterprise in the face of, say, the death of existing shareholders poses major problems. The issue revolves around the legal maximum of shareholders (50) *and* the inability to offer shares to the public. Existing shareholders either have to take up the new shares or new shares have to be placed with new shareholders if that is possible within the maximum limit. This placement process can be achieved by merchant banks and other intermediaries, but it is difficult as there is no 'free' market to transfer the shares and prospective investors fear a locking-in that minority holding could bring.

A fundamental issue that is present in the absence of a market on the shares is the price, which is why, in the case of Crown Corporations in the privatization process, the issue price has been a contentious issue. To establish the value today of a holding of a share traded on a secondary market, one merely has to check the price given by the market, which reflects all publicly available information (according to the semi-strong form of the efficient markets hypothesis we discussed in Chapter 3). In the absence of such a market, then, alternative measures of valuation, usually based on assets, are necessary to determine prices, and this occurs particularly when the death of a shareholder requires a valuation to be made for tax purposes. Ultimately a private company can choose to go public and raise finance, but this is an expensive and time-consuming step to take and can only be justified for the larger company.

If we now turn to *public* companies, then the distinction is between quoted and non-quoted, where we are referring to a quotation on a stock exchange. As we have mentioned already, to be quoted on the Official List or the main market, where 2,000 domestic equities are traded, a company must satisfy both at entry and subsequently an extensive set of requirements on disclosure. At least 25% of the shares must be available for sale to make the market and up to February 1990, a five-year trading history. From January 1991 this became three years to comply with EC directives (see Workbook).

The exchange itself is a secondary market, but its existence makes the issue of new securities, which can subsequently be traded, a more attractive proposition. It is a misconception to assume that public status automatically brings with it a stock exchange listing. This is not the case and many public companies either do not have a listing at all or are listed on the *unlisted securities market* (USM). This market developed in the 1970s operating under Rule 163(2) of the Stock Exchange and is similar to NASDAQ market in the USA except that NASDAQ has seen a very rapid growth. The USM began in 1980 and today, although still small (see details in Chapter 2 of the development of the USM), it has achieved a measure of success and has emerged as the biggest source of equity capital for small and medium-sized business with 450 companies quoted with a market capitalization of £9 billion in 1989.

For entry to the USM the ISE had *normally* required a three-year trading history, but this has been reduced to two years. A Third Market was established in 1987 and it had 70 companies traded with a capitalization of £0.6 billion in 1989. Eleven companies formerly in the Third Market moved to the USM. With the impending adoption of the Prospectus Directive of the EC in April 1991, the Third Market closed at the end of 1990 as the tightening of the requirements blurred the difference between this market and the USM. For Third Market companies that did not transfer, Rule 535.2 permitted members of the ISE to trade in securities that were not part of the market. The main requirements for the USM relate to the making of the market and only 10% of the company's equity need be offered.

The Big Bang (as discussed in Chapter 2) has brought about major changes in the markets, as has the harmonization of listing requirements within the EC. Trading in quoted securities has come under the umbrella of the Stock Exchange and the trading in unquoted companies under a separate regulating organization. The main determining factor of a full listing from the point of view of the market is that it should be possible to make a market in the shares. For the enterprise the problems are a function of the size of the enterprise, as maintaining a listing is costly and the raising of additional finance also costly due to the economies of scale. The requirements of the Exchange in terms of additional information have forced some enterprises to drop their quotation and/or not to seek a listing. The stock market has not been an effective vehicle for small enterprises as the institutional investors often fight shy of such investments since they impose additional costs on them in terms of monitoring performance. However, they may choose to invest by means of a private placement (as discussed in Chapter 2), which can give them a block of shares in one investment and probably influence the enterprise by means of the appointment of directors, etc.

Firms are not restricted to the issuing of shares and other securities on domestic markets, and the international equity market grew particularly between 1982 and the October 1987 crash. In 1989, however, it recovered with $15 billion equity issues. Japanese multinationals have been large issuers over this period with continental European companies also active. A major constraint for UK firms has been pre-emptive rights (see section 8.6), which have curtailed the attempts of many would-be international issuers. The attractions of such issues include a broadening of the shareholder base, the ability to raise large amounts of capital and the chance of obtaining the highest price possible as international investors may be more tempted to buy a new issue than the existing shares in their quest for international portfolio diversification.

The business enterprise that is quoted can raise finance by equity, preference and loan capital by four main methods (though the sale by tender is a variation of item 1).

1. offers for sale;
2. placing;
3. sale by tender;
4. rights issue.

The Russell Committee Report has made proposals for change in the initial Public Offers (IPOs). These proposals are reported in the Workbook and the details given in the text reflect the situation in the summer of 1990. The overall thrust of the report is to emphasize 'the overriding importance of flexibility to enable issues to be marketed in a way that meets the particular needs of the issuer' (Bank of England, 1990b, p. 247).

For initial equity financing, there are two main methods – *offers for sale* and *placings*. The offer for sale by tender was more common in the early 1980s. The data in the Workbook indicate both the number of issues by each method and the funds raised. The ISE currently requires for issues over £15 million (for the official list) and £5 million for the USM that these be made by an *offer for sale*. Between 1985 and 1989 nearly £6 billion was raised by this method. The offer for sale involves the selling of shares at a fixed price to the public by an issuing house, acting as an agent for the company. The issuing house may indeed buy the shares in toto and then sell them to the public – a public or prospectus issue, or what is referred to as a bought issue in North America. If they act as an agent, the issuing house can underwrite the whole issue by agreeing to buy any unsold shares. As lead underwriters, the issuing house will usually subcontract the risk to a number of sub-underwriters. If the shares are to be listed, the ISE has a set of rules to be followed and these are in line with EC directives. The costs are high as a prospectus has to be prepared, advertising placed and processing costs incurred, and there are also underwriting costs (on average 2%). The Bank of England estimates that for the period 1985–1989 the larger issues (£5–10 million) had costs of up to $7\frac{1}{2}$% and smaller issues 14% (far more expensive than for placings).

For *placings*, the issuing house generally buys the issue from the firm and arranges placements with investors, typically financial institutions. The issuing house acts in a distributing role and, where the issue is over £2 million, 25% of the issue has to be offered directly to the public or through another issuing house. The tables in the Workbook indicate that in the last five years there were 120 placings, raising £725 million. There are limits on the size of placings (generally £15 million), as was mentioned earlier, but the costs are lower than offers for sale. For placings of below £5 million, the Bank of England estimates the cost at $11\frac{1}{2}\%$, and for placings in the £5 to 10 million range it is $7\frac{1}{2}\%$.

The fundamental problem in new issues is the pricing of the shares. So how is the price of an issue determined? In Chapter 5 we did review some of the methods of valuing the shares of an enterprise. The stock market provides a basis for this as the price that a new security will realize will depend upon the prices of similar securities already issued. In theory, at least, this should lead to the accurate pricing of new issues. But as we argued in Chapter 5, share prices are based on *expectations* of future earnings. These will be influenced by the information contained in the prospectus and can be diverse, leading to an over- or undersubscription for the shares. In the case of the former, an allotment system has to be established which is often geared towards the small investor or the employees of the enterprise. The pent-up demand for the shares – often the result of stagging (which occurs when investors who are not potential long-term investors seek to profit from the price premium at the opening of trading) – will result in investors profiting from the mispricing rather than the enterprise. There have been many high-profile cases, such as the privatization of British Airways, British Telecom, Amersham International and British Gas, where very heavy oversubscriptions have occurred. This has confirmed to many the existence of systematic underpricing. A recent Bank of England (1990b) study focused on this issue and found that there was a continued tendency 'for issues to be priced at a discount to the price of which the shares subsequently trade' (p. 252). They also found the post-Big Bang period to the October 1987 crash to be a 'hot period', with premiums averaging 25% in the first week of trading. The Workbook covers this study in more detail.

To protect itself from the downside of an undersubscription, then, the enterprise can have issues underwritten. This incurs the cost of the commission which is really an insurance premium. Apart from placings, new issues (including rights – see section 8.6 below) are normally underwritten. But what of the underpricing? One method is to allow the market to fix the price by means of a tender issue. These were very popular in the early 1980s, but have not been used since 1986. A base or reserve price is fixed similar to an auction, and the strength of demand will fix the final price at which the market is cleared. What the issuing house cannot do is to use price discrimination. It has to set a price at which the whole issue is cleared and allow investors to enjoy any consumer surplus that arises. With keen competition for the shares the company reaps the benefit that would go with an oversubscription and subsequent opening premium to the investor. To protect the downside the issue can be underwritten at the reserve price.

For existing companies, the major form of raising external equity finance is by means of a *rights issue*, though recently dissatisfaction has been expressed about this reliance – not least that, unless the enterprise can obtain shareholder approval, it is denied access to the raising of share capital in the expanding euroequity market. The international equity market, as we have seen, has enjoyed a dramatic growth and will continue to grow in the future. Certainly the privatization process in the UK has seen the placement of some shares (a minority) abroad. This use of rights stands in contrast to the situation in some other countries, including the USA. The EC has issued directives but not all countries have complied. In the UK the Second Directive on Company Law of the EC (1979) was enacted into the Companies Act 1980 to give legal protection to shareholders in the case of rights issues. However, developments in international financial markets have led some firms to try and circumvent shareholder approval by issuing new shares abroad or obtaining shareholder approval in excess of 5% of authorized capital to do so. Some companies have been able to obtain approval and others have received well-publicized refusals. The ISE formed a committee in 1987 to issue guidelines reinforcing shareholder protection (note the agency issues here) by requiring shareholder approval on an annual basis. Notwithstanding this, the intention of the guidelines is also to allow:

> companies to broaden their shareholder bases and to make use of new issuing techniques in ways which should bring benefit to the companies as entities, while at the same time protecting the proprietorial rights of existing shareholders. (Bank of England, 1987, p. 549)

The costs of rights issues have been estimated at about $4\frac{1}{2}$% (see Wilson Committee, 1980). Because of their importance we devote the next section to the pricing of rights. This pricing will be influenced by the flow of new information from the enterprise. This will reduce the asymmetry in information between managers and shareholders but cause a fundamental reappraisal of the price of the underlying share and *ipso facto* the rights.

Turning to the issue of equity and other capital abroad, it can be said that the majority of issues in the past have been syndicated on what is now referred to as a flexible approach. Syndicate members were free to dispose of their allocations where a market demand was felt. More recently what is referred to as a 'ring fence method' has been used where the lead manager of the syndicate permits syndicate members to sell shares only in the country or region which has been allocated to them. Companies, particularly large multinationals, can have their shares quoted on more than one exchange (this raises interesting research questions of the 'efficiency' of cross-listings); and as the pace of international equity issues increases, cross-border delays and other problems arise. In time these problems will be resolved as these markets become increasingly integrated.

8.6   The pricing of pre-emptive rights

We referred earlier (section 8.3) to the importance of rights to the long-term finance of existing enterprises, and now we need to be more specific as to the nature, pricing and effects of rights convertibles and preference shares. However, because of the importance of rights issues we shall discuss these in more detail.

A pre-emptive right imparts a purchase privilege or an option to purchase to existing shareholders to subscribe to a new issue of shares in proportion to their current ownership, thus permitting them to maintain their share of ownership. In the absence of rights, any new shares issued would not only dilute that ownership but, if they were issued *below* the existing market price, would cause existing shareholders to suffer an economic loss, hence the opposition referred to earlier. As the objective of the enterprise is supposedly the maximization of shareholder wealth, it is clear why they are so commonly used, for as the number of shares is increased immediately, there may be a lag in the increase in the earnings, resulting in a dilution in the EPS. Once more this will impact on existing shareholders. The counter-argument to this is that by issuing shares to non-shareholders, particularly abroad, the firm may obtain a higher price than they would if they were issued as rights. With more capital to invest, firms can increase the overall wealth of the firm and therefore of the shareholders.

Let us take an example to illustrate the mechanics of a rights issue. ABC plc has 10 million shares outstanding and is considering the issue of additional share capital to finance an expansion plan. As Chapter 10 will reveal in more detail, the enterprise must ensure that the proceeds raised will at least return the same earnings as the existing equity base so as to preserve the capital of the shareholders, yet be an attractive proposition to obtain the additional finance. In other words, the shareholders should be no worse off from the issue of rights. Two questions stem from that — what the enterprise intends to do with the finance raised, and the discount rate used to capitalize those earnings.

The issue of rights can be attractive to the enterprise as costs, including underwriting costs, are lower. However, the critical factor is how they will impact on shareholders. In the UK, the subscription price of a right is generally set at a large discount on the market price and this discount then confers a value to the right. But as rights have a life of months, and as the *cum* or *rights on* the share price can be volatile because of market conditions, if it drops below the subscription price there is no incentive to subscribe. So, if we return to our example, ABC decides to raise an additional £10 million. Its current shares have been selling recently in the range of £6–7, and after negotiation with their brokers a subscription price of £4.00 is agreed as being one which will permit full subscription. To raise the £10 million, the enterprise will have to sell 2½ million shares, which will therefore mean that four rights will be required to purchase one more share at £4. Once the rights are announced, the share will trade cum rights or rights on (say £6.50) for a short period and then go ex rights.

Thus the price of the share is made up of two elements: the value of the share *per se* and the value of the option or right to purchase. The share price will fall by the intrinsic value of the right.

At some point the rights will expire. We can illustrate the two prices for the rights — cum rights and ex rights.

1. *Cum rights:*

$$\text{Value of a right} = \frac{\text{Share price (rights on)} - \text{Subscription price}}{\text{No. of rights required to purchase one share} + 1}$$
(VR)

In the case of ABC:

$$\frac{6.50 - 4}{4 + 1} = \frac{2.50}{5} = 50\text{p}$$

as the shares and rights then sell separately.

2. *Ex rights:*

$$\text{Value of a right} = \frac{\text{Share price (ex rights)} - \text{Subscription price}}{\text{No. of rights required to purchase one share}}$$
(VR)

The ex rights share price is unknown but as all the other factors are known then:

$$VR = \frac{6.00 - 4}{4} = 50p$$

Other things being equal the share price will drop by the amount of 50p — the value of the right on the ex-rights day. The shareholders can exercise the right by subscribing to the new shares or can sell them in the market, though sometimes a cash option is made available to shareholders.

If the shareholder has 100 shares, he or she now can buy another 25 at a cost of £4.00 each. The share price at the time of the rights offering is £6.50, so shareholder wealth is £650. The shares go ex rights, falling to £6.00 a share, and four rights are needed for each new share. But if shareholders do not take some action, either through neglect or because they are on a long holiday, then they will lose out. Otherwise the rights issue does not in itself change shareholders' wealth. We can prove this using the same example.

The investor who sells the rights had 100 shares before the rights and nets £50, which together with the £600 (100 shares × ex rights price of £6) retains his or her initial wealth before the rights offering of £650. If he or she subscribes, his or her wealth is now £600 + (25 × £6) = £750. The difference of £100, of course, is the price of the new shares (25 × £4). So the shareholder is neither better nor worse off provided he or she does something. If he or she fails to exercise or sell, his or her wealth falls to £600 — a loss of £50.

Once the share is ex rights then of course, until the exercise date, both the share and the right will trade separately, although the price of the right which is now an option is inextricably bound up with the price of the share. If the share price falls dramatically in this period, the rights become worthless and the underwriters will be left with the new shares. Of course, the share price could advance markedly and this would cause the price of the right to rise, too.

There are a lot of alleged myths surrounding the question of rights issues. We have illustrated how the shareholder does not lose. He or she should not as the underlying assets have not changed and, provided the new funds acquired earn at least the current rate of return (the same issue is raised in Chapter 10 with respect to dividends), the share price does not drop after the rights issue but he or she is compensated by the amount of the drop. Our previous discussion of market efficiency should therefore tell us that the effect of a rights issue is neutral. But practitioners often argue that the issue of rights will cause *price pressure* by virtue of the additional shares available. They also focus on the discount used in the issue which has the aura of cheapness. Whilst we have recognized that there may be a lag in the funds being used so that EPS may be diluted, this is only a short-run effect. Beyond that the crux of the argument will lie in the use to which the funds are put. The most thorough recent empirical study on rights issues is by Marsh (1979) and he finds no evidence of price pressure.

The same line of argument applies to a stock split or scrip issue. Companies use this to increase the number of shares outstanding in order to capitalize the retained earnings. The stock split should not change the wealth of shareholders since, if it is 1 for 7, the share price will fall correspondingly as nothing has happened to the earnings of the enterprise. However, there is an argument (not supported in the academic literature) that as the unit price has fallen the shares become affordable to the investor who has a smaller amount of capital to invest. If this were to be the case, we would expect an upward pressure on price due to this marketability issue.

8.7 New businesses

The presumption so far in the chapter is that we are talking about the raising of finance for existing companies. Each year new firms start up in business and many fail. In 1989 alone, there were over 10,000 insolvencies of companies, of which 4,000 were compulsory. In 1985 and 1986 the totals were over 14,000 for each year. One of the critical factors in their success or failure is the provision of finance or lack of it. Some of these new enterprises are the result of management buy-outs and generally these are well conceived and supported, for although the enterprise is technically new, the labour force, management, product line, etc., of the enterprise are existing and have a track record. But what of brand new firms? Most start up with an individual or individuals providing the equity capital and banks or others providing the short-term capital. The High Street banks in the UK have attempted through their marketing (with small business consultants in branches, and advertising) to develop and ensure a more supportive relationship with small business. Yet there is an almost ritualistic criticism of the banks by small firms which is borne out by study after study. Notwithstanding this criticism, the fact remains that banks provide around 90% of the financial requirements of this sector — £30 billion in 1989.

However, in recent years we have had a growth in the provision of venture capital (see Bank of England, 1990a) for companies in both the first and second stages of development. Indeed, although the concept has become part of the fashion in the finance area, there is no common theme to the range of investment opportunities supported (e.g. new technologies). The sums involved are generally in excess of £50,000 because of the management time involved in evaluation, and are provided by the large number of institutions involved (e.g. investment trusts, subsidiaries of pension funds, banks, insurance companies and some government agencies). The venture capital route is not, however, an easy option. A recent study indicated that 98% of proposals were ultimately rejected, with 60% being ruled out at the outset and a further 25% after a short investigation. The data available on funds provided point to use of venture capital funding to existing business rather than to start-ups. Palframan (1990) reports that 'of the £1.4 billion invested by the British Venture Capital Association's 90 members in 1988 ... only £130 million went to start-up and early-stage companies. The 1987 figure ... was £120 million out of a total of £1 billion' (p. 157). To safeguard their investment the investors normally have a very close working relationship with the enterprise. It is not just the provision of finance, but the whole management function that they are involved in. Their hope is that the venture will succeed such that, not only will their investment return them a profit, but the enterprise will go public and they can then liquidate their funds.

8.8 Interest rate and currency swaps

The uncertainties in financial markets of the early 1980s led to many financial innovations and new markets, one of which was the swap market — interest rate swaps and currency swaps. The advent of these swaps has led to a greater degree of management of longer-term liabilities, just as in Chapter 9 we refer to the management of short-term debt obligations.

The market in swaps has developed to such a degree that it is now a regular part of the enterprises' financing and one of the most widely used tools in corporate finance in asset/liability management. However, a note of caution is required here as swaps can be extremely risky and some local councils in Britain have lost heavily in speculative interest rates swap transactions. At the time of writing, banks (not all UK) are suing a number of councils, including Hammersmith, Fulham, Croydon, Brent, Tower Hamlets, Coventry, Welwyn–Hatfield, Hounslow, Merton, and Epsom and Ewell.

Just as there are many types of debt financing there are equally as many different types of swap arrangements. Swaps are not investment or funding vehicles; rather they are tools to provide a more optimal utilization of investment and funding sources. They can be used for speculative purposes too. Swap markets developed in 1981 and they are now utilized for several reasons: reduced funding costs, active asset/liability management, to gain access to alternative markets, and to hedge interest rates or currency exposure which emanates from the normal course of business. The global market for swaps in the beginning was around $3 billion, but the market has now mushroomed with the larger banks actively making markets and swaps. Data on the size and composition of swaps are given in the Workbook for 1988 and indicate a nominal value of $1,000 billion of interest rate swaps and over $300 billion of currency swaps. In addition, the Workbook contains an article on off-exchange instruments by Kodak.

Let us commence with 'interest rate swaps'. A swap is a transaction where two unrelated borrowers with identical principal borrowed over identical periods but from different lenders agree to exchange the cash flows relating to the interest expense of the borrowing. The key issue here is that it is only the cash flows which are swapped and not the debt instruments themselves. The swaps can either be arranged at the outset when the borrowings are done or subsequently on debt that is already in place. In essence it is really a privately negotiated forward contract.

We can expand further on the benefits of interest rate swaps:

1. Lower-cost financing: firms can through swaps maximize their savings by borrowing from their most cost-effective source, then swapping to an alternative, preferable, interest rate structure.
2. Asset/liability management strategies: swaps permit firms a number of financial strategies. For example, they can match the rate structure of assets and liabilities, they can hedge against interest rate movements and they can change the proportion of fixed and floating rate financing at will without incurring the cost of refinancing.

There are three main types of swap: coupon swaps, where the parties exchange fixed for floating rates; basis swaps from one floating rate to another floating rate; and cross-currency interest rates swaps, where fixed rate flows in one currency are swapped for floating rate flows in another currency.

An example will best serve to illustrate the essentials of swap transactions. Enterprise A is perceived by the market as a better credit risk and can therefore borrow both fixed rate (12%) and floating rate (10%) funds at a lower rate than Enterprise B (fixed rate 18% and floating rate 12%). Enterprise A decides to go for a fixed rate of 12%; Enterprise B goes for a float of 12% but agrees to take on 3% of the interest cost of Enterprise A. Both enterprises benefit from the arrangement. Enterprise A has an effective borrowing cost of 7% and Enterprise B 15% with Enterprise A having floating rate funds and B fixed rate funds. Fig. 8.1 illustrates this.

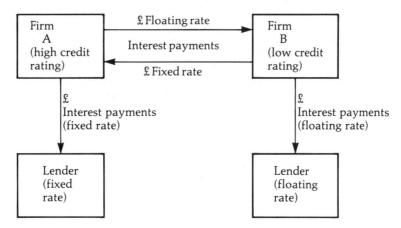

Fig. 8.1   Interest rate swaps.

For the swap to be mutually advantageous, it is *not* necessary to have different expectations of interest rates built into the decision to go fixed versus floating and the subsequent decision to swap. It can be purely the result of the pricing of risk and the rationing of funds in the market. Both enterprises still make their interest rate payments on their primary debt, but they settle the adjustment in the interest cash flows between themselves. Tax is deductible on the primary interest payments, and the cash flow from Enterprise B to A is deductible for B and classed as income to A. The case of swaps can go beyond the mutual savings on interest payments: it can extend into hedging against interest rate changes and can be used to take up speculative positions.

The logical extension of the interest rate swap is to include bonds denominated in different currencies that therefore involve a *currency swap*, where cash flows in different currencies on the debt are exchanged. Figure 8.2 illustrates this process. It is to be noted that generally it is interest and principal payments that are swapped. In the example given in the figure, Enterprise A in the UK agrees to swap its fixed rate obligation for UK sterling for a Swiss franc obligation of Enterprise B.

The reasoning for this sort of swap is to obtain a desired currency at a cheaper cost or to reduce the foreign exchange rate risks associated with the debt. So, say Enterprise A, a multinational which operates in Switzerland and which will have earnings in Swiss francs to service the debt, swaps its UK debt with Enterprise B which desires to be in a sterling debt. We have said earlier that if the arrangement includes the exchange of the principal too, then the relative involvement of the two currencies is critical. So, if in the year of the setting of the arrangement the exchange rate was £1 = 3 SwF, and at the maturity of the debt it has moved to £1 × 3 SwF, then if the original principal had been £100 million (300 SwF), Enterprise A will have incurred a loss on the transaction and Enterprise B a gain. Enterprise A will have to find 300 SwF (£150 million) yet Enterprise B will only have to find 200 SwF (£100 million).

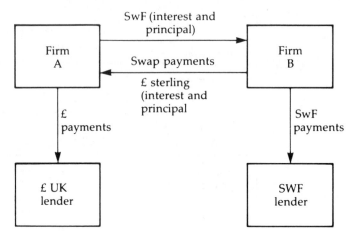

Fig. 8.2 Currency swaps.

Summary

In this chapter we have considered the raising of medium- and long-term finance by a business enterprise.

1. Most funds used to come from internally generated profits and not from capital markets. Since 1985 this has changed, with capital markets increasing the share and bank lending becoming increasingly significant.
2. We may take short-term financing to be up to one year, medium-term from three to ten years, and long-term over ten years. This chapter has been concerned with medium- and long-term finance.
3. Medium-term finance includes bank loans, hire-purchase and leases.
4. Long-term finance includes bank or other institutional loans, bonds, preference shares, equity (i.e. ordinary shares) and reinvested funds.
5. We saw how to issue ordinary shares, and how to price pre-emptive rights issues.
6. Finally, there was a discussion of interest rate and currency swaps, which are increasingly common, particularly for the larger firm.

Key terms and concepts

Here is a list of the key terms and concepts which have featured in this chapter. You should make sure that you understand and can define each one of them. Page references to definitions in the text appear in bold in the index.

- Term loan
- Hire purchase
- Financial lease
- Operating lease
- Rights issue
- Bond rating
- Burden coverage
- Sinking fund
- Callability
- Convertibility
- Foreign bond
- Pre-emptive rights
- Swaps
- Securitization

Further reading

The readings of Chapter 2 are again helpful here. Particularly useful are Rutterford (1983) and Peasnell and Ward (1985). It is especially important that you read a good financial newspaper such as the *Financial Times*, which has excellent articles on new developments in the financial markets. In addition, familiarity with its quotation system on the back pages is essential for you to claim an understanding of the capital markets. Various publications, such as the *Bank of England Quarterly Bulletin* and *Financial Statistics*, provide data and, in the case of the former, include excellent review articles. In addition, the Bank of England publishes a number of technical reports and working papers. The *Annual Report of the Bank for International Settlements* is an excellent source of up-to-date data and discussion of trends in international capital markets, as is the annual survey provided by the International Monetary Fund.

The Workbook material to accompany this chapter begins on p. 480.

9 Short-term financing and lending

Learning objectives

After studying this chapter you should be able to:

- understand the components of the short-term finance function of the enterprise and its interrelationships with the long-term borrowing and lending decisions;
- discuss the importance of cash management to the enterprise;
- understand the components of current assets and current liabilities, and the policies the enterprise can adopt to increase the flow of cash to the enterprise;
- consider the management of the liquid assets of the enterprise;
- discuss the overall financing needs of the enterprise and the disequilibrium behaviour the enterprise may exhibit due to the presence of external constraints;
- recognize that the size of a company influences both short- and long-term financing decisions.

9.1 Introduction

In the previous chapter where we considered sources of medium- and long-term financing, we made the point that, as they intertwine so much with the short-term financing decision, it is difficult to consider them separately. So in this chapter our focus will be on the overall financing needs of the enterprise, and we shall see how the needs for short-term financing and the opportunities for short-term investment arise.

Short-term debt is an integral part of the balance sheet and in recent years it has found an increased emphasis in enterprises as the highly volatile and uncertain interest rate environment has caused a shift into short-term debt. Organizations are having to be more astute in their handling of their total financing needs. Just as uncertainty in the capital-budgeting problem demands our attention, it is *uncertainty* that brings cash management to the fore in terms of:

1. the timing of payments and receipts — the permanent cash outflows (payments to vendors and employees) and cash inflows (collections from the sale of goods and services);
2. forecasts of the structure of interest rates;
3. forecasts of exchange rates;

4. defaults on payments extended and on securities in which funds are invested;
5. use of innovative financial instruments.

In previous chapters, we have portrayed the firm as investing in projects to produce net cash flows with an objective of shareholder wealth maximization. With the presence of uncertainty (risk) we have recognized that it cannot guarantee that the expectations it has at the outset of an investment will be realized. The investment may be more or less successful according to the impact of systematic and non-systematic risk (see Chapter 7). However, in any given period, an enterprise will have generated after-tax profits (or losses) from its past investments. These *income* flows can be supplemented by the sale of assets (the asset base of the enterprise), whether fixed or liquid, and they are available for distribution to shareholders in the form of dividends (see Chapter 10) or can be retained in the enterprise.

There are a number of reasons why enterprises need liquidity:

1. funds are needed to invest in projects that were agreed in previous time periods, or to take advantage of an investment opportunity that arises — this could, for example, be an acquisition;
2. they are needed for working capital — the need for this arises because of the time it takes to produce, sell and receive payments;
3. many enterprises need extra funds because they are in a seasonal business, with regularly varying sales levels through the year;
4. finally there are the underlying cyclical factors in the economy too, the boom and slump conditions which will affect a number of factors exogenous to the enterprise — sales, interest rates, etc.

If the total requirements exceed the capacity of the enterprise to finance from retained earnings *and* liquid assets, the cash deficit has to be financed externally — raising a mixture of short- and long-term funds as cheaply as possible. If there is a surplus of funds, these have to be invested, either short term or long term, so as to make the best use of them.

The enterprise may have excellent potential, with a strong product line, but account has to be taken of not just the balance sheet and the prospective profits from the investment in capital projects (positive NPVs), but the availability of cash. The enterprise may have accounting profits, but without cash it will fail. This cash is the life-blood of the enterprise and it has to be managed like any other resource in the enterprise. With high and volatile interest rates, it has become increasingly important for any business — small or large — to be more concerned about its management of cash. What is more, volatile exchange rates have meant that enterprises with overseas trade and/ or that operate overseas have an additional problem to consider.

Our focus is the financial plan of the enterprise which we develop in section 9.2. We shall assume that the objective(s) of the enterprise have been established (see our discussion in Chapter 1), and that:

1. the production plans (input needs and costs)
2. the investment plans and
3. the marketing plans (for instance, product mix, sales forecasts)

of the enterprise have been determined in the light of these objectives.

The ability of the enterprise to match the growth in demand for its products to the growth in production capacity will permit a balance in the growth of the enterprise. This can then be taken as given for the financial planning process. Of course, this presumes a sequential treatment of first investment plans and then financing. In practice it is unlikely that investment decisions would be taken independently of financing decisions. The actual and forecasted sales are a reference point, but it is the collection of accounts receivable that creates the operating cash inflows. As for input costs, these will involve payments some of which are fixed, others variable (see Chapter 4 of *Managerial Accounting: Method and Meaning*).

Thus the structure of this chapter will be as follows:

1. In section 9.2 we look at the financial structure of the enterprise: its balance sheet and sources and uses of funds.
2. In section 9.3 we examine short-term borrowing: bank finance, using bills of exchange, leases, hire-purchase, factoring and invoice discounting; then we look at short-term lending: in bank deposits, local authorities, bills of exchange and so on.
3. In section 9.4 we turn to look at the management of current liabilities — accounts payable and accruals. We look in particular at policies concerned with *different maturity periods* (that is, short versus long).
4. Section 9.5 is concerned with the management of current assets, in particular credit policy to customers, the size of inventories and managing cash.
5. Finally, in section 9.6, we consider portfolio aspects of these policies.

9.2   Balance sheet and sources and uses of funds

The enterprise commences a period, say January 19X8, with a given balance sheet or 'stock structure' which represents a historical snapshot. Throughout the next period — say a year — it performs its day-to-day operating activities, and thus by the end of that year, it has another stock position. The difference between these two stock positions can be portrayed via the flow of funds. These can then be examined in terms of the *sources* and *uses* of funds (see *Financial Accounting: Method and Meaning*, Chapter 8). Now, say the management reckons there are imbalances in this — for example, short-term borrowing is too high — then corrective policy action will be taken (the control loop of Chapter 1) via the flow elements. In this case, the enterprise will attempt to increase its long-term financing and retire its short-term financing.

Table 9.1(a) illustrates a simplified balance sheet of an enterprise and 9.1(b) a simplified statement of sources and uses of funds. Given that the title of this chapter is 'Short-term financing and lending', our primary concerns are the current assets and liabilities of the enterprise, and in sections 9.4 and 9.5 we examine these in detail. To make this concrete in terms of UK industry today it is helpful to know what the current situation is overall, and the recent data for the corporate sector are contained in the Workbook (pp. 534–7). In this section we shall focus on the cash surplus and deficit of the enterprise and, therefore, the management of this cash.

In Section 9.1 we said we would assume as given the production and sales forecasts and consequent cash needs, as well as the known commitments for funds including internal payments. Then the enterprise needs to:

Table 9.1   Simplified balance sheet and funds statement

| (a) Simplified balance sheet: | |
Assets	Liabilities and shareholders' equity
Current:	Long-term debt
Cash and marketable securities	Capital stock
Accounts receivable	Share premium
Inventories	Retained earnings
Prepaid expenses	
Total current assets	Current:
	Short-term borrowing
Fixed assets	Accounts payable
	Other liabilities and accrued expenses
	Total current liabilities
Total assets	Total liabilities

| (b) Simplified sources and uses of funds: | |
Sources	Uses
Funds provided by operations	Purchases of fixed assets
Decrease in cash and marketable	Decrease in accounts payable
securities	Increase in prepaid expenses
Decrease in accounts receivable	Increase in liquid asset holdings
Increase in short-term borrowing	
Increase in accruals	
Increase in long-term debt	

1. survey the sources of funds available to it, both internal and external;
2. estimate the costs of these various sources;
3. generate an overall forecast of cash needs extending, say, up to 18 months, including their incidence through time; for a merger active firm, these may be difficult, so additional liquidity and agreed bank financing may be planned for. Chapter 8 details the importance of cash in the acquisition process, particularly in 1988–9;
4. generate from this a forecast income statement;
5. generate a pro-forma balance sheet.

This step-wise process is illustrated in Fig. 9.1 in terms of a short-term finance function of the enterprise. Of course, the forecasts used are only tentative, but they do provide the enterprise with information and a better understanding of its likely financial position and the risks involved. They can also demonstrate the impact of changes in the assumptions on, for instance, profitability and liquidity. Thus they can provide a trigger for action — hence the inclusion of the control process and feedback loop referred to in section 9.1 and portrayed in Fig. 9.1.

To assist in this process, it is now possible to use computer software to develop interactive models of the planning process. Quite apart from its use in developing alternative scenarios, computer simulation can impart a deeper understanding to users of the financial relationships that exist within the enterprise.

Simulation can therefore demonstrate the impact of changes in the cash flow in terms of the cash inflows and outflows — this is illustrated in Fig. 9.2. The solid lines represent inflows of cash: the dotted lines, outflows. The financial manager is required to plan and control these financial flows to preserve adequate liquidity while at the same time establishing and monitoring each element to ensure, if not maximum profitability, at least a credible

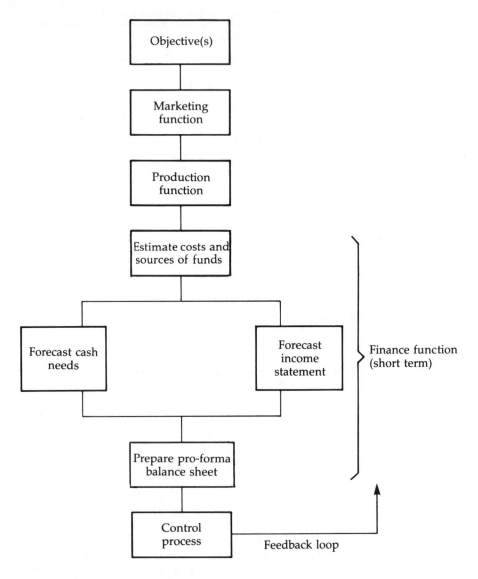

Fig. 9.1   Short-term finance function

profit. Some of these constraints can be incorporated into linear and goal programming models.

A fair slice of the cash management process is routine, and the banking sector can provide an efficient cash transfer system to concentrate cash from subsidiaries to the parent to minimize the overall financing needs and invest the maximum available surplus cash. In subsequent sections we shall examine the various aspects of the decisions to be made with regard to the cash flow cycle of the enterprise.

3. forecasts of exchange rates;

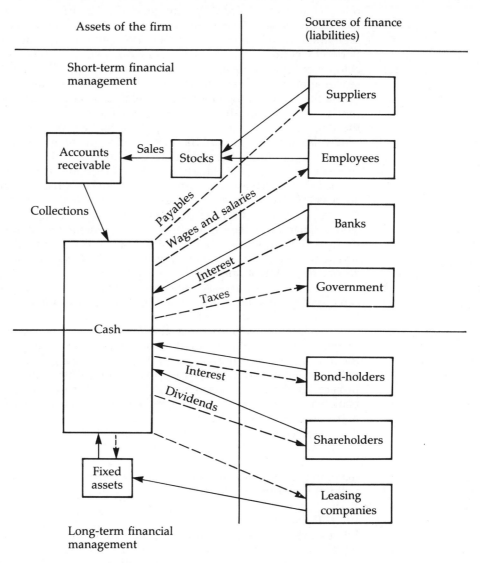

Fig. 9.2 The cash flow of the firm.
Source: Adapted from Smith (1979).

9.3 Forms of short-term borrowing and lending

(a) Short-term borrowing

(i) Bank finance
Bank finance in the form of overdrafts is a popular source of short-term funds for the self-financing needs of the enterprise. The overdraft is very flexible, with limits set by negotiation. It gives enterprises the scope to move freely within these limits and only be charged on the outstanding debit balance

(although small arrangement and commitment fees on undrawn balances are often charged). Overdrafts can generally be arranged quickly. They are technically repayable on demand (and occasionally banks give notice of repayment which can trigger insolvency); but they are usually rolled forward period by period, and in this way they can be used to finance the 'permanent' component of short-term needs. They can then be increased flexibly if seasonal or unexpected factors require additional funds.

The overdraft arrangement between a bank and an enterprise can develop into a strong relationship, so that a mutual trust builds up between them. On the one hand the enterprise supplies information to support the periodic renewals, and for its part the bank desires to maintain a strong customer relationship to retain the business (see Hodgman, 1963, for coverage of this). In some countries, e.g. Japan and West Germany, it is the strength of this relationship which is often seen as part of the set of reasons for their economic success. With the onset of more competition in the banking industry, this company–bank relationship takes on even more significance (see our discussion of disintermediation in Chapter 2). A major disadvantage of the overdraft — apart from the risk of a call by the bank — is that the rate of interest, which is bank base rate plus risk premium, floats so that the enterprise has to absorb this interest rate risk.

Whilst the overdraft is a convenient and flexible form of financing, the bank can also offer *term financing* at fixed or floating rates for short periods, usually tied to particular purchases.

In Chapter 8 we illustrated the rapid growth in recent years of bank financing, yet this is particularly risky when interest rates are so volatile. At the time of writing, the bank base rate is 15% (see Fig. W9.9 in the Workbook) with consequent higher rates for loans to represent the specific risk of the project. An interesting issue here is that, with the increase in securitization of bank loans, banks are trying to remove loans from their balance sheets and act more on a fee-for-service basis. While banks, particularly merchant banks, have been active as advisers and providers of funds in the takeover process, the growth of asset-backed securities, particularly in the USA and now in continental Europe, would appear to weaken the close relationship that can develop between a debtor and creditor to a looser advisory relationship. Time will tell how this develops.

(ii) Bill finance

Bill finance (or bills of exchange, as they are more properly called) is used for normal working capital purposes and also for trade financing. The terms of bills can be as short as 30 days or as long as 180 days, but generally they are for 90–1 days. There are two forms of bills — *trade* and *bank* bills.

1. In the case of a *trade bill*, an enterprise which is selling goods will draw up a bill of exchange which the buyer accepts, thus acknowledging the debt. The supplier of goods can then use the accepted bill to obtain finance by selling it at a discount. The buyer of goods and acceptor of the bill thus obtains trade credit.

2. The *bank bill* (or banker's acceptance, as it is referred to more generally) is a modified trade bill where a bank has accepted or put its name to the bill, which means that it guarantees payment. For this it receives a commission. Banker's acceptances are used extensively in financing foreign trade. The holders of these bills have an instrument in which the credit risk is transferred from the enterprise to the bank. This makes them a lot safer to

hold, of course. As a result, bank bills, when discounted by the enterprise, carry a lower rate of interest. Indeed, the rate is usually lower than overdraft finance. The data on the rates charged are contained in Fig. W9.7.

Bills also have the advantage that, once discounted, the enterprise has a known cost of finance; whereas the overdraft, as we have seen, is subject to interest rate risk. The use of bill finance in place of the overdraft frees up the latter for other working capital purposes in the enterprise.

(iii) Note issuance facilities (NIFs)

An NIF is a revolving financing facility of a medium-term nature, where the borrower issues a short-term paper generally known as a 'euronote' in its own name. The banks that underwrite these notes either are committed to purchase those that are unsold or provide financing. Although, strictly speaking, it is a medium-term facility of five to seven years and therefore more properly the domain of Chapter 8, because it is a revolving facility it is short term. In addition, maturities of less than one year are now common. Banks and others working as underwriters act as placers of notes which tend to have a face value of $500,000 or more. This market has expanded rapidly since 1985 and there are many varieties of notes. Fig. W8.4 illustrates the magnitude of issues ($7.8 billion in 1989) and the fact that the majority are in £ sterling.

(iv) Other forms of short-term finance

We mention briefly two other forms of short-term finance here:

1. *Leasing*, although used more extensively in medium- and longer-term finance (see Chapter 8 where the principles are discussed), is an appropriate form of finance for some more durable but short-term assets such as vehicles or office equipment.
2. *Hire-purchase* offers another convenient method of raising finance for the same sort of assets that can be leased: the enterprise, as with a lease, makes regular fixed payments and the ownership of the goods rests with the provider of this finance — usually a finance house — until the final payment is made.

(v) Factoring and invoice discounting

Bank and bill financing are used to meet the needs of the enterprise where it has advanced credit and thus created accounts receivable, or to purchase equipment and maintain inventories. If the enterprise can reduce the average maturity of the accounts receivable, it can reduce the amount of finance required. We shall discuss this in section 9.4 below. But there are other ways of achieving this, yet simultaneously advancing credit to suppliers.

1. The enterprise can *factor* the accounts receivable. Factoring is not a single service, but the most common type is where a financial intermediary, known as a factor or factoring house, purchases the accounts receivable and handles the collection for the enterprise at bank overdraft rates, to an amount up to 80% of each invoice raised, providing the balance at a later date. The client is not obliged to take all the financing provided. In addition, the factor provides a credit management role, assessing the credit worthiness of customers (both existing and potential), and can offer up to 100% protection. A factor will charge a fee of between 0.5 and 2.5%

of turnover, depending on the type of business transaction. Factors are also willing to take on overseas business, particularly in Europe. As has been mentioned previously, the data illustrate that factoring can be attractive to small companies by virtue of the source of finance, as well as the credit management role.

In 1988 the Association of British Factors, which accounts for the major share of the factorings, serviced over 6,000 companies with sales of £8 billion. Of these firms 85% had sales of less than £2 million and around 1,500 companies had a turnover of a £¼ million or less. Factoring has shown a strong growth over the past ten years and the High Street banks are very active in the market through their subsidiaries. Factoring is particularly strong in industry sectors where the goods and services supplied are not technically complex and are therefore not subject to contention. It is not surprising, therefore, to find that factoring has taken hold in the supply of raw materials and components to industry and the sale of consumer goods to wholesalers and retailers.

2. Invoice discounting is similar to factoring except that factoring is a continuing arrangement, whereas discounting is not. Large companies are sometimes active in selling a portion or the whole of their account receivables at a specific time. In this process the firm receives up-front cash, but it is still responsible for the collection of the accounts. The fees are therefore lower than for the full service of a factor. Clients can also take advantage of a protection scheme that is available in the factoring service whereby factors are willing, after due investigation, to insure the credit worthiness of some customers. Discounting accounted for £4 billion in 1988.

Although both discounting and factoring have shown a large growth in recent years, can be attractive to firms, particularly small firms, and can give flexibility in terms of the provision of finance and assistance in credit management and credit intelligence, they may impede the overall ability to raise overdraft finance because the bank, unable to take a floating charge on the accounts receivable, loses collateral in the enterprise.

(b) Short-term lending

Now we turn to ask: how does the enterprise deal with cash flowing through which will be relatively liquid for a while? It may decide to restrict its investments to immediately encashable assets in the form of till money (notes and cash) and current accounts at the bank. These can satisfy its needs for liquidity which may arise from, for instance, an expectation within a short time of needing cash to pay for new capital investment. However, this is unlikely as high interest rates can provide an incentive to switch into interest-earning assets. The total amount of funds invested in liquid assets by UK industrial and commercial companies was £78.6 billion at the end of 1989. In section 9.5 we shall examine the substitution between cash and other liquid assets, but for now we shall merely examine the range of assets available.

(i) Bank deposits
The banking sector can offer a range of investment media to corporate treasurers from overnight lending to term lending, certificates of deposit and eurodollar deposits denominated in sterling or foreign currencies. Most funds (around 90% of company sector portfolios) are invested in this way with the

monetary sector. Indeed bank deposits are a very convenient and popular form of investment, as they give the enterprise the flexibility to meet calls for funds from within its business activities, yet earn interest income. Where these calls are in foreign currencies, the deposit can be denominated in that currency and held either domestically or offshore. Enterprises can also invest in 'near banks' such as building societies, and appear to do so quite frequently when the rates are attractive.

(ii) Local authority temporary debt
Another popular investment channel, though in absolute terms quite small, is local authority temporary debt, which can be very short and extends up to fixed interest bonds. Generally corporate investors prefer the short end of the market. Whilst this lending is riskier than lending to the central government, and the uncertainties that occurred in the autumn of 1985 in the City of Liverpool have made it look riskier, to date there has not been a default.

(iii) Commercial paper
Enterprises can invest in the commercial paper issued by other enterprises. As we have referred to this in Chapter 2, we need not cover it further here.

(iv) Treasury bills and government bonds
Treasury bills and government bonds, particularly the short end of the maturity spectrum, are another form of investment for enterprises, though one not used extensively unless the yields are particularly attractive — say, at the peak of an interest rate cycle with the expectation of substantial capital gains. Gilt-edged securities are default-free and this can be a matter of consideration in the decision to invest. Holdings of T. bills in 1989 were high (£1.4 billion in December), although the holdings of government securities have fallen steadily over the past five years.

(v) Other media
There are a range of other investment media available in the short term, including commodities, options, etc., though generally enterprises will not utilize them. However, one channel that is used is that of certificates of tax deposit (CTDs), which are government instruments that can be exchanged for corporate taxes (mainstream and advanced corporation tax) and the petroleum revenue taxes (PRT) paid by oil companies. These are now quite significant (nearly £2 billion invested in 1989).

9.4   Current liabilities

(a) Accounts payable and accruals

Accounts payable represent the trade credit received from suppliers that have been invoiced. Accruals are taken here to be the payments due to be made to employees and to government (VAT, PAYE and National Insurance contributions); the term can also refer to amounts due to any other creditors not yet invoiced. Trade credit arises because suppliers usually allow a period of time from receipt of goods to the payment. Of course, the payables may be approximately matched on the asset side with accounts receivable if the enterprise also extends trade credit. It will be observed that this is not the usage of accounting (as in *Financial Accounting: Method and Meaning*), which is

governed by custom and has a different purpose from the way we are using it
here. It does nevertheless reflect a particular underlying situation.

(i) Accruals

Accruals occur because enterprises do not immediately pass on the deductions from pay to the government, and workers themselves give employers
credit since they work for a week, a fortnight or a month before receiving
payment in arrears. Both represent 'free' finance to the enterprise, and they
are often regarded as *spontaneous* or self-adjusting sources of financing. As
sales expand, both items will move upwards as the enterprise buys more raw
materials, takes on more labour and/or uses more overtime. The reverse
situation would be true in hard times (which makes them even harder). The
enterprises' policy on accruals will be dictated by custom or union agreement
in the case of wages and salaries, and by government regulation in the case of
taxes, etc.

(ii) Accounts payable

Accounts payable are a major source of finance and one which gives the
enterprise more scope for control and management. Although these payables
are determined by different credit terms and institutional practices, the
enterprise has to respond to these. We can argue that the enterprise should
utilize this credit as fully as possible within the constraints of not damaging its
credit rating or passing up favourable cash discounts.

For domestic purchases, most enterprises use an open account with an
invoice specifying the credit terms, which could be, say, net 30 days, i.e.
payment in 30 days following the sale. If there is a penalty for late payment,
the enterprise has to take that into account as this is then a charge for the
financing, but it may be cheaper than bank financing! If there is no penalty,
the enterprise has the opportunity to delay payments and benefit from more
zero-cost financing. Even when the penalties exist, some firms ignore them.
How long this can persist depends on the relative strengths of the supplier
and buying enterprises. If the latter is larger and has many alternative sources
of supply, it can be more aggressive in this respect without fear of retaliation
or damaging its credit reputation. If, however, it is small or there is only one
supplier, its options are more limited.

The average payment date in the UK is 78 days, yet the normal payment
term of business is 30 days. A study by Intrum Justitia, a credit management
group, estimates the cost of this as 5.7% of average turnover. Assuming a net
profit mark up of 10%, the cost of the delay is apparent. Some observers have
called for a judicial back-up to enable companies to enforce an interest charge.
This problem of payment was recognized in May 1986 when the Department
of Employment, with support from a wide range of business groups,
proposed a voluntary code entitled 'Payment on Time'. The Administration of
Justice Act 1982 provided for the enforcement of an interest charge, but the
'La Pintada' case illustrated a loophole whereby interest was disallowed if the
debt was repaid, no matter how late, prior to the beginning of proceedings.
The concern over late payment and the inherent costs to the providers of
trade credit has an impact on competitiveness, and it is likely that the
European Commission will seek to harmonize arrangements. Interestingly,
however, many European countries extend credit for larger periods, (e.g.
Italy and France, 60 days), but their collection record is proportionately better
than that of the UK.

The enterprise may be offered a discount for cash which substantially changes the consequences. This discount is an effective interest charge and the enterprise has to calculate the costs and benefits of taking or forgoing the discount. Let us take a typical example (Table 9.2) to illustrate this.

An enterprise has a £1,000 account payable net 30 days. In case 1, there is no penalty for late payment. In case 2(a), there is a late payment penalty (enforced) of 1.75% of the credit extended. If this is a fixed charge, then its effect is felt less and less, the longer the delay is made. However, it may be levied per month, in which case the cost would be that of case 2(b), namely 21.29% annualized.

For case 3, there is a cash discount of 2% if paid within 10 days. The enterprise now has an effective account payable of £980. If it now delays 30 days after the due date and loses the discount, the cost to it of the additional 20 days' financing is an annualized rate of 37.23%. As the delay in payment extends, and assuming no further penalty, the cost of losing the discount falls. The formula for this is:

$$\text{Cost of foregoing cash discount} = \frac{\text{Discount (£20)}}{\text{Purchase price} - \text{Discount}} \times \frac{365}{n}$$

where n = balance of days (20 in this case).

Another important consideration in this section is the fact that when accounts are paid they are items in transit until cashed by the payee. In the meantime the drawer has the use of the funds. There may be a policy of mailing by second-class delivery to extend the time period of the item in transit, and cheques in any event take time to clear and may not be presented for payment immediately. Thus enterprises have a float they can use. They can estimate the likely length of time they have these funds based on past experience and therefore play the float.

This can be risky, however. The enterprise receiving the funds can ask its bankers for 'special clearance', which means that funds that would take three days to be cleared are cleared in a day. The bank will make a fixed charge for this service, but if the cheque is large the service will be worthwhile because the interest earned in the extra two days the funds are available will be greater than the bank's charge. The enterprise 'playing the float' can therefore occasionally hit an awkward situation if the creditor has used the special clearance facility.

Table 9.2 The cost of trade credit with penalties for late payment and discounts for early payment

Case	Delay payment	Finance available	Cost %
1. No penalty	30, 60, 90 days, etc.	£1,000	0
2. Penalty:			
(a) single	30 days/60 days	£1,000	21.29/10.59[a]
(b) multiple	30 days/60 days	£1,000	21.29
3. Discount:			
(a) 2%	To normal credit period	£980	37.23
(b) 2%	To 30 days beyond	£980	14.9

Note: [a] The 1.75% on £1,000 is £17.50 on the basis of a 30-day delay. To calculate the annual cost (%) we divide the 1.75% by 30 to produce a daily charge (0.058) and multiply by 365 to derive the annualized cost of 21.29%. For a 60-day delay this is equivalent to a daily charge of 0.029% giving an annual cost of 10.59%. For 90 days it would be 7.1%, and so on.

These costs do not include the benefits of the credit granted on an account payable.

(b) Short-term debt

Short-term debt is a major component of the liabilities side of the balance sheet of enterprises, and it is one that has increased in importance in recent years. This development can be traced to the volatility of interest rates and the greater uncertainty surrounding the interest rate environment.

In the face of high interest rates and concomitant recession in the UK (and other industrial economies) in the early 1980s (15% base rate in 1989/90) enterprises generally did not borrow long whether by bonds or ordinary shares for a number of reasons. From the point of view of the borrower, high interest costs raised the cost of capital to the enterprise, which then eliminated some investment projects from further consideration. This short-term occurrence causing the non-investment in long-term projects has serious implications, of course, for both the enterprise and the economy. Those projects that the enterprise still wished to consider in its capital budget were often financed by short-term borrowing in the hope that a refinancing could occur once rates had fallen. For the investor, the uncertainty over the future movement of interest rates led many to go short (that is, deal in the short-term markets) and await the hitting of the eventual ceiling on rates, before returning to lend long. So reluctances to lend and borrow long both emerged. The net result has been a debt maturity structure which shortened considerably.

These events in the corporate sector of Britain and other countries were paralleled in sovereign borrowing by mainly non-oil developing countries (see IMF, 1986) and the resulting external debt crises of those countries. As we shall see, this can be a matter of concern for enterprises and for policy-makers in government, for it goes against accepted theory and practice which has dictated that short-term borrowings be matched, or at least strongly positively related, to short-term assets (inventories of raw materials and finished goods, accounts receivable and short-lived assets). Long-term borrowing and long-term assets (plant and machinery) should be similarly matched. If this is done then the enterprise does not have to run the risk of being mismatched when interest rates change.

For example, if an enterprise were to use short-term debt to finance long-term assets, the enterprise would face more financial risk due to a mismatch and uncertainty of cash available. The enterprise would have continually to roll the borrowing forward, and if interest rates rose, would face higher borrowing costs. If it financed its short- and long-term requirements with long-term financing then, because of the usual shape of the yield curve as depicted in Fig. 9.3, it would be paying r_2 instead of r_1 and therefore be paying more than it need. (Note, however, that the yield curve as portrayed can be misleading. Although a one-month rate is lower than a three-month or six-month rate, they have to be compared on an annual basis, so a one-month rate compounded monthly must be more than 10 basic points lower than an equivalent quarterly rate compounded quarterly to represent a lower cost. The yield curve does not always slope upwards. At the time of writing, with high interest rates, the yield curve is downward sloping; there exists a spread of 3 percentage points between the 91-day T. bill rate and that on long-dated (20-year) government bonds. This can be confirmed by reference to Table W9.6 in the Workbook.

If firms have borrowed long and some of that borrowing is maintained as surplus cash for any length of time, then its reinvestment in short-term assets will, given the yield curve in Fig. 9.3, not recoup its borrowed cost; but it will pay off well if the yield curve is downward sloping! All this analysis presumes

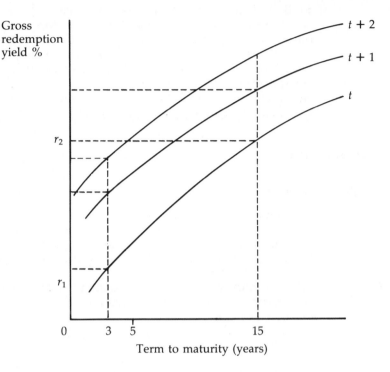

Fig. 9.3 The yield curve.

that the yield curve in t will hold for future time periods. If, however, the whole structure of interest rates is expected to move upward through time as portrayed by the new yield curves labelled $t + 1$ and $t + 2$, then serious thought has to be given to locking into longer-term financing in period t, perhaps even to cover many short-term needs. The reverse would be true for expectations of a downward shift in the curve where the enterprise would go short to cover both short- and long-term borrowing. The transition from a downward- to an upward-sloping yield curve produces an interesting time for investors and borrowers alike, and the level of rates that emerges will not necessarily revert to historical 'floors'. Timing is therefore of the essence if a firm wishes to lock in.

However, there is a clear temptation for the enterprise to mismatch and use short-term financing more aggressively beyond the typical self-liquidating transactions. The enterprise has balance sheet considerations, which would normally dictate the matching of the terms of assets and liabilities, and market interest rate considerations. In the past, it has been difficult to separate these, but with the changing environment of high and volatile interest rates, financial managers have been pushed into considering interest rate factors more than the balance sheet 'norms'. Innovations and developments in financial markets have, however, made it easier to take account of both, particularly with the distinction between fixed rate funds and term funds. The term funds, whether short or long term, can be priced either at a fixed rate or floating. Then, if the yield curve is very steeply sloping (positively) as portrayed in Fig. 9.3, and the enterprise which has long-term capital needs decides not to lock in at a fixed rate, it can still go long, but with a float at, say, a LIBOR (London inter-bank offer rate) based rate. Similarly, if the enterprise has short-term needs, say of one year, but does not wish to take the interest rate risk of borrowing successively every three months, it can borrow short at a fixed rate. Having made these decisions, the type of borrowing it could undertake is extensive, as section 9.2 revealed. If the borrowings of the enterprise involve a currency other than that of the country in which the enterprise is registered, then the agenda becomes wider as the volatility of the foreign exchange markets becomes another important consideration.

9.5   Current assets

(a) Managing accounts receivable

Although we have argued the case for the importance of cash, many enterprises do part or all of their business by extending credit, thereby creating accounts receivable in the current assets of the balance sheet. Likewise, as we saw on p. 228, the enterprise may expect to use credit itself in acquiring its purchases and thus have accounts payable in the current liabilities of the balance sheet. Although as a general maxim we can state that an enterprise should collect its accounts receivable as soon as possible, this is too simplistic an approach.

In granting this trade credit and managing the implications of this for the enterprise, two points emerge:

1. trade credit should be advanced to increase the sales *and* profitability of the enterprise;
2. the accounts receivable created are assets and require careful management in their creation and collection as they impact very directly on the cash position and solvency of the enterprise. In this respect, the literature (see, for example, Carpenter and Miller, 1979) has identified *customer payment patterns* as the key datum for monitoring and controlling accounts receivable.

If the enterprise can reduce the extension of credit, yet not sacrifice sales, then profitability can increase as the cash freed can be used to repay borrowing, thus reducing interest costs, and/or invested in, say, very short-term assets and earn interest income. Another approach is to attempt to identify potential bad debts earlier and thus prevent further extensions of credit and concomitantly press for payment at an earlier stage in the potential financial distress of the enterprise.

Such identification can also allow the enterprise to make provision for these potential bad debts. It may not have much latitude in its trade credit policy as industry customs and norms may well dictate not only that credit be extended (given the normal checks as to creditworthiness), but also the terms on which it is given. It can therefore be pulled in opposite directions — the need to advance credit versus the costs it incurs in doing this (including the bank finance often used to support the credit advanced). However, it can still attempt to model receivables so as to improve the control of these within the enterprise as well as to produce better forecasts of cash flows.

While high interest rates have had an important impact on firms managing their accounts receivable, much of the system currently in place is a paper-based system with inherent time delays. The introduction of fax machines can

Enterprise XYZ is contemplating the sale of a piece of equipment to a retailer which we assume has a cost to the supplier of £100 with a profit margin of £15. Three possible situations — a cash sale, and a credit with and without discount — are as follows:

	Cost price £	Sale price £	Profit %
(i) Cash sale	100	115	15
(ii) 30-day credit (cost of credit @ 10% = 82p on £100 = 2.7p per day)	100	115	14.18
(iii) 2% discount after 10 days (£2.30) (cost of credit @ 10% = 27p on £100)	100	112.70	12.43

Suppose the retailer requests a 30-day credit period. If we can assume that the opportunity cost of capital is 10%, then delaying 30 days in recovering the cost of goods sold would cost the enterprise 82p and this would reduce the profit to £14.18. We use cost of goods sold instead of the selling price since the former represents the investment the enterprise has in the appliance at the time the credit sale is made. However, if there is a speed-up in the payment of accounts receivable, the profit is also received sooner. This matter, as it applies to *existing* customers (who have, one presumes, established a track record of payment under a credit policy without a cash discount and now have a discount available), would require the sale price not the cost price to be a reference point for the incremental calculation.

Suppose that the supplier now offers the retailer a cash discount. Both parties in the transaction have to weigh up the costs and benefits to this. If the cash discount is taken up, the supplier obtains the cash sooner, but the amount is reduced by the amount of the discount. The retailer has to pay out sooner, too, and therefore incurs financing costs. If the retailer refuses the discount, then the supplier receives the full amount of the invoice price but later, and the retailer gets longer credit terms but at a price. If we modify the example used for a 2% discount after 10 days, the supplier will obtain £112.70 after 10 days instead of £115 after 30 days. The credit cost of 10 days is 27p plus the discount (£2.30), giving a total cost to the supplier of £2.57 compared to the 30 days (no cash discount) cost of 82p. So the granting of the discount is expensive to the supplier, and expensive for the retailer to sacrifice if the latter has a similar financing cost.

There may be compensating factors to the enterprise in granting a discount since, by obtaining the cash now, the supplier may feel less exposed to bad debts, as the potential loss after the 30-day period if the invoice is not paid is the £100 cost of goods sold and the credit cost up to the time when the account is written off as a bad debt. So the supplier may be willing to sacrifice some immediate profit to try and avoid these write-offs, although even with the incentive of a cash discount, there is no guarantee that it will be taken up, and the retailer may still not pay on the account.

Fig. 9.4   Cost of trade credit

still improve the efficiency of the paper mechanism, but the use of electronic storage and transmission can assist the production and delivery of quotations, purchase orders, invoices and payments.

(i) Credit policies

Unless the customs and practices of the industry fully dictate the credit policy to follow, an enterprise has to decide the terms on which it will advance credit. Granting credit is to be seen as an investment policy (cost of goods sold) with costs and benefits associated with it. So an enterprise, if it decides to relax or tighten credit, has to evaluate the incremental effect. If it relaxes credit, it will *ceteris paribus* increase sales since people who previously did not enjoy the credit are now receivers. The higher sales volume should raise profitability, but increase the average collection period as the likelihood of collection problems emerges. Models of accounts receivable would determine the division of the increase between sales growth and collection experience. The latter could be related not just to the relaxation of credit, but to seasonal or cyclical factors. The costs of these slower payments, the enterprise's time in managing these problem accounts, expenses of collection agencies, legal fees, etc., and potential write-offs of bad debts have to be estimated.

The credit policy requires the enterprise to specify the terms of credit, say 30 days, if a cash discount is to be made available and if so over what period, and the existence of other penalty charges for late payment. These terms may well differ by product and/or market. In setting the term, the granting enterprise has to evaluate the incremental gain/loss. Let us now consider the illustration given in Fig. 9.4.

The supplier, therefore, is exposed to a potential non-payment on the credit advanced and must be selective in granting it, just as the bank is selective in who it lends to or gives credit cards and limits to. The supplier must investigate its clients and only when satisfied give credit, establishing a *credit limit*. The traditional credit analysis follows a *sequential* analysis of investigating what information the supplier has in-house before moving outside to external sources.

For the latter, it can obtain information from various credit agencies who specialize in maintaining databanks of information on enterprises — their financial position, their credit record, etc. It may also try and obtain a reference from the bankers of the client, though this is often of limited value. Even with a mass of information, the supplier is not freed from the task of analysing this with the associated costs and then making a decision. The depth of analysis will depend on the size of the credit line.

For many credit decisions, particularly the use of credit cards, there is a simple credit scoring system used which is based on multiple discriminant analysis. This takes a series of criteria considered relevant for the credit decision *simultaneously* and weights them.

(ii) Collections

Once credit has been advanced, the supplier of credit has to monitor accounts receivable, and the state of technology is such that it is now possible to have an integration between the treasury management and accounting systems. With this an enterprise can produce accurate forecasts of payment cycles. The creditor will ensure that, if payment is not made when due, there is a collection policy to attempt to enforce payment. This can take various forms and follow a sequence of letters, telephone calls, personal visits, the involvement of collection agencies and, if necessary, legal action. This last possibility is expensive and provides no guarantee of recovering all sums owed anyway since it may cause bankruptcy. The accounts receivable, we have said, are current assets of the enterprise, but involve it in the opportunity cost of forgoing the funds. To replace these it can borrow from a bank using the accounts as collateral, or it can factor the accounts.

The recession that hit most industrial countries in the late 1970s and into the 1980s did cause many enterprises to re-evaluate their credit policy. Not only were enterprises facing a shortage of cash and seeing the average collection time increase, but interest rates were historically high, forcing higher credit costs on to them. As a consequence, where market power permitted, they tightened their credit terms by either refusing to grant credit or shortening the time permitted for payment and increasing the financial penalties for late payment. Typically, those caught up in this have been the smaller organizations that often find it difficult to raise finance and do not possess the market power to resist the tightening of credit on them, yet may have had to continue to grant credit to their customers.

(b) Inventories

Inventories of finished goods and raw materials represent a significant current asset of the enterprise. The decision to hold inventories and their level is thus an investment decision, though the proportion will vary depending on the nature of the business. Enterprises in the service sector, for example, will often have little need for inventories, whereas wholesalers and retailers will carry large inventories of finished goods. Manufacturers will usually carry inventories of raw materials, work in progress (particularly important in a manufacturing concern which has a very complex assembly process like shipbuilding or aircraft production) and finished goods. Inventories, however, tie up resources and require careful management, not just in their level, but in their composition. Moreover, they can add to the riskiness of profits and even threaten the survival of the enterprise.

The need for inventory arises from the very nature of the world that we live in. If manufacturers could receive raw materials each day, process them immediately and deliver the finished goods there and then, there would be no need for inventory. But inevitably time considerations enter in the form of delays in normal operations. Organizations do, however, have some discretion over the level of inventories they hold, and managements face a trade-off.

If they maintain high levels of inventories, they reduce some of the uncertainties in their operations. A car manufacturer, for instance, if it maintains a month's supply of component parts, can weather a shortage or delay caused by a strike at a suppliers or a transport disruption, continue production and not have to meet fixed costs (operating leverage) with little or no production. Large inventories may also attract quantity discounts if purchased in large orders. The holding of inventories may even yield additional profitability to the enterprise in a period of rising prices. If it maintains a supply of completed cars, it can immediately meet any sudden demand for new cars from special promotions or forces outside the enterprise and thus retain the goodwill of dealers and customers. There are also economic benefits from larger production runs or batch sizes at lower costs (less machine set-up costs) which are independent of the order received.

Of course, all these advantages are purchased at a cost, as the inventories are an asset which has to be supported by the earnings of the enterprise or by borrowing. If the inventories can be reduced, capital can be freed and used elsewhere in the business, or debt can be retired. And there are additional costs to holding inventories other than just the interest cost. Warehousing facilities and staff have to be available. Insurance is required. Stock may deteriorate if held for a time. Or it might require further work before it can be processed or sold. Or it may be subject to 'shrinkage' — that is, petty theft by employees. The enterprise also runs the risk that demand patterns will change so as to make it difficult or impossible to use all of the new materials or sell the finished goods at cost. It is possible to point to high inventory levels in many enterprises that have gone bankrupt, particularly in a recession. Indeed, Altman (1968) has developed an early warning model for business failure that has inventories as one variable. With all these costs the annual cost of carrying inventories can range between 10 and 40%.

So the financial manager has to balance the demands of his or her production and marketing managers who like large inventories to smooth out their operating functions and the financial control department which prefers lower levels to cut the costs. There may also be questions in the accounting realm as to the implications of stock valuation methods for declared profit — see *Financial Accounting: Method and Meaning*, Chapter 5.

The inventory system adopted by the enterprise may be extremely complex as there may be many suppliers of many products with many variations in the final products sold. Reflection on the example of the car assembler reinforces this. No doubt one should minimize the total cost of holding inventories so as to increase the profitability of the enterprise and hence its value. While we can present a simple intuitive approach to the problem, in reality the methods used are often very complex and all we can do is give a flavour.

Organizations require a detailed analysis of their past sales, sales forecasts, orders, production schedules, present inventory levels and their movement over time. From these data it should be possible to determine any systematic patterns of sales, such as seasonal factors, and the contribution particular product lines have to sales and inventories. The enterprise has to estimate the costs and benefits of holding inventories, and we can use the economic order quantity (EOQ) model to minimize total inventory costs. In its simplest form this recognizes three costs:

1. *ordering* (O) — the administrative costs of making orders;
2. *carrying* (C) — the warehousing, insurance, deterioration and interest costs;
3. *shortage* (S) — the costs to the enterprise of running out of stocks.

We shall make three simplifying assumptions: that the carrying and ordering costs are constant and that the demand is uniform. Initially we shall also assume that no safety stocks are held. The numerical example given in Fig. 9.5 illustrates the points we wish to make.

The model can be modified now to take account of safety stocks. Fig. 9.6(a) reveals that the stock level falls to 0 before it is replenished. If there are any unforeseen delays in delivery, or there are fluctuations in demand, etc., then the enterprise faces the problem of a *stockout*. To guard against this, it can choose to hold a safety stock. The latter is difficult to determine, but generally we can say that the greater the uncertainty, the greater the safety stock. Once more the enterprise has to balance the costs of this against the costs of a stockout.

If this is perceived to be a real problem for the enterprise, Figs 9.6(b) and

XYZ, a retailing enterprise, is currently selling 5,000 units of a product per annum. It would like to determine an ordering policy which specifies the quantity it should order (Q), and how many times it should place an order. Say that C = £25, O = £100.

Total carrying costs (TCC) = Average inventory × C

As there are no buffer stocks, then immediately before the order is received, inventories will be zero, so that the average inventory held will be $Q/2$. Therefore:

$$TCC = Q/2 \times C = \frac{QC}{2} \tag{9.1}$$

Total ordering costs = Number of orders placed (sales) (S) × Cost of order (O)

$$= (S/Q)O = \frac{SO}{Q} \tag{9.2}$$

Since total costs equal carrying costs plus ordering costs, so:

$$TC = \frac{QC}{2} + \frac{SO}{Q} \tag{9.3}$$

To minimize these costs, the enterprise could use a trial and error approach. This would look like Fig. 9.6(a). (Note the similarity to the Baumol model: Fig. 9.7 later.) Alternatively it can use the EOQ model, which involves differentiating equation 9.3 with respect to Q and setting this equal to 0 so:

$$EOQ = \sqrt{\frac{2SO}{C}} \tag{9.4}$$

In the case of XYZ, the EOQ would be 200 units with 25, that is:

$$\frac{5,000}{200}$$

orders a year. The graphical representation of this is given in the Workbook, p. 549.

Having determined the value, we can now plot this XYZ stock position over time with an order placed every 15 days, that is:

$$\frac{365}{25}$$

However, if there is a lead time for the order to be fulfilled, say five days, then XYZ will place the order when inventories reach the level of 67: that is, 200 × 5/15.

Figure 9.5   EOQ model for minimizing inventory costs.

(c) show how the introduction of a safety stock and the introduction of uncertainty in delivery times and demand affect the investing position.

The model will also be affected if there are quantity discounts. In the case analysed in Fig. 9.5, with an order of 200 the enterprise may only have to increase the order to 500 to obtain a discount. Once more, there is a balancing of price reduction against costs of additional holdings. This modification is examined in the Workbook, p. 550.

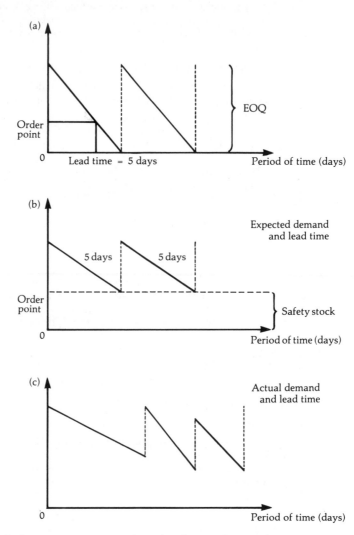

Figure 9.6   Inventory position with and without safety stock.

(c) Cash and marketable securities

Although we have emphasized the importance of *cash* to the enterprise, the concept of cash management also encompasses the investment in short-term marketable securities.

Organizations, like households, hold liquid assets (see Stone, 1971, for an analysis of this liquidity) for the three reasons originally propounded by Keynes (1930): *transaction, precautionary* and *speculative* (the data for the corporate sector in the UK are given in the Workbook, p. 538).

1. The transaction demand is present because of the non-synchronization of the outflows and inflows of 'cash'.
2. The precautionary motive comes from the possibility of a sudden unexpected cash requirement as a result, for example, of worse than expected collection.

3. Cash can also be held for a speculative motive which will be determined by portfolio management considerations of the enterprise. In particular we can cite the investment of temporarily idle cash, the switching between the investment in fixed plant and machinery within the enterprise and outside (by acquisition), and the range of near-cash securities (identified in section 9.2) and longer-term securities (covered in Chapter 8).

For smaller businesses this idle cash is likely to be minimal, particularly in an inflationary environment, as they are often less able to pass on increases in their costs in prices and therefore can face a liquidity problem from this source, quite apart from the problems discussed in Chapter 8 of the raising of finance for small business. They will not possess the professional expertise to utilize the money market, even if they had the funds. They will generally be more risk averse in their investment. Larger enterprises are not automatically less risk averse, but many are, and they possess a greater capacity to handle volatile cash flows and seek greater sources of funds to replace the cash.

Yet even here the enterprise, in its short-term portfolio management, is likely to wish to avoid accounting losses (and therefore forgo opportunities for profit) which are more readily reportable. The agency issue raised in the safety-first policy will be difficult to detect. The avoidance strategy could be one of hedging their investments to specific dates. If the enterprise is relatively free to pursue a portfolio policy, then it can identify a wide range of eligible assets to hold, it can adjust the average term of the portfolio in terms of its interest rate expectations *and* it can switch among the various securities. Generally, in choosing short-term securities financial managers will be looking for a maturity of a year or less, for marketability and for low default risk.

With a rising yield curve (as portrayed earlier in Fig. 9.3) these short-term securities can earn higher interest rates than time deposits or money at call, and although they may not be regarded as the main part of a commercial enterprise's business (as opposed to financial institutions'), they cannot be ignored. Many enterprises do have surpluses of cash to invest on a regular basis and sometimes they can be very sizeable, particularly when the interest rate structure is very high and the investment in fixed assets unattractive. In these circumstances, the business enterprise can become more like a financial institution.

In the periods when the enterprise has a surplus of sources over uses of funds, it can simply maintain this liquidity in very short-term assets, particularly with the bank, and thus avoid the excessive time and trouble involved in seeking more profitable, but less liquid, short-term investments. This can be even more attractive if interest rates are expected to rise in the future and/or if the enterprise has known future commitments in fixed capital investments. Of course, the converse of this situation requires borrowing, but let us assume that the enterprise has a horizon of a year or so to commit itself to investing funds, and the management is willing to balance the loss of liquidity against the potential profitability. If the enterprise invests in a one-year marketable security, its return will be:

$$R = \frac{P_2 - P_1 + I}{P_1}$$

(9.5)

where R = return

P_1 = purchase price of the security

P_2 = the expected sale price of the security in one year's time
I = interest paid.

This is a formalization of Chapter 6, p. 141.

Unless P_2, the sale price, is the par or maturity value of the security, it is an unknown, and the actual return can be greater or less than that expected. Of course, many short-term securities are expressed in nominal values and therefore their prices do not vary. Securities such as Treasury bills are sold at a discount on par and the return is the capital gain when the bill is redeemed.

If an enterprise is going to invest and trade in marketable securities, it will face the capital value risks, the transaction costs of the trading and the shortage costs incurred if cash is required (e.g. missed discounts on trade credit, costs of cashing in assets, etc.). Various models have been developed to handle the balancing of the costs of holding cash versus those of holding marketable securities. Although these are relatively dated now, and to some extent overtaken by events, it is still instructive to focus on them. We shall concentrate on two such inventory theoretic models:

1. the Baumol (1952) model;
2. the Miller–Orr (1966) model.

These are illustrated in Fig. 9.7.

1. The Baumol model, which dates from 1952, is basically a *certainty* model and has the enterprise's annual cash demand (D) as a steady net outflow which is accomplished by regularly withdrawing an equal amount (C) from marketable securities and paying a fixed transaction cost (b). In moving into cash the enterprise has to increase the transaction cost and loses yield (Y). So C is the optimal withdrawal to minimize total costs, which is:

$$C = \sqrt{\frac{2Db}{Y}} \tag{9.6}$$

   In holding cash the transaction cost is removed, but interest is forgone. So if D = £900,000, b = £90 and Y = 7%, then C = £48,000. In other words, the enterprise withdraws £48,000 each time. Since we know that it needs £900,000 each year, we can tell it will withdraw on average £900,000/48,000 = 18.75, say 19 times.

   Subsequently, the Baumol model has been modified by Beranek (1966) to recognize the greater discretion management has over cash outflows to inflows as well as applying a probability distribution to the latter.

2. The second popular model of the literature is that of Miller and Orr (1966). It is a stochastic inventory model with net cash flows occurring randomly over time. Control limits — upper and lower — are established as depicted by A and B in Fig. 9.7 and the enterprise targets the cash level of C. If cash reaches A then the enterprise invests in marketable securities, to the amount of $A - C$, and when the cash level falls to B the enterprise sells marketable securities to the amount of $C - B$. This sort of control model of the type discussed in Chapter 1 is very plausible, but the enterprise has to determine the limits. The lower limit of cash is a function of the management's attitude to risk. Those who are willing to take more risk will hold lower levels of cash. What Miller and Orr do is to set only the target level C and the upper limit A, namely:

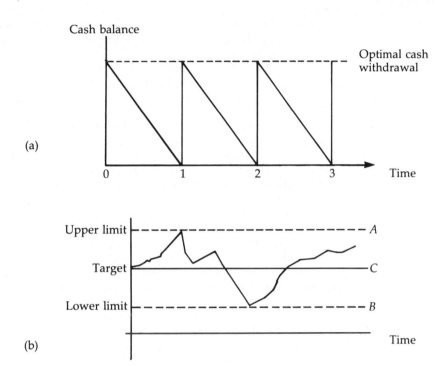

Figure 9.7   Inventory models: (a) Baumol, (b) Miller–Orr.

$$C = \sqrt[3]{\frac{3b\sigma^2}{4Y}} + B \quad \text{and} \quad A = 3C - 2B \tag{9.7}$$

where b = fixed cash cost per transaction
σ = standard deviation of daily changes in the cash balance
Y = daily yield on marketable securities.

Let us illustrate this model with an example. Suppose that the enterprise has determined the standard deviation, σ, to be £2,000 and the lower limit of cash to be £3,000, and that the market has a yield (Y) of 10.50% per annum (= 0.03% per day) and a transaction cost of £60. Then by substituting these values into equation 9.7 we would have a value of C of £11,434 — say £11,500, and hence a value of A of £28,500.

Both these inventory models and others that are available in the literature have their drawbacks. In the case of Miller–Orr, the fact that the enterprise has to estimate its variability of cash flow and provide a lower level of cash balance are two important factors. If the cash flow is not predictable over time, then the model is of limited use (see Daellenbach, 1974).

Beyond this the models are of limited practical use as they treat marketable securities as homogeneous. In section 9.2 we showed they were not. What the models give us is a framework within which cash can be managed in terms of the costs of trading and the opportunity cost of interest forgone. For many enterprises this is of limited value as they do not consciously follow an investment strategy or, if they do, it is very *ad hoc*. However, for those enterprises that do, guidelines are required and they are unlikely to follow the mechanical ones of the Baumol model; instead they will use either forecasts of the yield curve (often referred to as *riding the yield curve*) or portfolio theory as outlined in Chapter 6.

The allocation of liquid assets among the range of different financial claims is important, not just for the individual enterprise, but for the business sector more generally. A study by Owen (1982), using annual data for the period 1970–9, with a sample of 36 UK engineering companies, estimated demand functions for money and total liquid assets. He found that they were stable and had a scale (with respect to sales) elasticity greater than one, suggesting diseconomies in the holding of cash balances (as opposed to that predicted by the inventory approach examined earlier). He did not find interest rates (either short or long rates) a significant argument in the regressions. Although Owen stresses the caveats over the use of aggregated data in his work, his results are still instructive, since until then few studies had been performed on UK data.

More recently the Bank of England has published two studies. Jackson (1984) went beyond the limited brief of the Owen study to cover five categories of gross liquid assets — M1, short-term assets (sterling, time deposits, deposits with building societies, deposits with OFIs and local authority temporary debt), long-term assets (gilts and local authority long-term debt), foreign currency deposits with banks in the UK and tax certificates for the period 1972–82. These data included the period when the UK government eliminated exchange controls (October 1979), and a dummy variable was included to pick this up.

The mean proportions for these assets over the estimation period were 33%, 43%, 4%, 18% and 2% respectively, and representative interest rates (quarterly averages) were used. Beyond this we cannot cover the specific nature of the model for lack of space, but we may summarize its findings. Jackson found that the interest rate terms were statistically significant in the case of the holdings of M1: that is, as interest rates rose, holdings of M1 would decline. She could not find interest rate sensitivity in the holdings of time deposits, and perverse results were found for longer-term investments. The modelling of foreign money deposits was particularly unfruitful.

The latest and very comprehensive study was also undertaken by the Bank of England (Chowdhury, Green and Miles, 1986), which covered 700 UK-based companies, using published accounts. The model was a flow of funds. The *sources* identified were borrowing from banks (up to one year) and trade credit received. The *uses* identified were the acquisition of bank deposits and other liquid assets, and trade credit was extended. We may summarize the results as follows:

1. 40% of an increase in fixed investment was financed by short-term bank borrowing, 30% from a take-down in liquid assets and 30% from trade credit;
2. for stock-building they found that bank borrowing was important (40%) with 50% coming from trade credit;
3. increased profits were used to increase liquid assets rather than reduce bond borrowing;
4. when long-term finance was raised, 40% of it was used to repay bank borrowing;
5. they found relative interest rates to be important in the choice among liquid assets and liabilities. For example, they reported that when the

inter-bank rate rose, various changes occurred. Bank borrowing fell sharply and there were reductions in liquid assets. Enterprises also reduced the trade credit they extended.

9.6 Portfolio considerations

In this section we wish to draw together some of the threads of the earlier sections and Chapter 8 in order to understand the *overall* nature of the financing decision.

A significant function of the enterprise is the production and trading it undertakes. It is from this activity that the needs for financing and the availability of internal funds and the ability to raise external finance for investment emanate. What emerges is that the enterprise has both short- and long-term financing plans, so that it is aware of the expected month-to-month requirements for funds and the financing requirements over time. We illustrate the requirements for funds in Fig. 9.8. This section is based on Bridge and Dodds (1978).

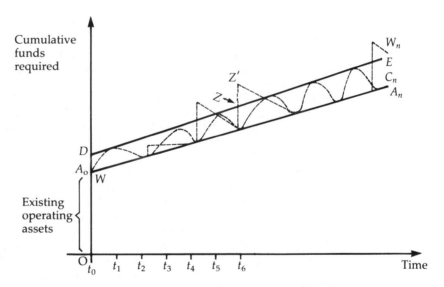

Fig. 9.8 Financing requirements.
Source: Bridge and Dodds (1978).

Figure 9.8 demonstrates that short- and long-run plans intertwine. Investment decisions will dictate long-term fund requirements from the range of alternative internal and external sources. The latter can be short-run expedients (particularly bank credit) or, more likely, liabilities to match the length of life of the assets (for example, corporate debt or permanent capital in the form of ordinary shares). The decision to go to the capital market is taken only at discrete intervals of time so that short-term financing may be used for a period, until an issue is made when short-term borrowing can be reduced or even eliminated. This point is illustrated in the figure where the enterprise is presumed to have a cumulative financing requirement as measured on the vertical axis. The enterprise starts at point t_0 in time and has total operating assets of OA_0. At a minimum it assumes that to finance its growth it requires cumulative finance as represented by the line A_0A_n. In addition it has short-term cash requirements which for the next time period t_1 are necessary for stockbuilding, etc. If we can presume that between t_0 and t_1 a similar pattern of short-term financing needs will materialize, and likewise to t_n, then we have a cyclical line A_0C_n in addition to the long-term needs. If only the funds to finance long-term growth were raised by retained earnings and/or external debt on equity issues, then the short-term requirements would have to be met by short-term borrowing and/or reductions in any holdings of liquid assets.

If the enterprise could raise all its finance by retained earnings or long-term capital, then we would have a line DE and there would be no need for short-term financing. In practice, the need for finance will be met by a mixture of short- and long-term sources. If the latter are based on retained earnings, then since those fluctuate in a cyclical fashion, the gaps will have to be met by short-term finance or recourse to long-term external sources. The latter, as we have already argued, are only used at discrete intervals. In practice what we might have, therefore, is more of a stepped long-term sources line (WW_n), which represents the enterprise's ability to back the cumulative demands. The stepped path will represent both the impact of variability of retained earnings and long-term issues. The gaps, for example ZZ', between the stepped relationship and the sum of the short- and long-term financing requirements permit the building up of liquid assets to act as a buffer for future periods. (Decisions concerning short- or long-term borrowing and the use of liquid assets as a buffer need to be analysed more fully — we shall do this later in this section.)

Let us now assume that the enterprise has determined an optimum balance sheet which specifies the desired relationships among the constituent parts of assets and liabilities. Adjustments towards this optimum take time because of frictional impediments such as transaction costs and information lags. In any given period t the enterprise may be in disequilibrium, but may still be presumed to take action via the flows identified earlier in the sources and uses of funds in an attempt to restore the equilibrium. If we allow for the continual change which pervades the business and its general environment, then the desired relationships will be subject to virtually constant reappraisal. Consequently, instead of a long-run steady-state optimum, towards which enterprises adjust period by period in varying degrees, the dynamic nature of business will bring about continual changes so that, in fact, the enterprise may have a kaleidoscopic view of long-run relationships.

Concentration on the equilibrium of the balance sheet *per se* can neglect the flow influences. Various approaches to the incorporation of both stock and flow elements are possible. The first major econometric model was developed by Anderson (1965) for USA manufacturing industry for the period 1948–60. The starting point was to assume that, in terms of the enterprise's present operations, plans for current production spending were fixed, as were its capital spending plans for the next planning period. With these autonomously determined, the finance function had to provide an optimal mix of long-term external finance and net liquidity (liquid assets and short-term borrowing) within specified maximum and minimum safe levels of debt and liquidity.

Thus, if a company commenced operations in period t near to the upper limit of its debt ratio, then the increased risk of further borrowing would tend to produce in practice an alternative form of financing: for example, running down liquid assets. The Anderson model appeared to indicate that these balance sheet constraints were effective, with financing behaviour responding to them. Certainly our previous discussions have indicated that we need to take explicit account of liquidity and gearing and the utilization of net income, comparing dividends and retained earnings (though the latter is covered more fully in Chapter 10, including the Workbook, where a flow of funds model is illustrated).

To develop a framework to incorporate these variables we need to have a consistent short- and long-term finance function. Recall that in section 9.2 we argued that the net difference (surplus/deficit) between the current sources of funds and the uses to which these could be put were in a sense predetermined by current and past production decisions and commitments to investment in fixed capital. We can represent the financing of this deficit (or the use to which a surplus could be put) in the following identity:

$$C \equiv \frac{\text{Long}}{\Delta E + \Delta D + \Delta LTA} + \frac{\text{Short}}{\Delta STB + \Delta TC + \Delta STA + \Delta S} \tag{9.8}$$

This relationship indicates the overall choice process which we can state as a series of alternatives, both short and long:

1. an increase in ordinary shares (by means of a rights issue, for example) (ΔE);
2. an increase or retiring of corporate debt (ΔD);
3. an increase/decrease in long-term external assets (ΔLTA);
4. an increase/decrease in short-term borrowing (ΔSTB);
5. an increase/decrease in net trade credit (ΔTC);
6. a build-up or reduction in short-term assets (ΔSTA);
7. a build-up or reduction in inventories (ΔS).

As portrayed the enterprise can switch *between* short- and long-term borrowing/investment as well as *within* the short and long alternatives. Presumably it will do so, as the discussion in previous sections has illustrated, if the expected return, net of transaction and other associated costs, signals a switch. With the use of interest rate swaps, the actual instrument itself is not exchanged so that the transaction element is minimized (see Chapter 8 for coverage of these swaps). So if, for instance, the enterprise expects interest rates to fall, it may borrow short and refinance later. Alternatively, if it has a surplus of cash, it may run down its short-term holdings of assets and increase its fixed capital (long) or invest in external long-term investments such as minority or even majority shares in another enterprise.

The enterprise does not have a completely free choice. Constraints within the enterprise in terms of desired balance sheet ratios can preclude freedom, unless management chooses to modify these ratios. But there are external constraints which are fully outside the control of companies. These are supply constraints caused by market imperfections and/or an unwillingness on the part of the lender to lend the amount required on the terms required. These blocks or impediments can exist because of government monetary policy: for example, in controlling the level, direction and cost of bank advances.

The ability to raise long-term finance is affected by the conditions in the capital market. These in turn are affected by the economic climate. In *bear* markets, with prices of securities falling, conditions are not favourable for new issues of ordinary shares or debentures. In *bull* markets the converse may be the case, with the funds available for investment outstripping the various demands by the industrial sector. This means the timing of borrowing (particularly long-term borrowing) is important, and whilst the enterprise may desire a particular structural change in the balance sheet (for example, by raising additional long-term finance), it may have to resort to short-term accommodation. Mindful of these constraints, let us explore some of the choices the enterprise has to make.

Suppose that the enterprise in question has a cash deficit which is currently financed by running down liquid assets, so that the enterprise's net liquidity (liquid assets less short-term liabilities) is negative. Reference back to the identity on p. 245 indicates the choices open to the enterprise. They are (given the cash deficit) essentially:

1. short-term borrowing and/or long-term finance;
2. sales of long-term investments;
3. reductions in inventories held;
4. reductions in net trade credit (shortening of accounts receivable and/or lengthening of accounts payable);

which we can consider in turn.

(a) Short-term/long-term finance

Assuming a free choice, the decision to go for short-term borrowing runs the risk of having continually to roll it forward. It involves the asymmetry argument that £1 worth of short-term borrowing is not seen as equivalent to £1 worth of liquid assets. Jackson's work (1984) referred to earlier is interesting again here. Her study was based on a survey of corporate treasurers. She found that there is asymmetry in the raising of bank finance and a reduction in liquid assets. The argument is that, although the monetary amounts may be the same, the holdings 'of financial assets probably give a company more flexibility and possibly more security than just an overdraft commitment' (p. 2). The choice of long-term debt or equity will depend on the safe gearing ratio of the enterprise, which itself will be determined by past profitability (and the variability of this) and the size of the enterprise. If the enterprise is near to the upper limit of its gearing ratio, it will have to attempt to raise equity capital.

We can portray the choice process for net liquidity and long-term borrowing as in Fig. 9.9, where the opportunity line (45° line) is CC'. The enterprise is on this line in period t by virtue of its inherited portfolio and cash surplus/deficit. We shall assume, in fact, that it is at point A, which indicates that net liquidity is negative. The enterprise can remain at this point or it could move up its opportunity line by raising more long-term finance, which enables it to increase its net liquidity.

Assuming that there are no supply constraints on either short- or long-term borrowing on this process, the choice it makes will be determined by its 'desired' portfolio. We said already that this will take the form of liquidity and gearing ratios, and we can illustrate the liquidity considerations in Fig. 9.9 by assuming that there is some desired level of net liquidity which represents a balance between short-term borrowing and holdings of short-term assets. Too low a level of liquidity can lead to insolvency; too high a level can bring a reduction in security because of possibilities of takeovers. (For further coverage of this, see Marris, 1964; Bridge and Dodds, 1978).

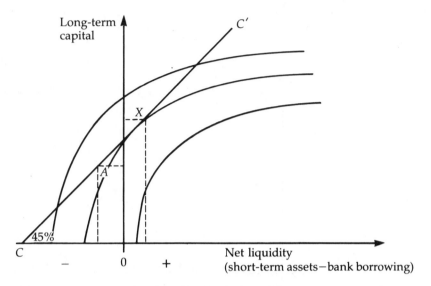

Fig. 9.9 Long-term capital and net liquidity (Adapted from A. D. Bain *et al.*, Figure 3.1).

Furthermore, the cost of raising additional long-term capital is likely to be higher than that of raising short-term borrowing. This is due not just to the transaction costs discussed in Chapter 8, but the fact that there is a term structure problem (see section 9.2), which may be due to the need to pay lenders a premium to cover their increased illiquidity. If management can successfully anticipate movements in the structure of interest rates, it may be able to raise long-term finance more cheaply by timing its issue of corporate debt to coincide with a trough in interest rates, though, as we have already suggested, in practice there may be few buyers at these low rates.

We can represent the preferences of the borrowing enterprise in terms of a family of indifference curves that slope upwards from left to right and are convex upwards. The company then faces a trade-off: to increase net liquidity by raising longer-term finance it has to meet the increased service costs. The point X in Fig. 9.9, where one of these indifference curves is tangential to the opportunity line, represents the optimum position. If there are market imperfections, or the company cannot raise this finance because of a perceived lack of creditworthiness, then it must settle for a non-optimal position. As Chapter 8 illustrated, there are transaction costs in raising long-term capital in terms of both management time and the costs of issue, although there are offsetting economies of scale here.

Given these considerations, companies raise their long-term finance in discrete amounts and this can cause further temporary disequilibrium in the balance sheets if, prior to the issue, companies have run down their liquid assets and increased their short-term borrowing and then, with the issue, repay some of this short-term borrowing and build up liquid assets. Quite what final choice is made will depend on individual circumstances, but enterprises may be tempted to retain some bank borrowing (some may be for fixed terms) in order to establish good relations with their bank so that in future periods when they may need acccommodation it is more readily forthcoming. This decision is illustrated in Fig. 9.10.

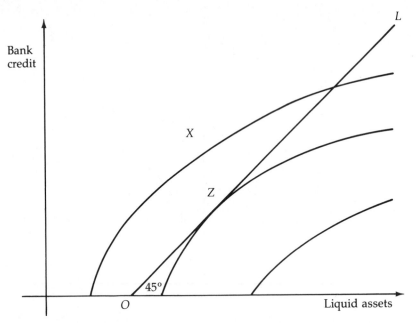

Fig. 9.10 Choice between liquid assets and bank credit. (Adapted from A. D. Bain *et al.*, Figure 3.2).

Say the enterprise was at a position X before the new issue. Then the influx of funds gives it the choice of several mixes of net liquidity. These are shown as an opportunity line OL, to which we can append our indifference mappings (which have the same characteristics as in Fig. 9.9. The enterprise will have a minimum safe level of liquid assets and a maximum safe level for bank borrowing — a level which may be externally given. The optimum point Z may not, however, be reached, as adjustment to this can take time, so that the enterprise may well be at some other point on the line and may be assumed to be adjusting to point Z in a sequential manner.

This leaves two matters unresolved:

1. the choice between corporate debt and ordinary shares;
2. the types of liquid asset purchased.

We have looked at both of these already, in Chapter 8 and in section 9.5(c) respectively. Taking these seriatim, two factors seem to determine the choice:

1. *The purpose of the issue.* If the issue is to enable the purchase of another company, equity finance (often by share exchange) will tend to be used and the wider joint equity base of permanent capital can then support debt capital in the future.
2. *The existing gearing ratio and the future expectations of earnings* (and their variability). The relative cost of the two types of issue will not in itself determine the choice, since debt finance is uniformly cheaper than equity. On strict economic criteria this might seem to signal a preference for debt over equity. However, debt capital often has a maturity date or a choice of conversion to equity that counts against it and, what is more, the market, as we have already seen, tends to set an upper limit to the level of gearing.

The choice of liquid assets will be determined by two considerations, which will in part be interrelated:

1. the degree of liquidity;
2. the return (and its variance).

Companies will need to maintain assets of differing degrees of encashability to meet expected outcomes (for fixed capital, inventories, tax payments, etc.) and any unexpected contingency. So we might expect the asset mix to include cash, bank deposits and short-dated securities, which can often yield a relatively high return to compensate for the short-term loss of liquidity. The deposits are fixed in nominal values, of course, but some of the securities which companies purchase can vary in their market price so that, if companies reckon they can anticipate future movements in security prices, they may be tempted into investing in them despite their illiquidity. The investment decision within the liquid asset set is thus a portfolio selection problem. Evidence tends to suggest that year by year companies make quite substantial changes in their bank borrowing (and thus in net liquidity) and in the composition of their liquid assets (see Table W9.3 for the data).

(b) Sales of long-term external investments

If the enterprise does have investments in longer-term securities, including the equity capital of other enterprises, it may choose to sell part or all of these. Of course, it may not be able to do this quickly: the market conditions might not be favourable. If its holdings are large, they may well require careful handling as the sale could turn even a strong market against themselves. Quite often the sale would be placed with another enterprise or with financial institutions. Although organizations tend to want to grow, and may hold securities in others as part of this strategy, the impact of the recession in the early 1980s caused many to re-evaluate such strategies, particularly in the light of the reorganization they undertook of closures, divestments, etc., which produced a slimmer and often differently focused enterprise.

(c) Reductions in inventories held

We have referred in section 9.5(b) to the issue of inventories and the need to manage them, particularly in times of high interest rates and recessions. Enterprises have taken a very close look at their stock levels of raw materials and finished goods and have when possible reduced them both. Where they have not done this, they have had to raise their borrowing, and, as we saw earlier, high stock levels are a frequent cause of business failure.

(d) Reductions in net trade credit

Again, we saw in earlier sections the importance of increasing the flow of cash to the enterprise. Increasing collections and delaying payments are two ways of achieving this. However, we did identify the limits that the enterprise may face in achieving a marked change in its policy. Nevertheless, the enterprise has to monitor the net trade credit carefully as well as the components, and where possible reduce it consistent with the overall objectives of the enterprise.

Summary

In this chapter, we have attempted to analyse several aspects of the short-term finance function and show the interrelationships with the long-term borrowing and lending decisions. We have argued that cash is a resource that has to be managed and that cash is held to make transactions and meet precautionary and speculative needs. It comes from the current operations of the enterprise, from a past endowment of liquid assets and from borrowing.

We have dealt with two questions:

1. how to manage the flow of cash through the enterprise;
2. how to determine the cash balance (including short-term securities) that an enterprise should have at a point in time.

Though looking at the current assets and current liabilities of the enterprise we have established the need for the enterprise to speed up the flow of cash in, slow down the flow of cash out, and minimize the resources held in cash rather than marketable securities. In pursuing these policies, the enterprise has to measure the gains and losses *and* associated risks. We argued that the high levels and volatility of interest rates have led enterprises to be more concerned with cash management. Also they have to manage their short-term needs when a cash deficit needs financing. But simply to separate the short-term financing decision (and lending for that matter) from the long-term decision is misplaced. Indeed, the enterprise probably has a preferred distribution of assets and liabilities, although adjustments towards this are unlikely to be instantaneous, and, in consequence, enterprises will generally be in permanent disequilibrium.

We focused attention on the need to combine short- and long-run financing decisions so that the enterprise knows in advance what its likely commitments will be period by period. Advance warning can then be given of the need to go 'long' before the maximum, safe, net borrowing position is reached. Within this is the decision to go for equity or debt, which may depend on the purpose of the investment and, more importantly, on the existing capital structure. The fact that, as we saw in Chapter 8, external long-term financing does not play a major role in most companies and that profits (and therefore retained earnings) follow a marked cyclical pattern throws a lot of the burden on to liquid assets (which can act as a buffer) and bank borrowing, all of which we examined in terms of desired portfolio relationships. The data we present in the Workbook for this chapter on the net acquisition of bank borrowing and liquid assets reveal marked fluctuations due, in the main, to the cyclical nature of retained earnings. But a contributory factor, which may cause changes within the short-term asset set, is the possibility of some investment behaviour by management to achieve the highest expected yield on short-term assets.

Key terms and concepts

Here is a list of the key terms and concepts which have featured in this chapter. You should make sure that you understand and can define each one of them. Page references to definitions in the text appear in bold in the index.

- Liquidity
- Trade bill
- Bank bill
- Banker's acceptance
- Factoring
- Invoice discounting
- Certificate of tax deposit
- Spontaneous financing

- Customer payment patterns
- Credit limit
- Economic order quantity model
- Stockout
- Transaction motive
- Precautionary motive
- Speculative motive
- Electronic communications/transfers

Further reading

A somewhat dated (and American) text is Orgler (1970). More recent is Hartley and Meltzer (1979). Although many of the general principles are relevant, some more specific practices are not because of the institutional differences between the USA and the UK. Have a look at Bass (1979) and, for a more specialized approach, Hudson and Butterworth (1974). For cash management models you cannot do better than return to the originals (Baumol, 1952; Beranek, 1966; and Miller and Orr, 1966). See also Mullins and Homonoff (1976).

The Workbook material to accompany this chapter begins on p. 533.

10 Dividend policy

The harder we look at the dividend picture, the more it seems like a puzzle, with pieces that just don't fit together. (Black, 1976, p. 5)

Learning objectives

After studying this chapter you should be able to:

- appreciate the multi-dimensional nature of the dividend decision, how it is part of the overall financing decisions of the firm and how it impacts on the enterprise and the shareholders and creditors of the enterprise;
- understand the theoretical approaches that have been taken in the debate and the empirical tests that have been employed to help unravel the dividend problem;
- analyse the impact of market imperfections on the controversy;
- outline the types of policy followed by organizations.

10.1 Introduction

In this chapter we raise two questions:

1. can dividends be used by management to influence the value of the enterprise?
2. what factors determine the division of the after-tax earnings of the business enterprise between paying them out in the form of dividends and retaining them in the enterprise?

As we have stressed in earlier chapters, these decisions are inevitably interdependent, since the enterprise has to balance not only its own needs for cash between the current period and future periods, but also those of its shareholders. Although the issue is often seen as a matter between the enterprise and its shareholders, the retention/distribution split does have a practical relevance to bond-holders and other creditors because any retentions in the form of fixed assets or liquid assets give them greater security.

Indeed, following our discussions on option pricing we can conceptualize shares as a call option on the assets of the enterprise. Dividends must then be seen as a dispersement of collateral. But other interest groups in the enterprise may also target on the decision, particularly the employees, who may see a dividend payment at a time of recession and lay-offs as a socially unacceptable policy. Dividends may thus be seen as a cross-subsidization of shareholders.

If the enterprise is a multinational then the complexity of the problem increases. There are two reasons for this:

1. the existence of different tax regimes;
2. because the dividend payments will be in local currency and subject to foreign exchange risk and possible restrictions on the ability of the multinational to transfer them out of the country.

Thus there is no simple answer to those two fundamental questions. The academic literature gives little guidance — though this is not for want of trying! The literature on dividend policy is prodigious, as we shall see. There is a fair degree of controversy in the theoretical stances taken (similar to that of the gearing debate — see Chapter 11). The debate does not rest there, because practitioners — investment managers and corporate managers — cannot themselves agree over the issues that surround the company's dividend decision either.

Clearly, given the amount of space devoted to the topic in the literature, and the attention paid to it by managers, 'dividend policy' is important, even though we may not have a consensus on how to measure that importance. Additionally, it has a public policy impact at a macro level, in terms of the supply of capital to companies (see, for example, Meeks and Whittington, 1976), and as a source of income to shareholders. It is no surprise, therefore, that governments have often legislated statutory controls on dividends.

Ultimately this is an empirical issue and the studies that have been performed have, as we shall see, focused on either:

1. a statistical analysis of the various time series data;
2. survey research by means of questionnaires. (One of the most recent and comprehensive studies done on dividend policy is to be found in Baker *et al.* (1985) for the United States, where a postal questionnaire was sent to 562 companies listed on the New York Stock Exchange from three industry groups — manufacturing, utility and wholesale/retail); or
3. modelling companies' financing decision using published accounts data see, for example, Devereux (1987) and the most recent study by Chowdhury and Miles (1987).

Although there is a wealth of empirical work, the statistical issues involved are complex, and as a result it has been difficult to find any resolution that satisfies the academic literature at least! Yet it would appear that dividend decisions are regarded as a matter of importance by the financial managers of enterprises and may be a constraint on their freedom of choice.

The structure of this chapter is as follows:

1. In section 10.2 we focus on the heterogeneity of enterprises and investors, and attempt to see what, if any, effect this can have on the dividend decision.
2. In section 10.3 we examine the theoretical stances — the two polar views of the irrelevance and relevance schools.
3. In section 10.4 we raise the issue of the market imperfections of transaction costs, clientele effect, taxes and the asymmetry of information between shareholders and managers.

4. The signalling properties of dividends are raised in section 10.5.
5. In section 10.6 we discuss the actual dividend procedures that enterprises can follow.
6. In section 10.7 we focus on the variations on cash dividends that are possible.
7. The international dimensions of dividend policy are raised in section 10.8.

10.2   Issues in dividend policy

In seeking to quantify the importance of the dividend decision we need to pose a series of fundamental questions relating to the heterogeneity of both enterprises and investors. Since enterprises differ in size and activity we need to ask: is the pay-out policy of an enterprise affected by size or the nature of the industry? Reference to the Chowdhury and Miles (1987) study discussed in Chapter 8 indicates that size of company does affect the dividend decision. They identified in their sample of 650 a more risk-averse behaviour among 'small' firms, which would make them more willing to cut dividends in response to a changed financial environment.

In turning to the investors and their financial advisers, there are even more questions to be asked. Not least among these problems is our inability to be fully aware of the factors that investors take into account when they value shares. How can we develop and test a theory of share valuation when we cannot measure directly the expectations of investors — say, with respect to the amount and risk of future dividends? These diverse expectations reinforce the fact that the risk of the *expected* dividend of a share is a subjective issue. Once the dividend is actually announced and paid, the risk of that particular payment clearly disappears.

We may, for example, attempt to use 'subjective probability' estimates, and investigate it by interviewing a sample of shareholders. Alternatively, we can attempt to infer the risk that shareholders are taking by examining their capitalization rate (or required rate of return) for these dividends. The higher the rate, the higher the subjective perception of risk. However, how can we measure the investors' risk estimate implied by this rate of return if they are not a homogeneous set? Shareholders differ for a number of reasons. For instance:

1. they belong to different marginal tax brackets;
2. they have different sizes of holding, which means they face different transaction costs;
3. some are speculative buyers hoping only for a capital gain, whereas others are looking to the investment for long-term returns in both dividend and capital growth.

With the growth of privatization, as Chapter 1 explained, there are now a large number of small investors — perhaps as many as 11 million, of which it is estimated that 60% own shares in only one company. Given their magnitude, their interests cannot be ignored and, as we have commented earlier, they are likely to be more risk averse. However, the institutional shareholders are still potent forces and, with a shareholding power which can be orchestrated together, they can change management policy. They can bring about change (even in the Coats Patons case they achieved some success) and can also side with a potential bidder (reference back to the Decca case is instructive in the issue of the loss of management control).

In raising this problem, we are aware that in Chapter 5 we argued that dividends were fundamental to the value of a share (go back and check our discussion of the Gordon growth model if you are rusty on this — see pp. 120–1). In this chapter, we need to see how dividends fit into market pricing of shares and, in particular, to focus on whether changes in the pattern of *expected* dividends affect the value of a share.

Using the basic share price model developed in Chapter 5:

$$P_0 = \frac{D_1}{k - g} \tag{10.1}$$

we know that if we do increase current dividends, specifically the next dividend D_1 (which may be an interim rather than a final dividend — see the discussion of Beedles in the Workbook, section W10.2), then this will increase the value of the share (everything else being equal). Although the equation is set in terms of a perpetuity, the investor does not have to, and is not expected to, hold it in perpetuity. As long as there are homogeneous expectations of g, the growth rate of dividends continuing in perpetuity, then the equation can still hold. If the share is held for ever, as it were, then the dividends are the only cash flows received. If sold, the investor's yield for the holding period will be a combination of dividend and capital gain/loss.

How shareholders perceive their investment — turning it over actively to achieve capital gains or holding to receive the income — may be of relevance here. Unfortunately, we know little about individual investors in themselves never mind their trading. Although we could, as a residual, obtain some measure of turnover by substituting the reported figure for financial institutions from the aggregate turnover figure, it is still imprecise and difficult to pinpoint as the residual will contain all other investors, including overseas, industrial and commercial companies, as well as trusts and households. For financial institutions, evidence to hand indicates that, for the United Kingdom, their portfolios are in the main actively traded, though there are marked differences among the financial institutions themselves (see Dodds and Dobbins, 1985). Thus what financial managers will be concerned about is how the change in the expected dividends will be perceived by the market — the *signalling* argument we referred to in Chapter 1 and shall refer to later (see pp. 265–6).

Of course, the firm could re-borrow the funds paid out in dividends from the capital market and thus preserve this growth. But this raises further complications over whether this borrowing is by debt or equity, and this raises the further issue of gearing. Additionally, the enterprise has to pay the transaction costs of issuing new securities (we indicated the size of these in Chapter 8).

Financial managers, therefore, are faced with a dilemma as they try to balance the competing demands of shareholders for income now and income in the future. If they can succeed in this, and achieve an optimal policy of dividends versus retentions, then they can achieve the maximum share value for the shareholders. However, as we shall see in this chapter, investors and professional analysts do not have access to the same flow of information as financial managers in enterprises and each operates to some extent in a separate vacuum. Investors are not privy to the internal information of the enterprise or its investment plans, and do not necessarily trust their agents, the board of directors, to act in the best interests of the shareholders, though the incentive signalling theory of Ross (1977) does link executive compensation to the value of the enterprise — presumably reducing the managerial slack in the enterprise.

The empirical evidence, too, is mixed on whether retained earnings are used more or less efficiently than funds raised in the market. Financial decision-makers in the enterprise for their part do not know how investors, and therefore the market, will react to a given policy change, and they are faced by capital markets that are not perfect, taxation systems that are often discriminatory in their impact on dividends, and (at times) statutory controls imposing limits on the dividends themselves.

In this world of imperfect and asymmetric information, changes in dividends can prove difficult for both managers and shareholders. As a result, as we shall see, there is a temptation to set an aspiration level of dividends, even if it is zero, and attempt to maintain it, only raising it through time. This enforced 'stability' of dividends is similar to that suggested by the classic study by Lintner in 1956. Managers are spared the need to make a dividend decision, and investors are spared the constant evaluation and re-evaluation of any changes in policy, including the signals they read into these decisions.

10.3   Theoretical viewpoints

The dividend policy decision involves, as we have seen, the determination of the amount of cash dividends (or their equivalent, such as share dividends) that should be distributed to the shareholders of the enterprise. The *theoretical* viewpoint as to the importance or otherwise of dividend policy has two main strands. These really are polar views, although reconciliation is possible, particularly if we allow for *market imperfections* such as taxes, consultation costs and so on, which we do in section 10.4. The two strands are as follows:

1. the *irrelevance* school, or pure earnings school, which has as part of its domain the *residual earnings theory*;
2. the *relevance* school, which has within it two arguments: that dividends should be low, and that they should be high.

Let us take the two viewpoints in order.

(a) The irrelevance school

We can summarize the irrelevance argument quite simply: it is argued that the value of a share is a function (*ceteris paribus*) of corporate earnings independent of dividends: that is, the split in the earnings between dividends and retentions does not affect the share value, so the enterprise and its shareholders are indifferent between financing new investment with retained earnings or borrowing. The enterprise has no need to identify the preferences of its shareholders with respect to either the investment policy or the time pattern of income they require. There is *no* optimum dividend policy.

The difficulty arises in actually portraying this, since academic rigour can itself involve a trade-off with understanding the essential policy prescription. In the text here we attempt a more intuitive approach; a proof appears in the Workbook (see pp. 567–8). See also Miller and Modigliani (1961).

The starting point for the irrelevance school is an idealized world of perfect capital markets and certainty, with wealth-maximizing behaviour, symmetric market rationality and with two parties, the *shareholders* and their agents, the *financial officers* of the enterprise.

Whilst these assumptions are clearly not all true of the real world, in Chapter 1 we argued the case for their use on methodological grounds as a guide to the sort of actions that would result in this artificial environment. Then we can relax some or all of them to assess the impact for policy. Now the capital investment decision (a decision which is independent of the dividend policy) is of primary importance as this will determine with certainty the future cash flows of the enterprise. Provided managers choose the optimal investment plan — not difficult when all projects and their outcomes are known — we can be sure that shareholders' wealth will be maximized. Recall that, in this world, there is a unique market rate of interest which is the borrowing–lending rate.

Enterprises will, therefore, know their cost of capital and will accept *all* projects with positive NPVs (though it is difficult to see how any would/could exist!). There is no capital-rationing constraint, as enterprises can borrow at the market rate and, provided they can at least earn the cost of capital, they will still add to shareholders' wealth. In this world then, provided the investment opportunities exist, we could conceive of zero cash dividends. Dividends would only be paid out if the eligible investment opportunities had been exhausted and there were residual funds left over. If shareholders require the cash, then as we show later (p. 259), they can make the dividends themselves by liquidating part of their holdings.

Thus the irrelevance school encompasses the *residual theory of dividends*. This is encompassed in Fig. 10.1 where the required amount of new investment is *OA*. If, after financing this from retained earnings, funds are left over, these can be distributed as dividends. If they were to be retained and not used to retire debt, then the enterprise and its shareholders would presumably suffer as a project with negative NPV would be accepted and shareholders could make more profitable use of the funds. Of course, reference back to the discussions on capital budgeting and the portfolio implications of this is relevant here. The enterprise may also have a target capital structure which includes debt financing, but as the Modigliani and Miller (MM) gearing thesis shows (see Chapter 11), with its simplifying assumptions, the use of debt does *not* produce a change in the market value of the enterprise.

Shareholders would be fully cognizant as to the reasoning behind their agents' decisions as they also have complete information on the available investment opportunities and the outcomes. They would, one presumes, sue their agents (and/or replace them) if all these projects with positive NPVs were not accepted, as clearly the agents would not be acting in the best interest of the shareholders. If for some reason shareholders wanted the cash now to make a consumption expenditure or to exercise a whim and invest in another company (in a world with no risk there is no need to diversify), then they could make that transfer of value themselves rather than rely on the enterprise. They could manufacture their own cash dividend payments by selling parts of their holdings, transferring the previously unrealized capital gain into a realized gain and current income. In reality this is not always possible, even ignoring transaction costs, because at the time a shareholder decides to sell, the stock market may be in a 'bear' stage and there will be little if any gain to liquidate.

There are other considerations too. The case of Coats Patons in the Workbook (pp. 574–80) highlights the issue of a dividend that is cut so as to retain funds and invest them in the enterprise. However, the Public Trustee's investment adviser indicated at that time that trust laws prohibited such a

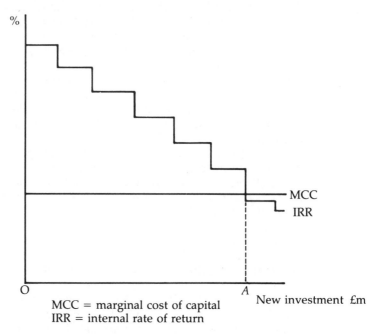

MCC = marginal cost of capital
IRR = internal rate of return

Figure 10.1 Investment opportunities.

strategy. Capital could not be distributed in place of income. In addition, even if a sale were allowed, it could involve the investor in a book loss which, for an institution that used book values for, say, its liquidity ratios and the like, might involve it in another set of problems.

The Fisher–Hirshleifer model could be applied here (see the Workbook, p. 567) to prove the MM argument. Just as enterprises are balancing the decision to invest or distribute involving an intertemporal choice, so the investor can do the same (see p. 259 below) and unravel any decision taken by management to distribute the time pattern of the present value of the earnings to his or her own choosing. Dividends can been in this light as forced liquidations of shares. We shall illustrate the whole process with the numerical example given in Fig. 10.2, in which we retain the original assumptions and further assume that the enterprise is all equity financed.

The irrelevance school can be generalized to include a world of risk where, although the amounts of future dividends are perceived to be uncertain, investors are able to assess the risk class of the enterprise and thus the stream of expected dividends. This risk class is determined by the riskiness of the investment projects and *not* by the division of earnings into dividends and retained earnings. Even if the investment plans change the risk class, this will be known to investors.

(b) Dividend relevance

The dividend relevance school stands in direct contradistinction to the irrelevance school, yet both would agree over the acceptance of those projects with positive NPVs at the enterprise's cost of capital (the unique market interest rate). Of course, enterprises can accept projects with negative NPVs

Suppose the enterprise has retained all its earnings until now and has 5,000 shares issued currently selling at 50p a share. Present shareholder wealth is £2,500 — the total value of the enterprise. The managers of the enterprise decide to pay a 10p cash dividend which is to be subsequently financed by a rights issue so as to preserve the ability to undertake the investment opportunities of the enterprise. The ex-dividend price of the share will fall to 40p and the value of the enterprise will fall also to £2,000. Shareholders' wealth per share after the dividend is 10p (dividends) + 40p (per share) = 50p.

The enterprise now issues more shares to raise the required £500, selling them at 40p each. The total market value of the enterprise returns to £2,500 and the unit price of shares remains at 40p. Shareholders who did not want the cash can buy the pre-emptive rights offered (see Chapter 8), and those who did can use the cash for consumption. Other investors will have to be found to take up the rights, or some existing shareholders may increase their holdings. The enterprise still has the £500 to invest in the same projects it has deemed desirable, but the enterprise has more issued shares, albeit selling at correspondingly lower prices.

The astute reader will have observed the many seemingly fatal flaws in the above analysis which we shall have to unravel later. Suffice it to say at this stage that the wealth position of the shareholder has not changed.

Figure 10.2

as we illustrated in Chapter 7 (section 7.6(b)). Where they differ is over the constancy of this required rate of return of investors, k_e. Gordon (1959) and Lintner (1962) in classic studies in the dividend debate argue that k_e rises as the dividend pay-out ratio is reduced, so that risk-averse investors are *not* indifferent between the capital gains and the payment of cash dividends.

The argument has two main strands:

1. Gordon in his 1959 study found the pay-out ratio and price–earnings ratio positively related. From this the conclusion was that the causal mechanism was from dividend to share value: in other words, high pay-outs meant high prices relative to current earnings.
2. The second strand is usually referred to as the 'bird-in-the-hand argument' — that £1 worth of cash dividends is worth more than the same £1 worth of retention because the dividend received is *certain*, but the reinvestment is *risky*. Shareholders are assumed to be risk averse (more so for the large number of small shareholders), future payments are uncertain and share prices can suffer extreme volatility. It is concluded that this means that, to offset a 1% reduction in dividend yields, an increase in g of more than 1% is required (to compensate for the shift into the future of the dividend). Modigliani and Miller were at pains to argue that this was fallacious because dividend policy was being confused with investment policy. However, see Wood (1975) for an extremely good defence of the 'bird-in-the hand' argument.

There is more to the argument than this, however. Dividends (both present and future) are measurable, being in cash, whereas earnings pose greater measurement problems (see also on this point *Financial Accounting: Method and Meaning*, especially Chapter 9). This may increase the accuracy (in the minds of investors) of performance evaluation. They can thus reduce their agency and monitoring costs. MM regard this as a fallacy, arguing that investors often reinvest their dividends in the shares of the same enterprise or enterprises of equivalent risk. Dividends can thus be seen to be less risky only if they are invested in, say, a risk-free asset. Taken to the extreme, if investors preferred cash in the form of dividends to shares in the form of retaind earnings, then investors would never purchase shares in the first place! We know that we do have a large body of investors and surely what they expect is a return which is commensurate with the risk taken.

Turning to the 'bird-in-the-hand' thesis, Gordon is arguing for positive liquidity premiums such that $LP_1 < LP_2 < LP_3$ to produce $k_{e1} < k_{e2} < k_{e3}$ and that these are market expected and, therefore, market determined. If an enterprise then retains more out of current dividends, we should expect to see a consequent fall in the value of the enterprise. The reasoning for this is that the dividends are reinvested at the enterprise's constant cost of capital, whereas the shareholder has an increasing capitalization rate.

However, as Brennan (1971) has pointed out, this produces an inconsistency of a constant cost of capital for an enterprise through time, with an increasing shareholders' capitalization rate. This argument is very persuasive, and if the two discount rates do not differ over time, as companies are sensitive to the preferences of investors and use discount rates that accurately reflect these capital market signals, then once more dividend policy returns as a *financing* issue. We are then back to the irrelevance school of MM, since the critical difference between the two approaches was over the constancy or otherwise of the investors' required return.

10.4 Market imperfections

Theoretical discussions on dividend policy typically take place in an 'idealized world' either devoid of uncertainty or, if uncertainty exists, where it can be reduced to risk, with all investors sharing the same information and expectations with respect to the earnings of the enterprise. The world we live in is not so convenient. Imperfections abound, and they can be broadly divided into the following:

1. transaction costs;
2. clientele effects;
3. taxes;
4. asymmetric information;
5. other imperfections.

These are discussed in turn below.

(a) Transaction costs

Once we allow for the costs involved (and discussed in Chapter 8 in detail), including those of underwriting the issuance of new shares, then the dividends are not equivalent to pre-emptive rights, since if the enterprise has to raise additional financing to undertake the investment plans it has available, it will have to issue more shares (i.e. undertake more dilution of earnings) to cover these flotation costs so as to end up with the same value. In addition, it has the problem we have seen earlier in the book (pp. 209–10) of pricing, and possibly underpricing, the issue. Retained funds are, therefore, not equivalent in cost to new share capital, but cheaper.

This should, if we retain the shareholders' maximization objective, lead to the payment of cash dividends as a residual and for investors to prefer, in consequence, *lower dividend to higher,* if the latter involves the raising of new finance. Even if the enterprise were to opt for debt financing, although this may be a cheaper form of financing than equity (see Chapter 8), this would once more involve issuance costs.

The existence of transaction costs is not restricted to those borne by the enterprise. Investors face these costs in two ways:

1. They incur costs of search in analysing information to choose their shares and monitor their portfolios. Whilst the growth of financial columns in the press has helped to contain these costs, nevertheless they are still not zero. The time and effort spent by an individual shareholder are not tax deductible, yet may be significant. Certainly these costs can be large for the large institutional investors, as they maintain research departments to undertake this analysis.
2. They incur costs of trading shares — the brokerage commission and stamp duty. These are particularly relevant to the 'home-made' dividend policy that is crucial to the MM/irrelevance school. In this process, the buying (if dividends are not required) and selling (if cash dividends are required) of shares is not costless. Indeed, these costs are differential in size and can be particularly prohibitive to the small investor (because brokers have minimum commission rates — see Chapter 2). The impact of this is that investors cannot costlessly switch at will, and therefore the time prefer-ence that they possess with respect to income now or income in the future will dictate their preference for dividends versus capital gains.

This can produce a 'clientele effect', where a particular segment of investors is attracted to the pay-out policy adopted by an enterprise. However, an enterprise, if it were to adopt a reinvestment alternative, could on the grounds of transaction costs alone cater for both sets of shareholders. Those who wanted cash could take the dividends and those who wanted to see the dividends reinvested could opt for this alternative.

(b) Clientele effect

Some shareholders do require regular and guaranteed income, and given the transaction cost raised above it is not always practicable or even possible with the existence of trust law for them to 'create' their own dividends. The Inland Revenue has estimated that for the period 1972–3, 40% of all recipients of dividends and taxed interest receipts were pensioners who, one presumes, would have a marked degree of liquidity preference (capital gains over, say, ten years would probably be of little use to them). Although this is a dated study, it is at least indicative. It is not possible in these statistics to separate dividend payments from fixed interest payments, but if we add to this the pensions and annuities paid out by life insurance companies and pension funds, which means that these institutions also have a regular income need, then we just reinforce the need for regular and guaranteed income. These institutions could, of course, use bonds to produce this regularity of income, and an examination of their asset holdings reveal that they do. But an overconcentration on debt would cause them to lose out on asset portfolio diversification and, more importantly, to lose on the protection that equity may give as an inflation hedge.

With these considerations in mind, it is known that some enterprises have made a consistent policy of paying dividends, and this should attract those investors searching for regular income. Indeed the prudential regulation as applied to financial institutions in some countries requires a dividend test rule before the share can be purchased. This is also true of the Trustee Investments Act 1961 in Britain, with a five-year dividend test rule. These enterprises may be in industries that face less volatility in their earnings. In the USA and Canada, for instance, this would be the case with utilities. We may, therefore, reasonably expect that if there is a clientele effect it will be industry based. Others who prefer capital gains will go for the low pay-out enterprises.

This time preference on the part of investors may be a result of their liability structure, e.g. a pension fund requires a regular income flow to pay pensions to those currently of retired age. But it may also be accentuated by the incidence of differential taxation on income and capital gains, and this is a point we pick up below. The existence or otherwise of a clientele effect requires the enterprise to appreciate and know its clients, and inevitably this can impose a constraint on the actions of the enterprise as the shareholders expect and can even require (given the shareholding position of large institutional investors) that the enterprise continue its dividend policy. What emerges is an implied contract between the enterprise and its shareholding body. Any departure, say a cut in dividends, will (or at least may) be seen as providing information to the shareholders that the enterprise is in difficulty even if this is not the case. The Coats Patons case in the Workbook (pp. 574–80) provides an illustration of this.

Despite the apparent appeal of such a clientele effect, the empirical evidence, perhaps surprisingly, does not fully support it on either side of the Atlantic. However, the tax position of some investors *must*, if rationality is assumed and if the advice of tax planners is taken in forming portfolios, condition shareholders' choice of securities, with low marginal taxpayers being attracted to high pay-out enterprises and vice versa, and for a coverage of tax induced clienteles, see De Angelo and Masulis (1980), Miller (1977) and Mayer (1986). Clearly this will not be the only factor, and investors have to take account of the fact that they may lose a measure of diversification by concentrating their investment in a particular type of enterprise or industry. In other words, the clientele effect is only one consideration along with others in the choice of securities purchased and sold, and so its effect may be masked by other factors which have contributed to a choice of securities held. Certainly the smoothing of dividend payments and the long lags of adjustment found by Chowdhury and Miles (1987) could be clientele introduced.

(c) Taxes

As with so many aspects of financial management, the existence of taxes, both personal and corporate, complicates the subject (but also makes it more interesting!). We have experienced a number of different corporation tax regimes in the UK since World War II. A review of these would reveal them to have been both *neutral* and *discriminatory* with respect to their impact on the division of earnings between retained and distributed. Most recently the 1984 Budget appears to have had a major impact on the financing decisions of UK firms with its return to greater neutrality.

Perhaps it would be interesting and instructive to look back to the 1950s when prior to 1958 there was a discriminatory tax regime and post-1958 it was neutral. However, for our present purposes it is necessary only to go back to 1966 when the so-called 'classical' corporation tax regime was introduced (as a result of the Finance Act 1965). Under this system, all profits were taxed at a single rate. If distributions were made, the shareholders were responsible for their own tax on these.

Thus, for instance, if an enterprise had before-tax earnings of £1,000, then in 1966 with a corporate tax rate of 42.5% the enterprise would have after-tax earnings of £575. If it chose to retain rather than distribute then there would be no further tax liability. But if it distributed the whole sum, investors would have to pay income tax at their own particular rate. The standard tax rate then was 41.25% — so the after-tax cash left in the hands of a shareholder who paid income tax at the standard rate would have been £337.81. This regime was *intended* to be discriminatory to encourage retention, and we might have expected an increase in retentions. However, the Briston and Tomkins (1970) study did not find an increase in retentions and Singh and Whittington (1968) have argued that a discriminatory tax regime may favour the more efficient and dynamic enterprises by providing funds for investment.

With the partial imputation system introduced in 1973, there is no discrimination in terms of total tax paid. Investors receive a tax credit equivalent to the standard rate of tax. The concept of an advanced corporation tax (ACT) was also introduced. This tax is paid within three months if the company pays a cash dividend. The actual rate of ACT depends on the basic rate of tax. Currently with a personal tax rate of 25% the ACT is $25/75 = \frac{1}{3}$ of the amount distributed. ACT is offsettable against mainstream corporation tax (MCT) provided the latter is paid. If not, this is referred to as tax exhausted. A high-geared capital structure can help in accentuating this exhaustion. Otherwise the firm can carry back the ACT to offset unused taxable profits from earlier years. If this does not exhaust the ACT then the unused portion can be carried forward to offset future taxable profits. For firms making trading losses — say, in a recession — the opportunity to offset may well lie long into the future. The extent of tax exhaustion has been estimated by the Institute for Fiscal Studies for their sample of firms to be 30% for the period 1975–9 and 35% for the period 1980–2 (see Bank of England, 1987; Devereux, 1987). The study found that a large majority of firms in their sample were tax exhausted at some point in the period after 1968.

1. The payment of the ACT deprives the enterprise of the use of the funds until it is recovered, if ever. As there is no interest paid to the firm on what is effectively a loan, not only does the firm lose the use of the money but it pays for this loss too! If dividends are not paid, the ACT is not levied and the shareholders should benefit from the use of the money in the enterprise in terms of improved earnings. In the Coats Patons case, this was an important consideration as it was a multinational, not all of the profits of which were subject to mainstream British taxes.

2. Another consideration for many enterprises has until recently (1983) been the 100% capital allowance available for new capital investment as an offset against taxable income. Those companies that have been growing by investment are not liable to pay any MCT until their taxable income exceeds the value of the capital allowance and stock relief, although stock relief was abolished in 1984. In these cases, dividend payments are penalized through the ACT.

3. A firm making a trading loss under the partial imputation system present in the UK faces an asymmetry. While profits create immediate tax

liabilities, losses do not create an immediate rebate. They are offsetable with a carry back of one year and carry forward provisions. The same situation as with ACT arises — that the firm may not be able to take advantage of the tax treatment of the losses and there is no indexation of them to reflect the lost interest.

Shareholders do not face the same *personal* taxes and there is a potential discrimination between capital gains and dividends, for the latter are treated as income whilst the former are only taxed when received. Book profits are not taxed until *realized*. Investors who have high marginal tax rates will favour capital gains as these are taxed at a lower rate (maximum 30%) than the equivalent amount of dividends, on which the tax could be 40%.

Some investors such as pension funds pay no tax on income or gain so that this would not apply, and hence we cannot be precise as to whether the tax implications lead to a strong clientele effect as we discussed above. Miller and Scholes (1978) for the USA did not support this. Some countries have tax-free allowances on income from dividends to assist the small investor, while others do not levy corporation tax for corporate investors on the dividends, or only do so at lower levels. Once again there are complications to cloud the issue.

(d) Asymmetric information

Managers have access to information not available to outsiders. But equally they are not privy to the decision-making process of investors. Both sets of economic actors, even if they have access to the same information, may diverge in their assessment of it, and its impact on them may differ because of tax and other considerations. Indeed, even within a group there may be different perceptions of the information (see *Managerial Accounting: Method and Meaning*, Chapter 1, for a discussion of this in the managerial context). In consequence, some investors may value particular dividend patterns more highly than others. Within the investing body they may not have the same access to the information or they may spend less time (and invest less cost) on analysing the information. Even with that time and effort, can investors, including professional analysts, be more accurate than naïve earnings forecasting methods? Empirical evidence says not (see Cragg and Malkiel (1968) for the USA and Lee and Tweedie (1981) for the UK). The net result is that investors have incomplete and unequal information. This leads to an area of dividend policy that has spawned a literature of its own, the *information content of dividends*, which is taken up in section 10.5 below.

(e) Other imperfections

There are other factors to take into account in framing a dividend policy. At the time the enterprise is wanting to raise outside finance to replace the funds paid out in dividends, it may face a hostile capital market with falling share prices at which it would not be possible (or would be extremely difficult) to raise finance. In other words, an enterprise can face a *supply constraint* irrespective of flotation costs. In addition, if it can manage to issue new shares, it faces a 'control problem' in that existing investors may not take up the rights offered to them and therefore may see their control being diluted as new investors are attracted and/or some existing shareholders increase their holdings. The reason for the investors not taking up the rights may be many and varied, but could include dissatisfaction over dividend policy. The net result would be that shareholders also liquidate their holdings and the enterprise risks the possibility of a takeover in which the managers themselves are often the major losers. Shareholders find abandonment a simple option because their shareholdings are either quite small or, as in the case of the institutional and overseas shareholders, are generally diversified, and hence they are only selling part. Managers, as full-time employees, are not able to do likewise.

So although this dividend decision is taken by managers, they, according to agency theory, have to take due cognizance of the wishes of the shareholders. They ignore them at their peril as many managements have found. Smaller, often closely held companies, will often not want to issue new shares as this may affect assets under the existing shareholders who may not consistently have the resources to maintain their ownership proportion. These companies will often be high retention companies. We may thus find that dividends are related to the size of the enterprise, as the Chowdhury and Miles (1987) study has found (see also an old, but still informative study by Bates (1964)) and the pattern of its shareholdings.

In summary we have discussed a number of factors that will affect the dividend decision; we cannot be definitive over their relative weights. We have argued for the importance of the investment plans and future growth of the enterprise, yet recognized that information is not perfect and investors differ in the way they evaluate the information they have at their disposal, or differ in their willingness or ability to search for new information. Tax and other imperfections present us with a mosaic in which investors may not be indifferent between gains and dividends, and managers cannot disregard this. Thus they have to frame a dividend *policy* rather than relying on, say, the residual theory. We can see that they do form policies, and in section 10.6 we shall consider what these might be.

10.5   Information content of dividends

Dividend announcements are often associated with movements in share prices beyond that expected between the cum- and ex-dividend price. This can result in confusion, for observers may assume that dividends affect share prices from this fact alone. What we have to do is to separate out the *information content* of the announcement from the intrinsic change in investors' wealth that results from the dividend. It is this information that affects the share price. We noted earlier (p. 264) that there is unequal information between management and outsiders, and therefore that the announcement can be taken as a signal by outside investors. One may presume that the larger the change, the larger the information content (see Baker *et al.*, 1985). Indeed, in a recent survey in the United States, it was found that on average the respondents stated that dividends were a *signalling device* of future company prospects. With some exceptions, empirical studies indicate that dividend changes do convey some unanticipated information to the market. However, the controversy still exists. The UK Stock Market is one which is 'fat' in terms of volume and is well analysed, in fact over analysed by some assessments!

If the incentive signalling approach holds, investors are looking to managers to give them 'accurate' information. The rationale is that, as enterprises are reluctant to cut dividends, a cut will convey a signal of poor earnings, even if a justification is given (see the Coats Patons case). An increase will lead to an anticipation of good future earnings. This forms an interesting case of 'he thinks that I think that he thinks that ...'. In the present case, shareholders are reckoned to believe that managers believe that they (the shareholders) will take dividends as signals. Because the shareholders expect this, they expect managers to act accordingly, and as a result they *do* take dividends as signals! Hence, if this psychology does hold, managers ignore it at their peril.

While there is empirical evidence in support of a signalling approach, this is not to say that the dividends contain *new* information *per se*, but rather that, if information is conveyed, this takes place through previous and concurrent earnings information. This past information issue has made it difficult to devise empirical tests (see Watts, 1973). However, as we saw in Chapter 3, the EMH would deny this, as the market has already anticipated the announcement and therefore impounded this into the share price through the well-developed capital markets and knowledgeable institutional investors. Thus the dividend announcement will not signal new information, but only confirm already known or forecast events. Should we be searching for hidden meanings or hidden information as some people do on popular records by playing them backwards? If we add to this the size issue (that larger enterprises either distribute more information or are more actively researched) then we can appreciate the difficulty of devising empirical tests.

Two methods have been used to test for this information content — the abnormal trading approach and the abnormal return approach.

1. The *abnormal trading approach* follows Beaver (1968) and focuses on the trading following the announcement of a dividend change. If the change causes some surprise on the part of investors and/or disagreement, then we would expect to see a flurry of trading activity in excess of the 'norm'.
2. The alternative and more popular test is the *abnormal return approach*. This attempts to see if there is an abnormal return where the abnormal component is taken to be proportional to the information content.

However, with both of these tests there are problems of prior information, the size of the change in dividend and the size of the enterprise — issues raised earlier. The abnormal trading test has many serious methodological problems associated with it, since the CAPM is often used to model the 'normal' returns. Taylor (1979) correctly pointed out that there is a joint hypothesis — tests of information content and the underlying model of security returns — the same problem raised in the empirical tests for the EMH (Chapter 3). In addition specific problems have been raised in the use of the cumulative average residuals themselves that form a part of most tests (see, for example, Brennan, 1971; Larcker *et al.*, 1980).

With this sort of empirical problem, it is perhaps not surprising to find conflicting evidence for the markets tested (for example, in the United States the evidence presented by Watts, 1973, 1976a, 1976b; Pettit, 1973, 1976; Ang, 1975; Laub, 1976; Charest 1978; and Aharony and Swary, 1980). Riding (1984), in a more recent United States test which covered a wide range of statistical techniques focusing on dividend decreases, found that 'neither dividend decrease announcements nor concurrent earnings proclamations seem to convey new information to the marketplace' (p. 174).

So, despite a battery of testing, we still have little in the way of usable evidence for policy-makers. If you think this is symptomatic of finance theory, then it can be regarded as either frustrating or exciting, depending on your point of view!

10.6   Dividend procedures

There are two polar procedures possible: 100% retention and 100% distribution. Both have their advocates. The 100% retention is justified on the grounds of taxes and transaction costs. The 100% distribution is put forward as a corporate control mechanism to force companies to submit their investment plans for market approval. Neither of these approaches tends to be followed in practice except that, as we shall see, dividend reinvestment schemes are a variant of the 100% retention procedure.

What we have illustrated so far is the difficulty of developing any dividend policies for an enterprise never mind an optimal policy. Despite the considerable degree of uncertainty surrounding share price determination, the management of the enterprise still has to make decisions and live with them.

If we rule out the two polar views, though not the reinvestment plans, then financial managers are still left with deciding on a mix of dividends and retentions. The procedures that have emerged are the result of either:

1. taking a particular share valuation model as valid, and developing a policy from that; or
2. ensuring that the procedure chosen does not run counter to observed general patterns of stock market behaviour, given the possible clientele effects and signalling aspects of dividends/retentions.

In both cases, given the objective of shareholder wealth maximization, the enterprise should only pay a dividend if the ex-dividend price plus the amount of the dividend is not expected to fall below the price prior to the announcement of the dividend. (For further development of this, see Porterfield, 1965).

(a) Constant or steadily increasing cash dividends per share

Some companies have been observed to set a constant monetary amount of dividends and pay this through 'thick and thin'. As Lintner (1956) argued, managers perceive that shareholders prefer a steady stream of dividends and therefore set a target pay-out ratio and adjust to that period by period. Thus instead of adopting an equilibrium level of dividends, given a particular year's or quarter's earnings, the enterprise is willing to attempt to smooth dividends in line with a long-run equilibrium pay-out. Once more we cite the Chowdhury and Miles (1987) study for evidence of their smoothing. Reference to the Workbook will indicate the impact of various economic 'shocks' to the firm on dividend policies (see Tables W10.2 and W10.3).

Thus we can think of an enterprise establishing a permanent dividend stream in line with its long-run sustainable earnings. Increases and decreases in the dividend which can be thought of in terms of transitory changes will then convey positive or negative information content. As referred to previously, because of the Trustee Investments Act (1961) which has a dividend test rule of five years these financial managers are probably reluctant to cut dividends completely. If there is a marked discrepancy between earnings and dividends in a given period (transitory income), then Lintner found this to be *the* most important determinant of dividend decisions. Thus, as Fama and Babiak (1968) have argued, the enterprise can then increase (or decrease) dividends if it feels that these earnings are now 'permanent', but there will be a lag. An examination of the time series data on dividends and earnings will illustrate that they do not fluctuate in the same manner.

As we have observed already in this book, the economy and therefore enterprises in it experience a cyclical tendency, and the ability to maintain stability of income may prove attractive to some investors (clientele effect) and may produce less price volatility in the share. If this cyclical movement has an upward path, then enterprises may be tempted to increase their dividends once the upward trend is assured. The enterprise can still maintain a target pay-out ratio, but can supplement the actual payment in lean times and increase the target once it is assured of growth subject to any statutory controls. However, if this stability is preserved in nominal terms then, with inflation, the real value will fall. The 1970s saw high inflation rates that eroded the 'real' value of dividends (for a discussion of dividend policy and inflation, see Kirkman and Nobes, 1976). Currently inflation rates are low, so real returns to investors can generally be positive.

(b) Constant pay-out ratio

A small number of enterprises will follow a policy of paying out a constant percentage of earnings. As the latter vary, although the ratio may be constant, the cash value will fluctuate. This will not help shareholders wishing to maintain a stable flow of dividends; nor will it help enterprises, as they will also face a fluctuating residual.

(c) Low interim plus final

As dividends in Britain are paid semi-annually, this gives financial managers some flexibility with respect to the timing of the dividend. An enterprise may declare a low interim hoping to follow with a higher final once it has a better picture of its earnings. Once more this can be fitted into the stability of dividend policy, though in the USA and Canada enterprises pay quarterly dividends. The whole question of how investors will regard the signal contained in an interim dividend is an interesting topic and is one of the many facets of the Coats Patons case in the Workbook.

(d) Government policy on dividends

We mentioned at the outset that dividends have a public interest aspect and that government policy has affected the dividend decision. This policy, when it has been utilized, has had a two-pronged approach to encourage investment and to counter inflation in the economy.

(i) Encouraging investment
Because governments have been concerned with the supply of capital to industry and the need to maintain and increase investment to promote economic growth, they have sought to assist in a number of ways. They have utilized policies of limiting the pay-out by statutory controls and taxation to encourage retention; they have utilized investment incentives in the form of grants and tax incentives; and they have at times controlled the access to the capital markets.

We shall examine some of this interaction briefly. Controls on the capital markets were retained into the 1950s once the more rigorous wartime controls were relaxed. While these controls were not the only cause of 'excess' liquidity in business enterprises in the 1950s and of the consequent takeovers, the fact that many enterprises did pay increases up to the legal maximum even where there had been a substantial decline in earnings is perhaps evidence of an attempt to maintain the purchasing power of dividends (see Ferris, 1962). It cannot have helped, nor can it have produced optimal investment in the economy, since the literature substantially agrees in condemning dividend regulation as an inefficient and ineffective way of regulating savings. For instance, the cash built up does not guarantee fixed investment and its efficient allocation, and could be used to acquire shares in other companies or to buy them outright.

(ii) Countering inflation

The 1960s saw the other facets of government policy become important. *Prices and incomes policies* developed, of which dividend control was often seen to be an essential element. During these incomes policies, dividends were at times 'controlled', with the last period of controls lasting for seven years ending in 1979 and restrictions on the size of increases being at three different rates — 5%, $12\frac{1}{2}$% and 10%. Although these policies are no longer in effect, the fact that they have been used in the past is an indicator that, notwithstanding their apparent overall failure (see, for example, Parkin *et al.*, 1973), they could nevertheless be resurrected. The evidence available on their effect finds that they did impose a binding constraint. The Chowdhury and Miles (1987) study referred to earlier found, contrary to the accepted view that companies paid what was legally permissible (perhaps more than they would have liked), that payments were reduced 'by 20% on impact leading to a 40% reduction on average over the longer term' (p. 264). The removal of controls in 1979 resurrected the problem for managers of deciding how much to distribute, and there is evidence to suggest that some firms started to adjust their payments of dividends to pay off a backlog, with the adjustment complete by 1984. (The taxation aspects of government policy have been treated already — see pp. 262–4).

In summary, government controls cannot guarantee an optimal allocation of earnings between dividends and retentions. They tend to block market controls, both at the level of the enterprise, which with a lower pay-out has more cash and less screening from the market, and at the macro level where the capital market cannot allocate funds on the criterion of efficiency.

10.7 Alternative policies

(a) Dividend reinvestment

In some countries, such as the USA, there are schemes for the automatic reinvestment of dividends in the enterprise similar in form to scrip dividends (see below). These are taxed as if the income had been received, but they have the advantage of lower costs. The shares supplied can be either new issues, sometimes at a discount, or outstanding shares purchased by a trustee from the market. If they are new issues of shares, then it is a way for an enterprise to raise new equity finance.

This approach can also improve the enterprise's relationship with existing shareholders. By offering a choice of dividend reinvestment or cash dividends, enterprises can cater for differing clienteles. They resolve the issue for the enterprise and place the onus on the shareholder. If, however, through time we see a preference for one or the other, then we may have to re-examine the question of the importance or otherwise of dividend policy.

(b) Non-cash dividends

As well as the payment of cash dividends, there are non-cash dividends which offer management a greater flexibility.

(i) Share dividends

In our discussion of the EMH (Chapter 3) we referred to share dividends and stock splits and showed that, although investors receive nothing of additional value, the use of these instruments may have an effect on the value of the enterprise. Once more the issue of tax is raised here, for the use of share dividends can save the company ACT. (An example of this is Cadbury-Schweppes, which offered shareholders a cash dividend or a scrip dividend. The former would have cost £22.3 million with an additional £9.1 million ACT. But share issues would have involved the enterprise in issuing 14.9 million new shares, increasing its share capital by 2.87%.)

Share dividends (scrip dividends) are used by some enterprises on a regular basis to replace or supplement cash dividends. They result in a shift within the capital funds (the shareholder equity) from retained earnings to equity capital. The net share price after the issue of the new shares will be prorated down so that the market share should remain unchanged, and the proportion of ownership of course also remains unchanged. The company may use these as a means of keeping the price of the share in what it considers a marketable range. In the United Kingdom, these scrip issues were used in part as an attempt to circumvent dividend controls under prices and incomes policies. Their main use, however, was to avoid tax (see the previous section), particularly for family controlled companies. This was very quickly stopped by taxing the scrip as if the amount had been distributed. However, this could be achieved (and more normally is) via share splits — and even reverse share splits — if the financial managers felt that the unit share price should be higher.

(ii) Share repurchases

Share repurchases are an alternative to cash dividends and are used more irregularly. Permission for UK companies to purchase their own shares came late (in the Companies Act 1981, since consolidated into the Companies Act 1985). They have been a feature of the US scene for many years, and are commonly used there. They are not part of dividend policy *per se*; rather they are regarded by some as investment or financing decisions. They are used to purchase shares for share option plans of employees, for companies going private, for enterprises avoiding a hostile takeover, or merely to reduce the number of issued shares and thus permit the enterprise to distribute excess cash to shareholders and hence produce a change in its capital structure. Just as increasing the number of issued shares results in dilution of earnings per share, so this does the reverse.

The effect on the enterprise of repurchase is to reduce its cash and to establish an asset account called 'treasury shares'. In the USA there have been some very sizeable cases of share repurchase. For example, IBM bought back $713 million and Gulf Oil $338 million. Shareholders need not take part in the repurchase, and not all shareholders may even be offered the option, but there are implications of this, particularly if the price paid, say, by tender or by a large share purchase from an institution or other large holder is greater than the previous current market value, thus placing the remaining shareholders at a disadvantage. There are tax implications for shareholders, too, as only the capital gain (if any) is taxed and not the total proceeds of the sale, whereas cash dividends are taxed at the investors' effective tax rates. They can thus be attractive to high marginal taxpayers.

10.8   International dimensions of dividend policy

For multinationals, a wider set of considerations is applicable to the dividend decision. Instead of just considering the payment of dividends to their shareholders in the parent country, multinationals operate subsidiaries in host countries and the payment of dividends is the most important way by which funds are transferred from the subsidiary to the parent. Zenoff (1967) identified three factors which would appear to determine the dividend policy of US affiliates in Europe. These were *tax, political risk* and *foreign exchange risk*:

1. The tax regime in the parent and host country will differ, and of particular relevance will be that operating in the host country (though bilateral tax treaties will often be present). There may be withholding taxes on dividends or there may be agreements operating as a result of the location of the plant in special economic zones. There may also be differential taxes on dividends and retentions. So, just as tax affects the normal dividend decision, the further dimension of international tax implications is added.
2. One reason for investing overseas is to produce international diversification and reduce risk. One of the risks is political — the chance of the appropriation of plant, the imposition of exchange controls and the uncertainty in the economy caused by political change. Because of the exchange risk the dividends in the hand of the parent are to be regarded as more desirable, although policies of this kind are not independent of political factors — they may precipitate the action they are avoiding.
3. As for foreign exchange risk, the volatility of currency rates that has occurred since the breakdown of the Bretton Woods system in 1973 has produced a clear need for rate forecasting. As intracompany dividends are an important source of income to a multinational, it has to take into account that these will be expressed in a currency other than that of the parent country. Although the enterprise can protect itself via the various instruments available in the foreign exchange markets (forwards, futures and options), the amounts and timing of these dividends has added significance because of the foreign exchange risk.

Summary

In summary, Lintner's thesis as to the importance of dividend continuity still holds today, thus supporting the notion that dividend pay-out affects share prices, even if we do not know why, other than that they may minimize agency and monitoring costs for investors and thus circumvent problems of asymmetric information. As the maintenance of share price is important to financial managers, dividend policy follows as an important restraint and we cannot assume that the subdivision of earnings into dividends and retentions is of no importance. Empirical evidence is mixed. From the survey data it would appear that managers are aware of signalling and clientele effects, and thus we find that we can explain the *aggregate* level of dividends by taking the current level of earnings and a lag. We end up with a smoothed relationship.

This is, however, at the macro level. when we come down to the industry or enterprise level, we still find it difficult to develop a predictive model. If stability of dividends is found in an enterprise, it is the result of the managers setting a target in line with their forecasts of long-run earnings. This so-called permanent dividend hypothesis may have a small transitory element if events really do change dramatically. Once a clear trend has emerged in long-run expectations, the enterprise will then change its dividend policy.

We can summarize this chapter as follows:

1. There are two fundamental questions: can management influence the value of the enterprise through its dividend policy; and what factors more generally govern the dividend decision?
2. The Gordon model is not much help to us for, although it gives a basis for valuing an enterprise through dividend growth, there are compensating factors in that increasing D_1 will decrease the future growth rate.
3. A key factor is *information asymmetry.* Managers know more about the internal situation of the enterprise than outsiders, and the dividen announcement will thus be taken as a signal by management to outsiders (since direct information may not be trusted).
4. Some have argued that dividends are irrelevant anyway because, for a given risk level, earnings within the enterprise will tend to be the same as earnings outside the enterprise by shareholders receiving the dividend and acting on their own. This is, however, a model that only holds under certain unrealistic assumptions (though it can form the basis for more complex theorizing).
5. Some argue that dividends should be high because shareholders like high dividends and, indeed, have a right to the dividends so they can dispose of them as they wish. This is linked to the 'bird-in-the-hand argument', that it is less risky to the shareholders to return the profits to them.
6. An alternative argument is that dividends should be low, with maximum retention, because this can reduce taxes and transaction costs. As a result, the shareholder will in the long run be better off.
7. A further strand of the argument is that some shareholders will prefer high pay-outs, others low pay-outs because they are in different positions as regards tax and liquidity preference. This is generally known as the clientele argument: it implies that companies should select a particular pay-out policy and stick to it.
8. All this may in any case be at the discretion of the company since dividends are politically visible and may be the subject of restrictive government policies, either through forced reinvestment for wealth purposes, or as part of anti-inflation packages.
9. Dividends other than cash can be made — for instance, scrip dividends.
10. The situation for the multinational is more complex still because of differential taxes, political risks and exchange risks among the countries in which it deals.

Key terms and concepts

Here is a list of the key terms and concepts which have featured in this chapter. You should make sure that you understand and can define each one of them. Page references to definitions in the text appear in bold in the index.

- Signalling
- Incentive signalling
- Residual earnings theory
- Bird-in-the-hand argument
- Clientele effect
- Neutral tax system

- Discriminatory tax system
- Information content (of dividends)
- Abnormal trading
- Abnormal returns
- Scrip dividend
- Treasury shares

Further reading

Original readings can be recommended here. The classic paper by Miller and Modigliani (1961) is still well worth reading, particularly since it is far more elegantly expressed than more recent and fashionable papers. A popular but eccentric view (from the standpoint of modern finance theory) can be found in Rubner (1966). Judge it in the face of the arguments you have been presented with here. A delightful and accessible summary of the Chicago approach can be found in the popularization by Miller (1986). Finally, you should try to understand the latest approaches by working through at least some of the recent literature: for instance, Litzenberger and Ramaswamy (1979) and Miller and Scholes (1978).

The Workbook material to accompany this chapter begins on p. 564.

11 Cost of capital and capital structure

Learning objectives

After studying this chapter you should be able to:

- understand how to calculate the specific cost of capital for bonds, preferred shares and ordinary shares;
- appreciate the concept of the weighted average cost of capital;
- know the difference between book and market values;
- outline the problems that a divisionalized enterprise structure can bring;
- understand the concept of the capital structure of the enterprise from both an empirical and a theoretical standpoint;
- appreciate that differing costs of capital across countries can give a competitive advantage to those companies that can access 'cheap' funds.

11.1 Introduction

(a) Link to previous chapters

In Chapters 8 and 9, where we looked at short-term, medium-term and long-term financing, we saw that we could classify capital sources into external and internal. In Chapter 10 we saw the interrelationship of the investment and dividend decisions. Like any other factor of production, capital, whether it be working capital or permanent capital, has a cost associated with its use. In our discussions of capital budgeting, we used the concept of the cost of capital. When calculating the NPV it was the rate of discount; and when using the IRR it was the hurdle rate with which we compared the IRR of a project to determine rejection or acceptance. This was done in a world of assumed certainty where the cost of capital is *the* market rate and the profit-maximizing enterprise will only accept those investments with returns greater than this. This cost of capital is an explicit one, but when we accept one investment, there is an opportunity cost expressed in terms of the next best investment, i.e. the investment forgone. So there is an implicit cost of capital too.

But we have also observed that, in a world of certainty with only the market rate, our assumptions were so restrictive as not to permit any investment with greater than zero NPV. So more realistically we have to cope with an uncertain world, yet we still have the same guiding principle — *the maximizing of the shareholders' wealth*. However, we cannot say with any degree of accuracy what an investor would freely pay for a particular investment, whether short or long, because we cannot say with any degree of assurance what the future flows of benefits will be for a given investment decision taken.

This chapter will attempt to unravel the difficulties that surround the cost of capital and the capital structure decision. These are critical decisions as in the past 20 years there have been very rapid changes in the economic environment that faces firms and it is important to study the impact of these on the corporate sector and how the latter has adapted. The sector swings between financial surplus (e.g. 1971–3, 1975, 1977–8 and from 1981 to date, with particularly large surpluses after 1983) and deficit (e.g. 1974, 1976, 1979–80). Inevitably the impact of this is felt on the short-term financing decisions before it affects longer-term financing and the capital structure. Evidence examining the impact on dividend policy and strategic debt is presented in Chapter W10 and readers are now recommended to examine the effects on debt of a series of parameter changes — gross profits, investment, financial assets, tax payments and interest payments.

In Chapter 10 we raised the issue of tax exhaustion and the widespread nature of this at some time in the life of many companies. The Chowdhury and Miles (1987) study covered the period to 1984. Since then the number of tax-exhausted companies has fallen (see Bank of England, 1987). We found that, with a policy of dividend smoothing, an adjustment lag was present. Inevitably tax exhaustion affects the incentive to use debt and therefore affects both the cost of capital and capital structure.

Paradoxically, perhaps, we shall have a lengthy discussion of the MM–traditionalist debate which is anchored in a world of certainty, because this has been a critical area of debate in the literature. Then we will switch to the real world and show how difficult it is to handle the issue in the presence of uncertainty. In a sense what we are doing is to recognize that the debate took place over a long period of time, but then bypass it, acknowledging that there is no general agreement following in the footsteps of the 'new finance' theory as developed in the 1970s.

(b) Design of this chapter

The structure of this chapter, then, is as follows:

1. In section 11.2 we briefly look at the concept and constitution of the weighted average cost of capital. This is a result of combining the costs of the various sources of capital.
2. These particular sources are analysed in section 11.3.
3. Having ascertained ways of calculating the cost of each individual source, we move on in section 11.4 to see how they are combined — that is, how they are weighted.
4. The fact that differences across countries exist in respect of cost of capital is raised in section 11.5.
5. All of the above has applied to the enterprise as a whole. In section 11.6 we turn to the constituent parts of all major enterprises, namely divisions, and the cost of capital for these.
6. Then, in sections 11.7 and 11.8 we look at the capital structure controversy. This is concerned with the optimal capital structure, and whether such a thing exists. In this sense it is similar to the dividend argument, since there are schools of thought that suggest it matters, and schools that argue it does not.

11.2   The weighted average cost of capital (WACC)

In the introductory section above and in Chapter 10, we stressed the linkage between the investment decision of the enterprise and the enterprise's value. We have argued that the enterprise has to accept projects which on average provide (expected) returns greater than its cost of capital to maximize the shareholders' wealth. This cost of capital is the minimum acceptable rate of return on *new* investments and can be calculated as a weighted average cost of the sources of new finance raised. So if we know the cost of debt (k_d), the cost of preference shares (k_p) and the cost of equity (k_e) then k_o — the overall cost of capital — is expressed as:

$$k_o = x_1 k_d + x_2 k_p + x_3 k_e \tag{11.1}$$

where x_1, x_2, x_3 are weights and sum to 1.

With this basic (and intuitively reasonable) model in mind, we turn to look at the way to find the cost of each of these sources of capital.

11.3   Cost of specific sources of capital

In Chapter 8 we identified the three external sources of long-term or 'permanent' capital of the enterprise as *bonds, preference shares* and *ordinary shares,* and the two internal sources of long-term finance as *retained earnings* and *depreciation charges*. We recognize, however, that there are alternative sources too from the public sector and from the use of leasing, etc. In this section we will analyse the specific cost of capital of each of these three external and two internal sources, though we stress now that even to commit oneself to a particular value is the result of numerous assumptions, which in itself shows the difficulties and delights of the whole operation.

(a) Cost of bonds

Long-term debt in the form of bonds costs the issuing enterprise interest payments. As we saw in Chapter 8 the bonds can be issued at a discount, at a premium or at par. The interest payments will generally be semi-annual and they are tax deductible (provided, of course, the enterprise is profitable). The value of this tax deductibility of interest costs to the firm is a function of the level of interest rates (the coupons contracted for the current level which would have to be paid on new issues), the rate of tax (and we have already made mention of the cut in corporate tax to 35% in 1986) and the tax position of the firm. Tax exhaustion, we have already said, reduces the incentive for debt finance. Devereux (1987) examines this issue in depth and is recommended for those readers interested in this particular aspect. The Bank of England (1987), in its survey of the corporate sector 1970–86, points to the emergence of more companies from tax exhaustion and therefore to a greater incentive to debt, notwithstanding the reduction in the tax rate itself.

After adjusting for the tax, the cost of debt (k_i) is therefore:

$$k_i = k_d(1 - T) \tag{11.2}$$

where k_d = before-tax cost (if the bond is issued at par = the coupon rate)
  T = the corporate tax rate.

So if there is a corporate tax of 50% and the before-tax cost equals 15% obtained from the current market rates for equivalent risk, etc., then k_i =

7.5%. The existence of this tax deductibility has a dramatic effect, in this case halving the cost of debt. But this is the cost of *new* debt. The existing debt coupons and interest costs are not relevant other than in their seniority of claim on assets and therefore enter into the assessment of the risk and coupon given. There would, of course, be flotation costs of this debt, but these are also tax deductible.

So to calculate the *before-tax* cost we need to take the bond evaluation method (see Workbook, pp. 587–91) and solve for the expected cost to maturity, substituting the net proceeds (after flotation costs, sale at discount or premium on par value, etc.) for the bond's market value following the Hawanini and Vora (1982) method of yield approximation:

$$k_d = \frac{I + \left(\dfrac{P - NPD}{n}\right)}{P + 0.6(NPD - P)} \qquad (11.3)$$

where I = annual interest (£)
P = par value
NPD = net proceeds from the sale
n = number of years to maturity
0.6 = a constant used in the approximation following the Hawanini and Vora approach.

Although the debt is a cheaper source of finance to the enterprise, what the shareholders have effectively achieved is the purchase of a *call option* from the bond-holders. (*Reminder:* Chapter W8 gives a brief overview of option pricing.) In issuing the debt and mortgaging the assets, the shareholders can recover the assets by paying off the debt. For the case of a liquidation, shareholders can simply walk away from the debt of the enterprise, including the debt to the bond-holders. In this respect the shareholder is exercising a *put option* on his or her assets. So to determine the before-tax cost, k_d, we have either the method discussed in Chapter 8, section 8.4, to value this return or we can use option pricing. Using the latter, we can obtain the riskless or default-free rate of return from equivalent government bonds and then value this put option. The exercise price of the latter is the cost of keeping the bond from default. The interest and principal payments and the maturity of the put are the same as that of the debt, so:

Market value of bond = Market value of default-free bond − Value of put

and:

Market value of bond = Asset values − Value of call on assets

So by assessing the value of puts and calls of an enterprise you are in a position to value debt and therefore place a value on the marginal cost of debt capital. Of course, what is possible in theory poses problems in practice and it is beyond the scope of this book to go further on this aspect.

(b) Cost of preference shares

The cost of preference shares is identical to the case of bonds except that, as we saw in Chapter 8, the final income (dividend) that companies have to pay to the holders is *not* tax deductible so that:

$$k_{\mathrm{p}} = \frac{D_{\mathrm{P}}}{NPD} \qquad\qquad (11.4)$$

where D_{p} = annual cash dividends paid on preference shares
NPD = net proceeds from the sale of preference shares.

(c) Cost of equity

Calculating the cost of capital for debt and preference shares was comparatively easy because they had a fixed income element. Though the riskiness of
the bonds clearly revealed problems and both are subject to price volatility,
the CAPM can be applied to estimating their costs too. But for equity capital,
which has no requirement to pay a dividend and which is, as we have seen,
the true permanent capital of the enterprise, we have a real difficulty in
producing accurate estimates. Yet we recognize the importance of having
them. Shares, by sharing in the good (and bad) features of the enterprise, are
necessarily more volatile than fixed income securities. Shareholders have to
form *expectations* as to the future value of the enterprise and its risk.

The cost of retained earnings will be formed on the same basis as that of
equity more generally, since retained earnings are shareholders' funds. After
all, the opportunity cost of retaining the past earnings of the enterprise is the
dividend forgone by the shareholders. However, costs differ for retained
earnings and new issues. We begin with retained earnings.

(i) Retained earnings

There are now a number of approaches to equity valuation. Two that have
reached prominence in the theoretical literature of recent years are the option
pricing approach of Black and Scholes (1973) and the arbitrage pricing model
of Ross (1976). For a number of reasons, not the least of which is the problem
of specification (for the Ross model in particular), we shall omit these and
instead consider three other approaches to estimating the cost of equity
capital for retained earnings/internally generated funds:

1. bond yield plus a risk premium;
2. dividend valuation model;
3. CAPM.

We will take these in order.

1 The bond yield method This method is very subjective. It takes the bond
valuation formula given in the Workbook (p. 587–90) and adds to it a margin
for the risk of equity. This can be used for the enterprise that has shares which
are not traded and/or that does not pay a dividend.

2 Dividend valuation method The dividend valuation method of Gordon (or
the DCF method as it is often referred to) is used widely. It was covered in
Chapters 5 and 10, but for the sake of completeness we reproduce the model
below:

$$k_{\mathrm{e}} = D_1/P + g \qquad \text{or} \qquad P = \frac{D_1}{k_{\mathrm{e}} - g} \qquad\qquad (11.5)$$

where D_1 = expected dividend
P = value of share
g = expected rate of growth (constant) on dividends.

Typically texts have assumed that the dividends are paid once a year and therefore the numerator D_1 would be the cash dividend expected one year from now. This is strictly incorrect as dividends in the UK are paid semi-annually, so the appropriate dividend to use would be the next one that is to be paid (see Beedles, 1984). The problem with this approach for the United Kingdom is that the interim and final are often seen as being related, so that an enterprise may pay a low interim followed by a higher final. For the USA, this would generally not be so, and the effect of the quarterly payment frequency cannot be ignored.

3 **CAPM** The CAPM (see Chapter 7) uses the security market line to show the relationship between the shareholder's required return (k_{ej} — the cost of existing equity capital) and the enterprise's systematic risk. Thus the k_{ej} will equal the risk-free rate plus a risk premium:

$$k_{ej} = R_f + \beta_j(E(R_m) - R_f) \tag{11.6}$$

where k_{ej} = enterprise j's equity cost of capital
       R_f = risk-free rate (e.g. Treasury bill rate)
       β_j = systematic risk or beta of the share, j
       $E(R_m)$ = expected market return, e.g. FT all-share index (this can be obtained by using *ex post* data or approximated by taking the Treasury bill rate and adding to it the historical risk premium of shares over bonds).

To summarize the three approaches we provide a numerical example in Fig. 11.1.

The shares of XYZ plc are sold for £10 each, the dividends to be expected (annual) are £1 and the expected annual growth rate in dividends is 8%. The bonds have a yield of 14% and the risk premium for shares has been estimated at 3%. The risk-free rate is 10% and the market return 8%. The beta of XYZ has been estimated to be 0.75. Using these data we can estimate the various estimates of k:

k_e (BYM)   = 14% + 3%   = 17%
k_e (DCF)   = 1/10 + 0.08   = 18%
k_e (CAPM) = 10% + 0.75(18% − 10%)= 16%

So we have three divergent estimates for the retained earnings.

Fig. 11.1   Three approaches to estimating cost of equity capital for retained earnings.

(ii) New issues
We now turn to the cost of new ordinary shares. These are identical to the cost of retained earnings except for the adjustments that arise from the mechanics of the issue. In selling new shares (see Chapter 8), companies incur expenses — flotation costs (F) and 'underpricing' at the sale. If we assume these issue costs are 5%, then if a share is sold for £10 the net proceeds of the sale $P(1 - F)$ will be £9.50. If we take the dividends and growth rate of XYZ provided in Fig. 11.1, then, adjusting for the flotation costs, the k_e rises to 18.05:

$$k_e = [D/P(1 - F)] + g \tag{11.7}$$
$$= [1/10(1 - F)] + 0.08$$

which constitutes a small increase of 5 basis points. But the more significant factor (as we saw with the rights issue) is the reduction in the share price resulting from the sale of the shares.

The usual approach to this is simply to lump the price reduction in with the flotation costs. So, if the price reduction were 10%, then we would have a total value of F of 15% with the result that k_e rises to 19.8%. The problems we have here are severalfold. We raised in Chapter 8, section 8.6, the issue of price pressure and rights issues and found empirical evidence against the institutional view of underpricing. We can go further than this if we argue that the use to which the funds have been put and the risk have not changed, merely the financing package. So why should we change the discount rate? However, as we have argued in the case of the rights issue, the effect is neutral: there is neither a loss or a gain, so that apart from flotation costs, which are small when taken across the whole equity base of the enterprise, the cost of new issues and retained earnings can be taken to be identical.

(d) Cost of depreciation

The inclusion of depreciation as a specific source of finance raises divergent views. A depreciation charge may be considered to be a means of maintaining capital intact so the enterprise can survive as a long-term entity, and depreciation provisions through time recover the original capital outlay which was itself financed by equity or debt or some combination of the two. They are neither debt nor equity finance in themselves. The provisions are thus bookkeeping entries to record this capital maintenance programme, and they can at times be very significant items in a sources and uses statement. Although they do not appear on the liability side of the balance sheet, they are not costless to the enterprise.

Instead we can regard their cost as being equal to the WACC, but note that they are *not* included in that calculation. This assumption is reasonable if the enterprise is maintaining the proportions of its sources of capital that are relatively constant through time, so that the cost of the provisions is an opportunity cost equal to the WACC. Of course, the enterprise is not obliged to maintain its equity capital including accumulated reserves, and it could distribute the accumulated provisions, thus slimming itself down in size.

11.4 The proportions used

Equation 11.1 utilized weights to establish an overall cost of capital (WACC). We still have to discuss the issue of capital structure, and we have hinted already in this book that the enterprise may well have a long-run target or optimal capital structure which is set as part of its overall operations (although circumstances may prevent the enterprise from achieving this).

Nevertheless, it may attempt period by period to adjust to its optimal balance sheet structure. Chapter 8 illustrated this quite fully. Of course, when we examine the financial statements of an enterprise we are not aware of the desired structure (the asymmetric information argument), though if there has been an apparent historical stability, we could infer that this is an optimal position for the enterprise. We may, therefore, use this *ex post* assessment *ex ante*. But we are still faced with the thorny issue of *market* versus *book* values as a basis for fixing the relative weights of the sources of capital. At times they do coincide, but there is no reason why they should. After all, we have argued throughout the book the difficult and slippery nature of valuation.

The case for *book values* is that the data are publicly available in the financial statements. In other words, the accounting numbers are telling us something! They also give relative stability to the weights calculated as they will not be subject to the volatility of interest rates etc. which will affect bond and share valuations. But beyond that we cannot really make a case for book values, though we recognize that they are still used extensively.

If we consider *market values*, then we are removed from the shackles of accounting numbers which will include such items as sunk costs (defined and discussed in *Managerial Accounting: Method and Meaning*, Chapter 4) and can focus on what is relevant *today* in a decision to invest in an enterprise or buy its bonds. This must be market returns and therefore market values, so that in calculating the WACC we need to use not only the current market rates (adjusted for any tax effects, for example, on bonds) but the proportions based on a market valuation. To produce these values is a little tedious, though a good calculator or microcomputer can easily handle the bond valuations. The frequency of the changes can be onerous: each time there is a price movement in shares or debenture stock this can produce a fluctuating set of market values which can lead one to wish for the more stable book values, despite the conceptual correctness of market values!

However, our argument would be that as they are conceptually correct we should not be deterred, and should therefore normalize the value to obtain a more operational set of values for use in calculating WACC. If financial analysts find it difficult and tedious to use these values, what of ordinary investors? Given that they have in front of them the financial statements or public information which contain book values, might we not conclude that if they use these to measure the financial risk of the enterprise (which we shall cover in more detail later in this chapter) then we have a case to resort to book values?

As market values fluctuate so much, it is difficult to think of financial managers being able to maintain an optimal capital structure, even if they wished to. Broad market movements that affect bond prices, and therefore yields and share prices, are beyond their control. If managers feel that there are bounds to these movements, then they may rely on a homoeostatic process and permit the gearing to fluctuate without the need to intervene. However, the limit of the upper bound will be 99.9% debt financing, which, as we shall see in section 11.8, may not be the desired upper level of management given the bankruptcy costs — or, indeed, one that the market is likely to permit. They are likely to set a lower target level which is consistent with an upper bound which is still below or even well below the liquidation limit. Then, if the bound is exceeded, corrective action can be taken to retire debt, float more equity or whatever.

In concluding this section on book and market values, we suggest that the safest method is to calculate both and highlight the divergence, if any. However, our argument would still be that market values must ultimately be used to calculate the WACC. A worked example of weighted average cost of capital is given in Fig. 11.2, based on both book and market values.

11.5 Differing costs of capital internationally

In the previous section we detailed the make-up of a cost of capital estimate, using the constant sources of capital, and in Chapter 2 we outlined the nature

On 31 December 1987 Fahy plc has a balance sheet that looks like this:

Various assets	£2,900,000

Represented by:	
1,600,000 shares of 25p issued and fully paid	400,000
11% preference shares	500,000
Share premium	400,000
Retained earnings	900,000
8% debentures 1995	700,000
Total	£2,900,000

You are given the following additional information:

The beta of Fahy's equity is estimated to be 0.85. The bonds were subject to issue costs of 6.5% of their face value. The issue expenses of the preference shares were 5.5%. Currently short-dated Treasury stock yields 9%, and historically the yield of equities has on average been 7.5% above the risk-free rate. Corporation tax is currently levied at a rate of 35%. Each £100 of the debenture issue is currently selling at £89 in the market; likewise the price of a £1 preference share is 96 pence. Each 25p equity share is quoted at £1.10.

Step 1
First we find the cost of each source of funds.

For equity we shall use CAPM:

$$k_e = 0.09 + 0.85[(0.09 + 0.075) - 0.09]$$
$$= 0.15375$$

Preference shares:

$$k_p = 55,000/(500,000 \times 0.945)$$
$$= 0.1164$$

Bonds:

$$k_d = \frac{56,000 + \left(\dfrac{700,000 - 654,500}{8} \right)}{700,000 + 0.6(654,500 - 700,000)}$$
$$= 0.0917$$

From which must be deducted the tax like this:

$$k_i = 0.0917 (1 - 0.35)$$
$$= 0.0596$$

Step 2
Next we must look at applying the weights which each source of capital bears to the total. We do this by setting out the percentage weights and applying these to the costs of each source. We shall first do this by means of book weights.

For equity we may combine the nominal value of the issued capital, the share premium account and the retained earnings, since all are effectively shareholders' funds.

For the other sources of capital the book value is straightforward. We then get the following calculation:

Source	Book value £	%	Cost of capital	Weighted cost
(1)	(2)	(3)	(4)	(3) × (4) × 100
Equity	1,700,000	58.62	0.15375	9.013
Preference	500,000	17.24	0.1164	2.007
Debt	700,000	24.14	0.0596	1.439
	2,900,000	100.00		12.459

This gives a WACC of about 12.5%. In fact, taking column 4 to the precision we have constitutes *spurious accuracy* given the estimation problems. We give it, however, for the sake of clarity in the example.

Now we repeat the exercise by weighting in terms of market values:

Source	Market value £	%	Cost of capital	Weighted cost
(1)	(2)	(3)	(4)	(3) × (4) × 100
Equity	1,760,000	0.615	0.15375	9.456
Preference	480,000	0.168	0.1164	1.952
Bonds	623,000	0.218	0.0596	1.297
	2,863,000	1.000		12.705

It will be seen that the result of 12.7% is close to but not the same as the result when weighting by book values.

Figure 11.2   Worked example of WACC.

of the UK financial system. Despite the moves to integrate financial markets, both within Europe and globally, differences in financial environments can militate against complete integration. The net result is that there appear to be structural factors which give rise to competitive advantage to some countries, such as Japan and West Germany.

The UK, along with the USA and Canada, for example, has a *capital market-based* financial system with funds allocated by market prices, whereas West Germany has a *credit-based* system dominated by *financial institutions* and Japan a *credit-based* system with *government-administered prices* (see Zysman, 1983). In the case of West Germany, a close customer relationship exists between banks and corporations where banks often take an equity position in a firm. In terms of our discussions in Chapter 1, this raises interesting agency issues. In Japan there is a clear national policy for development and cheap capital provided from a high savings ratio and from such institutions as the Post Office Savings Bank. Not only are costs of capital lower in West Germany and Japan, but firms have been permitted higher levels of gearing (leverage) because they are being freed from the vagaries of a financial market. It also permits firms there to take a longer view with respect to their investment policies. Although the issue of 'cheap' capital relative to 'dear' capital countries has been around for many years, a recent study by McCauley and Zimmer (1989) provides important empirical evidence. Not only do they conclude that there is indeed a lower cost of capital in Japan, but by breaking the cost of capital down into its constituent parts, they find that the advantage to Japan is both in debt and equity, whereas in the case of West Germany it is only debt. They also utilize a more rigorous weighting system for debt and equity. The data they provide (see Table 11.1) of cost of capital estimates are for various projects and take into account investment tax credits and depreciation allowances, as well as discounting the after-tax cost of funds. If we focus, say, on R & D projects with a ten-year pay-off, then the UK's cost of capital of 23.7% in 1988 is nearly three times that of Japan (8.7%); Germany, with 14.8%, still has a strong competitive advantage over both the UK and the USA.

Table 11.1   Cost of capital for various projects

	1977	1978	1979	1980	1981	1982	1983	1984	1985	1986	1987	1988
Equipment and machinery with physical life of 20 years												
United States	11.2	11.7	11.2	11.5	13.5	11.5	10.6	11.3	11.1	9.1	10.2	11.2
Japan	5.9	6.9	7.6	8.8	8.8	8.5	8.8	8.4	8.3	7.8	7.0	7.2
Germany	7.7	7.3	7.5	8.6	8.8	7.8	7.0	7.2	7.1	6.9	7.0	7.0
United Kingdom	8.8	10.8	9.8	12.7	10.3	10.7	10.8	9.3	9.4	7.8	8.2	9.2
Factory with physical life of 40 years												
	1977	1978	1979	1980	1981	1982	1983	1984	1985	1986	1987	1988
United States	10.0	10.4	8.9	9.3	10.1	12.4	10.8	12.8	12.6	9.3	9.0	10.2
Japan	2.8	4.2	5.1	6.2	6.8	6.6	7.0	6.3	6.1	5.8	4.8	5.0
Germany	5.5	5.5	5.6	7.0	7.4	6.3	5.4	5.7	5.5	5.2	5.4	5.4
United Kingdom	6.7	9.9	7.8	12.2	7.7	8.7	8.8	7.6	8.3	6.1	6.6	7.9
Research and development project with 10 year pay-off lag												
	1977	1978	1979	1980	1981	1982	1983	1984	1985	1986	1987	1988
United States	12.5	12.9	11.9	12.4	8.3	18.4	15.2	20.3	20.2	16.8	18.2	20.3
Japan	3.9	5.7	6.5	7.3	8.0	8.3	8.7	7.7	9.2	9.4	8.4	8.7
Germany	13.4	13.8	13.3	15.6	15.7	14.7	13.9	14.6	13.9	13.2	14.4	14.8
United Kingdom	18.2	28.4	21.1	33.4	24.2	29.5	29.2	24.4	25.4	18.9	20.6	23.7
Expensed item with physical life of 3 years												
	1977	1978	1979	1980	1981	1982	1983	1984	1985	1986	1987	1988
United States	39.5	40.6	42.4	43.3	38.5	40.5	39.3	39.6	39.1	36.7	39.4	40.4
Japan	35.0	35.1	35.4	36.4	36.1	36.0	36.0	35.7	35.6	35.3	34.8	34.9
Germany	34.7	34.7	34.7	35.4	35.6	35.1	34.7	34.8	34.8	34.6	34.7	34.8
United Kingdom	39.4	40.6	41.4	42.5	40.5	40.0	39.6	38.4	37.7	36.1	37.0	37.4
Land												
	1977	1978	1979	1980	1981	1982	1983	1984	1985	1986	1987	1988
United States	10.5	11.1	8.6	9.6	12.6	15.3	12.5	16.1	15.8	10.4	9.3	10.6
Japan	−5.6	1.3	3.2	4.4	7.0	7.8	8.4	6.6	6.0	6.5	4.8	5.4
Germany	3.1	3.7	3.0	5.5	5.6	4.6	3.7	4.6	3.8	3.0	4.3	4.7
United Kingdom	6.8	14.2	9.6	17.8	11.7	14.6	12.5	9.7	9.2	5.4	6.2	7.7

Source: McCauley and Zimmer, 1989.

Although these data appear to provide a stark confirmation of the 'cheap' and 'dear' capital countries, the assumptions that lie behind these estimates are critical. We would therefore urge students interested to read the original article, which covers the treatment of investment incentives and depreciation. The reason for this is that the authors go on to study the reasons for the differences and, although the high saving rates and close relationships that exist between governments, banks and firms are important, a major factor in their view is differences in rates of inflation and tax regimes.

11.6   Divisional cost of capital

The enterprise of neo-classical economic theory which produces a single product is typically not found in public companies today. The normal product life-cycle requires organizations to diversify in order to survive and grow. With often widely different product lines, the 'risk' as measured by the variability of earnings will not be the same within the enterprise. These intra-organization risk differences impact on the acceptance of new projects. In reviewing this the enterprise cannot just assume that each project will approximate to the overall risk of the enterprise, though presumably if sufficient were undertaken, the process of diversification would eliminate some of the total risk present in each project. The enterprise may be adding to its existing areas of operation or broadening into new areas. Generally the well-diversified organization will have a divisionalized structure — or 'M' form, as it is often referred to (see, for example, Williamson, 1970). The separate activities may compete for company funds such that the organization has an internal capital market of its own.

If an enterprise were to use a single cut-off or hurdle rate to evaluate capital projects in the face of differential risk, then something similar to Fig. 11.3 could occur. Use of a single discount rate (weighted average cost of capital) as a hurdle rate will reject projects that should have been accepted (e.g. project A) and accept projects that should have been rejected (project B). Project A has a higher return than the capital market line would suggest that a project of equivalent risk should command. The use of the single discount rate thus ignores the low risk in relation to the return, focusing instead on the lower return *per se*. Project B is accepted because its return is higher, yet comparison with the CML indicates that its return is below a comparable market return for the risk taken. It will thus lead to the under-allocation of funds to low-risk divisions and over-allocation to high-risk divisions.

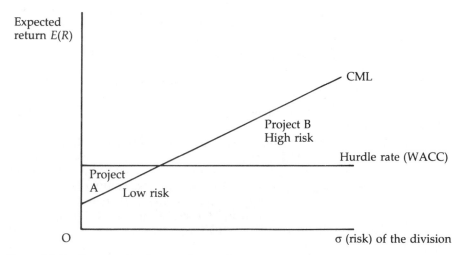

Figure 11.3   Divisionalized cost of capital.

The concept of fine-tuning the cost of capital to reflect the divisional risk is very appealing, but problems immediately arise. If the divisions traded as separate entities, then we could actually obtain objective measures of their risk by utilizing the CAPM and estimating their betas so as to come up with estimates of the equity cost of capital. Strictly speaking, we should do the same for the debt capital. In the absence of these, how can we estimate these risks? We have to use a little ingenuity and attempt to proxy these by finding a surrogate. The usual method is to identify one or more publicly quoted companies that are similar in product line and capital structure. We can also make use of the appropriate industry grouping from the stock exchange index. A measurable surrogate could be an individual enterprise, or the average of a group of enterprises or the index of the sector. Once decided, we can then obtain the beta and use this in the calculation using equation 11.6. We can then adjust this for the financial risk in the enterprise (assuming that the surrogate beta has the equivalent amount of debt) and this can be entered into the WACC for the division. But we cannot assume that the proportion of debt to equity will be the same in each division, so the adjustment to ungear the beta can vary by division.

11.7   Capital structure

We referred in Chapter 8 to the concept of capital structure of the enterprise, and we noted that there were substantial differences in structure between enterprises of different sizes and industries. Large enterprises appeared to be willing and able to accept higher gearing ratios than smaller enterprises. If we refer to a rather dated, but still important empirical study by Meeks and Whittington (1975) that was referenced in Chapter 8, we see that their findings illustrate the benefits which large companies have derived from debt financing. The 'giants' (top 100 companies) achieved their higher growth rates using external funds to a greater extent than 'the rest', and the capital market was thus willing to supply relatively more finance. The explanation offered by Meeks and Whittington is that the giants achieved a more stable performance over time, which you would expect through the diversification of assets: they made losses less frequently and they were able to operate at higher gearing levels. The average rates of return on equity capital stood comparison with the rest rather better than the return on net assets. The giants' high gearing may thus have helped their equity performance although Modigliani and Miller would, as we shall see, regard the benefit as compensation for financial risk. Furthermore, if one considers the tax exemption of debt interest (see section 11.8 of this chapter), it is apparent that these relatively highly geared companies have been able to derive direct benefits in the form of a lower proportion of income paid in tax.

More recent evidence (Bank of England, 1987) points to a debt ratio just over 20% (measured as net debt to capital base) for the period of the late 1960s and early 1970s. Interestingly, the Chowdhury and Miles (1987) study found that, for the period 1969–84, smaller companies increased their gearing while larger companies decreased theirs. In part this is explained by the overall financial surplus in the sector, reducing the need for external financing, particularly among the larger firms.

11.8   Capital structure theory

We have raised the multi-faceted issues that impact on the capital structure of firms and this calls for a modelling approach to the financial behaviour of enterprises. The financing mix — the subject of Chapter 8 and 9 — is one such approach, and this needs to be developed further in terms of the optional use of gearing and the capital-budgeting decision of the firm. In this section we shall examine the components of capital structure and then discuss the difficult issue of valuation.

What we have tried to stress throughout this book is that, although we can think of the enterprise in the context of a conventional comparative static framework in which the enterprise attempts to achieve equilibrium solutions, and in the context of this chapter, say minimizing the cost of capital, we are really perceiving the enterprise in a *dynamic* framework. In this respect we have an interdependence of decisions, both investment and financing, where the enterprise has constraints on these decisions both internal and external. It cannot freely switch its asset or liability structure around. Rather it uses its flows — the sources and uses of funds — to bring about changes in desired variables.

The capital structure of the enterprise is usually viewed in terms of permanent or long-term capital. Earlier in this chapter (pp. 276–80) we reviewed the *costs* of debt, preference shares and equity capital, and in Chapter 8 we examined their characteristics. What emerged from our earlier discussion was the apparent relative cheapness of debt capital. The question immediately springs to mind: why not use 100% debt financing? This is meant to be a rhetorical question, though given the issue we have raised earlier, tax exhaustion and the volatility of earnings, the answer is fairly obvious!

The issue of which proportion of each to use requires us to raise the issue of 'risk' again — the risk of the stream of returns (EBIT or NOI) generated by the normal operations of the enterprise. Earlier discussions focused on enterprise-specific risks which we identified as being *business or operating* risk from the type of business the enterprise is in, and *financial* risk from the gearing of the enterprise. So the enterprise in its capital-budgeting decisions impacts on the business risk, and the level of that risk at any moment in time is the result of those past decisions. The gearing issue is one of using *fixed cost* financing, which increases the variability of earnings that are available to shareholders, and thus increases the risk of bankruptcy borne by the owners. This means that cheaper debt is good news and bad news together, and an example in the Workbook (pp. 593–6) will seek to illustrate the effect of gearing on the distribution of the enterprise's EPS. Expected return is raised by introducing debt, but so too is the risk.

As we have stated repeatedly, the objective of business enterprise is taken to be shareholders' wealth maximization. Hence, in terms of capital structure, the question of an *optimal* structure relates to the combination of debt and equity that might minimize the enterprise's cost of capital and simultaneously maximize its market value. But we use the word *question*, and indeed the theoretical debate on the cost of capital has been one of the most notable in the finance literature. It has focused on two polar views — the traditional view and the Modigliani–Miller (MM) view — though inevitably we can detect middle ground between these two extremes.

In the *traditional* view, the cost of capital is a function of the capital structure such that the overall cost of funds can be reduced by a judicious use of debt finance. This also implies that there exists an optimal level of gearing which will minimize the cost of capital and therefore *inter alia* maximize the market value of the enterprise. An increase in gearing beyond this point will cause the average cost of capital to rise (because of the increased financial risk), giving rise to a U-shaped cost of capital function. That is, if a graph is drawn with the cost of capital on the vertical axis and the gearing level on the horizontal axis, then the function will be U-shaped. This viewpoint is entirely consistent with the neo-classical economic theory of the enterprise.

The other polar view is that of *Modigliani–Miller*, namely that in a no-tax world there can be no gearing effect on the market value, i.e. the cost of capital is independent of its gearing because *the advantages of using the cheaper debt are exactly offset by the disadvantages* (increased financial risk) *of that increased debt*. The introduction of corporate taxes, though it modifies the analysis, still does not produce an optimal capital structure.

(a) The traditional viewpoint

The traditional view of the use of gearing in capital structure utilizes a number of simplifying assumptions which, although they might appear restrictive, do not in fact stand in the way of the essentials of the argument. Rather, by holding many variables constant, they allow us to isolate the effects of changing gearing. The assumptions are:

1. no taxes, corporate or personal;
2. 100% dividend distribution;
3. a no-growth enterprise (i.e. a given investment strategy);
4. only debt and equity used in the capital structure;
5. no transaction costs, including those involved with a default of the issued bonds (bankruptcy costs);
6. constant business risk over time (i.e. the expected value and variance of EBIT is constant);
7. the increase/decrease in gearing occurs through the simultaneous issue and retirement of securities (i.e. an issue of equity is matched by a retirement of debt)

Starting from a 100% equity capital structure, then, there are three stages in the market reaction to the increase of gearing, although these stages can be smoothed to form continuous rather than kinked curves. We measure gearing as a ratio of the market value of debt to the total market value of the enterprise (market value of debt plus market value of equity).

In *stage 1* the use of low-cost debt more than offsets the increase in the equity capitalization rate, k_e. The latter rises because of the financial risk the gearing brings (see pp. 594–7 in the Workbook for a worked illustration of this). The bond-holders, too, are unlikely to require an increase in their coupon rates for the modest increase in gearing, so k_d is likely to remain constant (as is portrayed in Fig. 11.4(b)) and if it increases, it will do so only marginally. The overall effect then is that k_o — the weighted average cost of capital — will fall and the market value of the enterprise (P_T) will rise (Fig. 11.4(b)). Its components are derived from the market value of debt and equity.

In *stage 2* the enterprise has now attained a degree of gearing, and as this increases further, the additional financial risk requires k_e to continue to rise, but now the bond-holders require additional compensation in the form of

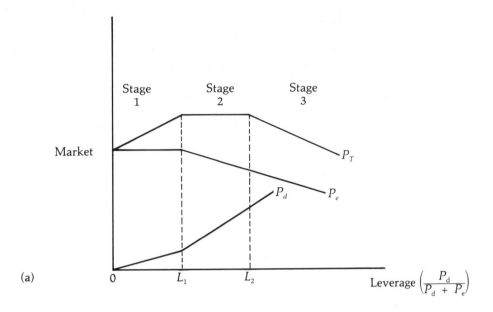

(a)

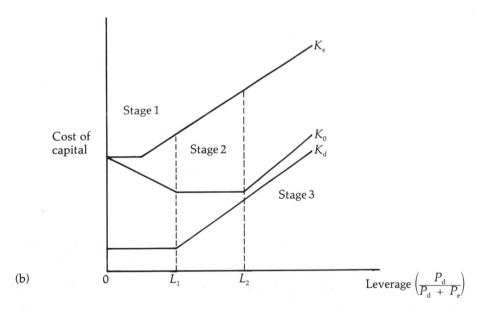

(b)

Figure 11.4 Traditional approach to capital structure: (a) market values of the firm for different levels of leverage; (b) cost of capital of the firm for different levels of leverage.

higher coupons and a discount on the issue price of the bond. If the relative cheapness of the debt is still able to cancel out the additional financial risk, then we can have a constant k_o (and correspondingly constant P_T). However, this may not be the case and the k_o may have a unique minimum, i.e. be U-shaped, and the market value of the enterprise a unique maximum. In this latter case, stage 2 does not really exist and the enterprise moves from stage 1 to stage 3. Figure 11.5 illustrates the U-shaped k curve and the optimal capital structure with optimum gearing, L^*.

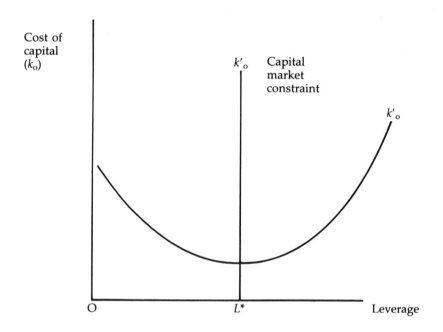

Figure 11.5 The optimal capital structure.

In *stage 3* further increases in gearing result in an increase in k_o and a decrease in the value of the enterprise.

So we can summarize:

1. k_d, the cost of debt, remains constant or relatively constant for the small or moderate case of gearing, but increases as the gearing becomes larger;
2. k_e, the cost of equity, remains relatively stable for low levels of gearing, but then increases;
3. the overall cost of capital, k_o falls and either levels and is constant or is U-shaped;
4. there is an optimum level or point of gearing (L^*) which will simultaneously maximize the value of the enterprise.

The clear conclusion from the above is that if enterprises do not use gearing and, if they do, that they are not tax exhausted to do so, then the shareholders are losing out. Presumably the latter are aware of this and once more the *agency* issue is raised as shareholders will pressure managers to adopt more gearing up to the optimum. Managers, on the other hand, may not be willing to oblige as they may be more risk averse and, as we have argued before, cannot diversify that risk whereas shareholders can. This is certainly true for institutional shareholders, though they have the ability to exert pressure on financial managers. The existence now of a large number of small investors who are not diversified adds a further dimension.

Whether stage 3 actually exists in practice is a matter of conjecture. The capital market and/or the prime debt-holders could set a constraint; that it is actually at L^* in Fig. 11.5, the optimal level of gearing, is unlikely given our discussions in Chapter 9 as to the difficulty of maintaining equilibrium relationships. However, theoretically it should be. This could cause k_o to be steeply rising and, if the constraint is binding, vertical. We show this in Fig. 11.5 with k_o' vertical.

We now turn to the Modigliani–Miller (MM) approach, which has two cases — the no-tax world and the with-tax world.

(b) Modigliani–Miller — no tax

MM's first study in 1958 excluded tax, but offered a theoretical argument with accompanying empirical validation which supported the view that the market value of the enterprise *and* its cost of capital are independent of the degree of gearing. This one paper was a landmark on the finance literature, and although modified in their second paper (1963) and developed and refined by others, it still demands attention and recognition today.

We can portray the MM approach in Fig. 11.6. We can observe from Fig. 11.6(b) that, as gearing increases, k_d remains constant and k_e rises immediately, but as the cost of debt (k_d) is lower than the cost of equity (k_e) the two offset one another so that we end up with a constant k_o. Thus there is *no* effect on the value of the enterprise (Fig. 11.6(a)) as the market value of debt rises (since more debt is issued) and market value of shares falls (since shares are retained).

The MM argument is contained in three propositions.

(i) Proposition I
The cost of capital and market value of an enterprise are independent of its gearing. Their proof of this is to capitalize the expected EBIT or net operating income at the rate k_o. How this is determined is a topic in itself, but it could be handled by normalizing the past data for EBIT. EBIT is assumed to be constant and is divided between bond-holders and shareholders. The former will receive $k_d P_d$, and the latter the residual, EBIT $- k_d P_d$, in dividends:

$$P_T = \frac{\text{EBIT}}{k_o} = P_e + P_d$$

and:

$$k_o = \frac{\text{EBIT}}{P_T}$$

(ii) Proposition II
The introduction of debt in the form of bonds into the financial structure (in practice, the debt would include preference shares and lease obligations) immediately increases the financial risk to shareholders, who require a premium to compensate. This exactly offsets the apparently lower cost of debt

Market value

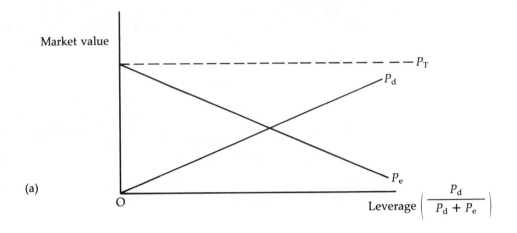

(a)

Cost of capital

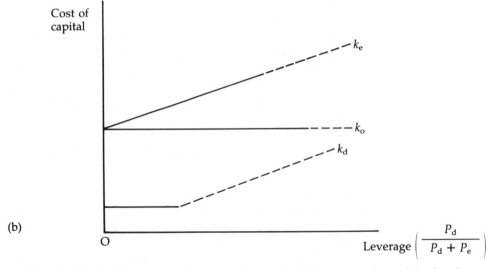

(b)

Figure 11.6   The MM approach to capital structure: (a) market values of the firm for different levels of leverage; (b) cost of capital of the firm for different levels of leverage.

and leaves k_o and P_T constant. As the debt is introduced, the market value of equity is given by:

$$P_e = \frac{\overline{\text{EBIT}} - k_d P_d}{k_e}$$

and the equity cost of capital by:

$$k_e = \frac{\overline{\text{EBIT}} - k_d P_d}{P_e}$$

We know from proposition I that $\overline{\text{EBIT}} = k_o(P_e + P_d)$, and therefore, through substitution, we can obtain:

$$k_e = \frac{k_o(P_e + P_d) - k_d P_d}{P_e}$$

and:

$$k_e = k_o + (k_o - k_d)\frac{P_d}{P_e}$$

The latter expression means:

> The expected return on the equity of an enterprise is equal to the expected return on a pure equity stream (see below) plus the financial risk premium proportioned by the ratio of debt to equity.

By 'pure equity stream' (k_o) here MM mean the return there would be on an enterprise without any debt at all, and we saw already in proposition I that this was independent of the amount of debt. This is, then, a straightforward linear function that increases the expected equity return linearly with the level of debt financing.

(iii) Proposition III

Projects to be accepted will have to have a rate of return (k^*) greater than or equal to the overall cost of capital k_o. To achieve the above, the MM hypothesis rests on an *arbitrage process* that exists in the simplified assumptions adopted. So if there are two enterprises X and Y, each with the same EBIT, they must be valued equally, whether the payments are made to shareholders or debt-holders. If they are not, then arbitrage profits can ensue.

We can show this with an example which appears in Dobbins and Pike (1982) and which is consistent with the example outlined in the Workbook in Table W11.1, p. 593. We can see from Fig. 11.7(a) that Z is 100% equity enterprise, Y has 20% debt and X has 80% debt. Their EBITs are identical. The market values of the enterprise differ. This contradicts MM: according to them, it is an irrationality that investors can exploit.

An example is given in Fig. 11.7(b) which takes a hypothetical investor in enterprise X with 1,000 shares. He earns £600 in income as the £120,000 cash flow for equity of Fig. 11.7(a) is distributed over 200,000 shares. He sells the shares for a total consideration of £4,000 (each share is worth £4). Then he takes on the same gearing (*home-made* gearing, we call it) as enterprise X by borrowing £16,000.

The investor now has £20,000 to invest which is placed in the shares of Z, paying £1.333 per share (15,000 shares). The investor receives £3,000 return on the equity and has to pay £1,600 in interest (assuming a 10% cost of capital). This leaves an income of £1,400, an increase of £800 or 75%. How can shareholders ignore such gains, you might ask. Of course, if they all recognized them and acted accordingly, the gains would disappear and the prices of the identical enterprises would be equal – the MM hypothesis. In other words, MM's argument revolves around the tendency for investors to do exactly that. They will perceive the profit to be made by using home-made gearing, and will undertake arbitrage processes until a new equilibrium is reached at which such arbitrage profits cannot be made. This is, of course, the stage at which the market values of the three enterprises (X, Y and Z) are all the same, regardless of gearing.

(a) Overvaluation of Firms A and B:

£000s	X Ltd 20E/80D £000s	Y Ltd 80E/20D £000s	Z Ltd 100%E £000s
Equity (£1 shares)	200	800	1,000
Debt (10% interest payable)	800	200	–
	1,000	1,000	1,000
Cash flow from trading	200	200	200
Less: Interest on debt	80	20	–
	£120	£180	£200
Equity market capitalization rate 15%			
Market value of shares	800	1,200	1,333
Market value of debt (par)	800	200	–
Market values (from Workbook)	£1,600	£1,400	£1,333

(b) Arbitrage to restore equality of values:

A shareholder owns 1,000 shares in X Ltd.

	£
Present income (all cash flows paid in dividends) 1,000(0.6)	600
	4,000

Step 1
He can sell for 1,000 (800/200) and borrow in the same proportion
and at the same rate as X Ltd (1:4)

	16,000
	£20,000

Step 2
He buys shares in Z Ltd: $\dfrac{20,000}{1.3333} = 15,000$ shares.

New income 15,000 (0.20)	3,000
Less: Interest at 10% on £16,000	1,600
	£1,400

He has increased his income by £1,400 – £600 | £800

A second shareholder owns 1,000 shares in Y Ltd.

Present income (all cash flows paid in dividends) 1,000(0.225)	225
	1,500

Step 1
She can sell for 1,000 (1,200/800) and borrow in the same proportion
and at the same rate as Y Ltd (4:1)

	375
	£1,875

Step 2
She buys shares in Z Ltd: $\dfrac{1,875}{1.3333} = 1,406$ shares.

New income 1,406(0.20)	281.25
Less: Interest at 10% on 375	37.50
	£243.75

She has increased her income by £243.75 – £225 | £18.75

Figure 11.7 Home-made leverage and the arbitrage process to restore equality of market values of firms.

Yet although, in the simplified world of perfect markets etc., we can think of these *arbitrage* models bringing about such an equality, in practice this will not be the case. To mention a few problems only:

1. We have to assume the equivalence of corporate and personal gearing. They may not be the same given the different legal status of the two sectors: for example, limited liability of enterprises.
2. Can we identify enterprises like X, Y and Z, group them together and think of them as identical?
3. Can individuals borrow at the same rate as companies? The answer is no, since, as we know, banks have base rates and load these with premiums for different classes of borrowers.
4. What of the tax shield available to enterprises but *not* to individuals? (This issue will be taken up in the MM hypothesis adjusted for tax below.)

Of course, these imperfections can limit the arbitrage process, but this does not destroy the essential message of the MM argument, that an arbitrage mechanism can exist. Whether it can work fully, though, depends on the degree of imperfection.

(c) Modigliani–Miller – with tax

The basic MM propositions change when corporation tax is brought into the picture because interest payments on debt qualify as an expense when corporation tax is being assessed. In other words, the greater the proportion of debt finance, the smaller the tax bill. Distributions to equity-holders do not bring any tax relief; indeed they accelerate the payment of corporation tax under the imputation system. At a 35% tax rate, the real cost of debt is only two-thirds of the coupon rate (i.e. the annual interest payable to debt-holders) because of the effect on the company's tax bill. This influences the propositions of the MM theorem because equity-holders no longer require quite such a large premium for a given degree of gearing (proposition II), and the reduction in the tax bill does effectively lower the cost of capital so that the latter is no longer independent of gearing (proposition I).

To calculate the presence of this tax shield – which is really a government subsidy on valuation – we return in the Workbook (pp. 593–6) to our three companies X, Y and Z, and illustrate how the market value will rise for the levered enterprises. So the MM after-tax view is similar to the traditional view that the cost of capital declines with gearing, except that they do not recognize an optimal point. Indeed, the use of debt in their after-tax model is even more dramatic as *there is no optimal level or point*. We can summarize the Modigliani–Miller approach before and after corporate tax in Fig. 11.8. There is the horizontal (before-tax) and falling (after-tax) overall cost of capital (k_o).

Shareholders will require managers to increase debt levels in the enterprise, but this tax shield has its limitations. The cut in 1986 in the UK corporate tax rate to 35% (from 50%) made a significant reduction in the value of the shield overnight. But more cogently, as we have argued earlier in this chapter, the tax shield is only of use to enterprises that pay the tax. Many enterprises do not, and if enterprises do use the debt and enter the market together, they will drive up the cost of the debt.

Nevertheless, the implication of not having an apparent theoretical limit on gearing levels and the pressure that shareholders can in theory bring on managers to increase gearing and thus their wealth has produced a solution both in the empirical and the theoretical world.

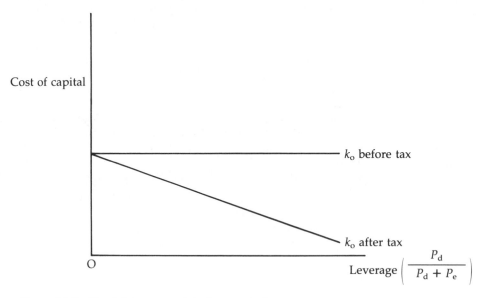

Figure 11.8 The MM approach before and after tax.

In practice the financial world has tended not to have extreme debt to total asset ratios but to use crude rules of thumb or guidelines to handle the judicious proportion of debt. For example, 'the proportion of debt must not exceed one-fifth of total financial assets' (measured either at book or current market value), or 'interest payments on debt must be covered four or five times by earnings'. Each case should, of course, be treated on its merits. Companies with stable profits, those which own highly marketable assets and those with sales covered by contractual agreements can reach higher gearing levels than their counterparts operating in unstable markets or involved in lease obligations.

For example, companies in the multiple retail business, e.g. breweries and restaurant chains, often have substantial freehold premises that can be used as collateral for debt finance (mortgage debentures). On the other hand, oil companies typically have substantial lease obligations which impair their credit status and reduce debt-raising capability. The traditional point of view is perhaps still worth heeding in that, if the use of debt finance by a company is not judicious but is carried to excess, its whole livelihood can be threatened, and this will be reflected in its market valuation as investors discount its earnings more heavily. The theoretical literature takes two different views on this. On the one hand, Warner (1977) argues that the value of the tax shields may still outweigh the bankruptcy costs; on the other hand, Haugen and Senbet (1978) argue that these costs are not relevant to the capital structure decision but only to the corporate liquidation decision.

More mainstream, however, is the approach (see Kraus and Litzenberger, 1973; Kim, 1978) which analyses the situation with respect to the potential liquidation of the enterprise if it cannot generate enough cash from its operations to meet its fixed cash obligations. This possibility of liquidation and the effect measured in monetary costs can be illustrated as in Fig. 11.9. The sort of liquidation or bankruptcy costs we are referring to are legal costs

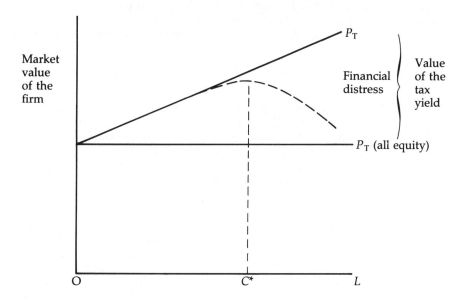

Figure 11.9 The MM approach after tax (but with bankruptcy costs) — the effect of leverage on the market value of the firm.

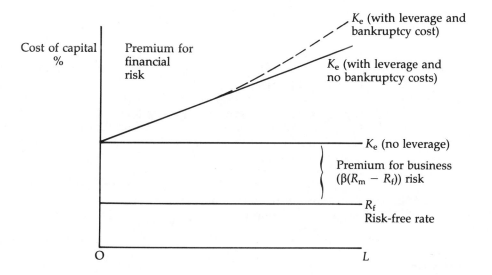

Figure 11.10 The MM approach after tax (but with bankruptcy costs) — the effect of leverage on the equity cost of capital.

and opportunity costs incurred from the interruption of business, etc. These costs are deadweight losses and cannot be eliminated, and as Fig. 11.10 shows, they increase the shareholders' required rate of return (k_e). So that now:

k_e = Risk-free rate + Premium for business risk + Financial risk + Bankruptcy risk

The impact of these bankruptcy costs differs between shareholders and managers. The former can benefit from the gearing up to the brink of bankruptcy, then sell out (if they can) and leave the bond-holder and other creditors to secure what they can from the assets of the enterprise. As we have argued previously, they too can diversify their risk of loss. The managers want to avoid bankruptcy as they would lose the security of their employment, and they will feel a responsibility for other interest groups in the enterprise too, particularly the employees.

Returning to Fig. 11.10, what we can observe is that there is indeed an optimal capital structure *and* a maximized value of the enterprise. This arises because of the tax shield. The continuity of that shield is removed by the presence of the financial risk discussed earlier. It is not gearing *per se* which is the real culprit here; rather it is the cyclical nature of the earnings which cannot support the gearing, and earlier we referred to the switch between financial surplus and deficit of the whole sector that can occur within a year. The later 1980s have, however, been a relatively profitable period for the sector and can support high gearing. In addition, the debt market itself, both within the UK and abroad, has recovered somewhat to be in a position to supply the funds.

Financial managers have a difficult tightrope to walk. They want to maintain the survival of the enterprise to protect their security. They therefore have to be careful not to allow the share price to fall to a point which makes the enterprise an attractive proposition for a takeover raider. To avoid this the enterprise can engage in various activities to load up the debt and/or load up the assets with ones of questionable security. Increasingly shareholders have become more vocal too, in putting pressure on financial managers, including action through the courts, to operate the enterprise in *their* best interests.

So even this theoretical development has its problems in seeking to explain the co-existence of debt and equity in a world of tax shields. And we can add to this the fact that shareholders gain from gearing in times of high inflation, which many countries have faced in the 1970s. The prior claim of debt capital is fixed in *nominal* terms so that the real return to debt-holders may fall, whereas equity-holders have a chance of being compensated, at least in part, for the decline in the value of money, particularly as the annual debt charge will, through the years, assume less and less importance and will be out of line with payments on recently negotiated debt if there has been a general rise in interest rates.

Summary

In this chapter we have illustrated the calculation of the cost of capital for the various specific possibilities of the enterprise as well as the overall weighted cost of capital. We have cautioned against the use of the latter for divisionalized organizations, arguing instead for the use of the CAPM to take into account both risk *and* return.

In Chapter 9 and Chapter W11 we have shown that enterprises raise both debt and equity, but typically do not have high gearing ratios. We tried to explain this through the theoretical framework available. We found that the traditional view pointed to the use of gearing to increase the market value of the enterprise up to an optimal point. This point would be market determined, and indeed if there is a binding constraint, the enterprise may have no opportunity to increase its gearing further even if it chose to do so. The MM approach, whether before or after corporate taxes, did not have an optimal capital structure, and therefore in theory an enterprise could push its gearing to 99.9%. In the before-tax world there is no effect on market value, but after tax the total tax market value of the enterprise increases indefinitely until the limit is reached of 99.9% gearing.

Without a natural stopping point, the MM approach clearly has difficulty accounting for the relatively low level of gearing experienced, unless bankruptcy costs are included. The argument here is that increased levels of gearing bring potential financial distress to the managers of the enterprise as they fear bankruptcy. Shareholders too may not perceive it in the same way, so we have an agency problem. Shareholders will demand more debt calls directly or through a modified arbitrage process. Financial managers may have to take more personal risk, which is non-diversifiable, to accommodate the wishes of shareholders. However, the latter have to incur agency costs to police the managers, and therefore the managers, even in the presence of asymmetric information, can have a level of gearing below that which shareholders may wish to maintain. The conservatism of financial managers is not just to protect their own security; they may feel a responsibility for the workforce too, so as to protect *their* security. Of course, at the point of bankruptcy, shareholders stand behind the debt-holders and other creditors to recover their retained earnings. Assuming that managers can get their way, we thus have an optimal capital structure on the lines of the traditional approach, and thus a co-existence of the two approaches.

Another explanation for the relatively low levels of gearing is that, if we use market values to value gearing, then with the increased volatility in interest rates and movements in the stock market, the gearing rates will fluctuate to accommodate the upward and downward movements in the gearing caused by these external factors which are outside the control of the individual enterprise. Indeed, if the debt is raised externally in a currency other than the domestic one, then unless the enterprise has some of its earnings in that currency it has a foreign exchange risk (see Chapter 8) and must take account of the volatility of exchange rates too.

Financial managers may well hold a target level of gearing which they regard as safe *within* the parameters that they think the market will move. If the level actually achieved is way off line, they can then step in and attempt to increase the debt or equity, or retire debt, or whatever is feasible. With these fluctuations in market values and the relative stability of book values we are aware once more of the difficulty of actually valuing an enterprise.

Thus we may summarize the whole chapter as follows:

1. The cost of capital, which was central to the capital-budgeting problems we looked at in Chapter 4 is best understood through the concept of the weighted average cost of capital. This acts as a pivot between financial stake-holders (shareholders, bond-holders, etc.) because it results from the interaction between the enterprise and the stake-holders in the markets,

and then gives a signal to the management as to the appropriate hurdle rate for investment.

2. It is found by taking the cost of each source of capital and weighting each by the appropriate proportion.

3. This proportion may be based on either book weights or market weights. The latter is to be preferred in principle, but may present considerable practical difficulties.

4. Turning to the *capital structure* problem, we found that there were two main approaches: the traditional and the MM (and post-MM) approach.

5. The traditional approach supposes that there is an optimal level of gearing: not too much and not too little debt mixed in with the equity.

6. The MM first approach (without tax) shows that, under perfect market conditions, the gearing level does not affect the value of the enterprise.

7. Since then it has been shown that, because of the tax shield, it should pay the enterprise to maximize its debt. However, this simple prescription is tempered by two factors. One is that, if all enterprises turned to debt in this way, they would force up the price of debt. The other is that liquidation costs have to be taken into account, together with the differential ability of shareholders and management to diversify their risks.

Key terms and concepts

Here is a list of the key terms and concepts which have featured in this chapter. You should make sure that you understand and can define each one of them. Page references to definitions in the text appear in bold in the index.

- Weighted average cost of capital
- Pure equity stream
- Home-made gearing
- Tax exhaustion

Further reading

We may begin by repeating that it is always desirable to go back to the original sources. The quality of argument in Modigliani and Miller's 1958 paper is exemplary. Look also at their 1963 correction. Miller's presidential speech to the American Finance Association (Miller, 1977) is already on the way to becoming a classic, and (believe it or not) is all but free of mathematics.

The Workbook material to accompany this chapter begins on p. 586.

PART

4 Overview and summary

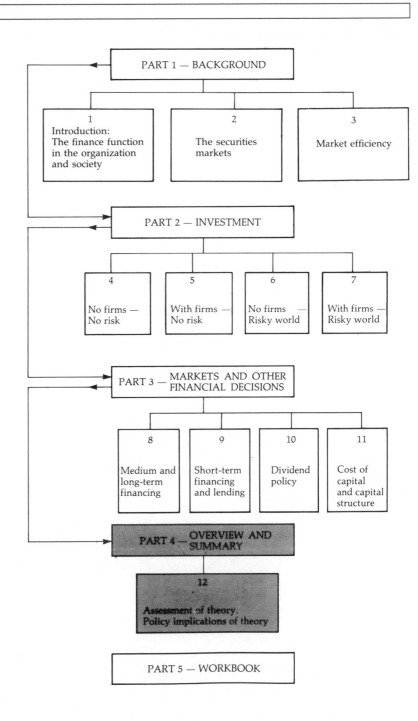

PART 1 — BACKGROUND

| 1 Introduction: The finance function in the organization and society | 2 The securities markets | 3 Market efficiency |

PART 2 — INVESTMENT

| 4 No firms — No risk | 5 With firms — No risk | 6 No firms — Risky world | 7 With firms — Risky world |

PART 3 — MARKETS AND OTHER FINANCIAL DECISIONS

| 8 Medium and long-term financing | 9 Short-term financing and lending | 10 Dividend policy | 11 Cost of capital and capital structure |

PART 4 — OVERVIEW AND SUMMARY

12 Assessment of theory. Policy implications of theory

PART 5 — WORKBOOK

Part 4   Introduction and overview

Part 4 consists of just one chapter. The body of the text has combined an attention to description both of the tasks of the financial manager and of the markets in which he/she is obliged to deal, and to theory concerning the ways these do — and should — operate. That theory has in the main been drawn from the considerable body of knowledge known as modern finance theory.

In this last part we consider in particular the limitations of the earlier parts, and the likely future that enterprises may find themselves in, in the light of current developments.

12 An assessment and a projection

Learning objectives

After studying this chapter you should be able to:

- reassess the nature of the problem of the financial manager;
- recap on the nature of modern finance theory, its supposed solution to the financial manager's problem and the way it has been used in this book;
- consider the weaknesses of this approach as a means of understanding the workings of the financial markets, both those stemming from its assumptions and those stemming from the testing of its conclusions;
- outline some possible implications of our conclusions about theory and practice as a whole for policy decisions in financial management.

12.1 Introduction

It is tempting, having worked through the knowledge that we have accumulated about the area of financial management, to conclude that it is a subject that is essentially concerned with enterprises and with markets. Most of the theorizing and virtually all the evidence has been developed in the context of the enterprise in the market. Our discussions of most of capital budgeting, of two-parameter theory, of efficient markets, of short-, medium- and long-term financing instruments, have all been couched in this context. Yet this would be misleading.

As we have emphasized, financial management is in the end concerned with the financial side of the more general organizational and economic problem. The economic problem is concerned with the configuration of wealth and income in society: it is concerned with economic growth and economic distribution. The organizational problem arises both from the economic problem and from the more general social problem of which the economic question is just a part, namely the way people relate to each other and to nature.

The separation of ownership and control that leads to the existence of the enterprise, to the multitude of financial instruments that are available and to the markets in which enterprises employ financial instruments is just a stage, albeit an important one, in the development of capitalist society. As a variety of people have recognized, from Marx on the one hand to libertarian economists on the other, capitalism is a remarkably powerful and resilient social structure for organizing social relationships and encouraging growth — albeit frequently with less fortunate social consequences that may or may not (depending on your political beliefs) arise from the intrinsic nature of the system itself.

In this concluding chapter we shall:

1. begin by going over the conclusions we have reached in the central chapters of this book;
2. revisit the structure and problems outlined in the introductory chapter; and
3. look more broadly at the future for enterprises, the financial management function and the financial markets.

12.2   The framework of modern finance theory

Modern finance theory (MFT) is a relatively recent development. It arises from a small number of, in many ways, separate developments. Notable ones are:

1. the development of modern portfolio theory by Markowitz, first published in 1952;
2. the findings of Kendall (1953) that there seemed to be no pattern in the movements of share prices (this had been noted by Bachelier for commodity markets at the turn of the century);
3. the challenge to the received folk-wisdom that capital structure could affect the enterprise's value by Modigliani and Miller in 1958 (and their later challenge to similar beliefs about dividends too);
4. the construction of the capital asset pricing model by Sharpe, Lintner and Mossin in the 1960s;
5. the creation of option pricing model by Black and Scholes in 1973, which laid the foundation for the expansion of both theory and practice in options trading.

In future years, we may look back to see Ross's arbitrage pricing theory and agency theory in the same light.

As a result of these disparate developments, a massive literature has arisen that has not just succeeded to some extent in bringing the threads of these theories together (particularly in the name of efficient markets) to integrate what were previously separate areas (see Rubinstein, 1973), but also been fiercely criticized. Let us look at some of this criticism of MFT.

The theory is concerned with the privately owned business enterprise, and most of it, indeed, is concerned with large, quoted companies with clear separation of ownership and control. It overturns previous ideas by suggesting that some commonly held beliefs by managers and participants in financial markets are probably mistaken: for instance, that shareholders are better off (and value enterprises more highly) with high-dividend pay-outs, that there is an optimal debt level for every enterprise, that NPV has to be positive in terms of historical cost of capital for a project to be desirable, and that skill in the financial markets consists in being able to outguess others in forecasting the future prospects of individual companies.

Certain factors are retained, in particular that value can be understood in terms of future benefits, whether it be the value of projects, enterprises or shares. But these are integrated into other frameworks so that, for example, CAPM or the arbitrage pricing model are put forward as better models to understand the pricing of a security than subjectively estimating future dividends, because the former are based on the consensual beliefs of traders in the markets who cannot be fooled through the manipulation of accounting or other information. To state a simple causal relation as forming the foundation of CAPM (that the return from the individual enterprise or portfolio of projects *will* change as a result of the market return and/or the risk-free return) may well be too simple. Certainly the testing problems for CAPM (which are effectively testing problems for efficient markets theory too) make a dependence on it distinctly problematic. Nevertheless, it has found powerful advocates in the academic world, and has (in the USA more than the UK) penetrated the everyday world of decisions by market participants.

Thus, returning to the fundamental fact that enterprises are only means by which investors can get to develop a portfolio of real projects, we can see the way finance theory has integrated the borrowing (treasury) decision and the intra-organization investment decision. This has meant not only that the recursion of:

Security investor → Enterprise → Project

has shown more clearly the need for NPV to be the criterion at every point; it has also meant that we can consider asset betas directly in understanding the appropriate discount rate in judging a project.

Yet information assymmetry cannot be ignored. The agency problem potentially creates serious problems in this world where enterprises are supposedly just agents for bringing the source of finance (the investor) together with the wealth-creating project. This has probably not yet been fully integrated into the more generally successful framework of an integrated financial theory through notions of efficient markets. It is, of course, true that an efficient market does not need perfect and certain information about the future — only that the information is common to all the participants in the market. Nevertheless, the extent to which information asymmetry means that the integrated picture does not hold is not yet clear, and indeed some of its normative propositions may be untestable since conditions of symmetry do not exist for experimental control purposes.

The policy implications for the financial manager considering an investment project are considerable. Now it is quite true, as the reading in the Workbook by King (pp. 411–21) suggests (and many others have made this point trenchantly), that the uncertainty surrounding forecasts of future cash flows is so great that elaborate theorizing to get to a cost of capital is of minimal practical use. Yet some conclusions of modern theory are at times startling. Thus the functional fixation that a new project has to return more than the historical overall cost of capital is, under the tenets of the theory, wrong. There are two reasons why negative NPV projects might be considered if MFT is accepted. One is that the project beta is low compared to historical asset betas. The other is that such an investment enables the enterprise to take advantage of a tax shield on debt.

Yet it is here that some of the prescriptions of MFT are at their weakest. When it comes to social welfare, finance theory has been quite silent. Whereas there has at least in conventional economics been a whole branch (albeit not always a popular one with professional economists) concerned with the welfare implications of various economic strategies, no similar research exists for financial economics (as financial theory can be considered).

There is general, but tacit, smugness that the size and efficiency of markets will itself have a profoundly beneficial effect on such welfare.

Yet the tax shield raises questions about this. Governments allow interest payments to be set against tax because they are a cost rather than a distribution (as dividends are). The tax shield substantially reduces the relative cost of debt compared to equity. It also means that projects which can be funded by debt are going to be accepted whereas, were the shield not there, they would be refused. Now ideally the operations of the markets are such that private gain would coincide with public benefit. But there is a danger that the tax shield will encourage projects that are not beneficial in terms of the various time-preference frameworks of investors. In other words, the capital market is being distorted by the tax benefit, and the loss to the Treasury of the tax forgone by making interest allowable against corporate tax assessment may be compounded by the welfare loss of non-economic projects being accepted. However, so long as theory remains at the level of the individual enterprise, it is hard to see how this might change, and indeed those who sponsor research into financial theory are generally those with a vested interest in the corporate gains rather than the macroeconomic national loss.

12.3   The problems of MFT

Moreover, even within a more restricted framework than social benefit, there are considerable problems with MFT.

1. It is concerned only with a limited number of long-term financial instruments. The post-MM developments of capital structure and dividend theory take only two types of security as being basic (equity and long-term debt). This ignores the increasing reliance that companies are placing on short-term borrowing such as commercial paper.
2. It has every appearance of being a theory for large private enterprise. It assumes that securities can be freely traded (which is not true even for some fairly large companies in well-developed markets). It assumes that there is no discernible reaction on price of unloading large amounts of shares or stock. It says nothing for other enterprises that operate in the financial world, such as local authorities (which are very important as short-term borrowers), nationalized industries (which are unquoted of course), co-operatives, companies subjected to management buy-outs, or unlisted enterprises such as small companies or partnerships.
3. Most of the evidence has been gleaned in the context of a one-country market (though some work has been done on the relationships among international capital markets, developing an international CAPM along the way, and, for instance, applying efficient markets theory to foreign exchange markets). However, it is now clear that financial markets have transcended national boundaries. This change has taken various forms. For example:
   (a) There are increasing tendencies for large companies to be quoted on the stock markets of more than one country. Arbitrage will to some extent even out differences among pricing of securities in different countries, but even that requires the theorist to take into account the massive information networks that have now been developed to internationalize capital markets.

(b) Large multinationals have made use of various mechanisms to manipulate funds worldwide and minimize tax liabilities, at the same time maximizing their access to new funds. For example, they own their own banks, or take advantage of differential asking rates for similar-risk securities in different world markets. Moreover, securitization (the bypassing of banks to issue commercial paper directly to lenders, which in many cases simply means doing deals among large companies using the bankers as resources of expertise only) differentiates the very large blue-chip from the rest, since only the very highest prestige companies can attract investment on commercial paper given the higher risk than is apparent to the lender when dealing with a well-known bank.

(c) New financial instruments are constantly being created by the financial markets to tap into the increasing internationalization of business itself, such as (to take one of many examples) the SCOUT (shared currency option under tender), which is designed for companies tendering for foreign contracts and provides certain rights for the buyer in the case of the tender to purchase the contract currency at a predetermined price (thus reducing currency risk).

Similarly there are at the time of writing developments in zero-coupon bonds (or deep-discounted bonds) which, as the name suggests, produce little or no income but provide for all the return to be in the form of a capital gain at the end of the contract period. They appear to have tax advantages, although special provisions were developed very quickly by the Inland Revenue to counter much of the advantage.

A third development has been the junk bond (more so in the USA than UK), which provides a high coupon because of the higher-than-average risk involved. Junk bonds appear to lie somewhere between equity and debt in the normal run of securities. They have a fixed yield as with any other bond, but offer risk more akin to equity (without the voting power).

4. The very largest companies cannot be seen to be subject to the same rules as the rest. For example, managing the treasury function in a large international company will involve *inter alia* making use of various hedging instruments in the foreign exchange markets, and going to the financial futures and currency options markets. The *very largest* companies cannot do this since (in the UK at present) they dwarf the markets themselves. Thus we can suggest that the whole structure of MFT is designed for companies that are large but not too large; smaller companies and multinational giants are excluded.

5. Finally, there is what amounts to a philosophical problem. The nature of evidence for or against any theory in economics or social science more generally is always open to doubt; the idea of proof or disproof is highly problematic. For example, suppose that a theory suggests that large capital markets are efficient (in one of the three forms). At what point is a capital market considered to be large? What type of statistical test is appropriate to the hypothesis? (We saw in the case of weak-form efficiency, for example, that both runs tests and serial correlation had been tried. Suppose they gave different signals?) Or again, in their original 1958 paper Modigliani and Miller claimed to have evidence for their leverage hypothesis from a linear regression in US utilities securities. Were utilities an appropriate market sector? Should not multiple regression have been tried (in case

other factors impinged on the dependent variable and their absence in the test distorted the coefficient and R^2)? Their hypothesis was that the function was linear rather than non-linear, yet non-linear regression was not attempted as a check. (This is not necessarily a personal criticism of MM: computing power was limited at the time, and econometric testing in the finance field was in its infancy.)

There are still further problems of this last kind. To understand these, let us distinguish between theoretical models based on assumptions, and the testing of such models.

It will have been evident throughout the book that the assumptions that have been made, like those of economic theory, are unrealistic. This is inevitable in order that manageable models might be created. Indeed, the models that have resulted have had the remarkable property, despite the complexity of arriving at them, of relative simplicity. Thus, for instance, NPV is a simple discounting model. CAPM is a linear model. So is MM's capital structure proposition II. Betas are linearly additive. The irrelevance of dividends (if true) means that no complex explanatory models of the consequences of dividend changes are necessary. The weak form of EMH merely says that price movements follow a random walk. The arbitrage pricing model, like CAPM, is a linear combination.

Without empirical tests, however, these models are, in the main, unacceptable precisely because their foundations are unrealistic. Thus the only saving grace for the models can be the results of empirical tests. Yet here the whole model starts to go awry. For example:

1. Testing CAPM and efficient markets theory beyond the weak form is a mutual joint hypothesis test. Each depends on the validity of the other. Hence it is conceptually flawed.
2. The tendency in the literature has been to accept market efficiency as essentially proven. Hence when tests are conducted that question market efficiency they tend to be labelled 'anomalies'. There is some evidence of papers being rejected by the referees of prestige journals because they do not find markets to be efficient. Hence, it is said, they *must* be flawed in their method. How many 'anomalies' are necessary before they stop being anomalies?
3. Roll (1977) has shown that CAPM cannot be tested because the problem of surrogates makes the whole testing process essentially meaningless. Thus CAPM is based on:
   (a) the total market portfolio, which cannot be observed since it would have to take in all world securities, paintings, gambles on horses and so on;
   (b) expectations of R_j, which similarly cannot be measured, so that past actuals have to be taken as surrogates;
   (c) beta that cannot be observed, only estimated from past data. Beta is fairly stable, but not wholly stable (it would be a dull business world if it were!) Others, such as Brennan (1970), have argued that without a dividend effect (for tax reasons) CAPM is insufficiently specified in any case. And so on.
4. Semi-strong market efficiency is also untestable because it is concerned with the incorporation of 'relevant' information. But the only way to decide what is relevant is to see what is incorporated! So, since there is no external definition of 'relevant', there is no real way of testing semi-strong

market efficiency. We are left with 'speed tests', which can remark on whether information is incorporated quickly (thus making abnormal profits impossible *after that speedy adjustment*) but not on whether it is incorporated appropriately, which, it could be argued, makes the *expression* 'market efficiency' over-optimistic and, indeed, misleading to the uninformed.

5. The mess we saw in testing dividend models and capital structure hypotheses likewise suggests that no adequately defined model is possible. Differential tax rates, transaction costs and liquidity preferences among shareholders suggest that no homogeneous general model relating them to the enterprise can ever be properly specified and tested. Clientele arguments have some validity in conception but, for the same reason, are impossible to test with certainty.

What we are left with, therefore, is a school of thought that is based on unreasonable assumptions and unacceptable tests! Not, perhaps, the best basis for financial decisions.

12.4   Policy implications for the financial manager

There is a view which suggests that, although managers cannot articulate and explain their actions well, they generally act very sensibly. Recent evidence, as we have seen, has to some extent rescued the managers who have stuck with payback rather than get involved in complex risk-adjusted techniques for investment appraisal, for instance. Again, whereas for many years theorists could not explain why enterprises stayed with certain debt levels rather than maximize them (as the revised post-tax MM theory suggested they should), an agency explanation has now been proposed in terms of voluntary bonding. A rediscovery of managerial 'rationality' seems to be under way.

And yet, there are serious problems with this view. The field of accounting, for example, is replete with anecdotes of managements who closed down whole areas of operation on the basis of full costings (cf. *Managerial Accounting: Method and Meaning*, Chapter 3). Similarly, a blanket approach to managerial rationality which supposes there are valid reasons for all managerial action would have difficulty in explaining why Bowater-Scott feels it necessary to turn to CAPM whereas apparently similar enterprises make do with more rule-of-thumb methods. Any explanation is likely to run into the 'special case' category: that *in this case* there was a particular pressure to do X. This shows no signs of predictive power for managerial action in the future.

But more importantly, perhaps, it says nothing in terms of *guidance* for the financial manager. Specifically, should the manager take on board the whole complex of general equilibrium models that MFT consists of? If so, then the financial manager's job will be very different from a more traditional approach to the function. In particular, as we pointed out in Chapter 1, the management problem is an integrated one that concerns all factors of production. Finance is only one of these. Once the participant model of the enterprise is accepted, the shareholders and lenders become just one constituent of an array that includes buyers, suppliers, workforce, environmental groups and so on. This means that the task of the financial manager must also be integrated in the more general managerial problem. We return to the implications of the participant model later in this section.

At first sight it is not clear how this contrasts or harmonizes with MFT and, indeed, with more traditional financial management activities. One answer may, however, be as follows. The general equilibrium assumptions of MFT assume that the market will adjust quickly and efficiently to differing conditions. This is, of course, the assumption in economic general equilibrium theory. In a dynamic world in which there are informational and other imperfections, this adjustment process will be flawed. Hence actions that would maximize the security-holders' wealth through exploiting short-term imperfections in other factor markets (such as labour or product markets) may in the longer term be both organizationally and socially undesirable. For example, the standard investment decision model supposes that expected return and estimated beta will be unaffected by the feedbacks that result from information about the wealth created by the investment decision. That is, costs and revenues are estimated, and it is supposed that they will thereafter be unaffected by the news of the surplus that — in an informationally efficient market-orientated world — will arise from adopting the asset. This, however, cannot be sustained. If indeed the project with a positive NPV exists (after, if necessary, adjusting for debt tax shield and so on), then this in itself is prima-facie evidence of market inefficiency. That such inefficiency should be exploited only by the owner participants rather than by all participants will be unacceptable to other participants, whose actions (bargaining up wages, bargaining down prices, increasing taxes, depending on which participant group it is) will then be devoted to gaining a slice of the benefit. This will affect both return and risk. *Hence the assumed wealth surplus for the security-holders will be self-defeating.* In these circumstances the use of conventional techniques without feedbacks of this kind are tendentious.

This brings us back, therefore, to the systems model with which we started. Financial management can only be properly exercised in the context of the whole managerial problem. Bolting on extras to the basic model (such as adjusting beta for expected labour unrest) is still, by virtue of being shareholder orientated, arguably questionable. Helpful though modern finance theory may be in so many ways in calling attention to problems, to frameworks and to possible solutions, it is distinctly doubtful whether it can operate fully under real market conditions to be a socially acceptable set of objectives and constraints for the enterprise decision process.

This becomes even more evident when we remind ourselves of the competing views of the nature of the enterprise. In Chapter 1 of this book — and in the first chapters of *Financial Accounting: Method and Meaning* and *Managerial Accounting: Method and Meaning* — we emphasized the participant view of the enterprise: the proposal that it should best be seen as a vehicle for the various participant groups to satisfy their needs within the context of a market. The theory we have reviewed, though not always completely internally consistent, has nevertheless taken shareholder wealth maximization as a starting point. It has, in other words, taken a unitary view of the enterprise.

It could, of course, be argued that this is an unfair criticism, particularly of agency theory, which does concern itself with all participants and their calculations of costs and benefits in the agency relationship. However, agency theory has some considerable flaws. For example, it is *reductionist*: it reduces all problems to economic ones, and to two-party negotiation over the agency contract as if it were taking place in a completely free market (at least in so far as any welfare implications are concerned). Moreover, to the extent that it has impinged on financial theory, it has taken only suppliers of financial capital and managers into account. It has said nothing about other participants.

We are still left, therefore, with the problem of the coalition approach to understanding the enterprise, and its implications for financial management. To give some indication of how it might differ from the unitary view, we shall briefly take two examples.

1. *The investment decision.* The prescription of post-CAPM theory is that a project should be accepted if it increases the value of the enterprise, given that the discount rate reflects the beta of the new project and hence the weighted effect it will have on the beta of the enterprise as a whole. The reason is orientated around the wealth of the providers of capital. Now if we ask about social welfare, in the context of the participant groups together, some different questions emerge. For example: how does the project interact with those of other enterprises? Suppose, for example, that the product or service concerned is already provided by other enterprises — is a further provision socially desirable? If the market philosophy is accepted, then the problem is solved by that mechanism because a new project would only have a positive present value if it were in demand by customers (for instance), and this would only be the case if the price charged were lower and/or quality higher (to simplify once again). This in turn would result from more 'efficient' production — and so would increase socioeconomic efficiency. However, this would be an excellent case for increasing the supply of heroin and cocaine, since there appears to be a market demand and there is currently monopoly rent by its suppliers. Few would argue that these drugs should be legalized and their production expanded. Yet they would provide positive net present values. Once this (extreme) argument is understood, and the principle consolidated, other less obvious cases are also called into question.

2. As a second example, take *the dividend decision.* According to the models we have seen, the welfare of owners based upon the market value of the enterprise is once again central, and policy prescription (for the dividend decision by management) is based on the maximization of that value. These models, however, distinguish between the financing and investment decisions: the latter are held constant in the MFT models concerned. There are doubts, moreover about the nature of managerial rationality, particularly where reinvested funds compared to externally raised funds are concerned. Because the cost of reinvested funds is less evident, and information asymmetry suggests that they may be less efficiently scrutinized by the market than externally raised funds (or at least, that managers may *perceive* this to be the case), different overall policies may result. In the context of the coalition theory of the enterprise this is clearly important. That approach takes bargaining as constant, and one input to it is the visible surplus available for distribution among the parties concerned. In this model, the dividend is a payment to owners in the same way that factor payments are to suppliers of materials, wages are to employees, and rent is to property-owners. The criterion is the long-run survival of the enterprise at a certain level of production, not the wealth of the owners as measured by the market value of the enterprise. If we had 'efficient' markets for information and factors, the two models (unitary and participant) would give identical results. In an imperfect world they do not, and the institutional structures that exist will result in different understandings of managerial decisions and different prescriptions for action by the participants.

All of this becomes clearer still when we return to the wealth maximization objective. This has had a stormy history in economics, and clearly there is no room (or need) to rehearse the arguments afresh here. One simple point will perhaps suffice. There are two models: that based on *financiers'* needs and that based on *all participants'* needs. Each of these may be based on *maximizing* or *satisficing*. Each of these, in turn, may be based on a reduction to *wealth*, or a broader concept of *all needs* (financial and non-financial). Thus the broadest concept, and arguably the one most in tune with the reality of decisions, is a satisficing model that takes all needs of all participants into account. The finance model takes only one or two participant groups, only one of their needs and assumes optimization. Whether this can ever become a satisfactory surrogate when, as we pointed out in Chapter 1, financial management is part of a total social process in the context of the financial function of the individual enterprise, must be judged very much open to doubt.

Summary

In this final chapter we have suggested the following:

1. Modern finance theory is a relatively recent phenomenon that has necessarily taken hold of both theory and practice in a far-reaching way.
2. It is based (in the main) on general equilibrium economics, and likewise is an all-encompassing theory based on fairly unrealistic assumptions that, its proponents would claim, are nevertheless susceptible to testing and hence verification/falsification.
3. However, its starting point (shareholder wealth maximization) is questionable, both as a prescription for what enterprises should be doing and as a description of what enterprises actually do.
4. Many of the other assumptions of the theory are likewise open to criticism, and their relevance to the modern world of international finance with its multiplicity of new financial instruments is uncertain.
5. The quality and, indeed, meaningfulness of most of the tests of the theory are doubtful.
6. Nevertheless, as a set of *general guidelines* it is possible to argue that many of the ideas of MFT are useful to the manager in day-to-day financial decision making within the enterprise.

Key terms and concepts

Here is a list of key terms and concepts which have featured in this chapter. You should make sure that you understand and can define each one of them. Page references to definitions in the text appear in bold in the index.

- Zero-coupon bond
- Deep-discount bond
- Junk bond
- Securitization

Further reading

An interesting paper analysing the rise of modern finance is to be found in Whitley (1986). The major finance journals appear to have tried to shut out criticism in recent years, but reference could be made to Friend (1973), Fouse *et al.* (1974), Ryan (1982), and Findlay and Williams (1980).

The Workbook material to accompany this chapter begins on p. 609.

P A R T

5

Workbook

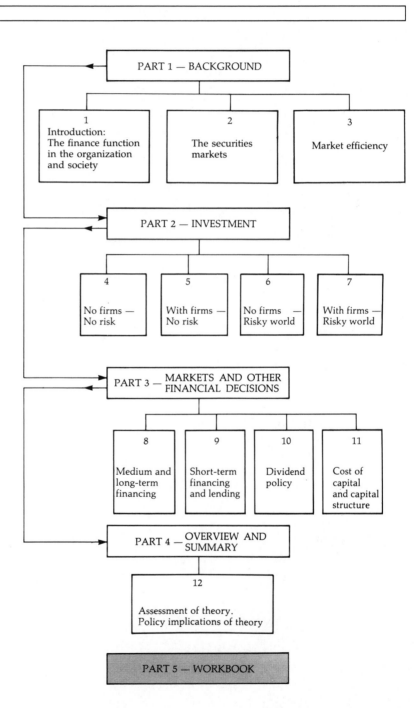

PART 1 — BACKGROUND

1	2	3
Introduction: The finance function in the organization and society	The securities markets	Market efficiency

PART 2 — INVESTMENT

4	5	6	7
No firms — No risk	With firms — No risk	No firms — Risky world	With firms — Risky world

PART 3 — MARKETS AND OTHER
FINANCIAL DECISIONS

8	9	10	11
Medium and long-term financing	Short-term financing and lending	Dividend policy	Cost of capital and capital structure

PART 4 — OVERVIEW AND
SUMMARY

12
Assessment of theory. Policy implications of theory

PART 5 — WORKBOOK

Part 5   Introduction and overview

The purpose of these Workbook chapters has been explained in the introduction to the book. They vary in their style and content depending on the nature of the chapter.

1

The finance function in the organization and society

W1.1 Introduction

In the chapter we present the financial world as one that is becoming increasingly more complex and interesting. We also use the term 'modern' when we refer to finance theory. We make the claim in the chapter that finance theory has a lot to offer in our understanding of the finance function of the firm and in the actual practice of financial management. There is no doubt that, in the area of investments and capital markets, finance theory has played a critical role in the development of new markets, e.g. through option pricing and techniques of risk management. Extensive econometric testing has deepened our understanding of the workings of financial markets, but it is in the area of corporate finance that the linkage between theory and practice is less obvious. You may care to reference an article by Smith (1985) which gives another view of the history of corporate finance. This can be read now to give a precursor of what is to come. We would recommend that you re-read the article each time one of the issues is discussed in the chapter. Finally, the article is a useful reference point at the completion of the book to draw the various strengths of the theory together.

In arguing that the financial manager operates in a very complex and changing world, it is apparent that various qualities are necessary for the successful management of the finance function. We have mentioned already that an understanding of the finance function gives a better overall view of the firm and in the chapter we have argued strongly that a thorough grasp of finance theory is useful to managers. It is claimed by some (see the article by Pietruski, reprinted on p. 320) that chief financial officers are good potential CEOs.

In the chapter we refer to the importance of *value*. Prices are one issue, value can be something else. We argue for the use of the 'economic value' model and the importance of cash, as this is measurable and thoroughly objective. It is our contention, and that of others, that investors, particularly institutional, can see through accounting biases. One problem here is that the shareholding body in Britain has changed quite dramatically, particularly with the privatization programme, and this has created a large number of small investors who are not diversified in their holdings. They do not fully understand the material that is supplied to them in financial statements and have been tempted out of a preferred habitat of building society investment to what has been revealed (after the 1987 stock market crash) as a risky environment and one in which the spectre of fraud and the unacceptable face of capitalism raises its head. The move to wider share ownership is a significant force in the British financial scene. While small investors can rely on the financial press and on the actions, sometimes in consort, of large institutional investors, the very existence of small investors will require more concerted effort by regulators and by firms, if this wider share ownership is to remain in Britain.

In the Workbook of this first chapter, we shall not be taking you through any methods of calculation. Instead we present three things. First, there are some general discussion questions. Second, there are some more practical assignment questions to give you the 'feel' of the subject. Each of them is concerned with a project using real-world data. It is good that you get used to this because there is a considerable amount of theory in this subject, and it is easy to forget, in the welter of symbols and assumptions, that the purpose of this theory is to describe and prescribe for the problems of financial managers facing real-world problems.

The third aspect of this Workbook chapter is the case studies. Each, for its proper solution, needs quite a sophisticated knowledge of the theory we just referred to. Of course you have not learned it at this stage, but we suggest that you work through the cases with your present state of knowledge, making notes on your understanding of the issues involved. Later, when you have studied the relevant theory, you can come back to your notes to see how differently you would have analysed the issues. (If there is no difference, then either you were a prodigy from the start or, alternatively, you have not understood the later chapters!)

W1.2   Discussion questions

Note: Some pointers on the first five of these questions are given in section W1.6 on pp. 347–8. They are not intended to be definitive, but we hope they will help. Try to make your own notes before turning to ours.

1.1 'Finance is emerging as the business function that holds the corporation together at the top management level.' Discuss in terms of the firm's finance function.

1.2 The shareholders are theoretically in control of the affairs of a company, so why do they actually have little input into the decision-making process?

1.3 Discuss the problem that the financial manager faces when the textbooks suggest that he or she should maximize shareholder wealth, yet the vast array of literature which deals with the motivational assumptions of firms rejects this unitary approach.

1.4 Models for financial management decision making generally take, as the basis for their objective function, the maximization of shareholder wealth. Do you consider the maximization of shareholder wealth to be an appropriate objective in this context in the light of theory and practice?

1.5 Discuss how the actions of investors can influence financial managers of firms and have an impact on the economic financial system.

1.6 Distinguish between a profit maximization objective as specified by the microeconomic theorist and value maximization as propounded by a financial theorist.

1.7 Do profits ensure the survival of the firm?

1.8 Can the management group act as an arbitrator among the various competing interest groups of the firm?

1.9 Why is it that to ensure that managers act in the best interests of shareholders the latter have to incur agency costs?

1.10 What remedies do shareholders have in pursuing their rights as the *de jure* controllers of the firm if they feel these rights have been threatened?

1.11 What policies can managers pursue to accommodate their own 'self-interest'? How relevant are the constraints and controls that may exist to limit such actions?

1.12 How might the interest of shareholders, bond-holders, management, employees and society coincide, and how might they be in conflict?

1.13 Profit maximization as an objective is often criticized for being non-operational, yet how is it possible to operationalize value maximization?

1.14 To pursue 'value' maximization a large number of assumptions are necessary, not least that the share price reflects the value of the firm. How do the decisions taken by the firm translate into the market price of the shares?

1.15 The shareholder retains the ultimate power of veto on a board of directors. Examine this fact with the emergence of large blocks of institutionally controlled shares.

1.16 The shareholder can diversify his risk of investment by holding at the very least a randomly selected portfolio share. The manager's interests by and large cannot be diversified. Examine the asymmetry that exists here.

1.17 Does and should social responsibility have a role in the formulation of objectives of the firm?

1.18 The risk of the shareholder is taken for granted, but the bond-holder is often exposed to risk. Illustrate how this occurs and what remedies are available to the bond-holder.

1.19 Discuss the differences between an 'economic value' model and an 'accounting value' model.

1.20 Financial policy can act as a mechanism which induces insiders to act in a way 'which is more nearly suited to outsiders' interests' (Edwards, 1987). Discuss.

W1.3 Assignments

1. Examine a selection of, say, 20 company reports at the very least and see if (a) there are statements of objectives, (b) there is disclosure of institutional shareholding. Discuss the findings in the light of course material studied.
2. Take at least one publicly quoted company share and perform the following tasks:

   (a) Graph its share price over an interval of one year, say weekly (take, for instance, the last Friday of each week for consistency).
   (b) Try and account for the price movements by separating those effects of the stock market in general: by comparing the movements against the

stock exchange composite index, say the FT All Share, the industry (the composite sector index of the FT) and the firm (what is left). For the latter, examine the impact of earnings and dividend announcements, new orders, major innovations, splits if any and the general good news and bad news of the firm.

All the data for the above are contained in newspapers such as the *Financial Times,* and back copies are available in libraries either in original form or on microfilm.

W1.4   Reading: global financial strategies

The new role of finance: what CEOs expect from CFOs

Reprinted with permission from the Business International Money Report, *21 December 1987, Copyright 1987, Business International Corporation, One Dag Hammerskjold Plaza, New York, NY 10017. All rights reserved.*

In recent years, the growing importance of finance has raised the corporate profile of the finance department and the CFO to new heights. The following article is drawn from an address by John M. Pietruski, Chairman and CEO of Sterling Drug to the Tenth Annual CFO Conference.

'As a key member of the Sterling Drug management team,' says Pietruski, 'my CFO must have all the characteristics I would look for in any other manager'. Three of these qualities are critical for success in any field: intelligence, motivation and a sensitivity to both people and situations. However, the following additional attributes are particularly essential for the CFO:

(1) Technical competence. A good CFO does not necessarily need to be an expert in high finance, but he must have a reasonably thorough knowledge of financial activities carried out within his department, from budgeting to tax. If he doesn't know the specifics, he must know how and where to get the needed information — fast.

(2) Objectivity and outspokenness. The CFO must be an impartial arbiter, open and candid in his evaluation of each situation. A chief executive officer is going to have a tough time if his CFO sits tight and waits to see which way the breeze is blowing. He wants the CFO to call it as he sees it.

(3) An ability to spot trouble in advance. The CFO must be able to anticipate problems — to be *proactive* rather than *reactive*. The CFO and the Finance Department must be able to spot trouble brewing early enough to allow the CEO to take action while the problem is still manageable. This applies to every aspect of a company.

(4) A 'watchdog' attitude. The word has a bad connotation, but no company can function without watchdogs alert for errors and overruns. Says Pietruski, 'At Sterling our internal audit function, under the leadership of our CFO, is both strong and effective. It not only ensures policies and procedures are being followed, but also makes constructive and cost-saving suggestions about operations.'

(5) A talent for playing the devil's advocate. A CFO must not be afraid to challenge expense and capital-funding requests. He is the steward of the company's assets, and he must guard them jealously.

(6) A vision of the 'big picture'. The financial function is inherently involved in an immense amount of detailed information, data reports and paper. But the CFO must never be blinded by all this detail. He must coordinate the data to present an accurate picture of the overall financial state of the company. In this way, he plays an important part in keeping everyone focused on improving the bottom line.

(7) An understanding of the P&L consequences of operating decisions. The CFO must be a predictor, not a record keeper. He must be on top of budgets, major projects and proposed changes in systems and procedures so he can estimate their impact on profit and loss. He must contribute to the decisionmaking and planning process. At Sterling, says Pietruski, 'my CFO and his VP of budgets and financial control attend every long-range operating planning meeting that I hold. I look to their counsel on matters in all areas of operations so that I am sensitive to the P&L and balance sheet impact of each proposed course of action.'

(8) The ability to train and develop people. A strong CFO must take the lead in counselling so that key managers in all areas of the business become more comfortable with financial information and more able to use it to increase their effectiveness. A strong CFO must also consider developing a cadre of successors. He must make sure that a good financial training program is in place and that opportunities exist for people within his department to be exposed to all its disciplines.

W1.5   Case studies

(a) Union Carbide

In 1984 poison gas escaped from a Union Carbide plant in India and killed some 2,000 people. Lawsuits were filed in the USA, and the share price dropped. In 1985 the US company GAF attempted to take it over. It bought 10% of Union Carbide, and soon after launched a bid for Union Carbide's shares of $68 each (in cash). Union Carbide's advisers told its board of directors that they estimated the company's true value at $85 per share as an operating company and as much as $100 per share if it were liquidated. The board recommended the shareholders to reject the offer, and it became what is known as a 'contested bid'.

To try to persuade shareholders not to accept the bid, Union Carbide made them a counter-offer: it would give them $20 in cash and $65 worth of loan securities per share for 35% of their shareholdings. It would, of course, have to borrow heavily to make good the offer.

GAF responded with a $74 cash offer. This still looked tempting to shareholders, so the Union Carbide board increased their offer: they would buy back 55% of the shares instead of 35% and promised to raise the dividend. To raise the funds for this they had to sell their most growth-orientated division. GAF could not match this and pulled out. To fight off the bid, Union Carbide had doubled its debt. The share price rose from $48 before the bid to a high of $76.

Brigham and Gapenski (1987, p. 734) comment:

> In defeat, GAF walked away with 3.1 million Carbide shares and a potential pre-tax profit of $135 million. Also, the investment bankers

and lawyers profited from the fight: GAF's investment bankers and lawyers garnered about $60 million in fees, while Carbide's bankers took in at least $14 million. It appears that Carbide's forced restructuring actually created value, and this value was shared by all the parties involved.

Questions

1. How could it be that the break-up value of Union Carbide was estimated at a value higher than the operating value?
2. If that were indeed the value, why did GAF not increase its bid up to, say, $90, then break the company up and realize $10 profit per share?
3. Do you agree with Brigham and Gapenski's claim that the incident had created value?

(b) Crown Cork Company Ltd

Note: The following draws upon the account of this case given by Brooke and Remmers (1970).

Crown Cork was a UK company 75% of whose shares were owned by a US parent, Crown Cork International. Thus the latter controlled Crown Cork's decisions completely. In 1963 the parent announced that it was going to suspend dividends so as to finance an expansion programme. Comment in the press and the House of Commons included the following:

> a decision like this would be difficult to justify in any circumstances; in those of the present case it is impossible to do so. First of all, Crown Cork is a subsidiary of a US company, Crown Cork International. Secondly, the last Crown Cork balance sheet showed loans to the holding company of £900,000. Thirdly, and even more weirdly, in September of this year, Crown Cork redeemed its £400,000 preference shares at a premium of 5s (25p) a share. If cash is needed for expansion, the way to get it is not to starve the minority holders.
>
> *Source: 'Lex', Financial Times, 1.11.63.*

> The cessation of dividends is unfair to the minority holders (71.5% of the equity is held by the US parent) and the Board is meant to represent all the shareholders. The amount involved is relatively small and so this devotion to 'primitive financing' by retentions alone is explicable only (though one hopes this is not the case) by a deplorable wish to squeeze out the minority.
>
> *Source: 'Lex', Financial Times, 12.11.63.*

> This sort of financing seems both stupid and unfair to the minority holders.
>
> *Source: 'Lex', Financial Times, 25.3.64.*

> Crown Cork is not going to be allowed to get away with its shabby treatment of minority shareholders scot-free . . .
>
> *Source: 'Lex', Financial Times, 25.4.64.*

and somewhat later:

> The firm, which has paid no dividends since 1962, invoked the British Treasury when it anounced it would make no payment for 1966. Crown

Cork said its decision was made 'after consultations with and in deference to the request of the Treasury'. Pressed to explain its stand, the Treasury said in a statement that it did not seem imperative to increase its distribution during a period of voluntary dividend standstill.

Source: New York Herald Tribune *(International Edition) 8.3.67.*

Questions

1. Why was it claimed that to withhold dividends from shareholders was 'shabby treatment'?
2. What could the minority shareholders do in the face of the parent's action?
3. The voluntary dividend standstill referred to was part of a restraint package by the government of the day. Restricting wage claims, it was argued that dividend growth should be similarly limited. Is this a valid argument?

(c) Decca: placing a value on the company

A bid approach for Decca, the defence, marine and consumer electronics company, was made on 18 January 1980 by the Racal defence electronics group. This bid ended the takeover rumours that had abounded since the previous September when Decca announced a pre-tax loss for the year 1978/9 of £384,000 (first half profits of £2.46m) on a turnover of £182.5 million (see Report 1 for the 1979 year results). This compared to a £16 million profit in 1974.

The 'Lex' column in the *Financial Times*, in commenting on the results, stated that:

Decca's decline has become downright alarming ... Yesterday, after falling 50p at one stage, the 'A' shares ended up 30p lower at 245p. There seems every justification for major shareholders to ask some hard questions of management; meanwhile the market in the shares is likely to be dominated more than ever by hopes of a bid. (14.9.79)

The firm had been approached many times in the past by potential suitors including GEC, but the fiercely independent chairman of 20 years' standing, Sir Edward Lewis, had always warned off the suitors with an asking price of well over 500p per share. This he was in a position to do by virtue of the capital structure. He had a personal holding of 9.6% of the 7.2 million voting shares (representing less than 40% of the total of 19 million shares) and with other holdings the board controlled over 17%; with the large nominee holdings, which usually voted with the board, they had over 50%. The institutions were effectively shut out.

The year-end results were a watershed for Decca as they gave the institutional shareholders further cause for concern. The pension funds in 1978 had set up an information watchdog committee, and following these new results the Prudential and Kuwait Investment Trust made direct approaches to Decca with a view to strengthening the management; even Sir Edward recognized the need for some minor change: 'a good bid for the [loss-making] television business, or some form of co-operative venture, might be considered'.

The potential bidders, but for the electronic heart of Decca, were already apparent in the form of Racal and GEC, particularly Racal. Indeed, by the time the Racal bid announcement was made, the share price of both companies had already reflected the probable bid approach. The bid approach coincided with Decca's interim results (see Report 2): further losses of £1.87 million pre-tax for the six months to 30 September 1979 with the expectation of a continuation of these pre-tax losses into the second half as a result of losses on consumer goods and the higher interest costs on the £50–£60 million (mainly bank debt) borrowing. The board also announced that interim dividends would be passed compared to a 3.3p total (interim, no final) for 1978/9.

Additionally Decca announced that Polygram, the record subsidiary of the international group of companies Philips and Siemens, had agreed to offer £9.5 million for the majority of the music division, namely the record list, particularly strong in classical, and the music-publishing subsidiaries.

While this would have given a welcome boost to the cash flow, particularly as there were provisions for up to £6 million on top of the deal if record sales were buoyant (but a penalty of up to £4 million if they were not), Decca also had to provide the estimated £2.5 million needed to pay for the 1,000 or so expected redundancies out of the 1,250 workforce. It also left the company with the remainder of the division (with a book value of £11.5 million), namely recording studios and pressing facilities. On top of the Polygram proposal, it was also announced that Decca's unprofitable television division was the subject of a bid negotiation with a joint approach from Binatone run by a Mr Gala Lalvani and an unnamed Far Eastern company, probably a South Korean concern. Binatone had bought from Sinclair Radionics their pocket television interests and sought the Bridgwater production facilities of Decca for this purpose. The asking price of £2 million was thought by Mr Lalvani to be too high.

The removal of the television and music interests would have left the radar and electronic warfare division, the main interest of Racal as well as other potential bidders. Decca had become market leader in many of these areas. In marine radar, for instance, it was pre-eminent, despite a fall in business reflecting the depressed shipping markets, but Decca's director of this division, Mr Charles Taylor, expressed optimism here particularly in the USA, despite competition from the US and Japanese companies. In its electronics warfare work, mainly for the UK Ministry of Defence, the potential was apparently present, and in its navigation division Decca was still a market leader, though it was weaker in the satellite systems.

The formal bid offer was made on 25 January after a week of negotiations (Decca was being advised by County Bank), and it received the irrevocable acceptance by Sir Edward who viewed the offer as 'very much in the interests of Decca and the UK electronics industry as a whole', and the unanimous recommendation of the Board, though the 8% holdings held by Dr J. Dimenstein's wife were not committed. With the Decca board agreement, Racal had 17.2% of the voting shares and 4.98% of its own holdings (costing it £4.5 million), which gave it useful leverage in securing the agreement of the other shareholders. The terms of the all-share offer were 5 Racal shares for every 3 voting shares and 3 for every 2 non-voting ('A') shares. This required Racal to increase its shareholding capital by 27.24 million (one-tenth of its capital), but the critical dimension of the offer was the market price of the Racal shares. The latter fell sharply to 206p but recovered to 226p, valuing Decca at £66.4 million (377p for the voting, 339p for the non-voting, compared with the market price of 360p and 325p respectively). This bid represented marginally less than the book value of the assets after allowing for the surplus on the disposals to Polygram.

The other arrangements of the agreed bid were for Sir Edward and Mr N.G.

Maw to join the Racal board as non-executive directors and for Mr E. Harrison, the chairman of Racal, to become the chief executive of Decca.

The Racal bid anticipated a quick recovery of Decca to its former profit levels (break-even by 1980/1), and it received widespread favourable press comment. For example, John Lloyd writing in the *Financial Times* (see Reports 3 and 4 for a brief summary of the Racal growth but also a hiccup in its 1979 performance):

> Decca has been seen as badly managed . . . Racal has, by contrast, grown over the past 15 years by ruthless concentration on the military tactical communications market . . . coupled with precise identification of growth markets . . . the two show an almost textbook compatibility. Racal has hard-driving, tough management which has snapped up export opportunities as an efficient production base; its strengths are in land-based radio communications. Decca has an apparently less effective top management . . . is strong in marine radar and navigation aids . . . (19.1.80)

and the 'Lex' column:

> this is a growth opportunity which Racal had to seize. [It is] acquiring valuable microwave technology which would have been highly expensive to develop independently . . . Whether this turns out to be a good buy, however, depends on how quickly Racal can pull Decca out of its decline . . . Continuing losses are bound to lead to further cash flow problems for Decca. Fortunately Racal's own balance sheet is strong, and by restricting itself to an all-equity deal it can preserve adequate resources to cope with Decca's high gearing. At least the take-over . . . will not require Racal to include a significant goodwill item in its balance sheet, as its previous electronics acquisitions have done.

On the basis of the Racal projections of a Decca turn-around, continued Lex:

> the initial impact will be to dilute Racal's own earnings per share by some 11% — but these should be growing quite strongly next year . . . It has to be said that Racal's record in previous acquisitions has been good. And the shares rose a little yesterday, apparently on belief that it did not pay much more than £60 million for Decca; there had been stories of a higher price. However, the deal carries obvious risks, and certainly will lead to a slow-down in earnings growth for the time being. With Racal's shares and prospective fully-taxed p/e of perhaps 16, and with £60m worth of shares to be issued if the deal goes through (as seems likely), there could be indigestion for a while. (26.1.80)

However, despite the apparent finality of the deal, the whole affair was re-opened when Morgan Grenfell announced on 1 February that GEC was about to make a bid. The market expected a cash offer given the £600 million cash and liquid assets GEC still had left over after their Avery acquisition. In the meantime, Sir Edward Lewis died and Mr N.G. Maw succeeded him as chairman.

The GEC bid valued Decca at £82.5 million in cash with the voting shares at 500p and non-voting at 400p. Whilst the bid was far in excess of Racal's offer and in cash, the company also offered an unspecified option of convertible unsecured loan stock for shareholders with capital gains problems and/or shareholders, particularly institutional that wanted to maintain a presence in the electronics sector. The bid seemed to some observers, to be marginally in excess of the net worth of Decca.

The bid also had a definite logic to it. Decca would become part of the largest electrical group with a £2 billion asset base, but more particularly it would become part of the GEC–Marconi group, a dynamic division to which Decca had already had some working contact on the Doppler navigational system and the Rapier missile. The two companies were largely overlapping, unlike Decca–Racal, though they were also complementary in many areas. It was the overlaps which the government via the Office of Fair Trading was concerned with. On the one hand, GEC strengthened by Decca would be a strengthened world force, particularly as GEC had cash reserves, whereas Decca with Racal would provide a 'second force' in the UK and be a competitive bidder to GEC for defence contracts. GEC indicated that if a reference were made to the Monopolies Commission it would withdraw. On top of this possible monopoly reference came the fear that GEC would be more ruthless with the restructuring of Decca, with inevitable redundancies.

Racal responded on 7 February with a mixture of cash and shares worth at the best £93.1 million. The cash alternative was the same as GEC's, but the share offer of 13 Racal for every 5 ordinary and 21 for every 10 'A' shares was an improvement on the GEC offer. It sent Decca shares to 550p for the ordinary, leaving the 'A' unchanged at 425p. It was also announced that Racal's share of the voting shares was now 6% and 9.1% of the 'A' shares.

Within ten hours of the Racal counterbid GEC announced it was intending to rebid, and its bid, when finally released, offered 550p for the voting and 450p for the non-voting shares of 585p nominal of 8.5% convertible unsecured loan stock (1990–2) for each ordinary share and 480p for each 'A' share. The bid was worth £97.9 million and it sent Decca's shares in the market to 580p and 440p respectively. Additionally, GEC gave a strong commitment to safeguard the present terms of employment at Decca. Concurrently with this revised bid Decca announced the sale of its half share in two European record companies (to realize £1.08 million to Mrs Sara Dimenstein and the daughter of Mr Maurice Rosengarten — a former director of Decca.

A week of intense lobbying followed until on 14 February it was confirmed that Racal's final bid had enabled them to secure 50.4% of the voting shares. They had already won the irrevocable acceptance of the Decca board (17.2%); they won over the 8% of the Dimenstein and 13% of institutional holdings, and with their own holdings (increased through the day by a further 6%) now 12.3%, this gave them control. To many this represented a shut-out bid which prior to April 1976 would have had to have been cleared by the Takeover Panel to ensure no known higher bidder existed. In the event the winning of control thwarted any further GEC bid.

The offer was 600p for the ordinary and 500p for the 'A' in cash (but not underwritten), valuing Decca at £101 million, or a share exchange of 3 in 1 Decca voting and 5 for 2 non-voting. On the current Racal share price this was worth 642p and 535p respectively. This final offer was a far cry from the 376p and 339p of the first agreed bid. Racal also announced that even if the bid was referred to the Monopolies Commission and subsequently cleared they would still renew the offer.

The immediate reaction was that, although Racal had won, its victory was hollow and it had to pay a price, the economics of which was based on shareholders taking the shares. Indeed, if the Racal share price were to slip to 200p, the share offer would equal the cash offer and lead to cash acceptances and an increase in Racal's borrowing. Racal's shares at the end of 1979 had fallen below 180p from a peak of nearly 260p in September/October to recover in time for the Decca bid.

This point about the crucial performance of the Racal share price was firmly made in the 'Lex' column on 6 March:

> if nobody asks for the cash terms, the combined Racal–Decca group will begin life with a reasonable balance sheet, despite Decca's present £60m debt burden: the group's indebtedness would be about £100m out of capital employed of roughly £300m. Significant cash elections would change this, however, the total cash at stake is £80m.
>
> So far all is well. Racal's share price dipped just 1p to 222p yesterday on the news that a few more worms have been discovered in the Decca can. Losses for the year to the end of this month will be more like £10m than the £6m originally anticipated. Some of 'the deterioration relates to the TV side which is to be sold. This will still leave Racal to cope with a deeply depressed marine radar business, but the view is still that Decca can be hauled back to break even in 1980–1. Meantime the worsening crisis at Decca will serve, at least, to make the Office of Fair Trading more reluctant to call in the Monopolies Commission.
>
> Only if the Racal price dips towards 200p will risks of large-scale cash acceptances become at all high. Even then, many institutions will not wish to reduce their exposure to the electronics sector. But Racal is taking a significant risk in order to achieve a considerable prize.

In the event by 1 April, with only one-tenth of the acceptances still to come in, the Racal cash liability from the deal amounted to only £8.6 million, with a probable total liability expected of £12 million. Additionally it was announced at the end of March that there would be no reference to the Monopolies Commission. This thus represented the end of the Decca bid saga.

REPORT 1

DECCA LIMITED

Directors
Sir Edward Lewis, *Chairman*
N.N. Graham Maw, *Deputy Chairman*
Dr Jack Dimenstein (*USA*)
Sir Martin Flett, KCB
W.L. Spalding

Secretary
W.L. Spalding

Registered Office
9 Albert Embankment, London SE1 7SW

Auditors
Mellors, Basden & Co., 38 Finsbury Square, EC2A 1SY

Solicitors
Rowe & Maw, 15 Devereux Court, Essex Street, WC2R 3JX

Registrars and Transfer Office
National Wesminster Bank Limited
P.O. Box 82, 37 Broad Street, Bristol BS99 7NH

DECCA LIMITED
Summary of Results
For the Year ended 31st March, 1979

	1979	1978
	£000	£000
Group turnover	182,500	186,300
Overseas turnover, including direct exports	104,900	112,300
Profit before interest	4,170	14,914
Depreciation	7,326	6,789
Interest payable less receivable	4,554	2,610
(Loss)/Profit before tax	(384)	12,304
(Loss)/Profit before special items	(2,353)	4,788
(Loss)/Profit after tax attributable to Decca Limited	(5,264)	4,095
Ordinary and 'A' Ordinary Dividends at 3.3p per share		
(1978 — 11.89643p)	621	2,238
Net cash flow	1,391	8,596
(Loss)/Earnings per share, after special items	(28.3p)	21.5p

DECCA LIMITED
Report of the Directors

The Directors submit to the Shareholders their Report and the Statement of Accounts for the year ended 31st March, 1979.

Principal Activities
Decca Limited is a Holding Company providing administrative services to the Group.

The principal activities of the Group are the design, manufacture, marketing and hiring of navigational aids, radar and other electronic equipment and the provision of navigational services (capital goods) and the manufacture and marketing of records, tapes, television, audio equipment, etc. (consumer goods).

Profits and Dividends	£000	£000
A summary of Results for the year is given above.		
The Group Loss after allowing for Taxation and amount attributable to Minority Interests as above amounts to		(2,353)
To which are added the special items referred to in Note 6 to the Accounts		(2,911)
Net Loss for the year attributable to Decca Ltd.		(5,264)
From reserves there has been appropriated:		
Dividends on the three classes of Cumulative Preference Shares	(50)	
Interim Dividend on Ordinary and 'A' Ordinary Shares of 3.3p per share	(621)	
		(671)
The Directors do not recommend a Final Dividend on the Ordinary and 'A' Ordinary Shares.		
Deficiency of the Year		(5,935)

Changes in Group's Reserves arising from
(a) effect of currency changes on:

Fixed assets of Overseas Subsidiaries	(611)
Reserves of Associated Companies	(175)
	(786)
(b) transfer from Deferred Taxation	9,259
Reserves brought forward	51,332
Reserves carried forward as Note 13 to the Accounts	53,870

The results for the year to 31st March, 1979 were disappointing. The change from a pretax profit in the previous year to a loss was mainly a consequence of three factors, namely the strength of the £, rising labour costs and higher interest charges.

Exports of £58 million represented 43% of UK output. In this important area the strengthening of the £ throughout the year — the US$ moved from 1.86 to 2.06 — created an increasing competitive disadvantage for Decca. We were unable to increase selling prices adequately and were indeed under pressure to reduce them despite rapidly rising costs.

The rising costs consisted in part of substantial increases in our UK wages and salaries. In addition, prolonged industrial action in some areas disrupted production with consequent loss of output and increased costs. Total UK wages and salaries for slightly fewer employees rose by nearly £6 millions to £39 millions.

The third major factor was the increase in UK clearing bank base rates which rose from 6½% to 13% during the year, at a time when bank borrowings rose partly to finance higher capital goods stocks and debtors less creditors. The resulting interest charge of £4.5 millions for the year was almost £2 millions more than during 1977–78.

The marine radar business was seriously affected by the strong £ and rising costs; as a result, total profits from radar were only marginally better than breakeven. Navigator profits, although somewhat lower, were satisfactory, while losses on the survey group were appreciably higher.

The TV and audio loss was similar to that of the previous year, while the record group changed from profit to loss. In particular, profits of the Nigerian record company, which had been an important contributor in the previous year, fell substantially; we incurred a small loss in the UK record company and also suffered losses in USA and Canada. Music publishing and printing both produced good profits.

The Board regret that the Group results for the past year do not justify their recommending payment of a final dividend on the Ordinary and 'A' Ordinary shares.

The Directors have adopted the treatment of Deferred Taxation recommended in the Statement of Standard Accounting Practice No. 15 and as a result have transferred £9,259,000 to Reserves.

During the first 5 months of the present financial year the three main adverse factors mentioned above have continued. The further strengthening of the £ in relation to the US$ and the Japanese Yen now represents a greater competitive disadvantage to Decca. Since 1st April, 1979 UK clearing bank base rates have moved up to 14% and industrial action continued in certain areas until August.

As a result of recent pay negotiations with the unions, restrictions have now been removed and we are engaged in discussions with the objective of increasing our productive effort and restoring profitability. Economies are being made throughout the group, especially where the demand for the products has fallen. We are also moving ahead with new developments, particularly in areas where increased demand and future profitability are foreseen, while modernization projects recently completed are producing higher output at lower costs.

The navigator marine rental business continues at a satisfactory level, while deliveries of our doppler equipment are expected to double during the present financial year with a further increase in 1980–81. Marine radar sales have been adversely affected in the new financial year both by the exchange rate factor and by the rise in the price of oil which has reduced sales to the US pleasure boat market. The radar company is building up its turnover in electronic warfare equipment as rapidly as possible. Survey contracts for oil exploration west of Ireland and off the coast of China represent new areas of activity. Orders on hand for capital goods are the highest yet achieved.

While profits from the sale of defence equipment are taking longer to materialize than expected, the Board believes that the steps being taken, the high technology of the group's products and their reputation form a firm basis for Decca's future.

The death on 21st May, 1979 of Sir Robert Adeane is deeply regretted. He had given most valuable service to the company since he became a director in 1962 and is greatly missed.

Mr Nigel N. Graham Maw, senior partner of our solicitors, Rowe & Maw, joined the Board on 12th April, 1979 and has been appointed a non-executive Deputy Chairman.

Turnover and Profits before Interest and Taxation
(a) An analysis of the Group Turnover for the year to 31st March, 1979, with comparative figures for the previous year, is shown in the following table:

	Capital Goods Electronics: Navigator, Survey Radar, etc.		Consumer Goods Records, Tapes, TV, Audio, etc.		Total	
	1979 £000	1978 £000	1979 £000	1978 £000	1979 £000	1978 £000
Overseas, including direct exports	75,500	73,000	29,400	39,300	104,900	112,300
United Kingdom	36,300	34,300	41,300	39,700	77,600	74,000
	111,800	107,300	70,700	79,000	182,500	186,300

Consumer goods turnover figures for the year to 31st March, 1979 exclude the turnover of Decca (West Africa) Limited which has become an Associated Company in which Decca's interest is now 40% (1978 £7,100,000).

The geographical analysis of the turnover was United Kingdom 42%, North America 17% and Rest of World 41%.

(b) Total Exports from UK companies amounted to £58,600,000 (1978 £59,400,000).

Exports do not include the value of equipments leaving the UK on hire rental but income from equipment rental and related services is included as are also royalties receivable from overseas.

(c) The year's profits before interest and taxation attributable to the major activities of the Group were as follows:

Capital Goods: £5,932,000 (1978: £14,413,000).
Consumer Goods: Loss £1,762,000 (1978: Profit £501,000).

Board of Directors
The Directors of the Company are as shown on page 327. Sir Robert Adeane, OBE, also was a Director until his death on 21st May, 1979.

Mr N.N. Graham Maw who was appointed a Director on 12th April, 1979 retires and, being eligible, offers himself for re-election.

The Director retiring by rotation is Mr W.L. Spalding who, being eligible, offers himself for re-election.

Directors' Contracts
None of the Directors has held any material interest, directly or indirectly, in any contract of significance in relation to the Company's business at any time during the financial year ended 31st March, 1979.

Directors' Rights to acquire Shares in the Company
At no time during the year ended 31st March, 1979, has there subsisted any arrangement to which the Company has been a party with the object of enabling any Director of the Company to acquire benefits by means of the acquisition of shares or debentures in the Company or in any other body corporate.

Directors' Interests
The Companies Act 1967 requires disclosure of a director's beneficial interests and interests as a trustee (other than as a bare trustee) in shares of the Company, interests of his wife and infant children (but not other members of his family) and interests of any company of which he controls at least one-third of the voting power.

The following statement shows particulars of Directors' interests in the Company's Shares as required by Section 16 (1) (e) of the Companies Act 1967.

Interests in Share Capital of the Company
In accordance with notifications received by 31st August, 1979 the following substantial interests in the Ordinary Share Capital of the Company subsisted as at that date:

Kuwait Investment Office		715,000	9.89%
The Prudential Assurance Co. Ltd		533,121	7.37%
Sir Edward Lewis — Beneficial	314,280		
As Trustee	375,000		
		689,280	9.54%
Dr Jack Dimenstein		593,000	8.20%

So far as the Directors are aware, the Company is not a close company within the provisions of the Income and Corporation Taxes Act 1970, as amended.

Fixed Assets
Particulars of the changes during the year are shown in Note 9 relating to the Accounts.

Group Employment and Remuneration
The average number of persons employed by the Company and its Subsidiaries during the year who worked wholly or mainly in the United Kingdom was 9,770 and the aggregate remuneration paid during the year to all such employees was £39,301,000. At 31st March, 1979, the total number of persons employed by the Group was 11,580 of whom 1,709 were employed by overseas subsidiaries.

Charitable and Political Contributions
During the year under review contributions by the Group for UK charitable purposes amounted to £21,000.

In furtherance of the causes of private enterprise a sum of £5,000 was paid by the Company to British United Industrialists.

Auditors
A resolution will be put to the Annual General Meeting proposing the appointment of Cooper Basden & Adamson as Auditors being the firm into which the practice of Mellors, Basden & Co. is to be merged on 1st October, 1979.

By Order of the Board,
W.L. SPALDING,
Secretary

31st September 1978

DECCA LIMITED and its subsidiaries
Consolidated Profit and Loss Account and Movements on Reserves
For the year ended 31st March, 1979

Notes		£000	1979 £000	£000	1978 £000
1(d)	**Group turnover**		182,500		186,300
2	**Balance from Trading Account** after charging Depreciation £7,326,000 (1978 £6,789,000)		3,820		14,527
2	Share of Results of Associated Companies		350		387
	Group Profit before Interest		4,170		14,914
3	**Interest payable** *less* **receivable**		(4,554)		(2,610)
	Group (Loss)/Profit before Taxation		(384)		12,304
5(a)	**Taxation**		(1,591)		(6,864)
	Group (Loss)/Profit after Taxation		(1,975)		5,440
	Attributable to Minority Shareholders in Subsidiaries		(378)		(652)
	Net (Loss)/Profit before special items		(2,353)		4,788
6	Special items		(2,911)		(693)
	Net (Loss)/Profit attributable to Decca Limited		(5,264)		4,005
	Dividends on the three classes of Preference Shares	(50)		(50)	
	Dividends payable on Ordinary and 'A'				

Ordinary Shares:		
Interim of 3.3p per share (1978 3.3p)	(621)	(621)
Final Nil (1978 8.59643p per share)	—	(1,617)
	(671)	(2,288)

(Deficiency)/Retained profits of the year	(5,935)	1,897

Changes in Group's reserves arising from
(a) effect of currency changes on:

Fixed assets of Overseas Subsidiaries	(611)	(776)
Reserves of Associated Companies	(175)	351
	(786)	(425)

(b) adjustments to reserves of Associated Companies	—	(43)
5(b) (c) transfer from Deferred Taxation	9,259	10,000
Reserves brought forward	51,332	39,993
13 **Reserves carried forward**	53,870	51,332

The profit dealt with in the Accounts of
Decca Limited is £1,264,000 (1978
£2,518,000)

7 **(Loss)/Earnings per share —**		
before special items	(12.8p)	25.2p
after special items	(28.3p)	21.5p

DECCA LIMITED and its subsidiaries
Consolidated Balance Sheet
As at 31st March, 1979

Notes		1979		1978	
			Issued and		Issued and
		Authorised	Fully Paid	Authorised	Fully Paid
	Capital	£000	£000	£000	£000
	3.5% Cumulative Preference Shares of £1 each	600	600	600	600
	11.2% Cumulative Preference Shares of 25p each	59	58	59	58
	17.5% Cumulative Preference Shares of 25p each	130	130	130	130
	Ordinary Shares of 25p each	1,807	1,807	1,807	1,807
	'A' Ordinary Shares of 25p each	2,895	2,895	2,895	2,895
	Shares of 25p each	750	—	750	—
		6,241	5,490	6,241	5,490
	Share Premium Account		3,833		3,883
13	**Reserves**		53,870		51,332
	Shareholders' Funds		63,243		60,705
	Minority Interests		1,745		2,918
5(b)	**Deferred Taxation**		2,583		13,211
	Prepaid Revenue				
	Equipment rental income	7,287		7,074	
	Advance payments against contracts	13,836		4,605	
			21,123		11,670

6% Unsecured Loan Stock 1980/85		4,500	4,500
14 **Secured Loans**		1,399	1,829
Current Liabilities			
Corporation Tax due 1st January, 1980	87	139	
Advanced Corporation Tax	1,061	1,845	
Current Taxation	1,678	2,129	
Proposed Final Ordinary and 'A' Ordinary Dividend	—	1,617	
Other dividends	621	624	
15 Bank loans and overdrafts	44,958	31,200	
Creditors	41,809	39,828	
		90,214	77,882
		184,807	172,224

Notes		At cost £000	Aggregate Depreciation £000	1979 £000	1978 £000
9	**Fixed Assets**				
	Freehold land and buildings	6,077	319	5,758	6,128
	Expenditure on leased premises:				
	Long lease	275	46	229	234
	Short lease	2,302	905	1,397	1,154
	Plant and machinery, vehicles and equipment	33,652	19,086	14,566	13,372
	Ships	1,474	751	723	1,194
	Navigator transmitting chains	4,732	2,468	2,264	2,250
	Apparatus for or on hire	30,190	18,111	12,079	11,653
		78,702	41,686	37,016	35,985
10	Trade Investments			2,708	2,456
11	Development Account and Goodwill			1,335	1,306
				41,059	39,747
	Current Assets				
12	Stocks and work in progress	68,790		60,734	
	Debtors and prepayments, *less* provisions	67,803		63,198	
	Short-term deposits and loans	999		1,997	
	Cash at banks and in hand	6,156		6,548	
			143,748		132,477
			184,807		172,224

DECCA LIMITED and its subsidiaries
Source and Application of Funds Statement
For the year ended 31st March, 1979

Source of Funds	1979 £000	1978 £000
(Loss)/Profit after taxation	(1,975)	5,440
Retained profits of associated companies	(339)	(20)
	(2,314)	5,420
Special items	(2,954)	(709)

	(5,268)	4,711
Net book value of fixed assets disposals	1,689	948
Net book value of trade investment sold	25	—
Sundries	4	1
	(3,550)	5,660

Adjustments for items not involving the use of funds

Depreciation	7,326	6,789
Goodwill	(23)	60
Provision for deferred taxation	(1,369)	5,493
Conversion of a subsidiary to an associate	(965)	—
	4,969	12,342
	1,419	18,002

Application of Funds

Dividends paid to shareholders	2,291	2,054
Dividends paid to minorities	575	384
Fixed Assets & Development Account	10,748	11,001
	13,614	13,439

Increase in working capital

Stocks	8,056	6,953
Debtors	4,605	3,836
Creditors	(1,981)	(1,379)
Taxation liabilities	1,287	4,574
Equipment Rental Income prepaid	(213)	(181)
Advance payments against contracts	(9,231)	(586)
	2,523	13,217
	16,137	26,656

Net outflow of funds (14,718) (8,654)

Represented by

Increase in bank borrowings	(13,758)	(7,659)
Decrease/(Increase) in secured loans	430	(724)
	(13,328)	(8,883)

(Decrease)/Increase in short term

deposits	(998)	1,090
(Decease) in cash at banks	(392)	(1,361)
	(1,390)	(271)
	(14,718)	(8,654)

DECCA LIMITED and its subsidiaries
Notes on the Accounts

1. Accounting Policies

(a) Basis of Consolidation
The Consolidated Accounts comprise the accounts of the Company and all its subsidiaries. Where because of local legislation or accounting practice an

overseas company has not complied with the Group's accounting policies, adjustments are made upon consolidation to ensure that the Consolidated Accounts are presented on a uniform basis.

The net excess book value of shares in subsidiaries over net attributable tangible assets of those subsidiaries at dates of acquisition is included in the Consolidated Balance Sheet under the heading of Development Account and Goodwill.

(b) Associated Companies
The Consolidated Accounts also include the Group's attributable share of the results and post-acquisition retained profits and reserves of associated companies based upon their latest financial accounts and, where appropriate, management accounts for subsequent periods, as indicated in Note 10.

(c) Foreign Currencies
All assets and liabilities and results in foreign currencies are converted into sterling at approximate rates current at the date to which the Company makes up its accounts, except that development expenditure and original capital of American subsidiaries up to 31st March 1949 are converted at US $4.03 to the £.

(d) Group Turnover
Group turnover represents the amount receivable from third parties for the supply of goods and services (after the deduction of trade discounts and agents' commissions) and income from licensees of the Group's patents, copyrights, trade marks and techniques.

(e) Research and Development and Recording Repertoire Expenditure

(i) Expenditure on the Group's research and development is charged against revenue as incurred.
(ii) Expenditure on recording repertoire is charged against revenue as incurred together with provisions for any expected future losses on current contracts: disposals are credited to revenue as they occur.

(f) Fixed Assets
Equipment manufactured by the Group is capitalised at the cost of direct labour, materials and manufacturing overheads.

(g) Depreciation

(i) Assets other than Freeholds comprising Navigator Transmitting Chains are amortised over periods of 10 or 14 years.
(ii) Freeholds are being depreciated over 50 years from 1st April 1977 or date of acquisition whichever is the later.
(iii) Expenditure on Leaseholds is amortised over the unexpired period of the lease or 50 years, whichever is the lesser.
(iv) Expenditure on purchase of 'know how' is amortised over six years.
(v) Depreciation on other fixed assets is provided on a straight line basis at rates estimated to write off their costs over their expected life, generally 10 years.

(h) Stocks and Work in Progress
Stocks and Work in Progress are valued at the lower cost (including manufacturing overheads) or net realisable value.

(i) Long Term Contracts (in excess of one year)

(i) Profits on manufacturing contracts are taken to revenue as part deliveries are made to the customer.
(ii) On other contracts, where selling prices are generally fixed by reference to costs, profits attributable to such costs are credited as the expenditure is incurred.

Where selling prices are not yet agreed only a conservative estimate of profit is included. Provision is made for any expected future losses.

(j) Deferred Taxation

Certain items of income and expense are reported in the Accounts in years which do not coincide with the years in which they are taxed or allowed for tax. The net future liability to taxation arising from such net timing differences and from the withdrawal of relief for increases in stock values is provided in accordance with the principles of the Statement of Standard Accounting Practice No. 15, no provision being made where there is a reasonable probability that no liability will arise in the foreseeable future. No provision is made for taxes which may become payable upon the distribution of profits retained by overseas subsidiaries or associated companies.

	1979	1978
2. Trading Account	£000	£000
The Balance from Trading Account is stated after charging:		
Audit fees	442	428
Hire of plant and machinery and the charter of ships	1,709	2,203
The Share of Results of Associated Companies includes interest received	56	56

	1979	1978
3. Interest	£000	£000
Interest payable:		
On loans repayable after 31st March, 1984	282	283
On other loans and overdrafts	4,686	2,768
	4,968	3,051
Less: Interest receivable	414	441
Total net interest payable for the Company and its subsidiaries	4,554	2,610

	1979	1978
4. Emoluments and Directors and Senior Employees of Decca Limited	£	£
Directors' Fees	5,400	5,267
Other emoluments	17,022	16,641
Pension to the widow of a past Director	2,404	2,401
	24,826	24,312
Particulars required under Sections 6 to 8 of the Companies Act 1967 are as follows:		
Emoluments of the Chairman	nil	nil
Emoluments of the highest paid Director	£16,627	£18,095
Number of other Directors in the following scales:		
£0–£2,500	two	two
£2,501–£5,000	one	one

Emoluments waived by five Directors (1978 five
Directors)   £13,050 £13,050
Number of senior employees in the following scales:
£10,001–£12,500   four   one
£12,501–£15,000   two   one
£17,501–£20,000   nil   two
20,001–£22,500   two   nil

5. Taxation

	1979		1978	
(a) The charge to Profit and Loss Account for taxation is made up as follows:	£000	£000	£000	£000
UK Corporation Tax —				
Current (including Advance Corporation Tax £291,000)	578		(Cr.) (320)	
Deferred	(Cr.) (1,086)		6,130	
		(Cr.) (508)		5,816
Double Taxation Relief		(133)		(1,032)
		(641)		4,784
Overseas Tax — Current	1,948		2,328	
Deferred	(Cr.) (2)		(Cr.) (374)	
		1,946		1,354
Associated Companies		172		238
Charge based on results of year to date		1,477		6,973
Prior years' adjustments		114		(104)
As Profit and Loss Account		1,591		6,864

(b) The provision made for deferred taxation in the Consolidated Balance Sheet in accordance with the principles set out in Statement of Standard Accounting Practice No. 15, after transferring to reserves £9,259,000 (1978 £10,000,000), is made up as follows:–

	1979 £000	1978 £000
Taxation deferred by reason of:		
Relief for increases in stock values	1,172	3,794
Timing differences (mainly accelerated capital allowances)	1,411	11,586
	2,583	15,350
Less: Advance Corporation Tax carried forward	—	2,139
As Consolidated Balance Sheet	2,583	13,211

(c) Had provision for deferred taxation been made in full, the total provison in the Consolidated Balance Sheet at 31st March, 1979 would have been £13,363,000 made up as follows:

	1979 £000	1978 £000
Relief for increases in stock values	10,296	

Timing differences (mainly accelerated capital allowances)	12,843	
		23,139
Less: Losses for tax purposes carried forward	7,360	
Advance Corporation Tax carried forward	2,416	
		9,776
		13,363

6. Special Items

	1979 £000	1978 £000
(1) Loss on reorganisation, cessation or disposal of business activities	(1,461)	(205)
(2) Net surplus on sale of trade investment	119	—
(3) Net loss upon realisation or revaluation of current assets and liabilities in foreign currencies outstanding at 31st March, 1978, less attributable minority interests	(1,569)	(488)
	(2,911)	(693)

7. Earnings per Share

The earnings per share have been calculated by reference to 7,228,024 Ordinary and 11,581,634 'A' Ordinary Shares in issue throughout the year on losses both before and after charging special items, less the cost of preference dividends.

8. Capital Commitments

	1979 £000	1978 £000
(a) Contracted for at 31st March by Subsidiaries	1,747	986
(b) Authorised at 31st March by respective Boards of Directors of Subsidiary Companies but not then contracted for	1,071	311

9. Fixed Assets — Summary of Movements

(a) Group	Total £000	Freehold Land and Buildings £000	Expenditure on Leased Premises Long Lease £000	Expenditure on Leased Premises Short Lease £000	Plant Machinery Vehicles and Equipment £000	Ships £000	Navigator Transmitting Chains £000	Apparatus for or on Hire £000
Cost								
As at 31st March, 1978	73,826	6,343	274	1,929	30,446	1,990	4,572	28,272
Disposals	(4,676)	(235)		(60)	(1,534)	(512)	(278)	(2,057)
Additions	10,741	160	1	444	5,363	7	472	4,294
Adjustment on currency change	(1,189)	(191)		(11)	(623)	(11)	(34)	(319)
As at 31st March, 1979	78,702	6,077	275	2,302	33,652	1,474	4,732	30,190
Depreciation Provision								
As at 31st March, 1978	37,841	215	40	775	17,074	796	2,322	16,619
Disposals elimination	(2,987)	29		(31)	(1,044)	(146)	(60)	(1,735)
Charge for the year	7,326	55	6	166	3,345	104	225	3,425
Adjustment on currency change	(494)	20		(5)	(289)	(3)	(19)	(198)
As at 31st March, 1979	41,686	319	46	905	19,086	751	2,468	18,111

(b) Company
Cost

As at 31st March, 1978	1,059	569	68	2	420
Disposals	(15)	(9)			(6)
Additions	56			16	40
As at 31st March, 1979	1,100	560	68	18	454

Depreciation Provision

As at 31st March, 1978	300	58	12	1	229
Disposals elimination	(9)	(8)			(1)
Charge for the year	43	11	2	4	26
As at 31st March, 1979	334	61	14	5	254

(c) The Navigator Transmitting Chains comprise the following assets:

	Cost		Provision for Depreciation	
	1979 £000	1978 £000	1979 £000	1978 £000
Freehold Land and Buildings	797	792	115	96
Expenditure on Leased Premises:				
Long Lease	17	17	17	17
Short Lease	317	311	192	183
Plant, Machinery, Vehicles and Equipment	3,601	3,018	2,144	2,028
Chains under construction	—	434	—	—
As at 31st March	4,732	4,572	2,468	2,322

10. Trade Investments

	Group		Company	
	1979 £000	1978 £000	1979 £000	1978 £000
Associated Companies — unquoted	—			
At cost *less* provisions	325	212	88	87
Share of post-acquisition reserves	2,212	2,048	—	—
	2,537	2,260	88	87
Others — unquoted, at cost (uncalled liability £90,000)	34	34	10	10
quoted, at cost	137	162	137	162
	2,708	2,456	235	259
Market value of quoted investments	766	475	766	475
In the opinion of the Directors the value of other unquoted investments does not materially differ from the cost of £34,000 Dividends receivable, including tax credit:				
Associated Companies	2	237	2	175
Other unquoted investments	5	4	—	—
Quoted investments	58	51	58	51

The principal Associated Companies in which the Group has a direct interest are:

Name	Country of Incorporation	Class of share	Percentage of issued equity shares held	Latest financial accounts
Decca Holding Limited	Liechtenstein	Ordinary	50%	31.12.78
Decca Holding Limited	Switzerland	Ordinary	50%	31.12.78
Communications Distribution and Export Co. (UK) Limited	England	Ordinary	50%	31.3.79
Communications Associates of Nigeria Limited	Nigeria	Ordinary	30.6%	31.3.79
*Record Merchandisers Limited	England	Ordinary	25%	30.6.78
*Record Manufacturers of Nigeria Limited	Nigeria	Ordinary	35%	30.6.78
Decca (West Africa) Limited	Nigeria	Ordinary	40%	31.3.79

* The results of these companies brought into the Consolidated Accounts are derived from management accounts and apportioned on a time basis to the year ended 31st March, 1979.

Decca Holding Limited Liechtenstein and Decca Holding Limited Switzerland (in both of which companies the remaining 50% of equity shares is beneficially held by Mrs Sara Dimenstein, wife of Dr J. Dimenstein) own respectively 50% of the issued capitals of Teldec International AG (TED AG) and Teldec Telefunken–Decca Schallplatten GmbH (TELDEC). Decca Holding Limited Liechtenstein also owns 51% of the issued capital of Decca Dischi Italia SpA. From 1951 until 30th June, 1977 Decca Holding Limited Liechtenstein and Decca Holding Limited Switzerland have, under arrangements for the mutual licensing of repertoires, participated in royalties receivable from sales in Germany and Italy of Decca repertoire records and tapes. On 1st July, 1977 the right to receive such royalties was vested in The Decca Record Company Limited but Mrs Dimenstein continues to participate therein through her holding of a special class of share in Decca Holding Limited Switzerland; such share carries no rights other than that of securing the continuation of her beneficial interest to the same extent as hitherto.

11. Development Account and Goodwill

	1979 £000	1978 £000
Excess of expenditure over income incurred by three subsidiaries in connection with the Decca Navigator system during periods ended on or before 31st March, 1952	601	601
Net losses from dates of formation or acquisition to 31st March, 1949, of other subsidiaries in USA and Canada	162	162
Goodwill at cost, including net premiums on acquisition of subsidiaries	417	391
Patent Rights and Trade Marks at cost, *less* amounts written off	1	1
Prototypes and design work for future production	1	1
'Know-how' at cost, *less* amortisation £219,000 (1978 £218,000)	—	—
Matrices at or below cost	50	50

Expenditure, other than £460,000 spent on dry wells, incurred to date by Dolphin Petroleum Ltd. in the exploitation of North Sea petroleum licences £202,000, *less* 4% minority interest therein

	103	96
	1,335	1,306

12. Stocks and Work in Progress

	1979 £000	1978 £000
Stocks and Work in Progress at 31st March were made up as follows:–		
Raw materials and work in progress	44,822	36,015
Finished Goods	26,742	26,675
	71,564	62,690
Less: Cash received on account	2,774	1,956
As Consolidated Balance Sheet	68,790	60,734

13. Reserves

	Group £000	Company £000	Subsidiaries £000	Associated Companies £000
As at 31st March, 1978	51,332	13,115	36,169	2,048
Effect of currency changes on:				
Fixed assets of Overseas Subsidiaries	(611)		(611)	
Reserves of Associated Companies	(175)			(175)
Transfer from Deferred Taxation	9,259	192	9,067	
(Deficiency)/Retained profits of the year	(5,935)	593	(6,867)	339
As at 31st March, 1979	53,870	13,900	37,758	2,212

Reserves of Subsidiaries at 31st March, 1979 include £100,000 reserves of certain overseas subsidiaries which are not distributable under present local legislation.

14. Secured Loans

Secured loans include loans repayable after 31st March, 1984 £129,000 (1978 £218,000) repayable by instalments, the latest of which is due in 2028 and the annual rates of interest currently payable are between 5% and 12%.

Loans repayable within one year amount to £205,000, between one and two years £200,000 and between two and five years £865,000.

15. Bank Loans and Overdrafts

The aggregate amount of bank loans and overdrafts at 31st March, 1979 shown in the Consolidated Balance Sheet includes secured loans and overdrafts of £3,197,000 (1978 £746,000).

Of the total of £44,958,000 bank loans and overdrafts £29,604,000 is repayable within one year, £9,754,000 between one and two years, £4,400,000 between two and five years and £1,200,000 is repayable after more than 5 years.

The Parent Company is contingently liable under guarantees of certain liabilities of Subsidiary Companies, one of which, if enforced, would bring an unsecured bank loan of £3,000,000 within the floating charge mentioned below. Group guarantees which relate to overseas bank loans could, if enforced, require payment in investment currency; the excess cost as at 31st March, 1979 of investment currency over ordinary rate currency £133,000 is not provided for in these accounts. There is a floating charge on the assets of and guarantees by the Parent Company to secure sums from time to time owing to bankers by the Company and five Subsidiaries.

16. Contingent Liabilities

	1979	1978
	£000	£000
In respect of bills receivable — Parent Company	1,274	1,723
Subsidiaries	803	2,191

Guarantees have been given by the Parent Company £200,000 (1978 £200,000) and two Subsidiaries £275,000 (1979 £225,000) in respect of bank advances to Associated Companies.

17. Contingent Assets

In an action against the US Government for infringement of a Decca patent the Trial Judge in the US Court of Claims has recommended that Decca Limited be awarded $39,355,715 up to 31st March, 1979, plus additional delay compensation at $5,436 per day from 1st April, 1979 till date of payment. The US Government has appealed against the recommendation.

18. Subsidiary Companies

At 31st March, 1979 the Subsidiary Companies which, in the opinion of the Directors, principally affected the results of the year and/or assets of the Group were as follows:–

Held by the Company	Country of Incorporation	Issued shares held
The Decca Record Company Limited	England	100%
The Decca Navigator Company Limited	England	100%
Decca Radar Limited	England	100%
Decca Survey Limited	England	100%
Internationale Navigatie Apparaten BV	Netherlands	50.1%
Held by Subsidiary Companies		
Decca Radio & Television Limited	England	100%
London Records Inc.	USA	100%
Deram Limited	Canada	100%
ITT Decca Marine Inc.	USA	50.125%

The financial year-end of Internationale Navigatie Apparaten BV was, at the time of acquisition, 31st December, in accordance with Netherlands custom and the Directors do not consider alteration of this date would significantly affect that company's trading results or assets included in the consolidated accounts of the Group.

Particulars of excessive length would be required in order to include details of all Subsidiary Companies.

DECCA LIMITED and its subsidiaries
Summary of Consolidated Results
Years ended 31st March

	Turnover	Depreciation	Profits before tax	Profits after Tax and Minority Interests	Profits Retained after tax	Preference Shares Dividends	Ordinary and 'A' Ordinary Shares Dividends	Number ranking	Dividends per Share
	£000	£000	£000	£000	£000	£000	£000		
1951	4,800	149	354	249	163	22	64	2,182,629	1/1½d.
1952	6,200	194	797	375	260	21	94	2,400,910	1/8d.
1953	7,200	227	943	381	235	21	125	2,600,928	1/9d.
1954	8,300	284	1,203	408	213	22	173	2,801,610	2/3d.
1955	9,600	342	1,141	538	235	39	264	5,253,018	1/9d.
1956	12,900	434	1,032	450	57	41	352	7,004,024	1/9d.
1957	17,100	599	1,403	581	117	41	423	8,404,829	1/9d.
1958	21,000	735	1,862	931	407	41	483	8,404,829	2/–d.
1959	21,800	881	1,953	1,031	475	41	515	8,404,829	2/–d.
1960	25,200	1,020	2,167	1,261	616	44	601	8,404,829	2/4d.
1961	24,500	1,134	2,310	1,249	604	44	601	8,404,829	2/4d.
1962	27,600	1,209	2,930	1,482	795	44	643	8,404,829	2/6d.
1963	28,000	1,298	2,958	1,444	714	44	686	8,404,829	2/8d.
1964	30,200	1,367	2,620	1,340	588	44	708	8,404,829	2/9d.
1965	36,900	1,584	3,939	2,167	1,321	44	802	8,404,829	3/3d.
1966	36,300	1,592	4,324	2,617	1,413	42	1,162	8,404,829	3/3d.
1967	40,000	1,847	4,451	2,578	1,070	72	1,436	8,404,829	3/5d.
1968	47,000	2,158	§3,765	†2,338	†795	72	1,471	8,404,829	3/6d.
1969	48,500	2,311†	3,011	1,581	38	72	1,471	*16,809,658	*1/9d.
1970	61,300	2,566	5,339	2,733	1,071	72	1,590	17,347,658	1/10d.
1971	66,700	2,740	3,004	1,548	(114)	72	1,590	17,347,658	9.1666p (1/10d.)
1972	81,800	2,727	7,063	3,859	1,762	72	2,025	18,809,658	11p
1973	116,400	2,996	15,082	9,224	7,631	72	1,521	18,809,658	8.085p (11.55p gross)
1974	136,600	3,620	16,286	‡7,506	4,848	50	1,528	18,809,658	8.125425p
1975	154,300	4,256	13,283	●4,613	1,768	50	1,631	18,809,658	8.67116p
1976	170,000	4,901	13,595	5,135	3,291	50	1,794	18,809,658	9.53827p
1977	181,400	5,574	15,888	6,620	4,566	50	2,004	18,809,658	10.65352p
1978	186,300	6,789	12,304	4,095	1,807	50	2,238	18,809,658	11.89643p
1979	182,500	7,326	(384)	(5,264)	(5,935)	50	621	18,809,658	3.3p

§ Excluding £987,000 devaluation revenue surplus. † Excluding £587,000 not devaluation revenue surplus.
* On 22nd October, 1968, each Ordinary Share of 50p and each 'A' Ordinary Share of 50p was subdivided into two such shares of 25p.
‡ Before deduction of exceptional taxation items £1,080,000. ● Before deduction of loss on 'Bed and Breakfast' sale of quoted trade investments £1,164,000. Profits for 1974 and subsequent years include the Group's share of the results of Associated Companies.

Source: Decca Ltd.

REPORT 2: INTERIM RESULTS TO 30 SEPTEMBER 1979[1]

	1979 £000	1978 £000
Capital goods	57,500	50,600
Turnover:		
Consumer goods[2]	28,800	35,000
Total	86,300	85,600
Trading profit	5,502	7,978

Depreciation and amortization	3,750	3,675
Leaving	1,750	4,303
Net interest payable	3,620	1,840
Loss before tax	1,868	[3]2,463
Tax	650	1,175
Net loss	2,518	[3]1,288
Minorities	120	131
Exchange losses	1,025	502
Surplus sale trade investment	750	—
Net costs[4]	193	144
Attributable loss	3,106	[3]511

[1] Excludes associates so not directly comparable with Report 1.
[2] Loss on the record division of £2.95m to 30 September, 1979.
[3] Profit.
[4] Of factory closure and loss on disposal of trading activity.

Source: Decca Ltd.

REPORT 3: RACAL'S FINANCIAL RISE

(a)	1975	1976	1977	1978	1979
			£ million		
Turnover					
(Group and associates)	53.98	79.97	122.26	183.33	226.69
Pre-tax profits	9.56	19.65	32.71	49.83	61.62
Assets	22.06	34.21	74.93	104.83	143.23

Source: Lloyd, J., Financial Times, 19.1.80.

(b) From the Extel Statistical (see *Management Today*, February 1980) Services, Racal showed the following growth record. (Ratio of profits before interest and tax to net capital employed.)

> 1974–78: ninth out of the top 200 with a 53.9% growth rate.
> 1969–78: fifteenth out of the top 200 with a 41.6% growth rate.

(c) The interim results for Racal announced 6 December, 1979 can be summarized from the 'Lex' column:

> The market reacted to the poor interim figures from Racal Electronics by cutting the share price 21p to 194p. Pre-tax profits are only 3.9 per cent higher at £25.3m compared with the rises of 30 per cent typical in previous years. Yet many bulls of the company have their faith intact, believing the setback to be temporary rather than a signal of any fundamental change of direction.
>
> The key problem is radio communications, where Racal has run into delays in landing several big potential contracts in the third world. As a result, turnover in this sector is static, although the company has ploughed ahead in production in order to retain its ability to deliver within eighteen weeks.
>
> Turnover in data communications is up about 27 per cent, helping to take the non-military activities form 50 to 60 per cent of the total. But whether the company recovers its growth pattern in the next year or two will depend to what extent there has been a once-for-all lengthening of the military electronics ordering cycle. There are signs currently of a generally upturn in orders from the Middle East and Racal sailed through the last world recession. But the company was much smaller in 1975 and Third World budgets are likely to be

squeezed so much that even military governments may consider old equipment good enough for the time being.

The market now expects full year profits to come out above £65m against £61.6m last year, for a fully-taxed prospective p/e of 14. That rating still leaves no room for any further disappointment.

Source: 'Lex', Financial Times, 7.12.79.

REPORT 4

(a) From the Extel services, GEC showed the following growth record:

     1974–78: 31.1%
     1969–78: 24.93%

(b) Its closing net capital employed was £1,483.40 million (1978)
    Its closing net profit before interest and tax was £409.8 million (1978).

(c) Its interim results were announced 6 December 1979 showing a fall in profit. We once more quote from the 'Lex' column:

> News that GEC's interim profits have fallen from £162.9m to £155.2m pre-tax sent the shares 19p lower to 317p yesterday. But there are specific reasons for the setback, and profits for the year could still rise from £378.4m to around £400m. More encouragingly for the longer term GEC says there are signs of an improving climate in industrial relations — and of better trends in productivity.
>
> In the first half, however, strikes have taken a heavy toll on profits — £20m or more; as a rough guide. GEC had to cope with internal disputes as well as the national stoppages, and the impact has been especially damaging on power engineering, components and the industrial side. The timing of some big deliveries has also worked against these figures, while the rise in sterling has brought a £5m write down on the cash balances held overseas and reduced overseas profits by perhaps another £3m.
>
> On the positive side, the order intake has held steady despite the absence of some lumpy export contracts which appeared in the comparable figures. The new US business is doing well, and so are electronics, automation and telecommunications — especially by contrast with Plessey and Racal. It is worth noting that two years ago the power engineering and industrial groups accounted for nearly two-fifths of interim profits, which totalled £145m. Now their contribution is down to about one-fifth.
>
> GEC's performance looks pedestrian by comparison with Hitachi, which also produced its interim statement yesterday, showing big gains on the back of a falling currency. But by UK standards, GEC remains outstanding for its balance sheet strength and its profit resilience. The interim dividend is up by a third, and the final ought to go up by at least that amount leaving a yield of 3¾ per cent.
>
> *Source: 'Lex', Financial Times, 7.12.79.*

Questions

1. Analyse the role of takeover bidders as trustees of the shareholders.
2. *Either* Analyse the auction for Decca from the point of view of the various interested parties.
   Or Place a value on Decca.
3. Critically appraise the role of institutional shareholders in achieving change in companies without a change of ownership.

W1.6   Suggested answers to discussion questions

1.1 We live in a capitalist society in which profits are fundamental to the system. That is why shareholders invest, and it is inevitable therefore that the finance function, being concerned as it is with policy towards shareholders (for instance, dividend policy and capital structure decisions), will be central. Moreover, the investment decision within the firm is the key to future profitability, and though the finance department relies upon management skill to develop new projects, or refine existing ones, and though it depends on other experts such as engineers and surveyors to place values of expected future cash flows, nevertheless it holds centre stage when decisions to proceed or not are made.

Whether this is desirable or not is a matter of opinion. The finance officer is not necessarily the most important or powerful manager (though he or she may be), but he or she is *central* to such decisions.

1.2 Shareholders hire managers to work for them, and making day-to-day decisions is part of that work. In general, therefore, they would not want to make such decisions. Anyway, they do not have the required skills, or the time to digest the information necessary to act.

The question makes the point that they are 'theoretically' in control. It is well known that managers/directors can frequently shut out the shareholders from even major decisions, such as those that come to general meetings of the shareholders. Some methods of doing this include:

(a) controlling the flow of information to shareholders, and making recommendations (for instance, as to who is elected to the board of directors);

(b) sending proxy forms to shareholders who cannot or do not wish to attend these meetings. The proxies generally give the directors power to decide on the way the shareholder's vote is directed;

(c) investing some of the pension fund in the company. The trustees of the fund are almost invariably directors or those who will act as they wish;

(d) relying on shareholder apathy or faith;

(e) tightly controlling the conduct of the meetings with the shareholders. (See, for instance, the entertaining accounts in Alex Rubner's angry book *The Ensnared Shareholder* of the way the chairman can switch off the microphone being used by any unhappy shareholder, or even have him or her ejected by commissionaires for 'disrupting the meeting'.)

1.3 There have been a number of approaches to this kind of problem. Economists have had to face it, and one solution has been to suggest that, though firms may not seem to be taking profit-maximizing actions, yet it would be hard to suggest different actions that would have returned higher profit.

There are clearly similarities between profit-maximization and wealth-maximization. There are both theoretical models suggesting that managers do not maximize the owner's wealth (for instance, those of Baumol, Williamson and Marris) and practical observations (can private aircraft really be squared with profit maximization?). The whole theory of agency starts from the proposition that the rational utility-maximizing manager will not maximize shareholder interests unless they coincide with his or her own.

What are we to conclude about managers' behaviour then? There is no 'correct' answer. Clearly we shall be working within this framework of 'unrealistic assumptions' for much of this book. Only the reader can decide if its comments are (a) descriptively true, (b) a proper prescription for action.

1.4 Again you must make your own judgement here. There are different models of the nature of the firm. The more conventional model is based on property rights. The shareholders own the firm and hence it should be run in their interest. Indeed, should they wish, they can apparently enforce this.

If, on the other hand, you subscribe to the coalition model of the firm which acknowledges that many parties come together to form the firm (creditors, managers, suppliers, customers, employees, for instance), then the prevalence of one party seems inequitable.

So far as the theory of the book is concerned, the coalition model is not only scarcely mentioned in the literature, but is also far more difficult to operationalize. But even if you wish to take a more conventional, 'investment-orientated' approach, a further consideration comes in: should the debt-holders as well as the shareholders share in this objective function?

1.5 This question is important in raising questions about the societal aspect of finance. In the models we look at, most variables are microeconomic with some notable exceptions (see, for instance, Miller's 'Debt and Taxes' presidential address in 1977). Now, financial managers like to see the prices of their shares high (we see why later). These prices are arrived at in the securities markets. If these markets work as smoothly as some theorists suggest they do (should), then good-quality investment will be encouraged and general wealth and welfare increase (although this says nothing about the *distribution* of wealth and welfare among members of society).

Other factors could be mentioned. Thus investors' perceptions of risk will affect their willingness to buy the company's securities, and hence affect its cost of borrowing. More expensive borrowing means fewer projects will be started (since some are marginal and will fail the profitability test when rates of return demanded get more stringent).

Learning objectives

This workbook chapter has the following aims:

- to develop your understanding of the operation of the securities markets;
- to strengthen your understanding of one market in particular, namely the UK over-the-counter (OTC) market;
- through the case studies, to give you the opportunity to consider the regulatory problems of the securities markets.

W2.1 Introduction

The text of Chapter 2 is lengthy. This Workbork chapter consists of one reading, three case studies and some self-study questions.

The reading is from 1987 and, on the face of it, a little out of date. However, it raises important questions, and the author is well placed to express opinions that are, perhaps, more trenchant than those permitted to textbook authors.

There are three case studies. The first describes the growth, decline and fall of the UK's over-the-counter market during the 1980s. Given that so much attention is focused on the major UK markets and the increasing globalization of capital markets, it is helpful to be reminded that small companies are important too, and markets such as these may well play a role in making capital available to them.

The second case concerns itself with a 'city scandal': the County NatWest affair. Although the dubious methods used are interesting, we have included the case at least as much because it shows, more vividly than any mere description could, how rights issues operate and the dynamics of the markets into which the issues are injected, as because it raises issues of City regulation.

The third case looks at the proposed takeover of BATs by a consortium led by Sir James Goldsmith. We do not give great emphasis to takeovers in the text, except the Decca case which is a capstone case for this book; and since contested takeovers are often interesting for the personalities involved, this may be a pity. However, a takeover illustrates admirably, albeit in a different way from the County NatWest story, how economic decisions and situations can be perceived differently depending on the point of view being taken. The other advantage of this case, consisting as it does of newspaper articles, is that it gives you, the reader, an opportunity to check that you are literate in the business-speak increasingly common in the financial press.

We hope you find the material interesting as well as informative.

W2.2   Under the skin of an image problem

The following article by John Plender appeared in the *Financial Times* on 15 June 1987.

The City of London is, for the moment, off the political hook. But in the aftermath of Mrs Thatcher's victory at the polls, the financial community has a problem with its image that all the wiles of the slickest advertising agency would do little to dispel.

While Labour failed to fire the voters' imagination with its attacks on City scandals, the electorate certainly did take an interest in another aspect of the sociology of the financial markets. The City yuppies, with their six-figure salaries, Porsche motor cars and liking for champagne bars, came to symbolize the ugly side of the Thatcherite revolution. On television and radio members of the public expressed unease at what they felt to be a climate of greed in the City.

Those who work in the Square Mile are no doubt tempted to dismiss this as a return to the politics of envy. Yet there is more to it than that. The times are surely out of joint when the cream of Oxbridge graduates are being offered starting salaries by UK investment banks of up to £25,000, equivalent to two-and-a-half times the rates on offer from some of Britain's top industrial concerns and more than five times the starting figure for student nurses; when the company that produces all those Porsche motor cars made more money last year from currency and financial market operations than from manufacturing the cars; and where the financiers are making more money than their customers in industry and commerce.

The public has intuitively diagnosed that something is up; and it is important to be clear what it is, because banking, finance and insurance now account for close on 10% of total employment in Britain and [reproduced here as Fig. W2.1] have constituted the fastest growing sector of the economy in terms of employment since Mrs Thatcher came to power.

Indeed, the rise in the financial sector's share of total employment from 7.1% in 1979 to 10% today (which ignores the spin-off generated by the sector's absorption of goods and services from the rest of the economy) suggests that the political debate on the City should have changed rather more than it has. So what is going on? And how can a service industry thrive when there are fewer and fewer manufacturers to service?

The short answer is that the fastest growing part of the City is providing a service mainly to foreign governments, corporations and financial institutions, not British manufacturers. Having established itself during the present economic cycle as the chief financial centre in the European time zone, London operates in a global market. That market is growing faster than most because it thrives on many of the instabilities that are contributing to low growth in the world economy. The City is taking a percentage cut of the huge capital flows that stem from trade imbalances and from financial volatility. It is thriving much as a drug company thrives in an epidemic.

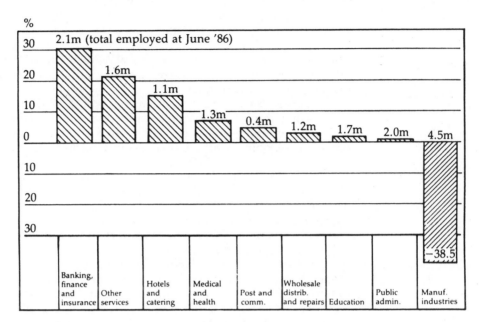

Figure W2.1   Increase in employment from June 1979 to June 1986.

Source: Central Statistical Office.

Put another way, the financial community has been a major beneficiary of the collapse of the Bretton Woods fixed exchange system and the widespread removal of exchange controls. The central bankers' traditional job of stabilizing currencies has, in effect, been privatized and the global financial system has increasingly taken on the role of an insurer against volatility.

A West German manufacturer like Porsche was able to make profits last year, despite the impact of the appreciating D-Mark on its exports to the US, precisely because it was able to hedge in the foreign exchange markets. At the same time multinationals such as General Motors or ICI engage in constant arbitrage through a host of new financial instruments such as swaps to minimize currency and interest rate risks and to reduce the cost of borrowing.

It follows that much of the City's international dealing is not so much anti-social as a symptom of a more fundamental economic malaise. That malaise has been exacerbated by the nature of recent technological development. Computer chips make no demand on the world's main commodity markets, which have been exceptionally depressed in the 1980s: they are made of cheap sand. Nor, as Brian Reading of International Advisory Associates has argued, do they do much to generate new consumer demand, compared with, say, the railway or the motor car. They chiefly change the workings of manufacturing processes and existing consumer products.

Yet the combination of computers and advanced telecommunications has transformed the financial world by reducing dealing costs by up to

90% and creating the potential for a plethora of new financial instruments that rely on complex mathematical formulae. All this contributes to the paradox of ballooning financial activity, high unemployment and low commodity prices across the world.

By diverting disproportionate human resources into financial activity Britain does, however, put itself in a rather peculiar position. Any international move to iron out payments imbalances, to bring back fixed exchange rates and capital controls, or to impose tougher financial regulations on the more casino-like games would, in the short run, have a damaging impact on domestic employment. By playing host to a foreign community whose pay rates reflect conditions on Wall Street, London inevitably contributes to the climate of social divison, and to the perception of a north–south partition.

This perception is a distinctive novelty of Mrs Thatcher's administration. For the City enjoyed a huge boom under Labour in the second part of the 1970s, as the international banks in London recycled the Organization of Petroleum Exporting Countries' petrodollars to Third World oil consumers. Yet it failed to attract envy on this particular score.

The growth of financial sector employment could none the less pose problems for any future Labour government. If Mr Roy Hattersley's proposals for increasing taxes on the rich had borne heavily on expatriates in Britain, for example, banking and securities business might have disappeared to continental Europe — though the risks tend to be exaggerated by those American bankers who were not working in London under the last Labour government.

This suggests that the City's international earnings are, as the financial analysts would say, of less than top quality. Then there is the question of how sensitive the financial system is likely to be to the needs of domestic businesses when its attention is fixed on distant horizons and the dealing habits of the international markets have been allowed to infect the domestic securities system in the wake of the Big Bang.

A domestic financial system has many functions. It exists to enable savers to minimize the excessive risk of direct investment in productive assets by offering a spread of portfolio investments. It allows people to trade earnings in their productive years for consumption in retirement and encourages households in financial surplus to recycle funds to those in deficit. It provides a payment mechanism across the country. Above all, it permits capital to be allocated to the most productive use.

On most of these points the City does a second job and deregulation of the financial markets has genuinely improved consumer choice. But on the final score it has recently come under fundamental attack from Professor Colin Mayer of the City University Business School — and the grounds are far more sophisticated than those offered by Labour during the election.

On the basis of an analysis of the financing of Britain's capital stock between 1970 and 1984, Professor Mayer points out, first, that only 4% of the corporate sector's total funding came from issues of new shares; and second, that if the non-financial sector's purchase of purely financial assets is stripped out of the picture, so isolating its investment in physical assets such as plant and machinery, the capital markets contributed nothing at all. He argues that the pursuit of efficiency in financial markets may be achieved at the expense of the more fundamental objectives of promoting investment and risk taking; and that it contributes to a lack of mutual commitment between investors and the company.

If Mayer's claims are right — and they certainly call for a serious response — they cast the City's domestic dealing activity in a curious light. In the year to June 1986 brokers were charging estimated commissions on equities of £572m, while the difference between the jobbing system's best buying and selling prices may, on tentative estimates, have been running to more than £1.5bn. These figures will have fallen sharply since the Big Bang. But they indicate what a high price has been paid in transaction costs to provide liquidity in a market that, in aggregate, finances no productive investment.

They also raise a question or two about Big Bang. To what purpose has equity market-making capacity been so heavily increased — at the cost, moreover, of creating a shortage of dealing skills that in turn inflates those yuppy salaries?

Of course, some of the casino aspects of the City will prove self-correcting. According to the OECD's latest issue of *Financial Market Trends*, international borrowing activity is slowing down and many forms of financial arbitrage are losing momentum.

But the paradox remains. By urging Big Bang on the City, the Bank of England has promoted increased liquidity in the capital markets. Yet more liquidity leads to less long-term commitment between the providers and users of capital — which happen to be none of the Bank's current worries. It wants fund managers to take a longer-term view and to monitor their stakes in the corporate sector more actively. Yet one of its own recent surveys suggests that a smaller proportion of investment institutions exercised their votes at company meetings than was the case with eligible voters at the general election. A strange way to exert control over British industry. What price liquidity?

W2.3   Case studies

(a) The over-the-counter (OTC) market in the UK

The history of the OTC market

The birth of the UK over-the-counter market in shares may be credited to M.J.H. Nightingale & Co. (now known as Granville), which began making a market in the early 1970s. An OTC market is one that operates outside a recognized stock exchange. It does not take place in a particular building: it consists of a network of dealers who contact each other by telephone.

The market was quiet in the 1970s, but it mushroomed in the 1980s. By 1986 there were estimated to be 160 companies traded, with total market value of £660 million.

At least four reasons have been put forward for the sudden growth at that time. First, there was the bull market of the early 1980s. In such an atmosphere of success, there is a greater propensity for companies to seek capital and a greater likelihood that investors will take higher risks. Second, there was the 'cult of the entrepreneur'. With the increasing influence of the Thatcher ethos, allied to the success of small start-up businesses in the USA, there was an acknowledgement that the commercial world was ready for innovation. Third, there was the government's Business Expansion Scheme, which provided in certain circumstances for tax relief on unquoted shares.

Finally, there were the hard-sell methods used by new dealers who sprang up. Although cold calling (that is, attempting to sell to a client who had not approached the seller) was not permitted, those with whom the new dealers did have relationships found themselves subjected to high-pressure selling, sometimes bordering on the unscrupulous.

Most OTC brokers acted on their own account: the investor would buy shares from them. Others (including Granville) did not: they invited buyers and sellers to contact them, brought them together and took a commission for doing so. This meant that the holder of shares might have to wait some time until a buyer could be found (if at all).

The US counterpart

Successful though the OTC market appeared to be from its growth record, it was small compared to the National Association of Securities Dealers (NASD) in the USA. Since 1971 the NASD had operated the National Association of Securities Dealers Automated Quotations (NASDAQ) system, which is a computerized system linking securities dealers throughout the USA (although it should be noted that NASDAQ is not synonymous with the US OTC market: there were and are OTC stocks outside the NASDAQ system). Terminals in the NASDAQ system provide all the prices being quoted by dealers with stocks to sell, just as on the ISE's SEAQ system.

The success of NASDAQ can be gauged by comparing its size with that of the New York Stock Exchange, which is the largest securities market in the world. In 1986 the annual trading volume was 80% of that of the NYSE, although in dollar terms it was only 28% (the average size of companies and deals is lower) at \$378 billion. This nevertheless makes it a very substantial market indeed.

The problems of the OTC market

Small businesses using the OTC market argued that there was frequently no other convenient source of capital for a growing company in the early 1980s. So far as investors were concerned, it might be argued that shareholders must have been aware that the risks were high and therefore had no basis for complaint if things went wrong. On the other hand, the complaints about the hard sell employed by some dealers suggest that many were not.

There were, indeed, many complaints each year about OTC market abuse. The market had intrinsic problems for those either in it or dealing with it. First, there was the problem of liquidity. Without market-makers and a large market size this would be a problem in the best circumstances. However, often a security was only dealt with by one dealer, which could exacerbate matters. Second, there was a high risk of corporate failure. Third, there was high price volatility. Fourth, the dealers tended to get a reputation for slow paperwork. Fifth, being unregulated, there was always a tendency to suspect that in some cases the dealers might, in recommending shares, be tempted to recommend those shares of which they had a large stock. Sixth, there was often little information on the companies whose shares were being offered. Finally, unlike for members of the ISE, there was no compensation fund if the dealer defaulted.

But the risks were not all on the side of the investors. In a bull market, it was not uncommon for investors to sell the same shares several times over to different dealers as the price went up, finally delivering to the one who paid the most.

The result
Regulation before 1986 was fairly minimal. Dealers had to apply annually to the Department of Trade and Industry for a licence to deal.

However, the Financial Services Act 1986 had a profound effect on the OTC market. It required that firms and individuals trading in securities must be members of a self regulatory authority that was overseen by the Securities and Investments Board (SIB). In the case of OTC dealers this meant the Securities Association (SA). The SA, in turn, was not prepared to accept as members those in whom it lacked confidence. The result was that the OTC market effectively died out during 1988. A small number of brokers were granted membership of the SA, namely Granville, Guidehouse, UTC, Fredericks Place and Baynard Securities. The other houses closed down, some voluntarily, some otherwise.

Granville is one of the few still to have any dealings outside the ISE: it now terms the set of shares it matches, and which it advertises daily in the *Financial Times*, the Independent Companies Exchange. The shares of many other companies, though still in existence, now lack any mechanism for dealing. This has led the *Investors Chronicle* to remark that 'the Government with its strong medicine is punishing the very investors it has sought to protect'.

The Investors Chronicle *investigation*
Some suggest that there were as many as 230 unquoted companies being dealt in the OTC market at the time of its demise. Concerned about the problems of investors who had been disadvantaged by the FSA, the *Investors Chronicle* in October 1989 traced 158 of them. The results were as shown in Table W2.1.

Table W2.1

	No.	%
In liquidation or receivership	40	25
Taken over	22	14
Moved to official stock exchange:		
Main market	3	2
USM	11	7
Third	8	5
'In limbo'	74	47
Total	158	100

The *Investors Chronicle* remarked that, although some companies had kept shareholders informed, others had not. Thus shareholders have been left in a situation where they cannot sell their shares and often cannot even trace the company to contact it, since companies are not required by law to give a trading address or business telephone number in their filing at Companies House. They do have to provide a registered address, but often this is little help.

Speaking to the *Investors Chronicle* about the shareholders left holding OTC shares, a dealer involved in the rump of the OTC market remarked that 'shareholders seem to have just given up the ghost'.

Questions
1. Given the problems of the OTC market, why might (a) companies and (b) investors have used that market rather than the established stock exchange before the advent of the Third Market?

2. As you saw from the text, the Third Market was set up specifically to attract the kind of company that might use the OTC market. Why do you think the OTC market survived a year or more beyond the formation of the Third Market (and indeed, through Granvilles, up to the time of writing)?

3. In describing the problems of the OTC market above, we wrote that it is subject to 'high price volatility'. Why do you think this is so?

4. Do you agree with the statement above that 'shareholders must have been aware that the risks were high and therefore had no basis for complaint if things went wrong'?

5. Explain the *Investors Chronicle's* remark that 'the Government with its strong medicine is punishing the very investors it has sought to protect'.

(b) Blue Arrow–County NatWest

This case has been distilled from public sources. Acknowledgement is particularly made to the summary of the case by J. Sully, 'County NatWest Limited, County NatWest Securities Ltd', Student Accountant, December 1989.

Blue Arrow, an employment agency group, was launched on the Unlisted Securities Market in 1984. By 1987 it had a market capitalization of £400 million. Manpower was an American company with a market capitalization of £600 million (US$ equivalent). In mid-1987 the chairman of Blue Arrow, Mr Tony Berry, discussed with Mr Nick Wells, an executive director of County NatWest, the possibility of bidding for Manpower. County NatWest was an ultimate subsidiary of the National Westminster Bank, one of the UK's largest clearing banks.

On 14 July a US investment bank, Dillon Read & Co., began to buy shares in Manpower on Blue Arrow's behalf, buying a further block of shares the next day. The two days' buying amounted to $7,548,025. Soon afterwards County NatWest made available a $9 million loan facility to Blue Arrow so that it could pay Dillon Read for these shares. The sum of $7,548,025 represented more than 10% of Blue Arrow's net assets. Under International Stock Exchange regulations Blue Arrow was required to make a public announcement of such transactions if they constituted more than 5% of its net assets. This was known as a Class II announcement.

Phillips & Drew Securities, who were Blue Arrow's stockbrokers, then asked the Stock Exchange for a waiver from the Class II announcement. In its letter to the Stock Exchange there were five statements that the Department of Trade and Industry's inspectors later claimed were untrue or misleading: the inspectors' interpretation was that the letter sought to give the impression that the Class II limits had not yet been reached. A further letter on 31 July enclosed a letter from County NatWest explaining why no announcement had been made. In neither case was the Stock Exchange satisfied that a waiver should be permitted. However, no public announcement was made.

On 4 August County NatWest announced the Blue Arrow cash offer publicly. Its press release stated *inter alia* that

> The Blue Arrow group owns 125,700 shares of Manpower Stock (representing approximately 0.8% of the Manpower Stock outstanding as at 31 May 1987) acquired at an average cost of (approximately) $60.21 per share.

At this stage Blue Arrow still did not make a Class II announcement.

Blue Arrow now proposed a rights issue of £837 million. County NatWest Securities, the stockbroking sister company of County NatWest, wrote a series of recommendations to its clients in the following weeks, including phrases such as 'now is the time to pile in' and 'we would recommend without hesitation the rights to be taken up'.

Immediately the offer was announced, the share price of Blue Arrow fell from 216p to 184p (a drop of nearly 15%). The same day (4 August) they bought a further 750,000 shares at 180p. County NatWest bought 2.5 million shares the next day.

On 24 August, Blue Arrow and Manpower announced the signing of a definite merger agreement, including the terms under which Blue Arrow would buy the remaining equity for cash. Three days later Blue Arrow held an Extraordinary General Meeting at which a resolution was approved of the Manpower offer and an increase in the company's authorized share capital.

On 7 September, County NatWest declared the Manpower offer unconditional and announced that the rights issue was to go ahead at a price of 166p. The market price of the shares, in a generally weak market, had by then fallen to 165p.

The rights issue was underwritten by various City institutions. County NatWest was the principal underwriter, but found others willing to sub-underwrite only up to 74.4% of the issue (and this was mainly Phillips & Drew, with 64.6%). Thus County NatWest was left to take up the balance, which might potentially be £214 million.

The closing date for applications was 28 September. On the previous Friday (25 September) Mr Nick Wells of County NatWest had attended a meeting of analysts and salesmen at County NatWest Securities. He indicated at the meeting that the take-up of rights was expected to be 70%. However, by the close of business on the 28th, the Registrars found that only 38% of the rights issue had been taken up. Phillips & Drew believed they could place a further 36%; this left 26% for the underwriters.

Three parties (County NatWest, Phillips & Drew and Dillon Read) then, at the last moment, took up parts of the rights issue between them amounting to about 10.9%. This was done after the official 3 p.m. deadline on 28 September. Lloyds Bank, the registrar, counted these as part of the take-up despite the late time.

This meant that the next morning 258 million shares had to be sold. The sales staff of Phillips & Drew and County NatWest began to place them at 7.30 a.m. By 10 o'clock demand had slowed, and Phillips & Drew and County NatWest took a further 5 million shares each. At 10.51 a.m. on 29 September they announced that the rights issue was a success, with 48.9% taken up, and that the remainder of shares had been sold.

County NatWest now owned 13% of the shares. As we have already seen, any shareholder holding over 5% of a company's equity must disclose the fact. The shares were then parcelled up: County's corporate advice department held 4.99%, County NatWest Securities (who were market-makers) held 4.43%, and 3.9% were held by Phillips & Drew. Holdings over 5% do not have to be disclosed by professional share-dealing firms.

At the beginning of October Phillips and Drew negotiated that the Union Bank of Switzerland should take 4.5% of Blue Arrow at a price of 166.25p. An indemnity stated that if the price fell by the end of the year, County NatWest would reimburse UBS for the loss. If it rose, County would receive 70% of the gain.

On 19 October the market crashed. On 16 October the price had been 167p; a week later it was 112p, and after another week it had dropped to 80p. Every penny change in the price meant a potential loss to Blue Arrow of almost £1 million. County NatWest had to pay UBS £30 million under the indemnity. By the end of November the chairman of National Westminster Bank was aware of the potential loss totalling almost £40 million.

On 17 December National Westminster announced that it was injecting £80 million into County; a second press release stated that County NatWest had notified the board of Blue Arrow that it had become interested in 9.5% of its issued share capital. The press release mentioned neither the total interest of the NatWest group in Blue Arrow, nor the UBS indemnity.

The Blue Arrow–County NatWest affair was investigated by inspectors from the Department of Trade and Industry, whose report was issued on 20 July 1989. The report was critical on a number of counts. The *Observer* of 23 July 1989 commented that it was 'the most damning attack on a UK clearing bank and its investment banking subsidiaries ever written' and noted that

> Ten senior city figures, including three NatWest main board directors, have their conduct described as 'falling well below that expected from responsible executives' . . . The Serious Fraud Office and City of London Police have been called in. The Bank of England, the Securities and Investments Board and the Securities Association are all considering what action should be taken over the breaking of their individual rules. The City's self-regulation is once again firmly in the spotlight.

Questions

1. Why do you think the share price of Blue Arrow fell on the announcement of the planned acquisition of Manpower? Why did County NatWest buy on 4 and 5 August?

2. What are the consequences if a rights issue is not substantially taken up?

3. Why might Blue Arrow not wish it to be known that it owned more than 5% of the shares in the early stages of the bid?

4. Why after 29 September might County NatWest have wished to avoid disclosing its 13% holding of Blue Arrow?

5. In what respects would you say the case as described shows conduct that falls 'well below that expected from responsible executives'?

(c) The Hoylake bid for BATs

Waiting for the barbarians

'I have never seen a good company succumb to a hostile bid,' said Sir James Goldsmith shortly after launching a very hostile £13 billion ($21 billon) bid for BAT Industries, the second-biggest takeover bid ever. Is he right? What makes a company good or bad? And which is BAT?

Sir James and two rich henchmen, the elegant Mr Jacob Rothschild and the Australian Mr Kerry Packer, believe good companies concentrate on what they do best. By this reasoning conglomerates are self-evidently bad companies, created by managements more interested in size and deep-pile carpets than value. Conglomerates pay a premium to shareholders in companies they acquire rather than hand it over to their own shareholders. Their biggest gains from acquisitions are the one-off kind that flow from kicking out an acquired firm's managers and eliminating waste.

Once such profit has been made, it soon becomes painfully clear that the parts of a conglomerate are worth more separately than together. Consider SCM, a conglomerate that Hanson, a recognised master of company break-ups, bought in January 1986 for $930 million, then thought to be more than a fair price for a troubled company. By the end of 1988 Hanson had raised $1.3 billion by selling all SCM's business except its core one of making typewriters. That is thought to be worth around $5 billion now.

It is in this sort of spirit that the trio led by Sir James has launched an attack as much on the idea of the conglomerate as on BAT. 'This exercise is all about the defective architecture of very large companies,' says Mr Rothschild. He should know. He built a financial-services conglomerate in the mid-1980s and then dismantled it. That begs the question: in what way is BAT defective?

The burly Mr Patrick Sheehy, a tobacco man who has worked for BAT for 39 years, has guided the company's strategy since 1982, when he was made chairman. His brief was straightforward: the tobacco business is stagnant but provides stable and strong cash-flow. BAT, the world's largest tobacco company (Benson & Hedges and Kool are two of its better known cigarettes), was well positioned in the market. It has a near-monopoly in several fast-growing markets for cigarettes in poor countries. Mr Sheehy had to work out how to invest third-world profits in safe first-world economies. Like his peers at Philip Morris and R.J. Reynolds, he chose diversification.

With the benefit of that infallible strategist, hindsight, it is easy to say that shareholders would have been better off if the tobacco companies had just handed back their excess cash in dividends. But no management likes doing that: it is hard to keep staff motivated when they are just managing a declining asset.

Nor did Mr Sheehy fall for the honey-trap of synergy, unlike R.J. Reynolds, which bought Nabisco saying it could use its brand-marketing skills on food just as well as on cigarettes. Now Kohlberg, Kravis, Roberts, the leveraged buy-out kings, are busily unbundling that empire.

Instead Mr Sheehy bought into three unrelated areas — paper (Wiggins Teape), retailing (Argos-to-Saks Fifth Avenue) and insurance (Eagle Star-to-Farmers Group). Mistakes were made in the last two fields, and the whole thing lacked a little lustre. But it was an honest and thoughtful attempt to build businesses, and despite some past blunders BAT's return on equity is well above the average for British companies. The company's earnings per share have started to recover from stagnation between 1984 and 1987.

Then along comes Sir James with one fact that wreaks havoc with the logic behind this diversification strategy. Over the past ten years BAT has spent £7 billion on acquisitions. At the end of last year, before bid speculation boosted the value of its shares, its market capitalization was roughly the same amount. The break-up value of BAT is at least £16 billion, probably closer to £20 billion. This steep discount reflects what the bidders see as BAT's basic flaw: 'The conglomerate that has been created makes no managerial sense,' says their offer document. The way the market puts it is that Mr Sheehy and his colleagues are worth less than nothing to their company.

Much the same charges could be laid at the door of high-flying Hanson. It, too, trades at a steep discount to its net asset value, which Drexel Burnham Lambert calculated to be between £14.6 billion and £16.6 billion compared to a market capitalization of £7.9 billion just before Hanson's £3.5 billion bid for Consolidated Gold Fields in late June. Sir James decided not to accept Lord Hanson's long-standing offer to send a car round to pick up anyone who offered enough money for his company.

The bidders have a tough battle ahead. They are offering BAT shareholders a mix of £6.5 billion secured-loan notes; $6.4 billion in increasing-rate notes (otherwise known as junk); and £2.6 billion of loan stock exchangeable into shares in their bidding vehicle. Without any ready cash, a less formidable team making such a bid would be dismissed without a second thought.

With grotesque amounts of cash chasing big deals, finding a cash alternative should not be a problem. Convincing the Bank of England that the result will not be too highly geared might be harder. BAT will be good at seeking establishment protection: its non-executive directors include Lord Armstrong, a former cabinet secretary, and Sir Michael Palliser, former head of the Foreign Office. The bidding trio, by comparison, are City outsiders. Whatever the outcome, few of Britain's big companies — good or bad — will be able any longer to feel immune from hostile bids.

The intriguing question is whether Anglo-Saxon habits like takeovers are going to spread to more peaceful parts of the world. Hostile bids are still almost unheard of in West Germany and Japan, where banks' shareholdings in companies make them difficult. Sir James suspects that this may change. Most of the companies that have been raided in America and Britain, he says, were so old they were 'rotting away' while their West German and Japanese rivals were 'reinvigorated by bombing'.

Nearly 45 years later the reinvigoration is showing few signs of wearing thin. Lack of pressure from financial markets gives West German and Japanese companies the freedom to pursue long-term strategies and to concentrate on making better products at a lower cost. Partly as a result, their share of world markets continues to grow while that of their Anglo-Saxon rivals shrinks.

The Japanese see little reason to change the way their system works, though they may be setting a time bomb for themselves with the torrent of convertible bonds now being issued so complacently. In Europe, the advent of the single market may force West Germany to adopt some foreign financial customs. Bankers and consultants are convincing themselves they can see signs that West Germany too will eventually succumb to the urge to restructure, though not too many West German industrialists are ready to believe it. Either way, Sir James by then will have won or lost BAT and it will be up to a younger Visigoth to take up the cudgels.

Source: The Economist, *15.7.1989.*

BATs: the defence

BAT Industries' defence against the £13.5 billion junk bond financed break-up bid from Sir James Goldsmith's Hoylake enterprise will make its appearance at the start of business tomorrow morning.

With the Takeover Panel looking down from high, BATs' chairman

Patrick Sheehy and his co-directors have inevitably proved tight lipped in respect of their defence strategy, but expectations are that Sheehy will concentrate on demonstrating that the BATs' conglomeration — far from being a failure as Goldsmith contends — has paid off.

Sheehy, who must be careful to conserve his ammunition, will almost certainly call Goldsmith's bluff and respond, with not a little force, to the provocative introduction to Hoylake's offer document.

As Goldsmith put it: 'If BATs is able to demonstrate that its programme of diversification has been well founded, that the companies acquired have been strengthened by joining its group and that shareholders have benefited as a result, then there is little purpose in this offer. You would be well advised to refuse it despite the immediate financial advantages that are offered to you.'

This week BATs will seek to demonstrate that Sheehy has led the company in a 'clear and logical' multi-billion pound diversification away from tobacco towards the creation of a combine that should not be broken up.

BATs argues that:

- Total returns to shareholders in terms of dividends and share performances have been good (irrespective of the spark in BATs' shares lit by Kohlberg Kravis Roberts' $25 billion leveraged break-up bid for RJR/Nabisco late last year).
- BATs is a highly focused conglomerate which, over the past five years, has sold off even profitable businesses in order to concentrate on its four core activities: tobacco, paper, financial services and retail.
- The interchange of management, products and techniques in various world markets has yet to be fully exploited.

Such are some of the positive factors which BATs can be expected to preach. The negative, knock-Hoylake, aspects of BATs' defence are likely to touch on the following:

- Hoylake is offering unquoted, unattractive debt paper of dubious value.
- Goldsmith and his partners — financier Jacob Rothschild and Australian industrialist Kerry Packer (along with numerous other investors best known for their respective wealth) — would reap an inordinate proportion of the rewards from a break-up, or 'unbundling' of BATs, at the expense of shareholders, should the bid succeed.
- Hoylake faces significant regulatory hurdles in the US, while a powerful anti-Hoylake campaign has been launched on Wall Street — not least by those who still smart from Goldsmith's foray into Goodyear Tire.

Meanwhile the BATs camp has established — with City Takeover Panel Blessing — that Hoylake's junk bonds cannot be properly valued and so, under Panel rules, Hoylake is prevented from purchasing BATs' shares through the market.

David Verey, deputy chief executive of Lazard Brothers, BATs' lead advisers, argues: The current offer is dead in the water. So what can Goldsmith do? To create any credibility he will have to underwrite a cash alternative at a substantially higher price. But can he do that? Will the banks give him the time of day when he has major regulatory problems overhanging him? Maybe they will, but we estimate that the upfront cost of underwriting the package could be of the order of £250 million to £300 million, against Hoylake's current net worth of £100 million. Can Goldsmith afford to take this risk?

Thursday brought confirmation that the Securities and Exchange Commission will review Hoylake's bid following the call by 200 Congress leaders for the SEC to assert its jurisdiction. BATs earns around 50 per cent of its pre-tax profits — struck at £1.6 billion last year — from its US operations where it employs some 55,000.

The SEC review will seek to establish whether Hoylake has violated US takeover or other securities laws and avoided US jurisdiction.

As for the US tobacco lobby, the message from one prominent tobacco union boss is: 'We've looked at Goldsmith's track record. People do not count in their (Hoylake's) calculations.'

Such antipathies aside, one of the key factors — which the Goldsmith camp has acknowledged from the off — is whether Hoylake will clear American insurance regulatory hurdles within the 81-day deadline imposed by the Takeover Panel. Bearing in mind the fact that the US insurance commissioners have the power to withdraw the licence of BATs' insurance off-shoot Farmers, parallels are inevitably drawn with Minorco's defeat in its quest for ConsGold at the hand of Judge Mukasey in the New York courts.

As it is, the battle for BATs is still at the phoney war stage. Hoylake can be expected to raise its offer and underwrite a cash alternative should it sense a chance of victory. Goldsmith and Co.'s first shot — a sort of Mickey Mouse salvo — is widely recognised as little more than a professional manoeuvre to test the regulatory/market waters.

But the slings of Goldsmith's rhetoric and the arrows of Hoylake's attack have served to wound rather than merely scratch BATs. The Goldsmith/Rothschild duo have derived more than a little amusement from BATs' decision to call in PR Sir Gordon Reece — the Westminster ranger who worked for Guinness under Ernest Saunders' reign, is closely associated with Mohamed Fayed (star of the unpublished House of Fraser report) and, of late, plied his wares on behalf of ConsGold. Reece's arrival on the scene suggests that Sheehy is intent on attempting to strengthen BATs' image — an image which, until Hoylake appeared, was not perceived to require Reece's special brand of expertise.

In the words of one leading fund manager: 'A traditional defence from BATs, based on its earnings and dividend record, would not be enough to answer the unflattering comparisons of BATs' performance with other focused businesses. At the same time we would not consider accepting the bid in its present form.'

So this weekend, at the Hoylake nerve centre in St James's Place — where 'Jimmy' and 'Mr Jacob' occupy neighbouring houses (owned by the latter) — concern is more likely to focus on the City's cool reaction to Goldsmith's junk than the pending arrival of what is likely to prove a relatively restrained initial defence document from BAT.

Inquiries by The Observer strongly indicate that City fund managers are distinctly uncomfortable with the characteristically complex corporate takeover structure created by Goldsmith which, to all intents and purposes, is designed to ensure that some 30 per cent of the value of any BAT break-up flows in the direction of himself and his supporters.

Nor has the highly leveraged aspect of Hoylake's £13.5 billion take-over proposal been well received in the City which remains exceedingly sceptical over the attractions of junk — the commodity indelibly associated with investment bankers Drexel Burnham Lambert who just happen to be one of Hoylake's advisers.

Just to add piquancy, news came last week of three junk-bond defaults at the same time as a new study — carried out by the Bond Investors' Association — revealed that junk bonds have accounted for more than two-thirds of US corporate bond issue defaults since 1980.

On Monday, Seamans Furniture announced that it had missed a debt repayment. The following day Zapata Corp, the oil drilling enterprise founded by President George Bush, let it be known that it would miss an interest payment. Tuesday also brought news that despite rescue attempts by Drexel, Integrated Resources, a financial services firm which has long been teetering on the brink, will miss an interest payment and is now set for reorganisation and, alas, liquidation.

The Bond Investors' Association's study found that junk bonds accounted for 70.1 per cent — or $21.1 billion — of $30.1 billion worth of corporate bond issues that have defaulted over the past nine years.

A total of 631 corporate bonds defaulted during the period, while the average settlement was 49.6 cents on the dollar. This put the default rate over the period at 11.2 per cent.

Leveraged buyouts and restructurings have fuelled the phenomenal growth of the junk-bond market — courtesy of the likes of Michael Milken, former king of junk at Drexel and now the subject of fraud and racketeering charges.

The doubtful value of the unlisted loan notes which BATs share-holders are being tempted with is underlined in Hoylake's offer document, which admits that the values and marketability of the junk bonds cannot be assured.

Yesterday the Times reported that some 1,200 Lloyd's names who hold BAT shares as part of their deposit at Lloyd's may have to find up to £50 million should Hoylake's bid prove successful.

According to the Times, the names have been informed by Lloyd's that Hoylake's paper will not be acceptable as part of their deposit should the bid succeed.

Meanwhile, Hoylake may have made something of a public relations gaffe in enlisting the support of a bevy of glitzy international rich — a cabal gazed upon with more than a little cynicism by the dark-suited professionals who manage funds in the City and Charlotte Square.

Ironically, the Hoylake camp — which chose Tim Bell to peddle its PR — saw the glitzy names, embracing the likes of Gianni Agnelli and Lord Weinstock, as powerful picture cards in the public relations game — witness the leak, within days of Hoylake's appearance, of the above's respective participation.

Now the fear, for those with fees to play for, is that the little rich boys may prove to be the jokers in the pack.

Not a few of Goldsmith and Rothschild's carefully assembled monied cast — who have given maximum commitments to subscribe for shares in the Bermuda-based Hoylake in the event of Goldsmith gaining control of BATs — are also conspicuously tax sheltered, as indeed is Goldsmith. Unfortunately the dark-suited reaction is: too-clever-by-half.

As one City operator bluntly put it: 'The caribbean white trash factor — with admitted exceptions — has hardly helped Hoylake's cause.'

He added: 'The Goldsmith camp has used such words as "play", "fun" and "game" to describe its BATs operation. People may giggle at first but eventually they should consider that 155,000 people work for BATs — a matter which should not be the subject of fun and games.'

It is a matter of common knowledge that Weinstock was not best pleased at the high profile publicity which GEC's support generated — support to the tune of £30 million via its Zipbond off-shoot.

Individual rich boys include the art-dealing Duke of Beaufort who, via his Nassau-based investment company, is down for up to £10 million. Multi-millionairess Barbara Flick of Mercedes fame and fortune is on side for as much as £15 million, via Liechtenstein, while Baron Philippe Lambert, a banker and private investor based in Switzerland, has committed up to £1 million. Maurice Dwek, through Pragma Holdings International, a Swiss-based investment company, has pledged £9.25 million, while Agnelli, of Fiat, has committed up to £15 million via his family's IFI International holding enterprise, based in the Virgin Islands.

Meanwhile, the BAT-men, led by Sheehy, deputy chairman Brian Garraway and finance director David Allvey, go into battle armed with an inch-thick manual listing the names and numbers of their not inexpensive advisers. On side are Lazards, S.G. Warburg and Wall Street powerhouses Goldman Sachs and Shearson Lehman, along with joint brokers BZW and Cazenove, lawyers Herbert Smith and Freshfields and American law firms Cravath, Swaine Moore, and Le Boeuf.

At BATs' curiously vulgar brown granite and pink columned head-quarters (owned and decorated, to BATs' distaste, by the Norwich Union) in London's Victoria Street, the £452,255-a-year Sheehy, who has framed the cashed cheques bearing his signature, which he used to pay for the company's billion pound forays out of tobacco, insists: 'BAT Industries has rationale. It may not be self-evident to some, but the evolution of the business has followed a clear and logical pattern.'

He adds: 'Our whole strategy adds value for shareholders by building coherent businesses. Hoylake's bid is only going to enrich the predators at the expense of the shareholders. It is significant that throughout their 160-page offer document there is nothing about building the businesses — and so long as the threat hangs over our businesses, the net effect on them can only be negative.'

Such is the state of play as Sheehy mounts his defence.

Source: Observer, *20.8.1989.*

BATs: talk about talks

A week in the life of BATs is, under the present circumstances, a long time. As every merchant banker and his compliance officer knew, BATs was set to unveil its defence against Hoylake on Monday morning.

But it was Sir James Goldsmith, star of Cavenham, *Now* and Goodyear Tire, who just happened to make the headlines in that morning's papers. On Sunday, Goldsmith felt compelled to invite Patrick Sheehy, BATs' chairman, to hold talks regarding Hoylake's £13.5 billion offer.

In a letter delivered to Sheehy (and the Press) on the Sabbath, Goldsmith pointed out that BATs extended a similar invitation during its £2.9 billion battle for control of Farmers, the US insurance combine, and wrote: 'In the same spirit, I and my associates issue an invitation to you and your colleagues to sit down and negotiate with us an offer, all aspects of which are open to negotiation.'

Sheehy & Co. promptly rejected Goldsmith's overtures and a reply — sent c/o Hambros Bank, Hoylake's advisers — suggested that if Goldsmith had a 'significantly different' offer in mind, he should put it to shareholders.

Just for good measure, BATs informed Goldsmith that it saw the bid as 'destructive asset-stripping, motivated by the wishes of a small group of people to enrich themselves at the expense of BAT Industries' shareholders'.

Goldsmith, presumably with tongue in cheek, subsequently declared: 'It would seem more appropriate for Mr Sheehy and his colleagues to seek the best terms available for BAT shareholders rather than initiate, at shareholders' expense, an intense and extensive political and legal campaign, which would deny shareholders their right to reach their own decisions about their own company.'

Such was the manner in which Goldsmith held the stage on Sunday. Something of a spoiling attempt? Who knows? In the event, Goldsmith can be expected to claim — either privately or publicly — that BATs' management has refused to hold talks with him.

Strange that Sheehy should have taken such a decision. I mean, surely the gentlemanly thing to do when you receive such a letter on a Sunday is to drop everything, telephone a few co-directors and one of your advisers from Lazards or Warburgs and let someone like Sir James know that as soon as you have advised shareholders to ignore his asset stripping inclinations and junk bond currency you would like to avail yourself of the opportunity for a constructive chat.

Not, of course, that such a chat should be on a one-to-one basis — a point that Goldsmith conceded. Sheehy and his colleagues would obviously relish the chance to listen to Kerry Packer's philosophy in respect of the regeneration of British industry in general and the reasoning that motivates his desire to destroy BATs in particular. There are, after all, a great many lessons to be learned from the state of corporate Australia. Unfortunately, Packer has chosen to keep such thoughts bottled up.

And, should Hoylake choose to embark on a retreat after an amicable exchange of corporate view-points, all would not necessarily be lost. Could not Jacob Rothschild be tempted to join BATs' board as a non-executive director where his management skills (which he has always kept hidden under a bushel or a Pissarro) could be shared with Sheehy's cigarette-puffing brethren? And, once Hoylake retreated and Rothschild joined BATs' board, a prince or a frog or Kerry Packer could come along and kiss Sir Mark Weinberg who would once again turn into a real person and, at long last, would be able to discuss all the events that have been going on around him. Alas, a chance missed.

Instead, Sheehy published BATs' defence document in which he agreed to take up Goldsmith's challenge to demonstrate that BATs' programme of diversification has been well founded and that shareholders have benefited as a result.

Sheehy and Lazards, it has to be said, did rather a good job. The delicately worded advice to shareholders was: 'Do not give up your valuable investment in return for junk bonds and a strategy based on asset stripping.'

As for benefits to shareholders, BATs pointed to:

- Compound growth in earnings per share: 18.5 per cent per annum since 1980;
- Compound growth in dividends: 19.8 per cent per annum since 1980;
- Total return to shareholders: 38 per cent compound per annum since 1980; while
- £100 invested in BATs on 31 December 1980 grew to £1,547 eight and a half years later.

BATs argues that since 1983 — the period highlighted by Hoylake in its offer document — £100 invested in the company would have generated a total return of 33 per cent compound, growing to £555. This puts BATs at the top of the UK's 'Big Ten' corporate league, in terms of market capitalization, and outstrips runners up Hanson and BTR, both of which just happen to be conglomerates.

On the basis of a £1 billion increase in Hoylake's value, BATs estimates that the Goldsmith camp would take £360 million, while the Anglo Group minority would take £32 million. All of which would leave a maximum £605 million for BATs' shareholders.

Sheehy also chose to bring forward BATs' mid-year results for 1989, which revealed a 20 per cent rise in pre-tax profits of £811 million (compared with City expectations of around £750 million) on turnover up 23 per cent to more than £10 billion. Earnings per share rose 20 per cent to 32.07p, while the dividend was raised 22 per cent to 9.30p per share.

All in all, an appropriate response to what was always a non-offer from the Goldsmith camp, designed to test the regulatory clime. Goldsmith duly retaliated with Wednesday's revelation of Hoylake's plans to sell Farmers to Axa Midi, the French-based insurer, for $4.5 billion, but whether this development will help or hinder Goldsmith's cause as far as US insurance regulators are concerned is debatable.

Goldsmith is currently pressing the Takeover Panel for an extension of the 60-day timetable and, in the not too distant future, Sir Gordon Borrie must recommend whether the Goldsmith/BATs affair should go to the MMC.

The unenviable problem for Sheehy is that although he can laugh Goldsmith's funny money out of court, the stuff has done wonders for BATs' share price.

Source: Observer, *27.8.1989.*

Questions

1. What is a conglomerate? Why might there be a difference between the aggregated value of a conglomerate and its break-up value? If the break-up value is higher, why does the existing management not break the company up?

2. The package being offered by Hoylake was somewhat complex. According to the first article, 'without any ready cash, a less formidable team making such a bid would be dismissed without a second thought'. Why? What is meant by 'without any ready cash'? Why is the fact that Hoylake's is a 'formidable team' relevant?

3. At the end of the first article, *The Economist* suggests that the Japanese 'may

be setting a time bomb for themselves with the torrent of convertible bonds now being issued so complacently'. In the context of the article, what might be the outcome of the issue of these convertible bonds?

4. Why should problems in the USA (for instance, the second article refers to the fact that 'a powerful anti-Hoylake campaign has been launched on Wall Street') affect a bid for BATs, a British company?

5. The second article informs us that 'Hoylake's junk bonds cannot be properly valued'. Explain this statement.

6. The second article suggests that 'Hoylake can be expected to raise its offer and underwrite a cash alternative should it sense a chance of victory. Goldsmith and Co.'s first shot — a sort of Mickey Mouse salvo — is widely recognized as little more than a professional manoeuvre to test the regulatory/market waters.' Why should an initial bid be of this kind?

7. Look at the paragraph in the second article beginning 'In the words of one leading fund manager . . .' and explain why the speaker could be at the same time critical of BATs' performance and yet adamant that the current bid was unacceptable.

8. The second article tells us that fund managers in the UK are sceptical of junk bonds. It gives recent US experience of junk defaults to back this up. But why might Hoylake's bonds be considered 'junk' when they would, after the bid, be part of the financing of one of the UK's largest, and very profitable, companies?

9. The second article suggests that the City is unhappy with 'glitzy' names being involved as potential shareholders in Hoylake. Why? Is it because this affects the maximization of shareholder wealth which we have suggested is the purpose of financing? Or are there other reasons?

10. In the third article, we are told that BATs saw the Hoylake bid as 'destructive asset-stripping, motivated by the wishes of a small group of people to enrich themselves at the expense of BAT Industries' share-holders'. Using the information throughout the three articles, explain how Hoylake might achieve this, given the ownership structure of Hoylake.

11. Towards the end of the third article, the strengths of BATs' performance since 1980 are listed. Earnings, cash and share price have all risen very significantly. Contrast this with the picture painted halfway through the first article in the paragraph beginning 'Then along comes Sir James . . .'. How do you reconcile these two pictures of the company? How might you judge them comparatively were you a shareholder of BATs?

12. Explain the last paragraph of the third article.

W2.4 Discussion questions

Note: Suggested answers to questions 2.1–2.5 are given in section W2.5 on pp. 368–70.

2.1 Is it true that investing in shares is gambling in just the same way as betting on horse races or greyhounds, or as in poker?

2.2 Was the Big Bang inevitable?

2.3 Who do you think gains from the Big Bang? Who loses?

2.4 Explain Plender's argument in the context of his remark that 'a domestic financial system ... permits capital to be allocated to the most productive use'.

2.5 How might the City's activities be justified even though it were shown that it had little or no benefit to industry through new issues?

2.6 Go back to Fig. 1.3 (p. 12). It was suggested in the text that this was a fundamental model linking investors to projects. What is the place of a financial intermediary in this model? What are the implications of the internationalized role of the City for the model?

2.7 Why might a UK investor buy shares in a UK company on a foreign stock market?

2.8 What were the implications of the abolition of exchange controls for the development of the UK financial services industry? Do you think some of the developments around the Big Bang would have happened if exchange controls had remained?

2.9 Examine the advantages and disadvantages of the post-1986 financial system for the financial manager of a manufacturing company when compared to the pre-Big Bang system.

2.10 What are (i) bonds; (ii) bank loans; (iii) commercial paper? Why might you use one rather than another as a financial manager?

2.11 Why does the issue of bonds and short-term paper take place in the euro-currency markets when there are domestic markets in the same securities?

2.12 Is it possible that the price of ICI's shares might be different in New York from that in London?

2.13 Why might you consider entering the options or futures markets? How would you choose between them?

2.14 What is 'disintermediation'? Why has it arisen?

2.15 In the text we pointed out (p. 55) that some evidence suggests the Unlisted Securities Market has consistently underperformed the main market since its inception. If this is so, why do you think it still finds willing investors?

W2.5 Suggested answers to discussion questions

2.1 The best way to answer this is to make a distinction between the situation facing the *individual* making a choice of investment, and the level of the economy as a whole. So far as the individual is concerned, there are many similarities between investing in securities and gambling.

First, both require a present outlay for a risky future inflow. Second, both offer the possibility of either loss or gain. Third, both offer an interest over and above the risk itself. In the case of securities, there is their relationship to the economy and development — for instance, choosing to invest in electronics because the growth of new technology is itself an interesting topic to observe. In the case of gambling on, say, horses, there is the interest in the career of a particular jockey or owner, or the success of a particular bloodline. Fourth, both offer a selection of levels of risk. Just as the gambler can choose a short-odds favourite or a long-odds outsider, so the investor can choose the safe security (BP, ICI, government bonds) or the risky one (a small newcomer to the Unlisted Securities Market selling rustproofing for hot-air balloons, for instance).

So far as the economy is concerned, there is more of a difference, albeit a debatable one. Both generate employment, but it may be argued (on moral grounds at least) that real investment in a factory is more beneficial to the community than the establishment of a new casino or greyhound track.

2.2 Some change in the operation of the London stock markets was probably inevitable. Whether it would have had to take precisely the course the Big Bang did is less likely.

Change was inevitable because London is linked into international markets quite separately from the Stock Exchange. This linkage means that international development inevitably affects the London markets. Had the City not changed, then to an increasing extent it would probably have been bypassed as institutional investors sought the most efficient markets in which to invest. This may have been more difficult if, say, the exchange control regulations had not been abolished. But even so, there were other domestic investments available to large funds, over and above the International Stock Exchange. Some of them were mentioned in the text (see section 2.2, pp. 36–41): old masters' paintings, gold coins, rare stamps, real property, for example. In addition, with the development of new technology, the same pressures might have existed as they did in the USA, where NASDAQ, with the advent of computer trading, began to pose a serious threat to the New York Stock Exchange, and hence forced down commissions.

In any event, whatever the political colour of the government, the restrictive practices of the Stock Exchange would almost certainly have been challenged.

2.3 This is contentious, and your own judgement is essential. The dealers on the market have gained, in the form of high salaries and commissions but there is now a downturn. The partners of Stock Exchange firms bought out in the pre-Big Bang rush of institutions from abroad certainly gained substantial amounts from selling out. Probably large institutional investors will gain from the lower commissions they can bargain for. Indirectly this will benefit those on whose behalf they deal: policy holders, pensioners and so on. Finally, there would appear to be a steady job for those employed by the regulatory bodies that will oversee the Stock Exchange in the years to come under the umbrella of the Securities and Investments Board.

Small dealers may lose, being pushed out by the competition of the large market participants. Nomura has already been reported as saying that it will sustain losses for several years, if necessary, so as to obtain market share. Industry may lose; it is not certain what the implications of the changes in the market will be for the ease with which funds can be raised in new issues, or whether it will or will not entail a rise in the average cost of capital facing industry. Certainly the massive sums quoted by Plender as dealing and similar commissions have to come from somewhere.

2.4 Plender seems to be saying this: in any economy we have capital markets so as to channel funds from savers to investment projects. If information is of good quality, then those savers will wish to place their money with those who are shown to use it best, and, given the competitive nature of the markets, this will be those who have in the past used funds most successfully — made the most profit, in other words.

But crucially this requires that the financial intermediary should have an interest in the efficiency of the allocation process. The financial markets act because they are rewarded for acting, and that reward is based on the way they ease the communication between investor and the enterprise, and the way they move those funds smoothly between saving and spending sectors.

The City of London currently does not have this interest. It is geared to foreign governments and foreign investors. It could almost be on a desert island, given the evidence that it does not function at all to aid British manufacturing to raise new funds. Hence the gist of Plender's argument is to show that the City is currently ignoring the needs of British industry because it is more lucrative to look outside the UK for profitable work. As a result, there are doubts if the UK's economy — or, at least, the allocative efficiency of that economy — benefits from the expertise and talent currently in the City.

2.5 Any primary market requires a secondary market. People and institutions are prepared to buy new securities issued by an enterprise because there is satisfactory potential liquidity; because a secondary market exists in which, should they need to, they can dispose of their holdings.

Thus, even under the circumstances of this question, the City's markets would be justified so long as they were seen to provide a ready and efficient market-place where holdings of shares and bonds could be liquidated.

3 Market efficiency

W3.1 Introduction

There are probably three ways you can approach a securities market. One is the chartist's way: you suppose that, solely on the basis of graphing the movements of a share, some prediction can be made of its future price changes. A second is the fundamental analyst's way: you believe that by looking at all the socioeconomic factors that affect the enterprise, you can make better predictions of the company's future than other people. The third approach is the one to which we have devoted most space in this chapter: a belief in the efficiency of markets and hence a belief that the chartist and the fundamental analyst must be wrong.

To give a flavour of the chartist's approach, we give below an introductory article from *The Accountant* of 7 August 1985, intended to introduce chartism to accountants unversed in its mysteries. It is important to consider the chartist's point of view. Having read the extensive statistical evidence, you may feel that chartism just cannot work, but this would not explain why intelligent people ignore the random walk evidence and continue to draw charts (and invest good money as a result).

Chartists Fly the Flag
Clara Furse

Forecasts, whether of currency or interest rate movements, play an important role in influencing treasury strategy. There are many different approaches to making forecasts, but the two major schools of thought are the technical (or Chartist) method, based on determining trends in market behaviour, and the fundamentalist method, based on an analysis of economic data.

Few investors and no technical analysts would argue with the statement that the US dollar has in the last four years been a spectacularly good example of a bull market. While the vast majority of fundamental analysts argued hopelessly the case against the dollar (which has indeed been an increasingly strong one), it has continued nevertheless to put in a stellar performance. Despite what many see as the recent 'turn' in the market, technical factors still suggest that the growing forecasts of an imminent dollar collapse are premature if not presumptuous.

The technical analyst has played an increasingly important role in influencing investors' trading decisions in the last decade, although this is still considerably more obvious on Wall Street than in the City. It can even be argued that the dollar would never have reached its peaks without the technical analysts' insistently bullish forecasts.

The basis on which the Chartist operates is that history repeats itself. He is concerned with the fact that if a pattern of price movements becomes familiar to the market, then this pattern may repeat itself. The Chartist has therefore defined many signals which, when observed, will predict a further directional move in the market. The fact that a market may have broken on the upside or the downside is more important than the reason for the break. Additional price-related data also play an important role in judging the relative strength of the break.

All Chartists' observations are based on a fundamental belief. This is that a price represents the consensus of all fundamental factors and the market's view of these factors.

In making his observations and forecasts of a market's behaviour, the technician will use what is normally referred to as the rule of multiple techniques. This suggests that he should use as many techniques as possible based on the same data. The number of techniques successfully used to point in the same direction yields a further piece of information: a good indication of the market's strength or weakness.

A starting point for any lesson in the technician's art is 'the trend is my friend'. Those investors who heed this simple maxim will have been on the 'right side' of the dollar's rampage since 1980.

At this stage it is also worth describing the 'players' in the foreign exchange markets: those who create and sustain a trend. There are basically two influential foreign exchange markets. One is the interbank market whose power is centred in London, the other is the futures market, whose power base is at the Chicago Mercantile Exchange.

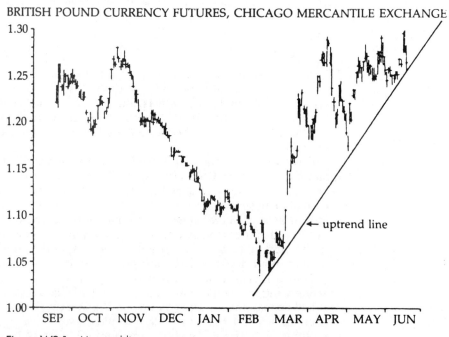

BRITISH POUND CURRENCY FUTURES, CHICAGO MERCANTILE EXCHANGE

Figure W3.1   Uptrend line.

To some extent the strength of the dollar became self-generating, certainly in the months before it reached its peak last February, and this has led to talk about a speculative bubble, which is, we are told about to burst.

Such a bubble, if that is indeed what it is, is based not on 'real' demand, i.e. commercial demand, but on purely speculative demand. There is undoubtedly some basis to this theory of the strength of the dollar's rise which will only be proved if there is a collapse in the dollar when it breaks through important chart points which then turn dollar charts bearish and trigger waves of selling. If this is indeed what happens, the technicians will play a major role in calling and indeed creating the change in the market's mood.

The technician's most basic tool is his line and bar chart, probably the most commonly used form of graph. The 'line' joins all prices traded in the course of the day and the bar is drawn at the day's settlement price. The line and bar chart illustrated shows an uptrend in sterling which originated in February [Fig. W3.1]. The uptrend line is considered to be a support for the market and therefore limits its setbacks.

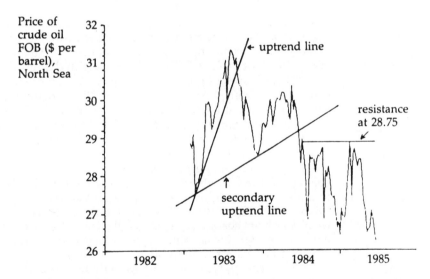

Figure W3.2   Trend lines.

A break of the uptrend lines, e.g. a close below the line, would be a bearish signal expected to generate additional selling. A good example of this is seen on the crude oil chart [Fig. W3.2] where the break of the first major uptrend line towards the middle of 1983 was followed by a collapse in oil prices. A secondary uptrend line was broken in mid 1984. This not only preceded a further collapse but has since provided a major ceiling to prices (resistance level) at $28.75. Two rallies to this level failed, thereby reinforcing the bearish chart picture.

There are several major chart formations, the most famous of which is probably the double top or bottom. These are often referred to as M or W

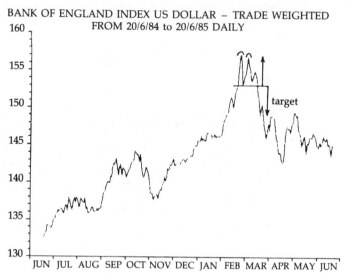

BANK OF ENGLAND INDEX US DOLLAR – TRADE WEIGHTED
FROM 20/6/84 to 20/6/85 DAILY

Figure W3.3   Double top formation.

patterns and are considered significant in that they tend to call either the top of a market (double top) or its bottom (double bottom). Although rather imperfect in that there is an additional small 'shoulder' to its right, the chart of the US dollar trade-weighted index [Fig. W3.3] shows a double top formation at its recent peak. We can see that the downward retracement from the initial high was followed by another bull move which peaked within a short distance of the initial high.

To complete and confirm the double top, another downward leg to break the previous setbacks' lows was required. This did happen following another small upward blip (which slightly distorts what would otherwise have been a perfect double top). The measurement rule applied to a double top (conversely for a double bottom) would be that a measure from the breakout below the low reached in the setback following the first peak will be equal to the distance from the two peaks to the low in the intermediate rally. In other words the market is expected to fall by as much again. This it did (and more!), thereby reaching targets for the double top formation.

Another major type of chart formation is the triangle [Fig. W3.4]. These consist of at least two lower tops and at least two higher lows about which you would draw two trend lines as demonstrated on the Canadian dollar/US dollar chart.

Once defined, the Chartist awaits the breakout to confirm the formation. This is crucial because it is the direction of the break which defines whether the pattern is a base, top or merely a consolidation phase.

The flag [Fig. W3.5] is the next most important chart pattern. It is a variation on the theme of triangles, being another sideways consolidation pattern which must consist of at least two highs and at least two lows when being formed. It may also be formed in either an ascending or descending market. However, unlike a triangle it only forms part of a consolidation phase.

Figure W3.4 Triangle formation.

Figure W3.5 Bear market flag formation.

The flag will 'wave' in the opposite direction to the trend and is consequently termed a 'corrective' consolidation. The first point to note about a flag is that the preceding move is always very steep. This forms the 'flagpole' from which the flag waves. Once the flag is drawn, the Chartist awaits the break.

The target is establised by measuring the distance between the high and low points and then measuring an equal distance from the breakpoint. This chart formation is particularly familiar to currency traders: many a potential rally in the major currencies traded against the US dollar has been a flag formation.

Clara Furse BSc (Econ) is an executive with Phillips & Drew Futures Ltd (a wholly owned subsidiary of Phillips & Drew). She specializes in financial futures and currency hedging.

W3.2 Discussion questions

Note: Suggested answers to questions 3.1 and 3.2 are given in section W3.6 on p. 382.

3.1 With which of the following statements from the above article would a modern financial theorist agree?

1. 'The basis on which the Chartist operates is that history repeats itself.'
2. 'The Chartist has therefore defined many signals which, when observed, will predict a further directional move in the market.'
3. 'All Chartists' observations are based on a fundamental belief. This is that a price represents the consensus of all fundamental factors and the market's view of these factors.'

3.2 If everybody believed what chartists say, would this not make them right, since their predictions would become self-fulfilling prophecies?

3.3 Toss a coin 50 times, and plot your own price chart by taking the graph up for heads and down for tails. Now look at the chartist's formations given in the article and see if you can spot any on your graph.

W3.3 The securities market: a case study

Before we turn to efficient markets theory proper, it is useful to consider a case study of market operations. The Piggly Wiggly case is entirely true, and though it happened in the USA much earlier in the century, some principles are true of markets to this day. We give here the first part of the case. There are further parts which are available in the teachers' manual.

Part I

This story is true. It concerns Piggly Wiggly Stores Inc., a company founded in 1919 by Clarence Saunders. Saunders gave the world two things. One is well known to all of us: Piggly Wiggly was the world's first supermarket chain. The other is the story told in this case study: of Piggly Wiggly and the Bear Raid.

By the autumn of 1922 there were more than 1,200 Piggly Wiggly stores, around 650 being owned by Piggly Wiggly itself, the rest franchised. The franchisees paid royalties to use the Piggly Wiggly name. Piggly Wiggly itself had become a force to be reckoned with in retailing, and its 200,000 shares were quoted on the New York Stock Exchange.

In November 1922 some companies that had operated Piggly Wigglies through franchises failed and went into liquidation. Being only franchises their failure hardly affected Piggly Wiggly itself, but some bears in the market spotted an opportunity to make a profit and, apparently, simultaneously began to sell Piggly Wiggly short on the New York Stock Exchange and spread rumours about its financial situation being precarious. They seemed to be successful. The price of Piggly Wiggly, which had been $50, dropped below $40. Clarence Saunders, who still ran the chain, was not very pleased.

W3.4   Reading: anatomy of an analyst

The following are three extracts from an interview with a New York investment analyst and consultant, conducted by one of the authors and a colleague. The replies have been numbered to help you trace the context of questions asked at the end of the passage.

Question: If you look at the whole of accounting as it's used, how do you see it being adequate for the sort of purposes you're concerned with, which I guess is as an investment manager? I wonder if you could talk about the things which you see about it, both in terms of what's good and what's not so good about it.

Analyst: (1) If I had to generalize, I would say that financial statements are very adequate most of the time. In fact, I think many of us don't appreciate the extent to which we're spoiled because, compared with most other countries, accounting and disclosure standards here are very high. So the amount of information we have is relatively speaking very good. It still varies a lot from company to company. As a general rule, I think the larger the company is, the more effort it puts into making data available. Most large American companies have extensive investor or analyst relation programmes. They may have one or two people — junior executive types — whose only function is to deal with analysts. And they provide all sorts of additional information and so-called fact books. They have meetings, sometimes as often as quarterly, for analysts to come to. They answer phone enquiries. I guess they see it as beneficial. So for that kind of company there's a lot of effort goes into making the reports understandable and meaningful.

Question: So you would really be able to contact specific individuals in specific companies if you've got some question you want.

Analyst: (2) Absolutely. On the other hand, when you get into smaller companies, that tends to disappear. The smaller the company, the less likely it is that they will have someone whose only job is to — You'll wind up speaking with the treasurer or the financial V–P or sometimes the president of the company, who may or may not be interested in telling you anything. Some companies don't really care to talk to you.

Question: Really, if a person like you is approaching you'd have thought they'd want to take it seriously because somebody's interest —

Analyst: (3) It varies. Some companies do, but some — particularly where management or a controlling family owns a lot of the stock — they tend to act more like a private company and they won't even send you the annual report sometimes. You can always get it from the files of the SEC, but some companies are just totally indifferent. I'm not sure if it's exactly that, or the fact that they don't have the expertise, but the annual reports of these companies tend to be less informative. I think they rely more on the auditor to just put out the financial statements, and the explanatory material will be very skimpy. For example, I remember a few years ago asking a company treasurer about a year-end inventory adjustment and he said, 'Well, I don't really understand it myself, but that's what the auditors told us to do.' So I think, as a general rule, large companies are much better that way in terms of providing information. But on the whole, I won't say that they're — Well, if you asked me to talk about where I think improvements are needed, I think it's mainly in explanatory information. Companies too often just give you what we call boiler plate responses. I don't know if you know that term?

Question: No, I've never heard that.

Analyst: (4) Boiler plate means just a sort of standard response, which doesn't really tell you anything. 'Sales went up because we sold more goods' — that kind of thing. Just really a disclosure which doesn't tell you anything that you didn't already know. And what's really needed, particularly for complex companies, is discussion of their different lines of business, discussion, for example, of their financing plans, why their business was good, why it was bad, how they expect it to change: what we call softer information as opposed to how much cash was in the bank ...

Question: Do you believe that the market can see through the way that people adjust their accounts?

Analyst: (5) Well, actually that's a good question. I think you can take the efficient markets theory too far. I guess I mean that in two ways. One is the distinction I made between larger firms and smaller firms. The smaller firms, I don't believe the flow of information is such that there is a truly efficient market. For an IBM, or General Electric, or General Motors, I think you've got a reasonably efficient market, but you go into the over-the-counter market and I very much doubt it. Then I'll slice the other way. When you go to accounting variations which I think are reasonably understood, such as depreciation methods and inventory methods, I think the market is again reasonably efficient in understanding the differences. I'm not sure it's true in more difficult areas, where the data isn't very good — for example, pensions. That might be an example. The problem with efficient market literature is that it's been tested really only in a Fortune 500 type of context. I think the smaller the firm and the more arcane the accounting, the less efficient — I think that, if you were to poll the membership of the Financial Analysts Federation, you would find that most people — virtually everybody — are aware of it. But a minority could really explain it to you. The people who use it are a very small minority ...

Question: On the last round of interviews one of the persons we talked to was also an analyst who had a similar sort of interest in that kind of issue. He said he believed that analysts in a sense did not want better accounting, because the better the accounting was, the more clear it was that anyone could do their job, whereas so long as the accounting wasn't so good, then they had a comparative advantage in their own particular industrial sector. And he saw almost a split mind between good and bad information in that sense. Would you think he was right, or do you think he was just speaking for himself, about the way that most analysts think?

Analyst: (6) I understand what you're saying. I'm not sure.

Question: Would it be true to say that a good analyst is one who, in a sense, does not need the accounts, because he is so *au fait* with the industrial sector and keeping in touch with the companies that he —

Analyst: (7) No, I wouldn't agree with that. I think that you need the accounting information to help you to decipher the true results as opposed to perhaps what management would like you to think the results were. But I think there is some truth in the way you phrased it the first time, in that — and maybe this goes back to the issue of accounting versus disclosure — for some analysts a disclosure is enough because they can adjust the financial statements. But on the other hand, there are many analysts who just use the reported numbers and don't even look at the footnotes, who don't understand the footnotes. And if the stated numbers need adjustment, they lose out. It's a sort of a problem. There is a tension there among analysts. There is this whole debate about who financial statements are meant for; whether they're meant for a mythical Aunt Jane from Iowa who doesn't really understand anything, who just looks at the earnings. That's one of the continuing debates: what level of expertise should one have to be able to understand financial statements?

Questions

1. Towards the end of answer (1), the analyst seems to be taking the same attitude towards generally available 'fact books' and meetings with analysts and individual telephone conversations. Is that reasonable, given that the first two are generally available and the third is not?

2. Look at answers (2) and (4). If the conversation between the analyst and the company representative is useful, and particularly if line of business information is given that is not in the financial statements, is this breaking confidentiality (i.e. would it constitute insider information, thus leading to insider dealing)? If it is not useful, why hold the conversation? In other words, why should the analyst ever ring the company at all, if he or she wishes to act honestly?

3. Based on the first three passages, consider the reasons why the company might or might not wish to talk to an analyst. They want to put the best interpretation possible on the company's progress. This makes such a discussion similar to public relations. Why should the analyst believe what they say? If the analyst cannot believe what they say, why speak to them at all?

4. Consider this analyst's attitude to the efficient markets hypothesis.

Discuss his two reservations (large versus small companies; better understood versus less understood accounting methods).

5. Look at the end of answer (5). Why might analysts feel they can operate with little knowledge of EMH, if we suppose it to be correct? Why might analysts feel uncomfortable with efficient markets theory, and have a vested interest in arguing that it is incorrect?

6. Be sure you understand the point made by the questioner immediately before answer (6). Do you think it would be true that, were financial statements to be far better than they are, there would be fewer jobs for analysts?

7. In answer (7) the analyst says 'there are many analysts who just use the reported numbers and don't even look at the footnotes, who don't understand the footnotes. And if the stated numbers need adjustment, they lose out.' Does this lack of understanding by those who advise investors constitute valid evidence against efficient markets theory?

8. Following from question 7, why might such 'inefficient' analysts still remain in their jobs? In other words, is there an efficient market in analysts?(!)

W3.5 Discussion questions

Note: Suggested answers to questions 3.4–3.6 are given in section W3.6 on p. 382.

3.4 'Tests have tended to show that the market does not react to information received in the form of current cost accounts. Since they contain information that was not available before, it is clear that this is evidence that the market is inefficient.'

'No, you have it all wrong. I agree about the findings of the tests, but that only shows how efficient the market was in impounding that information before the companies published it.'

Who is right?

3.5 If it is true that the market is efficient, then no investor can have a positive NPV. How is it, then, that companies can apparently have positive NPVs on projects?

3.6 If I had bought shares in 1975, when the market stood at around 150, I would consistently over the following ten years have made profits, since the market index was then over 1,000. Does this consistent profit making invalidate the EMH?

3.7 Does the efficient markets hypothesis mean that all investors have the same expectations?

3.8 A company's financial manager explains to you that he only issues new securities when his share price is riding high. This maximizes the funds he raises per share. Is this a sensible strategy?

3.9 If a share tipster recommends an investment, is this just a reworking of existing information, or does the very recommendation itself constitute new information?

3.10 Does the evidence that unit trusts cannot outperform a passive strategy suggest that you should avoid using them?

3.11 Here is an extract from *The Economist* of 14 June 1986. Consider Mr Winan's fate in the light of the strong form of the EMH.

> *Insider Trading*
> Outside which law?
>
> *Washington, DC*
> On what issue of current interest in America might a senior fellow of the right-wing, free-market Cato Institute and the editor of a liberal magazine like the *New Republic* find themselves in agreement? For different reasons, neither is happy with the insider-trading laws.
>
> Since last month's accusation by the Securities and Exchange Commission (SEC) that Mr Dennis Levine, an investment banker formerly at Drexel Burnham Lambert, had amassed $12.6m of illegal profits from insider trading, the subject has hardly been out of the newspapers. Mr Levine has pleased guilty to four charges, has disgorged over $11m into a fund held by court-appointed receivers, and is co-operating with federal prosecutors. Two Wall Street analysts have pleaded guilty to insider trading in an apparently unrelated case, as have two other members of their alleged ring. A fifth defendant, from the prominent law firm of Paul, Weiss, Rifkind, Wharton and Garrison, has pleaded not guilty. On June 3rd, two Italian investment bankers in another case were found guilty of insider trading.
>
> The proliferation of insider-trading cases, with the prospect of more to come, has focused attention on the fact that hardly anybody knows what the offence is. The SEC rule which proscribes it (though not by name) is notoriously imprecise. It is one recent, and wide, judicial interpretation of insider trading that has drawn fire from both the Cato Institute and the *New Republic*.
>
> On May 27th, an American apeals court upheld the securities-fraud conviction of Mr R. Foster Winans for insider trading. Mr Winans, a reporter on the *Wall Street Journal*'s share-tipster column, had leaked its contents to a couple of stockbrokers, who traded on his information.
>
> Nobody doubts that Mr Winans was guilty of a breach of a fiduciary duty to his employers — or criticises them for firing him for it. But Mr Winans owed no fiduciary duty to anybody else — certainly not to the stockholders of the companies that were traded. Had he been a 'quasi-insider' — say a lawyer or investment banker to those companies — the trading would probably have been illegal. But so removed was Mr Winans from the companies involved that the appeals court found the *Wall Street Journal* itself could legitimately have traded on the information.
>
> So Mr Winans was convicted of a securities fraud (and sentenced to 18 months in jail) because he breached, to his profit, an entirely internal duty owed only to his employers. One of the judges dissented vigorously from this novel doctrine. Mr Winans will appeal.
>
> The real argument here has less to do with the healthy regulation of a market than with the way in which regulations are made. Had

a similar case been tested first in the civil courts (through an action by the SEC for disgorgement of profits), it would probably have been uncontroversial, lawyers say. Instead, the Winans case has extended criminal law into hitherto uncharted territory. The danger is not — or not only — that such prosecutions will scare off legitimate market activity. It is that the prosecution of insider trading itself will come to look ludicrous.

W3.6   Suggested answers to discussion questions

3.1 It is interesting that chartists and financial theorists can agree on some factors yet interpret them in opposite ways.

1. Modern finance theory (MFT) would not disagree with the claim that history repeats itself. It would deny that you can *predict* when history will repeat itself. For instance, a share may go from £4.50 to £5.50 in 1988, and six years later also go from £4.50 to £5.50. But MFT would argue that no chart (or anything else) could predict that this would happen.
2. MFT would disagree completely with this statement in so far as the 'signals' are only market movements. MFT would not disagree with the statement if it were intended more generally, because some signals (such as stock splits) will tend to cause a price movement: they constitute new information.
3. We do not think any modern finance theorist would disagree with this statement. But the MFT interpretation is that the consensus arises because of a consensus view, and this very fact means that prediction based on that consensus cannot be better than the consensus.

3.2 The logic behind this statement is that, for instance, predictions of a market fall will lead people to sell, and that will indeed make the market fall. But there are problems with such a simple statement. For instance, it assumes that all chartists agree on the interpretation of charts. But this is not so: chartists will argue over whether a formation is a double top or not (they are often not so neat as the article's pictures). Chartists pride themselves on their skill that has been built up in interpreting the charts, but so long as there are different views among chartists, people will still act differently faced with the same formation.

3.4 Both statements seem to be right, and there is no real way of choosing the correct one based on either theory or evidence. Both the theory and the evidence are on test, and the evidence is ambiguous. This should raise doubts in your mind about the use of evidence, not just in efficient markets research, but also in finance (and, indeed, in other disciplines) more generally.

3.5 The first part of the statement is true: in the efficient market all investors have a zero NPV. This is not at variance with positive NPVs within the enterprise once it is accepted that the projects that arise within the enterprise are not part of an efficient market structure. For instance, projects that are profitable to ICI might not be profitable to Dow Chemical (because they link to other facilities the company has).

3.6 No, it does not, because that rise could not have been foreseen before it started; nor, at any time during the rise, could an investor have been sure that it would continue.

4

A risk-free model for investment

W4.1 Introduction

In this chapter of the Workbook we shall spend more time consolidating the presentation of the principles of compound interest as given in the text, and extend this. This *must* be understood because discounting is the basis for almost all finance theory. There are, however, some elaboration sections in this Workbook, and those whose mathematics is not especially strong may omit these sections. Subsequently we shall explore further the notions of NPV and IRR using these principles, and similarly there will be some questions we shall asterisk that need the calculus.

Before we begin let us go over again the purpose of this chapter. All financial decisions involve the flow of funds through the enterprise. Decisions have to be made about these funds. Thus individuals have to choose whether to save or spend on immediate consumption. If they save, by investing in real projects (probably through the agency of a business enterprise), they have to decide what projects to invest in. This means all expected future flows of funds have to be converted to a similar basis. That basis is *present value*. You cannot compare £100 today with £105 in three months' time without some idea of the opportunity cost of funds, and your own personal time preference between savings and consumption. The best starting point, therefore, is to make all expected flows into their *current equivalents*. This is why we discount.

This explains the first part of the chapter in both the text and this Workbook. The second part is concerned with using these ideas of dicounting to make financial decisions. These principles are again *general ones*: they apply whether you are considering an individual or a business enterprise.

Thus the structure of this Workbook chapter follows that of the text pretty closely. Unlike most of the other chapters it is more like a programmed text: you will be invited to read a sub-section, and questions to test your understanding will follow. Do try the questions! It is almost the only means you have of checking you have understood.

Note: In the sections which follow in this chapter, questions introduced as *worked* problems have model solutions provided on pp. 395–402, whereas those questions introduced as *further* problems have no such solutions provided. Those questions and other material marked with an asterisk involve rather detailed mathematics and may therefore be omitted.

W4.2   What is the rationale of compound interest?

(a) The rate of interest

Donald (1970, p. 1) defines a rate of interest like this:

> The amount contracted to be paid in one unit interval of time for each unit of capital invested.

You will note a number of characteristics of this definition:

1. It is a very general one: it says nothing about the economic notion of opportunity cost.
2. It does not state that the rate is an annual rate — for it need not be, and, especially for government bonds, rarely is.
3. Though not explicit in the definition, the rate of interest is really a secondary matter, for the force of interest is the fundamental mechanism at work, the rate being just a discrete manifestation of it.

Compound interest (in contrast to simple interest) assumes that when interest is received it can be reinvested at the same rate as the original sum (there was a long debate over this many years ago, when some unfortunately crude arguments to the contrary were put forward). Thus, if we are considering the growth of £100 over five years, and accumulating it at a rate of interest of 12% per annum, we are assuming that when the first receipt of £12 arrives after one year, that too can be invested at 12% per annum. This may or may not be true, and we shall delve more deeply into the implications of this problem when we come to compare NPV and IRR later.

Let us begin with the *perpetuity*. If there is no redemption date to a contract for the payment of interest, then it must be assumed that the interest will be paid for ever. A building society account is like this: the investor lends to the building society, and does not specify a date at which the money must be returned. Nor does the building society define such a date. Thus, so long as the investor leaves the funds with the society, it will pay him or her interest.

A perpetuity is valued very simply. Since the interest payable on the principal £P is £I at a rate of interest r, then we can say that:

$$P = I/r$$

To put this another way, we can *capitalize* the periodic interest by dividing it by the appropriate interest rate. This is illustrated in the simple example given in Fig. W4.1.

Dr Foster is offered the right to receive £400 in perpetuity (that is, for ever). If the ruling rate of interest for risk-free investments is 13%, what sum should he be prepared to pay for this right?

Solution:

£400/0.13 = £3,077 (to the nearest £)

Figure W4.1   Simple example of a perpetuity.

Now try the following problems based on the above and on section 4.2(a) in the text.

Worked problems

4.1 You wish to borrow £500 to buy a new moped. Your father agrees to lend you this, charging just 3% interest. He asks that when you complete your studies in three years' time you repay him. How much will you then need to do so?

4.2 Fred will receive £4,000 when he is 25, under the terms of his aunt's will. If he has just turned 18 and he wishes to sell his right to a broker, then, if the broker discounts the right at 18%, how much will he offer Fred?

4.3 You invest £800 in a bank, receiving £74 per annum interest. What is the annual interest rate being paid by the bank?

4.4 Claudia, like Fred, will come into money when she reaches 25. She is presently 19, and instead of a capital sum, she will be the beneficiary of a trust that expects to be able to pay her an annuity of £1,500 in perpetuity. Were she to be able to sell the right to this annuity now, and were the interest rate applicable to be 16%, how much should she expect to receive?

Further problems

4.5 'Thank you for your deposit,' You are told by the building society manager. 'Since the present rate of interest we pay is 9.75%, you will receive £292.50 at the end of each year.' How much did you deposit?

4.6 You would like to buy a small car (second-hand, of course) in two years' time. If you intend to buy a car that will cost £1,200, and you calculate that you will need to deposit £1,010 now, what rate of interest are you being offered?

4.7 Five years ago Mandy won a sum of money through holding premium bonds. She invested it with an insurance company under a contract that would pay her nothing until the present, but would as from today pay her an annuity in perpetuity of £400. If the interest rate used was 12%, how much did she win?

4.8 Your ancestor bought your present house 160 years ago for £200. At the time he could have bought government stock instead yielding 4% p.a. payable yearly in arrears, together with an opportunity to reinvest the interest receipts at a guaranteed rate of 4%. The government stock has just matured, and an expert has valued the house at £100,000. (i) In terms solely of these financial values, did he make a wise investment decision? (ii) In answering this question, what factors other than these monetary values do you believe to be relevant?

(b) The present value of a series of receipts

A simpler way of deriving the expression for $a_{\overline{n}|}$ that we developed in the main text is to see a finite series of receipts as a perpetuity valued now, less a perpetuity valued now that begins after the finite series ends. This is illustrated in Fig. W4.2.

Taking the perpetuity $\frac{1}{i}$ at t_0

t_0	t_1	t_2	t_3	t_4	t_5	t_6

—————————————— ∞

deducting the perpetuity $\frac{1}{i}$ at t_4

				t_4	t_5	t_6

—————————————— ∞

leaves the series to t_4

t_0	t_1	t_2	t_3	t_4

Figure W4.2   Finding $a_{\overline{n}|}$ by deducting perpetuities.

As we have seen, the value of the perpetuity a of 1 per period will be:

$$a = 1/i$$

The value of the perpetuity after time t_n will *at time t_n* be:

$$a = 1/i$$

that is, the same quantity. To find the value of the latter at time t_0 it must be discounted by v^n, which will give:

$$v^n(1/i)$$

and hence the value of the finite annuity up to and including the sum due at time t_n will be one less the other, that is:

$$1/i - v^n(1/i) = \frac{1 - v^n}{i}$$

which is the expression we found in the text (see p. 94).

The next set of problems will test your understanding of the manipulation of series of payments. We shall progressively make these problems more complex, and you are advised to attempt them all, looking carefully at the solutions since these extend somewhat the examples in the main text.

Worked problems

4.9   Suppose Claudia (see question 4.4) were entitled to the annuity of £1,500 in perpetuity immediately. What would be its present value?

4.10 Using the expression for $a_{\overline{n}|}$ of which you are aware (or alternatively, the tables at the back of this book), calculate the present value of a series of receipts of £1,500 for six years at an interest rate of 16%.

4.11 Compare your answer to question 4.10 with the answer to question 4.9 less the answer to question 4.4. Explain what you find.

4.12 You decide to place £200 each year in a building society. If the society pays interest at 8% per annum, to how much will your investment have grown after seven years if you put in these sums (i) at the end of each year, (ii) at the beginning of each year?

4.13 One more question about Claudia. Suppose that after she has received the annuity from the trust fund for ten years, the trustees propose to hand over to her the capital sum. What will be the present value of her rights? (It is suggested that you answer this by finding (i) the value of the annuity from the age of 25 to 35 right now; (ii) the value of the capital sum at age 35 by capitalizing the infinite series of sums still due; (iii) discounting the amount in (ii) back to the present; (iv) adding the result of (i) to the result of (iii).)

4.14 Compare the result of question 4.13(iv) with the result of question 4.4. Explain what you find.

Further problems

4.15 Sandy starts to save £350 a year in a Post Office account paying 6% interest. What will it have grown to at the end of eight years (assuming that the payments are in advance — that is, the first instalment is paid in immediately, and the last deposit she makes is at the beginning of the eighth year)?

4.16 Sandy begins as described in question 4.15, but after four years' saving she increases the amount she is saving by a further £100 for the remaining four years' deposits. Now what will she have in her account at the end of the eighth year?

4.17 (An extension of questions 4.15 and 4.16.) What sum of money at the very beginning of the period would be equivalent to the sums invested over the period? You should calculate this in two ways, showing they give the same result: (i) by finding the present value of the sum of money that represented the answer to question 4.16; (ii) by discounting the series of deposits that Sandy makes.

4.18 Christopher pays £10,000 to an insurance company. He wants them to pay him an annuity from the age of 65 to 75 (that is, ten instalments), beginning on his 65th birthday. If he is just 40 today, and the ruling rate of interest is 12%, what amount per annum should he receive? (Assume the sums will be paid at those dates irrespective of whether or not he is alive to receive them.)

4.19 According to the product life-cycle theory, a product's sales will at first grow but then, after reaching a plateau, will experience a decline. Generally cash inflows will be negative in the initial years as more cash is spent on developing and promoting the product than is recouped from sales.

Suppose that a product has the following pattern of sales and costs:

1. *Sales* are expected to be £150,000 in the first year and to grow by 15% per annum for the next eight years. They are then expected to decline by 5% per annum for a further four years, after which the production machinery will be worn out and production will cease.
2. *Costs* will begin high, because of promotion costs. The immediate expense will be a launch budgeted at £80,000, and purchases of machinery at £220,000. After that, starting from year 1, operating costs to manufacture the product will be £70,000 per annum, growing by 6% a year until the product is discontinued.

What is the NPV of this project if the current cost of financing it is 11%?

(c) Continuous compounding

(a) Payments at intervals other than yearly

The important point to grasp about this is that compounding can take place with any unit of time. We think in terms of years simply because we know from everyday experience that so much growth or decay is given in years — for instance, annual inflation rates, annual interest rates, annual rises in world population or GNP. But this is just one example of a general model in which compound growth occurs, and the critical factor is the *period of compounding*. For instance, when a government stock is stated to be compounded (or *converted*) half-yearly, it means that each half-year an interest payment is made. Hence this sum is available for reinvestment.

The reason for confusion is that, despite the fact that interest may be payable at periods other than a year, people tend to refer to the instrument (a treasury bond, for instance) as if it were yearly. Thus if interest is really 4.5% per half-year, it is often — even officially — called a 9% bond compounded half-yearly. The 9% label is generally called the nominal rate of interest. The easiest way to avoid this confusion is to repeat to yourself that *this 9% label has no meaning at all other than as a convenient label*. It has no meaning so far as the nature of the bond is concerned. Nominal rates are only labels, nothing more.

Worked examples

4.20 Margaret buys £1,000 in corporate debentures with a nominal interest rate of 13% that pay interest every half-year. If she can reinvest at the same rate, what will her investment have grown to after 15 years?

4.21 Alex buys £1,000 in corporate debentures with a nominal rate of 13% that pay interest every half-year. As he receives the interest, he invests it at the best rate he can obtain, which is 11% p.a. What will he be worth after 15 years?

4.22 Samantha, an actuary, is considering the future of her new-born baby Lydia from a purely economic viewpoint. She believes that a private education only will result in her daughter's going to Oxford, and that the annual cost of the education will be £4,000 per annum (payable in advance) from Lydia's 11th to her 18th birthdays (inclusive) and £3,000 for her stay in Oxford from her 19th to 21st birthdays (inclusive). This will result in benefits to Lydia of an earnings increment from her first year of work (aged 22) onwards until she is 60 of £8,000 per annum. You may take the rate of interest applicable to be 13% throughout.

1. If Samantha were to deposit a single sum immediately that would pay for the schooling and university education, how much would she now have to give an insurance company that specialized in such contracts?

2. Is the extra cost of the schooling from age 11 to 21 worthwhile in purely economic terms?

3. If, instead of a single sum, Samantha paid for the schooling in equal quarterly instalments in advance from now until Lydia left school on her 19th birthday, what would the quarterly payment be?

4. If, instead of the above plan, Samantha dropped the whole idea of private education and saved the sums she would otherwise have paid for schooling until Lydia's 22nd birthday, how much could she give her in cash on that date?

5. If, instead of the single cash payment in 4. above, Samantha decided

to buy Lydia an annuity payable from her 22nd birthday to her 59th birthday (inclusive), how much would the annuity be?

Further problems

4.23 Sally saves £10 each week from her salary and puts it in her building society account which is paying 9.25% p.a. How much interest will she have earned after four and a half years?

4.24 Bert has been given bonds that pay a nominal interest rate of 14% convertible quarterly. They mature in six years' time, when he will receive the nominal value of the bonds, which is a capital sum of £18,000. If the current interest rate for such an investment is 11%, what is the present value of these future receipts?

(b) The exponential function*

There are two reasons why the exponential function is important in the study of compound interest.

1. It has a practical application for all those sets of receipts and payments that are continuous, or approximate to being continuous;
2. It supplies the theoretical underpinning for discrete interest functions (which is what rates of interest are).

A moment's thought will make the second point clear. Think of a rate of interest. It seems that throughout the period (for instance, the year) the amount involved does not grow at all. Then on the last instant of the period it becomes bigger by the amount of interest. Now this may be the way interest is credited or charged. For example, credit card companies only charge interest if a balance is outstanding on the balance of the account at the end of each month — in effect, no interest seems to accrue to an outstanding balance until that date, and hence the card-holder who pays at the last moment is receiving free credit from the company. But this is not a logical way to understand the earning of interest, for as long as a party in an economic world has money, that person can earn interest on it (and conversely, so long as someone lacks money, there is an opportunity cost of not being able to use it).

Thus interest accrues continuously, as in Fig. W4.3. It will be seen from this figure that the discrete rate of interest only 'catches up' with the true accrual at the date of the attachment of the interest.

As we pointed out above, there is a practical reason for using continuous compounding too. Institutions such as life assurance companies and banks are receiving and paying out funds daily: and compounding 365 times per year is as near as makes no difference to a continuous stream. Some large industrial enterprises too may be receiving payments from debtors daily (for smaller firms the 'lumpiness' of receipts at the end of each month, when debtors draw their cheques, makes this less true — this is smoothed out for the larger firm, since the larger number of debtors typically have different systems of settling debts).

We can now extend the discussion of exponential functions from the case of the single payment compounding (or being discounted) to the case of continuous payments or receipts being compounded/discounted. Although the exposition necessarily seems arduous, the resulting expressions are not difficult to manipulate.

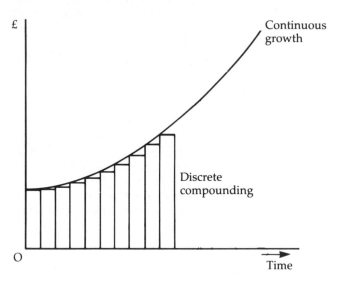

Figure W4.3 Continuous compounding (A).

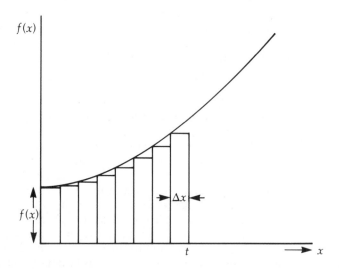

Figure W4.4 Continuous compounding (B).

We are now considering the case where *both the payments and the compounding are continuous*. To do this we begin from the case where the amounts are discrete but the compounding is continuous (in this section we draw upon Cissell and Cissell, 1973. We suppose that time is denoted by x, and hence the amount of funds is a function of time (since it grows with time); thus it can be denoted by $f(x)$. Now suppose that payments are made over a long period of time (t). Since the payments are discrete we can define a finite number of such payments over the time t — suppose there are n such payments. In these circumstances we find a picture as in Fig. W4.4.

Since the total time t is divided into n units, the length of each unit (the length of time between payments) will be:

$$\Delta x = t/n$$

Now consider any rectangle in Fig. W4.4. The sum to which the flow has grown by that time is $f(x)$ and the time that sum exists is Δx. Hence the rectangle $f(x)\, \Delta x$ represents the total quantity of funds in that period. The present value of each of these amounts will therefore be:

$$[f(x)\, \Delta x] e^{-\delta t}$$

and thus the present value of them all will be:

$$\sum_{i=1}^{n} f(x_i)\, \Delta x_i e^{-\delta x_i}$$

Now as the period of compounding Δx decreases, n becomes very large, and at the limit the present value tends to

$$\int_0^t f(x) e^{-\delta x} dx$$

If we now let the cash flow be $f(x) = A$, then the present value becomes:

$$\int_0^t A e^{-\delta x} dx$$

and integrating gives:

$$A \int_0^t e^{-\delta x} dx = A \left[\frac{-1}{\delta} e^{-\delta x} \right]_0^t$$

$$= \frac{-A}{\delta} (e^{-\delta t} - e^0)$$

$$= \frac{A}{\delta} (1 - e^{-\delta t})$$

Let us illustrate how all this works by means of an example, given in Fig. W4.5.

A company has contracted to have a new factory constructed at a cost of £2,500,000. If the current interest rate is 6.5% per annum, what is the present value of the cost of the factory under the following conditions?

1. The construction company will require payment on completion in two years' time.
2. The construction company will require equal stage payments in one year's time and two years' time.
3. The construction company will require constant funding as it has to pay its own costs and accrue profits for its own shareholders. Thus it will require the £2.5 million to be paid continuously over the next two years.

Solution:

1. £2.5m $\times v^2_{6.5\%}$ = £2,204,150
2. £1.25m $\times a_{\overline{2}|}^{6.5\%}$ = £2,275,780
3. $\dfrac{£1.25\text{m}}{0.065} (1 - e^{-0.065 \times 2})$ = £2,344,320

Figure W4.5 *Examples of present value calculations.*

Worked problem*

Since the material of the previous section is not essential to much of the material in the rest of this book, we give only one worked problem. It is similar to question 4.19 for continuously compounded amounts.

4.25 Floria Ltd are planning a new product. The initial period's net cash flow is £1m. This is expected to grow by 10% p.a. for five years and then to decrease by 8% p.a. for seven years. It will then be scrapped. Funds arrive continuously. At a ruling interest rate of 11%, what is the present value of this investment?

W4.3   Bond valuation

We treated bond valuation fairly simply in the text. There were just two complications: understanding the meaning of interest being paid other than yearly (which we already discussed in an earlier section); and understanding the resulting difficulties when we speak of nominal and real interest rates.

There are other complications in the real world of bond purchases. One of particular interest is the *reinvestment rate assumption*. We shall not give any mathematics here — it gets very messy — but you will appreciate that very often an investor receiving his or her half-yearly interest cannot reinvest it at the coupon rate. It might be more, it might be less. That depends on the current state of the market. This in turn means that the compounding, which we simply plugged in as a single rate with the assumption that funds would always be reinvested at the rate named, would in fact be far more complicated than that.

Since we do not propose to go into the mathematics of this here, we only make the point that, whereas we did our calculations on the basis that it would be possible, it often is not — and this in turn means that the *effective* rate earned by the investor may well not be the rate we have just discussed.

We now give one further problem on bond valuation (only one because you have already come across some examples in section 4.2(c) on compounding other than yearly).

Worked problem

4.26 On 1 July 1982 XYZ plc issued a 12% straight bond with a term of 20 years and an issue price of 97. The bond is redeemable at par. Interest is paid half-yearly in arrears.

1. What was the redemption yield of the bond at the time of issue (take this to one decimal place)?
2. Suppose it is now 1 July 1991. If current rates for such bonds are 17%, what price would you expect to pay for this bond now?
3. Bond prices become less volatile in relation to ruling interest rates as they near their redemption date. Explain why, giving a numerical illustration to demonstrate your point.

W4.4   Investment appraisal methods

(a) NPV and IRR

The logic behind each of the two investment appraisal methods detailed here is quite straightforward. The *net present value* method leads the user to invest in a project if the present value of the inflows is greater than the present value of the outflows (i.e. if the *net* present value is positive). The *internal rate of return* method leads the user to invest in a project if the rate of return from the project is greater than the criterion discount rate.

You will need little extra practice via this Workbook in calculating net present values: this is essentially an application of the compounding techniques we have been examining. It will be beneficial, however, to give some attention to the calculation of internal rates of return (IRRs). The following problems should help to give you practice in calculating IRRs.

Worked problems

4.27 'Twice your money back!' says the advertisement. It goes on: 'If you invest with us, we give you twice — yes, twice — your money in return. If you invest £1,000 with us, for instance, we will give you £250 a year for the next eight years!' What internal rate of return is this company offering? If you could borrow money at 13%, would you invest in this offer?

4.28 Joe sells hamburgers. He reckons that if he spent money on improving the appearance of his stand, it would increase profits. He recognizes, though, that it will begin to look shabby again before too long, so he judges that if he spends £800 on the stand now, the increased net cash flows for the next four years will be £400, £300, £200 and £100. What would Joe's internal rate of return be?

4.29 Complete the following statement:

The internal rate of return of a project is found by equating the present value of the ＿＿ to the present value of the ＿＿ of the project by the use of a unique ＿＿ of ＿＿ and comparing the resulting ＿＿ to the cost of ＿＿ or other personal discount rate.

4.30 To invest in Scotch whisky you invest now and realize your return in a lump sum in eight years' time. If you invest £5,000 and receive £11,000, what is your internal rate of return?

Further problems

4.31 What is the IRR of each of the following sets of cash flows?

Year	Project A £	Project B £	Project C £
0	(8,000)	(350)	(23,000)
1	2,000	150	(10,000)
2	3,000	300	10,000
3	4,000	—	15,000
4	5,000	—	20,000

4.32 Fiona would like to invest in a laundrette. She is told that the cash flows she would receive for the next five years if she did so would be £400 for the first year, increasing by £150 each year for the remainder of the investment. If she had to borrow £1,500 to take up this offer, what would be the maximum rate of interest she would be prepared to pay on the loan?

(b) The relationship between NPV and IRR

It is important to study the graph given in Fig. 4.13 (p. 109) of the text. Do understand that *the NPV is the residual after discounting at any given rate*, and hence just one rate will give a NPV of zero and thus be the internal rate of return.

We emphasize in the questions that now follow the importance of seeing how NPV relates to IRR, and especially the implications of the crossover point that can happen with two projects (as happens in Fig. 4.15). At high rates of discount the project with the more distant cash inflows loses out.

Worked problems

4.33 Bill is considering investing in a proposal that will return him £500 each year for seven years. The outlay will be £2,200. Work out the NPV at the following rates of interest: 0%, 5%, 10%, 15%, 20%. Map this project on to a graph and trace the curve of the project. What is the approximate internal rate of return according to your sketch?

4.34 Tracy can invest in one of two projects. Their cash flows are as follows:

Year	Cash flow A £	Cash flow B £
0	−3,000	−3,000
1	2,000	0
2	1,000	0
3	500	1,000
4	500	2,000
5	—	3,000

Map each of these on a graph and comment on what you find.

W4.5 Discussion questions

Note: Suggested answers to these questions can be found in section W4.6 on pp. 402–4.

4.1 Why could we write in the text that 'when just one project is being considered, both methods [that is, NPV and IRR] must always give the same accept/reject signal'?

4.2 Suppose a director says the following to you: 'I cannot accept the superiority of net present value over the rate of return. When I consider an investment I want to know what my return will be — and that's a percentage. After all, we talk about profitability rather than profit, don't we? We do not say that ICI is a better investment than the corner shop. We see which is giving a better return on investment — a rate in order words. Net present value is just a sum, like profit. So it is meaningless.'
How should you respond?

4.3 We have seen that as the discount rate gets higher, so the NPV gets lower. This is to be expected because the future cash flows become subject to division by progressively higher denominators. The graph in Fig. 4.13 shows this well. But now look at Fig. 4.14: for part of the curve the NPV *increases* as the discount rate goes up. How do you explain this?

4.4 Here are four sets of cash flows, and four types of project. Which do you think is a likely set of cash flows for: (i) a purchased annuity certain from a life assurance company; (ii) a corporate bond nearing maturity; (iii) commercial paper; (iv) a successor to Rubik's cube?

| Year | Cash flow | | | |
	A £	B £	C £	D £
0	−10,000	−10,000	−10,000	−10,000
1	2,000	3,000	230	11,000
2	9,000	3,000	230	
3	3,000	3,000	230	
4		3,000	14,000	

W4.6   Answers to questions

(a) Answers to worked problems

(i) Answers to problems 4.1–4.4

4.1 The amount to be repaid will be:

$$£500 \times (1.03)^3 = £546.36$$

Note: In answering like this, you are assuming that everything takes place at the end of a year. Unless we state otherwise, we always assume this in questions based on the rate of interest.

4.2 It is necessary to discount the future receipt of £4,000 by $v^7{}_{18\%}$. That is (where PV is present value):

$$PV = £4,000 \times v^7{}_{18\%}$$
$$= £4,000 \times 0.3139$$
$$= £1,255.70$$

4.3 Since $P = I/r$, then $r = I/P$. So the interest rate must be:

$$(74/800) = 0.0925$$
$$= 9.25\%$$

4.4 It is best to approach this question in two stages. First, find the value of the perpetuity on her 25th birthday. Second, discount this back to the present (that is, by six years).

The value of the perpetuity on her 25th birthday will be (assuming that the first receipt is one year later; that is, on her 26th birthday):

$$£1,500/0.16 = £9,375$$

The present value of £9,375 six years hence is:

$$£9,375 \times v^6 = £9,375 \times 0.4104$$
$$= £3,847.90$$

(11) Answers to problems 4.9–4.14

4.9 This is straightforward — in fact we found it as part of question 4.4. It is simply:

$$PV = 1{,}500/0.16 = £9{,}375$$

4.10 This should also be simple. Using the expression for $a_{\overline{n}|}$ we have:

$$£1{,}500 \times a_{\overline{6}|} = 1{,}500 \left(\frac{1 - (1/1.16)^6}{0.16} \right)$$
$$= £5{,}527.10$$

4.11 First, we can see that the result of deducting the answer to 4.4 from 4.9 is indeed 4.10, as follows:

4.9:   £9,375.00
4.4:   £3,387.90

4.10:   £5,527.10

This illustrates the point made in the Workbook, p. 386. Question 4.4 was concerned with an annuity payable at a future time, while question 4.9 was concerned with an immediate annuity. Deducting the one from the other leaves the finite annuity-certain for n years — in this case, six years.

4.12 1. This part is quite straightforward, and we can use the expression for $S_{\overline{n}|}$ that we developed in the text. Hence the amount we require is:

$$200 \times S_{\overline{7}|} = 200 \, \frac{(1.08)^7 - 1}{0.08}$$
$$= 200 \times 8.9228$$
$$= £1{,}784.56$$

2. This requires a function we have not yet discussed — but you should have been able to work out the answer from first principles. When an annuity or sum is paid in advance it is known as an *annuity-due* and represented by $\ddot{a}_{\overline{n}|}$ or $\ddot{S}_{\overline{n}|}$. The latter (which we need here) can be found in one of two ways, but we shall only consider one of them here.

   Since $S_{\overline{n}|}$ represents sums payable in arrears from t_1 to t_n, and the same function in advance will represent sums payable from t_0 to t_{n-1}, it should be clear that the latter is just the former shifted back by one year — that is, receivable/payable one year earlier. Here the series in advance can be found simply by taking $S_{\overline{n}|}$ and multiplying it by $(1 + i)$:

   $$\ddot{S}_{\overline{n}|} = (1 + i)S_{\overline{n}|}$$

Thus, working from the previous answer, we can see that the answer can be found as:

$$£1{,}784.56 \times (1.08) = £1{,}927.33$$

4.13 As suggested in the question, we shall take this in stages.

   1. This will be:

   $$v^6 \times a_{\overline{10}|} \times £1{,}500 = 0.4104 \times 4.8332 \times 1500$$
   $$= £2{,}975.31$$
   assuming that the first receipt is on her 26th birthday.
   2. This is just the perpetuity we have met before, namely £9,375.
   3. The sum in part 2. was due, we shall assume, on her 35th birthday (the series of annuity payments having ended the previous year).

Since she is now 19, this amount must be discounted by v^{16}: that is, 0.0930.

This gives £(9,375 × 0.093) = £872.25.

4. £2,975.31 + £872.25 = £3,847.56.

4.14 Allowing for minor rounding errors, this is obviously the same as the answer to question 4.4. Having worked through to the solution you should quickly see why: we have once again taken a perpetuity (in 4.4) and valued it at the end of the finite time requested in the present question (when Claudia will be 35). Clearly, assuming that the ruling interest rate will still be the same, we can suppose that the principal due to her at 35 will represent the perpetuity on that date, and hence when this is deducted from the perpetuity in question 4.4 it will leave us with the annuity in part 1. of this question.

Note, however, the implication of this question that, making the crucial assumption of similar discount rates, Claudia would be indifferent (in terms of present value, and ignoring her liquidity preference) as to whether the trust fund was broken up or not.

(iii) Answers to problems 4.20–4.22

4.20 The reinvestment assumption is important here, as we shall see later. Given that it can be assumed, the solution is simply:

$$1,000 \left(1 + \frac{0.13}{2} \right)^{(15 \times 2)} = 1,000 \, (1.065)^{30}$$
$$= £6,614$$

4.21 It is tempting to proceed in this question as follows: the interest received each half-year is £65; this is reinvested at 11%, which also needs to be adjusted for the fact that we are converting half-yearly; hence the solution is to add the accumulated interest to the original sum invested thus:

$$65 \times S_{\overline{30}|}^{5.5\%} + 1,000 = 65 \left(\frac{(1.055)^{30} - 1}{0.055} \right) + 1,000$$
$$= £4,708 + 1,000$$
$$= £5,708$$

This would be correct if we knew that the reinvestment attracted interest convertible half-yearly of 11%. We are not told this, however, and we proceed best by splitting the receipts of £65 per half-year into two groups: those received on the half-year mark and those received at the end of each year. Each is treated as an annual accumulation at 11%, and they are added to obtain the result (one series being enhanced by a half-year's additional accumulation). This is further illustrated in Fig. W4.6. This gives:

$$65 S_{\overline{15}|}^{11\%} + (65 S_{\overline{15}|}^{11\%})(1.11)^{0.5} = (65 S_{\overline{15}|}^{11\%})(1 + (1.11)^{0.5})$$
$$= 2,236.35 \times 2.05$$
$$= £4,592$$

and adding the original £1,000 gives us £5,592.

This throws light also on the assumption we made in answering question 4.20, since we implicitly assumed that Margaret could reinvest at a rate of interest convertible half-yearly.

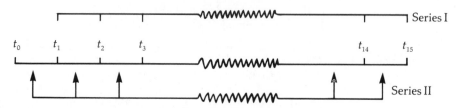

Series II is enhanced by $(1.11)^{0.5}$ to bring it to its growth at t_{15}

Figure W4.6   Part-answer to worked problem 4.21.

4.22 1.

		£
PV(School) = £4,000 $a_{\overline{8}}$ v^{10} = £4,000 × 4.7988 × 0.2946 =		5655
PV(University) = £3,000 $a_{\overline{3}}$ v^{18} = £3,000 × 2.3612 × 0.1108 =		785
		6440

2. To answer this we need to compare the answer to 1. above with the present value of the earnings increment.

$$PV(\text{Increment}) = £8,000\, a_{\overline{38}}\, v^{21} = £8,000 \times 7.6183 \times 0.0768$$
$$= £4,681.$$

(Note that 38 + 21 = 59 years. We assume the last increment on the first day of her 60th year, that is, her 59th birthday.) Since £4,681 is less than £6,440, it is not economically worthwhile.

3. Since the payments are in advance, we multiply the whole expression by v. There will be 76 payments so the quarterly payment is found by spreading the answer to 1. over 76 periods.

The *effective* interest rate is 13% so the quarterly rate is
$$\sqrt[4]{1.13} - 1 = 0.0310 = 3.1\%.$$

Thus the quarterly payment is
$$\frac{£6440}{a_{\overline{76}}^{3.1\%}} \times v_{3.1\%} = \frac{£6440 \times 0.9699}{29.0886} = £214.72.$$

4. This is simply £6,440 × $(1.13)^{22}$ = £6,440 × 14.7138 = £94,757.
5. We use the answer to part 4. and spread it over 38 years:
$$\frac{£94,757 \times v}{a_{\overline{38}}} = \frac{£94,757 \times 0.8850}{7.618} = £11,008.$$

(iv) Answer to problem 4.25*

4.25 In the exposition above we derived the expression:

$$f(x)\, e^{-\delta x} dx$$

before substituting $A = f(x)$. Now if we have an increasing function rather than the static A, we simply set:

$$f(x) = Ce^{kx}$$

where C is the initial amount and k the growth rate. Hence the present value of the growing cash flows is:

$$PV = \int_0^t Ce^{kx}e^{-\delta x}dx$$
$$= C \int_0^t e^{(k-\delta)x}dx$$
$$= \frac{C}{k-\delta}[e^{(k-\delta)x}]_0^t$$

So in this case it is:
$$\frac{1,000,000}{0.1 - 0.11}[e^{(0.1-0.11)x}]_0^5 = -100,000,000(0.951 - 1)$$
$$= £4,880,000$$

Now we turn to the decreasing period. The expression is similar, but incorporating a decay rather than growth factor, and the present value *at* $t = 5$ is:

$$C \int_0^t e^{(-0.08-0.11)x}dx = \frac{C}{-0.19}[e^{0.19x}]_0^7$$
$$= (C/-0.19)(-0.73552)$$

Now C will be $(£1m)e^{kt} = 1,000,000e^{0.1 \times 5}$
$$= £1,648,721$$
and substituting into the previous expression gives a present value at $t = 5$ of £6,382,459.

At $t = 0$ this will be:
$$\frac{6,382,459}{e^{\delta t}} = \frac{6,382,459}{1.7333} = £3,682,359$$

So the total PV will be:
$$£4,880,000 + £3,682,359 = £8,562,359$$

(v) Answer to problem 4.26

4.26 1. This has to be done by trial and error. We need to solve the following for i:

$$(100/(1 + i)^{40} + 6((1 - (1/(1 + i)^{40}))/i) = 97$$

It turns out that the redemption yield is approximately 12.4% per annum as follows:

$$100/(1.062^{40}) + 6((1 - (1/1.062^{40}))/0.062) = 97.065$$

2. As the text pointed out, the history (issue price and initial yield) is irrelevant. Thus, based on future receipts, the price is:

$$£6(a_{\overline{22}}) + £100 \, v^{22} = £6 \times 9.8098 + £100 \times 0.16617 = £75.48$$

3. This is best explained through a simplified example. Suppose that interest rates fall from 15% to 12%. There are two bonds, each of which bears a coupon of 9% payable annually and is repayable at par. Bond A matures in two years' time, bond B in ten years' time. The market prices before and after the fall in rates will be as follows:

Bond A (before):

$$£9(a_{\overline{2}}^{15\%}) + £100v^2{}_{15\%} = £9 \times 1.626 + £100 \times 0.7561$$
$$= £14.63 + £75.61 = £90.24$$

Bond A (after):

$$£9(a_{\overline{2}}^{12\%}) + £100v^2{}_{12\%} = £9 \times 1.690 + £100 \times 0.7972$$
$$= £15.21 + £79.72 = £94.93$$

Bond B (before):
$$£9(a_{\overline{10}|}{}^{15\%}) + £100v^{10}{}_{15\%} = £9 \times 5.019 + £100 \times 0.2472$$
$$= £45.17 + £24.72 = £69.89$$

Bond B (after):
$$£9 \ (a_{\overline{10}|}{}^{12\%}) + £100v^{10}{}_{12\%} = £9 \times 5.650 + £100 \times 0.3220$$
$$= £50.85 + £32.20 = £83.05$$

This can be summarized, with percentage changes, as follows:

	15% £	12% £	Diff £	% Diff
Bond A	90.24	94.93	4.69	5.2%
Bond B	69.89	83.05	13.16	18.8%

You will see that both the absolute and the relative differences are greater for the longer bond. The shorter bond is 'anchored' by the fact that the redemption is to take place soon. The difference in discounting rates is less important since the bond-holder can be sure of receiving the redemption sum soon. It is the proximity of the receipt that makes the price less volatile.

(vi) Answers to problems 4.27–4.30

4.27 The internal rate of return is 18.7%. Trial and error methods are not necessary here, of course, since the receipts constitute an annuity. All you need do is to solve the equation:

$$1{,}000 = 250 \times a_{\overline{8}|}{}^{i}$$

which reduces to:

$$a_{\overline{8}|} = 1{,}000/250 = 4.00$$

and this can easily be solved by running your finger along the row of a set of discount tables for various rates of interest until one is discovered that gives a value for $a_{\overline{8}|}$ of nearly 4.00. Since the value for 18% is 4.078 and for 19% is 3.954, the IRR clearly lies between these two rates, and can be approximated by linear interpolation.

Thus, according to the simple rules we have developed, you will find it worthwhile to borrow to invest. Whether you would trust anybody who placed an advertisement like that with your money is another matter!

4.28 At 12% the NPV is £2.21; at 13% the NPV is −£11.13. Thus the internal rate of return is 12.1%

4.29 Inflows; outflows; rate; interest (or discount); rate; borrowing.

4.30 This is simple. It is just a matter of solving the equation:

$$5{,}000 = 11{,}000v^{8}$$

for i, that is:

$$5{,}000 = 11{,}000/(1+i)^{8}$$

so that:

$$(1+i)^{8} = 11{,}000/5{,}000$$

and hence:
$$i = \sqrt[8]{11/5} - 1$$

which gives:
$$i = 0.1036 \text{ or } 10.4\%$$

(vii) Answers to problems 4.33–4.34
4.33 The net present values are:

%	£
0	1300.00
5	693.19
10	234.20
15	(119.80)
20	(397.70)

The graph of this project is shown in Fig. W4.7. The IRR is found by the rate at which the curve cuts the horizontal axis (because at this point the NPV is zero), and this turns out to be just over 13%.

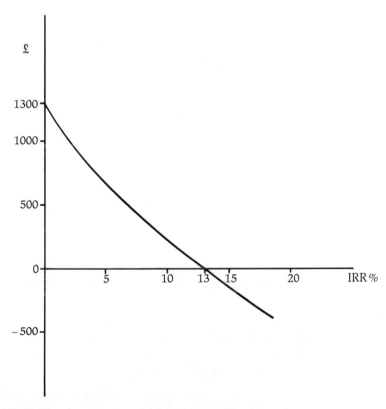

Figure W4.7 Part-answer to worked problem 4.33

4.34 The net present values at various rates of interest are as follows:

%	A £	B £
0	1,000	3,000
5	655	1,860
10	362	980
15	110	292
20	−108	−251
25	−299	−686

and the internal rates of return are about 17.5% for both projects. Mapped on to a graph these appear as in Fig. W4.8.

Now we saw in the text (pp. 110–11) that one project might be preferred at certain discount rates, but another at other rates. *This is not true in this case* because neither project would be desirable if its NPV were negative! So for all the positive values of NPV, project B is to be preferred.

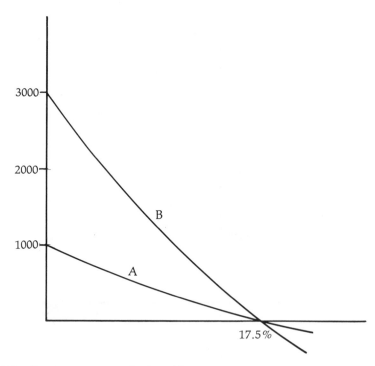

Figure W4.8   Part-answer to worked problem 4.34.

(b) Suggested answers to discussion questions

4.1 The NPV of a project is positive when cash inflows are greater than outflows where discounted at the cost of capital. In general, the higher the discount rate, the lower the NPV. This means that, as the discount rate is raised above the cost of capital, the NPV will decrease. At some point it will become zero. Thus the IRR — which means the rate at which the NPV is zero — must be higher than the cost of capital for a desirable project. Thus a positive NPV must always correspond to an IRR greater than the cost of capital.

4.2 This can be best answered in three stages. Let us take the director's first statement. This is indeed quite reasonable: a rate of return is intuitively helpful. However, the problems of multiple rates of return and the slight difficulty of calculating it make the IRR less desirable. The second statement is also reasonable. If you have a project of £100,000 giving a NPV of £15,000, this is possibly not as good as one of £1,000 giving a NPV of £800. But this can be sorted out by scaling them so they are comparable — and we shall see how that is done in Chapter 6. The glaring error comes with the final statement. This is not a valid conclusion to draw. NPV is a sum, but it is not meaningless: it represents the immediate amount by which the investor is better off by investing in the project — an increase in present wealth, in other words.

4.3 Although the investment shown here is credible, it is not typical. Look carefully at the cash flow represented by this example. First there is a positive, then a negative, then a positive flow. This could, for instance, be a project where a government grant is received immediately, payment for the capital goods is delayed until some time after inception so they can be shown to be working correctly, and then the whole project is sold for refinancing purposes, giving a final positive outflow. Remember, the axis shown is v, not i.

We have here an unusual situation. One discounted amount is an inflow, one is an outflow. As a result, between the points where the curve lies between NPV = £15,200 and its minimum, NPV falls as v increases, which is the same as saying that NPV falls as i falls. As i falls, this affects the one-year negative return more than the two-year positive return. For instance, here are the figures when the discount rate drops from 40% to 30%:

Cash flow	Discount factor 40%	(A) × (B)	Discount factor 30%	(A) × (D)	Difference (C) − (E)
(A) £	(B)	(C) £	(D)	(E) £	£
−35,000	0.714	(24,990)	0.769	(26,915)	1,925
20,000	0.510	10,200	0.592	11,840	(1,640)
15,200	—	15,200	—	15,200	—
200		410		125	285

The drop in the negative amount for the first year (a gain of £1,925) has more than offset the drop in the positive flow of £1,640.

4.4 1. A purchased annuity certain is one in which a person pays over a single amount to receive a series of (usually) equal smaller amounts in the future. Pattern B corresponds to this.
   2. A corporate bond pays a series of interest amounts to the owner, and at maturity a much larger amount, corresponding in some way to the initial investment payable. Pattern C is of this kind.

3. Commercial paper is of a period less than a year, and pays no interest (the profit lies in the difference between the buying and selling prices). Pattern D appears to be like this.
4. A product like Rubik's cube will rise quickly in popularity and die out within a small number of years. This means that the cash flows will also follow this pattern. A is like this: the peak is in year 2, after which the product goes into sharp decline.

Thus the most likely correspondences are:

A	4.
B	1.
C	2.
D	3.

5 Enter the enterprise: the risk-free model

W5.1 Bringing in the enterprise

The starting point of Chapter 5 of the text is to allow the business enterprise into the picture and emphasize the distinction between the investor–enterprise relationship and the enterprise–project relationship. In fact, there are both differences and similarities between these relationships.

They are different in that the investor–enterprise relation is an *arm's length* relationship. There is no direct control between the investor and the enterprise's management. (The sanction of the general meeting is really quite a weak one, and financial institutions have a history of being quite wary of direct intervention in management — in the UK, at least. Thus there is normally considerable separation of ownership and control; the large public company can have some hundreds of thousands of shareholders (millions since the privatizations of the 1980s). This means there is an asymmetry of information between them: managers know things about the enterprise that investors do not know. Moreover, even if the managers try to tell some of these things to the investors, there is reason to suppose they will not always be believed. This is the basis of *agency theory*, of course, which we saw in Chapter 1 and have referred to already a number of times since.)

Yet there is also an agency-type relation among some managers within the enterprise, and this has implications for the enterprise–project relationship. In one sense this second relationship is very different from the first because the people involved know each other, and there is a direct control relationship involved. This, indeed, was the basis of the 'market failures' literature from which agency theory derives, but which took a different turn in the 1960s with its development by, in particular, Oliver Williamson (see Williamson, 1975). The emphasis in this work was on the *hierarchy* within the enterprise that replaced the market under certain conditions. A key aspect of that hierarchy (which distinguished it from the market it replaced) was that there was a direct control relationship between, say, a parent board of directors and a divisional manager.

In many ways agency theory has abandoned this special relationship, and taken the contract to be the basis of the director–divisional manager relationship (for instance) just as it is outside the boundaries of the enterprise. They have in common such things as:

1. *contractual relationships* — the management/enterprise more generally is contracted to the investors to perform on their behalf. Similarly, the employment contracts of managers are evidence of a principal–agent relationship between the individual manager and the organization;

2. *monitoring devices* — just as investors receive accounts to monitor the management more generally, so the directors and senior managers receive internal financial reports about the performance of more junior managers. Indeed this monitoring relationship is not confined to the senior–junior hierarchical relationship; all managers monitor each other, even at the same level of seniority.

Looked at this way, there is no more trust within the enterprise than there is outside it.

A particular similarity between the investor–enterprise relationship and the enterprise–project relationship, as we pointed out in the text (p. 114), is that identical principles of discounted benefits apply in each case. The investors wish to maximize their utility (which we take to be the maximizing of their wealth). The enterprise seeks to maximize its value. Both are conceived in terms of NPV, and hence the recursive relationship we discussed applies.

Of course, agency theory would suggest that information asymmetry applies equally outside and within the enterprise. This is because divisional managers have direct access to information that senior management does not have, and in their own interests may not be truthful about affairs. Senior managers are aware of this and treat information circumspectly, in just the same way that shareholders and markets more generally are wary of declared information by an enterprise's management.

To summarize then: there are differences and similarities between these two relationships, but the similarities seem to outweigh the differences.

W5.2   Valuing shares

Having emphasized the distinction between the two relationships, we turn first to the investor–enterprise relationship — and this means the market. It is the interactions in the market that govern the (market) valuation of the enterprise. To enquire into this valuation we need a model through which we can tackle individual share valuation.

Share valuation is always a tricky business. When a company is unquoted, valuation involves a great deal of analysis of the company and its prospects, though even then the valuations in the market for similar companies can act as a helpful yardstick. For quoted companies, models such as the Gordon growth model given in section 5.2 of the text can be helpful. Try using the Gordon model for the Amersham case given in Fig. 2.1. With the sparse information available to you, what is the implicit cost of equity capital for companies in Amersham's risk class? A possible answer is given in Fig. W5.1, but remember this is based on:

1. the Gordon model (which makes assumptions that may or may not obtain);
2. approximate numbers -— for instance, we have assumed that the growth has been taken by the market to be roughly continuous between 1976–7 and 1981–2, and we have also, of course, assumed that the profit forecast will turn out to be correct!
3. pre-tax figures.

Now try some further examples.

(a) The case of Amersham International.

OBSERVER BUSINESS
Melvyn Marcus City Editor
THE AMERSHAM HORROR

It is very easy, with the benefit of hindsight, to declare that the £71 million Amersham offer for sale, which attracted applications worth £1.75 billion, was pitched too cheaply.

With such benefit I believe it was — but I do not share Labour MP Tam Dalyell's conviction that the Government has 'defrauded' the taxpayer of millions of pounds.

Nor (tempting as it is) do I feel inclined to castigate Rothschild (who acted for the Government), Morgan Grenfell (who acted for Amersham) or Cazenove, broker to the issue.

Amersham is, admittedly, a glamour stock which, under the wing of the Atomic Energy Authority, specialized in radioactive chemistry with a bias towards diagnostic products. But the profit record hardly inspires: pre-tax earnings were down from £4.8 million in 1976–77 to £4 million in 1980–1 — although a doubling of £8.3 million has been forecast for 1981–82.

But at the offer price of 142p, the shares have been sold at almost 19 times earnings (think about the historic multiple) and the forecast dividend yield is a mere 3.5 per cent.

A wrong decision? Yes, but it is an error of judgement which is dwarfed by the De Lorean fiasco — an affair which Dalyell might be better employed worrying about.

Wait now for cries of 'tenders' instead of offers for sale. A tender (never popular with jobbers) was initially considered for Amersham but the reality is that tenders are far more complex and only accentuate the advantage for *professional* investors.

But, in the wake of £500 million worth of applications for British Aerospace and £1.2 billion for Cable and Wireless (along with handsome profits for the 'stags') the privatization of BNOC's oil production operation, Britoil, will clearly give rise to some in-depth analysis.

As it is, the uproar in the Commons has served to ensure Amersham stags a very substantial premium when deals start on Thursday.

Source: The Observer.

(b) An approach to Amersham International.
To apply the Gordon model:

$$R = \frac{D_1}{P_0} + g$$

we need to estimate D_0 and g. We already know that $P_0 = 142$ (all sums will normally be measured in pence in this example).

1. We begin by estimating g. Although the actual figures for earnings growth are negative (£4.8m down to £4.0m) the implication of the forecast is that this will change. The bullishness of the market implies that it thinks so too. So we shall take the earnings forecast of £8.3m for 1981–2 as being the best information we have, and assume also that it is the best that the *market* has. This means that the growth rate can be estimated from:

$$4.8(1 + g)^5 = 8.3$$

so that:

$$g = [8.3/4.8]^{0.2} - 1$$
$$= 0.116 \quad \text{or, say, } 11.5\%$$

2. We are not told the dividend as such, but we know that the yield is 3.5% and the share price is 142 pence. Thus we can calculate the dividend D_0 as 142p × 0.035 = 5p.
3. It is now possible to estimate the expected return on such a share from the Gordon model as:

$$R = \frac{5 \times 1.115}{142} + 0.115$$
$$= 0.154 \quad \text{or about } 15.5\%$$

Figure W5.1

Worked problems

Note: Answers to the following problems are given in section W5.8(a) on pp. 433–4.

5.1 A company's profits have grown at 6% a year for the past few years and are expected to continue doing so. If the current market price is £2.35 per share and its last dividend was 20p, what is the return that shareholders seem to expect for a share of this kind?

5.2 You are valuing a company's shares. Its dividends have in the past five years been 65p, 67p, 70p, 69p, 74p (the last amount being paid last month). If the expected return from shares of this kind is 13%, at what price would you value the shares?

5.3 Budge plc is forecast by an influential stockbroking firm to grow at an average 11% per annum for the foreseeable future. If the current expected rate of return for such a company is 9% and the next expected dividend is 82 pence per share, at what price do you expect the market to value the company's shares?

5.4 Simon Industries plc is considering the cost of its equity capital. A discussion at a board meeting included the following:

'We are doing well. At the current rate of growth of our dividend it should reach £1.26 in five years' time. It was only half that five years ago.'
'What is the current share price?'
'Yesterday it was around £9.25.'

Use the Gordon growth model to estimate the cost of equity capital.

Further problems

Note: No answers are provided for the following problems.

5.5 Stock analysts Drillit & Phew claim that the growth of Smudge plc's earnings will be somewhat between 5% and 7% for the foreseeable future. Smudge is in a high-risk industry where the expected rate of return is about 16%. If next year's dividend is expected to be somewhere between 82p and £1 per share (with the latter estimated to be twice as likely as the former), what price would you expect Smudge's shares to sell for?

5.6 In February 1986 Wellcome, one of the UK's leading pharmaceutical companies, went public floating 25% of its shares on the Stock Exchange. The merchant bankers Robert Fleming were asked to advise on the flotation price. After careful assessment, a price was fixed which, in the words of Anthony Hilton, city editor of the *London Standard*, 'put the company on a rating just a fraction less than Glaxo, which by common consent is the leader in the sector'. At the time, Hilton observed, one of Wellcome's supposedly key executives had left and interest rates were on the upturn.

Supposing that the pricing of the shares of a market leader is a useful touchstone against which to judge a company's flotation price:

1. do you think the price was possibly correct, too high, or too low?
2. what further information would you like before making a judgement of what the price should have been?

5.7 'As you well know', said the chairman, 'our dividend was a mere 22p per share ten years ago. For six years it grew at a magnificent 20 per cent each year. It is true that since then the growth rate has dropped to only half that. All the same, I think — and I believe that shareholders agree with me — that the average growth sustained over those ten years will be achieved in the future. Hence, I believe that the current share price of £27 shows investors' confidence in us'.

From the above information, what rate of return would you infer that investors require on the company's equity?

W5.3   Project valuation within the enterprise: the alternatives to DCF

In this section we shall cover three matters:

1. we shall work through some examples to consolidate our understanding of payback and accountant's rate of return, at the same time reminding ourselves of the discounting methods we looked at in Chapter 4;
2. we shall give a series of three articles that some years ago attempted to explain the reluctance of managers to use DCF methods;
3. we shall consider further the desirability of using non-DCF methods, and use the ideas of agency theory so as to provide a more recent possible explanation of their use in practice.

(a) Risk-free project evaluation in the enterprise

It is conventional to argue, as we have done in the text, that discounting methods are superior to non-DCF methods. The reasons have been given and are quite straightforward. So long as the *defined objective* is wealth maximization, and that is measured in NPV terms, then disounting must be the standard by which methods are judged. However, since payback and ARR are so frequently encountered, we must work through some examples to be sure of understanding them.

Worked problems
Note: The answer to these problems can be found in section W5.8(b) on p. 434–6.

5.8 You are presented with the three projects below. Calculate the payback period, ARR, NPV and IRR of each. Take the cost of capital to be 10%. Show the rankings of the projects given by each of the four methods.

Period	Project A £	Project B £	Project C £
0	(5,000)	(5,000)	(5,000)
1	900	700	2,000
2	900	800	2,000
3	900	900	2,000
4	900	1,000	1,000
5	900	1,100	
6	900	1,200	
7	900	1,300	
8	900	1,400	
9	900	1,500	
10	900	1,600	

5.9 You are considering four projects that are expected to produce cash flows as follows:

Year	Project A £	Project B £	Project C £	Project D £
0	−31,000	−60,000	−25,000	−40,000
1	6,000	20,000		30,000
2	6,000	20,000		25,000
3	6,000	40,000		
4	6,000	10,000		
5	6,000			
6	6,000			
7	6,000			
8	6,000			
9	6,000			
10	6,000		80,000	

The cost of capital is 12%. You only have £120,000 to spend on these projects. Assuming they are independent of each other and all infinitely divisible, which projects would you choose? Show the resulting net present value of the combination of projects you select.

5.10 As finance director, you have been asked to compare two possible investment projects, here called projects A and B. This is what you are given:

Year	Project A £	Project B £
0	(20,000)	(25,000)
1	7,000	2,500
2	7,000	5,000
3	7,000	10,000
4	7,000	20,000

Since the company has historically used multiple criteria for project evaluation, you are asked to compare these two projects on the following bases: NPV, IRR, ARR, payback period, discounted payback period and profitability index. Take the cost of capital to be 13%

Further problems
Note: No answers are provided for the following problems.

5.11 Nudge Ltd can select among four projects. Buying a new lathe will generate extra earnings of £400 per annum for an outlay of £1,200 during the life of the lathe, which is expected to be five years. Replacing an old grinding machine will cost £2,300 and generate savings of £600 in each of the next eight years. Neither of these is likely to have any scrap value. Investing in a robot for assembly work will cost £11,000 and save labour costs of £3,500 for each of the next four years, at which time it is expected to be sold off for £1,500. Placing £9,000 in a bond will generate no income until the end of the fifth year, when it will mature with a redemption value of £13,000.

If the cost of raising funds is 12%, which of these projects is worth investing in, using the criteria of payback, ARR and NPV?

5.12 Fezziwig Ltd is presented with the following mutually exclusive proposals for a mini-computer. The outflows are the costs of the two possible computers; the 'inflows' are the cost savings they are expected to generate.

	National Business Machines (NBM) £	National Computer Ltd (NCL) £
t_0	(95,000)	(105,000)
t_1	30,000	35,000
t_2	40,000	45,000
t_3	50,000	70,000
t_4	20,000	

Take the cost of capital to be 14%
Which project is better under the NPV criterion? Does your judgement alter when the duration (unequal lives) factor is taken into account?

(b) Why do managers not use DCF methods?

It has been widely observed that managers either do not use DCF techniques or, if they do, that they combine them with other methods in a way that does not fit the prescriptions of finance theory. We saw in the text (Figs 5.1 and 5.4) that such techniques are used, more than they were when the articles we give below were written. Yet the principle remains that managers are frequently unconvinced that NPV has all the answers.

The following article discusses some of these issues. It is followed by a critical comment, and a rejoinder by the original author.

IS THE EMPHASIS OF CAPITAL BUDGETING THEORY MISPLACED?
PAUL KING
Fellow of Queens' College, Cambridge
(Received October 1973; revised August 1974)

The Basis of Capital Budgeting Theory

Since the early writings of Joel Dean [1] a large body of literature has developed on the subject of capital investment decision making. The majority of this literature [2] implicitly adopts as its foundation the scientific model of the decision-making process. The scientific approach, or as it has been variously called the synoptic, rational or comprehensive model, prescribes that all possible courses of action should be listed together with their consequences under each possible 'state of the world'. The decision process is then seen to consist of choice from among the possible actions through evaluation of their consequences.

Schon [3] considers that the scientific model of the decision-making process, the development of which can be traced through the writings of Plato, Aristotle, Locke, Hume, Bentham, Kant and others, owes its origins partly to the displacement of the concept of a balance. The most overt use of a metaphor stemming from this displacement of concept is probably the 'scales of justice' but other phrases have an obvious association with the idea that decisions are made by weighing the evidence. Examples include 'weighing the arguments', 'tipping the scales in favour of', 'the decision is in the balance', 'on a knife edge', etc.

An examination of the history of capital budgeting theory shows the progressive development and sophistication of project appraisal procedures. The early literature exhibited a concern with the need to develop a valid weighing technique. Arguments [4] raged over the correct method of evaluating a project as between payback, rate of return, or discounting calculations. Once general agreement had been reached on the appropriateness of discounting procedures, attention was directed towards the development of the concept 'cost of capital' [5] so that the balance might be calibrated and individual projects compared with a standard. Recent work has been directed towards enriching the description of 'states of the world'; interest has centred on the treatment of uncertainty [6] and interdependence [7].

Schon goes on to ask [8] 'given the presumptive evidence for the role of the scale in theories of deciding, what assumptions would we expect to find associated with it? Because the scale has been treated since the seventeenth century as a special form of Newtonian machine, it shares with other mechanical systems some of the assumptions to which its displacement gives rise'. In particular 'objects are brought to the scales. They do not have to be invented to be weighed.' 'The issue is not how they come to be but how much they weigh in comparison with one another.' The literature of capital budgeting for the most part fully accepts this implicit assumption. As Bromwich says in his review [9] 'some mechanism outside the capital budgeting process is assumed to highlight the firm's opportunities and weakness, and generate search for alternative projects to exploit opportunities and remedy weaknesses'. Projects are assumed to be ready awaiting evaluation. Schon goes on, 'As far as the sales are concerned, an object goes out as it came in. If changes occur, the weighing does not cause it' [10]. 'When a process of deciding answers the question, "should I do this or that?" and answers it by listing and evaluating advantages and disadvantages of two courses of action, its conclusion is a decision to do this or that, or neither; not a change in the formulation of the alternatives' [11]. Capital budgeting theory has been concerned to develop ways of evaluating projects. The definition of the form of a project is assumed to be given for evaluation.

Of course it is freely admitted that the scientific model of the decision-making process is an idealization, that not all information will be available, and that in practice any analysis will be partial rather than comprehensive. But, implicitly the literature on capital budgeting argues that effort expended in attempting to follow the ideal will be worthwhile. Decision makers should strive to obtain all necessary information and to carry out full analysis of projects. Good capital investment decision making is seen as synonymous with good evaluation.

Weaknesses of the Scientific Model

Braybrooke and Lindblom [12] examine in detail what they call the synoptic model of the decision-making process. They identify many weaknesses of the model as a normative statement in that it is in no way adapted to

'1. man's limited intellectual capacities
2. his limited knowledge
3. the costliness of analysis
4. the analyst's inevitable failure to construct a complete rational-deductive system or welfare function
5. interdependencies between fact and value
6. the openness of the systems to be analysed
7. the analyst's need for a strategic sequence to guide analysis and evaluation' [13]

They go on to argue that the inevitable failure in any practical situation to follow the procedure for decision making specified by the scientific model calls into question the desirability of adopting it even as an ideal.

Recently I have completed two case studies of large capital investment decisions in a major British company. Both case studies attempted to follow the process of decision making from conception through to fruition. The formal decision-making procedures of the company require that a written case be presented to top management in support of any major capital investment project. The case must include a full financial evaluation incorporating discounted cash flow calculations. The rationale for this procedure stems directly from capital budgeting theory and the scientific model of decision making. The control of capital investment is seen to be a function of top management which may be fulfilled through the choice of an optimum set of investment projects. In both case studies it became apparent that the weaknesses of the scientific model identified by Braybrooke and Lindblom were of considerable importance. The formal procedures of the company provided a framework for analysis for only a small proportion of the process of decision making. Below I shall describe a tentative descriptive model of the decision-making process from which I conclude that the current emphasis in capital budgeting theory is misplaced.

A Model of the Process of Decision Making

The model suggested by the case studies is illustrated in [Fig. W5.2]. It has been developed in the context of large-scale investments in a diversified hierarchical organization; its appropriateness in other contexts has yet to be tested. The model divides the decision-making process into six stages, namely, triggering, screening, definition, evaluation, transmission and decision. Each stage is described separately below although, of course, in practice they are overlapping and interactive.

Triggering
The existence of a set of capital investment projects from which choice may be made is taken as given by capital budgeting theory. In practice each opportunity for investment must be identified and exploited. Opportunities for capital investment arise in many ways, for example, growth in demand, worn-out plant, the invention of new products or processes: the recognition of such opportunities will, however, be by no means automatic. Choice situations are often viewed by those involved in them as potentially laborious and painful. The sponsors of an investment project incur a high level of personal risk with perhaps little tangible reward; if the project goes sour, it will be viewed as a black mark against them but if it goes well, they have merely done their job. Human beings employ a whole host of personality defence 'mechanisms'

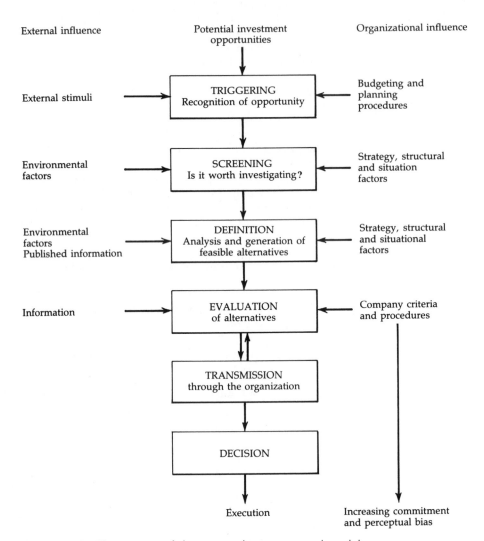

Figure W5.2 The process of decision making: proposed model.

[14] to protect themselves from unpleasant thoughts and information. One powerful 'mechanism' is denial. In its simplest form we see this 'mechanism' operating every time we put off an unpleasant task until tomorrow. Similarly, the recognition of an opportunity for capital investment will frequently be denied by those directly responsible until the need becomes pressing, that is, until some form of trigger is provided. For example, the need for additional capacity in my first case study was apparent for many months before any attempt was made to investigate the possibility of further investment. The recognition of the necessity for action was only triggered by a period of overcapacity working as a result of which little time remained for deliberation and investigation; investment was felt to be urgently required. Given the likelihood of denial, the triggering stage is usually marked by the

occurrence of some form of stimulus from a source external to those directly involved. Such stimuli will tend to occur naturally as when an old piece of machinery finally has a major breakdown or an important customer removes his business because of poor delivery but by definition they occur at a late stage.

Screening

The triggering stage provides for the recognition of an opportunity for investment but it does not guarantee evaluation. If information had no cost associated with it and copious human resources were available, all opportunities would be pursued as is implicitly assumed in the scientific model of decision making. In reality each opportunity will be screened to decide whether further work is justified. Such screening decisions will be made on the basis of readily available information, precedent, strategic considerations and environmental factors; comprehensive analysis will be avoided. Bower [15] in a study of four investment decisions in a company he chose to call National Products developed a model of the process of decision making based on three concepts — definition, impetus and context. Under context he identifies situational and structural factors as the major components. Each of these factors will influence the screening process. The sort of questions that will be asked at the screening stage will be — has this type of activity got a good profit record, does it fit corporate strategy, are the resources available to execute the project, what risks are we running in sponsoring this investment, etc. A decision by those involved to pursue the investigation of a nascent project marks the first stage in their developing commitment to the success of the project. If the project fails to be approved or is dropped during evaluation, it will reflect on their initial judgement.

Definition

At the end of the screening process the barest outline of a project exists. The definition stage covers the articulation of the project to meet the needs which have been identified. The limited problem solving capacity of organisations and individuals requires that not all the possible forms of the project are put forward for evaluation. The definition stage entails imaginative search for possible forms of the investment which meet the needs identified and the reduction of this list to perhaps two or three forms to be evaluated. The process of search will be interactive; the needs identified will be amended as possible means are found. Again choice in the definition stage will be based on limited information and restricted criteria. 'Context' will be important. During this stage commitment begins to be generated. This process is admirably described by Y. Aharoni [16], 'the very act of collecting information creates many individual commitments, and often organizational ones as well. In order to collect information, it is necessary to communicate with people, to make certain decisions, and often to give tacit promises. In this process commitments are accumulated until a situation is created which leads inevitably to investment.' Criteria are developed by those who carry out the definition phase in order to guide the search for alternatives and for information. The creation of such criteria of itself will generate further commitment to the emerging project in that any criticism of the form of the project will be taken as implicit criticism of the choice of operating criteria. Built into the definition of the project will be many of the necessary assumptions concerning risk, uncertainty and change. In summary, definition is concerned with developing the form and content of the project; its execution requires both innovation and imagination.

Evaluation

For the scientific model of decision making evaluation is the alpha and the omega: the merit of each alternative is assessed and choice follows. In this model evaluation is seen as only part of the decision process. The descriptive separation of definition and evaluation, although in practice they are heavily linked, serves to emphasize the difference between the choice of the form of a capital investment project and the evaluation of that form against company criteria. Much of the work performed in the evaluation stage could, perhaps, be more appropriately labelled justification. The nature of this validating process is illustrated by a remark made in the course of the decision meeting for my second case study: the originator of the project described how the tentative choice of equipment was made and went on to say 'everything we have found has confirmed our original choice'. Many companies lay down a specific formal sequence for project appraisal and for the presentation of information; these will be the procedures used in the evaluation phase. Typically the stage will include the collection of further information and the quantification of previously qualitative judgements. When required company capital application forms will be completed including all necessary calculations such as discounting. Specific allowance for uncertainty may be incorporated in the evaluation. The end product of the stage will be a formal case in support of a particular form of an investment project.

Transmission

The descriptive model, here proposed, was developed in the context of a divisionalized hierarchical organization in which the final authority for sanctioning projects rests with top management. In such an organization, capital projects will usually be developed at company level and must be communicated through division to the corporate team. The transmission stage is intended to cover the process of communicating the project to division and then to corporate level. Informal transmission during the earlier stages will obviously occur and will provide a major source of criteria and assumptions for screening and definition. Formal transmission requires the consolidation of the evaluation phase into a coherent case which can be understood by higher levels of management whose specific knowledge of the business environment is likely to be restricted. The transmission stage, however, covers more than just the transfer of information. For the company management formal communication of a case to division represents the final stage in their commitment to it. They can expect to be judged both on the presentation of the case and on the outcome of the project if approved. The divisional management in their turn must commit themselves to the project before communicating it to the corporate team. Bower considers that 'impetus' is central to the process of decision making. 'Impetus, the force that moves a project towards funding, has been defined as the willingness of a general manager at the division president's level, or one level below, to commit himself to sponsor a project in the council of division officers and before division general management. In making this decision, he puts his reputation for good judgement on the line. Therefore, he is careful in computing the costs and benefits to *him* of making such a commitment. His usefulness as a manager depends upon maintaining or increasing the confidence with which his superiors, colleagues, and subordinates hold his judgement' [17]. In essence the transmission phase is political, the worth of the project must be argued and sponsors found.

Decision

The last stage in the process of capital investment decision making occurs when an application for funds is brought before the corporate team. Normally the application will consist of a written case which may be supplemented by a verbal presentation by division or company management at the formal meeting. The decision phase appears to serve three distinct purposes. First, it allows the overall strategic considerations of the firm to be specifically incorporated in the evaluation of the project through the judgement of the corporate team. Second, it provides an opportunity for the corporate team to make an assessment of the management which will be responsible for the execution of the project and finally the process of adjudication formalizes that management's commitment to the success of the project. It is important to note, however, that severe limitations are imposed on the decision-making body by the formal stage. Usually a single alternative will be presented which they may accept, reject or refer back. To do other than accept the project is to cast doubt on the ability and judgement of the operating managers whose knowledge of the particular project will be far greater than that of central management. A study of the history of capital applications in the company in which I conducted my case studies showed that applications for funds were rarely, if ever, rejected and very infrequently referred back. Bower summarized his findings in National Products as 'The definition of a project did not change. In fact, the response was typically "go" and, as noted earlier, the last level at which projects were turned down with any frequency was the division' [18]. The decision phase is therefore normally a process of endorsement rather than judgement at which commitments are formalized.

It is probably best to summarize the main features of the model before considering its implications for capital budgeting theory. First it is observed that the potential for capital investment will not automatically be recognized. Choice situations are often viewed by those responsible as a threat which causes them to deny the need for action. Some form of external trigger is required to start the decision-making process. Limited resources both financial and managerial preclude the possibility of assessing every potential opportunity for investment. Some form of screening process will take place based on readily available information and crude criteria to decide whether a project merits further investigation. A definition stage follows screening during which the technical and economic characteristics of the proposed investment are chosen. This choice process requires active search and the bilateral adjustment of needs and means. Implicit in definition is an evaluative process which is used to choose among potential forms of the investment. Limited resources and human competence require that such evaluation is not exhaustive but again based on readily available and comprehended information and crude criteria. The formal evaluation stage seeks to develop a case to justify the form of the project chosen during definition. Increasing commitment towards the project will be a normal occurrence and will lead inevitably to bias in the information generated for evaluation. In a hierarchical organization the case for investment has to be transmitted upwards through the organization. This will be an essentially political process during which the proponents of the project seek higher level sponsors. Choice in the decision phase is restricted. Rejection of a project will be seen as repudiation of the judgement of those involved. Empirical evidence suggests that acceptance is normal.

Why is the Emphasis Misplaced?

Capital budgeting theory is primarily concerned with the optimal choice of capital projects. It has sought to achieve this aim by developing sufficient statistics (e.g. net present value) with which projects may be evaluated and compared. By adopting the scientific model of decision making, capital budgeting theory has naturally accepted that evaluation is central to optimal choice. Throughout the literature two assumptions, inherent in the scientific model of decision making, are tacitly accepted. First, projects are assumed to exist ready for evaluation and second, the act of choosing among articulated projects is presumed to be sufficient to obtain an optimal allocation of capital.

Except for the repetitive and the trivial it is apparent from both my case studies and those reported in the literature that capital projects do not begin life in a filing cabinet awaiting only the tedious collection of the information necessary for their evaluation. They must be created. The choice of the form of a project occurs at the screening and definition stages where information is limited, search required and analysis sequential. Capital budgeting theory and the scientific model offers no help to those who struggle to articulate a project and to gather relevant information. Their only guide to action exists in the formal and symmetrical structure of exhaustive lists of alternative policies, consequences and values. No indication is given as to how these lists might be created or shown to be exhaustive. It is little use to direct a manager to assess his subjective probability estimates for each possible outcome if some of those outcomes consist of consequences he cannot reasonably foresee. Capital budgeting theory therefore makes no contribution to how screening and definition should be conducted, how the search process should be directed, except by holding up an ideal towards which those involved are impugned to aim. The ideal is 'be comprehensive' but as Braybrooke and Lindblom point out, after listing the limitations imposed on any human attempt to be comprehensive, no guide is given as to the direction of the path towards this ideal.

Perhaps the problems associated with traditional capital budgeting theory in practice can best be described by analogy. Consider that each potential investment opportunity is represented by a mountain. The facility managers are situated in their several valleys surrounded by these mountains. The occurrence of a trigger prompts the recognition of the fact that it would be desirable for the company to establish a base on one of the mountains. The value of the base to the company may be measured by its height up the mountain and the stability of its position on the mountain. The ideal, which can never be obtained, is to place the base securely on the summit. Capital budgeting theory has sought to develop and refine measures of height and stability so that the worth of each base to the company can be measured. To guide a manager in his assault on a mountain the scientific model suggests that the manager should investigate all possible routes towards the summit and compare them. Except for the well-known mountains with many bases on them already no maps will exist. From the summit looking down all routes may be seen but from below only a general impression of one face is available. The manager will begin by screening the mountain to decide whether the potential value of a base outweighs the risk and effort associated with the climb. He may decide that some form of reconnaisance is required in the hope that the information so obtained will more than cover the cost. He may seek the advice of local guides but of necessity his questioning of them will suffer from his lack of knowledge of the right questions to ask and their preconceptions of what he wishes to hear. He will then try to pick out a few potential routes on the basis of what he can see from the bottom and begin his ascent. As he goes up the mountain other routes will come into view and his perspective may change. He may be able to change course or even go down and start again but the higher he gets the more he will become committed to his chosen route. When he feels he can go no further he attempts to describe and evaluate the position he has reached.

Central management is faced with a series of requests from managers to establish bases at the positions they have reached. They have before them the information supplied by the managers and their knowledge of the general topography. Their aim is to establish an optimum distribution of bases. Their freedom of action is, however, severely restricted. They can say go down or go back and try another route but given the effort expended by the manager they are likely to say, yes, establish a base. Capital budgeting theory helps them to judge the height and stability of the bases but, unless they are seated on high, they will never know what other bases might have been established, or what information is lacking from their descriptions.

If they wish to influence the quality of the bases, they must attempt to influence the triggering of the recognition of mountains and lay down guidelines for searching out routes towards the summit. Capital budgeting theory offers no guide to those who wait at the bottom from whence they can only see a part of the mountain. It is little help to them to point to the summit and say that is the ideal or to say investigate all the routes. The climbing process entails a sequence of decisions; research is required on how this sequence of decisions should be directed and controlled.

Conclusion

The above analysis leads to a somewhat paradoxical conclusion. In seeking to improve capital budgeting, corporate management should strive to develop a process of decision making which in the end allows them to merely rubber stamp the majority of capital investment proposals.

Capital investment decision making in a large organization consists of a process of investigation not a single act of top management deliberation. The process is essentially one of search; search for ideas, search for information and search for decision criteria. Of necessity these search processes occur at many points in the organization and are spread out over time. They lead ultimately to the creation of a proposal for capital investment which may be accepted or rejected by top management. If the process of decision making has been 'good', then a proposal should typically be accepted.

In the above model, the crucial stages in the process of decision making are seen as triggering, screening and definition. Corporate management must seek to influence these stages so that they fully reflect corporate strategy. A requirement that each major proposal should be discussed with top management before detailed evaluation commences would provide an opportunity for corporate consideration before commitment and bias begin to develop. Whatever procedures for decision making are chosen, they must seek initially to stimulate creative thought, and also ultimately to stimulate commitment to what is chosen by top management as the 'one right thing to do'.

Capital budgeting theory has progressively sought to improve techniques for the evaluation of capital projects. This article has argued that evaluation is only a part of the process of decision making, the majority of which remains largely unexplored. Research is now required to develop an understanding of the relationships between organizational structure, decision-making procedures, creativity, commitment and bias, not on how to process and condense information which only God could provide.

References

[1] Joel Dean, 'Better Management of Capital Expenditure through Research', *Journal of Finance*, **VIII**, 1953.
[2] A good review of the literature has been provided by M. Bromwich, *Journal of Business Finance*, **2** (3).
[3] D.A. Schon, *Invention and Evolution of Ideas*, Tavistock Publications, 1963.
[4] A good textbook summary of the arguments is provided in Ch. 9 by A.J. Merrett and Allen Sykes, *Capital Budgeting and Company Finance*, Longman, 1966.
[5] The concept 'cost of capital' is exhaustively analysed in Ezra Solomon, *The Theory of Financial Management*, Columbia University Press, 1963.
[6] See, for example, Pierre Massé, *Optimal Investment Decisions*, Prentice-Hall Inc., 1962.
[7] See, for example, and for references, John S. Hughes and Wilbur G. Lewellen, 'Programming Solutions to Capital Rationing Problems', *Journal of Business Finance and Accounting*, **I** (1).
[8] D.A. Schon, ibid., pp. 119–20.
[9] M. Bromwich, ibid.
[10] D.A. Schon, ibid., p. 121.
[11] D.A. Schon, ibid., p. 121.
[12] D. Braybrooke and C. Lindblom, *A Strategy of Decision*, The Free Press of Glencoe, 1963.
[13] D. Braybrooke and C. Lindblom, ibid., p. 113.
[14] See R.S. Lazarus, *Personality and Adjustment*, 1964, p. 23, for a listing of these 'mechanisms'. Prentice-Hall, 1964.
[15] J.L. Bower, *Managing the Resource Allocation Process*, Harvard, 1970.
[16] Y. Aharoni, *The Foreign Investment Decision Process*, Harvard, 1966.
[17] J.L. Bower, ibid., p. 68.

[18] J.L. Bower, ibid., p. 65.

Bibliography

Y. Aharoni, *The Foreign Investment Process*, Harvard, 1966.
J.L. Bower, *Managing the Resource Allocation Process*, Harvard, 1970.
D. Braybrooke and C.E. Lindblom, *A Strategy of Decision*, The Free Press, 1963.
C.W. Churchman, *Challenge to Reason*, McGraw-Hill, 1968.
C.E. Lindblom, *The Intelligence of Democracy*, The Free Press, 1965.
D.A. Schon, *Invention and the Evolution of Ideas*, Tavistock, 1963.
A. Wildavsky, *The Politics of the Budgetary Process*, Little Brown, 1964.
H. Wilensky, *Organizational Intelligence*, Basic Brooks, 1967.
B.R. Williams and W.P. Scott, *Investment Proposals and Decisions*, George Allen and Unwin, 1965.

Source: Journal of Business Finance and Accounting, *Vol. 2, No. 1, 1975, pp. 69–82.*

A SHORT NOTE ON 'IS THE EMPHASIS OF CAPITAL BUDGETING THEORY MISPLACED?'
A.M. TINKER*

In the Spring 1975 issue of this journal(1), Paul King concluded that 'the current emphasis in capital budgeting theory is misplaced' ... It is reassuring that this accords with the conclusions reached by W.W. Haynes and Martin B. Solomon, Jnr thirteen years earlier, (from whom I assume Paul King obtained inspiration for the title of his publication) (2). It is rather unfortunate however, that far from cementing some of the methodological 'cracks' that appear in Haynes and Solomon's earlier analysis, Paul King's reliance on more recent, 'popular' socio-political ideas has produced a number of 'San Andreas Faults' in what would otherwise be a reasonable assessment of the state of capital budgeting literature. The main 'faults' in his argument are in two forms: the first relates to his analysis of the problem and the second concerns his approach to its resolution. Both 'faults' seem to flow from the same source; Paul King's (and others') conception of 'the scientific model'.

Paul King relies heavily on the work of Schon (3) and Braybrooke and Lindblom (4) in his analysis of the problem. The main contention of this analysis is that by overplaying the 'scientifically rational' aspects of 'scaling and weighing' given alternatives, 'facts' about human decision-making behaviour are neglected. Thus, the 'scientific' or synoptic model neglects 'man's limited capacities', 'interdependencies between fact and value', 'human motives and selective perceptions', etc. The implication is that decisional behaviour is essentially 'irrational' relative to 'the scientific model'. The fallacy in this argument lies in the assumption that science has only one conception of man (i.e. the scientific model). Yet through their references King (2), Bower (5), Lindblom (6) and others acknowledge the existence of other scientific conceptions of man; e.g. psychological man (7), economic man (8), (9), social man, political man (10) etc. The poor state of capital budgeting theory cannot be blamed on the scientific model in general, but on the dominance of a particular scientific view of man in capital budgeting, that of economics. This model regards as non-problematic (and thereby ignores) many of the

Dr Tinker is a lecturer in the Division of Economic Studies, University of Sheffield. (Received June 1975).

characteristics of the human or social systems that affect choice. Thus man is not 'irrational' relative to the scientific model, but only in relation to a particular scientific model. Explicit recognition of this distinction initially (in both Haynes and Solomon's as well as Paul King's articles), might well have led to a somewhat different approach to resolving the problem.

Paul King's (alternative) model of the process of decision-making is similar to that of Haynes and Solomon in that it consists of a series of stages; triggering, screening, definition, evaluation, transmission and decision. Although Paul King states that this model (represented by the above categories) was 'suggested by the case studies ... has been developed in the context of large-scale investments in a diversified hierarchical organization', the empirical status of the model (i.e. the extent to which it is capable of producing empirically testable propositions) seems rather doubtful. Although Paul King refers to 'two case studies of large capital investment decisions in a major British Company' ... it is by no means clear in what sense this evidence 'tests' the validity of the perspective elaborated by King. Indeed, the general character of Paul King's model suggests (rather ironically) that it suffers from precisely the same deficiencies as the synoptic paradigm he is concerned to replace, i.e. as G.P. Clarkson has suggested, 'it seems capable of explaining everything and predicting nothing' (11). This derives from a Popperian argument that a scientific model should be refutable (12).

Given the thirteen year advantage over Haynes and Solomon, Paul King has not really done justice to the many developments in theories of organizational decision-making and their application to capital budgeting. Much of this work has been elaborated and exposed to more rigorous empirical tests than that of Paul King. The works of G.P. Clarkson (13), March and Simon (14), Hage and Aiken (15) and E. Carter (16) are but a few examples.

REFERENCES

(1) P. King, 'Is the Emphasis of Capital Budgeting Theory Misplaced,' JOURNAL OF BUSINESS FINANCE AND ACCOUNTING, Spring 1975.
(2) W.W. Haynes and M.B. Solomon, Jnr, 'A Misplaced emphasis in Capital Budgeting'. QUARTERLY REVIEW OF ECONOMICS AND BUSINESS, February 1962.
(3) D.A. Shon, INVENTION AND THE EVOLUTION OF IDEAS. (Tavistock Publications), 1963.
(4) D. Braybrooke and C.E. Lindblom, A STRATEGY OF DECISION. (The Free Press), 1963.
(5) J.L. Bower, MANAGING THE RESOURCE ALLOCATION PROCESS. (Harvard), 1970.
(6) C.E. Lindblom, 'The Science of "Muddling Through".' PUBLIC ADMINISTRATION REVIEW, Vol. 19, Spring 1959.
(7) H. Simon, MODELS OF MAN. (Wiley), 1958.
(8) K. Boulding, 'Economics as a Moral Science'. AMERICAN ECONOMIC REVIEW, 1961.
(9) H. Simon, 'Theories of Decision-making in Economics and Behavioural Science'. AMERICAN ECONOMIC REVIEW, Vol. 49, 1959.
(10) A. Pettigrew, THE POLITICS OF OGANISATIONAL DECISION-MAKING. (Tavistock), 1973.

(11) G.P.E. Clarkson, 'Verification and the Function of Laws in Micro-economics'. INDUSTRIAL MANAGEMENT REVIEW, 1962.

(12) K. Popper, SCIENTIFIC DISCOVERY. (Hutchinson).

(13) G.P.E. Clarkson, PORTFOLIO SELECTION: A SIMULATION OF TRUST INVESTMENT. (Prentice-Hall), 1962.

(14) J. March and H.A. Simon, ORGANISATIONS. (Wiley), 1958.

(15) M. Aiken and J. Hage, 'The Organic Organisation and Innovation'. SOCIOLOGY, Vol. 5, No. 1, January 1971.

(16) E. Carter, 'The Behavioural Theory of the Firm and Top-Level Corporate Decisions'. ADMINISTRATIVE SCIENCE QUARTERLY, December 1971.

Source: Journal of Business Finance and Accounting, *vol. 3, no. 2, 1976.*

'A SHORT NOTE ON "IS THE EMPHASIS OF CAPITAL BUDGETING THEORY MISPLACED?"': A REPLY
PAUL KING

In the Spring 1975 issue of the *Journal of Business Finance and Accounting*, I suggested (1) that the majority of the literature concerned with capital budgeting had implicitly adopted the scientific model of the process of decision-making as its normative foundation. The scientific model prescribes that all possible alternative courses of action should be listed together with their consequences under each possible 'state of the world'. Choice of the most preferred alternative follows through the evaluation of each consequence against a set of objectives. Within the context of this model of decision-making, the central theoretical problems are associated with the choice of objectives and the development of techniques for evaluating the worth of alternatives. Capital budgeting theorists have, therefore, been preoccupied with the development of more refined techniques for measuring the worth of a set of projects. By postulating a descriptive model of the total process of decision-making, I sought to argue that the emphasis of the work conducted by these theorists should be shifted towards the problems associated with controlling the process of decision-making as it is actually performed by human decision-makers. I noted that human decision-makers could not follow the prescriptions of the scientific model because they suffer from limited intellectual capacities, knowledge, etc. Obviously if they could follow its prescriptions, if man were 'economic man',[1] no change in emphasis would be required.

In his note on my article Dr Tinker (3) stated that my argument rests on a fallacious premise 'that science has only one conception of man (i.e. the scientific model)'. The argument does not rest on this premise, indeed, such a premise would be ridiculous.[2] The scientific model is not a conception of man; it is simply a set of prescriptions of what constitutes rational decision-making. The model does not concern itself with the characteristics or motivations of the 'actors' who carry out the process of decision-making.[3] I argued that any attempt by a human actor to carry out the prescriptions of the model would result in failure because of his limited intellectual resources, knowledge, etc. Such failure does not, however, imply that his behaviour is irrational with respect to *the*[4] scientific model, nor does it imply that the prescriptions of the model are wrong. Irrational behaviour occurs if, for example, the 'actor' lists all the alternatives and chooses one which fails to meet his specified objectives, but not if he fails to list all the alternatives simply because of the magnitude of the task.

Dr Tinker, in his second paragraph, appears to think that I believe capital budgeting theory to be in a poor state. Not so. The theory has provided valuable techniques designed to facilitate the choice of capital projects. My argument is that we know man will fail in his attempt to follow the precepts of the scientific model. We, therefore, know that both the definition and description of the available projects will not be perfect. Should we expend further effort on refining our techniques for evaluating the worth of projects, or should the energy of capital budgeting theorists be channelled into developing ways of improving the process of decision-making?

In order to answer the above question, we need to have a picture of that process so we can judge whether significant problems exist in the control of the total process, or whether optimal choice is indeed the central problem. The model presented in the article was intended to provide such a picture. It was a *descriptive* model of the total process and was in no way intended as an alternative to the scientific model as Dr Tinker suggests.

In the article, I did not attempt to provide empirical substantiation of the model as this was not the purpose of the article. I would, however, take issue with the suggestion that the model 'explains everything and predicts nothing': it does neither. Several predictions follow directly from the model, which can be empirically tested. For example, opportunities for investment will not usually be recognized unless an external trigger is provided, the process of decision-making will often be rushed, the presentation of available information will tend to be biased in favour of the project, and rejection of proposals by top management will be infrequent.

Turning to Dr Tinker's final paragraph, I had no intention of belittling the many developments in organizational decision-making theory. My article was prompted by the fact that I see little evidence that capital budgeting theorists are synthesising these developments into their own work. I, therefore, conclude that the current emphasis of this work is misplaced. This is indeed a similar conclusion[5] to that reached by Haynes and Solomon (4) thirteen years earlier. Perhaps the next thirteen years will see a change of emphasis in capital budgeting theory towards tackling the stages of the decision-making process where judgement is important.

NOTES

1. 'Economic man has a complete and consistent system of preferences that allow him always to choose among the alternatives open to him; he is always completely aware of what these alternatives are; there are no limits on the complexity of the computations he can perform in order to determine which alternatives are best; probability calculations are neither frightening nor mysterious to him' (2).
2. Science as such cannot have a conception of man; individual scientists, who work in a common scientific discipline, may well share a common conception of man. The existence of more than one discipline, let alone the multiplicity of scientists, will ensure the existence of many conceptions of man.
3. Only if we take the scientific model as descriptive of human

decision-making behaviour do we, by implication, create a conception of man. This conception would have to accord closely with Simon's conception of 'Economic Man'. Simon notes, however, that 'Economic Man' possesses considerable normative interest but little discernible relation to the actual or possible behaviour of flesh-and-blood human beings' (2).

4. In his second paragraph, Dr Tinker suggests that it would have been valuable if I had initially clearly distinguished between *the* scientific model and a particular scientific model. Paragraph one of my article clearly states what I understand to be the prescriptive content of the scientific, or as it has been variously called, synoptic, rational, or comprehensive model. Dr Tinker offers no justification for the implication contained in his synopsis that this statement constitutes a caricature of the scientific model.

5. The conclusion reached is similar, but it is important to note that the context is very different. Haynes and Solomon (4) studied small businesses; they noted that their conclusions might not apply to large firms. The model presented in the article was developed in the context of large firms. Haynes and Solomon's conclusion is therefore confirmed, but in a different context and for somewhat different reasons.

REFERENCES

(1) Paul King, 'Is the Emphasis of Capital Budgeting Theory Misplaced?', JOURNAL OF BUSINESS FINANCE AND ACCOUNTING, Vol. 2, No. 1, Spring 1975, pp. 69–82.
(2) H.A. Simon, ADMINISTRATIVE BEHAVIOUR, The Macmillan Company, 2nd Edition, 1957, p. xxiii.
(3) A.M. Tinker, 'A Short Note on "Is the Emphasis of Capital Budgeting Theory Misplaced?"', JOURNAL OF BUSINESS FINANCE AND ACCOUNTING, Vol. 3, No. 2, Summer 1976, pp. 23–26.
(4) W.W. Haynes and M.B. Solomon, Jnr, 'A Misplaced Emphasis in Capital Budgeting', QUARTERLY REVIEW OF ECONOMICS AND BUSINESS, February 1962, pp. 39–46.

Source: Journal of Business Finance and Accounting, *Vol. 3, No. 2, 1976, pp. 23–6.*

(c) Agency theory and a defence of payback

We outlined agency theory in Chapter 1. If you need a refresher, go back to section 1.4(d) where we discussed it, and then try question 5.13 below.

Worked problem
Note: No answer is given to the following problem.

5.13 Try to imagine how agency theory might be applied in explaining why managers (agents) use payback as a criterion for investment decisions.

W5.4 Dealing with inflation

Worked problem
Note: The answer to this problem will be found in section W5.8(c) on p. 436.

5.14 'Look', said the finance director to the project accountant, 'I pointed out that we would have to face inflation of maybe 7% over the next few years. Your estimates of returns from this project ignore inflation. Now is it a good investment or is it not?' The accountant had in fact estimated returns of £7,000 each year for the next six years, with an outlay of £27,000 immediately. Given that current return for such companies is 15%, what should the project accountant reply.

Further problem

Note: No answer is given to the following problem.

5.15 A project accountant in a different enterprise from the one in question 5.14 above got even further. He proudly presented his calculations which showed clearly that the project concerned should go ahead because it had a positive NPV of £8,600. But it turned out that he had used monetary cash flows with a real rate of interest. The incoming cash flows were estimated at an even £23,000 p.a. over four years, and the initial investment was £63,000. Given an inflation rate of 9%, what should the NPV have been? Was the 'accept' decision correct?

W5.5 Tax considerations

Since we bring tax into our DCF calculations in the course of this chapter, it makes sense to take time out to look briefly at the basic nature of the current corporation tax system in the UK.

The UK tax system does not use company profits as such as the basis for tax calculations. Certain items that are deducted in the income statement from profits (such as depreciation) are not allowed. On the other hand, other allowances (such as capital allowances, which are the Inland Revenue's substitute for depreciation) are given. The conventional method of calculating a tax liability is to begin with the annual profit, add back those items that are not allowable against tax, then deduct the allowable items. The tax rate is then applied to the resulting figure. In the examples of this book we shall ignore these complications and assume that the net cash flow is the basis for the tax calculation. On the other hand, capital allowances will also be brought into the picture since they can be quite substantial. For instance, for many years through the 1970s and 1980s the first year's allowance was 100%. This meant that the whole of the expenditure on capital items could be deducted from the year's profit in the year the capital equipment was bought. This encouraged the purchase of capital equipment. It also made the payment of corporation tax all but voluntary, and many companies paid little or no tax for some years.

Once an amount of tax is agreed, two further issues must be covered. One concerns the time when the tax must be paid. The other concerns the extent to which tax liability depends on dividend payments.

Under the imputation system these two matters are interlinked. If no dividend is paid, then the tax is payable some months after the end of the year to which it relates. The rules governing this can be quite complex, but in this book we make the simple assumption that they are paid one year after the end of the accounting year.

If a dividend is paid, then part of the corporation tax becomes due immediately. This is known as advanced corporation tax (ACT). It varies pro rata to the dividend and is based on the personal tax rate. The reasoning behind it concerns the income tax due on the dividend. To clarify what is happening, we shall assume that the income tax rate is 25% (which it has been since April 1988). Suppose a company has profits of £2,000, and pays its sole shareholder a dividend of £750. The shareholder *receives* a cheque for £750. Now this turns out to be a net dividend: the shareholder does not actually pay tax on it, because his or her tax liability on the dividend has been *imputed*, and it is effectively paid over to the Inland Revenue on his or her behalf by the company.

If the net amount received by the shareholder is £750, what would be the equivalent gross amount (that is, before deduction of tax)? Clearly it must be £1,000 because, if £1,000 were received by the shareholder gross, he or she would pay 25% tax, leaving £750 net — which is the amount of the dividend cheque sent. Thus to find the imputed tax, we take the dividend amount and multiply by $\frac{25}{75}$: that is, $\frac{1}{3}$. Because it 'would be due' from the taxpayer, who has received the benefit straight away, the company has to pay it immediately too (as ACT). But this amount of ACT will later be deducted from the final tax bill due on the £2,000 profits (known as 'mainstream corporation tax').

Thus the calculation is as follows (from the company's view):

	£
Taxable profit	2,000
Dividend	750
ACT due: $\frac{1}{3} \times 750$	250
Mainstream tax: 35% × 2,000	700
Less ACT already paid	250
Payment due for mainstream tax	£450

and the total tax paid is £700, in two stages. Since the area of taxation is highly complex, little more will be said here. One thing must be said, however, since it can be important to some of the theory later in this book. If a company makes no profits (including, of course, the case where it makes a loss), no tax is payable, since tax is levied on profits. However, companies are free if they wish to pay dividends in years when no profits have been earned, provided there are cumulative profits available from earlier years. If a company chooses to do this, ACT will be payable, there will be no mainstream tax from which to deduct it, and hence effectively there *is* tax payable even in a loss-making year.

Worked problem
Note: The answer to this problem will be found in section W5.8(c) on p. 436.

5.16 Schutz Ltd is considering a project with an outlay of £160,000 and cash inflows of £40,000 p.a. over six years. If the appropriate discount rate is 10%, capital allowances are 25% and the rate of corporation tax is 35% payable one year in arrears, should Schutz accept the project? Assume the asset has no scrap value, and is disposed of at the end of this period.

Further problem
Note: No answer is given to the following problem.

5.17 Scarlatti plc has been offered a partnership in a new venture which is expected to generate £20,000 for it at the end of the first year, which will increase by £10,000 each year until the seventh year when it will reach £80,000. After that no further inflows will be forthcoming. Suppose the corporation tax rate is 35% and the current cost of capital is 15%. Given that capital allowances are currently 25% on the outlay of £140,000, the asset being sold for £60,000 at the end of the period, should Scarlatti go ahead?

W5.6 Case study: the Ford Pinto

Finally, try the following case of the Ford Pinto. What do you learn about the extent to which NPV calculations are appropriate in management situations, and its implications for the way management should use NPV?

The case study is based upon contemporary newspaper reports. It is not intended to imply criticism or blame of any of the parties concerned.

Introduction

In 1978 a Californian court awarded more than $128 million to Richard Grimshaw — a sum then worth £66 million — in compensation and punitive damages against the Ford Motor Company. Grimshaw had been a passenger in a Ford Pinto, a car never sold in the UK. It was a 'sub-compact' car and the jury found that Ford had sold two million such cars knowing that they were of a dangerous design.

A key aspect of the case was an internal memorandum of 1972, part of which is reproduced in Fig. W5.3.

BENEFITS:
Savings — 180 burn deaths, 180 serious burn injuries, 2,100 burned vehicles.
Unit cost — $200,000 per death, $67,000 per injury, $700 per vehicle.
Total benefit — 180 × ($200,000) + 180 × ($67,000) + 2,100 × ($700) = $49.5 million.
COSTS:
Sales — 11 million cars, 1.5 million light trucks.
Unit cost — $11 per car, $11 per truck.
Total cost — 11,000,000 × ($11) + 1,500,000 × ($11) = $137 million.

Figure W5.3   The arithmetic that cost £66 million.

On the basis that Ford considered the savings of $49.5 million to be less than the cost of altering the cars and light trucks to conform with safety standards then being proposed by Congress ($137 million), it was concluded that no design change should be made.

It was felt by Grimshaw's lawyers that the massive damages were punitive and were a result of the jury's dissatisfaction with Ford's attitude, as evidenced by the testimony given and the memorandum reproduced in Fig. W5.3.

The events

On 28 May 1972 Richard Grimshaw, then 18, was offered a lift in a new Ford Pinto by a friend of his family, Mrs Lily Gray. They were heading for the southern California desert resort of Barstow on Interstate route 15 when Mrs Gray's Pinto stalled because of a faulty carburettor and was hit from behind by another car. The Pinto's petrol tank, located only seven inches behind the rear bumper, was ruptured by the impact. Fumes from the petrol that escaped mixed with air in the passenger compartment, a spark ignited the mixture and the Pinto was enveloped in flames.

Lily Gray was so badly burned that she died in hospital two days later. Richard suffered 90 per cent burns: he lost his nose, left ear and four fingers. Miraculously he survived. After 52 operations he now has a new nose and ear, but his face will always be a mass of twisted scar tissue and there are more operations to come. He has also been awarded £66 million in damages, the highest ever personal injury award. 'I don't want to sound like I'm ungrateful', he said last week after his award was announced, 'but if I had a choice of whether to take this money and go through all these burns and stuff or just lead a normal life, then I'd lead a normal life'. (Mrs Gray's family was awarded about £340,000.)

It was more than five years after the crash that Richard's suit against Ford came up in the Santa Anna Superior Court, and by then his lawyers could fall back on several case histories. A court in Florida had awarded $3.3 million damages (about £1.6m) against Ford in 1975 following an accident in which a Pinto's petrol tank had exploded. A year later, an Alabama jury had awarded $1.2 million to the plaintiff in a very similar Pinto crash. And as Richard's case began, a Virginia court ordered Ford to pay $625,000 following another incident of a Pinto's petrol tank going up in flames.

In none of those cases, however, were punitive damages sought against Ford. Richard's lawyers were determined to press for a punitive judgment, which would involve convincing the jury that Ford had 'consciously and wilfully' disregarded the safety of people who bought Pintos. They knew that Ford's central defence in Richard's case would be that Mrs Gray's Pinto had, at the time of the accident, conformed to all existing government safety regulations and that the leaking petrol was not necessarily the major factor in the tragedy.

Richard's legal team had access to valuable background material before the case began. The hazards presented by the design and positioning of the Pinto's petrol tank had been investigated by several independent organizations since the model went into production in August 1970. A study in 1973 by the University of Miami's accident analysis unit, examining four years of car crashes, had singled out the Pinto for comment. Under the heading 'Gas Tank Integrity/Protection (Ford Pinto)', the Miami unit observed: 'In each case the gas tank was buckled and gas spewed out. In each case the interior of the vehicle was totally gutted by the ensuing fire. It is our opinion that three such conflagrations (all experienced by one rental agency in a six month period) demonstrates a clear and present safety hazard to all Pinto owners'.

Shortly before Richard's case began, Dr Leslie Ball — former safety chief for the NASA manned space programme and founder of the International Society of Reliability Engineers — had publicly asserted that 'the release to production of the Pinto was the most reprehensible decision in the history of American engineering'. Ball was particularly scathing about the design and location of the Pinto's petrol tank. There were, he said, a large number of European and Japanese cars in the same price and weight range as the Pinto which were more safely designed. Most used a 'saddle style' petrol tank placed above the car's back axle, out of the line of direct impact. The basic patent on the saddle-tank, Ball noted, was owned by Ford.

A lot more was required to win punitive damages — and Richard's lawyers got it. The production of Ford's own confidential documents and the cross-examination of senior Ford executives about their contents made an enormous impact upon the jury. And the greatest damage to Ford's case was done by its own analysis of the price of building greater safety into Ford cars against the expected benefit derived from saving Ford owners from death or injury by burning.

The evidence to the court

The figures were buried in a seven-page report from the company's 'Environmental and Safety Engineering' division, which was circulated under the title 'Fatalities associated with crash-induced fuel leakages and fires'. Ford's experts doubted the government statistics of between 2,000 and 3,500 such deaths every year; their research suggested that most of the deaths in 'fire-accompanied crashes' were due to injuries caused by the impact not the flames. They concluded that between 600 and 700 fire deaths a year 'is probably more appropriate'.

The report pointed out that the chance of petrol spilling from a ruptured tank was significantly greater when a car was hit from behind than from the front, side or after being rolled over. None the less, Ford's engineers based their calculations of the sums at stake if proposed new regulations were adopted, on the less common hazard of 'static rollovers'.

Some common measure was required to make the comparison. The memo noted: 'the measure typically chosen is dollars'. Ford's calculations of the value of a human life were based on a 1972 study by the National Highway Traffic Safety Administration (NHTSA), which sought to establish the cash cost of death in a car crash by breaking down and valuing ten separate components. 'Future productivity losses' were so much, medical costs so much, insurance administration and legal expenses so much: there was even a figure — $10,000 — for 'victim's pain and suffering', though the NHTSA steadfastly refused to say how it had been arrived at. The overall 'societal cost' came to $200,000. Ford also allowed a figure of $67,000 for non-fatal burn injuries.

From official statistics Ford extracted the figure of 180 deaths per year from burns in rollover accidents. Where some experts disagree with Ford is in their further estimate that numbers emerging alive from such accidents, but suffering severe burns, would also be 180 a year. Some authoritative studies have put this figure ten times higher at 1,800 a year.

Based on the benefits of saving 180 lives and preventing another 180 people from being burned, with an allowance for the cost of damaged cars, Ford put the total benefit of a design change at slightly less than $50 million. That was set against the costs — $11 worth of modifications per Ford vehicle sold — of $137 million. That, Ford's engineers observed, was almost three times greater than the benefits, 'even using a number of highly favourable benefit assumptions'. They could not envisage any developments which 'would make compliance with the rollover requirement cost effective'.

On the heels of that memo, the Santa Anna jury heard something of the background to Ford's decision to place the Pinto's petrol tank in such an exposed position. First, Richard Grimshaw's lawyers produced their star 'defector', Harley F. Copp, a senior design engineer with Ford for 20 years, now retired. Against a stream of objections from Ford's team of lawyers, Copp demonstrated with blackboard, wall chart and models to the evident discomfort of his former employers. (He was helped by occasional indulgence from the bench: 'I will allow hearsay' the judge declared at one time, 'provided it is reliable hearsay'.)

Copp had worked on Ford's successful Capri range in which the petrol tank rode, saddle-style, above the back axle; he was certain that this was the safest design (Ford had, in fact, considered using the Capri design on the Pinto). What could a designer like him do, Richard's lawyers asked, if 'corporate management' specified the location of the petrol tank? 'Follow corporate policy', Copp replied. Had Ford's top management, in fact, issued a design directive for the Pinto's tank? 'Behind the rear axle, beneath the floor.' Could he estimate how much extra it would have cost to place the Pinto's tank above the axle? 'About $9 more per car.'

Copp's testimony was reinforced by more memos from Ford's confidential files, demonstrating, Richard's lawyers argued, how Ford had disregarded danger signals in its rush to get the Ford on to the lucrative US small car market (the company's share of this market had been declining at an alarming rate in the face of competition from European and Japanese models). Shortly after Pinto's production began, several Capris with saddle-style tanks came through crash tests with flying colours; next day, Capris with modified tanks placed, like the Pinto's, behind the rear axle were crash-tested and leaked petrol in every case.

Like every company in the ferociously competitive small car market, Ford was exceedingly price conscious. A Ford engineer told the US magazine *Mother Jones* that the Pinto was rigidly governed by 'the limits of 2,000' – it was not to weigh more than 2,000 pounds and not to cost more than $2,000 (the magazine was the first to publish some of the Ford documents used in Richard Grimshaw's case). A $25 increase in production costs could price a compact out of its market; so could a marginal reduction in sales features such as the size of the boot. 'Do you realize that if we put a Capri-type tank in the Pinto you could only get one set of golf clubs in there?' another Ford engineer told the magazine.

The result

It took the jury in Richard Grimshaw's case one minute to reject Ford's argument that the speed at which Mrs Gray's Pinto had been hit – from 50 to 65 m.p.h. – was the chief cause of the tragedy rather than any deficiency in the design of its petrol tank (the jury concluded that impact speed was 35 m.p.h. at the most).

Ford's position is that every Pinto it manufactured had met or surpassed the government safety standards applicable at the time, and Pintos produced since September 1976 meet the revised rear-impact standards introduced since Richard was involved in his accident.

Mr Grimshaw was awarded punitive damages of more than $128 million against Ford. Ford announced that it would appeal.

Questions

1. Should non-financial factors be taken into account in making corporate investment decisions?
2. If so, should an attempt be made to quantify them so as to express all features of a decision in a common and comparable form? Should this form be financial?
3. The error to avoid here is blindly applying the growth model formula. This, of course, forecasts a future share price of:

$$P_0 = D_1/[r - g]$$
$$= 82p/[0.09 - 0.11]$$
$$= - £41$$

Clearly a negative share price is impossible. In any case such a high growth rate would hardly be linked to a 'low' price such as a negative price! If you return to the model that derived the formula, you will see that it depends on r being greater than g. If g is greater (as it is here), the derivation just will not work – you will see in the text that we pointed out that it would result in an infinite share price. But that price cannot be arrived at by applying the formula.

The answer is, then, not some valuation, but the conclusion that the influential stockbroking firm is mistaken. The formula requires that the 11% should apply through perpetuity, but that is clearly unrealistic.

It is helpful to consider here a famous mathematical puzzle known as the 'Petersburg Paradox'. It is so named because it was first propounded by the mathematician Bernouilli in a paper read in St Petersburg. It runs like this. Suppose that Peter and Paul are playing a wagering game. Peter proposes a game as follows. He will toss a coin. If it comes down heads, he will pay Paul £1. If it comes down tails he will pay nothing but play again, so that in the next round the stakes will be doubled: that is, if it comes down heads he will pay Paul £2 and if not, play again. This will carry on until the coin comes down heads. How much should Paul be prepared to pay to participate in this game?

According to the simple laws of probability, the expected value of the first toss is £1 multiplied by the probability of winning, that is £1 × 0.5 = 50p. The probability of heads on the second toss will be $0.5^2 = 0.25$. Hence the expected value of the second toss is £2 multiplied by the probability of winning, which is 2 × 0.25 = 50p. In the same way the expected value of each successive toss is 50p and hence the value of the game is:

$$50p + 50p + 50p + \ldots$$

which of course sums to infinity. The implication that Paul should pay an infinite amount of money to play this game violates all common sense and has troubled mathematicians ever since. No rational person could be found who would pay an infinite sum to play (nor could they afford to!). Now, no fully accepted solution has ever been found to this paradox, and its implication of an infinite future stream leading to an infinite price to pay to play the game is clearly suggestive of the share valuation problem with a forecast growth that is higher than the discount rate.

W5.7 Discussion questions

Note: Suggested answers to questions 5.1 – 5.3 are given in section W5.8(b) on pp. 437–8.

5.1 In making pragmatic assumptions to estimate a growth rate to plug into the Gordon growth model, we suggested taking the average growth over the previous five years or so. What other possibilities for using past performance to predict the future might there be? How might you justify one method as compared to another?

5.2 Say that, in recent years, a company's profits have been declining rather than increasing. What are the implications for using the past to assess value through the Gordon model?

5.3 List the good and bad features of non-discounting methods of investment appraisal. Why might you use them? Why do you think managers use them?

5.4 Is the ranking of profitability indices a useful method of allocating resources if there is no capital rationing?

5.5 Why might it be particularly tricky to incorporate ACT into a NPV calculation?

5.6 What relevance do the discounting methods we have been looking at have to the new financial instruments and markets that we surveyed in Chapter 2?

W5.8 Answers to questions

(a) Answers to worked problems

(a) Answers to problems 5.1–5.4

5.1 We know that:

$$P_0 = \frac{D_1}{r - g}$$

and so:

$$r = \frac{D_1}{P_0} + g$$

so that:

$$r = [20(1.06)]/235 + 0.06$$
$$= 0.15 \text{ or } 15\%$$

5.2 We estimate the growth rate using the method described in the main text (we used it for Amersham, too). Taking the growth in dividends as being roughly steady, we have:

$$g = [74/65]^{0.25} - 1$$
$$= 0.033 \text{ or } 3.3\%$$

This can then be plugged into the growth model to give:

$$P_0 = 74(1.033)/(0.13 - 0.033)$$
$$= £7.88$$

5.4 The dividend will have doubled in ten years. So the growth rate is:

$$(1 + g)^{10} = 2$$

so

$$g = \sqrt[10]{2} - 1$$
$$= 1.072 \text{ or } 7.2\%$$

So the current dividend D will be

$$D(1.072)^5 = £1.26$$

that is:

$$D = £1.26/(1.072)^5 = 89p$$

Using the model of $D_1/(r - g)$ we have:

$$r = D_1/P_0 + g$$

that is:

$$r = [89(1.072)]/925 + 0.072$$
$$= 0.175 \text{ or } 17.5\%$$

(b) Answer to problems 5.8–5.10

5.8 The payback periods are as follows:

A:	5.56 years
B:	5.42 years
C:	2.50 years

The accounting rates of return are found like this:

A: $\dfrac{900 - (5,000/10)}{(5,000/2)} = 16\%$

B: $\dfrac{1,150 - (5,000/10)}{(5,000/2)} = 26\%$

C: $\dfrac{(7,000/4) - (5,000/4)}{(5,000/2)} = 20\%$

The NPVs are given in the following table:

Year	Discount factor	A	B	C	A	B	C
0	1.0000	−5,000	−5,000	−5,000	−5,000.00	−5,000.00	−5,000.00
1	1.1000	900	700	2,000	818.18	636.36	1,818.18
2	1.2100	900	800	2,000	743.80	661.16	1,652.89
3	1.3310	900	900	2,000	676.18	676.18	1,502.63
4	1.4641	900	1,000	1,000	614.71	683.01	683.01
5	1.6105	900	1,100		558.83	683.01	
6	1.7716	900	1,200		508.03	677.37	
7	1.9487	900	1,300		461.84	667.11	
8	2.1436	900	1,400		419.86	653.11	
9	2.3579	900	1,500		381.69	636.15	
10	2.5937	900	1,600		346.99	616.87	
		4,000	6,500	2,000	530.11	1,590.33	656.72

The IRRs are as follows:

A:	12.4%
B:	16.0%
C:	16.5%

Thus the rankings can be summarized like this:

	Payback	ARR	NPV	IRR
1	C	B	B	C
2	B	C	C	B
3	A	A	A	A

5.9 This is a straightforward application of the ideas in the text, as follows:

Year	Discount factor	Project A £	Project B £	Project C £	Project D £
0	1.000	−31,000	−60,000	−25,000	−40,000
1	1.120	5,357	17,857		26,786
2	1.254	4,783	15,944		19,930
3	1.405	4,271	28,471		
4	1.574	3,813	6,355		
5	1.762	3,405			
6	1.974	3,040			
7	2.211	2,714			
8	2.476	2,423			
9	2.773	2,164			
10	3.106	1,932		25,758	
NPV		2,901	8,627	758	6,716
Profitability index		0.09	0.14	0.03	0.17

Thus taking the PI as the criterion, the funds are applied as follows:

Project	PI	Outlay £	Accumulated outlay £	Accumulated NPV £
D	0.17	40,000	40,000	6,716
B	0.14	60,000	100,000	8,627
20/31 × A	0.09	20,000	120,000	1,872
Total NPV				17,215

5.10 Project A can of course be solved using a_n. However, we shall discount individual cash flows here so as to be consistent with B, which, of course, has varying cash flows. It also helps in calculating the discounted payback.
The NPV is found as follows:

Year	Project A £	Project B £	Discount factor	Project A discounted £	Project B discounted £
0	−20,000	−25,000	1.000	−20,000	−25,000
1	7,000	2,500	0.885	6,195	2,212
2	7,000	5,000	0.783	5,482	3,916
3	7,000	10,000	0.693	4,851	6,931
4	7,000	20,000	0.613	4,293	12,266
				821	325

It is straightforward from this table to calculate the NPV and iterate to find the IRR.
The accounting rate of return for A is found as:

$$\frac{((4 \times £7,000)/4 - £20,000/4)}{£20,000/2}$$

and that for B can be found similarly.

The payback period for A must be slightly under 3 years, since £21,000 has been received after 3 years and it was only necessary to recover £20,000. Thus the payback period is 2⁶⁄₇ years.

For B, it must be some time in the fourth year, since only £17,500 of the £25,000 has been received after 3 years. To this, therefore, must be added £7,500/£20,000: that is, 0.375.

The discounted payback can be calculated from the NPV columns. For instance, for A, £16,528 has been recovered after 3 years. Thus the fraction of the fourth year must be (£20,000 − £16,528)/£4,293 = 0.809.

The profitability indices for A and B respectively are £821/£20,000 and £325/£25,000.

The criteria required can thus be summarized as:

NPV	£821	£325
IRR	15.0%	13.5%
ARR	20%	25%
Payback	2.857 yrs	3.375 yrs
Discounted payback	3.809 yrs	3.974 yrs
PI	0.041	0.013

(c) Answer to problem 5.14

5.14 The first step is to discover the real rate of interest. From the text (section 5.7) we find that the real interest rate r can be expressed as:

$$[(1+m)/(1+f)] - 1$$

where m is the market rate of interest and f the rate of inflation. In this case, therefore, the real interest rate is:

$$[(1.15)/(1.07)] - 1 = 0.0748 \text{ or } 7.5\%$$

We then plug the rate of 7.5% into the NPV calculation in the usual way:
$$\text{NPV} = 27,000 + 7,000a_{\overline{6}|}^{7.5\%}$$
$$= -27,000 + 7,000 \times 4.6938$$
$$= £5,857$$

(d) Answer to problem 5.16

5.16 The solution here is straightforward, and follows closely the example given in the text. Note that, because there is no scrap value, the total of the capital allowances at the end of the project is equal to the total investment: in other words, the final capital allowance of £37,969 is a balancing figure to make the total of the column equal to the total investment.

Year	Net cash flow £	Cap All'ce £	Taxable surplus £	Corp'n tax £	CT lagged 1 year £	Cash flow after tax £	Discount factor	Discounted cash flow £
0	(160,000)					(160,000)	1.0000	(160,000)
1	40,000	40,000	0			40,000	0.9091	36,364
2	40,000	30,000	10,000	3,500		40,000	0.8264	33,058
3	40,000	22,500	17,500	6,125	3,500	36,500	0.7513	27,423
4	40,000	16,875	23,125	8,094	6,125	33,875	0.6830	23,137
5	40,000	12,656	27,344	9,570	8,094	31,906	0.6209	19,811
6	40,000	37,969	2,031	711	9,570	30,430	0.5645	17,177
7					711	(711)	0.5132	(365)
Total		160,000						(3,395)

The conclusion must therefore be that the project should be rejected.

(b) Suggested answers to discussion questions

5.1 Think first of what we are doing here. We cannot be precise, since both the figures to be entered into the model and the choice of the model itself are inevitably arbitrary: that is, a matter of judgement. Hence it is also a matter of judgement, depending on the circumstances observed, as to what pattern to suppose is likely in the future. After all, the Gordon model assumes growth into the infinite future. This is pretty optimistic.

One alternative to assuming continuous growth is to assume that the current dividend will stay constant. In a way this is what the standard Stock Exchange method does, in giving prominence to the P/E ratio. The price is the current price (as it is with the Gordon model), the earnings the last reported earnings. Thus to use this you would make a further assumption about how long it would last, then use $a_{\overline{n}|}$ (if you assumed a finite term of years) or divide the earnings by the current appropriate discount rate (if you assumed a perpetuity).

A further possibility is, like the previous method, to assume a constant amount, but instead of just the immediate past dividend, to take an average of the last few years' dividends. This would smooth out any oddities in one particular year's trading.

Thus we emphasize that different people will make different judgements in facing the uncertain future. None of the methods is 'right': in the end, the methods are just there to help one come to a sensible conclusion.

5.2 Let's try. Suppose we have a series of dividends like this: 50p, 48p, 47p, 45p, 44p. The discount rate is 11%. Then the growth rate will be found, as before, by supposing we can take the first and last amounts and assume smooth decline (particularly appropriate to British industry, perhaps). Then the negative growth is found, as before, by:

$$50(1 + i)^4 = 44$$

which becomes:

$$i = \sqrt[4]{\frac{44}{50}} - 1$$

$$= -0.032$$

This gives a Gordon solution of:

$$P_0 = \frac{50(1 - 0.032)}{0.11 - (-0.032)}$$

$$= £3.41$$

This seems reasonable. So there is no reason the model cannot be used for negative growth rates. It should not need to be said that this should only be used with care and judgement, as with any other valuation estimation.

5.3 The advantages of payback are:
(a) it is easy to understand;
(b) it is simple to compare projects;
(c) it incorporates an element of risk aversion;

(d) It may lead managers to accept the projects that shareholders would expect them to accept.

Its disadvantages are:

(a) it ignores the time value of money;
(b) it ignores cash flows after the payback date in its main version;
(c) the figure presented means very little in itself: it can only be used with any confidence when one opportunity is being compared to another.

The advantages of ARR are:

(a) it is easy to understand;
(b) it is probably the same method (effectively, return on investment) that will be used subsequently to assess whether the investment was a success, and thus like is being compared with like;
(c) projects can be easily compared.

Its disadvantages are:

(a) it ignores the time value of money;
(b) item (b) of the 'advantages' above is limited. This is because ROI *ex post* will vary from year to year, as the depreciated value of the investment decreases. ARR assumes an *average* of the denominators. (For further discussion of ROI in the context of performance measurement see *Managerial Accounting: Method and Meaning*, Chapter 10.)

It can be said of both methods that they are openly approximations. DCF methods have an air of accuracy that may well be spurious given the estimation errors of the future cash flows.

Managers would use the methods for the reasons given above, of course. It can only be a matter for conjecture as to why they use multiple methods, and the way they do so can vary from company to company. Typically a project or projects will be put forward by divisional/departmental managers. They will use their own criteria to decide which ones are 'worth' putting forward. Then they go to senior management to make the final decision, often based on capital rationing.

The result is that, if divisional managers use a different criterion, the project has to pass two different methods. If they use the same criterion, senior management have in a sense, little choice, since they are only ever presented with good projects!

Procedures other than the rational maximizing methods suggested by theory may obtain. For example, one of the authors was involved with one of the UK's largest companies some years ago. He was told by head office that their major problem was getting managers to spend the funds they were allocated. That is, bids for funds were made each year, and funds allocated to bidders, but the company had found that frequently the funds were not spent quickly, and lay around in divisional coffers earning bank interest. This was bad because the funds could have been allocated to other competing managers who would have used them. Thus their rules had developed so that the managers proposing projects were more likely to be successful if (a) they had been successful with previous projects, and (b) they had spent the funds allocated to them previously as they had promised. In each case, the company's heuristic was a response to uncertainty.

6 Portfolio theory

W6.1 Introduction

The structure of the argument, and the assumptions underlying each chapter, cannot be ignored at any time, and you are advised to remind yourself constantly that the essential feature of this and subsequent chapters is that *risk is now being brought explicitly into the picture*.

Since arguments are in many cases best developed through simple cases, with more realistic elaborations coming later, it is understandable that we begin with the two-investment case. It would be very rare that a real-world investor would be given only two project opportunities, yet the essence of all the later argument can be found in the two-parameter exposition.

The whole of the text chapter is concerned with one particular approach to handling risk: the two-parameter model. In the first section below we look at an alternative approach: that of *stochastic dominance*.

W6.2 Stochastic dominance

(a) The two-parameter model

The two-parameter model has certain strengths. In particular, it can be pretty easily manipulated. Indeed, that has arguably been its chief attraction. Once the assumption has been made that the two parameters are the basis on which investment decisions are or should be made, the reasoning of the chapter can continue so as to lead to the conclusions we have observed concerning the desirability of spreading risk, and the way in which a portfolio should be constructed. This is of course very far-reaching; the prescription that we ended with — that all investors should hold the market portfolio adjusted by borrowing or lending at the risk-free rate (see p. 162) — is both counter-intuitive and powerful.

Also, it can be argued that the starting point at least *is* acceptable intuitively. In other words, most people would not quibble with the argument that:

1. return matters to the investor, and that the mean expectation is a reasonable way of measuring it;
2. risk is important to the investor, and dispersion is a reasonable way of measuring it.

And yet, some of the assumptions that have to be made after this are not so intuitive, and depend on the faith that is customarily reserved for religion and economic arguments.

Francis and Archer (1971, p. 7) give the following as the assumptions of portfolio theory:

1. all investors maximize one-period expected utility also, the increase in wealth they expect from investment has diminishing marginal utility;
2. the investors' estimates of project risks are proportional to the spread of the expected returns;
3. only their expected return and risk are important to their investment decisions;
4. for any level of risk, investors will prefer higher to lower returns; and for any level of return they will prefer lower to higher risk.

With this careful formulation, doubts arise. For a start, can a person really put prior expectations on risk and return — actually quantify what is expected? Try it for yourself. It is not easy. Is nothing except expected return and risk important? What about moral considerations? Can the one-period model be extended beyond, to multiple periods? And in response to item 4., can we really be sure that there are no risk-takers who would want more risk even for the same return, rather than less?

Since these concerns are very real ones, we might wish to look for a basis for investor assessment of risk that avoided making too many assumptions. We would find it with *stochastic dominance*. Stochastic dominance looks at this, makes fewer assumptions and comes out with an approach that is also intuitively appealing.

(b) Stochastic dominance

Table 6.1   Two securities

Security A		Security B	
Probability (P)	*Return*	*Probability (P)*	*Return*
0.25	10	0.25	5
0.25	20	0.25	10
0.25	30	0.25	15
0.25	40	0.25	20
$X_A = 25$		$X_B = 12.5$	
$\sigma_A = 11.18$		$\sigma_B = 2.24$	

Take a look at Table W6.1. We have two securities. A offers a higher return — in fact double that of B — but a higher risk. Can we choose? By the two-parameter model, no, as we need to know the risk preference. Different investors will have different risk preferences (as we saw in Fig. 6.11). However, the rules of stochastic dominance do enable us to choose. There are two approaches to stochastic dominance: first order and second order (FSD and SSD respectively from now on).

By the FSD rule A is preferred since the chance of earning higher returns is always greater with A and B. To see this we first need to work out the *cumulative probabilities*, and these are given in Table W6.2. We can then list the returns available and the cumulative probabilities of receiving them. These are given in Table W6.3 and graphed in Fig. W6.1.

Table 6.2   Cumulative probabilites of returns

	Security A			Security B	
P	Cum. p.	Return	P	Cum. p.	Return
0.25	0.25	10	0.25	0.25	5
0.25	0.5	20	0.25	0.5	10
0.25	0.75	30	0.25	0.75	15
0.25	1.0	40	0.25	1.0	20

Table 6.3   Ranked cumulative probabilities
of returns

Return	Cum. p_A	Cum. p_B
5	0	0.25
10	0.25	0.50
15	0.25	0.75
20	0.5	1.0
30	0.75	1.0
40	1.0	1.0

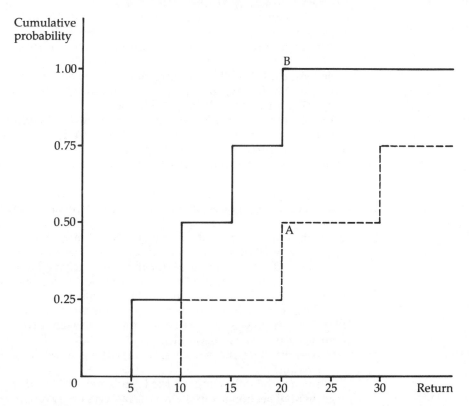

Figure W6.1   Mapping of cumulative probabilities of A and B.

From Table W6.3 and Fig. W6.1 can it be inferred that investment A is preferable because, in every state of nature (in other words, at every point), it dominates B. To see this, run your finger along the returns and look at the chance of each one. For instance, try a return of 20%. You will see that there is a 50% chance that investment A will give a return higher than that. But it is *certain* (cum. p. = 1.0) that B cannot exceed it.

However, this case is not very likely as Hillier, Hiltz and others have pointed out. Usually one will be dominant at some points, the other at other points. For this there is second degree dominance as the two distributions intersect. This involves taking the difference between the two cumulative probability distributions — provided it is non-negative — over the whole range of the return. Provided that, say, A on balance is greater than B (the positive difference between the two distributions exceed the negatives) then, invoking the risk-aversion criteria, we can say that B dominates A.

Although stochastic dominance has appeared in the literature of finance to some moderate extent, it has not formed anything like as large a base as the mean-variance criterion. For the rest of this Workbook we shall concentrate on expanding upon the two-parameter model in the text. We begin with the two-investment case.

W6.3   The two-investment case

The basic notion of the mean-variance model is a very simple one: *that it pays to diversify so long as the investor is risk averse and so long as the investments are not perfectly correlated*. In section 6.2 of the text we turned to the mechanics of calculating risk–return for two-investment portfolios. In section 6.3 this was extended to more than two investments — a more realistic case.

The mathematics of this section are not really at all complex; they can be a little tedious. It is highly recommended, however, that you work through the exercises that follow, since familiarity with the way the numbers behave helps in gaining an understanding of what is happening.

In one sense, it could be argued that the Markowitz portfolio model is doing nothing more than expressing the old adage that you do 'not put all your eggs in one basket'. In fact it says a great deal more. Not only is it precise about the relationship between different risks and covariances and the resulting portfolio risk, it also links the risk profile to return — something not envisaged in the adage. For the institutional investor, its lessons are perhaps minimal. This is because institutions such as pension funds, insurance funds and large unit trusts tend to have such large funds at their disposal that diversification is inevitable. The market simply could not provide all the opportunities they wanted should they attempt to invest in just one or two securities. On the other hand, for those unit trusts that promise to specialize in one particular sector (say, a 'fashionable' sector such as electronics has been in the past) the theory has a clear warning. This becomes clearer still in the context of CAPM (Chapter 7), where these can be seen to be potentially high-beta or low-beta portfolios, and in the context of efficient markets theory, where it is made clear that in almost all cases expertise cannot consistently 'beat the market', so that there is no long-term advantage in specializing.

Now try the following worked problems to see if you understand the argument of section 6.2 in the text. (Answers are given in section W6.7 on pp. 450–3.)

Worked problems
Are the following statements true or false?

6.1 The two-parameter model assumes that the investor is interested in only two things: the risk and the variance of returns on a project.

6.2 The risk of a project is the same thing as the variability of returns.

6.3 If two risky projects are perfectly negatively correlated, it must be possible to avoid risk altogether.

6.4 You can only benefit from diversification if the returns of two securities are either uncorrelated or negatively correlated.

Now try the following questions.

6.5 (It is helpful to use a spreadsheet to solve this if you have access to one; it is not, however, essential.) The market prices of securities X and Y have at the end of each of the past seven years been as follows:

Year	X pence	Y pence
1	120	180
2	130	190
3	170	120
4	110	150
5	120	140
6	70	140
7	140	170

X paid a dividend of 8p in year 1, which was increased by 1p in each of the first three years (i.e. until year 4) and has since remained static. Y has paid no dividends at all.

1. Calculate the annual return from holding each investment.
2. Say you want to create a portfolio by holding equal amounts of the two investments. Create a further column to show the annual returns from holding the combination.
3. Calculate the mean and variance of the new portfolio directly from your new data.
4. Check this by calculating the two parameters for X and Y and applying the appropriate expressions for mean and variance of a two-security portfolio.

6.6 You are offered two investments. One (call it A) has an expected return of 24% with a standard deviation of past returns (surrogate for risk) of 18%. The other (B) has an expected return of 17% with a risk of 13%. If the correlation between them is 0.2, what are the risk and return of the following portfolios:

1. 0.2 invested in A
2. 0.5 invested in A
3. 0.75 invested in A?

6.7 Suppose you are offered two securities, one (security A) offering an expected return of 12% with a risk of 10%, the other (security B) offering an expected return of 20% with a risk of 4%. Suppose further that the correlation between the two is zero. Now suppose you choose to invest half your funds in each security. Call the resulting portfolio C.

1. What are the expected return and risk of C?
2. Compare this to the investment in B alone. Which is better?

3. Graph this by setting up axes of expected return and risk, mapping on to it the investments A, B and C.

4. We have learned that it is better to diversify than to hold just one security. In the light of this, how do you explain the result in 2. above?

The following are more difficult. Those who cannot do the first in particular are strongly advised to follow the explanation in the suggested answers.

6.8   Suppose an investor is risk averse. He is to invest in two projects, and wants that combination that gives the least risk. Advise him how to find it. (*Hint:* You are minimizing the risk of the portfolio; and we know that by definition $w_b = 1 - w_a$.)

6.9   Use the result of question 6.8 above to give the minimum variance of a portfolio where the standard deviations of the two investments are 9.3 and 25.8 and the correlation between them is -0.7. What proportion of each investment is required?

6.10   Similarly, use the result of question 6.8 to give the proportions of the same two projects in a minimum variance portfolio if the correlation between them is 0.7. Fully explain the answer you get.

W6.4   Portfolios of more than two projects

In question 6.10 it was seen that, if there is a correlation that is not very significantly different from unity between the two investments, then the curve joining them is not very different from the straight line joining them (which is, of course, the curve where correlation is perfect). Now at the end of Chapter 6 we derived the capital market line that joins a particular point on the curve to a point on the vertical axis (i.e. where risk is zero). If you sketch a curve such as that in question 6.10 (see Fig. W6.7 later), it will be clear that no such line could in many cases be drawn.

In fact the advantages of diversification beyond two investments means that this is not a problem: as more than two investments are available and used, the envelope curve gets progressively 'fatter'. Figure W6.2 illustrates a surface resulting from three investments with a highly (and unrealistically) negative correlation. A similar shape for the efficiency frontier would result from a larger number of investments, albeit not so significantly negatively correlated.

There are two points to reinforce concerning the text of section 6.2 here. The first and less important, concerns the mathematics of finding the curves that combine to form the surface. The second concerns the nature of the surface of investment possibilities itself.

Matrix notation, which we have used at this point in the text for the first and last time, has two advantages. It is a compact way of writing the expression — which can run into hundreds of terms once there are more than a few investments (see, for instance, p. 166 where we show that for 20 investments this would entail 210 correlations). Also, it shows clearly in the central matrix the way the variances of the individual investments relate to the many covariances. This is also, incidentally, the reason that covariance rather than correlation is central. It is covariances that are relevant to the mathematics, since it is they that form the core of the equations:

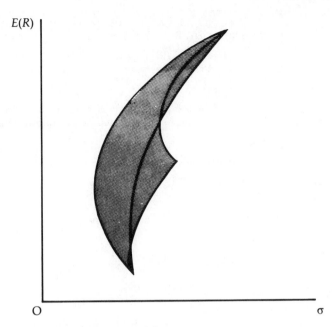

Figure W6.2 A three-investment portfolio.

correlations are merely normalized covariances that are more intuitively manageable.

The nature of the central matrix of equation 6.3 in the text shows, through the symmetry about the diagonal, that the expansion of equation 6.3 will always involve pairings of covariances since obviously $Cov(a,b) = Cov(b,a)$. Because the mathematics are either excessively time consuming (if you do not have a computer) or unilluminating (if you do), we give just one example (in Fig. W6.3) for a single point on a surface where there are four investments to be combined in the portfolio.

The example given in Fig. W6.6 leads us quite well into the second of the two important matters we referred to: a full understanding of the nature of the opportunity space indicated by a situation such as the one in Table W6.1. To further an understanding of this, try the following worked problems. (Answers are given in section W6.7 on pp. 453–6.) Since they are concerned with matters that are related to diversification more generally, we consider them in the next sub-section about diversification beyond three investments.

W6.5   More than three projects

Worked problems

6.11 Suppose you have invested in two projects that are imperfectly correlated with one another, thus gaining the benefit of diversification. You are offered the chance to diversify into a third project. Would you reduce your risk in doing so?

6.12 Say the new, third project were perfectly correlated with both the existing projects. Would it be worthwhile diversifying into it?

6.13 What is the envelope curve?

Suppose Mr A. Stafford has derived the variances and covariances for the investments A, B, C and D as follows (all in percentages terms):

$$\begin{bmatrix} 117 & 16 & -17 & -106 \\ 16 & 86 & -7 & -25 \\ -17 & -7 & 119 & 59 \\ -106 & -25 & 59 & 113 \end{bmatrix}$$

and he wishes to place twice as much of his funds in A and B as in C and D. What will be the risk (measured as standard deviation)?

Solution:

The weights are A = 0.33, B = 0.33. C = 0.17, D = 0.17. Hence we have to solve:

$$[0.33\ 0.33\ 0.17\ 0.17] \begin{bmatrix} 117 & 16 & -17 & -106 \\ 16 & 86 & -7 & -25 \\ -17 & -7 & 119 & 59 \\ -106 & -25 & 59 & 113 \end{bmatrix} \begin{bmatrix} 0.33 \\ 0.33 \\ 0.17 \\ 0.17 \end{bmatrix}$$

which reduces to:

$$[22.98\ 28.22\ 22.34\ -13.99] \begin{bmatrix} 0.33 \\ 0.33 \\ 0.17 \\ 0.17 \end{bmatrix} = 18.32\%$$

This is clearly a very considerable reduction from the individual variances of 117%, 86%, 119% and 113%.

As you might suppose, the fact that this is a quite massive reduction from the individual risks results from the fact that some of the covariances are negative, and some of them substantially negative too. However, a good reduction in risk can be achieved even if all the covariances are positive. For example, if the covariance matrix is changed to the following:

$$\begin{bmatrix} 117 & 16 & 0 & 52 \\ 16 & 86 & 68 & 25 \\ 0 & 68 & 119 & 59 \\ 52 & 25 & 59 & 113 \end{bmatrix}$$

then the solution is a portfolio variance of 51.98% — much greater than the 18.32% just derived, it is true, but still significantly lower than the individual securities' variances.

Figure W6.3   An example with a four-investment portfolio.

6.14 What is the efficiency frontier? Explain, using indifference curves to illustrate your point.

6.15 Is the following proposition true or false? 'Certain people (such as retired people on low incomes) need a steady and low-risk income, and hence should place their funds in a set of low-risk investments. Others prefer more risk, and should thus build a portfolio of high-risk stocks.' (Assume that only risky securities are available.)

The final topic of this part of the chapter is the notion of systematic risk versus unsystematic risk. Systematic risk is a cornerstone of modern finance since, as the text points out (p. 158–60), all unsystematic risk can generally be diversified away through building a portfolio. This suggests that in the development of the theory (which will be continued in Chapter 7) the total risk we have so far considered becomes irrelevant. Only that part of the individual investment's risk that cannot be diversified away can be said to matter.

Worked problem

6.16 'No need to worry about the risks in this scheme,' says the broker smoothly, as he tries to sell you over-the-counter shares in a company formed to turn base metals into gold. 'Modern finance theory shows that only the systematic risk matters. Since the success or failure of this company is related to technical discovery and not general market trends, there is virtually no systematic risk. Hence the risk is irrelevant and this is a good investment.' Would you accept this logic?

W6.6   Combining risky and risk-free assets

The key point made in this section is the straighforward one that, once a risk-free asset is available to the investor, a better risk–return (that is a higher indifference curve) can be reached by mixing a proportion of a riskless asset, such as a short-dated government stock, with one particular mixture of risky assets, namely the market portfolio. We explain more extensively why the market portfolio in equilibrium is the appropriate risky asset mix in Chapter 7 when we derive the capital asset pricing model. For the moment it is only necessary to indicate that this offers maximum diversification *by definition*, since it composes all available assets.

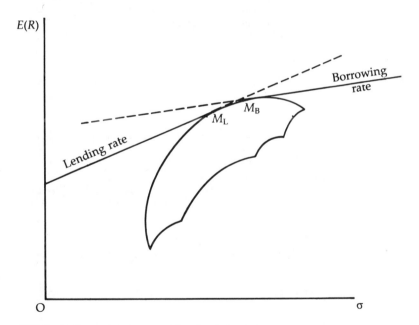

Figure W6.4   Different lending and borrowing rates.

We expand here on just one point in the text. It was explained (pp. 161–2) that funds could be shared between risky and riskless assets, and it was stated that, were the investor to prefer a high risk–return, this could be achieved by moving up the capital market line to a point higher than the point

Mr Lyon has invested £100 in Jumbo Ltd. He does so in the expectation that, at the end of the investment period, there are equal chances that his investment will be worth £90 and £130. Hence the expected return on the investment is:

$$(0.5) \left(\frac{130 - 100}{100} \right) + (0.5) \left(\frac{90 - 100}{100} \right) = 10\%$$

The risk is:

$$\sigma_p^2 = (0.5)(0.3 - 0.1)^2 + (0.5)(-0.1 - 0.1)^2$$
$$= 0.02 + 0.02$$
$$= 0.04$$

Thus:

$$\sigma_p = (0.04)^{0.5}$$
$$= 0.2$$
$$= 20\%$$

Now suppose Mr Lyon borrows £100 and uses this to invest in Jumbo. He has now moved into the borrowing zone of the map (i.e. the sector of the CML above the market portfolio). If the borrowing rate for the period is 5%, then the risk and return will be as follows.

First, find the outcomes probable with the given probability values of 0.5 for each outcome:

	Alternative A £	Alternative B £
Original equity in Jumbo	100	100
Borrowed to invest in Jumbo	100	100
	£200	£200
Return at end of period from Jumbo	180	260
Less Loan repayment: principal	(100)	(100)
interest	(5)	(5)
	£ 75	£155

Hence the expected return is:

$$0.5 \left(\frac{75 - 100}{100} \right) + 0.5 \left(\frac{155 - 100}{100} \right) = (0.5)(-0.25) + (0.5)(0.55)$$
$$= (0.5)(0.30)$$
$$= 0.15 \text{ or } 15\%$$

The variance is:

$$(0.5)(-0.25 - 0.15)^2 + (0.5)(0.55 - 0.15)^2 = (0.5)(0.16 + 0.16)$$
$$= 0.16$$

Thus:

$$\sigma_p = (0.16)^{0.5}$$
$$= 0.4 \text{ or } 40\%$$

Figure W6.5 A numerical example.

tangential to the efficiency frontier. In this position the investor is borrowing at the risk-free rate. (We are making the assumption here that such borrowing is indeed possible and, unrealistically, that borrowing and lending rates are the same. If they are not, the capital market line is curved between the two points where it meets the envelope curve — see Fig. W6.4. This will not be pursued here, and does not affect the theory presented.)

Although most students are happy at the notion of sharing funds between risky and risk-free assets so as to achieve some linear combination of them, the notion of borrowing on the higher part of the line can sometimes cause problems. Figure W6.5 gives a numerical example (adapted from Francis and Archer, 1971) to show how this can be done.

Further problems

Note: No answers have been provided for the following questions.

6.17 Colonel Kaye has been offered two investments. One is in a Welsh gold mine which has an expected return of 28% and risk estimated at 48% (measured as variance). The other is a Bolivian tin mine with an expected return of 40% but risk of 74% (variance). If the success or failure of each of these is reckoned to be unrelated to the success or failure of the other, calculate some appropriate values for different combinations of the two investments and use these to draw the curve of the two-project portfolio.

6.18 Draw an opportunity set of investments together with an indifference curve touching it at some point on the efficient frontier. Call this point A. Now indicate a point within the opportunity set that is lower than, and to the left of, the point at which these curves touch. At this point, both return and risk are lower than at point A. Call this point B. Does the theory we have developed claim that an efficient point is preferable to an inefficient one? And if so, how can it claim that point A is preferable to point B when we do not know if in fact the investor would prefer the lower risk and hence be prepared to accept the lower return as a price for this?

6.19 (This question is based on an account by Brooks (1971).) The Haloid Company, which made photographic materials, was looking for new products soon after World War II. It bought the rights to an embryo copying process from a research institute. Over the next ten years it invested $75 million on researching a new machine, which was double its profits in that period. In other words, it raised massive amounts of funds by the issue of new bonds and shares. In effect, all its eggs were in one basket. The product, moreover, was unproven either in technology or market. The result was the plain paper copier, and Haloid changed its name to Xerox. The Xerox story then became one of the most remarkable in business history. Sales of the company in 1959 when the machine was launched were $33 million. In 1966 they exceeded $500 million. A shareholder would have seen the value of his or her investment grow between 1955 and 1967 by 180 times. It was a classic story of perseverance and risk taking that paid off with massive profits.

Clearly the Xerox corporation's actions were in direct contrast to those put forward in this chapter. Should you conclude that the notion of portfolio diversification is flawed?

W6.7   Answers to worked problems

6.1 False. The variance is a measure of risk.

6.2 False. The past variability may be the best guide to future risk, but it is not the same thing. Future risk relates to uncertainty of returns to be received; the variability of past returns is not uncertain — on the contrary, it is known exactly.

6.3 True. The proportions of each will vary from case to case, but there will always be some combination that has no risk whatever.

6.4 False. You can benefit from any correlation that is not perfect: that is, which is less than unity.

6.5 (a) The table given in Fig. W6.4 was a printout from a spreadsheet solution to this problem. The first and fifth columns repeat the given data in the question concerning the market prices of X and Y. The second column gives the dividend paid by X. The return on X, given in the third column, is the result of both the capital gains on X and the dividends received, since return is a combination of the two. For example, the return in period 2 (a percentage) is found as $((130 + 9 - 120)/120) \times 100$. The return for security Y just reflects the capital gain since there is no dividend. Thus the annual returns are to be found in columns 3 and 6.

Table W6.4   Spreadsheet answer to question 6.5

X (1)	Div. (2)	Return (3)	(4)	Y (5)	Return (6)	(7)	Portfolio return (8)	(9)
120				180				
130	9	15.83	29.84	190	5.56	17.16	10.69	0.44
170	10	38.46	294.65	120	−36.84	1,463.42	0.81	111.19
110	11	−28.82	2,511.98	150	25.00	556.37	−1.91	175.99
120	11	19.09	4.86	140	−6.67	65.27	6.21	26.44
70	11	−32.50	2,894.02	140	0.00	2.00	−16.25	762.00
140	11	115.71	8,914.80	170	21.43	400.64	68.57	3,273.80
Mean		21.30			1.41		11.35	
Var			2,441.69			417.48		724.98
SD			49.41			20.43		26.93

Cov(X,Y) = 20.37
Corr(X,Y) =   0.02

(b) Column 8 gives the equally shared return from the portfolio; for instance, the first calculation is simply $(15.83 + 5.56)/2 = 10.69$.

(c) Hence the expected return of the new portfolio is the mean of the returns in column 8: that is, 11.35%. The risk is calculated using:

$$\text{Var(portfolio)} = E(r - \bar{r})^2$$

and the figures of columns 4, 7 and 9 are the respective values of $(r - \bar{r})^2$. These are averaged at the bases of the columns, giving a value for the portfolio risk (measured as standard deviation) of 26.93%

(d) In a similar way, the expected return and variance of X and Y can be found. They can then be combined in the usual way, using a linear combination for the return and the text equation 6.1 for the risk:

Mean   =   11.36
Variance = 724.78
SD   =   26.92

6.6 This is simplest answered by using the expression for expected risk given in the text as equation 6.1 and the simple linear combination for calculating the expected return. Of course, we have to substitute for the covariance in 6.1 since it is not given directly.

The answers are then:

	Mean	SD
(a)	18.40	11.67
(b)	20.50	12.11
(c)	22.25	14.50

6.7 (a) Using equation 6.1 for risk and a linear combination for return we have:

Risk   = 5.39%
Expected return = 16%

(b) The combination C offers a worse expected return than B (16% compared to 20%), and higher risk (5.39% compared to 4%). Clearly investing in B is better than diversifying.

(c) This is graphed in Fig. W6.6.

(d) You may have puzzled over this for a while! The answer is very straightforward. We have already agreed that the nature of the market is such that expected returns from investments will be higher if the perceived risk is higher. If there is no market, then those without higher expected returns will get no takers. If there is a market, then the market price will adjust itself to reflect the expected inflows and risk so that the expected return is indeed higher for higher risk. But in the case of the two investments here, one (A) already offers a worse return coupled with a higher risk. Thus it would not even be considered as a one-off offered investment, or if the expected return resulted from a market valuation, the valuation would not have made the figures seen here possible at all.

Thus there is nothing wrong with the theory of diversification given the two-parameter assumption: the numbers given were merely unrealistic in a real-world context. This can be seen by looking at the slope of the straight line joining the two individual investments. Reflection will make it clear that this should slope in the opposite direction.

6.8 This is solved by the standard technique of minimizing a function using the differential calculus (in this case, using partial differentiation). The function to be minimized is the portfolio variance; the salient variable with respect to which the function is to be minimized is the weight of one or other of the projects, since that is the only thing we can control in our investment policy.

Now we know that:

$$\sigma_p^2 = w_a^2\,\sigma_a^2 + w_b^2\,\sigma_b^2 + 2w_a w_b \sigma_{ab}$$

and since $w_b = 1 - w_a$ we can substitute to get:

$$\sigma_p^2 = w_a^2\sigma_a^2 + (1 - w_a)^2\sigma_b^2 + 2w_a(1 - w_a)\sigma_{ab}$$

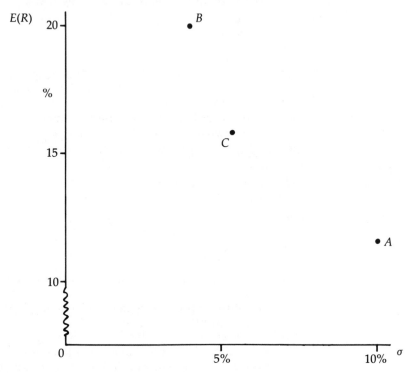

Figure W6.6 Answer to question 6.7(c).

For simplicity of terminology, we shall abbreviate w_a to w. The above equation can then be differentiated with respect to w:

$$(\sigma_p^2)' = 2w\sigma_a^2 + 2w\sigma_b^2 - 2\sigma_b^2 + 2\sigma_{ab} - 4w\sigma_{ab}$$

where we use the 'prime' (') to denote a differentiated function.

Setting this equal to zero and dividing by 2 gives:

$$w\sigma_a^2 + w\sigma_b^2 - \sigma_b^2 + \sigma_{ab} - 2w\sigma_{ab} = 0$$

Hence:

$$w(\sigma_a^2 + \sigma_b^2 - 2\sigma_{ab}) - \sigma_b^2 + \sigma_{ab} = 0$$

and thus the minimum point for w is:

$$w = \frac{\sigma_b^2 - \sigma_{ab}}{\sigma_a^2 + \sigma_b^2 - 2\sigma_{ab}}$$

This is not just important for helping to draw curves for given covariances between projects (that is, telling us where the curve turns back on itself), but also because that point defines the end of the efficiency frontier. The efficient set of investments, in other words, lies on the set of outermost points between the project with the higher risk and return and the turning point just defined.

6.9 This is now just a matter of substitution. In this case we have:

$$w = \frac{(25.8)^2 - (9.3)(25.8)(-0.7)}{(9.3)^2 + (25.8)^2 - 2(9.3)(25.8)(-0.7)}$$
$$= 0.77$$

Thus the proportions are 0.77 and 0.23.

This gives a variance of:

$$(0.77)^2(9.3)^2 + (0.23)^2(25.8)^2 + 2(0.77)(0.23)(9.3)(25.8)(-0.7) = 27.00$$

This compares with variances of 86.49 and 665.64 for the individual projects.

6.10 This question shows the danger of blindly following a formula: always think of the *meaning* of the question in terms of real investment projects. The first stage, as with question 6.8, is of course to calculate the minimum variance using the expression we derived in question 6.7. This gives the following proportion for w:

$$w = \frac{(25.8)^2 - (9.3)(25.8)(0.7)}{(9.3)^2 + (25.8)^2 - 2(9.3)(25.8)(0.7)}$$
$$= 1.20$$

At first sight this is counter-intuitive: you would expect w to lie between 0 and 1. This proportion seems to imply investing more than 100% of funds available in one project and a negative amount in the other. Let us first understand what is happening. Remember that the usual assumption when we are creating a portfolio is a curve such as the one in Fig. W6.7(a). Here the lowest variance is to the left of both the underlying investments. But if the covariance is not greatly different from 1, the curve looks more like Fig. W6.7(b). There is still a benefit from diversifying, but still all variances lie between the variances of the individual projects.

Now this is, of course, just part of a full curve that continues as in Fig. W6.7(c). We do not usually consider this because the normal course of events supposes that we can only invest *in* projects, not borrow from them. Hence we consider only the curve between the points of the two projects. But the mathematics of differentiation do not know we have made this supposition, and hence they dutifully tell us of a point beyond one of the project points. Thus what is happening is that we have to use our sense of what is *really* happening in financial investment and not rely blindly on the mathematical answer.

Thus if (as is normally the case) we can only lend money to projects (that is, invest in them), then we have to ignore the curve beyond the two investment points. This means that the best point is the existing project with the lower of the two variances (in this case, that with a standard deviation of 9.3). If we could borrow (that is, sell the investment short in some way), then the solution of (1.20, -0.2) would, of course, hold true.

6.11 Probably but it depends on the proportions you invested in each. Go back to Table 6.11 of the text (p. 160). It might well be that the extra benefit from risk reduction was not justified by the effort (and maybe the transaction costs) of selling part of your existing portfolio and buying into the third project.

6.12 The third project could be perfectly correlated with one or other of the current projects, but not with both of them (unless they themselves were perfectly correlated). Think about it. Hence the question does not make sense.

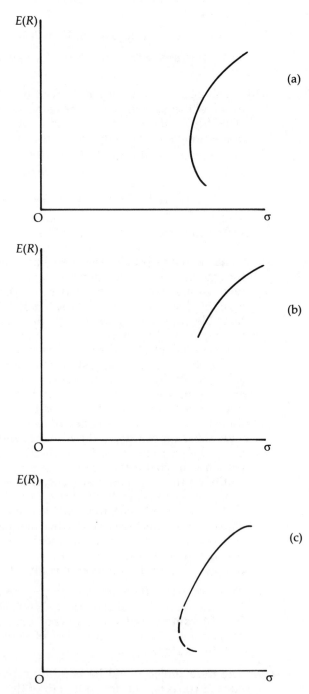

Figure W6.7   Illustration for answer to question 6.10.

John and Mary each have portfolios of three shares, and have each shared their money equally among the shares they have. John prefers to take less risk than Mary, and so has invested in shares A, B and C that have in the past had a low spread of returns, as measured by their standard deviation. Mary is more willing to take risk to obtain a higher expected return and has invested in shares D, E and F, all of which have higher risk and return than A, B and C. Are these sensible policies?

Solution:

We can show quantitatively that their approach is misguided. The prices of the six shares are as follows:

	A	B	C	D	E	F
Share	210	120	76	230	45	92
prices	215	126	78	250	48	84
	222	128	78	269	52	78
	213	119	74	270	39	83
	200	118	72	290	37	89
	212	121	76	240	46	96

These result in the following period-on-period returns:

	A	B	C	D	E	F
% changes	2.4	5.0	2.6	8.7	6.7	−8.7
in	3.3	1.6	0.0	7.6	8.3	−7.1
price	−4.1	−7.0	−5.1	0.4	−25.0	6.4
	−6.1	−0.8	−2.7	7.4	−5.1	7.2
	6.0	2.5	5.6	−17.2	24.3	7.9

The resulting *ex post* risk and return that have persuaded John and Mary to buy them are as follows:

	A	B	C	D	E	F
Std devn	4.6	4.1	3.8	9.8	16.4	7.4
Mean	0.3	0.3	0.1	1.4	1.8	1.1

As you can see, the return and risk of Mary's shares are all higher than those of John's. However, the key to the risk (variance) of the portfolios that result from these policies is the covariances between the period-on-period returns on the shares. The resulting portfolio variances for each, using the method of equation 6.3 in the text, are:

$$[0.3\ 0.3\ 0.3] \begin{bmatrix} 21.1 & 13.1 & 15.4 \\ 13.1 & 16.8 & 13.1 \\ 15.4 & 13.1 & 14.3 \end{bmatrix} \begin{bmatrix} 0.3 \\ 0.3 \\ 0.3 \end{bmatrix} = 15.02\%$$

and

$$[0.3\ 0.3\ 0.3] \begin{bmatrix} 95.3 & -71.6 & -43.5 \\ -71.6 & 268.0 & -26.8 \\ -43.5 & -26.8 & 55.1 \end{bmatrix} \begin{bmatrix} 0.3 \\ 0.3 \\ 0.3 \end{bmatrix} = 14.57\%$$

Thus John has a higher portfolio risk than Mary, even though the risks of the individual shares in his portfolio are lower. The reason is, of course, that Mary's choice of shares included negative covariances, whereas John's did not. In other words, the effect of the relationships among the shares was greater than that of the risk expected in the shares themselves.

Figure W6.8 The effect of covariances on portfolio risk

6.13 When an investor is presented with a set of more than two investment opportunities, a surface can be mapped that represents all the risk–return opportunities available to that investor. The envelope curve is the set of investment opportunities that lie at the boundary of the opportunity set.

6.14 The efficiency frontier is a subset of the points that constitute the envelope curve. Given that the envelope curve will almost certainly turn back on itself, so that there are a large number of combinations of securities that will lead to different levels of expected return for a particular level of risk, the efficiency frontier is that part of the envelope curve which dominates the other. That is, a rational investor will prefer a higher to a lower expected return for a given risk level. Hence the points on the efficiency frontier are the optimal set of points for the rational investor.

6.15 This has sometimes been referred to as the 'interior decorator fallacy'. The error is to suppose that, taken together, the portfolio of high-risk stocks will *necessarily therefore* have a higher risk than the portfolio of low-risk stocks. In fact, if they are chosen judiciously to have low common covariances, and the covariances of the low-risk stocks are quite high, then the resulting risk of the set of risky investments could actually be lower than the risk of the 'safe' investments. Put another way: what matters is not so much the individual variances as the covariances.

Another way to appreciate this is to return to the central matrix of equation 6.3. There are far more covariances than variances as the number of investments increases. For instance, for a ten-share portfolio there are ten variances but 45 covariances (each of which is promptly doubled since it appears twice). Thus the relationships among the investments are far more important than the characteristics of the investments alone. Understanding this is important, so in Fig. W6.8 we give a fuller illustration.

6.16 The key factor to remember is that, although we have spotlighted risk a great deal in this chapter, it is only one of the two salient parameters. What is the likely return from this scheme? Clearly there is a very low probability of success since alchemists through the centuries have tried and failed. What is significant is the mixture of risk and return. If this investment has a very low expected value, this will drag down the average expected value of the portfolio as a whole, and the fact that the risk is orthogonal to the rest of the portfolio is little recompense.

This is quite a complex chapter, and probably the one that relies most on mathematics for much of its substance. We begin therefore by summarizing the gist of the argument of the development of CAPM in the order presented in the text, but without the derivations.

W7.1   Summary of the argument of the chapter

The first part of the text's argument extended the discussion of the capital market line (CML) to consider its equation. The CML describes the equilibrium optimum set of investment opportunities for investors, whatever their particular indifference functions. The line is concerned with an independent variable (risk) and a dependent variable (return). The locus of the line represents portfolios that are mixtures of risky and risk-free securities, and the dependent variable is thus the return the investor requires for a given amount of risk. Put another way: there is always a trade-off between risk and return (the higher the risk, the greater the return demanded for funds to be made available).

Sharpe (1985, p. 153) explains the nature of the CML very well. In taking on a risky asset you are doing two things. You are putting off consumption, and you are bearing a risk. The intercept at R_f is the reward for waiting. The slope of the CML can be viewed as the reward per unit of risk borne. So the 'interest rate can be thought of as the *price of time*, and the slope of the capital market line as the *price of risk*'.

The question becomes therefore: how does the expected return vary with the risk involved? The equation of the CML that satisfies this answer turns out to be that in equation 7.5:

$$E(R_p) = R_f + \frac{E(R_m) - R_f}{\sigma_m}\sigma_p$$

Hence if there is no risk, the portfolio return is R_f, the risk-free rate. If there is risk, then the expected return increases in a linear relationship with the portfolio risk. As risk goes up, so does expected return in proportion, and the slope of the line is $(E(R_m) - R_f)/\sigma_m$. At any point in time all these are quantities defined by the state of the market: they can be discovered through the use of commercial database services.

We then turn to use this equation in a one-period model with a substantial number of assumptions (given on p. 172). By doing so (and the derivation is given in full detail on pp. 173–5) we arrive at a new expression that, in equilibrium, claims to explain the forces determining the *expected return from any individual security*. As with the CML this turns out to be a linear function. As with the CML its intercept is at the risk-free rate. However, unlike the CML the dependent variable is the return on a given security, and the independent variable is the security's *beta*. The line relating them is known as the *security market line* (SML), and its equation is given in the text as equation 7.12:

$$E(R_i) = R_f + \beta_i(E(R_m) - R_f)$$

This gives a powerful tool for predicting the expected return and hence the price of a security in the market *if the CAPM holds true*. For any share we only need some elementary market information (the current rates on risk-free securities and on risky securities as a whole — though, note, this is just a surrogate for the 'true' total set of risky investments available to the lender) together with the security's beta, and a rate for the security can be calculated. This does not in itself, of course, provide a suggested security price. However, the expected return can then be plugged into another model that is deemed appropriate — such as the Gordon model — to arrive at a price.

Beta is thus, according to the model, a fundamental property of a financial market. It corresponds to the covariance between any risky security's price movements and those of the market as a whole. This can be taken a step further. Any investment that involves risk can covary to a greater or lesser extent with the market. An enterprise is (as we have emphasized in the earlier chapters of this book) just a bundle of investment projects. This means that each investment will have its own beta, and the beta of the enterprise is determined by these project betas. If there is no debt, the enterprise's beta will be merely the average of the project beta weighted by their relative size. This we can call the asset beta. If there is debt this will be modified to take account of the financial risk inherent in raising debt, and the debt and equity betas can be related to the overall asset beta by a simple linear function, given as equation 7.14 on p. 181, which is:

$$\beta_A = \beta_E \left(\frac{\text{Equity}}{\text{Equity} + \text{Debt}} \right) + \beta_D \left(\frac{\text{Debt}}{\text{Equity} + \text{Debt}} \right)$$

There is a further implication of going back one stage, reducing the enterprise's problem of beta to the individual project betas. A major task of the financial manager is to advise on whether to accept a new project or not. Following the logic that the new project should enhance the NPV of the enterprise, we have in Chapters 4 and 5 taken the basic rule that the NPV of the candidate project should exceed zero. With risk taken into account this is no longer true. This is because a new project affects *both* the expected return *and* the risk of the enterprise as a whole. Even without the apparatus of CAPM it had been clear to financial analysts that the weighted average cost of capital of the enterprise would be changed by a new project and hence that the historical WACC was not appropriate as a hurdle rate (unless by chance the raising of funds to finance the new project took place in precisely the same proportions as the existing capital structure). We shall meet this in detail in Chapter 11. This problem is compounded by the probability that any new project does not offer an identical risk to the bundle of projects already in existence. Hence we see that the old NPV acceptance rule changes to the rule on p. 181, namely that we accept a project *j* if:

$$\sum_{t=0}^{n} \frac{k_{jt}}{(1 + R_f + \beta_j(E(R_m) - R_f))^t} > 0$$

The structure of the expression is the same as that for the risk-free NPV criterion, but the appropriate discount rate is now governed by the CAPM.

For the remainder of this Workbook chapter we shall concentrate on one essential: an elaboration of some of the issues discussed so far so as to deepen our understanding of the nature of CAPM and beta. But first, here are some worked problems. Try the questions and look at the answers given in section W7.5 on pp. 462–7 before continuing.

Worked problems

Note: Answers to worked problems are given in section W7.3 on pp. 462–3.

7.1 Look at Fig. W7.1. Would an investor invest in:

1. security A?
2. portfolio B?
3. portfolio C?
4. security D?

7.2 Explain the divergence of security A from the market portfolio M in Fig. W7.1 in terms of systematic and unique risk.

7.3 Below are some factors that can result in changes in the return on the equity of a motor manufacturer. They are, in other words, the kinds of factor that make investment risky. Which will tend to govern systematic risk, and which unique risk?

1. a shortage of supplies of special steel;
2. labour dissatisfaction in the company's special components division;

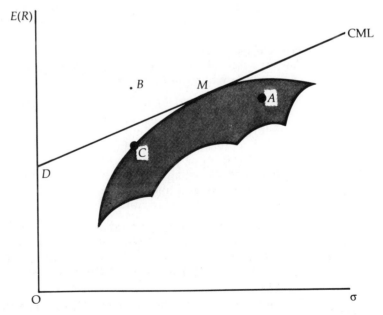

Figure W7.1   Worked problem 7.1.

3. inflation;
4. government controls on the money supply;
5. the publication of an opinion poll giving the main opposition party a 10% lead;
6. the discovery of economic quantities of oil below Lanarkshire;
7. the abandonment of speed limits on all roads.

W7.2   Further issues in CAPM and beta

Next we turn to a further examination of beta and systematic risk. We have seen that beta and systematic risk are both essentially measures of the covariance between the risk of an individual security and the risk of the market as a whole. We saw that the expression for the beta of a security i was:

$$\beta_i = \frac{\sigma_{im}}{\sigma_m^2}$$

and for the systematic risk of a security i it was (see p. 178):

$$\sigma_m^2 \beta_i^2$$
or: $\sigma_i^2 \, \rho_{im}^2$

We shall concentrate on the expression for beta and the first expression for systematic risk. Each of these, it will be seen, incorporates the market variance, which can be taken as given for any particular market, and a function relating the security i to the market through the covariance of their returns, which will of course be different depending on the security concerned. Since we are therefore concerned with relating a security to the market, we can clearly graph the relationship between the security's return and that of the market.

To see how this works, go through the next set of exercises interactively, trying each question and checking its solution before proceeding to the next. You will find the solutions in section W7.3 on p. 462.

Worked problems

7.4 Suppose a share has a positive beta. Would you expect its price to go up or down when the market moves up?

7.5 We are interested in the share's return and the return of the market. Ignoring dividends, an upward movement in price implies a positive return. Thus we can consider price changes to be effectively the same thing as returns on holding the security (or, in the case of the market, securities). Now set out two axes on a graph, the vertical axis for the return on the share, the horizontal axis for the return on the market. Given the assumptions of CAPM, would you expect the graph relating the two to be linear or not?

7.6 To draw the graph mentioned in question 7.5 above we need to know two things: the point at which it cuts the vertical or horizontal axis, and the slope. First, consider the point of intercept with the axes. Would you expect the graph to cut the vertical axis above or below the horizontal axis?

7.7 Would you expect the gradient of the function to be positive or negative — that is, would you expect it to slope up or down?

7.8 Take the intercept with the vertical axis to be greater than zero, and sketch a line that relates the share's return to that of the market.

7.9 Now imagine that you are observing a number of returns on this share, and the corresponding market returns. Would you expect them to lie perfectly along the line we have just drawn?

7.10 Draw some imaginary observations about the line you have drawn. Normally, of course, you would never be able to start with the line. You would begin with the observations and later estimate the line through the technique of linear regression. Under what special conditions would all the observations lie exactly along the line, with no random error?

7.11 Is the slope of this line the beta of the share?

7.12 We observed in the introduction to this section that there are two equivalent measures of systematic risk, namely $\sigma_m^2\beta_i^2$ and $\sigma_i^2\rho_{im}^2$. Prove they are equivalent.

7.13 In discussing R^2 we considered its meaning. Prove, using $R_i^2 = (\sigma_m^2\beta_i^2)/\sigma_i^2$, that it can also be expressed as ρ_{im}^2. Discuss the meaning of this latter expression in relation to the meaning of R_i^2.

7.14 Here are two columns, the first containing security prices and the second, the all-share index.

Period	Share	Index
0	345	1,890
1	326	1,790
2	340	1,980
3	317	1,860
4	305	1,788
5	298	1,699
6	320	1,810

1. Calculate the return on each.
2. Create a scatter graph of the returns on each.
3. Regress the security price on the index, thus finding the beta of the security.
4. What is its alpha?
5. How might you interpret the meaning of such an alpha?

7.15 The unique risk of Belladonna plc is 13%. If the correlation coefficient between Belladonna and the market index is 0.346, what is the total risk of the share?

7.16 Hengist plc and Horsa plc merge. Hengist had just one activity, and was ungeared. Its beta was 0.85. Horsa had equity with a market value of £8m together with £3m debt. Its equity beta was 1.3. If the debt of the merged company is still £3m, and Hengist was twice the size of Horsa, what would you expect the beta of the assets of the merged company to be?

Further problems
Note: No answers are given for the following questions.

7.17 Kernel plc has two divisions. Division X is 20% bigger than division Y, but has a beta 30% lower. The market value of its equity is twice the market value of its debt. If the beta of division X is 0.9, and the beta of the debt is 0.1, what is the beta of the equity?

7.18 The current average rate of return on risky securities is 18%, which is 7% greater than the risk-free rate on short-dated stocks. The market standard deviation is 12%. Wotan plc correlates 0.4 with the market, and has a standard deviation of 26%. What would you expect its return to be?

W7.3   Answers to worked problems

(i) Answers to problems 7.1–7.3

7.1   1. By diversifying, the investor can attain a better return for a risky portfolio for the same risk at a point directly above point *A* that lies on the efficiency frontier at *E* (see Fig. W.7.2). This can be improved still further by investing in the total market portfolio and borrowing to lever the investment up. The appropriate level of borrowing will take the investor to point *F*.

   2. It is not possible to attain this point. It lies outside the feasible region of risky investments (that is, portfolios of risky securities that cán be combined in all possible ways) and cannot be achieved by mixing these with other risk-free assets since that must result in a linear combination which is, in fact, the CML.

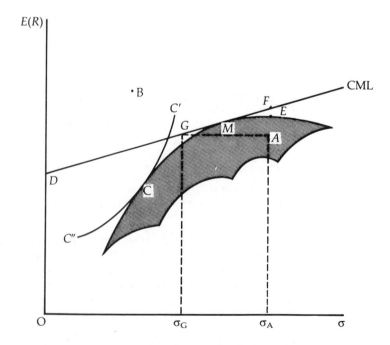

Figure W7.2   Answer to worked problem 7.1 (1.)

3. Although this is an optimum point for some investor(s) with in-difference curve *C'C''* (see Fig. W7.2) *if only risky investments are available*, this will not normally be the case and, as in 1. above, the situation can be improved by a movement up to the CML.
4. This could be an optimal strategy for the investor who wishes to take no risks at all. It is hence a perfectly feasible strategy.

7.2 The risk attaching to security A is composed of both unsystematic and systematic risk. The unsystematic risk can be diversified away by invest-ing in the market portfolio; by definition all that remains is the systematic risk. Hence the divergence of A from M is explained by the un-systematic risk. This can be generalized: *the reason every security in the feasible region is more risky than the corresponding point on the capital market line (cf. point A with point G where $\sigma_A > \sigma_G$) is that it includes some avoidable unsystematic risk.*

7.3 1. Unique risk.
2. Unique risk.
3. Probably both.
4. Mainly systematic risk, though if the controls took the form of specific restrictions on credit that affected the purchase of motor cars, it would affect unique risk too.
5. Systematic risk.
6. Both, though more systematic risk since there is no reason, given the political nature of oil prices, that the increase in the supply of oil should force the price down thus affecting the motor industry directly.
7. Unique risk.

In all the above, whether the discussion has been hedged around or not, it will always remain true that the socioeconomic structure is complex and highly interrelated, so that it will always be difficult to disentangle one effect from another.

(ii) Answers to problems 7.4–7.16
7.4 Up. If the beta were negative, it would slope downward to the right.

7.5 We would expect it to be linear. We have already established that, subject to a scale factor, beta is equivalent to covariance. Since covariance will be given for all values of the returns on the share and on the market, it follows that the slope of the curve (for that is what it is) must be constant. A constant slope for all values of the independent variable is, of course, a defining characteristic of a linear function.

7.6 It could be either. Consider the meaning of this intercept point. It is the expected return on the security when the expected return on the market is zero. Now for any set of observations, some securities will perform better than the market, others less well than the market. If market participants earn nothing in a particular year, then it would be expected *if the model held up for that period*, that holders of a share with a positive intercept would profit more than those holding the market portfolio. The converse would obviously be true if the intercept were at a negative return on the share.

7.7 Positive because, on the logic already discussed, for a positive beta we have a positive relationship between the share and the market. Hence if one goes up, the other will, and that means a positive gradient.

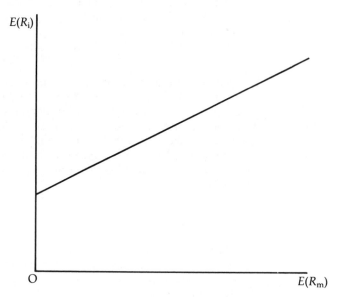

Figure W7.3   Answer to worked problem 7.8.

7.8 A possible such sketch is given in Fig. W7.3.

7.9 No. There will always be a random error process at work, and so the individual observations will deviate from the line (called the 'characteristic line').

7.10 When the correlation coefficient is exactly unity. In all other cases there would be random variations about the regression line. Now you will know from your study of statistics that the correlation coefficient can be squared to obtain the coefficient of determination, or R^2. In regression terms, this represents the proportion of the variation in the dependent variable that is explained by the variation in the independent variable. Thus in the case we are looking at, the R^2 represents the proportion of the variance of the returns on the individual share that is explained by the variance of the market returns. For instance, if the correlation coefficient were 0.7, we would say that 49% of the variation in the share was explained by changes in the market. It is essential that the implications of this are not confused by the interpretation of beta. Beta tells us by how much we should expect the share price to move for a given movement in the market. On the other hand, R^2 tells us how reliable statistically the estimate of beta is. To put this another way: we may find R^2 for a share i as:

$$R^2 = 1 - \frac{\sum_i e_i^2}{\sum_i (y_i - \bar{y})^2}$$

so that it is a function of the error term e_i in the regression equation. Intuitively this should make sense: if the error term is zero, all observations lie exactly on the regression line, and from the expression $R^2 = 1$ (because substituting $\sum e_i^2 = 0$ makes the entire second part of the expression equal to zero). This ties in with our observation above in the first sentence of this answer.

7.11 Yes. However, there is now a danger of confusion in your mind between the line just discussed and the SML. They are not the same thing at all, and the three linear functions we have considered in this chapter — the CML, and SML and the characteristic line — must be clearly distinguished from one another. We described the CML–SML difference in the text (see pp. 170–7). The characteristic line relates the return on a share to the return on the market. That relationship — the coefficient of the independent variable which defines the slope of the curve — is beta. Beta is then graphed against the expected return of the share to give the SML. Hence the characteristic line relates to just one security and the market. The SML puts many shares' betas together to form a curve that describes different betas as they relate to different expected returns of different securities. Note, if this is still in any way confusing, that the axes for the SML and characteristic line are totally different, and that the *result* of the calculation of the characteristic line becomes data in forming the SML, then return to the text, p. 167, where the characteristic line is first introduced.

7.12
$$\sigma_m{}^2 \beta_i{}^2 = \sigma_m{}^2 \left[\frac{\sigma_{im}\ \sigma_{im}}{\sigma_m\ \sigma_m{}^2} \right] = \frac{\sigma_{im}{}^2}{\sigma_m{}^2} \qquad (i)$$

Now:

$$\rho_{im} = \frac{\sigma_{im}}{\sigma_i\ \sigma_m}$$

Thus:

$$\sigma_{im} = \rho_{im}\ v_i\ \sigma_m \qquad (ii)$$

Substituting (ii) in (i) we have:

$$\frac{\rho_{im}\ \sigma_i\sigma_m\ \rho_{im}\ \sigma_i\ \sigma_m}{\sigma_m{}^2} = \rho_{im}{}^2\sigma_i{}^2$$

7.13
$$\frac{\sigma_m{}^2 \beta_i{}^2}{\sigma_i{}^2} = \frac{\sigma_m{}^2}{\sigma_i{}^2} \left[\frac{\sigma_{im}{}^2}{\sigma_m{}^4} \right]$$

$$= \frac{\sigma_{im}{}^2}{\sigma_i{}^2\sigma_m{}^2} = \left[\frac{\sigma_{im}}{\sigma_i\sigma_m} \right]^2 = \rho_{im}{}^2$$

Correlation measures the extent to which two variables covary: that is, are similar in the direction and quantity of changes in their values. R^2 measures the extent to which the change in the dependent variable is explained by a change in the independent variable. Intuitively you would expect that, if two variables were more highly correlated, one would 'explain' the other better. The relationship we have demonstrated underscores this.

7.14 1. The returns are as follows:

Share returns	Index returns
−5.51	−5.29
4.29	10.61
−6.76	−6.06
−3.79	−3.87
−2.30	−4.98
7.38	6.53

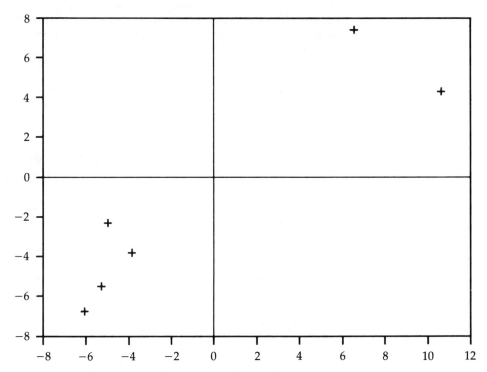

Figure W7.4 Graph plotted from worked problem 7.14.

2. See Fig. W7.4.
3. and 4. You may have to check out a statistics text if you are rusty on this. Alternatively, most spreadsheets have a regression function now, and this affords a good opportunity to practise work on a spreadsheet. The regression equation turns out to be

$$R_j = -0.745 + 0.723R_m$$

so that the alpha is −0.745 and the beta, 0.723.

Of course, the latter can be confirmed by calculating the covariance (31.11) and dividing by the variance of the market returns (43.03).

5. The meaning of alpha can be derived by looking at the graph. It is the return on the security that, on average, might be expected when the market as a whole is producing no return at all. On this particular share it is negative (i.e. on average one would make a loss on this share under those conditions).

7.15 We know from the text (section 7.5 (b)) that unique risk can be expressed as:

$$\sigma_i^2 - \sigma_m^2 \beta_i^2 \tag{i}$$

that is, as total risk less systematic risk. However, we already know that an alternative way to depict systematic risk is:

$$\sigma_i^2 \rho_{im} \tag{ii}$$

Substituting equation (ii) into equation (i) and bringing σ_i^2 out of the brackets gives unique risk (U) as:

$$U = \sigma_i^2 (1 - \rho_{im}^2)$$

Thus total risk σ_i^2 is:

$$U/(1 - \rho_{im}^2) = 0.13/1(1 - 0.346^2) = 0.148 \text{ or } 14.8\%$$

7.16 The asset beta of Horsa is found using the expression from the text:

$$\beta_A = \beta_E [E/T] + \beta_D [D/T]$$

where $T = E + D$. We must assume, in the absence of other information, that $\beta_D = 0$. This means the beta of the asset is:

$$1.3 [8/11] = 0.95$$

The asset beta of the merged company will be the linear combination of the asset betas of Hengist and Horsa weighted by their relative sizes, that is:

$$\beta_{Hengist} \times 2/3 + \beta_{Horsa} \times 1/3$$

that is:

$$0.85 \times 2/3 + 0.95 \times 1/3$$

which is 0.88.

W7.4 Discussion questions

Note: No suggestions are given in answer to the following questions.

7.1 Risk is dimided into two kinds: unsystematic risk and unique risk. True or false?

7.2 Why is it said that the market portfolio is not the set of securities that are available through a major stock exchange?

7.3 Why might we take short-dated government stocks as representing R_f as the risk-free rate instead of, say, long-term risk-free securities?

7.4 At times the market is more uncertain and volatile than at other times. Hence at these times investing in the market as a whole is more risky. The theory of CAPM states that beta is the significant risk measure. Does beta for the market change with market risk? In other words, if you chose to invest in the market as a whole, would your risk measure change under these circumstances? Explain and discuss the significance of your answer.

7.5 An investor who prefers higher risk will, according to CAPM, be sensible to develop a portfolio of high-beta securities. Does this square with

Chapter 6 where we argued that such a person moved higher along the capital market line?

W7.5   Reading: Bowater-Scott Corporation

The final item in this Workbook chapter is a study of the use of CAPM by a UK company, as a basis for estimating the hurdle rate for capital investment decisions (reproduced, with permission, from J. Sizer and N. Coulthurst, *A Casebook of British Management Accounting* (ICAEW, London, 1984).

BOWATER-SCOTT CORPORATION LTD
The use of the capital asset pricing model for developing hurdle rates for capital investment decisions in a jointly owned disposable paper products business.

1. INTRODUCTION
Bowater-Scott Corporation Limited was formed in 1956, a joint venture between Bowater Corporation Limited and Scott Paper Company of the USA, two of the world's largest paper manufacturers.

Bowater-Scott manufactures and markets a wide range of disposable paper products in both the consumer and away-from-home markets. It is the market leader in many of the market segments in which it is represented, including the £200 million per annum toilet tissue market, where its flagship brand, Andrex, outsells its nearest rival by 3:1.

The Company has two main production sites, at Barrow-in-Furness, the largest tissue manufacturing complex in Europe and at Northfleet, Kent. From these locations Bowater-Scott supplies over one third of the UK soft tissue requirement. Bowater-Scott employs some 3,500 people, with a turnover in excess of £160 million. It operates in a highly capital intensive industry, where a single capacity step costs in the region of £20 million.

Making the right investment decisions is therefore vital for Bowater-Scott and in 1982 a working party, with members drawn from both Financial and Marketing disciplines, was formed to update its method of Capital Appraisal. This case study is drawn from their findings.

2. THE PURPOSE OF THE CASE STUDY
The key to satisfying a company's investors is the setting and achievement of appropriate financial returns for the company as a whole and for its constituent parts.

If a company has set its targets too low it may have undertaken considerable capital investment which may not satisfy its investors' expectations. Earnings may not be high enough to cover interest payments and/or give an adequate return on equity shareholders' investment. The banks will call for guarantees and eventually refuse to lend any more. The shareholders may not wish to invest any more funds when they are already achieving an inadequate return upon their present funds. The business may contract, not be able to afford essential capital expenditures, and finally, may be taken over by someone else or closed down.

If a company sets its targets too high it may turn down potentially profitable business ventures, growth might be stifled and contraction in the business may take place. It may be the case that it is satisfying its investors, however, it will certainly not be maximising its potential earnings.

In both situations of course much depends upon investments turning out as planned.

The purpose of this case study is to describe the approach that has been taken within Bowater-Scott to establish the company's cost of capital and further establish financial criteria for the assessment of the viability of individual capital investment projects, taking into account the relative risks of such projects.

3. DESCRIPTION OF THE SYSTEM

3 a) Determining the Average Cost of Capital

3 a) i) *Introduction:* It is important to stress at the outset that determination of the Cost of Capital for a jointly owned company such as Bowater-Scott is an especially difficult problem, because of the unavailability of market information on investors' attitudes to the company. Nevertheless the Company has attempted to use the Capital Asset Pricing Model in order to estimate the cost of equity capital. This is then weighted with the cost of debt capital according to the finance mix, in order to determine an average cost of capital for the company.

3 a) ii) *The Capital Asset Pricing Model:* The basis of this model is that the Stock Exchange is the 'market' for risky assets and that the pricing mechanism for these assets takes account of both Risk and Expected Returns.

The Capital Asset Pricing Model indicates that this relationship between Risk and Return is composed of two parts: a *Risk Free Rate*, which represents a fixed minimum level of return to investors, and a *Premium*, which is proportional to the level of risk associated with one particular investment. This can be expressed as follows:

$$\text{Cost of Equity Capital (\%)} = \text{Long term Risk Free Interest Rate (\%)} + \left(\text{Risk Premium on shares in General (\%)} \times \text{Variability of the Company's return in relation to the Stock Market as a whole [factor of 1]} \right)$$

The risk free rate is taken to be the rate of interest available from Government Securities. As can be seen from the above formula the risk premium is a function of the *average* premium available from quoted shares and the *relative* riskiness of the share in comparison with the average of the stock market. The higher the risk the higher the premium [see Fig. W7.5].

The company regards this as a commonsense approach. If an investor does not wish to take any risk, he can invest in 'Gilts' and obtain the prevailing interest rate (X). For an average risk investment (Y) — such as a widely based investment trust — he will expect average returns, and for any other degree of riskiness, according to the nature of the investment made, a relatively higher or lower return than average will be required. The relative riskiness (termed Beta) of any quoted company can be found from a variety of specialist reports and that for a private company, subsidiary or business unit, by comparison with similar quoted companies in the appropriate business sector.

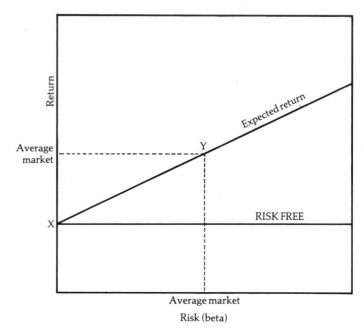

Figure W7.5

3 a) iii) *The Cost of Equity Capital:* Bowater-Scott, in their exercise to determine an appropriate cost of equity capital using the capital asset pricing model, took as the risk free rate, the long term treasury bill rate (in 1982 this was 12% representing a real return of 2–3%). The average risk premium as measured by the London Business School from work on the London Stock Exchange (1970–1981) was 9.6% after tax. The risk premium for the individual company will depend upon the riskiness of the returns of that company in relation to the market average.

The average market Beta is defined as 1.0; both Bowater and Scott were regarded as riskier than average with Betas of 1.1. Comparable industry groupings were in the range 1.1 to 0.9 and given the narrowness of Bowater-Scott's product range and geographic dependence its Beta was taken as 1.1.

Putting these figures into the capital asset pricing model equation produced the following result:

$$(12 \times 0.7^*) + (9.6 \times 1.1) = 19\%$$
* Personal Tax rate

3 a) iv) *The Cost of Debt Capital:* The cost of debt capital depends upon expectations of interest rates (affected amongst other things by future inflation) and tax allowances. It is outside the scope of this case study to detail the Company's expectations in this respect.

3 a) v) *The Weighted Average Money Cost of Capital:* Once the costs of equity and debt capital had been separately determined these were then weighted according to the proportions of equity and debt capital used in

the finance mix. The Company's policy regarding optimum capital structure is also outside the scope of this case study.

For the sake of illustration, an equity/debt ratio of 80/20 and an after tax money cost of debt capital of 8% will be assumed. The weighted average money cost of capital thus becomes:

Equity	80% × 19% =	15.2%
Debt	20% × 8% =	1.6%
		16.8% (say 17%)

3 b) Different Rates for Different Projects

3 b) i) *Rationale:* In capital investment appraisal within Bowater-Scott the financial worth of a project is measured by comparing the Internal Rate of Return (IRR) of its net cash flows with a hurdle rate derived from the company cost of capital. In order to determine Bowater-Scott's cost of capital the Capital Asset Pricing Model was used as illustrated above in order to determine a cost of equity capital and was combined with the cost of debt capital according to the company's gearing ratio. This represented a starting point for the establishment of hurdle rates for appraising individual projects, taking into account their relative risks. Just as shareholders expect different rates of return for companies with different degrees of risk, Bowater-Scott considers it reasonable for management to use different hurdle rates for projects with different risk characteristics. The logic of this argument can be demonstrated by the following example [see Fig. W7.6].

With a single hurdle rate, project A, with an expected return below the hurdle rate, will be rejected and B accepted. However A is a low risk project whose return is in excess of that normally demanded for a share

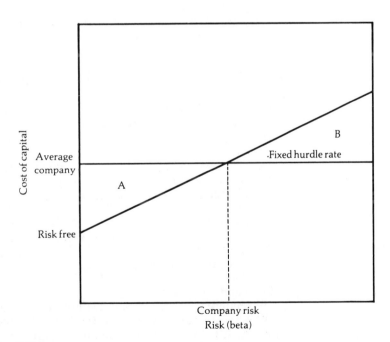

Figure W7.6

of equivalent risk, whilst B's return would not be considered high enough to compensate for its higher risk. The use of a single hurdle rate will therefore tend to reject low risk 'bread and butter' cost-saving projects and accept high risk, perhaps speculative ventures. Over a period of time this may:

a) Increase the riskiness of the company, and therefore its cost of capital, without a commensurate increase in the rate of return.
b) By neglecting cost-saving projects, harm the overall competitive position of the core business.

For these reasons the Company determined to adopt a range of hurdle rates which would reflect the intrinsic risk of the project being appraised. The problem then was how to estimate the riskiness of individual projects. To obtain risk-adjusted rates of return from the Capital Asset Pricing Model, one needs some measure of relative riskiness. Estimates of company risk can be obtained from statistical studies of the Stock Exchange, which are updated on a regular basis by a number of institutions. When estimating the project hurdle rates, however, measures of riskiness are more difficult to obtain as there is no 'market' for individual projects and hence no readily available source of risk measurement. To estimate project risk, therefore, one must apply an understanding of the nature and causation of risk to the characteristics of the project in question.

3 b) ii) *The Nature of Project Risk:* Risk means that more things *can* happen, than will happen. In other words, if only one result is possible, there can be no risk, the outcome is certain. Risk, then, involves uncertainty, the variability of possible outcomes, and the wider the range of these outcomes, the higher the degree of risk.

The outcome of a capital project is defined in terms of its cash flows. These can be separated into two major categories, each subject to differing degrees of uncertainty:

Fixed Cash Flows
Those that reasonably can be expected to occur if the project goes ahead, i.e.:
  Initial capital expenditure
  Working capital for a product launch
  Test market expenses
  Incremental overheads
  1st year advertising and promotional expenditure
  Tax allowances/charges associated with the above
These tend to occur at the beginning of a project.

Variable Cost Flows
Those that are subject to some uncertainty as to their size, timing, duration or even occurrence, i.e.:
  Scale of Cost Savings
  Volumes
  Price and Cost Levels
  Subsequent advertising and promotional expenditure
  Tax allowances/charges associated with the above
These tend to occur later in the life of a project.
  The variability of a project will therefore depend upon both the

proportion of the cash flow that is reasonably certain — Operational Gearing — and the potential volatility of the remaining variable flows — Revenue Sensitivity.

3) b) iii) *Operational Gearing:* Basically an extension of break-even analysis, this uses Net Present Values (NPVs) instead of profit and loss, in order to adjust for timing differences. It is calculated by simply dividing the variable cash flow by the sum of the fixed and variable flows.

$$OG = \frac{V}{V + F}$$

This measure is based on the concept that the larger the proportion of fixed cash flows the higher the risk of the project.

For instance, as illustrated in Appendix 1, a project with twice as much variable flows as fixed — Operational Gearing of 2 — could suffer a 50% reduction in its variable flows and still break-even. A similar reduction to a project with a ratio of $1\frac{1}{2}$:1 — Operating Gearing of 3 — would result in a 50% loss.

3 b) iv) *Revenue Sensitivity:* This is a measure of the likelihood of the variable cash flows being materially different from those forecast.

Unfortunately, unlike Operational Gearing, *there is no simple method for quantifying Revenue Sensitivity.* Statistical techniques — such as regression analysis — might be applicable for those projects where reliable historical data is available. However the time and cost involved in data collection and processing would be prohibitive for all but the largest projects. In addition, such techniques can only reflect historic relationships, thus ignoring the vital element of future uncertainty.

Management must therefore make qualitative decisions about the uncertainty of the variable cash flows. This requires the identification of those factors which are critical to their size and timing, e.g.:

Unit revenue — Cost levels
              — Efficiencies
              — Competitive pricing
Unit volume — Market Size — Consumer spending
                        — Substitute products
                        — Growth rate
              — Market Share — Success of marketing platform
              — Nature of Cost Savings — Fixed/Variable

(Note: it will be appreciated that many of these factors are inter-related.)

In general:

Volume adding projects tend to have a higher revenue sensitivity than cost saving ones.
New products tend to have a higher revenue sensitivity than existing ones.
Premium products tend to have a higher revenue sensitivity than price brands/own label.
Luxury goods tend to have a higher revenue sensitivity than essentials.

However, the *Revenue Sensitivities of projects must be judged on their individual characteristics, not 'rules of thumb',* (see Appendix 3 for examples). It is vital that these judgements are made in a disciplined and systematic manner. A checklist, covering the more important factors, has been issued in order to assist in this process.

The judgemental nature of this approach should not be regarded as a drawback; the process of forecasting is itself very subjective. One of the major advantages of this measure is the way in which it focuses management attention upon the critical issues.

3 b) v) *The Project Hurdle Rate:* To adjust a project's hurdle rate for its intrinsic risk, an estimate of that risk is required. It has been demonstrated that project risk is dependent upon both the relationship between the fixed and variable cash flows and the uncertainty associated with the variable flows.

Project Risk = Operational Gearing × Revenue Sensitivity

The Company recognised that if they could determine to what extent changes in the variable cash flows of the project would affect its outcome — Operational Gearing — and could estimate how variable those cash flows might be — Revenue Sensitivity — then they would have a measure that describes the total risk of the project (Appendix 2).

However, because there is no reliable method of *quantifying* Revenue Sensitivity this technique cannot provide an *absolute* value for project risk. But it is also true that the company Beta, or risk, is similarly a product of its own Operational Gearing and Revenue Sensitivity.

Company Risk = Co. Operational Gearing × Co. Revenue Sensitivity

Therefore the *absolute* level of project risk can be determined by reference to its *relative* Operational Gearing and Revenue Sensitivity, (in comparison to the average for Bowater-Scott).

$$\text{Project Risk} = \begin{matrix}\text{Relative}\\\text{Operational}\\\text{Gearing}\end{matrix} \times \begin{matrix}\text{Relative}\\\text{Revenue}\\\text{Sensitivity}\end{matrix} \times \text{Company Risk (Beta)}$$

Project and Company Operational Gearing can be easily calculated from the cash flows.

For Revenue Sensitivity it was decided that the following broad categories of variability should be used:

Category	Relative Revenue Sensitivity
Low	$\frac{1}{2}$
Medium	1
High	2
Very High	>2

The use of sensitivity and scenario analyses for key variables can provide a useful guide when determining the appropriate category. These bands of Revenue Sensitivity are consistent with the risk classifications of companies on the Stock Exchange.

3 b) vi) *Recommendations:* The following are the recommendations arising from one of the exercises regarding project hurdle rates carried out by the Working Party.

'Each project submitted for appraisal should be measured against a hurdle rate depending upon the risk characteristics of the project itself.

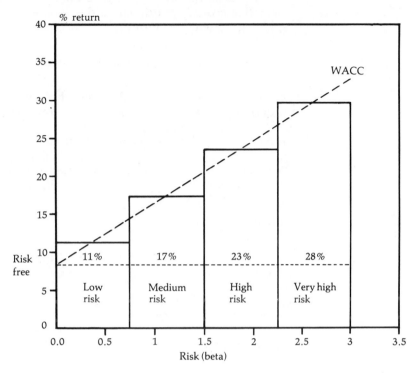

Figure W7.7

Risk matrix
Relative revenue sensitivity
(cf. average Bowater-Scott)

	Low ½ av B*S	Medium ½–1½ × av B*S	High 1½–2½ × av B*S	Very high 2½ × av B*S
Low ½ av B*S	Low risk 11%	Low risk 11%	Medium risk 17%	High risk 23%
Medium ½–1½ × av B*S	Low risk 11%	Medium 17%	High 23%	Very high risk 28%
High 1½–2½ ×av B*S	Medium risk 17%	High 23%	Too high? >34%	Too high? >34%
Very high 2½ × av B*S	High risk 23%	Very high risk 28%	Too high? >34%	Too high? >34%

Relative operational gearing

Figure W7.8

The project risk should be determined by calculating the relative Operational Gearing, estimating the relative Revenue Sensitivity and applying these to the formula:

$$\begin{array}{ccc}\text{Relative} & \text{Relative} & \text{Bowater} \\ \text{Project Risk} = \text{Operational} \times \text{Revenue} \times \text{Scott} \\ \text{Gearing} & \text{Sensitivity} & \text{Beta} \end{array}$$

The project hurdle rate should be found by reading the rate of return appropriate to the level of project risk, from the following chart [Fig. W7.7]. This should be compared with the most likely IRR of the project.

The risk matrix [Fig. W7.8] should be used by General Management as a guide to the range of hurdle rates that will be applied.

We believe that it is essential for Bowater-Scott to adopt a comprehensive Capital Appraisal System which explicitly recognises the relationship between risk and return.

APPENDIX 1

	Operational gearing	
	Project A NPV	Project B NPV
Fixed cash flows	100	200
Variable cash inflow/unit	4	4
Variable cash outflow/unit	2	1
Expected NPV	100	100
Operational gearing	2	3

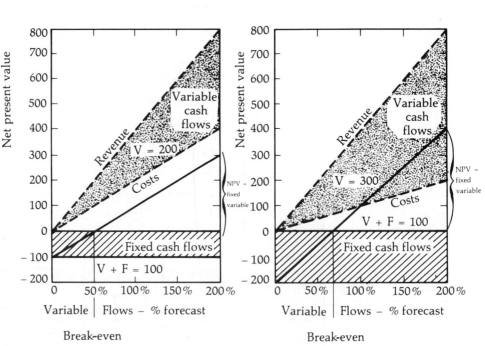

Variable cash flows % forecast		Range of NPVs
0	−100	−200
50%	0	−50
100%	100	100
150%	200	250
200%	300	400
Range	400	600

APPENDIX 2

From the example in Appendix 1, Project A appeared to be less risky than B, because of its lower Operational Gearing.

The effect of Revenue Sensitivity on project risk can be demonstrated by applying differing probabilities to the variable cash flows of the two projects.

% Achievement of forecast:−	Project A	Project B
	Probabilities	
Nil	0.1	
50%	0.2	0.15
100%	0.4	0.70
150%	0.2	0.15
200%	0.1	
Variability (s.d.)	0.35	0.27
Revenue sensitivity	2	1

Probability distribution of project N.P.Vs

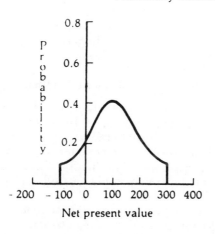

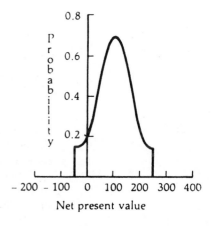

Variability (s.d.)   1.10   0.82

The risk-variability of project A is now $\frac{1}{3}$ greater than that of project B

$$\left(\frac{1.1}{0.82} \right)$$

This is exactly as predicted by the model,

$$\text{Risk A} = \text{OG(A)} \times \text{RS(A)}$$
$$\text{Risk B} = \text{OG(B)} \times \text{RS(B)}$$

$$\frac{\text{Risk A}}{\text{Risk B}} = \frac{\text{OG(A)}}{\text{OG(B)}} \times \frac{\text{RS(A)}}{\text{RS(B)}} \quad \left\{ \begin{array}{l} \text{Relative} \quad \text{Relative} \\ \text{Relative} = \text{Operational} \times \text{Revenue} \\ \quad \text{Risk} \qquad \text{Gearing} \qquad \text{Sensitivity} \end{array} \right\}$$

$$= \frac{2}{3} \times \frac{2}{1}$$

$$= \underline{\underline{1\frac{1}{3}}}$$

APPENDIX 3

Estimating Revenue Sensitivity

These simple examples may serve to illustrate the process of estimating relative Revenue Sensitivity.

1. *Fixed Cost Saving*

   e.g. EDP device to save clerical labour.

   The outcome of this type of project depends on two variables, the *real* cost of labour and the continuing need — without the project — of those clerical tasks.
      There must be a very low probability of the cost of labour inflating in a materially lower way than general product costs. If the clerical tasks are truly fixed, they will be unlikely to vary with small changes in the scale of the enterprise.
      A project in this category would therefore be regarded as one with a particularly low Revenue Sensitivity.

2. *Variable Cost Savings*

   e.g. Energy saving device for the most efficient paper machine.

   The benefits of this project again depend upon two variables, the *real* value and the expected duration of the savings.
      Energy costs are unlikely to reduce significantly in real terms, and the chances of the lower cost machine being surplus to requirements must be viewed as remote. Another low Revenue Sensitivity project.
      This does not, however, imply that all cost saving projects have low Revenue Sensitivities, i.e.:
   a) Energy saving device for the highest cost machine, which, after the saving, still remains the least efficient.
         Obviously, a much higher variability of earnings, as presumably, in times of low demand, this would be the first machine to close. Perhaps a medium classification.
   b) *A Dual Fired Boiler*
         Particularly sensitive to very small differences in the inflation rates

of the alternative fuels — a cost saving project with high Revenue Sensitivity.

c) *Packaging Savings*

The scale of these savings will depend very much upon product volumes. Depending on the stability of the product concerned, a medium to high Revenue Sensitivity project.

3. *Volume Adding Projects*

e.g. Launch of new Premium Grocery Product.

The variable cash flows of this type of project are dependent upon a far larger number of factors; i.e.:–
a) Differences between product cost and price inflation.
b) Changes in Market size.
c) Changes in Market share.
d) Changes in Market Growth Rate.

Changes in the economy are likely to be particularly important to this type of project, i.e.:

Changes in Real Disposable Income — this may affect the extent to which product cost inflation can be reflected in the price.

Changes to the Real Price (vs RSP) — likely to cause fluctuations in the size of the premium sector in particular and the market size in general.

The existence of substitute products could exaggerate this sensitivity and the possibility of the presence of next generations products in the future may threaten the premium positioning.

In addition, if there is no sustainable competitive advantage — such as patentable technology — there is a significant possibility of strong branded or Own Label competition, affecting product pricing, marketing spends and/or market share.

In view of all these factors, this type of project would be regarded as one with either high or very high Revenue Sensitivity.

8 Medium- and long-term financing

Learning objectives

The aims of this chapter are to:

- demonstrate the rather artificial distinction that exists between short- and long-term financing;
- explain how medium- and long-term funds can be raised from both *internal* and *external* sources, and recognize that differences exist in the financing decision between 'small' and 'large' firms;
- outline the sources of medium- and long-term finance;
- explain the characteristics of company securities – corporate debt (including convertibles), preference shares and ordinary shares;
- explain the methods of raising ordinary share finance and appreciate the difficulty of pricing new share issues;
- indicate the mechanics of the pricing of pre-emptive rights;
- discuss the problems that may arise in the provision of finance for new businesses;
- explain the nature of interest rate and currency swaps.

W8.1 Introduction

We shall use this Workbook chapter to do two basic things: first to summarize and expand on certain areas of the text, and second to provide some discussion questions.

This chapter and the one that follows examine the borrowing decisions of the enterprise. These decisions cannot be divorced from the capital requirements of the enterprise as discussed in Chapter 1, which include the decisions on capital structure (Chapter 11) and dividend policy (Chapter 10). The fact that the borrowing takes place in financial markets adds further dimensions to the supply of this borrowing, its price and other features, including the denomination of the currency. In this chapter we examine the medium- and long-term borrowing of business enterprises mainly through the provision of instruments that are available. In Chapter 9 we examine some of the borrowing strategies of business enterprises.

It is apparent from the outset in the chapter that we find it difficult to time-date borrowing. We take the stance, following the Bank of England, that up to three years is short, three to ten years is medium and over ten years is long, but this still is an arbitrary distinction and you can find short defined as up to 18 months, medium up to 15 years and so on. The issue of time *per se* is not really of that much importance in the sense that enterprises now are footloose across time maturities, so there is no definite segmentation and no need to be that specific about the time. Rather we can think of 'short' and 'medium' and 'long' in the context of areas along the maturity spectrum of debt. Floating rates on a longer-term loan make it essentially a series of short-term loans, and swaps can permit firms the opportunity to switch when the need arises.

The division between the internal and external finance of enterprises has been a thorny issue for a long time. The ability to raise funds from outside the enterprise has existed for centuries. However, the apparent lack of provision of finance for small companies was first recognized in the Macmillan Report of 1931 and raised again in the more recent Wilson Committee Report of 1980. This apparent shortage of funds for small business is not shared by all concerned as there have been many attempts to make more provision, particularly with the growth of specialist financial institutions and venture capital, management buy-outs, etc. It is a matter of degree – how small is small? Are we talking about start-up capital or small unquoted or quoted companies? In the text we refer to the Meeks and Whittington study (1976) and the importance of external finance in the growth of companies, so clearly there would not appear to be a shortage there. So what we are saying is that the issue is not resolved.

In the first edition of this book it was clear that, in the aggregate, enterprises relied on internal sources for around 70% of finance, though it varied, as we might expect since earnings themselves will vary. Whether this reliance was completely out of choice or forced by market factors we could not generalize on. However, the most recent data to 1989 paint a rather different picture, with some overall increase in capital issues and a significant increase in bank borrowing – in 1989 accounting for 38% of identified sources of funds. On the issue of size, it is worth noting that the Department of Trade and Industry does make available data on the 'large' industrial and commercial companies which can in part give a better picture of their current assets and liabilities and how they might differ from the smaller companies. Data on the liquidity of large firms are to be found in *Financial Statistics*, table 8.6. A further point on the issue of large *vis-à-vis* small is relevant here. In the 1985–9 period, £16.7 billion were raised in the 15 privatizations, which represented 71% of all sums raised by initial offers. Many of these were large issues and have resulted in a shift in the composition of the private company sector towards a greater dominance of large firms as measured by capital employed. There are important public policy issues that arise in this context, but these are not in the domain of this book.

W8.2   Medium-term financing

The point is made in the chapter that we are concerned with two main sources of medium-term credit – *banks* and other specialist brokers which provide various kinds of credit principally in the form of a *term loan*; and *leasing* and institutional credit. Let us take these in order.

(a) Term credit

Term credit can be at fixed or variable rates and really the question is, who wants to take the interest rate risk? A fixed rate prevents the downside risk of an upward movement in rates, but of course borrowers cannot benefit from the upside potential of a fall in rates. This is the whole essence of a hedged position on rates – hedging is against profit and loss. The reasoning for a term loan is to give stability to the source of credit so it can be matched (hedged) against the life of the assets acquired. These could be plant and machinery or 'permanent' working capital. In Chapter 9 we shall see how the use of short-term finance in these cases involves the rolling forward of credits, and there are associated risks involved in this. Term loans thus give a safety-first position, and if complete safety is required, the borrower can attempt to secure a fixed rate.

(b) Leasing

Lease financing developed as an important form of finance after the 1970–2 changes in the tax regime of investment, where there was a switch from grants to tax allowances. In the latter case those enterprises with taxable profits could deduct 100% of most capital investment in the year in which it occurred. In the case of enterprises formed without sufficient taxable profits, their investment was no longer subsidized. However, these changes assisted the leasing industry in two major respects:

1. the leasing company, provided it had taxable profits, could claim the 100% offset and share it with the lessee who had not sufficient profits itself;
2. the benefits of tax allowances are only felt after the year end, so purchases made early in the year have to wait for up to a year. By employing subsidiaries with various year ends, leasing could circumvent this and offer a lease not only to those in 1. above, but to any enterprise. To the latter it would have the advantage of bringing the shared benefit of the allowance forward.

The growth has been quite dramatic and the data given below reveal this to the extent that, by 1984, financial leases alone accounted for about 10% of total investment. However, just as one tax regime provides the impetus for growth, so another is likely to cause a diminution in its growth and importance. In 1984 the government announced budget changes which reduced the corporation tax rate from 52% to 35%, and the 100% first year tax allowance was replaced by a 25% writing-down allowance (that is, the allowance was spread over a number of years instead of all being deducted from taxable profit at once).

In this chapter we examine leasing as a source of finance and we make the distinction between operating leases and financial leases (full pay-out leases). The *operating lease* is generally short term and is suitable for a range of assets where ownership is not required or an advantage. Such leases are generally quite expensive, but they are cancellable and free working capital that can be used elsewhere in the business. They can free other resources too, e.g. labour (as the equipment often carries a maintenance contract). They thus impart greater flexibility to the enterprise. But the loss of ownership means that any tax advantage that ownership would bring is lost to the enterprise. This is true for the *financial lease* too. The latter can be regarded as a straight substitute for a medium-term loan in that it is not cancellable and the lessee is normally responsible for maintenance. Financial leases are referred to as *full pay-out leases* as the lessor expects to recover the cost of the purchases of the asset from the lessee and make a profit. The period over which this is achieved is often referred to as the primary period of the lease. Once it is past the lessee can generally then rent the equipment at a lower cost for an indefinite period. The length of this primary period will obviously be a function of the economic life of the asset as well as the negotiation between the two parties. The source of the lease finance lies with finance houses and specialist finance leasing subsidiaries or associates within the monetary sector.

The Bank of England now publishes data on leasing in addition to the *British Business* data published by the Department of Trade and Industry. What these data reveal is that the greater part of the expenditure on capital assets is leased out under financial leases. Apart from leases, enterprises can also enter into instalment credit arrangements such as hire-purchase to acquire the asset.

The whole area of leasing is an important growth area with many ramifications for the enterprise. We touch on some of these in the chapter. We can summarize these again:

1. What impact do leases have with respect to financial reporting?
2. What impact do they have on other claimants to the enterprise – bondholders, debtors, etc.?

As leases are a fixed charge and we have argued that they are really a substitute for medium-term capital, they add to the leverage of the enterprise. As some leases can be long term – where there is a sale and leaseback involved – then once more they add to the long-term leverage of the enterprise, with the implications we shall discuss in Chapter 11 (see also Myers *et al.*, 1976; Franks and Hodges, 1978). However, it would appear that the market views these implications differently, as at times leasing can avoid the capital rationing problem (see Fawthorpe and Terry, 1976).

W8.3   Long-term financing

When one thinks of long-term financing, generally one thinks of issued securities. Increasingly banks and other lenders have entered the market to lend to the corporate sector with long-term loans at both fixed but more generally floating rates. The data given in the text show how successful they have been. However, one issue which is raised, albeit briefly, in the text of the chapter is that of *securitization*. Bank lending is balance-sheet intensive to banks and is an incentive for banks to arrange loans (with the issue of asset-backed securities) between borrowers and lenders direct and collect a fee for service. The other parties can benefit in the process too, as borrowers and lenders can share in the intermediary margin previously earned by the bank, which is the difference between borrowing and lending rates. Banks increasingly, particularly abroad, have been 'selling off' some of their existing loan portfolios to investors. This is in terms not just of Third World debt, but of other loans, particularly household. This trend to a greater market presence in the financing of firms is likely to continue as financial markets become increasingly integrated. The first signs of this are now apparent in the UK and continental Europe.

What this section does is to provide a brief overview of the sources of long-term capital which also extend to that provided by government and supra-government agencies. The main focus is on company securities and the issue of term loans from banks and others. (The associated risk is picked up in

Chapter 9). One issue that is raised is that of rights issues, and section W8.4 does cover this in more detail. We can expand on the nature of rights issues as attention has focused on them in terms of the trends that have occurred in the past decade. We argued in the text that they dominate the issue of new ordinary shares and reference to Table 8.2 confirms this. Yet as we can see in Table W8.1, the dominance is less pronounced expressed as a percentage of *net* issues.

Table W8.1   Rights issues 1981–1989

	Rights as a % of net issues of ordinary shares	Rights as a % of net issues of listed public companies
1981	98.6	98.7
1982	74.5	61.6
1983	93.0	75.7
1984	89.2	73.7
1985	93.3	78.0
1986	74.2	66.4
1987	70.2	68.1
1988	95.2	73.3
1989	117.9	62.8

However, we can cite an article by Wolff (1986) in this context. It is difficult to relate fully the data he gives with what we represent in Table 8.2 in the text as his data are not for calendar years. Nevertheless, we give his in Table W8.2 and attempt a synthesis.

The data are all from issues of UK seasoned (therefore listed) companies for 1983–4. An examination of the data reveals that they can fit into the data series given in the text (see p. 200) and that they give a more complete picture of the trends that are occurring. What they show is that the rights issue is declining. This matter has aroused considerable debate, particularly in the financial press. The debate centres around whether shareholders perceive rights as a fair means of raising new capital or whether the alternatives of placing – as they can offer lower transaction costs and speed of issue – are better for the shareholder. These issues are addressed in later sections, in particular in section W8.4.

Table W8.2   Cash proceeds from various categories of seasonal equity issues by UK companies, October 1983–September 1984

	Proceeds £	% of total proceeds	Number of issues	Average proceeds £
Rights issues	1,343.6	61.8	93	14.4
Vendor placings	394.4	18.1	101	3.9
Placings and offers	200.7	9.2	26	7.7
Employee share plans and other issues	236.4	10.9	n.a.	n.a.
Total	2,175.1	100.0		

Source: Wolff, 1986.

W8.4   Characteristics of company securities

This section goes into more detail about the nature of the various financial claims, which are taken in the order they are treated in the text.

(a) Bonds

This is the generic term for long-term fixed interest corporate securities. Unlike government bonds, they are subject to *default risk* and one aspect of the chapter examines how to measure this risk. The point is made that in North America there are bond-rating services which remove the need of investors to do it themselves. Of course, these are not perfect predictors and investors may still feel the need to do some of the work themselves, but generally this is not necessary. So there is a great saving in transaction costs of time to investors. As these services continually monitor bond issues and reassess the risk, major shifts are reported in the financial press and the information becomes public very quickly. We give in Table W8.3 a typical bond-rating category used in the USA.

Unfortunately this is not done in the United Kingdom and it is not the investor who is the only loser. The rating can help the enterprise that is making the issue price its bond more accurately. Of course, there are negative features for enterprises too, in that no enterprise likes to be downgraded as it will raise its borrowing costs next time around.

Table W8.3   Bond rating categories

Moody's	Standard & Poor's	Description
Aaa	AAA	Highest rating – has extremely strong capacity to pay principal and interest.
Aa	AA	High grade – has a strong capacity to pay principal and interest, but lower protection margins than Aaa and AAA.
A	A	Upper medium grade – has many favourable investment attributes, but may be vulnerable to adverse economic conditions.
Baa	BBB	Medium grade – generally adequate capacity to pay interest and principal coupled with a significant vulnerability to adverse economic conditions.
Ba	BB	Somewhat speculative – has only moderate protection during both good and bad times.
B	B	Speculative – generally lacks characteristics of other desirable investments. Interest and principal payments over any long period of time are not safe.
Caa	CCC	Poor quality – in danger of default.
Ca	CC	Highly speculative – often in default.
C		The lowest rated class of bonds – extremely poor prospects.
	C	Income bonds on which no interest is being paid.
	D	Issues in default with principal and/or interest payments in arrears.

Source: Adapted from *Bond Guide* (Standard & Poor's Corporation); *Bond Record* (Moody's Investor Services). Used with permission.

Some bonds are secured on the assets of the enterprise; others are not, but stand before the claims of preference and ordinary shareholders. The trust deed mentioned in the text (see p. 201) can give a lot of additional security to the bond-holders. It can set limits to the debt incurred by the enterprise in terms of interest cover, it can set restrictions on major asset disposals and it can limit the use of non-mortgaged assets as security for further loans. If the debenture has a floating charge, it can specify minimum levels of investing and place restrictions on factoring accounts receivable. Even if the bond is secured, an agency problem exists. Bond-holders have to take account of what the enterprise is up to in its financial management policy. For example, its dividend policy, as this chapter points out (and which is developed further in Chapter 10), represents a dispersal of collateral. Bond-holders presumably would prefer higher retention as the assets acquired by these funds can be liquidated and the proceeds paid to bond-holders if the need arises. On capital structure decisions (Chapter 11) too, the bond-holders cannot stand idly by. The tax shield available on debt may encourage high debt levels with increased risk of bankruptcy in which the bond-holders can stand to suffer. In addition, as more and more debt is issued, there is the question of how this affects the *original* bond-holders, who may have security provisions built into their bonds, yet still might feel an increased risk exposure. They will face a capital loss as the price rises and a net benefit from the increase in yield.

As well as the issue of default risk, which will be handled in terms of a risk premium on the yield compared to default-free government bonds, there are a lot of other interesting aspects of corporate bonds. The point is made that they are generally shorter in term. One of the reasons for this is that they lack marketability and therefore are often bought to hold to maturity. There is some turnover in them, but the market is not a fat one, particularly once the term shortens. Institutional investors such as pension funds and life insurance companies prefer the longer-dated issues.

Corporate bonds can possess special features that are not as prevalent in government bonds, such as call features and sinking funds. But one particularly interesting feature is the convertibility available with some bonds. What we have is a hybrid bond with an option added to the baseline fixed interest element. This aspect is developed in sub-section (b) below, and the whole issue of option pricing implied there is developed later in section W8.5. A good example of the use of convertibles to lower an enterprise's cost of capital was Woolworth. In May 1985 it issued a convertible loan stock on a rights issue with an 8% coupon. This compared with a $12\frac{3}{4}$% bond base rate and $11\frac{1}{2}$% equivalent loan stock redemption yields!

(b) Valuation of convertible bonds

If we take a convertible bond with a conversion price to equity of £10 per share with a par value of £100, the *conversion ratio* is 10, i.e. each bond can be converted to ten shares. As this bond is a hybrid, the bond has a baseline value – that of the identical coupon bond without this conversion feature *plus* the value of the option to convert. Following the formula from the text for a bond (see p. 100), with a 10% coupon and a 20-year life and a yield to maturity of 12%, the bond will sell for £85.06:

$$P = \frac{10}{(1.12)} + \frac{10}{(1.12)^2} + \ldots + \frac{110}{(1.12)^{20}}$$

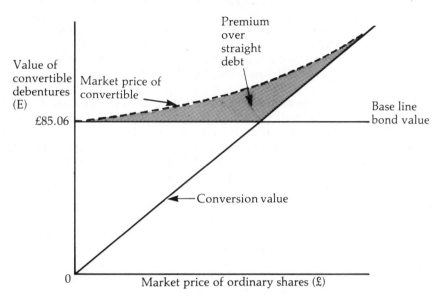

Figure W8.1   Convertible security price determinants.

The £100 is an annuity, so from the present value tables we would have 10(7.469), and the £100 is discounted with a factor of 0.1037, giving a total value of £85.06.

This is the baseline price of the bond, and if it sells for more then we are pricing the conversion option for a given yield. If the yield changes, say, to 13%, the price will move down and vice versa. That itself has a particular valuation approach.

Conversion value = Conversion ratio × Market price of the share

So as we know, the conversion ratio is 10, and if we assume a current market price of £11 then the conversion value = 10 × 11 = £110. If the market price of the share is £8 then the bond can still sell for £85.06 plus whatever speculative premium someone is willing to pay. If the price is £15 the value will be £150, and so on. The relationship of the bond-due plus the option is shown diagrammatically in Fig. W8.1.

Convertibles usually sell at prices higher than either the baseline bond value or the conversion value, as follows.

(i) Premium over bond value
We can see from Fig. W8.1 that, when the market price of the share is quite low relative to the conversion price, the premium over the bond is quite small. As the market price rises, the premium rises too, until it becomes quite large. Investors are willing to pay this based on the upside potential they see associated with the growth of the share price.

(ii) Premium over conversion price
The conversion premium (i.e. the amount the market price exceeds the conversion value) is high when the share price is low because the bond has a built-in downside protection. It cannot decline below the value of an

equivalent straight bond. However, you have to remember that, as we have indicated earlier, these bond prices are themselves subject to change as interest rates change. Returning to the case in hand of the conversion premium, as the stock price rises, the premium decreases until it disappears as conversion is about to be forced. (For further reading on the issue of premiums, see Jennings, 1974.)

Another hybrid is a *warrant*. This does not raise funds for the enterprise as such, but is usually used as a sweetener with a debt (or preference share) issue. A warrant is a long-term option on the ordinary shares, giving the right to purchase at a given price within a particular time span of years. Through time warrants are detachable and can be traded.

On the sinking funds provision, the idea is a reasonable one as it is really like a mortgage which is amortized over its life. The text argues that the security this gives to the investor is bought from the enterprise in terms of its having continually to find the principal payments. If the fund is one that builds up by compound interest to repay the issue at its maturity date, this can be one aspect of the security given to investors if the principal repayment is used to redeem the bonds. This may or may not be attractive. If the trustee enters the market and purchases, this gives some liquidity to holders as there will be a market in the bonds. But if there is retiring of bonds by ballot, then bond-holders may be less inclined to view this as a positive feature as they may be forced to sell.

The data given in Table 8.2 on the net issues show that debt is still a lot smaller than shares as a source of finance, but the growth of *leveraged buy-outs* has seen a great increase in debt in particular companies (though the debt used is generally not issued capital, but long-term loans). These buy-outs have started to become popular in Britain, having really caught on in the

Table W8.4 Type and currency structure of international bond issues ($US bn)

	Announced gross new issues				Net new issues				Stocks at end
	1986	1987	1988	1989	1986	1987	1988	1989	1989
Straight fixed rate issues	147.4	121.3	161.3	150.1	108.6	68.9	99.4	89.0	864.0
of which: US dollar	67.3	29.8	47.3	54.5	45.9	10.7	26.6	25.9	307.6
Japanese yen	21.4	21.9	19.0	22.3	18.9	18.4	11.9	14.5	125.0
Swiss franc	16.8	16.8	18.5	5.7	11.0	2.0	1.1	−3.9	97.7
Deutsche Mark	11.9	12.9	21.2	9.4	7.3	1.5	14.0	6.2	96.8
Ecu[a]	5.7	7.2	10.8	11.7	4.7	7.2	9.5	7.4	51.4
Pound sterling	5.4	9.2	11.7	12.1	4.9	8.2	10.4	11.0	46.2
Other	18.9	23.5	32.8	34.4	15.9	20.9	25.9	27.9	139.3
Floating rate notes	47.7	12.1	22.6	23.4	28.7	0.6	3.6	7.8	164.5
of which: US dollar	38.2	3.9	6.6	8.1	19.0	−7.1	−10.2	−1.6	106.5
Pound sterling	5.4	2.2	10.2	7.3	5.5	2.2	8.7	5.4	27.8
Other	4.1	6.0	5.8	8.0	4.2	5.5	5.1	4.0	30.2
Equity-related issues	27.4	43.7	42.1	85.2	22.4	38.3	34.1	74.7	223.8
of which: US dollar	16.8	29.5	29.0	65.1	14.1	26.1	26.2	60.4	153.6
Swiss franc	6.0	7.1	8.3	13.6	4.5	5.4	4.3	8.8	42.0
Other	4.6	7.1	4.8	6.5	3.8	6.8	3.6	5.5	28.2

Note: [a] Excluding bonds issued in borrowers' national markets.
Source: BIS Annual Report 1990, p. 141.

USA. They involve investors, often management, buying perhaps an offshoot of a large enterprise. There will be a high level of debt (hence the word leverage) and a small amount of equity held by the management. Providers of the debt are generally institutions and banks. Sometimes the equity is held by the management only with preference shares held by the providers of the debt. If problems arise, the preference shares become ordinary shares so that the debt-holders have some security.

The international nature of bond markets is touched on in the text. This has been a growth market, with many enterprises beginning to use both the bond market and the swap market (section 8.8). Tables W8.4 and W8.5 give the recent data on the market in terms of type of issue and currency and nationality of bond issuers.

As far as United Kingdom enterprises are concerned, they have increasingly used the eurosterling market, raising, for example, over £20 billion in 1989. Generally, United Kingdom enterprises prefer the fixed rate to the floating, and some issue zero-coupon bonds.

(c) Preference shares

There is not much to add to the brief coverage of preference shares in the text. They can take many forms and generally they are more expensive than debt finance. With the reduction in the rate of corporation tax, the value of the tax shield for debt is correspondingly lower, which may provide a basis for an upsurge in new issues. Also the issue of convertible preference shares can be attractive.

Table W8.5 Nationality of international bond issuers ($US bn)

Issuers		New issues				Stocks			
		1986	1987	1988	1989	1986	1987	1988	1989
Japan	A	31.8	42.7	50.8	96.7				
	B	27.0	36.8	40.3	83.9	17.7	153.5	184.2	266.0
United States	A	41.6	22.5	16.6	16.4				
	B	32.6	11.4	5.4	−0.3	36.0	163.6	165.6	162.7
Canada	A	17.9	9.0	13.1	13.3				
	B	13.6	2.2	5.9	4.1	41.4	92.6	97.4	100.9
United Kingdom	A	20.2	11.2	26.3	23.0				
	B	17.5	9.5	19.6	20.2	11.1	64.3	82.4	96.5
France	A	13.4	8.5	16.5	13.5				
	B	5.7	3.1	10.1	9.4	18.4	58.3	65.8	74.5
Other developed countries[a]	A	74.8	60.5	77.0	68.2				
	B	53.5	36.3	47.9	40.7	67.3	295.2	329.1	364.7
Developing countries[b]	A	3.0	2.2	3.9	2.6				
	B	0.4	−0.9	−1.0	−1.0	18.0	34.1	32.2	29.9
Eastern Europe	A	0.6	0.6	1.2	2.0				
	B	0.6	0.5	1.2	1.9	0.6	2.0	3.2	5.2
International institutions	A	19.1	19.9	20.6	23.1				
	B	8.7	8.8	7.7	12.7	48.8	142.9	141.0	152.0
Total	A	222.4	177.0	226.0	258.7				
	B	159.7	107.8	137.1	171.6	259.1	1,006.6	1,101.0	1,252.3

Notes: A = announced gross new issus; B = completed new issues, net of repayments.
[a] Other BIS reporting countries plus non-reporting developed countries. [b] OPEC and non-OPEC developing countries.
Source: BIS Annual Report 1990, p. 145.

(d) Ordinary shares

Ordinary shares are, as we say in the text, the true permanent capital of the enterprise. Shares can be issued, as we shall see, by a variety of means. However, the importance of the rights issues to existing shareholders is still paramount. The ordinary shareholders take the largest risk of all the providers of capital. Their share of profits is a residual one either through dividends or retained earnings. The data on the new issues of ordinary shares given in Table 8.1 shows that they are more important than debt and preference shares, but are swamped by the retained earnings and bank financing. In relation to the holdings of these shares, in Chapter 1 we have mentioned the growth of the institutional shareholders, and the Wilson Committee (1980) and various other published studies (e.g. Dodds and Dobbins, 1985) have confirmed the 'dominance' that institutional share-holders have in terms of holdings, net acquisitions of ordinary shares and the trading activity. This dominance has been modified somewhat with the privatization programme, which has led to a wider share ownership. The implications of this were raised in Chapter 1.

The text refers to the need for ISE to take account of harmonization measures within the EC. Table W8.6 presents the major EC directives which impact on securities markets.

Table W8.6   Major EC directives affecting securities markets

Number	Name and description	Proposed by commission	Compliance
79/279/EEC	*Admissions Directive* Sets out the conditions that a company must satisfy before its securities can be listed on a European exchange	1975	June 1983
80/390/EEC	*Listing Particulars Directive* Requires a company to publish a document called 'Listing Particulars' prior to its admission to listing. It sets out the required contents of the document, which is intended to provide investors with reliable information on newly issued securities and on the company issuing them	1972	August 1982
82/121/EEC	*Interim Reports Directive* Sets out the information to be published regularly by companies which have been admitted to listing on a European stock exchange	1979	June 1983
87/345/EEC	*The Mutual Recognition of Listing Particulars Directive* Requires that once listing particulars have been approved by one member state, they will be recognized by all member states	1987	January 1990
89/298/EEC	*Prospectus Directive* Requires a prospectus to be published when securities are offered to the public, whether or not a stock exchange listing is sought. An exception is made for wholesale issues	1980	April 1991

Source: Bank of England, 1990b, p. 244.

Also in the text we referred to new issue markets and recent data. We give these data in Table W8.7.

Table W8.7   Initial public offers

(a) Total sums raised[a] via initial public offers (£m)

Year	Offers for sale	Tenders	Placings	Privatization	Total
1985	603	103	8	–	714
1986	2,375[b]	258	70	5,434	8,138
1987	1,021	–	271	3,488	4,779
1988	643	–	296	2,500	3,439
1989	1,213[c]	–	80	5,239	6,532
1985–89	5,855	361	725	16,661	23,602

Notes: [a] Includes sums raised for existing shareholders.
[b] Includes £1.5 billion flotation of TSB, which had many of the characteristics of a privatization but was unique in that the funds raised were retained by the company not the government.
[c] Includes the Abbey National flotation, which raised £975 million.

(b) Initial public offerings 1985–1989

Entry method	Number	Size of issue (£m)		Proportion of equity capital	
		Mean	Median	Mean (%)	Median (%)
Offers for sale	94	62.3	11.4	35.6	33.5
Tenders	11	32.8	12.2	32.2	27.0
Placings	120	6.0	5.3	31.6	28.0
Privatizations	15	1,110.7	848.8	99.8	100.0

(c) Entry methods to the ISE Official List

Year	Offers for sale	Tenders	Placings	Privatization	Introduction[a]	USM transfers	Total
1985	29	6	3	–	2	10	50
1986	37	5	17	1	5	27	92
1987	12	–	46	3	18	25	104
1988	11	–	39	1	11	19	81
1989	5	–	15	10	7	7	44
1985–89	94	11	120	15	43	88	371

Note: [a] A company can obtain a quotation for its existing shares without issuing new shares provided it has 100 shareholders or more.

(d) Sums raised by issue size (£m)

	1985		1986		1987		1988		1989		1985–89	
	Number	Amount	Number	Amount	Number	Amount	Number	Amount	Number	Amount	Number	Amount
Up to £3m raised:												
Offers for sale	1	2.9	–	–	–	–	–	–	–	–	1	2.9
Tenders	–	–	–	–	–	–	–	–	–	–	–	–
Placings	3	8.3	9	23.9	10	19.6	3	6.3	3	5.7	28	63.8
£3m–£5m raised:												
Offers for sale	3	12.8	4	18.4	1	4.1	–	–	–	–	8	35.3
Tenders	3	12.8	1	4.3	–	–	–	–	–	–	4	16.9
Placings	–	–	3	13.2	14	56.0	10	38.9	5	20	32	128.1

	1985		1986		1987		1988		1989		1985–89	
	Number	Amount	Number	Amount	Number	Amount	Number	Amount	Number	Amount	Number	Amount
£5m–£10m raised:												
Offers for sale	16	110.5	12	78.9	2	14.2	–	–	–	–	30	203.6
Tenders	1	9.7	1	7.2	–	–	–	–	–	–	2	16.9
Placings	–	–	4	21.6	16	116.9	16	115.7	6	42.1	42	296.3
£10m and more raised:												
Offers for sale	9	477.1	21	2,277.6	9	1,002.4	11	643.4	5	1,212.8	55	5,613.4
Tenders	2	80.4	3	246.5	–	–	–	–	–	–	5	326.9
Placings	–	–	1	11.7	6	78.4	10	314.8	1	12.1	18	237.0
Privatizations	–	–	1	5,434.4	3	3,487.8	1	2,500.0	10	5,239.2	15	16,661.4
Total by issue method:												
Offers for sale	29	603.3	37	2,375.0	12	1.020.7	11	643.4	5	1,212.8	94	5,855.2
Tenders	6	102.8	5	258.0	–	–	–	–	–	–	11	360.8
Placings	3	8.3	17	70.3	46	270.9	39	295.7	15	79.9	120	725.1
Privatizations	–	–	1	5,434.4	3	3,487.8	1	2,500.0	10	5,239.2	15	16,661.4
Total	38	714.4	60	8,137.6	61	4,779.4	51	3,439.1	30	6,531.9	240	23,602.5

(e) Direct costs of initial public offerings[a] (£m)

	1985		1986		1987		1988		1989		1985–89	
	Number	Amount	Number	Amount	Number	Amount	Number	Amount	Number	Amount	Number	Amount
Up to £5m raised:												
Offers for sale	7	14.3	5	13.4	1	12.8	–	–	–	–	13	13.8
Placings	3	12.7	12	10.9	24	10.9	13	11.0	8	13.9	60	11.4
£5m–£10m raised:												
Offers for sale	17	10.1	13	10.4	2	8.6	–	–	–	–	32	10.1
Placings	–	–	4	8.3	16	7.9	16	7.8	6	6.8	42	7.7
More than £10m raised:												
Offers for sale	9	6.8	24	6.8	9	7.5	10	6.9	4	5.7	56	6.9
Placings	–	–	1	9.2	6	4.3	10	6.6	1	5.5	18	5.9
Total by issue method:												
Offers for sale	33	10.1	42	8.7	12	8.1	10	6.9	4	5.7	101	8.8
Placings	3	12.7	17	10.2	46	9.0	39	8.5	15	10.5	120	9.3
Total	36	10.3	59	9.1	58	8.8	49	8.2	19	9.5	221	9.1

Notes: [a] Only private sector issues are included. Privatizations are not comparable. The costs borne by the privatized company, as recorded in the prospectus, are very small as a proportion of the issue.
All investment trusts are excluded from the figures.
Figures relate to full listings on the London Stock Exchange and exclude issues on the USM and Third Market.
No secondary issues, relistings, reverse takeovers, etc. are included.
Only initial public offerings of ordinary shares are included; debenture, bond or preference share issues are excluded.
Source: Bank of England, 1990b, pp. 245–9.

The changes that are recommended by the Russell Committee are referred to in the text. The following synopsis of the committee's report is quoted directly from the Bank of England (1990b, p. 247):

The trend towards greater use of placings raised the question of whether the limit of £15 million, and £5 million for the USM, established at the time of Big Bang, was appropriate. Moreover, the ISE thought it useful to review more generally its requirements for IPOs to ensure that its rules did not impose unnecessary costs on the issuers or their agents. The report emphasises the overriding importance of flexibility to enable issues to be marketed in a way that meets the particular needs of the issuer. Nevertheless the market objective of achieving fair distribution of shares and a liquid market after the issue was seen to require some rules.

The committee recommended that the ISE should adopt new limits on the size of particular types of offer. It was suggested that sponsors should be allowed to place small issues (defined as up to £10 million) with clients subject only to a tranche being reserved for market makers and the sponsor achieving a minimum spread of shareholders. (Issues by companies that are already listed on another exchange can of course be made entirely by placing because the need for an active after-market is already satisfied.) The current requirement to use a second distributor was not thought to work well because the second distributor often did not feel committed to making a market in the shares or actively following the company after the issue.

The committee proposed the introduction of an 'intermediaries' offer' to facilitate medium-sized issues (of £10 million–£20 million). They proposed that up to £10 million (or 75%, if less) of such issues could be placed, with the remainder either being offered for sale or sold through an intermediaries' offer. The latter was intended to be a quicker method of issue, which was one of the principal advantages of a placing over an offer for sale, but one still accessible to most investors. In this method sponsors would invite intermediaries (such as ISE members and possibly other authorised investment businesses) to subscribe for the issue on behalf of their customers. This would be particularly attractive to customers whose funds were managed on a discretionary basis by securities firms. The closest parallel is perhaps the American system of distribution of IPOs where retail securities firms buy new issues on behalf of customers. The committee hoped that the development of such channels of distribution in the United Kingdom would encourage retail interest in shareholding.

For large issues (over £20 million), the committee considered that the offer for sale procedure remained most appropriate. They suggested, however, that the sponsor should be able to place up to half of the offer. Such hybrid offers have been permitted in large privatisation issues.

Although the committee recommended the retention of offers for sale as the main technique for large issues, it suggested a number of cost-reducing changes in the rules governing offers for sale. The committee indicated that it thought it was unnecessary to require the full prospectuses to be published in national newspapers and that greater use of mini-prospectuses and box advertisements should be encouraged. The committee emphasised instead the principle that sponsors should ensure that potential investors had a reasonable chance of knowing when an offer was to be made and of participating in it. These proposals have been published in a consultative document.

One point raised in the text is that, although attention is often focused on the shares of quoted companies — that is, those with a Stock Exchange quotation — the majority by number of enterprises are not quoted. This causes a problem of pricing their shares and of trading. Some, however, use a half-way house — the *Unlisted Securities Market* (USM). The Bank of England (1983) gives an excellent discussion of the origin and main features of this market, and for our part here we can comment on its achievements. Table W8.8 gives the recent data on the capital issues in the USM. We can see that it has been a source of equity finance and the companies in the market are small expanding ones.

Table W8.8 Capital issues and redemptions on the USM 1985–89

	1985	1986	1987	1988	1989
Gross issues:					
Rights	87	76	567	227	296
Total	181	320	967	632	767
Redemptions	–	1	–	4	–
Net issues — total:	181	319	967	628	767
Ordinary shares	163	284	826	509	628
Other	18	35	142	119	139

Source: *Financial Statistics*, table 12.2 (CSO).

Entry to the market can be via placings (about two-thirds come this way now), offer for sale (including by tender) and Stock Exchange introduction. The companies are not all from the United Kingdom. There are enterprises from the USA, Canada, France and Bermuda. The market does offer investors some liquidity because turnover has increased, and it has proved a vehicle for full listing. But as the market has matured, it has become less open to the brand new company. The latter has now had to seek out the OTC market.

In reviewing the methods of raising finance by ordinary shares, the most popular method used for existing quoted companies is the rights issue as we shall discuss in more detail later. The concept of private or Stock Exchange placings is appealing for enterprises, given the costs, because even if they are underwritten, the costs are lower. But another method not yet available in the United Kingdom is *shelf registration*. This was introduced in the USA in March 1982. Quite simply it allows an enterprise to register with the Securities and Exchange Commission (SEC) — the major statutory US regulator for securities — a single registration certificate covering all the securities it is expecting to issue over a two-year period. It is then free to choose the amount and how much it issues over the period. In essence it is a standby facility giving the enterprise great flexibility, and in the USA it has proved a cheaper source of finance.

(e) The pricing of new issues

The pricing of new issues is raised as a particular problem in the text. Issuing houses have the role of advising a fixed price or, in the case of a tender, the base or strike price. The problem here is that the houses often act in a lead underwriting role, whether it be an offer for sale or a placing, and it is clearly in their interest to have a lower price to clear the market. As agents, however, they are acting on behalf of their clients, who desire the highest price possible! The tender offer appears to give firms a method of exacting the most return from the market, but apart from a few years, this method has not endured.

The point is raised in the text that there appears from casual empiricism a systematic underpricing of new issues. The Bank of England (1990b) study is referred to. With permission, we quote their study direct:

> In addition to the direct costs of going public, there is an indirect cost either to the original owners of the firm or, where new finance is raised,

to the company itself, if the shares are sold for less than investors would be willing to pay. There will always be a suspicion that this was the case where shares are sold for less than the price at which they subsequently trade. Such systematic discounting has been observed in the United States and in the Bank's earlier study on the United Kingdom, with, on average, shares immediately trading at a considerable premium over the issue price. This study reports some research into measuring these discounts. In order to remove the impact of any general movement in share prices, the extent of any discount or premium was measured relative to the FT-Actuaries all-share index using the formula:

$$\text{Discounting} = (P_{t+s}/I_{t+s} - P_t/I_t)/P_t/I_t$$
$$= (P_{t+s}.I_t/P_t.I_{t+s}) - 1$$

where

P_t	=	the issue price of the share
P_{t+s}	=	the share price s days after the listing date
I_t	=	the FT all-share index on the listing date
I_{t+s}	=	the FT all-share index s days after the listing date

This formula measures the extent to which the rate of return on a newly issued share exceeds the rate of return earned on the stock market as a whole. Of course any company-specific or industry-specific news which emerges after trading begins will reduce the accuracy of this correction for developments after the issue price is fixed, although over short periods such influences are likely to be small. In order to minimise such problems, while at the same time allowing the after-market to settle down following the often highly active initial trading, the measure of discounting used here compares the price prevailing at the end of the first trading week with the issue price. In fact, the choice of period does not seem to matter, as [Table W8.9] shows. IPOs tend to jump in price on the first trading day, and thereafter move, on average, with the overall market.

Table W8.9 Analysis of returns on companies seeking a full listing, 1985–89 (%)

	1985	1986	1987	1988	1989	1985–89
After:						
1 day	7.5	8.4	22.6	7.3	10.7	11.9
1 week	6.6	8.1	24.4	6.7	11.3	12.1
4 weeks	5.9	7.1	22.9	6.2	11.7	11.3
13 weeks	4.3	7.9	23.9	10.3	13.7	12.6
Number of firms	36	57	57	47	30	227

The average discounting of new issues was around 12% for the sample as a whole. The standard deviation of the first week discount is 16.4%, and the distribution is positively skewed ... While the 10% most overpriced issues fell in price, on average, by 12.6% by the end of the first week, the 10% most underpriced issues rose in the after-market by 46% on average over the same period. Almost half of all new share issues rose in price by more than 10% within the first week.

The discounting of placings and offers for sale
As noted above, since 1986 many more IPOs have been conducted via a

placing of the shares, with offers for sale being restricted, increasingly, to large issues. Estimates of discounting by type of issue are presented in Table W8.10. Overall the discounting of placings in the sample was about 5.7 percentage points more than the discounting of offers for sale but this result is partly attributable to the variation of the discounts over time. Around 40% of the placings in the five-year period were made in 1987, when discounts on both offers for sale and placings were exceptionally large: 19.5% and 25.4% respectively after the week. This 'hot issue' period is discussed further below ...

Table W8.10 Discounting the initial public offerings (percentages in italics)

	1985		1986		1987		1988		1989		1985–89	
	Number	Discounts	Number	Discounts	Number	Discounts	Number	Discounts	Number	Discounts	Number	Discounts
Up to £5m raised:												
Offers for sale	7	*7.0*	5	*8.2*	1	*23.4*	–	–	–	–	13	*8.7*
Placings	3	*−0.1*	11	*1.5*	22	*23.9*	10	*11.8*	8	*12.5*	54	*14.1*
£5m–£10m raised:												
Offers for sale	15	*3.1*	13	*9.3*	2	*33.0*	–	–	–	–	30	*7.8*
Placings	–	–	4	*9.7*	15	*29.0*	16	*5.8*	6	*7.4*	41	*14.9*
More than £10m raised:												
Offers for sale	11	*13.1*	22	*10.1*	8	*15.7*	11	*2.3*	5	*−1.9*	57	*8.8*
Placings	–	–	1	*12.9*	6	*22.0*	9	*8.9*	1	*4.1*	17	*13.4*
Privatizations	–	–	1	*8.8*	3	*28.1*	1	*1.3*	10	*19.9*	15	*19.6*
Total by issue method:												
Offers for sale	33	*7.2*	40	*9.6*	11	*19.5*	11	*2.3*	5	*−1.9*	100	*8.5*
Placings	3	*−0.1*	16	*4.2*	43	*25.4*	35	*8.3*	15	*9.9*	112	*14.3*
Privatizations	–	–	1	*8.8*	3	*28.1*	1	*1.3*	10	*19.9*	15	*19.6*
Total	36	*6.6*	57	*8.1*	57	*24.4*	47	*6.7*	30	*11.3*	227	*12.1*

Notes: The estimated discounts compare the trading price one week after issue to issue price, corrected for movements in the overall market index.
The offers for sale figures include both fixed price offers and tender offers. The small number of the latter precluded a reliable separate analysis.

There was significantly less downside risk for investors who took up placings in this period: only 12% of all placings fell in price and even for these the average fall was only 5.4%. In contrast, 29% of offers for sale fell in price, by an average of 7.5%. Risk-adjusted returns to investors could, of course, be equal for placings and offers for sale if the distributions followed a similar pattern for the most underpriced issues. In fact the reverse is true: for example, the most discounted 10% of placings in the example rose in price by the end of the first week by an average of over 52%, whereas the corresponding offers for sale rose by around 38% on average. There thus appears to be a large risk-adjusted return to investors in IPOs, especially those who can obtain placings.

When the sample is broken down by issue size, there seem to be few systematic differences in the extent of discounting. Over the whole sample period, placings were discounted to a greater extent on average for both small issues and large issues alike, although again this seems to be partly attributable to the preponderance of placings in 1987. The overwhelming feature of the data is that the extent of discounting is only marginally influenced by size of issue but tends to be dominated by the timing of issue. Such serial dependence of new issue premia has also been reported in studies of new issues in the United States [see Ibbotson and Jaffe, 1975].

1987: a 'hot issue' period

1987 stands out as a year with a substantially greater degree of discounting. Table W8.10 shows that the average discounting of IPOs coming to the market in 1987 was around three times that of companies going public over the remainder of the sample period. Such 'hot issue' periods have also been observed in the United States, and have been the subject of various Securities and Exchange Commission investigations. In particular, during the periods 1959–61, 1968–69 and 1980–early 1981, IPOs in the United States seem to have traded at abnormally large premia over their issue prices, although in the latter period this was apparently associated almost exclusively with issues made by companies in the natural resources sector [see Ritter, 1984].

While it is not possible to identify the beginning of the 1987 hot issue period in the United Kingdom clearly (indeed by their very nature such phenomena tend to develop gradually) it might be reasonable to choose October 1986 — the date of Big Bang — as a starting date . . . At its peak in the second quarter of 1987, IPOs were trading on average at 28.7% above their issue prices. As might have been expected, the October 1987 stock market crash seems to have signalled the end of such exceptional premia. The hot issue period in the UK market of 1987 was one in which equity prices rose rapidly: the FT-Actuaries all-share index rose by nearly 50% between December 1986 and July 1987. Pricing decisions may have been more difficult against a background of rapidly changing prices which might have encouraged conservative estimates of demand.

(f) The pricing of pre-emptive rights

In the text we refer to the costs of rights issues. The fixed costs calculated by Marsh (1977) as a percentage of funds raised are given in Table W8.11.

Table W8.11 UK rights issues: fixed costs as a percentage of funds raised

Issue size (£m as at June 1975)	Mean issue size (£m as at June 1975)	Fixed issue costs (%)
0.0–0.2	0.16	4.45
0.2–0.4	0.27	2.01
0.4–0.6	0.52	1.79
0.6–0.8	0.70	1.51
0.8–1.0	0.90	1.30
1.0–2.0	1.41	0.88
2.0–3.0	2.45	0.79
3.0–4.0	3.45	1.00
4.0–5.0	4.59	0.53
5.0–10.0	6.54	0.57
10.0–20.0	14.78	0.70
20.0–50.0	28.45	0.71
Over 50.0	99.15	0.44

Source: Marsh, 1977.

The institutional and legal framework in the United Kingdom has enshrined rights as the normal method of raising new equity finance. This is the case in most of the articles of association of companies, in the 1985 Companies Act and in the Stock Exchange listing requirements. Quotations from the Wolff (1986) article that discusses both of these are given below:

1985 Companies Act Sections 89–96
Rights are to be the general rule, viz.:

> ... a company proposing to allot equity securities ... shall not allot any of them on any person unless it has made an offer to each person who holds relevant shares or relevant employee shares to allot to him on the same or more favourable terms a proportion of those securities which is as nearly as practicable equal to the proportion in nominal value held by him or relevant shares and relevant employee shares ...

Exceptions are recognized through:

1. non-cash issues;
2. issues under an employees' share scheme;
3. through a single majority vote of shareholders at a general meeting;
4. through the articles of association of the company which approve the non-use of rights;
5. for private companies.

As Wolff claims:

> Exception 1 allows acquisition issues and vendor placings, while exceptions 3 and 4 open the door to circumvention of pre-emptive rights in general, provided that a majority of shareholders or the articles of association approve. (p. 7).

(g) Stock Exchange: admission of securities to listing

Paragraph 15 of Chapter 2 (Section 1) of the *Yellow Book* reads:

> Issues for cash of securities having an equity element must, in the absence of exceptional circumstances, be offered in the first place to the existing equity shareholders in proportion to their holdings unless the shareholders in general meeting have agreed to other specific proposals.

Provided that shareholders' approval is obtained, shares can be brought to listing by any one of the methods described under the heading 'Methods of issuing new equity' (p. 7). The Stock Exchange has relaxed the rules on new issues such that the limit on the issue of equity, previously around 10–15%, has now been removed.

The issue of rights to existing shareholders should cause an effect on the price of the share in exact proportion to the value of the rights. In other words, shareholders neither benefit from nor lose out from a rights issue. This requires the demand curve facing the enterprise doing the issuing to be perfectly elastic. If it is inelastic, then the argument would be that to sell more shares, the enterprise has to lower the price (see Fig. W8.2). This is the argument for price pressure following a rights issue and for giving discounts in placings. Marsh (1979) does not find evidence of price pressure, but the case of discounts on placings is more telling in that it is quite simple to illustrate the transfer of wealth argument from existing to new shareholders. Fig. W8.3 provides a numerical example.

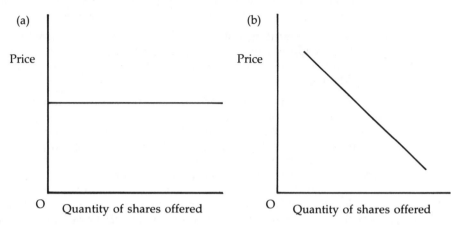

Figure W8.2 Demand curves facing the firm issuing new shares: (a) elastic; (b) inelastic.

XYZ plc is an all-equity company with 150 shares, each currently selling for £12. Fifteen new shares are placed at £10 each.

Value of enterprise before placing = £1,800 (150 × £12)
£150 received in cash
Value of enterprise after placing = £1,950
Value of each share 1,950/165 = £11.82

Figure W8.3 Transfers of wealth following discount on placing

The new shareholders are better off than the existing ones. Of course, we have used an extreme example here with a large discount, but the principle is the same. Why the discounts should be given and tolerated is not clear. One line of reasoning is that they are expected so as to be able to sell the volume of new shares, and they create a wider interest in the shares which can help future marketability. A more sinister argument refers to the motives of institutional shareholders. The argument here is similar to that raised in Chapter 1 of *inside* and *external* shareholders, except that the insiders here are institutions. The issue is placed with them and they effectively buy the rights at a real discount. Proposals put forward by Wolff to protect the wealth of existing shareholders include:

1. the setting of a maximum discount;
2. a bidding system for the placing.

Still staying with rights, we make the point that rights issues are generally underwritten, which is equivalent to a put option by the enterprise exercisable if the issue fails. Underwriting will cost the enterprise $1\frac{1}{4}$% of the issue and the question is: is it worth the cost or insurance premium? Marsh (1980) examines 539 such underwritten rights issues for the United Kingdom using an option-pricing framework. We can quote his findings:

> Sub-underwriting appears to have been a very profitable activity, . . . with underwriting fees pitched, on average, at roughly twice the level required to ensure underwriters earn a 'fair' reward for the risk involved.

The alternative if an enterprise fears the failure of an issue is to offer a deep discount, and Marsh finds that these would be less expensive than underwriting issues. Of course, the Marsh study was published in 1980 and in the aftermath of the Big Bang there will be more competition in the underwriting business from foreign companies. In consequence we should find the fees fall to a level commensurate with the risk involved.

Another development in the issuing of rights has been the issue of *vendor rights*. This is a variant on a vendor placing where shares issued normally with a merger are placed by a broker. The first example of vendor rights was Systems Designers International (SDI), which purchased a US software company. The shares issued to the target company were offered back to SDI shareholders through a rights issue instead of being placed with the market.

W8.5   Option pricing

Options provide investors with the right to trade securities, but not the obligations to do so, at a fixed price (exercise price) within a given period (the expiration date). European options only allow the exercise at the expiration date, while American options permit exercise up to and including the expiration date. Investors can hold options to hedge to offset risk or to take a speculative position. The options markets allow the management of risk rather than the creation of risk *per se*. Put and call options permit the redistribution of the risks that are inherent in an investment, and the strategies available allow an investor to use options in both high- and low-risk ways. *Call* options are the right to purchase and *put* options the right to sell. The seller of a call option or the buyer of a put option is effectively reducing the exposure from the fall in the market and therefore in the price of the underlying share(s). He or she has to pay a price for the insurance. The counterpart who assumes the risk does so for the opportunity it gives of interest income and leverage (this last point will be developed later — see pp. 511–13). What the option market does is to balance actual and potential gains and losses. There are now organized markets to trade options. In London it is the London Options Clearing House (LOCH), in the USA the Chicago Board Options Exchange. In the United Kingdom options have been slow to catch on compared to the USA.

There are two sides to an option contract — a new buyer or investor in the put/call and a writer of the put/call. We give in Fig. W8.4 a typical set of option quotations taken from the financial pages of a newspaper. What we can see is that there are a series of expiration dates. Options expire in one of three different quarterly cycles, though only the three recorded are available for trading at any one time:

1. January, April, July, October;
2. February, May, August, November;
3. March, June, September, December.

LONDON TRADED OPTIONS

	Series	Calls Jul	Calls Oct	Calls Jan	Puts Jul	Puts Oct	Puts Jan
Alld Lyon	460	48	67	80	3	10	15
(*498)	500	18	40	57	16	21	27
	550	3½	19	32	55	55	55
ASDA	100	19	21	26	1½	4	5½
(*117)	110	10	13½	19	3½	7	8
	120	4½	9	14	7	10	14
Bass	1000	107	-	-	3	-	-
(*1092)	1050	65	-	-	7	-	-
	1100	29	-	-	24	-	-
Boots	280	22	33	41	4½	8	11
(*296)	300	9	21	29	12	15½	19
	330	2	9	17	37	36	38
Brit Air	180	39	46	50	1	2	4
(*216)	200	20	29	34	1½	5½	7½
	220	6	16	22	9	13	15
BP	300	32	39	46	1½	5	7½
(*326)	330	8	19	28	8	14	17
	360	1½	8	-	34	34	-
Brit Steel	130	20	20	23	¾	2	3
(*150)	140	10	12½	15½	3	4½	6½
	160	¾	3½	6½	18	18½	19
C & W	500	50	72	90	4	11	15
(*547)	550	14	40	60	21	30	34
	600	2	-	-	62	-	-
Com Union	460	68	79	95	2	7	11
(*521)	500	34	48	72	7	17	21
	550	8	23	42	31	41	42
Courtauld	297	76	87	-	1	2½	-
(*365)	327	47	60	-	2½	5	-
	357	22	-	-	7	-	-
GKN	360	53	59	72	1½	7	9
(*410)	390	27	41	50	6	15	18
	420	9	20	33	17	28	30
Grand Met	600	75	95	114	1½	8	13
(*668)	650	29	53	80	8	20	27
	700	7	28	50	37	43	45
ICI	1150	61	87	129	13	35	42
(*1182)	1200	30	59	100	33	59	64
	1250	10	39	75	70	90	94
Kingfisher	300	55	65	76	1	3½	4½
(*357)	330	27	40	50	3½	7	11
	360	9	20	34	13	19	23
Ladbroke	300	40	52	60	2	5	10
(*335)	330	14	30	41	7½	13	17
	360	3½	-	-	27	-	-
Land Sec	460	49	67	80	1	6	7½
(*497)	500	15	38	53	9	17	22
	550	2	15	28	50	52	50
M & S	200	41	49	55	1	3	5
(*238)	220	23	32	39	3	6	8
	240	9	18	26	10	13	17
STC	260	5	14	23	20	25	28
(*244)	280	2	7½	14	38	42	43
	300	1	4	10	58	62	64
Sainsbury	260	26	36	46	1½	4	6
(*284)	280	11	24	32	6	10	12
	300	3½	13	21	20	21	23
Shell	420	48	58	75	3	7	9
(*460)	460	15	32	47	11	20	23
	500	4	15	28	43	43	43
Smkl Beech	500	46	64	80	3	9	15
(*538)	550	12	32	50	20	30	34
	600	2½	13	28	66	66	67
Storehse	110	19½	24	28	2	3	5
(*129)	120	10	17	21	4	7	8½
	130	4	11	16	8	10½	13
Trafalgar	280	43	55	62	1½	5	10
(*318)	300	26	40	47	4	10	18
	330	7	24	30	19	25	33
Ultramar	300	40	50	65	2	5	8
(*333)	330	16	30	45	9	15	20
	360	5	17	30	27	32	33
Unilever	600	96½	16½	133	2	4½	7¾
(*690)	650	48½	74	92¼	3¾	9½	15¼
	700	12¼	40½	60¾	18¼	28¾	34½
	750	2	-	-	62¼	-	-
Utd Bisc	300	67	73	82	1	2	3½
(*369)	330	37	46	57	2	7	9
	360	13	26	36	9	16	19

	Series	Calls Aug	Calls Nov	Calls Feb	Puts Aug	Puts Nov	Puts Feb
BAA	360	90	103	-	1	2	-
(*446)	390	62	75	85	2	5	10
	420	34	55	65	8	11	17
BAT Ind	587	73	-	-	3	-	-
(*645)	637	38	60	-	13	23	-
	687	10	32	-	47	50	-
	737	4	15	-	100	98	-
BTR	390	52	60	75	3	9	11
(*431)	420	28	40	55	9	19	21
	460	8	19	33	33	40	42
Brit Aero	460	78	88	-	3	9	-
(*524)	500	47	60	78	10½	22	26
	550	17	32	52	37	45	50
Brit Tele	280	23	31	38	4½	7	10
(*299)	300	8½	19	27	14	16	18½
	330	1½	7½	-	39	40	-
Cadbury	300	62	70	81	1½	3½	5½
(*359)	330	33	47	58	5	11	12
	360	13	26	40	16	22	24
Guinness	650	157	175	200	1½	3	3
(*792)	700	112	132	155	2½	5	9
	750	67	92	120	6	15	20
GEC	180	23	27	31	2½	4½	6½
(*200)	200	7½	13	20	11	14	16
	220	2½	6	11	28	29	30
Hanson	200	48	55	-	1	1	-
(*243)	220	29	37	39	1½	2¾	5½
	240	13½	22½	26	5½	9	13
LASMO	367	57	70	-	4	7	-
(*410)	400	32	47	-	11	17	-
	433	13	29	-	28	30	-
P & O	550	00¾09½		-	2	4½	-
(*637)	600	54	67	87¾	5	14½	17½
	650	19¼	34	55¼	22¼	35	36½

	Series	Calls Aug	Calls Nov	Calls Feb	Puts Aug	Puts Nov	Puts Feb
Pilkington	180	35	42	48	2	4½	5½
(*209)	200	18	29	34	7½	11	13
	220	7	16	22	17	18	21
Polly Peck	382	69¼	87¼	-	2½	6½	-
(*439)	418	39½	60	-	8¾	15¾	-
	460	16¼	36¼	48¾	29¼	35¾	40
Prudential	200	37	40	47	2½	3	6
(*228)	220	19	24	33	4	8	10
	240	8	14	21	13	17	19
Racal	200	15	24	33	7	12	14
(*206)	220	6	15	23	20	22	24
	240	2	8	15	38	39	40
RTZ	500	77	93	110	2	6	8
(*563)	550	36	56	76	11	18	22
	600	13	30	50	42	47	49
Scot & New	300	33	43	52	6	10	15
(*327)	330	14	28	33	20	23	29
	360	5	16	23	42	45	47
Tesco	200	21	26¾	34½	2	4¼	5½
(*216)	220	7¼	13¾	21	9½	11½	12½
	240	2	6¼	12¾	27½	27½	27½
Thames Wtr	120	35	35	-	1	2	-
(*154)	130	25	25	29	2	4	6
	140	15½	17	22	6	9	12
	160	5	8	13	19	20	22
Wtr Package	1500	70	90	160	120	130	190
(*1520)	1550	40	80	140	160	170	220
	1600	30	50	120	210	210	260
	1650	20	40	100	260	260	300

	Series	Calls Jul	Calls Sep	Calls Nov	Puts Jul	Puts Sep	Puts Nov
Ferranti	35	3½	6½	8	1¼	2	3
(*36)	40	2	4	5	4½	6	7
	45	¾	-	-	9½	-	-
Lucas	140	21	25	26	1	2	3½
(*158)	160	5	11	12½	7	9	12
	180	1	3½	6	24	24	25

	Series	Calls Jun	Calls Aug	Calls Oct	Puts Jun	Puts Aug	Puts Oct
Reuters	1150	49¾	83¼	-	10½	22¼	-
(*1275)	1200	10½	147	-	21¼	36	-
	1250	77¼	115	50¾	38½	54½	65¼

	Series	Calls Jun	Calls Sep	Calls Dec	Puts Jun	Puts Sep	Puts Dec
Abbey Nat	180	30	33	-	2½	4	-
(*203)	200	15	20	25	8	9½	12
	220	6	11	14	20	22	24
Amstrad	60	13	15	19	2½	3½	4½
(*68)	70	6½	10	13½	6½	7½	9
	80	3½	5½	8½	12½	13	14
Barclays	357	57	67	-	6	8	-
(*403)	393	28	43	-	17	18	-
	429	12	22	-	37	37	-
Blue Circ	200	60	66	-	1	3	-
(*249)	220	41	48	-	3	7	-
	240	24	34	43	7½	13	15
	260	13	23	31	18	21	24
Brit Gas	180	44	46	-	1½	2	-
(*221)	200	25	28	33	3½	6	7
	220	9½	17	20	11	14	15
	240	3	7½	10	26	26	27
Dixons	120	35	38	-	2	3	-
(*150)	130	26	30	32	4	6	7
	140	18	23	25	8	10	12
	160	8	13	16	17	19	21
Glaxo	700	132	-	-	4	-	-
(*802)	750	92	104	130	11	21	29
	800	52	74	100	30	39	47
	850	30	49	73	54	64	75
Hawker	600	105	110	-	9	22	-
(*668)	650	63	70	80	28	43	55
	700	27	45	65	55	60	70
Hillsdown	240	50	57	-	2½	4½	-
(*280)	260	33	42	52	6	9	10
	280	21	29	40	12	17	18
Lonhro	236	25	35	-	7	10	-
(*252)	255	14	25	-	14	18	-
	273	6	16	-	27	30	-
Midland	280	33	47	55	8	11	15
(*298)	300	22	35	45	17	22	28
	330	12	23	29	38	38	45
R-Royce	160	61	63	-	½	1½	-
(*215)	180	42	46	-	1½	2½	-
	200	25	30	39	4	7	8
Sears	100	8	12	15	5½	7	8
(*99)	110	4	7½	10	11½	13	14
	120	2½	-	-	22	-	-
THF	260	53	56	-	3	6½	-
(*301)	280	36	43	49	5½	10	12
	300	21	30	37	12	18	19
Thorn EMI	700	85	102	-	12	18	-
(*777)	750	47	70	92	25	34	38
	800	23	42	60	55	60	60
TSB	130	13	17	21	3	5½	8
(*137)	140	8	12	15	9	11	13
	160	2	5	8	24	25	27
Vaal Reefs	60	11	12	14	4½	7	10
(*$64)	70	6	8	10	12	14	13
Wellcome	600	47	72	92	32	41	50
(*600)	650	27	47	67	64	70	74
	700	14	30	47	107	107	107

FT-SE INDEX (*2369)

	2200	2250	2300	2350	2400	2450
Calls						
Jun	189	139	94	52	22	8
Jul	210	167	128	93	64	43
Aug	250	207	167	125	97	70
Sep	273	230	190	153	120	93
Dec	315	-	238	-	170	-
Puts						
Jun	1½	3	7	16	38	88
Jul	11	15	24	40	57	85
Aug	18	24	33	50	67	95
Sep	24	28	40	56	75	100
Dec	34	-	57	-	88	-

June 21, 1990 Total: 28391 Calls 21382 Puts 7009 FT-SE: Calls 1383 Puts 2304

*Underlying security price.

Source: The Times, *22.6.90*

Figure W8.4 Option quotations.

There is a standardization of exercise prices, contract size (normally 1,000 shares of the underlying security), guarantees for the buyer of the option against default by the writer, and a secondary market (as the prices given reveal) in unexpired options.

(a) Call options

A call option is the right to sell an underlying security at a specified price (the exercise or strike price) on or before a specified date (the expiration date). If we survey the data given in Fig. W8.4 and pick the Allied Lyons July 460, an investor has the right to buy 1,000 shares at a price of 460.

The buyer of the call is long in a call and clearly expects the price of the underlying security to rise, just as the seller or writer expects it to remain stable or fall. The investor in the call may expect the share price rise to be permanent, temporary or just very volatile, so that the investor thinks it will rise quickly, but for a very short period.

We can note that for the Allied Lyons call option 460, 500 and 550 there are three prices, as shown in Table W8.12. These prices follow a systematic time profile of being higher the longer into the future the option has to run, and lower for the higher exercise price. If we take the closing price to be 498, then the intrinsic value of all of the three options for a strike price of 460 is 38p, so the premiums are 10p, 29p and 42p respectively. The intrinsic value is the difference between the share price and the strike price. If the share price rose to 485p, the intrinsic value would be 25p and so on.

Table W8.12   Allied Lyons call option prices

	460	500	550
July	48	18	$3\frac{1}{2}$
October	67	40	19
January	80	57	32

The factors that cause the premium to be what it is are:

1. time to expiry;
2. volatility;
3. dividends;
4. interest rates;
5. market sentiment.

Taking these in order, the *time factor* is an important one. Options have a non-negative time value, so that even if an option is out of the money, there is always the chance that the share price will rise to yield a profit. There are plenty of examples around to prove the point that, even on the last day of the life of an option, events can change. The longer the time to expiry, the greater the chance for the share price to rise (or fall). On the issue of *volatility*, as some shares are more volatile (and therefore have higher betas), the premium for these shares will be higher for calls (and puts) to reflect the greater opportunity

investor wants the dividend, he or she must exercise the call at the cum-dividend share price. When *interest rates* are high, we might expect calls to have a higher premium, as investors are often long on calls, but have their funds invested in short-term deposits. They benefit from the high interest rates and have the calls to protect themselves if the market rises. The final factor, *market sentiment*, is the psychology of the market — the bull/bear issue. For a bull market the premium on calls will be higher.

(b) The seller (writer of calls)

The writer of calls believes that shares will not rise appreciably or will fall. However, even he or she can protect a position by hedging. Many writers are institutions with holdings of shares, so when they write calls they have a covered position. They cannot freely trade all of their shares for the reasons discussed in the text, so they buy protection by holding the shares and writing calls. The exact relationship can be derived to produce a *risk-free hedge*.

Let us assume an investor holds shares which have a current market price of £10, but feels that there are two possibilities over the next year — a price of £12 and one of £8. If there is an option on the shares at an exercise price of £10, we can set out the consequences as follows (remember, this is a writer of call options):

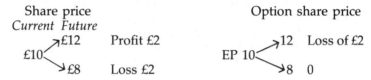

To derive a hedge we need to know the ratio of shares to be held to calls written and this is equal to:

$$\frac{\text{Difference in possible end-of-period option values}}{\text{Difference in end-of-period share value}} = \frac{2 - 0}{12 - 8} = \frac{1}{2}$$

The investor should therefore write two calls and hold one share. We can explore this relationship further. The end-of-period wealth of the investor will be £8 whatever the outcome of the share price:

1. *Share price rises to £12 from £10:* profit of £2 on the share, loss of £4 on the two calls = £8.
2. *Share price falls to £8:* loss of £2 on the share, call expires = £8.

The investor therefore has a risk-free investment worth £8 in one year's time. The question is: what would he pay for that investment today? If the risk-free rate is 7%, the investor should pay at least £8/1.07 = £7.48. This is the total outlay. As the share price is currently £10, the writer should sell the two calls for £10 − £7.48 = £2.52 or £1.26 each. If he sells for that, there is a guaranteed return risk-free of 7%. If the price is higher, the return is greater, but of course in an efficient market this should not be the case!

(c) Option pricing theory

To develop the option pricing argument further with the Black and Scholes (1973) pathbreaking article, we provide a reading from Hemmings (1982):

The study of option pricing has a long history, stretching as far back as the turn of the century, but it was the now almost legendary paper by Fischer Black and Myron Scholes published in 1973 which produced the real breakthrough, in the form of the famous Black–Scholes Option

Valuation Formula. The derivation of this formula involved a rather hard and somewhat obscure branch of mathematics (Stochastic Calculus) which is not readily accessible to the non-specialist, or conducive to intuitive thought, but stripped of the mathematics in essence option pricing theory is quite easy to understand. This is the approach taken here, beginning with a simple numerical example. Suppose that the current price of a share is 100p, and it is known that after one month has passed this will be either 110p or 95p (i.e. either up by 10 per cent or down by 5 per cent) but which is not known in advance, and that no dividend will be paid in that time. This simple example thus captures the characteristic that the future price of a share is uncertain beforehand. Consider a call option written on this share which expires in one month with an exercise price of 98 — an in-the-money option. Option pricing theory seeks to determine what such an option is worth now, that is what its market price ought to be. It is not too difficult to establish bounds within which the value of the option must lie. For the purposes of this example let us assume that the rate of interest is 2 per cent per month.

Since the option can be converted into a share only on payment of the 100p exercise price, it is clearly less desirable than owning the share itself, so the option could not currently be worth any more than the share. Therefore the current share price, which is 100p, must be an upper bound on the value of the option. It has already been observed above that since exercising the option is at the holder's discretion (at worst the holder gets nothing), its current value cannot be less than zero. Thus the price of the option must lie somewhere between zero and 100p. Can this be narrowed down any further?

Let C_0 = current (as yet unknown) option price, and consider the return at the end of one month from buying one option and depositing 98 pence/1.02 in the bank to earn interest at 2 per cent per month. By the end of the month the bank deposit will have grown to 98p. This money can then be used to exercise the option if it is worthwhile to do so, i.e. if the price of the share turned out to be 110p — the investor would not have to find any more money following his initial investment. On the other hand if the share price turned out to be 95p, the investor would be better off not exercising the option. Thus the combination of option and bank deposit is at least as good as the share itself, and may be superior, from which it may be concluded that

$$C_0 + \frac{98}{1.02} \geq 100$$

i.e. $C_0 \geq 100 - 96.08 = 3.92$

This further narrows the range within which the option value must lie to somewhere between 3.92p and 100p. The great contribution of Black and Scholes was to discover a method for finding the exact value of the call option. The ideas lying at the heart of their discovery can be explained in terms of our simple example as follows. Assuming the option is still in existence at the end of the month, it will be exercised if the price of the share turns out to be 110p for a profit of 110p − 98p = 12p, or allowed to expire unexercised if the share price turns out to be 95p in which case the profit will be zero. The option then provides a return of either 12p or zero at expiration. The Black-Scholes insight was that the return from the option could also be obtained from a holding of the underlying share if this was partly financed by borrowing. In this example, were an investor to purchase 4 shares at 100p partly financed by borrowing $\dfrac{380}{1.02} = 372.55$, this would cost the investor 27.45p. The return from the investment would be

either $4 \times 110 - 380 = 60$

or $4 \times 95 - 380 = 0$

This is precisely the same as the return which would have been obtained from five call options on the shares. It may be inferred that in a reasonably efficient market the cost of these investments would therefore have to be equal, i.e. the price of 5 call options would have to be 27.45p, that is 5.49p per option.

To see how the previous argument was constructed, it is important to notice first that the return from the option and the return from the share are directly related, as follows:

Return from:	Share		Option
Either	110	and	12
or	95	and	0
Difference	15		12

There is a difference of 15 between the possible returns for the share, and 12 for the option. It follows that the difference between the possible returns from four-fifths $\left(\dfrac{12}{15} \right)$ of one share will be 12, the same as for the option that is

$$\frac{4}{5} 110 - \frac{4}{5} 95 = 88 - 76 = 12$$

This can be converted into exactly the same return as is obtained from the option by arranging to pay out 76 at the end of a month. This is easily done by borrowing 76/1.02 at the beginning. The total cost of this package to an investor would be

$$\frac{4}{5} 100 - \frac{76}{1.02} = 5.49$$

Above this was multiplied by five to avoid involving fractions of shares.

The ratio, h $\left(= \dfrac{12 - 0}{110 - 95}$ in our example $\right)$ of the differences in the returns on the option and the share is known as the hedge ratio. The reason for this name is that a riskless hedge involving only the share and the call option can be formed by buying a proportion h of one share and writing one call on the share. The cost of and returns from this in our example are as follows:

Cost	Return
$0.8 \times 100 - C_0$	Either $0.8 \times 110 - 12 = 76$
	or $0.8 \times 95 - 0 = 76$

Since the return is the same whatever happens and therefore riskless, it may be inferred that the investment will be priced so as to offer a rate of return equal to the rate of interest, that is

$$(0.8 \times 100 - C_0)(1.02) = 76$$
whence $C_0 = 5.49$

Since the intrinsic value of the option is $100 - 98 = 2$ it will not be exercised immediately, since it is worth more 'live', so the option would be sold rather than exercised. Providing the interest rate is greater than zero, it is shown below that this will always be the case for a call option on a non-dividend paying share, i.e. it will never be exercised prematurely.

If it is known that the share price at the end of the month will be either 110p or 95p, and the riskless interest rate is 2 per cent per month, then the share price, P_0, at the beginning of the month must lie somewhere in the range

$$\frac{95}{1.02} < P_0 < \frac{110}{1.02}$$

Otherwise there would be obvious opportunities for making a riskless return in excess of the rate of interest from the share combined with riskless borrowing or lending only, exploitation of which would drive the share price back inside the limits. Table W8.13 shows the theoretical option value corresponding to integer share prices in this range.

Table W8.13

Share price	% increase	Option value	% increase
94		0.69	
95	1.06	1.49	115.9
96	1.05	2.29	53.7
97	1.04	3.09	34.9
98	1.03	3.84	25.9
99	1.02	4.69	20.6
100	1.01	5.49	17.1
101	1.00	6.29	14.6
102	0.99	7.09	12.7
103	0.98	7.89	11.3
104	0.97	8.69	10.1
105	0.96	9.49	9.2
106	0.95	10.29	8.4
107	0.94	11.09	7.8

Two points are worthy of comment. First the extreme volatility of the option price relative to the underlying share price. The ratio of the percentage change in option price to the percentage change in share price ranges from 8 to 109. Secondly, the relative volatility is very much greater the lower the share price, when the option is out-of-the-money. Buying options is clearly a very much more speculative venture than buying shares.

It is a straightforward matter to extend this approach to more than one period. For example, suppose the dynamics of the share price over two periods are as follows:

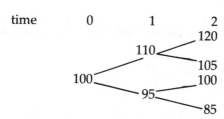

Let us consider a call option written on this share which expires after two months, with an exercise price of 98 and assuming the rate of interest is 2 per cent per month as before. At expiration the return on the call option will be:

$$\left. \begin{array}{l} 120 - 98 = 22 \\ \text{or } 105 - 98 = 7 \\ \text{or } 100 - 98 = 2 \\ \text{or zero} \end{array} \right\} \quad \text{depending on the share price.}$$

Working backwards to time 1, if the share price at time 1 turns out to be 110, then the outcome at time 2 must be

	Share	Option
Either	120	22
or	105	7

The relevant hedge ratio h_1^+ will then be

$$h_1^+ = \frac{22 - 7}{120 - 105} = 1$$

so that by the previous argument the price of the option at time 1 in this event, C_1^+ will be given by

$$(110 - C_1^+)(1.02) = \left\{ \begin{array}{l} 120 - 22 \\ \text{or} \\ 105 - 7 \end{array} \right\} = 98$$

whence $C_1^+ = 13.92$

On the other hand, if the share price at time 1 turns out to be 95, then by analogous reasoning the relevant hedge ratio h_1^- will be

$$h_1^- = \frac{2 - 0}{100 - 85} = \frac{2}{15}$$

so the price of the option, C_1^- will be given by

$$\left(\frac{2}{15} \cdot 95 - C_1^- \right) (1.02) = \left\{ \begin{array}{l} \dfrac{2}{15} \cdot 100 - 2 \\ \text{or} \\ \dfrac{2}{15} \cdot 85 - 0 \end{array} \right\} = 11\tfrac{1}{3}$$

whence $C_1^- = 1.56p$

The theoretical value of the option at time 0 can now be determined in the same way using the derived option values at time 1 The hedge ratio h_0 is

$$h_0 = \frac{13.92 - 1.56}{110 - 95} = \frac{12.36}{15} = 0.824$$

so the price of the option at time 0 is given by

$$(0.824 \times 100 - C_0)(1.02) = \left\{ \begin{array}{l} 0.824 \times 110 - 13.92 \\ \text{or} \\ 0.824 \times 95 - 1.56 \end{array} \right\} = 76.72$$

from which $C_0 = 7.18p$

It will be observed that the price of this two month option is higher than the price of the otherwise identical one month option considered above (5.49p) as would be expected from a priori consideration.

As long as the price of the underlying share on which the option is written follows a discrete, two-step, process as assumed in the above example, this procedure can be used to value an option which expires after any number of periods by working backwards from the expiration date period by period, using the relation

$$(hP_t - C_t)(1 + i) = \left\{ \begin{array}{l} hP_{t+1}^+ - C_{t+1}^+ \\ \text{or} \\ hP_{t+1}^- - C_{t+1}^- \end{array} \right\}$$

the share pays no dividend assuming this relation can be used to determine the value of the call option at each point in time given the price of the share on which it is written. This is possible, if the interest rate is greater than zero, because the option's intrinsic value will always be less than its 'live' value, as the following proof shows.

Assume $i > 0$, let E = exercise price and note that the share price at the time t must satisfy the condition

$$\frac{P_{t+1}^+}{1 + i} > P_t > \frac{P_{t+1}^+}{1 + i}$$

(If this condition did not hold, there would be opportunities for profitable and riskless arbitrage requiring only the share and borrowing or lending at the riskless interest rate.)

If $h = 1(E < P_{t+1}^-)$ then

$$C_t = P_t - \frac{E}{1 + i} < P_t - E$$

If $0 < h < 1(P_{t+1}^+ > E > P_{t+1}^-)$

If $h = \dfrac{P_{t+1}^+ - E}{P_{t+1}^+ - P_{t+1}^-} > \dfrac{P_{t+1}^+ - E}{P_{t+1}^+ - \dfrac{P_{t+1}}{1+i}} > \dfrac{P_t - E^*}{P_t - \dfrac{P_{t+1}}{1+i}}$

Therefore $h \left(P_t - \dfrac{P_{t+1}^-}{1 + i} \right) = C_t > P_t - E$ as required.

(The case $h = 0$ is trivial since both the exercise value and the live value of the option are zero.)

because $\dfrac{p}{q} > \dfrac{p-a}{q-a}$ if $p > q$

since $\dfrac{p-a}{q-a} = \dfrac{p\left(1-\dfrac{a}{p}\right)}{q\left(1-\dfrac{a}{p}\right)} < \dfrac{p\left(1-\dfrac{a}{p}\right)}{q\left(1-\dfrac{a}{p}\right)} = \dfrac{p}{q}$

At no time therefore during the life of the option would premature exercise be worthwhile, so that recursive application of the above relation will yield the current option value.

This does not necessarily follow if the share pays dividends during the life of the option. To illustrate, suppose that in the previous example the dividend yield of the share is 12 per cent, that the share will be ex dividend when the option expires at time 2, and that share prices in the example are cum dividend. From the standpoint of the option buyer, who will not benefit from the dividend at expiration, the share price dynamics look like this:

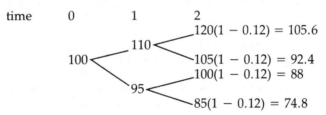

```
time        0          1          2
                                  120(1 − 0.12) = 105.6
                          110
      100                         105(1 − 0.12) = 92.4
                                  100(1 − 0.12) = 88
                          95
                                  85(1 − 0.12) = 74.8
```

If the share price at time 1 turns out to be 110p, then the value of the option live, C_1^+, will be given by

$$\left(\dfrac{7.6}{13.2} \times 110 - C_1^+\right)(1.02) = \dfrac{7.6}{13.2} \times 105.6 - 7.6$$

since $\qquad h_1^+ = \dfrac{7.6}{13.2}$

so that $\qquad C_1^+ = 11.18\text{p}$

In this case, the option will be worth more if it is exercised prematurely at time 1, since the exercise value is

$$110 - 98 = 12$$

Thus premature exercise of a call on a share which pays a dividend before the call expires may occur, since the value of the prospective dividend is included in the share price before it is paid, and the option buyer will lose out on this if the option is held unless the shares go ex dividend. This is not, however, a foregone conclusion, as the value of the option live may well still exceed the intrinsic value even so. This would have been the case had the dividend yield been, say, 10 per cent rather than 12 per cent (in which case $C_1^+ = 12.86$, so the option would not be exercised).

The procedure for valuing an option can still be adapted to cope with the problem of dividend payments by substituting the exercise value for the live value of the option in the calculation whenever premature exercise would be optimal. Thus in the above example 11.18p would be taken as the option value corresponding with a share price of 110p at time 1 in order to calculate the theoretical option value at time 0.

Dividend payments and the consequential possibility of premature exercise which this raises present more of a problem for the application of an option valuation formula. If it is assumed that the price of the underlying shares follows some well defined stochastic process over time, then it may be possible to obtain an explicit formula which relates the current equilibrium price of the option, to the current price of the share, the exercise price and expiration date of the option, the interest rate and certain parameters of the stochastic process which generates share prices. This can be done for the discrete two-step process considered here if it is assumed for example that the percentage by which the share price moves up or down is the same each period. The resulting Binomial Option Pricing Formula appears in Cox, Ross and Rubinstein, 1971.

In the examples used earlier it was suggested that the time intervals were one month long. Clearly the two-step pattern of share price movements assumed would be somewhat contrived over month long intervals. However, there is nothing in the approach which precludes the choice of a shorter interval, perhaps a day, or an hour or even less. The shorter the interval, the less objectionable and more realistic this representation of the way share prices develop over time. In the limit, as the interval length approaches zero, the share price follows a continuous stochastic process, and in order to derive the value of the call option written on the share, the hedge must also be adjusted continuously rather than at discrete intervals as in the previous examples. Though the mathematics involved in its derivation are formidable, this is the basis of the Black–Scholes option valuation formula which has received so much attention.

The option value produced by the recursive procedure described here gives results which converge rapidly to that given by the Black–Scholes formula as the step length is shortened. In addition the recursive procedure is very much more flexible and can cope easily with problems like premature exercise, which are very difficult to handle using the Black–Scholes formula.

It may also be remarked that since it is based on an arbitrage argument, the relationship between the value of the call option and the value of the share on which it is written is not dependent on any assumptions about the risk preferences of investors. Profitable riskless arbitrage opportunities would be created if the relationship did not hold, from which any investor regardless of preferences could benefit. For this reason also it is unnecessary to assign probabilities to the up or down movement in share price at each step. Regardless of what these probabilities are the option value will be the same given the price of the share.

The valuation of put options can be approached in much the same way as call options, and this can be illustrated using the same numerical example as above.

Consider a put option which expires at time 1 with an exercise price of 98. The return on the share and the put at time 1 will be as follows:

	Share	Put
Either	110	0
or	95	$98 - 95 = 3$

The hedge ratio defined as for a call option is 3/15. The return on the put can be reconstructed by a short sale of one-fifth of a share and a loan of $\frac{1}{5} \times \frac{110}{1.02} = 21.57$. The return from this will be

$$\text{either} \qquad -\frac{1}{5} \times 110 + \frac{1}{5} \times 110 = 0$$

$$\text{or} \qquad -\frac{1}{5} \times 95 + \frac{1}{5} \times 110 = 3$$

$$\text{and the cost is } \frac{1}{5} \times \frac{110}{1.02} - \frac{1}{5} \times 100 = 1.57$$

It may be inferred that the value of the put option should be 1.57 at time 0. As for a call option this procedure can be extended to any number of periods. In the case of a put option, however, premature exercise may be optimal. For example, if the share price was 95, the value of the put live would be

$$\frac{1}{5} \times \frac{110}{1.02} - \frac{1}{5} \times 95 = 2.57$$

whereas the exercise value would be $98 - 95 = 3$ so that it would be optimal to exercise the put at time 0. In the case of a put option dividend payments on the share act in the opposite direction from a call to diminish the likelihood of early exercise. This is because the holder of the put will benefit from the drop in price when the shares go ex dividend.

(d) Put options

A put option is the right to *sell* an underlying security at a specified price (the exercise or strike price) on or before a specified date (the expiration date). Using the data given above, if you hold put options on Allied Lyons July 460 you have the right to sell 1,000 shares at a price of 460.

The buyer of the put is long in a put, but why does a buyer buy and a seller sell? Taking the point of view of the buyer — he or she will have formed an expectation that shares in Allied Lyons are going to fall in price. We can set up three scenarios:

1. *Permanent decline* — buying a put can provide what we call a highly levered (or geared) way of profiting from the fall in price.
2. *Temporary decline* — buying a put can profit from this provided the time is right. However, the investor may be a holder of the underlying shares so the put can provide a hedge to protect the downside risk if they do decline.
3. *Volatile shares* — if Allied Lyons had gone through a period of volatility, but currently had increased in price and is expected to continue, then by buying shares and the put as a hedge the investor is protected both ways.

We can illustrate this as follows. Suppose the investor is appraising the current economic trends and anticipates that the stock market will decline with Allied Lyons falling too. He or she buys an October 460 contract in June at 10p, when the current closing price is 468p. The put option is really worthless (out of the money) in terms of what we referred to earlier as intrinsic value. No rational investor would sell for 460. However, there are nearly four months to go before the option expires. If the share price does drop to, say, 450p, and the price of the put rises to, say, 30p (it has an intrinsic value of 10p), then the profits look like this:

		£
Put purchase: 1 contract at 10p	=	100
Put sale: 1 contract at 30p	=	300
Gross profit before expenses	=	200

A profit of 200% on the original outlay has been made as a result of a 10% decline in the share price. We show this diagrammatically in Fig. W8.5.

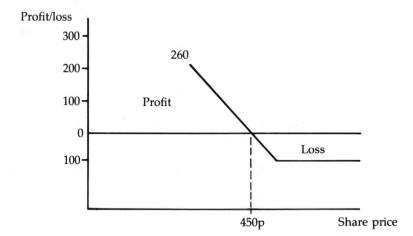

Figure W8.5   Put option.

The maximum loss the investor can make is the £100 invested (plus the expenses), even if the price rises to 550p. He or she starts to recover the investment once the share price falls to 450p. The put option is really the mirror image of the call option.

Just as in the case of the call option, there are premiums on top of the intrinsic values: time periods, volatility, dividends and interest. Taking these in order:

1. *Time.* The same reasoning for calls applies for puts — the further away the expiration date, the more chance a share price will move; in this case the hope is for a decline. The closer to the expiration date the smaller the premium over the intrinsic value.
2. *Volatility.* Volatile shares will trade with higher premiums (or calls and puts) than the more stable shares because of the greater opportunity of profit.
3. *Dividends.* The effects of dividend payments on puts and calls are opposite. As shares drop in price after a dividend (ex-dividend share price) this enhances the value of the put.

4. *Interest*. High interest rates have the effect of reducing the value of the option. The reasoning for this is that puts are often held as a hedge, so the investor is long in the put and long in the share too, and therefore does not have free cash to take advantage of the higher rates.

The other factors are combined in various option pricing models, but elsewhere in the text we have argued that the value of anything is the result of the interaction of supply and demand in the market, and market sentiment (the pulling power of bulls and bears) can affect the premiums too. For the puts it should be a bear market that gives the higher premiums.

(e) Selling (writing) puts

If an investor thinks the market will remain stable or rise, he or she can sell puts to add to his or her cash flow. This creates a liability, and he or she may have to buy the shares at the exercise price at any time. That might have been one of the objectives in selling the put — the acquisition of the shares at a lower price at a later date. This is a strategy followed by many institutional investors. Space precludes a fuller coverage of the writing of puts to acquire shares or for income.

(f) Straddles

A straddle is a put and a call option on the same share with the same exercise price and expiration date. This strategy can be followed by an investor who expects a major price change, but does not know the direction. This could be the case with a commodity share and/or a share which has risen in price as a potential acquisition victim but where the takeover might not occur.

We can illustrate this for a share in ABC. It is January and it has risen over 30% in the wake of bid rumours (from 30p to 40p). An investor has estimated that if the bid does materialize, the share price could rise to 50p or 60p. The other scenario is that the share price could fall back to 30p if the bid does not materialize. The investor could hedge — buy the shares and a put option — but this would limit the downside loss while preserving the upside potential of profit. A straddle can give a position of profit no matter which way the share finally moves.

Suppose there is a call option (February, 30p) available and a similar put available — the call has a price of 5p and the put 3p — and the investor buys a contract of each. We show the profit/loss position in Fig. W8.6. The break-even points (note that no commissions are included) for the investor are 38p (the exercise price of 30p plus the combined cost of the two contracts) for the call option to start to give a profit, and 22p for the put option. The writer of the straddle obviously expects the price to remain relatively stable. If it does then the writer profits from the price paid for the option as it expires. However, if it does rise or fall, then the writer stands to lose on either the put or the call,but clearly not both. If, for example, the share price rises to 45p, the investor who holds the straddle will make on the call option and the put will expire. The writer, of course, will lose on the call, receive the premium on the expired put, but still lose overall. This highlights the risk undertaken. If the price rise is only to 35p then the investor loses overall; the writer gains.

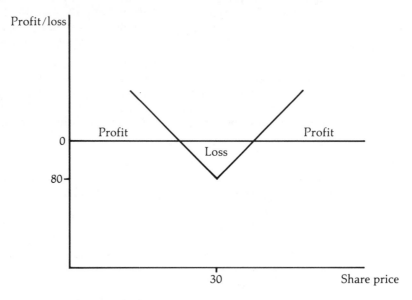

Figure W8.6   Risk–reward of a straddle.

W8.6   New businesses

At the outset of the chapter we talked about the apparent shortage of finance for small business. There is another class of small business — the new business. Governments of many countries, not least the United Kingdom, have claimed that an important factor for the economic recovery out of a recession would be the emergence of new businesses. The fashionable topic now is the provision of venture capital to these new enterprises. Some are new only in the sense of being spun-off from another enterprise with, say, a management buy-out, and we have mentioned those already. Others are literally brand new. For a fuller discussion of venture capital finance see Bank of England (1982, 1984) and Treasury (1985).

W8.7   Interest rate and currency swaps

With the advent of swaps, enterprises can now have a flexibility of debt management of term, interest rate and currency which was unheard of even several years ago. Arnold (1984) provides an excellent coverage of interest rate swaps. To provide an example of them in action, the following extract is taken from *The Economist* of 12.7.1986, p. 78.

Why Treasurers Swap

Paris

Profits from one activity over the past three years at Gaz de France (GDF), the French state-owned gas company, have just topped FFr1 billion ($143m). These profits have not been made by installing new gas fires in Parisian homes nor by discovering new gas fields in Bordeaux. They have been made, instead, in swaps.

Swaps (together with other state-of-the-art financing techniques involving futures and options) allow companies to manage their debts actively. A company can, for example, shift its debt from floating-rate to fixed, or from dollars to yen. This enables the company to match its debts with its assets: i.e., if a company starts making more profits in dollars it may want to have its debts in dollars. For a good debt manager like Mr Jean Reboul, treasurer of GDF, playing with swaps can also mean raising profits.

Three years ago, GDF decided to reduce its dollar debt by swapping into European currencies. Mr Reboul correctly foresaw that the dollar would rise. The soaring dollar in 1984 and 1985 meant that GDF's swaps out of the dollar became profitable, because swaps — like securities — have a value in the secondary market.

Sounds complicated? This is how one of Mr Reboul's currency swaps worked. In March 1984, he swapped $44m of 13¾% debt for 50m of European currency units (ecus) at 11% at an exchange rate of $10 to 1.1375 ecus. In eight years' time, GDF was to pay its swapper 50m ecus and receive $44m. These payments would redeem each company's original bond issues from which the debts derived. For the life of the swap each would meet the other's interest payments. Thus, while each could service its underlying debts, both companies had effectively switched out of those debts for eight years.

Six months later, the dollar had risen against the ecu. This was good for GDF. The ecu was worth less in dollar terms, so the size of GDF's debt was reduced. If the exchange rate at that time of $1 to 1.275 ecus stayed the same until the swap expired, GDF could buy the 50m ecus for less than $44m; its swapper would need more than 50m ecus to buy $44m. However, Mr Reboul reckoned that the dollar might not stay above the exchange rate fixed into the swap for long, so he decided to cash in the swap's profit. He was able to do this because banks provide a secondary market in swaps. Mr Reboul sold — i.e., he reverted to the original debt structure — for a cash payment (effectively a profit) of $1.4m.

In 1985, Mr Reboul continued to swap out of the dollar and then to sell later in the secondary market. By doing this he netted tens of millions of dollars in profit. His powers of foresight were not infallible, however. In the autumn of 1985 he made further swaps out of the dollar, believing it would climb back to its early 1985 peak. The dollar, alas for him, continued to fall. After three months, Mr Reboul decided to cut his losses and take out short-term cover against the dollar falling further. He bought options to sell the dollar at exchange rates of FFr7.25–7.50 to the dollar.

Another good move. The dollar is now below FFr7. These contracts are profitable and mostly compensate for the losses incurred on the swaps out of the dollar. If Mr Reboul believes the dollar is about to move up again, he can cash in the options and then benefit from the swaps if the dollar does rise.

Not all companies like playing with swaps, or active debt management of any kind. Treasurers, some argue, are unlikely to predict interest-rate and currency movements correctly more than half the time. Companies take enough risks in their main businesses without taking on additional financial risks. But to the likes of Mr Reboul — and their number is fast increasing — the advantages seem obvious. Hanging on

Swapping it all back home

Currency composition of debt (%)

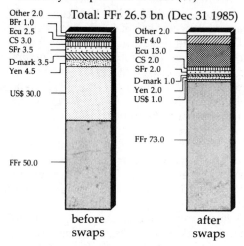

Total: FFr 26.5 bn (Dec 31 1985)

before swaps

Other 2.0
BFr 1.0
Ecu 2.5
CS 3.0
SFr 3.5
D-mark 3.5
Yen 4.5
US$ 30.0
FFr 50.0

after swaps

Other 2.0
BFr 4.0
Ecu 13.0
CS 2.0
SFr 2.0
D-mark 1.0
Yen 2.0
US$ 1.0
FFr 73.0

Source: *The Economist*

Figure W8.7 Swapping it all back home: Gaz de France.

to one form of debt is like buying a bond and holding it whatever happens to the price. Swapping debts in today's volatile markets is no more speculative than leaving them alone.

W8.8 Privatization

The privatization of parts of the public sector in the United Kingdom has had a significant impact on the financing plans of companies as there is more competition for funds. Reference has already been made to the amount of funds raised in the privatization programme, and to some of the public policy issues arising in terms of the increased concentration of the corporate sector. Although there are still plans for further privatization, at the time of writing some of these are still in doubt: for example, British Coal.

W8.9 Discussion questions

Note: Suggested answers to questions 8.1–8.5 are given in section W8.12 on pp. 528–31.

8.1 'Investment good, consumption bad!' Discuss this statement.

8.2 Outline the kind of factors that may cause a gap in the provision of finance for small business, particularly business start-ups.

8.3 Examine the reasons for the growth of financial leases in the United

Kingdom paying particular attention to the tax regime, particularly the 1984 tax changes.

8.4 Leasing can be argued to be equivalent to using borrowed capital. Suggest how the commitment to future leasing rentals could be shown in a company's accounts.

8.5 What risks does a leasing company face? How might it prepare against adverse contingencies?

8.6 Discuss the reasons why the shareholders' privilege of having first call on any new equity issued is circumvented in a growing number of cases.

8.7 When a company makes a rights issue, how does the subscription price affect shareholders' net worth?

8.8 Appraise the importance of issuing costs in terms of the scale of finance and the frequency used.

8.9 When a company makes a placing at a discount, how does it affect the net worth of the existing shareholders?

8.10 Discuss the various risks to an investor associated with holding a share or a bond.

8.11 Discuss the price/yield relationship that might exist between corporate and government bonds.

8.12 What are the advantages and disadvantages of an enterprise's issuing preference shares?

8.13 Discuss the 'characteristics' of ordinary and preference shares and bonds.

8.14 Why are call features sometimes present in bonds?

8.15 Why do companies often include sinking fund provisions in bond issues?

8.16 What effects might sinking fund provisions have on the price of the bond?

8.17 Why and in what way might borrowers and investors in Britain gain from a system of bond ratings?

8.18 Consider the constraints on a company's ability to raise long-term capital.

8.19 What is the Unlisted Securities Market?

8.20 Discuss the dangers of financing long-term capital needs by short-term instruments.

8.21 In the eurosterling market zero-coupon bonds have been issued. What is the rationale for these?

8.22 'The main purpose of an option market is to manage risk, not create it.' Discuss.

8.23 Discuss the term 'securitization'.

8.24 Provide a critique of the privatization programme in the UK from the point of view of public policy issues.

W8.10   Worked problems

Note: Answers to problems 8.1–8.5 are given in section W8.13 on pp. 531–2.

8.1 Calculate the value of a right for a one-for-ten issue with a subscription price of 80p and cum-rights price of £1.

8.2 Taking the data on yields from *Financial Statistics* or the *Bank of England Quarterly Bulletin*, plot the index of corporate bonds against the representative yield on gilts, say, 15 years, for, say, 5 or more years, using quarterly data. Attempt to explain the relationships you have found.

8.3 Examine the financial pages of one of the leading national dailies for a few consecutive Mondays and select one or more new issues of shares. Follow it through from the press comment prior to issue until after the issue itself. Try to identify and account for any apparent mispricing.

8.4 Take a small sample of rights issues and follow the share price through from pre-announcement to announcement and finally until the exercise date has passed. Do the prices follow what one would expect *a priori* from theory (and common sense)? Do you detect any price pressure?

8.5 A share sells at £2 cum rights and a one-for-ten rights issue is made. Prove that with a subscription price of £1.50, the existing shareholders should be no worse off.

8.6 Taking the option price data given in the Workbook for RTZ (see p. 501) and with the closing price of 563p, explain the price patterns that emerge across time and with the two different exercise prices for both calls and puts.

8.7 Given the following data, determine the value of the call options at their expiration dates:

Option	Market price per share at the expiration date £	Exercise price of the option £
A	10	12
B	25	21
C	48	52
D	7	5

8.8 Two companies, X-G Company and X-T Company, have both actively traded options on their shares with the same exercise price, £30. Moreover, the current market prices of the two shares are the same, £27 per share. Yet the current market price of the X-G option is £2.25 while that of the X-T option is £3.90. How can this difference in option prices occur?

8.9 Gloria X is considering writing a 30-day option on VS Corporation, which is currently trading at £60 per share. The exercise price will also be £60 per share, and the premium received on the option will be £3.75. At what share price will she make money, at what price will she begin to lose money, and at what prices will she lose £5 and £10 on each option that is written?

8.10 The shares of ABC Company and XYZ Company are expected to have the following probability distributions with respect to market price per share six months hence:

Probability of occurrence	ABC £	XYZ £
0.15	34	22
0.20	38	28
0.30	40	36
0.20	42	44
0.15	46	50

Options exist for each of these shares, and both have an exercise price of £38 and an expiration date six months from now.

1. What is the expected value of market price per share six months hence for the two companies?
2. What is the expected value of option price for the two options at expiration, assuming the options are held to this time?
3. Reconcile your answers to 1. and 2.

W8.11   Case study: FBS Services

This case study is meant to illustrate the difficulty of raising finance for a very small business and therefore stands in contradistinction to the relative ease with which quoted companies can raise finance. The data are taken from a real-life situation, but the industry and names have been changed.

FBS Services is a four-man partnership, and is concerned with providing repairs and other services to the engineering industry. The four partners are Fred Small whose previous position was of production director and who has had 25 years' service in the engineering industry; Joe Wright who has a degree in mechanical engineering and who has also had some experience in management; James Grimshaw and Charles Quimby, both of whom have had considerable experience in the engineering industry.

The company is situated on an industrial estate and is very well placed to serve the numerous enterprises in the local area. It is estimated that their catchment area extends up to a radius of 20 miles. Entry to the repair and services industry does not require a high capital outlay. In the case of FBS, £10,050 had been sufficient to establish the business, though the partners had secured bank support. Of the £10,050 only £3,000 had been introduced as cash. An overdraft of £4,500 from the ND Bank Ltd had been granted. As part of the loan sanction the bank had not only wanted security but projections of the cash flow prospects of the firm for the forthcoming year. These are provided as Tables W8.14 and W8.15.

The firm, after a ten-month trading period (see Tables W8.16–W8.18) had established good sales contacts and customers' confidence had increased. It had increased its plant capacity and this had enabled it to increase its sales.

Table W8.14   Projected cash flow forecast for 12 months to 30 June 1986 (£).

	Jul.	Aug.	Sep.	Oct.	Nov.	Dec.	Jan.	Feb.	Mar.	Apr.	May	Jun.
Cash introduced: Partners	3,000											
Bank	4,500											
Sales		750	3,190	4,250	3,500	4,880	5,630	6,370	6,910	7,430	7,950	8,502
Cash in hand b/f												1,212
Cash deficit c/f	911	2,657	2,666	2,322	5,106	4,806	5,588	3,955	2,338	651		
	£8,411	£3,407	£5,856	£6,572	£8,606	£9,686	£11,218	£10,325	£9,248	£8,081	£7,950	£9,712
Purchases	636	1,593	2,232	2,739	3,153	3,600	3,762	3,984	4,302	4,614	4,935	5,100
Plant and machinery etc.	5,000				2,000		1,500					
Lease	1,250											
Rates	195				390							
Rent	330			330			330			330	390	
Power			125			125			125			125
Telephone and postage	10	10	70	10	10	70	10	10	70	10	10	70
Carriage and packing		13	20	25	29	33	38	41	44	47	50	50
Advertising	60			60			30					
Stationery	40	40	12	12	12	12	12	12	12	12	12	12
Repairs and renewing			50			50			50			50
Bank charges	45	45	45	45	45	45	45	45	45	45	45	45
Capital repayment	125	125	125	125	125	125	125	125	125	125	125	125
Professional charges		150										30
Sundries	80			40			40			40		
Insurance	120											
Motor expenses	170	170	170	170	170	170	170	170	170	170	170	170
Drawings	350	350	350	350	350	350	350	350	350	350	350	350
Cash in hand c/f											1,212	3,585
Cash deficit b/f		911	2,657	2,666	2,322	5,106	4,806	5,588	3,955	2,338	651	
	£8,411	£3,407	£5,856	£6,572	£8,606	£9,686	£11,218	£10,325	£9,248	£8,081	£7,950	£9,712

Table W8.15   Trading account to 30 June 1986 (£).

	Jul.	Aug.	Sep.	Oct.	Nov.	Dec.	Jan.	Feb.	Mar.	Apr.	May	Jun.	Total
Sales		2,120	3,190	4,250	4,880	5,630	6,370	6,910	7,430	7,950	8,500	8,500	65,730
Opening stock		636	957	1,275	1,464	1,689	1,911	2,073	2,229	2,385	2,550	2,550	19,719
Purchases	636	1,593	2,232	2,739	3,153	3,600	3,984	4,302	4,614	4,935	5,100	5,100	41,988
Less Closing stock	636	957	1,275	1,464	1,689	1,911	2,073	2,229	2,385	2,550	2,550	2,550	2,550
Gross profit		£848	£1,276	£1,700	£1,952	£2,252	£2,548	£2,764	£2,972	£3,180	£3,400	£3,400	£26,292
Lease amortization	52	52	52	52	52	52	52	52	52	52	52	53	625
Rates	65	65	65	65	65	65	65	65	65	65	65	65	780
Rent	110	110	110	110	110	110	110	110	110	110	110	110	1,320
Light, heat and power	42	42	41	42	42	41	42	42	41	42	42	41	500
Telephone and postage	30	30	30	30	30	30	30	30	30	30	30	30	360
Carriage and packing		13	20	25	29	33	38	41	44	47	50	50	390
Advertising	60			60			30						150
Stationery	40	40	12	12	12	12	12	12	12	12	12	12	200
Repairs and renewals			50			50			50			50	200
Bank charges and interest	45	45	45	45	45	45	45	45	45	45	45	45	540
Professional charges	150											30	180
Sundries	80			40			40			40			200
Insurance	10	10	10	10	10	10	10	10	10	10	10	10	120
Motor expenses	170	170	170	170	170	170	170	170	170	170	170	170	2,040
Depreciation	266	267	267	294	294	295	339	340	340	339	340	340	3,721
	1,120	844	872	955	859	913	983	917	969	962	926	1,006	11,326
Net profit/(loss)	(1,120)	4	404	745	1,093	1,339	1,565	1,847	2,003	2,218	2,474	2,394	14,966
	—	£848	£1,276	£1,700	£1,952	£1,252	£2,548	£2,764	£2,972	£3,180	£3,400	£3,400	£26,292

The partners had refrained from drawing too heavily on the enterprise, but they were hoping that soon the business would provide them all with a living. To this end they were seeking further expansion and were proposing to make a further application to the ND Bank for an increase in overdraft facilities.

Appraise a further loan application.

Table W8.16 Trading and profit and loss account for 10 months ended 30 April 1985.

	£	£
Sales		19,811
Purchases	10,638	
Less: Closing stock	885	
		9,753
		10,058
Less:		
Motor expenses	1,214	
Rent	1,100	
Rates	650	
Insurance	96	
Light, heat and power	344	
Stationery and postage	54	
Repairs and renewals	182	
Telephone	155	
Sundries	377	
Bank overdraft interest	264	
Bank loan interest	631	
Bank charges	71	
Professional charges	155	
Depreciation:		
Plant and machinery	1,032	
Fixtures and fittings	21	
Motor vehicles	1,300	
Lease amortization	476	
		8,122
Net profit for the period		£1,936

Table W8.17 Balance sheet at 30 April 1985.

	Notes	£	£
Fixed assets	1		13,144
Lease consideration	2		524
Current assets:			
Stock		885	
Debtors		8,526	
Cash		21	
		9,432	

	Notes	£	£
Current liabilities:			
Bank overdraft		2,656	
Creditors		5,231	
		7,887	
Net current assets			1,545
			15,213
Less: ND Bank Ltd loan			4,831
			£10,382
Financed by:			
Partners' capital accounts	3		10,050
Partners' current accounts	4		332
			£10,382

Table W8.18   Notes to the Accounts for period ended 30 April 1985

1. Fixed assets:

	Total £	Plant and machinery £	Fixtures and fittings £	Motor vehicles £
Cost:				
Additions	15,497	7,447	250	7,800
30 April 1985	15,497	7,447	250	7,800
Depreciation:				
Charge for period	2,353	1,032	21	1,300
30 April 1985	2,353	1,032	21	1,300
Net book value at 30 April 1985	£13,144	£6,415	£229	£6,500

The depreciation rates used are estimated to write off the cost of fixed assets over their useful lives as follows:

Plant and machinery — 20% of cost
Fixtures and fittings — 10% of cost
Motor vehicles   — 20% of cost

2. Lease consideration:

The cost of the lease is amortized equally over the period of letting of the related property.

	£
Cost	1,000
Less: Amortization	476
	£524

3. Partners' capital accounts:

	Total £	F. Small £	J. Wright £	J. Grimshaw £	C. Quimby £
Capital introduced	£10,050	£2,950	£2,000	£3,250	£1,850

4. Partners' current accounts:

	Total £	F. Small £	J. Wright £	J. Grimshaw £	C. Quimby £
Net profit for the period	1,936	484	484	484	484
Less: Drawings	1,604	410	410	392	392
	£332	£74	£74	£92	£92

How corporations use off-exchange instruments

By Lawrence R. Quinn

When it comes to structuring new debt financings, Eastman Kodak Co. applies the same sort of creativity that goes into its new product development and marketing.

Keep the product high quality, easy to use and understand — 'user friendly'. Perhaps most important, push innovation; add a few new bells and whistles that improve technology and keep buyers excited.

Do all that and, if production, marketing and distribution costs are lowered at the same time, so much the better.

'Over the last year or two we at Kodak have used quite a few bells and whistles to enhance the value of our debt issues,' says Alfred Wargo, a financing specialist at the company. 'It's safe to say that almost every one of our deals last year had at least one bell or whistle.'

Among recent offerings from Kodak: a 9% coupon note containing five $470.60-strike call options — hardly the stuff of traditional Fortune 100 bond financings.

'We'll be exploring a lot of alternatives and tools having features like that,' says Wargo. 'We're going to be focusing on interest rate risk, exploring a lot of alternatives and tools (like the ones in that offering). If these bells and whistles are available to us and if our investment bankers can use them to help structure a deal, we're going to take advantage of them.'

Kodak may be the most aggressive and innovative corporate user of what are called 'off-exchange-traded hybrid financial instruments'. Hybrids are tools that treasury executives use in order to make their securities more attractive to the potential purchasers. In some cases, they can be used to lower the cost of the issuance to the corporation.

Another type of corporate hybrid is less common: transactions that contain both futures and forward contract aspects. Cash-settled forward contracts between companies would be one example.

Hybrids enhancing securities offerings usually offer much more to buyers than the benefits typically associated with most corporate issues. Historically, bond buyers have expected nothing more and asked for nothing more than a safe investment in an AAA- or higher-rated company, offering a guaranteed return over an agreed-upon period.

With hybrid instruments attached, however, the bond becomes a much more dynamic financial instrument, with return tied to the performance of a particular commodity or financial index over the bond's life.

Oil-indexed units

One of the best-known examples involves Standard Oil of Ohio. In the mid-1980s, the company, now part of BP America, issued a new kind of security that it called oil-indexed units. These securities consisted of eight debentures totaling $8,000 in face amount and two notes totaling $2,000 in face amount.

Each unit earns contingent interest pegged to increases in the spot price for West Texas Intermediate crude oil, allowing holders to benefit from oil price volatility or diversify their exposure to energy costs — while still receiving a guaranteed return of principal at maturity.

Conceivably, investors could receive, either at maturity or redemption, as much as $2,550 for notes due in 1990 and $3,000 for notes due in 1992, depending on increases above $25 per barrel in the price of West Texas Intermediate oil.

Response to the initial offering, totaling $250 million, was strong enough that the company increased it by $50 million four days later.

The offering does not need to be pegged to just a single commodity to be considered a hybrid.

One brokerage firm, for example, tied the rate of interest it paid on a bond issue to the volume of shares traded on the NYSE.

'They argued that, if the volume went up, they were going to make some money so they could pay more interest,' says Jim McConnon, a consultant with RXR Capital Management Inc., a hedge consulting and money management company based in Stamford, Conn.

Nor are these the only varieties of hybrids. In some instances, the buyer may be able to choose the form of payment at maturation — cash or the physical commodity to which the bond's performance is attached (most common with gold or silver).

In addition, investors may have the opportunity to 'cash in' before maturation if the performance of the underlying commodity reaches an agreed-upon level that would make early redemption desirable.

In early 1980 before the silver crash, at least one mining company put together a hybrid issue to attract investors who might otherwise have stayed away. Dallas-based Sunshine Mining issued several series of 15-year, silver-indexed bonds. Each series was indexed to either 50 oz. or 80 oz. of silver. Investors had the option of being paid either in silver or dollars. If the value of the silver was higher than the face value of the note at maturity, buyers would be paid the higher amount. The call amounts were paid either semiannually or annually.

In one of the most interesting provisions, if the indexed amount of the bonds at any time exceeded two times the face value and stayed at that high for a specified period, an optional call would be made.

In addition to metals and financial indexes, currencies also have been used as a peg.

Tying yield to dollar

In 1987, the Student Loan Marketing Association offered $100 million of five-year, fixed-rate notes for which the yield to investors increased if the dollar appreciated against the yen and decreased if the dollar fell.

Semiannual interest payments on the notes, at a coupon rate of 10.875%, will be made. Principal at maturity will be paid in dollars; the amount of the principal will be tied to the prevailing dollar/yen exchange rate at that time. In putting the bond issue together, the association simultaneously hedged its currency risks.

Many of these deals, regardless of what bells and whistles are attached, may offer significant tax advantages to investors. If what the investor will receive at maturation isn't a fixed amount of dollars, depending instead on commodity or index performance, investors pay tax only on the capital gain realized at maturation, not on interest payments received over the bond's life.

'The tax benefits are substantial because the investor is getting interest income tax deferred,' says Edward Paules, a New York banker who has analyzed extensively the tax advantages to both investors and corporations. 'After five years, it's especially significant because of the time value of money. My contention is that tax benefits frequently outweigh the economic benefits. I have seen benefits of as much as 200 basis points over 10 years.

'For example, let's suppose there is no way to hedge the price of gold 10 years forward. Under original issue discount regulations (a section of the tax code), if the amount the investor gets back at maturity is, in fact, uncertain, then the coupon, whatever it may be, is not considered income.'

While these hybrids may offer a substantial payoff to savvy investors, the benefit to corporate issuers is no less noteworthy. In general, with securities hybrids, those benefits can be broken down into these categories:

- The corporation may be able to pay a below-market coupon.

'Let's say the issue and what it pays is tied to gold (prices),' Paules says. 'In the past, the corporation might have issued 10-year debt at 10%. But, if the return is tied to gold, the corporation might get away with a 6% coupon if, in fact, the par value at maturity has gone up because the price of gold has risen.'

Adds Lilly M. Palmieri, a vice president with Emcor Eurocurrency Management in New York, a corporate hedge consulting firm, 'If you attach a bunch of options, as Kodak has to its issues, investors put a higher value on the issue, and it ends up costing Kodak less.'

- For corporations that have difficulty obtaining 'traditional' types of financings because of poor credit ratings, adding hybrid characteristics to an issue may attract investors who otherwise wouldn't touch the company's securities.
- Hybrids may attract a type of investor who previously has not been interested in that particular company's securities.

'You could be a very good credit risk and still looking for a new type of investor,' Palmieri says. 'You might do a foreign currency debt issue, as an example, do a swap and end up with synthetic dollar debt that is more favorable than what could have been gotten on a domestic basis.'

In some instances, issuing a hybrid bond might help two corporations that have an interest in the same commodity but for entirely different reasons.

'Hypothetically, let's say that United Airlines wanted to issue long-term debt. Obviously, the company's very sensitive to the price of fuel oil,' Paules says. 'Another corporation like Mobil might be on the other side of a deal — it's long fuel oil.'

Inverted relationship

'Could United issue a bond where its price is related to that of fuel oil?' he asks. 'You would have an inverted relationship where, if the price of fuel oil goes down, the maturity goes up. That's exactly the kind of instrument Mobil might want to own because it is in the oil business and has the opposite interest.'

Conceivably, not-so-obvious counterparties might join in a transaction.

Paules, who structured deals similar to these while he was an executive at Bankers Trust in New York, says a drug company expressed interest in being the counterparty in an oil debt issuance deal similar to the United Airlines–Mobil Oil example.

'The drug company had a fertilizer subsidiary. It was short oil and needed petroleum distillates to make the fertilizer. So it would have made a natural counterparty' in such an arrangement, Paules explains.

While hybrid securities sound as though they might be attractive to both corporations and investors, few companies have put together these innovative financings to date. Part of the problem is that, until earlier this year, the legal status of such off-exchange-traded financial instruments was unclear. Futures exchanges charged that all off-exchange-traded instruments were illegal under the Commodity Exchange Act and CFTC regulations.

Moreover, which agency would regulate these products, the CFTC or the SEC, was unclear.

Few financial executives and attorneys familiar with hybrid products believe, however, that these regulatory and legal skirmishes have kept corporations interested in issuing hybrid securities out of the market.

'The bottom line is that I doubt there were many hybrids corporations wanted to do that they did not do,' says Edmund R. Schroeder, a partner of Barrett Smith Schapiro Simon & Armstrong in New York and an expert in hybrids law.

If corporations have been slow to embrace hybrids, it's because the way they traditionally put together debt packages leaves little room for incorporating them, Kodak's Wargo says.

'When a lot of companies aproach the debt markets, they look at interest rates as the major issue,' Wargo says. 'They'll look at the rates and decide that today is a good day to do the debt issue. They then go to two or three investment banks and say, "We want to do a 10-year treasury financing and we want you to bid on that," and what they're bidding on is the interest rate'.

'We take a different tact,' Wargo says. 'We have decided that, rather than picking the maturity and letting the investment bankers bid on the interest rate, we pick the lowest interest rate that's acceptable to us over the long term ... Then we tell our investment bankers to give us the longest maturity date they can with that coupon.'

'What that does,' he says, 'is give the investment banker an opportunity to engineer a transaction rather than just bid on a number. That's where the opportunity to bring in a lot of bells and whistles comes in. They really like this approach because it gives them an opportunity to be creative rather than biting the bullet and taking a loss on the rate. They've told us how unusual this is.'

Even if investment bankers are given the liberties that Wargo suggests Kodak enjoys, putting together a deal may be incredibly difficult.

Paules, for example, struggled to find ways to hedge the risks for a debt issuance where the principal due at maturation is contingent on a commodity or index, while still giving investors the tax breaks available only if the risks could not be hedged.

'The difficulty in structuring deals like these is that the financial intermediary — in my case, Bankers Trust — never wanted to be at risk, so we needed to find someone who would take it,' Paules says.

Liquidity scare

Other financial executives and consultants worry that hybrids, if they grow too complex, may actually scare away investors, reducing liquidity. US exchanges invariably mention the possibility of default in off-exchange-traded transactions.

'These are great ideas,' says RXR's McConnon, 'but what happens when the investor wants to sell the bond to the rest of the world? Will you be able to sell it?'

'Nine out of 10 people will say they are not interested because they don't understand these things,' he adds. 'If it's too esoteric, it will limit its marketability and defeat the original purpose of going through the gymnastics to achieve the most attractive security to the end investor.'

McConnon and others agree that, if use of 'bells and whistles' by corporations grows, it will be gradual, tempered primarily by the conservative nature of treasurers and the difficulty of selling these packages to senior management and boards of directors.

As Palmieri says, given a choice, 'Corporate executives would rather keep their debt financings simple.'

Regulators settling their differences

Federal regulators won't stand in the way of corporate treasurers interested in attaching hybrid 'bells and whistles' to debt financing packages. Nor will they mind if treasury departments tie into an automated, over-the-counter system for trading and clearing options on US government securities.

Indeed, treasury executives should welcome decisions made by both the CFTC and the SEC during the first two weeks of January. After years of studying hybrid financial instruments and off-exchange trading systems, these agencies have clarified who will regulate instruments that have look-alike or hybrid types of products attached to them.

Equally important, the regulators have stated that they do not consider off-exchange trading systems illegal violations of the Commodity Exchange Act and CFTC regulations, as some US futures exchanges, particularly the CBOT, have argued.

The SEC's decision regarding off-exchange trading may have the most immediate impact on treasury departments. The SEC approved a plan, first proposed by Security Pacific National Bank more than two years ago, to establish an automated, over-the-counter system for trading and clearing options on US government securities.

Specifically, the SEC's approval allows New York-based Delta Government Options Corp. to become the first registered clearing organization for these over-the-counter options. Designed to meet the trading, hedging and arbitrage needs of primary dealers of government securities, commercial banks and large institutional investors, the Delta system enables users to trade on screen while prices are updated continuously.

RMJ Options Trading Corp., a subsidiary of RMJ Securities, an interdealer broker of government securities, will broker trades on the system. A sophisticated margin system and $200 million of credit enhancements from Security Pacific National Trust Co. and Capital Markets Assurance Corp., a subsidiary of Citicorp, will protect users against the risks that a counterparty will default.

'I think the potential corporate market for the Delta system is well-defined,' says Stephen Lynner, president of RMJ Options. 'Many of the tools currently used by treasurers — floors, ceilings, swaptions — are nothing more than options, or they incorporate options of one sort or another.

'Interest rates — the cost of funds — are very much on the minds of corporate treasurers,' he continues. 'Since US treasuries are the peg used by everyone to determine what those will be, I would think tying into a system like this would be a natural for companies.'

Separately, the CFTC's decision regarding regulation of debt instruments with hybrids attached may result in a gradual increase in their use by corporations.

Generally, the ruling exempts hybrids that are debt or depository instruments that have option components attached to them. Securities registered under the Securities Act of 1933, commercial paper, certain insurance policies and annuity contracts, some private placements, time deposits offered by Federal Deposit Insurance Corp.-insured banks and government securities are all eligible for exemption, provided the futures and options components attached to them meet specified CFTC criteria.

In some instances, at least, treasury executives will still find themselves dealing with the nation's futures and options on futures regulator. Many of the corporate debt issues with options and futures attached have been 'detachable' from the security to increase investor interest. Those issues, alas, will continue to be subject to CFTC scrutiny.

Source: Reprinted from *Futures* magazine, 219 Parkade, Cedar Falls, Iowa 50613, USA.

W8.12 Suggested answers to discussion questions

8.1 Present consumption can be postponed to the future and that this will involve the 'saving' decision of the household. We could perhaps go further and argue that the saving decision is an investment decision, although we have to be a little careful here. In everyday parlance people equate saving to investing. They say they are investing in the stock market, for example. However, investment in the economics context means the purchase of fixed capital or inventories. In macroeconomics the savings and investment decisions are normally seen as separate decisions undertaken by different people. Although this does not have to be the case — a saver can save directly through his or her own business or in a partnership — generally the presence of intermediaries separates out the decision.

In addressing the issue of good or bad to investment and consumption, it is really a matter of concern at the margin. The economic system is there to satisfy the wants of people. These wants can carry an intertemporal factor in that they are often very heavy in early adulthood and decrease with middle and old age. There is a cycle of income too which is not even and which forces borrowing, e.g. mortgage in early life and the repayment and saving for retirement. People who spend everything they earn and borrow on the strength of future income have to be balanced against people who save, otherwise the borrowers could not borrow! Whether this is bad is a value judgement and we try and avoid this. What has to be recognized is that investment in fixed plant machinery and working capital is necessary to permit the continuation of production through time. We cannot therefore consume everything in the current time period. Hence countries that can mobilize capital investment can grow through time, and that is why government policy is often geared to the provision of incentives for investors in industry through grants, tax allowances, etc. In this sense we can say investment is good in that it is necessary. However, this has to be qualified. Is all investment good — what of the divisions between public and private, and what of the need to appraise it against some accepted criteria as discussed earlier in the book (Chapter 4)? Without consumption, firms would not sell what they produced, so we need consumption too. There are charges that we consume too much, that we live in an acquisitive society, that we overproduce in certain areas and underproduce in others (e.g. welfare, health, etc.). This can be discussed in terms of the Galbraith work as well as others. The issues of value judgements have to be dealt with somehow by politicians. An argument which could be used to illustrate the problem of spending *vis-à-vis* investment is that, in aggregate, we can allow for the spendthrift *and* the miser. The ultimate long-term success of a country and the corporate sector within it will rely not just on investment *per se*, but on investment which will maximize the wealth of shareholders and *ipso facto* society. If it is investment in the public sector, it should maximize a social welfare function, yet not ignore the opportunity costs issues (setting the discount rate) of the transfer of funds from the private sector.

8.2 This question is addressed to the long-established myth or reality of lack of finance for small business. Originally it was dubbed the Macmillan Gap. The more recent Wilson Committee also commented upon this apparent gap in the provision of finance.

We have tried to argue that, in any commitment of funds, we are concerned with *risk* and *return*, so lenders to small business have to evaluate their loans in terms of these criteria. So we can pose two questions:

1. are risks any higher than with, say, larger firms?
2. are returns any lower or higher, than with larger firms?

Taking these in order, one of the problems of trying to handle 'risk' is the lack of past information. Of course, this is only relevant if the past is a guide to the future. Assuming that it is, often small firms do not have that history to provide us with information. We cannot go back 5–10 years and assess trends. We may have one or a few years of data only. Also there is the question of how one evaluates the data. Quite often small firms are single product firms relying on a single technology and the expertise of a small number of people. Investors are often wary of this and feel it is too risky. They are 'gambling' on a particular product (as opposed to a large firm which is usually diversified) *and* on the personnel. Indeed the key to investment in many small businesses is the quality of the owners/ managers or whatever. With such a reliance it must be more of a risk.

Of course, if you intend to invest in small business, either you combine it with investment in other size segments of industry, or you diversify your investment across a number of small businesses in an attempt to reduce the risk. However, as Chapter 2 illustrates, if there are common factors at work (e.g. the small-firm effect of the type referred to above), you may not achieve as much diversification as you would like. Some investors have separate 'venture capital' portfolios in which they hold these investments.

The question of whether the returns are higher is fairly straightforward. If the risks are higher, which they would appear to be, the returns must be higher to compensate (given risk aversion) unless they obtain a subsidy of some sort. The need for greater returns is not due solely to the risk element. Many investors will ignore small businesses and concentrate on standard investments. These are well researched and, given their diversification, do not offer much difference to a market return. The very essence of small firms is that they are not diversified and therefore, if they succeed, their success can be very dramatic. Of course, their failure can be a disaster. As we have argued previously, to beat the market you cannot hold it! But many investors cannot or will not take the risk. Hence small business as a sector is often starved of finance.

8.3 A lease involves the client (the lessee) obtaining the use of an asset from a leasing company (the lessor) in return for the payment of a series of rentals with the lessor. In this question we are concerned with a financial or full pay-out lease, i.e. one to amortize the capital outlay *and* give a profit.

It is a fact that financial leases have grown in size since the early 1970s, coming from practically all sectors of the economy, with approximately half in the hands of three or four firms, the impetus coming from the switch in 1970–2 from grants to tax allowances.

The decision to use a lease will depend on the financial effects upon the business, although there are non-financial reasons too. Evidence is available from four UK studies on why lessees lease, and we cite some of the evidence below as compiled by Taylor (1982). The studies found that the reasons are not those you would expect *a priori* from theory. The oft cited reason, conserving cash flow, can only apply if leasing displaces debt on less than a one for one basis, or if leasing is cheaper than debt. Taylor argues that the increase in leasing may be the result of supply-side influences — particularly marketing. Since his article was published, there have been major changes in tax treatment, including:

1. lower CT rates;
2. 25% writing-down allowance in place of 100% first year tax allowance.

Both of these are likely to cause a reduction in the attractiveness of leases.

8.4 Financial leasing obliges the lessee to pay, over an obligatory period, specific payments to amortize the capital outlay and give a profit to the lessor. In this respect, it is identical to a bond. The issuing firm has to make interest and sinking fund payments to amortize the bond and presumably give the borrower a return of capital and a profit.

The financial leverage of a bond is clearly shown in the accounts and normal debt equity measures would pick this up. Financial leases are almost identical, except their life will generally be shorter. How can we show this and take account of it?

We do not take this issue up directly in the text. However, a reference to the *Financial Accounting* text will reveal that we cannot treat it as an off-balance sheet item. The PV of the lease payments is a *liability*, and the value of the asset on the asset side is then amortized over its useful life, producing:

1. a reduction in reported income;
2. adjustment in the liability side.

8.5 The leasing company will grant both *operating* and *financial* leases and the risks it faces will be different across these two kinds of lease.

The concept of a financial lease is that it is a full pay-out lease in which the original outlay is recovered and a profit made. As the lease is written so as to provide a profit, the risks presumably emanate from a miscalculation of the assumptions underlying the lease. How could this occur?

1. As the major lessors are banks, they have offset their substantial profits from banking against the depreciation allowance on equipment purchased for leasing. Presumably this could be disallowed (see 2. below).
2. The lessee may miscalculate his or her costs and margin.
3. Even though it is a full pay-out, lease ownership still rests with the lessor. In the case of a default by the lessee, the assets are reclaimable; but can they be released or sold? In periods of recession, this would be debatable.
4. The tax regime is important for both lessor and lessee.

The issue has been one of the lessor being able to take advantage of tax allowances or capital expenditures not available to the lessee and pass on some of these benefits (see 1. above). This can, of course, change.

In operating leases the asset is not wholly amortized over the period leased, so the lessor does not rely on his or her profit from a single lease contract. A case in point would be car hire, which could be as short as a day. In these contracts the leasing firm has to charge a rate that will reflect utilization. The lease becomes more of a rental. The risks involved here include:

1. risk of under-utilization — rates which are based on some arranged costs underestimate the actual experience;
2. the reverse situation, over-utilization, really an inventory problem resulting in having to turn customers away. This is an issue we discuss in Chapter 9.

W8.13   Answers to worked problems

8.1 $\dfrac{100 - 80}{10 + 1} = 1.82p$ (see p. 518).

8.2 You should find that the corporate yield is always above the government bond yield to reflect the default risk. However, fluctuations will occur which can reflect differential supply and demand factors; different perceptions of the corporate sector (and its leverage) *vis-à-vis* the government sector. This is mispricing which arbitrage (because of limited marketability of corporates) cannot fully reconcile.

8.3 NA.

8.4 NA.

8.5 The value of the share cum rights is 2.00. We can separate out the value of the rights:

$$\frac{\text{Cum rights} - \text{subscription price}}{\text{Exercise ratio} + 1} \quad \text{i.e.} \quad \frac{2.00 - 1.50}{10 + 1} = 4.545\text{p}$$

The price ex rights is therefore 1.95455. We can check the price of the rights as it is:

$$\frac{\text{Ex rights} - \text{subscription price}}{\text{Exercise ratio}} = \frac{1.95455 - 1.50}{10} = 4.5455\text{p}$$

The rights can sell for this, which is the difference between the price of the share ex rights *and* the cum-rights price.

Short-term financing and lending

Learning objectives

The aims of this chapter are to explain:

- the components of the short-term finance function of the enterprise and the interrelationships with the long-term borrowing and lending decisions;
- the importance of cash management to the enterprise;
- the components of current assets and current liabilities and the policies the enterprise can adopt to increase the flow of cash to the enterprise;
- the management of the liquid assets of the enterprise;
- the overall financing needs of the enterprise and the disequilibrium behaviour it may exibit due to the presence of external constraints;
- the way that the size of firms can affect their financing decisions.

W9.1 Introduction

Although Chapter 9 is entitled 'Short-term financing and lending', it is intended to bring together the medium- and long-term financing of Chapter 8 with the short-term aspects of the chapter itself. These are integrated because, with the volatilities of interest rates and currencies, and the evolving nature of financial markets, it is no longer possible to split the finance function into the simple categories of short and long term. Enterprises are now footloose across the maturity spectrum of borrowing and lending as well as between fixed and floating rates.

The key word in the chapter is *cash*. It is the inflows and outflows of cash that are the concerns of the short-term finance function. Organizations find that the inflows of cash receipts do not coincide exactly with cash disbursements. Typically in some periods cash reserves build up because receipts exceed outlays. In others there can be a sharp reduction in the cash balance, as expenditures outstrip receipts. Holding cash reserves can bridge the gap between receipts and payments and permit the enterprise to maintain its planned expenditure independently of cash inflows in a particular period.

Maintenance of cash reserves (in cash as opposed to marketable instruments) involves a cost to the enterprise of interest on borrowed funds or interest forgone — the opportunity cost of holding cash instead of using it for capital investments or lending it out. In periods of high interest rates, these costs can be significant. The more cash the enterprise can retain, the lower its borrowing needs, or the more it can invest in various financial securities.

Conversely, as cash resources fall, the enterprise has to sell its investments and increase its borrowings.

The institution of the 'money market' has evolved to meet the needs of the enterprise. the more the enterprise can forecast its cash needs and inflows, the better it can manage its borrowings and investments. In other words, it has a portfolio and debt management problem of its capital investments and other investments and of its borrowings. These will be reflected in its balance sheet structure, and in section W9.2 we illustrate a simplified balance sheet and sources and uses statement for the enterprise The actual data on the sources and uses of funds are given in Chapter 8 (Table 8.1), and in this chapter of the Workbook we give actual balance sheet data for the corporate sector.

W9.2   Balance sheet and sources and uses of funds

In Tables W9.1 and W9.2 we give some balance sheet and sources and uses data for the corporate sector. The information comes from *Business Monitor* and is meant to be for illustrative purposes only. The data are not directly comparable with those given in Table 8.1.

Table W9.1   Balance sheet data for the corporate sector: all companies (manufacturing and non-manufacturing) 1986 and 1987 (£m)

Balance sheet at end of accounting year	All industries		All industries excluding oil		Manufacturing industries		Non-manufacturing industries excluding oil	
	1987	1986	1987	1986	1987	1986	1987	1986
Fixed assets:								
Gross tangible assets	328,308	296,026	268,287	235,692	125,388	117,811	142,899	117,881
Deduct: Accumulated depreciation	106,829	100,548	82,232	76,211	48,575	46,630	33,657	29,581
Net tangible assets:								
Land and buildings	102,686	86,448	100,139	83,815	34,097	30,522	66,042	53,293
Plant and machinery	99,245	90,906	69,397	60,079	35,819	33,809	33,579	26,270
Fixtures, fittings, etc.	13,089	10,705	12,852	10,444	4,475	4,694	8,377	5,750
Payments on account and assets in the course of construction	6,460	7,418	3,666	5,142	2,422	2,155	1,244	2,987
Total net tangible assets	221,479	195,477	186,054	159,480	76,812	71,180	109,242	88,300
Intangible assets	10,333	8,379	7,484	4,407	3,002	2,424	4,482	1,983
Investments, of which:	24,323	21,617	20,071	17,942	12,920	11,222	7,151	6,720
British government securities	712	402	712	402	342	393	370	9
Local authority loans	227	16	227	16	15	16	212	–
Total net fixed assets	256,136	225,473	213,609	181,830	92,734	84,826	120,875	97,003
Current assets:								
Stocks and work in progress	98,068	96,941	92,390	90,942	48,398	49,139	43,991	41,803
Debtors due within one year:								
Trade debtors	87,550	78,070	81,733	72,178	43,893	40,306	37,841	31,872
Due from group companies	5,416	5,002	5,243	4,841	3,732	3,393	1,511	1,448
Due from related companies	3,165	2,492	2,489	1,831	713	603	1,776	1,229
Amount receivable under finance leases	1,977	1,412	1,977	1,411	892	408	1,085	1,003
Other debtors	16,608	11,263	15,442	9,906	5,677	4,948	9,765	4,957
Prepayments and accrued income	9,648	7,934	8,730	7,049	3,109	2,776	5,621	4,273
Total debtors due within one year	124,362	106,172	115,615	97,216	58,016	52,434	57,599	44,782
Debtors due after more than one year:								
Trade debtors	804	1,299	794	1,289	366	608	428	681
Due from group companies	296	237	241	227	199	199	42	28
Due from related companies	89	91	71	73	33	15	38	57
Amounts receivable under finance leases	1,807	1,317	1,807	1,317	808	466	999	852
Other debtors	1,347	1,703	1,104	1,262	631	883	473	378
Prepayments and accrued income	533	440	285	205	110	118	176	87
Total debtors due after more than one year	4,876	5,088	4,302	4,373	2,147	2,290	2,156	2,083
Government grants receivable	17	4	17	4	2	4	15	

Table W9.1   Continued

Balance sheet at end of accounting year	All industries		All industries excluding oil		Manufacturing industries		Non-manufacturing industries excluding oil	
	1987	1986	1987	1986	1987	1986	1987	1986
Investments	12,443	12,523	10,540	9,812	6,793	6,642	3,747	3,170
Cash at bank and in hand	44,095	37,242	41,110	33,609	21,943	18,553	19,166	15,056
Total current assets	283,863	257,968	263,974	235,956	137,300	129,062	126,675	106,894
Current liabilities:								
Creditors and accruals								
falling due within one year								
Debenture loans	1,610	1,202	1,401	767	426	526	975	241
Convertible loans	5,068	4,191	4,088	3,490	1,648	1,395	2,440	2,095
Bank loans and overdrafts	33,287	32,239	31,282	30,683	14,044	14,506	17,239	16,177
Payments received on account	5,024	4,233	5,002	4,208	3,308	2,752	1,694	1,457
Trade creditors	66,511	62,342	62,653	58,415	27,075	24,736	35,578	33,679
Bills of exchange payable	3,803	2,871	3,782	2,855	1,980	1,519	1,803	1,336
Due to group companies	12,308	10,943	11,926	10,379	4,615	4,503	7,311	5,876
Due to related companies	2,441	2,260	1,458	1,003	899	537	559	466
Indebtedness to directors	1,586	1,315	1,586	1,315	132	124	1,454	1,191
Net obligations under finance leases	757	491	723	470	395	351	328	120
Social security	2,155	1,833	2,133	1,797	1,005	914	1,128	883
Other creditors	24,844	18,110	22,165	15,742	9.056	8,118	13,109	7,624
Accruals and deferred income	20,555	17,697	18,541	15,614	10,192	8,758	8,350	6,856
Total creditors and								
accruals falling due within one year	179,950	159,727	166,740	146,738	74,773	68,738	91,967	78,000
Dividends due and unclaimed	8,196	6,850	6,763	5,530	3,848	3,030	2,915	2,500
Interest due on loan capital	2	6	2	6	1	3	1	2
Current taxation:								
UK and overseas taxation	27,778	24,398	24,693	21,294	13,139	11,463	11,554	9,831
Deduct: act recoverable	1,757	1,734	1,697	1,655	812	838	885	818
Total current taxation	26,021	22,664	22,996	19,639	12,327	10,626	10,669	9,013
Total current liabilities	214,169	189,247	196,502	171,913	90,950	82,397	105,552	8,516
Net current assets	69,693	68,721	67,473	64,043	46,350	46,664	21,123	17,378
Total net assets	325,828	294,194	281,081	245,873	139,084	131,491	141,997	114,382
Net assets financed by:								
Shareholders' interest								
Ordinary shares	39,508	33,998	36,822	32,347	19,462	16,982	17,360	15,365
Preference shares	4,213	3,532	4,144	3,468	1,631	1,445	2,513	2,023
Other shares	188	129	188	129	71	12	118	117
Capital fund account	74	72	74	72	67	65	7	7
Reserves	181,393	159,705	157,698	135,305	75,902	71,033	81,796	64,272
Total shareholders' interest	225,376	197,436	198,926	171,321	97,133	89,536	101,793	81,785
Minority shareholders' interest	6,824	9,669	5,896	5,786	4,151	4,366	1,745	1,420
Provisions	21,868	22,428	13,820	13,822	9,615	9,691	4,205	4,131
Creditors and accruals								
falling due after more than one year:								
Debenture loans	13,836	11,827	13,177	10,983	4,130	3,451	9,046	7,532
Convertible loans	20,959	18,683	17,102	14,845	9,052	9,093	8,050	5,751
Bank loans and overdrafts	21,351	20,350	19,346	17,710	9,185	10,152	10,161	7,558
Payments received on account	494	406	494	396	488	388	7	7
Trade creditors	210	625	198	603	66	95	132	508
Bills of exchange payable	59	162	59	162	11	148	48	15
Due to group companies	2,938	1,994	2,642	1,832	1,678	977	964	854
Due to related companies	1,723	1,201	507	312	162	92	345	220
Indebtedness to directors	691	710	691	710	78	59	613	651
Net obligations under finance leases	1,617	1,346	1,392	1,206	839	902	553	304
Social security	6	29	6	29	2	1	3	28
Other creditors	6,726	6,353	6,051	5,500	2,043	2,202	4,008	3,298
Accruals and deferred income	1,149	975	774	657	449	337	325	320
Total creditors and accruals								
falling due after more than one year	71,760	64,661	62,439	54,944	28,184	27,898	34,255	27,046
Total net assets	325,828	294,194	281,081	245,873	139,084	131,491	141,997	114,382

Source: Business Monitor MA3.

Table W9.2   Sources and uses of funds: all companies (manufacturing and non-manufacturing) 1986 and 1987 (£m)

	All industries		All industries excluding oil		Manufacturing industries		Non-manufacturing industries excluding oil	
	1987	1986	1987	1986	1987	1986	1987	1986
Income and appropriation account								
Gross trading profit	73,024	58,502	65,294	52,059	33,638	27,806	31,655	24,253
Investment income	2,825	2,698	2,363	2,407	1,683	1,810	680	597
Other revenue income	5,070	4,869	4,411	4,168	2,420	2,294	1,991	1,874
Prior year adjustments (other than tax)	13	7	13	7	6	7	7	–
Total income	80,931	66,076	72,081	58,642	37,747	31,917	34,334	26,724
Deduct: Interest on bank and short-term loans	8,981	8,642	8,283	8,104	3,568	3,765	4,715	4,339
Gross income	71,950	57,435	63,798	50,538	34,180	28,152	29,618	22,385
Appropriation of gross income:								
Depreciation provisions:								
Leased assets	587	444	563	426	287	284	277	142
Owned assets	18,239	17,777	15,756	14,740	8,124	7,780	7,632	6,960
Amounts written-off intangible assets	708	1,312	171	142	91	77	80	65
Other amounts written-off	22	20	21	16	11	6	10	10
Taxation:								
UK corporation tax	14,528	11,844	13,227	10,652	6,670	5,606	6,557	5,046
Act recoverable	−173	−176	−180	−184	−164	−132	−15	−52
Double taxation relief	−809	−765	−784	−741	−698	−656	−86	−84
Deferred taxation	−695	−929	−432	−604	−199	−210	−232	−394
Overseas taxation	3,797	2,588	3,149	2,740	2,652	2,295	497	445
Prior year adjustment	−254	−129	−254	−123	−111	−89	−143	−35
Total taxation	16,394	12,433	14,726	11,740	8,149	6,314	6,577	4,926
Dividends								
Ordinary	12,245	10,282	10,257	8,279	5,883	4,807	4,373	3,472
Preference	282	211	277	206	107	86	170	121
Total dividends	12,527	10,493	10,534	8,485	5,990	4,892	4,543	3,592
Interest on long-term loans	2,227	2,504	1,929	2,122	1,091	1,064	839	1,059
Minority shareholders' interest	1,144	854	918	748	711	573	207	175
Retained income	20,102	11,597	19,180	12,118	9,726	6,664	9,454	5,455
Total appropriation of gross income	71,950	57,435	63,798	50,538	34,180	28,152	29,618	22,385
Sources of funds								
Proceeds from issue of share and loan capital:								
For cash:								
Ordinary shares	8,627	4,334	6,939	3,929	3,878	2,099	3,060	1,830
Preference shares	756	384	750	384	277	467	473	−83
Long-term loans	5,939	5,357	5,801	5,232	2,135	2,479	3,666	2,753
Total	15,322	10,075	13,490	9,545	6,290	5,045	7,200	4,501
In exchange for subsidiaries								
Ordinary shares	2,774	2,208	2,732	2,154	1,172	773	1,560	1,381
Preference shares	672	–	672	–	69	–	603	–
Long-term loans	83	3	83	3	10	3	73	–
Total	3,529	2,211	3,487	2,157	1,250	776	2,236	1,381
Other capital fund accounts	2	6	2	6	2	6	–	–
Total receipts from issues	18,853	12,292	16,979	11,708	7,543	5,827	9,436	5,881
Increase in amount owing to banks	1,691	1,337	1,880	2,006	−1,422	1,712	3,302	293
Increase in short-term loans	736	122	675	−77	−107	−160	782	83
Increase in creditors and accruals due after more than one year	1,573	−476	1,168	−169	607	−489	561	320
Increase in creditors and accruals due within one year	17,997	9,240	18,308	11,414	6,974	5,196	11,334	6,218

Table W9.2   Continued

	All industries		All industries excluding oil		Manufacturing industries		Non-manufacturing industries excluding oil	
	1987	1986	1987	1986	1987	1986	1987	1986
Gross income	71,950	57,435	63,798	50,538	34,180	28,152	29,618	22,385
Exchange differences (unrealized)	−169	−9	−27	−475	203	−336	−230	−138
Other capital receipts	−2,932	1,081	240	1,034	−601	733	841	301
Total sources of funds	109,700	81,022	103,021	75,980	47,377	40,635	55,644	35,344
Use of funds								
Payments out of income:								
Taxation	14,340	11,387	12,079	8,496	6,952	5,070	5,127	3,425
Dividends	11,258	8,632	9,379	6,815	5,138	4,070	4,240	2,745
Interest on long-term loans	2,229	2,518	1,931	2,136	1,093	1,079	838	1,057
Total payments out of income	27,827	22,537	23,388	17,447	13,183	10,220	10,205	7,227
Expenditure on:								
Tangible fixed assets	42,539	25,404	37,255	23,486	19,544	12,655	17,711	10,831
Intangible assets	5,207	2,667	5,799	1,714	2,827	873	2,972	841
Acquisition of subsidiaries	11,535	10,870	10,773	10,154	5,458	5,116	5,315	5,038
Adjustment due to consolidation	−339	−180	−328	−159	−401	−63	73	−96
Other expenditure on capital account	35	165	36	156	−372	85	408	70
Total expenditure on fixed assets, etc.	58,978	38,926	53,535	35,352	27,055	18,667	26,479	16,685
Increase in current assets and investments (fixed and current)								
Stocks	1,215	7,387	1,542	9,613	−2,108	3,125	3,650	6,488
Debtors due within one year	15,369	3,100	15,586	5,161	4,505	2,507	11,081	2,654
Debtors due after one year	−533	15	−392	−77	−141	196	−251	−273
Investments	627	2,050	2,475	1,679	1,772	1,257	704	423
Cash at bank and in hand	6,215	7,007	6,885	6,804	3,111	4,663	3,774	2,141
Total increase in current assets and investments (fixed and current)	22,895	19,559	26,097	23,180	7,139	11,748	18,959	11,432
Total uses of funds	109,700	81,022	103,021	75,980	47,377	40,635	55,644	35,344
Estimated number of companies	337,341	331,121	337,302	331,081	51,002	49,844	286,300	281,237

Source: Business Monitor MA3.

W9.3   Forms of short-term borrowing and lending

The enterprise can use the banking sector and/or it can use the 'money market'. These are markets (note the plural) for short-term credit instruments such as Treasury bills, commercial paper, banker's acceptances and negotiable certificates of deposit (CDs).

(a) Borrowing

We stress the importance of bank loans, particularly via overdrafts, though now there are more bank instruments available. One point we must emphasize is the importance of a strong bank–customer relationship. It is a two-way street benefiting both parties, and reducing the asymmetry of information. Borrowers probably feel more secure in the expectation of future borrowing, and banks (the lenders) not only obtain a more secure lending opportunity, but often obtain more information on which to base their lending decision.

It is difficult to test the strength of this relationship and quantify it. Yet it does seem to exist and to cloud the issue of yield differentials. For example, we cannot presume that a lower rate on bills will prompt a complete or significant movement from bank finance to bills. Likewise, when the cash surplus of the corporate sector increases, we cannot presume that an enterprise will reduce its borrowings pro rata by the amount of the increase in the surplus. In both situations, the strength of the customer relationship can be such as to blunt the expected reaction of the corporate sector.

(b) Bill finance

Banks can act as advisers on bill finance, and discount houses are specialists in this area. In the case of *trade bills* the rate of discount charged will be determined by the perceived risk — which will reflect the nature of the goods concerned but more particularly the credit standing of the traders. It is possible for these bills to be guaranteed by a credit insurance company, and in consequence the rate of discount will be correspondingly lower as the risk is lower.

For *bank bills* the point is made in the text (p. 224) of their importance in financing overseas trade. They are used extensively in foreign trade as well as domestically to finance working capital. We can outline the advantages of bill finance:

1. they are competitive with bank overdrafts — often even cheaper;
2. they *may* free overdraft facilities for other uses, which is particularly useful when there is external capital rationing in the long-term market;
3. when bills are accepted by a bank or discount house there is a known cost of capital as opposed to a floating rate on overdrafts.

(c) Short-term lending

We made the point earlier in the Workbook that 'cash' has costs — the borrowing of funds to maintain liquidity, the tying up of funds and the opportunity cost of lost interest. A rational enterprise will minimize holdings of cash *per se*, including current accounts. The banks and money market can help in absorbing a large volume of transactions in a quick and convenient way, ranging from cash lent overnight to generally 90 days or less, but it could be up to a year. Table W9.3 gives the data on selected liquid assets for the corporate sector, though these are not reconcilable with the balance sheet data given in Fig. W9.1. The data reveal the importance of *bank deposits* — over 94% in December 1989 of the total identified liquid asset holdings. Most are held in sterling, and it is perhaps surprising that the holdings of the other five currencies have not increased over the period 1983 to 1989. In fact, an inspection of Table W9.3 will indicate that between these two dates there has been a decline in such holdings.

(d) Certificates of deposit (CDs)

(i) Domestic
Negotiable CDs issued by United Kingdom banks are large denomination, time deposit liabilities with lives ranging from two weeks to twelve months. There is a secondary market in them.

(ii) Dollar
A dollar CD is a dollar-denominated instrument with maturities ranging from thirty days to five years, though shorter terms are the norm.

Table W9.3   Selected liquid assets of industrial and commercial companies: amount outstanding at end of period (£m)

	Deposits with banks				Deposits with building societies	Sterling Treasury bills	Tax instruments	British government securities	Local authority temporary debt	Local authority longer-term debt	Total identified	Bank advances
	Sterling certificates of deposit	Dollar certificates of deposit	Other sterling deposits	Other foreign currency deposits								
1983 Q1	1,023	683	17,398	7,511	341	364	1,932	1,650	352	123	31,377	46,880
	1,017										31,371	
Q2	940	589	18,448	7,193	422	367	1,918	1,910	307	112	32,206	47,176
Q3	1,076	728	19,079	7,745	652	307	1,934	2,080	290	110	34,001	48,586
Q4	729	898	21,086	9,481	583	218	1,916	2,080	232	101	37,324	49,006
1984 Q1	849	603	20,431	9,779	649	341	1,653	2,060	284	98	36,747	50,136
Q2	851	374	21,019	8,056	623	404	1,840	2,200	276	92	35,735	52,604
Q3	1,103	170	22,346	8,838	512	351	1,592	1,880	331	98	37,221	53,247
Q4	501	949	24,248	10,098	486	225	2,201	1,980	276	93	41,057	57,938
1985 Q1	544	541	24,844	9,674	451	253	2,344	1,850	353	106	40,960	58,197
Q2	552	516	24,885	9,484	449	309	2,394	1,720	333	103	40,745	58,398
Q3	1,237	882	26,187	9,280	458	318	2,358	1,510	342	101	42,673	59,600
Q4	670	1,044	27,148	9,496	454	170	2,620	1,570	250	101	43,523	60,889
1986 Q1	712	826	28,511	9,701	476	260	2,314	1,330	207	103	44,440	63,158
Q2	826	895	30,987	10,476	494	245	2,443	1,220	160	102	47,848	64,259
1986 Q3	1,653		33,717	11,020	507	193	2,526	1,310	199	98	51,223	67,188
Q4	886		34,820	10,656	606	226	2,614	1,360	176	96	51,440	69,532
1987 Q1	1,504		34,636	10,982	605	427	2,062	1,020	162	101	51,499	72,525
Q2	2,203		36,615	9,553	611	573	2,254	930	148	97	52,984	74,601
Q3	2,370		39,717	8,883	607	611	2,236	980	161	84	55,649	77,935
Q4	2,915		41,968	8,728	478	770	2,234	1,070	104	83	58,350	79,742
1988 Q1	3,056		41,441	8,783	526	626	2,039	780	134	81	57,466	86,980
Q2	3,335		42,088	8,537	535	556	1,870	740	92	73	57,826	96,325
Q3	3,942		45,566	9,040	496	368	2,164	720	77	69	62,442	104,332
Q4	4,974		46,432	8,898	484	664	1,837	650	60	62	64,061	109,835
1989 Q1	6,132		47,384	8,267	482	575	1,739	500	72	60	65,211	119,693
Q2	6,500		49,960	10,530	484	1,234	1,768	490	58	56	71,080	130,375
	7,304		50,488		249						72,177	130,534
Q3	7,939		51,522	10,157	248	1,322	1,873	303	79	52	73,495	142,912
Q4	8,459		53,837	12,007	215	1,403	1,967	516	103	51	78,558	147,381

Source: Financial Statistics, table 8.4 (CSO).

(e) Treasury bills

T. bills are a convenient, marketable and safe investment for the enterprise. However, a literature has developed to suggest that enterprises can use financial futures to increase the return on T. bill investments. Although this evidence is from the United States, it is instructive for us to review the main ideas.

A number of United States studies have pointed to the inefficiencies in the futures markets: for example, that of Elton, Gruber and Rentzler (1983a). They found:

1. systematic overpricing on futures on T. bills;
2. trades can be made which can exploit discrepancies between T. bill prices and futures to earn an excess return.

Another article by the same authors (1983b) illustrates the use of T. bill futures and develops a decision model to exploit the abnormal returns. We utilize some of their material below, converting their dollars into sterling for the sake of illustration.

(i) Using T. bill futures

In order to illustrate the use of T. bill futures by a corporate financial manager we shall start with a simple example which will then be generalized. To avoid complexity we will assume away the problems of indivisibility, transaction costs and daily settlement of gains and losses (marking to the market). The effect of these latter two influences will be explained below and will be considered in the empirical section. Indivisibility is not a problem as long as the sum being invested is sufficiently large.

Assume that a financial manager is considering buying a T. bill which matures in 30 days and is now valued at £999,000. Since T. bills are pure discount instruments, this bill will be worth £1,000,000 at maturity. This is a return of 10/990 or 1.01% over the 30 days.

Now assume that a futures contract exists for delivery of a 91-day T. bill in 30 days. No money changes hands when a futures contract is bought (or sold), but an agreement is entered into requiring the holder to purchase (and the seller to deliver) a particular maturity T. bill at a particular price on a particular date. Assume that the price of this futures contract is £969,700. Also assume that a 121-day T. bill now exists with a price of £960,000. These represent actual cash prices not discount prices quoted by financial services.

The financial manager could manufacture a 30-day investment by buying the 121-day T. bill, writing a futures contract and in 30 days, at the maturity of the futures contract, delivering the then 91-day T. bill to fulfil the futures contract. This would return £9,700 (969,700 − 960,000) on an investment of £960,000 for a return of 1.01%. Thus whether the financial manager invests in a 30-day bill directly or manufactures one by selling a futures contract and buying a 121-day T. bill, the same return is earned.

We shall analyse the case where the financial manager is assumed initially to be holding a T. bill, but considers switching to a longer bill and a futures contract, and perhaps back again if the return warrants it. In general a switch may be profitable any time the following instruments offer a different rate of return:

1. an n-day T. bill;
2. a $(91 + n)$-day T. bill combined with the sale of a futures contract on a 91-day bill for delivery in n days. We shall call this a 'pseudo T. bill'.

There are two influences which may limit the ability of a financial manager to make a profit when the return on the cash T. bill and the pseudo T. bill are not the same. The first of these is transaction costs. If a financial manager held T. bills, he or she would incur transaction costs when switching into pseudo T. bills and prices could differ by the amount of these transaction costs without a swap being profitable. These costs involve the sale of a T. bill, the purchase of another T. bill and the sale of a futures contract. Reasonable estimates of these transaction costs are £40 on a one-way transaction for the short-term bill, £60 on a one-way transaction for the long-term bill and a £25 round trip for the futures contract. In all tests they use £175 as an estimate of transaction costs in switching from a pseudo T. bill to a cash T. bill or vice versa. This is an overestimate of transaction costs, which have an average value of £82.50 (30 + 40 + 25/2). These estimates of transaction costs are conservative. If we find positive trading profits with these overstated values, we can be sure they will be even larger under a more realistic estimate.

The second influence affecting the profitability of a swap is the cash flows associated with futures contracts being marked to the market daily. Marking to the market is the basic difference between a futures contract and a pure forward contract. Under daily marking to the market, at the end of each trading day the holder of a future contract must compensate the seller or be compensated by the seller for any change which takes place in the settlement price. Fortunately this results in a very small cash flow. Cox, Ingersoll and Ross (1981) have argued on theoretical grounds that it should be extremely small and Elton, Gruber and Rentzler (1983a) have demonstrated empirically that it is quite small (average value of −£4 on a £1 million contract).

Just considering a single swap, it will not pay a manager to swap if the T. bill and pseudo T. bill differ by less than transaction costs and the effect of marking to the market. However, empirical studies have shown that there are much larger price differences between the two instruments. If large price discrepancies exist but tend to disappear over time, one should be able to earn an excess return by trading against these discrepancies. Elton *et al.*'s (1983b) paper tests whether the differences which have been noted are sufficiently large to allow a profit to be earned by trading against them. The viewpoint taken is that of a corporate financial manager who starts with a sum of money committed to T. bills but is willing to switch between T. bills and pseudo T. bills with the same effective maturity. Likewise if the financial manager has swapped to the pseudo T. bill, we assume a willingness to swap back if the differential shrinks sufficiently. Since the T. bill has a finite life, this is a case of repetitive decision making over a fixed horizon. As such the problem is amenable to modelling via *dynamic programming*.

(ii) Optimum swap rules
We assume that the financial manager starts with a position in cash T. bills. Several times a day he or she is able to observe prices on T. bills and futures contracts and based on these observations calculate an expected profit from a swap into the pseudo T. bill. Once the financial manager swaps into the pseudo T. bill he or she continues to examine prices to see if a swap back into bills is profitable.

Even though the analysis of prices in Elton, Gruber and Rentzler (1983a) shows that if one is going to hold only one instrument the pseudo T. bill is generally the more profitable instrument, multiple swaps are still potentially profitable. For example, it might be profitable to incur a £100 loss in swapping from the pseudo bill to the bill in anticipation of a much higher profit in swapping back to the pseudo bill as the difference between the prices of these two instruments once again widens. It is the potential for multiple swaps that makes this a dynamic programming problem.

The other securities, such as local authority or government bonds, etc. are discussed in the text (p. 227) and do not require further elaboration.

W9.4   Current liabilities

Although these represent debts of the enterprise, they are a source of credit. The enterprise generally is not a spot trader, buying and paying for its raw materials, etc., on receipt. Any delay in payment represents credit to the enterprise, although the credit is shown as a liability.

(a) Accounts payable and accruals

These represent the major short-term commitments of most enterprises as they represent the liability to make payment for the goods and services that the enterprise uses. The *accruals*, although a commitment, represent a source of credit to the enterprise: that is, it can owe wages and salaries to its staff, and it can owe to the government the deductions from these wages and salaries, and its own commitments for National Insurance, VAT, etc. The accruals are thus a revolving credit line within the parameters of which the enterprise operates. Obviously if it pays its workforce monthly in arrears, then the accruals will be larger than if it pays bi-weekly or weekly. This finance is normal and 'free' to the enterprise. Once it steps outside the boundaries set, problems will arise which can damage its reputation and in some cases lead to fines being imposed.

The *accounts payable* are another major source of credit to the enterprise in which there is more scope for the enterprise to negotiate and influence the terms on which it buys its raw materials. Ideally, the enterprise would like to defer payment for as long as it can so that it can use the inputs in generating sales revenue. However, there is symmetry in the accounts payable element in the enterprise as the accounts payable of one enterprise are obviously the accounts receivable of another enterprise. So stretching this on the liabilities side may bring an equivalent demand from other enterprises for a stretching on the receivables side, in which case the net effect balances out in the aggregate. Unfortunately this balancing does not always occur at the level of the individual enterprise. The negotiated terms on which credit is given and accepted will depend on the relative power of the enterprises concerned. Small enterprises in particular can find themselves squeezed to settle their accounts payable quickly, sometimes spot (cash and carry), yet find that their debtors (the accounts receivable) extend for quite long periods. A mini-case study to illustrate is given in section W9.9.

With some accounts payable there may be penalties for late payment and discounts for early payment. The point made in the text is that it is a cost–benefit decision for the enterprise, though the costs are not always straight tangible financial costs: for instance, how do you measure 'reputation'? Persistent late payments cannot only have penalty costs, but damage the chances of being granted further credit or raise the cost of the credit, say from a bank.

We shall illustrate the two cases of with and without discounts by means of a full numerical illustration. What we can see is that there are several key dates in the process of creating the account payable and settling it:

1. the ordering of the goods in question;
2. the receipt of the goods;
3. the receipt of the invoice;
4. the date on which the payment by cheque is posted;
5. the date on which the cheque is cashed and the account of the enterprise debited.

This is illustrated in Fig. W9.1.

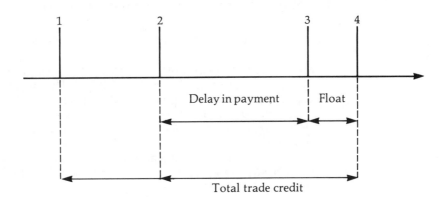

Figure W9.1   The time profile of trade credit.

For ease of illustration we shall assume a £10,000 order on a net 30 days account with a 12.5% cost of capital. We will assume that mail (second class) and clearing times average 5 days. There is no incentive for the enterprise to settle the account early unless it is trying to impress its supplier with this policy. We shall examine policies of:

1. paying on time;
2. delaying payment beyond the 30 days to 45 days, without penalties;
3. delaying payment to 45 days with a penalty of 2% monthly on unpaid balances.

Table W9.4

	Credit	Cost		Value of credit
1. 30 days	£10,000	0%		£102.74 + £17.12 = £119.86
2. 45 days: no penalty	£10,000	0%		£154.11 + £17.12 = £171.23
3. 45 days: 2% penalty	£10,000	24%	annual 0.99% for 15 days	£154.11 − £98.625 + £17.12 − £32.88 = £39.73

The figures in Table W9.4 have been calculated as follows:

1. 30 days' credit is worth at 12.5%:

$$£10,000 \times 0.125 \times \frac{30 \text{ days}}{365} = £102.74$$

The 5-day float is worth:

$$£10,000 \times 0.125 \times \frac{5}{365} = £17.12$$

so the total value of the credit = £119.86.
2. 45 days' credit:

$$£10,000 \times 0.125 \times \frac{45}{365} = £154.11$$

The 5-day float is the same at £17.12 so the total = £171.23.
3. Late payment charge of 2% on unpaid balances:

$$\left(£10,000 \times 0.125 \times \frac{40}{365} \right) - 2.0\% \text{ penalty}$$

The 2% penalty per month is equivalent to a single annual rate of 24% so the daily charge is 24%/365 = 0.0006575. The delay in payment is by 15 days so the interest charge is $15 \times 0.0006575 \times 10,000 = £98.625$. But there is a further delay of 5 days, so $5 \times 0.0006575 \times 10,000 = £32.875$. We can see that this extra 5 days is crippling as it costs the enterprise £32.88 yet it saves only £17.12.

The enterprise is still ahead on the 45 days' extension (+ 5 days' float), but it has to weigh up the possible additional cost of 'bad' reputation for delay.

If we introduce a discount of, say, 2% if settlement is made within 10 days, we can then modify the cost–benefit analysis, as now there is an incentive to settle early which effectively reduces the price of the goods purchased. So we now have £9,800 as the cost of goods purchased.

Table W9.5

	Credit	Cost	Value of credit
1. 10 days	£9,800	0%	£33.44 + £16.78 = £50.22.
2. 30 days	£9,800	24.8%	£(189.93) + £16.78 = £(173.15)
3. 45 days: no penalty	£9,800	16.55%	£(184.897) + £16.78 = £(168.12)
4. 45 days: 2% monthly penalty	£9,800	33.2%	£(204.90) + £16.78 = £(188.12)

Explanations of the figures in Table W9.5 are as follows. In case 1., of paying within the 10 days' grace, we can see that the benefit is:

$$£9,800 \times 0.125 \times \frac{10}{365} = £33.44$$

plus the five days of the float of:

$$£9,800 \times 0.125 \times \frac{5}{365} = £16.78$$

giving a total benefit of £50.22.

Once the enterprise delays beyond the 10 days, problems emerge. The £200 discount has been forgone, but the enterprise still benefits from the delay as its cost of capital is 12.5%. For the normal 30-day period we would have a percentage cost of:

$$\frac{200}{9,800} \times \frac{365}{30} = 24.8\%$$

and a loss in financial terms of:

$$£980 \times 0.125 \times \frac{30}{365} - 200 = £(189.93)$$

For a 45-day period, the percentage cost will be:

$$\frac{200}{9,800} \times \frac{365}{45} = 16.55\%$$

with a loss in financial terms of:

$$£980 \times 0.125 \times \frac{45}{365} - 200 = £(184.897)$$

If there is an interest rate penalty of 2% per month, and assuming it is not prorated per day, then the cost would be:

$$£980 \times 0.125 \times \frac{45}{365} - 200 - 20 = £204.90$$

The cost of the 2% penalty is:

$$\frac{20}{980} \times \frac{365}{45} = 16.6\%$$

So the % cost is 16.6 + 16.6 = 33.2%.

(b) Short-term debt

We make the point in the text (p. 230) that short-term debt has increased in importance in recent years, and we discuss the problems of enterprises continually having to roll forward their borrowing. If this can be done, the enterprise can benefit or lose by this maturity policy.

It is observed that financial managers have to consider these interest rate factors in place of balance sheet norms of matching short-term assets/ liabilities, etc. We also refer to the fact that, with the advent of fixed and floating rates for both short- and long-term funds, the enterprise has an added dimension to its choice in that short-term borrowing on a float can be effectively short–short and longer-term borrowing on a float is effectively short term. The point is also made about the exchange rate dimension. These issues will receive further consideration later in the Workbook.

W9.5   Current assets

(a) Accounts receivable

As noted in the previous section, enterprises are not generally spot traders unless they are in the retail sector. Just as enterprises receive trade credit, so they are often called upon to grant it too. This involves the need to establish procedures for:

1. credit terms;
2. analysing credit risk;
3. monitoring customer payment patterns;
4. collection policies.

What we illustrate in the text is that once more it is a cost–benefit exercise involving the enterprise in balancing a series of other policy areas within the enterprise, principally inventory policy, production capacity, and operating financial leverage. We make the point forcibly that trade credit can be used to increase both sales and profitability, yet the enterprise may operate within the constraints of the industry norms which lead it to extend credit beyond what it would normally freely choose to do. Once credit accounts are advanced, for whatever reason, they have to be managed as they are an asset of the enterprise just like any other short-term asset. The quicker they can be collected, the more cash enters the enterprise to reduce short-term borrowing and/or invest in other short-term assets.

(i) Credit terms

The enterprise, assuming it grants trade credit, enters into a 'game' with its creditors which can be illustrated as in Fig. W9.2. In this matrix a + indicates a gain for the enterprise. For instance, if the enterprise grants credit and the creditor defaults, the enterprise loses. If it grants credit and the creditor pays on time, it was correct to grant credit, it has a sale, and it gains.

Creditor Enterprise	Pays on time	Delays	Defaults
Gives credit	+	+?	−
Rejects credit	−	+?	+

Figure W9.2   Credit pay-off matrix.

Now in the case of four of the cells of this pay-off matrix, the outcome is clear — a gain or a loss. In the case of delays that may occur, it is less clear whether the enterprise would gain from a policy of granting credit or not doing so. The issue would depend on the delay in question. If it were short and did not involve the added costs of collection agencies, etc. on top of the interest costs of extending the credit, then the enterprise might still find it worthwhile extending the credit. For the rejection of credit strategy, the converse would be the case. The credit decision is still a matter of judgement and if granted, as we saw in section W9.4(a) above with regard to accounts payable, the enterprise can adopt various credit terms, including discounts, etc., to encourage early payment.

The judgement side can often be removed by using *credit scoring*, and this is discussed in the text (p. 234). This is used in particular for consumer credit, though, rather than trade credit. The key to the decision will be the amount of information possessed on a potential customer and the assessment of what the information means.

However, the decision to grant credit does not stop there as the pay-off matrix tells us that problems may arise over payments. This information should:

1. trigger action to follow up for payment;
2. feed into decisions on whether to cut off the future credit lines.

It is in this area that the use of computers can help the enterprise in providing an updated assessment to help monitor and manage the accounts receivable and assist in the *collections*. A cost–benefit approach is also necessary — to compare the cost of collection to the size of the account. However, the enterprise may randomly select small accounts and pursue them vigorously to act as a deterrent to others. Otherwise small creditors will systematically escape without payment.

Perhaps the major theme of this section is that the policy of accounts receivable is not separate from the other areas of the enterprise — such as production, marketing and financing. Thus if a policy decision is taken to produce and sell more, the enterprise has to expect more collection problems. If this can be borne and *profitability* still increases, then it is worthwhile to pursue this policy. Information is the key item to permit the management of the receivables, to reduce the delays and bad debts and to bring the cash into the enterprise as soon as is possible.

We illustrate this diagrammatically in Fig. W9.3 where we show a base line of bad debts due to a given credit policy. That base line can increase or decrease depending on how tight the enterprise wants to be. The objective then should be to reduce the bad debts to this base line, but this will incur additional collection expenses.

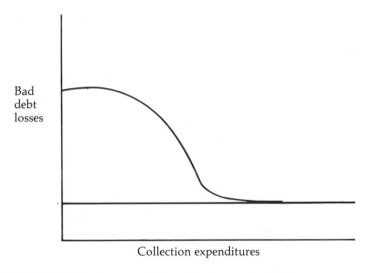

Bad
debt
losses

Collection expenditures

Figure W9.3 Bad debt losses and the collection expenditures.

(b) Inventories/stocks

Once more we have a cost–benefit exercise here in that the enterprise has to balance the level of inventories against the cost of maintaining them or not maintaining them (running out of inventory). The production function would like to have high levels of inventories of raw materials present to accommodate any sudden increase in demand. Likewise the marketing function would like a similar cushion of inventories of finished goods so they can sell from stock and not lose customers. Both policies are expensive, and we make the point in the text that excessive inventories can lead to bankruptcy, so we need an optimal or near-optimal policy. The model discussed is the EOQ. The example used in the text we replicate below, but let us first examine the inventory question in more detail.

The literature informs us that it is possible to rank the composition of inventory (see Fig. W9.4) in order of decreasing value per item. This is sometimes referred to as the ABC method of stock control:

> *A items:* a *small* percentage (say 20–30%) represents a *large* share (over 80%) of the total investment in inventories.
> *B items:* 10–20% represent a small (say 10–15%) share of total inventory investment.
> *C items:* a large percentage of items but at a small cost.

This simplistic approach would then predict that controls are more stringent on type A items rather than type B or C, though clearly costs *per se* are not the only consideration, as in a production process a small cost item can often be critical. However, it is a start on which to base further evaluation.

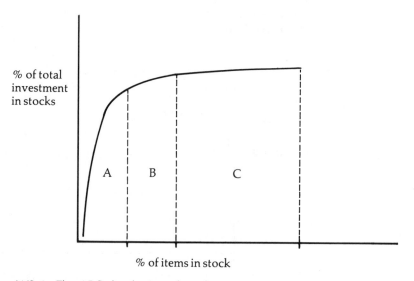

Figure W9.4 The ABC distribution of stocks.

The inventory process involves three interrelated items;

1. customers — within and outside of the enterprise;
2. storage — warehousing space, etc.;
3. sources of stocks — within or outside of the enterprise.

If we are searching for an optimal policy we require one that minimizes costs or maximizes profit.

(i) Costs

1. Cost of inputs or cost of product ready for sale.
2. Costs of purchase of inventory — raising orders, etc. — and if purchased from within the enterprise, any production set-up costs.

3. Holding or storage costs, including warehousing, insurance, and interest cost on funds tied up in inventory.
4. Costs of lost orders, if sales lost through shortages — shortage costs.

(ii) Revenues
These are simply the proceeds from the sale of goods, which could be increased if:

1. goods can be supplied quickly from inventory;
2. profit margins can be increased by doing so.

The costs of concern to use are 2. to 4. and initially only 2. (order costs given as O in the text), and 3. (storage costs given as C in the text). From the text (p. 236), the total ordering costs are SO/Q and the total carrying costs are $QC/2$ so:

$$\text{Total costs} = \frac{QC}{2} + \frac{SO}{Q}$$

If we follow what is referred to as the trial and error approach, we would have Fig. W9.5, which would map out the costs and show the minimum total cost. However, we make the point in the text that we can move to a direct method — differentiate equation 9.3 to arrive at the optimum value of Q:

$$EOQ = \sqrt{\frac{2SO}{C}}$$

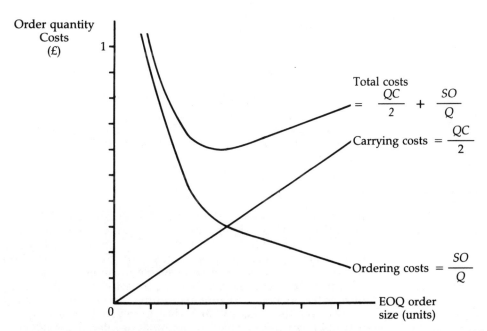

Figure W9.5 Determination of the minimum total costs and economic order quantity.

So with the example of the text we have:

$$\sqrt{\frac{2(5,000)(100)}{25}} = \sqrt{40,000}$$

$$= 200 \text{ units}$$

with 25 orders (i.e. 5,000/200) a year every 14.6 days.

If we add in the problem of lead time (in the case in the text it is five days), then XYZ will place an order when inventory reaches a level of 68 units so that this will be exhausted when the shipment arrives. We can show this to be 68 units by examining the sales per day. There are 5,000/365 = 13.7, so for a five-day delay we have 13.7 × 5 = 68.5. To guard against uncertainties, delays in delivery, increases in sales, etc., a safety stock can be carried as shown in Table W9.6.

We raised the issue of *quantity discounts*. If these are available, say 15p per unit on orders over 500 then we can take account of this. Once more it is a trade-off — savings in price if the discount is taken, but increased carrying costs and reduced ordering costs. With the discount of 15p, the savings on the total order of 5,000 units = £750.

(iii) Carrying costs
If the required quantity for the discount is given the notation Q' then the carrying costs are:

$$\frac{Q'C}{2} - \frac{EOQ(C)}{2} = \frac{(500)25}{2} - \frac{(200)25}{2}$$

$$= 6,250 - 2,500$$
$$= 3,750$$

(iv) Ordering costs

$$\frac{SO}{EOQ} - \frac{SO}{Q'} = \frac{(5,000)100}{200} - \frac{(5,000)100}{500}$$

$$= 2,500 - 1,000$$
$$= 1,500$$

The net cost to XYZ is £3,750 − £1,500 or £2,250. The savings on the discount are only £750 and the additional costs are £2,250, so XYZ should forgo the discount.

(c) Cash and marketable securities

In Chapter 9 we refer to the demand for 'cash'. Opportunities now exist for enterprises to make significant returns and this requires a strategy involving investment both at home and abroad. The banks play a key role in the process in transferring funds to pool funds. We give an illustration below of the history of the techniques now available for international cash management.

For many enterprises, though, the investment of 'cash' is a domestic affair utlizing the sorts of instruments outlined in section 9.3. What we discuss in the text are the risks of illiquidity involved in tying up 'cash' in longer-maturity securities against the potential profitability — given the usual shape (rising) of the yield curve. Investing is one thing, but trading or being forced to sell is another. This involves transaction costs and these are discussed via two models in the text — the Baumol and Miller-Orr models. We make the point that these are simplistic models, but they permit us to identify conceptually the problems involved. Of more specific interest to us is the allocation of funds across the range of assets that can be held. We refer to the Jackson (1984) study and more particularly the study by Chowdhury *et al.* (1986). We also give some interest rate data taken from a recent issue of the *Bank of England Quarterly Bulletin* to illustrate some of the different rates available for investors in short-term assets (see pp. 558–9).

W9.6   Portfolio considerations

Although the Chowdhury *et al.* article is concerned with portfolio considerations in the short-term investment decision, this section in the text was aimed at attempting to focus on the *stock* (balance sheet) and *flow* (sources and uses) elements so as to show the interrelationships. What we illustrate is that, given the existence of market constraints, the enterprise finds it difficult to achieve a desired equilibrium, so it builds up, say, short-term borrowing until it goes to the market. It then has a surplus of funds until it allocates these into long-term capital investment. Although we argue that the enterprise will have *desired* stock relationships, it is through the flows that it seeks to achieve these. So we have a surplus/deficit of 'cash' which has to be invested or financed.

We discuss some of the choices the enterprise has to make. There are two in particular:

1. the choice between long-term capital and net liquidity;
2. the choice between liquid assets and bank credits.

These are discussed at length as are the other choices that have to be made. The issue of the international dimension is not covered in the text and we turn to it now.

(a) International cash management

Dow Chemical in 1963 bought an interest in Bank Mendes Gans, a small Amsterdam bank, and this bank developed a service to receive payment for customers throughout Europe using correspondent bank accounts. The bank received Dow's export remittances and converted foreign currencies to dollars at attractive spreads. Transfers of funds between European banks were credited without value dating float.

The giant European company Philips Gloeilampen wanted to develop a programme to improve the movement of funds in Europe, focused on its subsidiaries. Bank Mendes Gans developed a service called multilateral netting, and a system was successfully implemented.

In 1977 Manufacturers Hanover Trust Company purchased an interest in Bank Mendes Gans and began to offer its international cash management services to Manufacturers Hanover's corporate customers. Bank Mendes Gans now specializes in international cash management and acts as a service agent for a number of the world's largest corporations.

In the early 1970s several New York banks began to offer European money transfer and cash management services through branch networks. These service efforts have been expanded. In fact, a recent research report indicates that international corporate cash management is one of the fastest growing non-credit bank services of United States major centre banks.

While the most important service efforts have been developed in New York, regional US banks, without extensive overseas branch or correspondent networks, are also entering the field by providing advice on international corporate cash management. For example, one bank in Chicago is well known for studies of cash management procedures in Latin American countries, and a bank in Philadelphia has successfully developed studies of the cash management problems pertaining to exports and imports.

In addition to American banks, services are being developed by multi-national banks in many countries. Canadian and Japanese banks now offer global cash management services to their corporate customers, and two British banks recently announced the formation of cash management departments focused on corporate cash management in the United Kingdom.

The current status of this newly developing field was catalogued in the 1980 Harris/Blanc Research survey of the bank services utilized by large multi-national companies operating in the United States and Europe. The most important services can be divided into three categories: international money movement services, information services and advisory services.

(b) International money movement services

Here we survey the major services and techniques for handling international transfers, especially for collecting and concentrating funds.

(i) Concentration-pooling services
The Harris/Blanc Research survey indicates that the most widely used technique is the concentration or 'pooling' of subsidiary cash at a single bank, either within a country or on a regional level at a money centre. Often European-wide systems are established at a bank in London or Amsterdam while Asian systems are established at a bank in Hong Kong or Singapore. Funds in the accounts of cash-rich subsidiaries are used to fund deficit subsidiaries. Funds may be allocated by a special bank procedure in which credit balances are used to offset overdrafts at the end of each day. Alternatively, more complex schemes can be used involving zero-balance accounts. Excess funds are reported daily to the company. Generally, amounts over target balances are invested.

(ii) International transfer support
Another frequently utilized service is the special handling of US dollar international money transfers. Companies incur high costs and delays when funds are transferred across country borders. Therefore, companies work out special service arrangements, with their banks having international branch or correspondent bank networks. These services include same-day settlement, settlement of payment transactions between branch accounts for a company, and settlement between correspondent bank accounts on a bank's books.

(iii) International lockbox
An international lockbox is a lockbox collection procedure involving the interception of customer payments on behalf of a company in a foreign country. Payments denominated in a foreign currency are settled in the country where the currency is legal tender. This within-country collection

avoids cross-border cheque clearing. Besides mail delays, cross-border cheques mean collection delays of several days and even weeks, quite apart from the collection costs, which can amount to as much as 1% of the face value of the cheque. Organized services are offered for intercepting foreign currency payments in a bank branch, collecting the cheques and reporting transaction information to the company. US dollar cheques are generally sent by courier to the United States.

(iv) Netting arrangements

A fourth major international money movement service is intracompany netting. Many international corporations have large sums of money tied up in their intra-company transactions. With transactions that are intracompany, one subsidiary's payables are another subsidiary's receivables. In an intra-company netting system, each company subsidiary provides a list of its payables by currency either to the company's treasury organization or to a designated bank. This list is converted at current exchange rates into a common currency and matched against the payables in the same currency of other subsidiaries. The netting service includes a monthly calculation of amounts to be paid by each subsidiary, the settlement of the net payments between the subsidiaries on a same-day basis, and the reporting of the payment transactions to each subsidiary and to the headquarters, typically via time-sharing terminals. This service is offered by the Bank Mendes Gans/ Manufacturers Hanover and several other American banks. It is estimated that more than 100 multinational corporations have installed such a system. Some countries (for instance, Japan and Italy) prohibit netting.

(c) Information services

A variety of computer-communication techniques are used to provide information to support cash management. Here we review the major types of service and technique.

An important development for serving multinational corporations is the operation of international banking communications networks that facilitate payments both within countries and across borders. A world-wide service called SWIFT (Society for Worldwide Interbank Financial Telecommunications) operates through an organization owned by more than 90 international banks. SWIFT service began in 1978 from Europe to the USA and Canada. It has been extended recently to several countries in Asia and Latin America.

SWIFT facilitates the standardization of international funds transfer instructions and other international banking messages. SWIFT enables transactions to take place almost instantaneously at relatively low cost. Previously, numerous messages were sometimes required to ensure completion of a complex money transfer transaction.

Automation of country payment systems is also proceeding in a number of countries. In most cases, these systems are being interconnected to SWIFT. In New York, major US banks operate a computer system called CHIPS (Clearing House Interbank Payments System) for settling international dollar payments. On an average day, approximately 100 banks settle more than $100 billion via CHIPS.

These communication-transfer systems move money between accounts at international banks, thereby enabling these banks to provide corporate customers with computerized money transfer services. Systems are now being developed for major corporations. Competition is increasing among banks in providing a variety of terminal-based communication-transfer services.

Corporate cash managers use treasury terminal systems in several important ways for international cash management:

1. *Balance reports*. Treasury terminals can be used for daily monitoring of international accounts just as with domestic balance reporting systems.
2. *Money transfer*. The terminal can be used to initiate transfer instructions to draw these accounts down to target levels or to fund accounts. The payment instructions to the bank can be transmitted on the same terminal.
3. *Message delivery*. Banks use a company's treasury system(s) to send messages to and from SWIFT or CHIPS networks as required.

Almost all of the top 1,200 industrial corporations in the United States now use a terminal reporting service for banking accounts in the United States. Many of these corporations are receiving regular statement information via terminals from the overseas bank branches of their US banks. This is a growing area of international cash management because many companies recognize a need for much more overseas financial information delivered in a timely way. Companies want a regular flow of overseas cash information to enable daily management of global cash positions and forecasts.

(d) Advisory services: international consulting

The implementation of new international cash management systems is sometimes affected by organizational issues. Often subsidiary controllers either cannot or will not provide the headquarters treasury staff with day-to-day information about local banking relationships, and senior management is reluctant to require new procedures that might tend to reduce the accountability and independence of local operations without good justification. To study the need and justification for new overseas banking procedures and cash management techniques, companies frequently make use of consultants, especially from the bank advisory services.

(i) Country studies

New advisory services now offered by banks focus on studies of subsidiary cash procedures. They supplement the traditional services that evaluate foreign exchange exposure measurement and management.

These studies are called intracountry studies, a term that is often shortened simply to country studies. These are growing rapidly in importance to corporations and are one of the major areas of consulting in international cash management.

Intracountry studies provide background information on the use of cash management procedures in particular countries where subsidiaries are operating. The countries most frequently studied are Spain and Italy in Europe, Venezuela, Brazil and Mexico in Latin America, and Taiwan, the Philippines and Korea in Asia.

In the typical country study, a team of bank and company representatives visits the company subsidiary, analyses current cash management procedures and recommends steps for improvement. Study results typically include recommendations on reducing the number of banks and negotiating improved value dates as well as educating company staff about cash management procedures.

(ii) Microprocessor-based treasury systems

With the increasing use of terminal-based services that include both domestic and international cash management information, it is apparent to many companies that computerized information should be integrated into the companies' internal treasury systems so that global cash forecasts can be maintained and updated. Banks are developing 'customized' terminal services that incorporate the specific requirements of a company for processing bank information. Some of the newest services include the use of microprocessors to receive bank information and to support automation in the financial manager's office. Although microprocessor-based services are still in a very early stage of development for international cash management, there is strong corporate interest in their use.

(iii) Export remittances

A number of companies also report the use of advisory services for improving overseas export remittances. Such studies are typically called 'export cash management'. They review the remittances of overseas customers and make recommendations for improving remittance handling by both the company and its banks. These studies typically involve both the international treasury and credit management functions. Recommendations frequently include the use of direct collections with exporters filling out collection forms to eliminate mail time to the bank, reducing the number of banks receiving remittances, and the use of the bank courier services for sending and receiving documents overseas.

(iv) Netting systems

Companies also use banks for studying the feasibility of establishing intra-company cash management systems such as the use of multilateral netting or reinvoicing companies. Banks familiar with the netting process can look at a sample of intra-company payments and determine projected savings in foreign exchange commissions and float costs. Moreover, systems design guidelines and advice on how to obtain central bank approval of a netting system on a country-by-country basis and can often be a valuable part of the consulting services offered in the netting/reinvoicing area.

(e) Synthesis and conclusion

Establishing international cash management techniques is typically a long and difficult process for multinational corporations that now operate decentralized overseas operations. The typical company may have separate manufacturing and overseas sales subsidiaries reporting to regional offices responsible for international business. These regional operations may have accounting functions which are relatively independent. Only decisions relating to policy issues such as long-term financing are handled by headquarters. Therefore, establishing more centralized daily information flows and controls over international cash management functions usually requires organizational changes.

Key steps in establishing more centralized international cash management typically involve organization of personnel matters, establishing a cash concentration and account funding framework, information systems support and a systematic approach to banking relations.

As improvements in technology allow banks to support a variety of new global information services, more multinational corporations will place increased emphasis on international cash management because of the very significant potential for improving the utilization of global cash assets.

W9.7   Discussion questions

Note: Suggested answers to questions 9.1–9.5 are given in section W9.10 on pp. 560–1.

9.1   What are accruals and why are they an attractive source of finance to a enterprise?

9.2   In what way is the cash discount affected by the enterprise's opportunity cost of short-term funds?

9.3   Explain the cost-benefit approach to the taking of cash discounts and the extending of credit terms.

9.4   Who pays the cost of credit — the seller or the buyer? In what way?

9.5   By referring to the short-term interest rate structure, show how commercial paper can be an attractive form of short-term borrowing for the enterprise. Then evaluate the purchase of this paper from the point of view of the investor.

9.6   'Financial managers of enterprises have had to consider interest rate factors more than balance sheet norms.' Discuss.

9.7   Discuss what is meant by an enterprise's credit terms and what they determine.

9.8   If an enterprise were to increase its cash discount period, what would the effect be?

9.9   What is the trade-off among inventory turnover, costs of holding inventory and shortage costs?

9.10   'Inventories are an investment.' Discuss.

9.11   What is the relationship between inventories and accounts receivable? If credit terms were relaxed, what effects would this have on the levels of inventory?

9.12   Explain what the EOQ seeks to do and provide a critique of it.

9.13   What effect would a rise in the structure of interest rates have on levels of inventory, accounts payable/receivable, etc?

9.14   Discuss the factors that affect the transactions demand for cash by enterprises.

9.15   'The great advantage of short-term assets, given risk aversion and an uncertain world, is that they facilitate the utilization of new information about the environment as it becomes available over time' (J. Hirshleifer). Discuss.

9.16   Discuss the Chowdhury, Green and Miles article from the point of view of the interrelationship of the financial position of the enterprise *and* the general economic environment.

9.17   What role does the holding of 'cash' and marketable securities have in achieving the objective of shareholder wealth maximization?

9.18 Discuss the trade-off of profitability and illiquidity in the holding of marketable securities.

9.19 Outline the practical problems involved in using the Baumol and Miller-Orr models.

9.20 'The separation of the short-term and long-term financing decisions is misplaced.' Discuss.

W9.8 Worked problems

Note: Answers to problems 9.1–9.4 are given in section W9.11 on pp. 561–3.

9.1 An enterprise has a total wage bill of £8 million twice a month with a 13% cost of capital. Calculate the benefit to the enterprise of changing to a monthly pay cycle.

9.2 Take the interest rate data given in Table W9.6 and plot some simple yield curves for November 1989 to March 1990. Explain their shape, then compare the yields with:

(a) the yields on debentures and loan stocks
(b) dividend yields

and discuss your findings.

9.3 Take the short-term money rates in Table W9.7 and attempt to explain the yield structures that are present.

9.4 Fred Davies is a finance director of a large industrial products enterprise. The enterprise offers debtors a 2% discount for payment within 10 days. The average collection period of the enterprise is 28 days. Fred contends that the discount should be dropped. His estimates are that the average collection period would only increase to 30 days, and the enterprise would save 3% on all accounts taking the discount. (Thirty per cent of the enterprise's customers currently take the discount.) The marketing manager estimates that sales would drop from 21,000 to 20,000 units. The enterprise has a 20% required rate of return on investments. If the selling price per unit is £22, average cost per unit is £20 (at the current sales volume) and variable cost is £17 per unit, should the enterprise discontinue the discount?

9.5 Select any quoted enterprise and utilizing its financial statement on the Moody Cards for a number of years compare the interrelationships that exist between short-term assets/liabilities and long-term assets/liabilities. Then for the data period covered attempt to explain what you have found in terms of the yield structure and the state of the capital markets (e.g. whether they are in a bull or bear situation).

9.6 XYZ plc is attempting to evaluate whether the enterprise should ease collection efforts. The enterprise repairs 72,000 carpets per year at an average price of £32 each. Bad debt expenses are 1% and collection expenditures are £60,000. The average collection period is 40 days, the average cost per unit is £29 (at the current sales level) and the variable cost per unit is £28. By easing the collection efforts, XYZ expects to save £40,000 per year in collection expense. Bad debts will increase to 2% of

Table W9.6   Security yields (per cent per annum except for index number in right-hand column).

	Government stocks				Company securities (FT-Actuaries indices)			
	Short-dated (5 years)	Medium-dated (10 years)	Long-dated (20 years)	3.5% War Loan	Debenture and loan stocks	Industrial ordinary shares (500 shares)		
	Calculated redemption yields			Flat yield	Redemption yield	Dividend yield	Earnings yield	Price index (10 April 1962=100)
Last working day								
1989 Nov.	11.37	10.71	10.15	9.81	12.12	4.28	10.21	1241.05
Dec.	11.06	10.41	9.85	9.56	12.00	4.18	9.88	1310.62
1990 Jan.	11.80	11.11	10.50	10.13	12.68	4.36	10.20	1269.30
Feb.	12.34	11.63	11.04	10.60	12.86	4.58	10.72	1225.01
Mar.	13.05	12.52	11.60	11.20	13.66	4.72	11.02	1215.52
Mondays								
1989 Nov. 6	11.12	10.53	9.97	9.66	11.94	4.37	10.36	1202.03
„ 13	11.03	10.49	9.92	9.61	11.82	4.33	10.24	1216.03
„ 20	11.25	10.63	10.07	9.76	12.09	4.41	10.45	1201.67
„ 27	11.25	10.62	10.03	9.78	12.05	4.36	10.37	1217.15
Dec. 4	11.43	10.78	10.20	9.90	12.03	4.24	10.10	1254.20
„ 11	11.26	10.56	9.96	9.72	12.13	4.17	9.94	1283.79
„ 18	11.20	10.50	9.90	9.64	12.11	4.22	10.07	1280.94
„ 27[a]	11.07	10.44	9.86	9.56	12.03	4.17	9.97	1295.85
1990 Jan. 2[b]	11.13	10.45	9.87	9.56	11.99	4.17	9.86	1319.17
„ 8	11.23	10.60	10.05	9.72	12.11	4.15	9.81	1325.87
„ 15	11.67	10.90	10.27	9.86	12.28	4.28	10.06	1292.92
„ 22	12.05	11.18	10.51	10.14	12.61	4.39	10.33	1258.10
„ 29	11.76	11.05	10.40	10.07	12.70	4.36	10.23	1268.48
Feb. 5	11.92	11.25	10.64	10.24	12.72	4.34	10.16	1274.99
„ 12	11.99	11.28	10.65	10.26	12.75	4.43	10.38	1248.64
„ 19	12.25	11.49	10.92	10.45	12.73	4.45	10.50	1250.87
„ 26	12.16	11.45	10.84	10.37	12.91	4.58	10.74	1219.70
Mar. 5	12.75	12.19	11.22	10.83	13.09	4.64	10.80	1211.55
„ 12	12.96	12.44	11.48	11.14	13.20	4.67	10.88	1207.74
„ 19	13.01	12.41	11.45	11.03	13.45	4.67	10.87	1217.10
„ 26	12.99	12.48	11.54	11.16	13.57	4.61	10.77	1239.80

Source: Financial Statistics, Table 13.8, June 1990 (CSO).
Notes: [a] Wednesday.
       [b] Tuesday

sales, and the average collection period will increase to 58 days. Sales will increase by 1,000 repairs per year, and can be met from present excess capacity. If the enterprise has a required rate of return on its investments of 24%, what recommendation would you give the enterprise? Use your analysis to justify your answer.

9.7   Polson Brothers have sales of £200,000, a gross margin of 20% and an average age of inventory of 45 days.

(a) What will be the change in the average investment in inventory if the enterprise's inventory turnover ratio changes to 7?

(b) If the enterprise's required rate of return on investments is 18%, what additional profits (or losses) result from the change in (a)?

9.8   Cantreal plc uses 10,000 units of a raw material per year on a continuous basis. The enterprise estimates the cost of carrying one unit in inventory is £0.25 per year. Placing and processing an order for additional inventory costs £200 per order.

Table W9.7   Short-term money rates (per cent per annum).

		Sterling Treasury bills		Commercial bills: discount market buying rates (discount rates)	Selected retail banks		Interbank sterling		Sterling certificates of deposit 3 months
		Average discount rate for 91-day bills	Yield 91-day bills	Prime bank bills 3 months	Trade bills 3 months	Base rate	Call money	Overnight lending	3 months
Last Friday of period										
1986 Dec.		10.65	10.94	10.69	11.31	11.0	10.75	10–11.5	11.31–11.34	11.00–11.13
1987 Dec.		8.21	8.38	8.38	9.03	8.5	8.13	8.38–11	8.75– 9.00	8.81– 8.88
1988 Dec.		12.51	12.91	12.63	12.63	13.0	12.75	11.75–13.13	12.69–13.19	12.94–13.00
1989 Dec.		14.48	14.66	14.53	15.19	15.0	14.88	14.63–14.88	15.13–15.16	15.03–15.09
1988 May	27	7.15	7.28	7.34	7.97	7.5	7.38	6.75– 9.00	7.56– 7.75	7.50– 7.56
Jun	24	9.03	9.24	9.00	9.75	9.0	7.50	5.00–10.50	8.94– 9.44	9.06– 9.13
Jul	29	10.26	10.53	10.38	11.06	10.5	9.75	7.50–11.50	10.63–10.94	10.56–10.63
Aug.	26	11.49	11.82	11.66	12.38	12.0	12.00	8.50–13.00	11.31–12.25	11.88–11.94
Sep	30	11.39	11.47	11.63	12.25	12.0	11.00	9.00–14.00	11.75–12.19	11.81–11.88
Oct	28	11.50	11.84	11.66	12.38	12.0	11.75	5.00–12.25	12.00–12.25	12.00–12.60
Nov	25	12.58	12.98	11.69	12.34	13.0	12.25	5.00–12.75	12.13–13.00	13.00–13.03
Dec.	30	12.51	12.91	12.63	12.63	13.0	12.75	11.75–13.13	12.69–13.19	12.94–13.00
1989 Jan.	27	12.31	12.70	12.53	13.16	13.0	12.88	10.00–18.00	13.00–13.13	12.94–13.19
Feb.	24	12.51	12.91	12.63	13.25	13.0	12.81	12.00–14.50	12.94–13.19	12.94–13.06
Mar.	31	12.39	12.79	12.52	13.21	13.0	12.75	7.50–13.00	12.94–13.13	12.94–13.00
Apr.	28	12.23	12.62	12.41	13.16	13.0	10.50	8.00–14.00	12.88–13.38	12.75–12.88
May	26	13.27	13.35	13.25	14.13	14.0	12.00	13.50–13.75	13.81–13.88	13.69–13.81
Jun.	30	13.62	13.71	13.58	14.31	14.0	13.00	13.88–14.13	14.19–14.25	13.94–14.06
Jul.	28	13.24	13.32	13.37	14.00	14.0	14.00	13.94–14.00	13.81–13.88	13.78–13.84
Aug.	25	13.35	13.44	13.39	14.03	14.0	13.63	14.13–14.25	13.88–13.94	13.81–13.88
Sep.	29	13.44	13.53	14.10	14.88	14.0	13.75	13.50–13.63	14.63–14.69	14.13–14.38
Oct.	27	14.44	14.54	15.13	15.63	15.0	14.88	15.50–15.63	15.63–15.75	15.50–15.63
Nov.	24	14.45	14.62	14.50	15.16	15.0	14.88	14.81–14.88	15.03–15.06	15.00–15.06
Dec.	29	14.48	14.66	14.53	15.19	15.0	14.88	14.63–14.88	15.13–15.16	15.03–15.09
1990 Jan.	26	14.45	14.63	14.54	15.16	15.0	14.75	14.75–14.81	15.13–15.19	15.00–15.16
Feb.	23	14.34	14.45	14.53	15.19	15.0	14.75	14.63–14.75	15.09–15.13	15.00–15.06
Mar.	30	14.59	14.69	14.62	15.25	15.0	14.88	14.75–14.88	15.22–15.25	15.13–15.19
Apr.	27	14.62	14.73	14.69	15.34	15.0	14.81	14.75–14.88	15.28–15.31	15.19–15.25
May	25	14.46	14.56	14.49	15.13	15.0	14.75	14.88–15.00	15.03–15.09	14.97–15.03

Source: *Financial Statistics*, Table 13.8, June 1990 (CSO).

(a) What are annual ordering costs, carrying costs and total costs of inventory if the enterprise orders in quantities of 1,000, 2,000, 3,000, 4,000, 5,000, 6,000 and 7,000 units, respectively?

(b) Graph ordering costs and carrying costs (y-axis) relative to quantity ordered (x-axis). Label the EOQ.

(c) Based on your graph, in what quantity would you order? Is this consistent with the EOQ equation? Explain why or why not.

9.9   JBC has four divisions, each of which maintains its own separate transactions cash account. Transactions cash expenditures over the next month for each division are expected to be £40,000. An examination of the enterprise's records has revealed that the basic EOQ cash order model provides a reasonable description of the enterprise's transactions payment patterns. The enterprise has estimated that every £1 of cash held in the divisional transactions cash accounts will have an opportunity cost of £0.04 per month. The fixed cost per cash order for each division is estimated to be £50.

Management is contemplating the consolidation of the divisional cash accounts into a central account which will be accessible to each division for its transactions payments. Would you advise JBC to take this action? Explain.

9.10 ABC plc makes 30% of its sales to the USA, invoiced in dollars, and 10% to West Germany, invoiced in deutschmarks. Evaluate the foreign exchange exposure by taking a six-month period and plotting spot foreign exchange rates. Compare the strategies the enterprise has in the light of the *ex post* data on spot, forwards, options and futures contracts.

W9.9   Mini case study

ABC Limited has just secured a contract which requires additional stocks of raw materials and work in progress of £1.5 million for about a year. It has net assets of £4.0 million and pre-tax profits of £800,000. It has an overdraft facility of £500,000 which at present is not in use. Its accounts receivable are £1.5 million, inventory £2 million and accounts payable £1.4 million.

ABC will need additional finance to be able to take on this contract. Set out the position before and after this proposed financing.

W9.10   Suggested answers to discussion questions

9.1 Accruals are taken to be payments made to employees and other agencies, particularly the government, but which are not made immediately and therefore involve the granting of a form of credit to the firm. The nominal cost is zero, but there is a positive benefit in terms of a saving on other financing. The main types are wages and salaries — employees generally give their labour and receive payment a week or even a month in arrears — and deductions from the wage bill which are to be passed on to the government or elsewhere (PAYE, National Insurance contributions, pension contributions) but not immediately. VAT can be another source.

They are attractive because they are a free and spontaneous source of financing, increasing when the activity of the firm increases. There are other examples of accruals that occur in certain types of business, e.g. auction houses. They receive payment for the goods sold and then a week or so later they make the payment to their clients. In the meantime, they have the use of the money. In times of high interest rates this could make a considerable difference to their profits.

9.2 We make the point in both the text and Workbook that the giving and taking of a cash discount is based on a cost-benefit calculation. The granting firm loses the value of the discount by reducing the price, but will do so to speed up collections so as to reduce its need for financing or to use the cash for short-term assets. We also make the point that the granting of a discount may be expensive and outweigh the strict financial benefit of the opportunity cost. However, the supplier may feel it can get a better grip on its potential bad debts, i.e. reduce uncertainty by offering an incentive to get the cash in — the bird-in-the-hand argument.

There may be some merit to this, but presumably a potential bad debtor will not even bother with the discount. For the taker of the discount the same calculations apply. To pay early requires financing on the use of funds that could be employed elsewhere — the opportunity cost. Unless the firm wants to establish a good reputation by paying early, it will only take the discount if it is worth its while. Unless the opportunity costs are different, it is unlikely to be simultaneously in the interests of the supplier and taker.

9.3 This answer draws heavily on that for question 9.2 with the exception of credit terms. Although we argue for a cost–benefit approach, we make the point in 9.2 that it is unlikely both parties will benefit from the arrangement. It may be that the supplier does give discounts because this is the norm in the industry, in which case it cannot follow a strict cost–benefit approach. The taker of the discount is likely to follow a cost–benefit approach.

9.4 There is no such thing as a free lunch! A supplier of trade credit chooses to do so either because it has to match industry norms or because it makes a conscious choice to increase trade. It hopes that the cost will be recouped in terms of a higher sales volume. However, it can build these costs into its profit margin — just like the allowance for bad debts, thefts, etc. So the cost could be shared by supplier and receiver. We cannot assume that it is free to the receiver, although it appears that way. If the supplier gives a cash discount, then we can see that the receiver actually pays in terms of a higher price by not taking the discount.

9.5 In Table W9.7 we supply some data on short-term money rates. However, you may well wish to use more recent data or another data set. In essence what we wish to show is that if the enterprise can issue bill finance — only the larger enterprises can generally do so — it will usually be a cheaper form of finance compared to bank borrowing. If we compare the bill rates (choose either the bank bills or trade bills), quite often these are lower than the base rate. As most enterprises pay base rate plus a margin, the bill finance can be cheaper. Actually in the data set given, long-term borrowing is also cheaper in some months!

The lender has several alternative short-term investments. Commercial bills are better (in return) than T. bills, but have the added risk, although eligible bank bills have little risk. In some months they are higher than CDs and local authority deposits.

W9.11 Answers to worked problems

9.1 With certain assumptions, e.g. fixed workforce, we can assume that the wage bill accrues at a constant rate. With £8 million fortnightly the average financing provided by the workforce is half that, i.e. £4 million. With a monthly wage bill of £16 million the average financing would be £8 million. We would therefore have a benefit of (£8 million − £4 million) × 13% = £520,000.

9.2 The choice of the data in Table W9.6 is deliberate as it shows the following:

(a) Over the whole period there is a downward sloping yield curve. The data are plotted for three sets of yields, short, medium and long. The $3\frac{1}{2}$% War Loan is a perpetuity and is at the tail end of the yield curve. You will see it is lower (always) than the 'long'-dated 20-year bonds.

(b) How you interpret these findings depends on your knowledge of term structure — expectations (unbiased), liquidity preference and market segmentation. These are too extensive to go into here.

(c) For the inclusion of corporate bonds, you can observe that the yield is *always* above the 20-year government bond rate and above the short rate even when there is a downward-sloping yield curve. However, if we do a comparison with the 20-year and the corporate, we will observe that the premium can differ quite significantly. On just a casual basis take:

6 Nov. 1989: we have 9.97 and 11.94, a difference of 1.97 = 19.76% *
8 Jan. 1990: we have 10.05 and 12.11, a difference of 2.06 = 20.50% *
26 Mar. 1990: we have 11.54 and 13.57, a difference of 2.03 = 17.59% *

* of 20-year bond rate.

(d) Once we include dividend yields, we have what is called a reverse yield gap. Dividend yield, of course, is simply dividends (pounds) divided by the share price. The latter will fluctuate daily, and as interest rates fall generally we would expect the stock market to improve. Whilst this can also improve dividends, the immediate effect is on the share price. So with a fixed numerator, we would expect the dividend yield to fall. Likewise with falling interest rates, with the fixed coupon on bonds their yield will fall (price rise). Note equities are perpetuities and bonds have a fixed term with the return of the principal. Also equities do not have to carry a dividend (see Chapter 10).

9.3 This is really a question of default risk, though you could also examine the yield through time on, say, T. bills and other instruments to assess how the premiums vary over time.

If we stick with a single time period, say 30 March 1990, then we see the following structure:

T.bills (91 day)	14.69	Classed as the risk-free rate.
Bank bills	14.62 ⎫	Commercial bills of exchange. We
Trade bills	15.25 ⎭	would expect bank bills to carry a lower yield because of the reduced risk.
Base rate	15.0	The bank lending rate on which risk premiums are added to reflect the risk of different borrowers.
Call money	14.88	Short-term lending in the money market, often to a discount house. It could be as low as one day.
Interbank £s:		
Overnight	14.75–14.88	This rate can vary dramatically: see, for example, May and June 1988.
3 months	15.22–15.25	These rates depend on supply and demand. You would expect a close relationship with the same term CD rate.
Sterling CDs	15.13–15.19	

9.4 Benefits (no discount):

$$(0.03)(0.3)(21,000)(22) = £4,158$$

Cost (lost sales):

$$(22 - 17)(1,000) = £5,000$$

One could stop here. Since costs exceed benefits, one would not discontinue the discount. However, to be complete, one should consider the additional financing of the Accounts Receivable (A/R) of two additional days.

$$\text{Average investment in A/R} = \left(\frac{(20,000)(17)}{360} \right)(30) - \left(\frac{(21,000)(17)}{360} \right)(28)$$
$$= £28,333 - £27,767$$
$$= £566$$

Cost of investment in A/R = £566(0.20)
$$= £113.20$$

Total costs = £113.20 + £5,000.00
$$= £5,113.20$$

Total benefits = £4,158.00

Reject the policy, since the total costs exceed the total benefits.

10 Dividend policy

Learning objectives

The aims of this chapter are to:

- consider the multi-dimensional nature of the dividend decisions of enterprises and how it impacts on the enterprise and the shareholders and creditors of the enterprise;
- understand the theoretical approaches that have been taken in the debate;
- understand the impact of market imperfections on the controversy;
- appraise the types of policy followed by enterprises.

W10.1   Introduction

In Chapters 8 and 9 we discussed the raising of finance; as part of this we raised the importance of internal sources of funds. So how can an enterprise decide what to retain and what to distribute, and how does an investor who owns both retentions and dividends react? In the quotation given below it is clear that dividends are important, and given that they exist and persist, they are in a sense an institution.

> A cow for her milk, An orchard for fruit,
> A hen for her eggs, Bees for their honey,
> And a stock, by heck, And stock, besides,
> For her dividends. For their dividends.
> (Lorie and Hamilton, 1973)

This chapter will reveal that the whole area of dividends policy is surrounded by a controversy in the academic literature and among practitioners. This is perhaps surprising for, as we have remarked above, there appears to be irrefutable empirical evidence that dividends are relevant to share valuations.

W10.2   Issues in dividend policy

Dividends can be paid in cash or in shares. In the United Kingdom they are typically paid after six months as an interim and six months later as a final payment. In North America they are paid quarterly. This timing aspect is important if we wish to use the Gordon valuation model. This point can be illustrated further here using an illustration from Beedles (1984).

Beedles takes a security which has declared and paid a $100 quarterly dividend (it is American), with an expected growth rate of 10% (2.41% quarterly). The data are given in Table W10.1. He then takes a 20% annual required rate of return (4.66% quarterly). To quote (pp. 246–7):

> The *typical* procedure to find value involves dividing the total dividend to be received during the next year (= $4.247) by the difference between the required return and expected growth (= $k - g = 0.2 - 0.1$), which results in a price of $42.47 (= 4.247/0.1). The *proper* procedure reflects the actual quarterly frequency. Using the actual next dividend and quarterly discount and growth rates results in a price of $45.47 [= 1.024/(0.0466 − 0.0241)].
>
> All of this is important when an attempt is made to *estimate* the owners' required return. Since for this illustration the price and growth rate are known, on the (erroneous) annual basis the estimate is:

$$k = D/P + g$$
$$= 4.247/45.47 + 0.1$$
$$= 0.1934$$

This 19.34% value is in contrast to the *actual* value of 20%.

To summarize, the *proper* method first involves using the next quarterly dividend and a quarterly growth rate:

$$k = 1.024/45.47 + 0.0241$$
$$= 0.0466$$

Table W10.1 Expected dividends, quarterly growth

Months hence	Expected dividends	Yearly sum
3	$1.024	
6	1.049	
9	1.074	
12	1.100	$4.247
15	1.127	
18	1.154	
21	1.182	
24	1.210	4.673
27	1.239	
30	1.269	
33	1.300	
36	1.331	5.139

Source: Beedles, 1984.

Investors when they invest in shares expect a return on their investment. This can be in the form of income (dividends) and/or in the capital gain/loss when the share price moves. The ability of an enterprise to pay dividends is *inter alia* determined by its profitability in a given period. But there is no exact proportional relationship and dividends have been less cyclical than profits, reflecting reluctance on the part of enterprises to cut them when profits fall, and to increase them in proportion when profits rise.

We can illustrate this briefly for the recent past in the United Kingdom where there has been a marked recovery in profits — they doubled between 1980 and 1984 — but dividends increased by only 60% (although this is still a substantial rise and greater than other forms of personal income over that period). However, a word of caution. As dividends had experienced statutory controls in the 1960s and 1970s, and as the major recession of the late 1970s had hit corporate profitability hard, including dividends, then it can be misleading to take a four-year period such as this solely on its own and out of context of the longer-term trends.

The fundamental questions raised in Chapter 10 of the text are:

1. can dividends be used by management to influence the value of the enterprise?
2. what factors determine the division of after-tax earnings of the enterprise between paying them out in the form of dividends and retaining them in the enterprise?

How the enterprise decides to split its earnings into dividends and retained earnings is the crux of the debate. The impact of the split between retention and distribution has important implications for the enterprise, the shareholders and other creditors. Let us examine each of these in turn.

(i) The enterprise
The split will have an immediate effect on the financing and investment plans of the enterprise. If the enterprise has projects which it has evaluated and feels it should accept, and there are insufficient retained funds by virtue of a dividend payment, then either it has to forgo some of them, or it has to borrow and incur the transaction costs and market scrutiny. On the latter aspect, more retention can involve higher agency costs given the asymmetry of information, since the enterprise will not have to come to the market as often and release more information. There is the added effect that retained earnings will improve the debt/equity ratio.

We can show the interactive relationship of dividends to other financial decisions by using a flow of funds identity, namely *sources* of funds must equal *uses* of funds. Thus we can have:

$$\Delta I_t + D_t \equiv \Delta O_t + \Delta B_t + E_t$$

where: ΔI_t = net change in investment in period t
  D_t = dividends in period t
  ΔO_t = net change in equity finance in period t
  ΔB_t = net change in debt finance in period t
  E_t = earnings in period t.

With earnings given, there are four major management decision areas:

1. dividend policy;
2. debt policy;
3. investment policy;
4. equity policy.

Yet management can only determine three as the other will fall out as a residual.

(ii) The shareholders
We cannot assume that shareholders are homogeneous with respect to their preference for income now or in the future, and certainly their tax status will differ. Compounding these issues is the asymmetry of information, which

requires investors to attempt to deduce from the enterprise what a dividend increase or cut really means — the signalling approach.

(iii) Other creditors

Bond-holders will not welcome a greater distribution as opposed to retention since they will lose out on the capital security aspect of their bonds. In fact, shares are a call option on the assets of the enterprise. Other creditors, too, who would look to the assets of the enterprise on liqiidation to meet their claims, will also prefer a large retention ratio.

(iv) The government

Dividend controls have often been used by governments, and in the United Kingdom statutory control was lifted in July 1979 ending seven years of continuous operation and a longer period — since 1961 — of various persuasive and statutory controls. Reference to a Bank of England (1980) study reveals that the limits were largely adhered to.

W10.3   The theoretical controversy

We have presented the theoretical controversy in the text. Our starting point is the polar views of the theoretical literature — the relevance and irrelevance schools. The latter as propounded by Miller and Modigliani (1961) is cast in a neo-classical framework with very simplifying assumptions. How can we quibble with their arguments given the simplifying assumptions used? There is perfect substitutability of dividends and retentions on the part of the enterprise and shareholder. The enterprise would be failing in its duty of maximizing shareholders' wealth if it did not invest in all the profitable projects it could, even if this meant no dividends. If for some reason the shareholders require present income rather than future, then they simply make the dividends themselves by selling some shares and taking out as income the capitalized value of the dividends. So the driving force in the enterprise is its investment policy *not* the financing policy. The further relevance of this argument is found in Chapter 11.

However, given the simplifying assumptions, particularly certainty, how could there be any projects with greater than zero NPVs? Why do we need an enterprise to exploit these projects, since with certainty individuals presumably could undertake the same investments? Enterprises and individuals would compete and we would end up with projects yielding at best just the cost of capital, which is a single borrowing–lending rate of interest. For the sake of completeness we show the MM view in the Fisher-Hirshleifer framework as developed by Fama and Miller (1972).

The Fisher-Hirshleifer model is shown in Fig. W10.1. The straight line $c'c$ is the market line of borrowing–lending showing the reward for postponing consumption in the present period to the next period. The crucial difference here is that we broaden the investment opportunities to include 'real' assets, and returns from these are shown by the curved line $r'r$, and this is tangential to the market line $c'c$ at point x. With the objective of shareholder wealth maximization, the enterprise will invest ar in real assets. If the enterprise has only br in cash from, say, its operations, it can raise the difference ab by, say, a rights issue (see Chapter 8, pp. 210–13). There would be no dividends paid in this case.

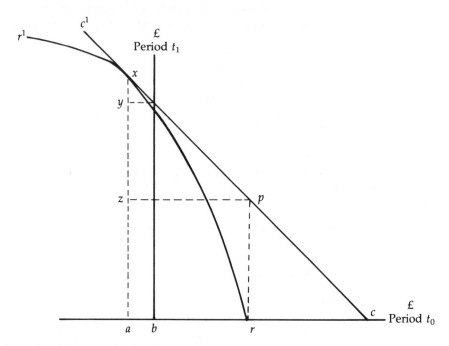

Figure W10.1   MM dividend irrelevance.

If the enterprise decides to pay dividends, the amount it pays has to be balanced by additional shares issued. Let us take the two cases — no dividends and dividends.

(i) No dividends
Here the enterprise issues shares to the value of ab in period 0, which will require a return to new investors of xy. Current shareholders will have a return of ay, which has a present value of bc.

(ii) Dividends paid
If these were of the order of br in period 0, investors who subscribe to new shares will have to provide ar, requiring a return in period 1 of zx. Current shareholders have an investment of rc, which has a future value of pr. Current shareholders have a wealth position of $br + rc = bc$, i.e. dividends (br) and shares (rc), which is exactly the same as the no dividends case.

It is when we change the assumptions of the MM model that we can find differences in the theoretical and practical implications. If we relax the assumption of *certainty* and hold the other assumptions constant, then we enter a world of risk. The MM argument can still be proved to hold provided there is constancy of risk between new and old investments and shareholders and managers have identical preferences with respect to the risk-adjusted rates of return. Once we drop this latter assumption, the dividend decision in an uncertain world becomes a behavioural issue, as Lintner (1956) argued. He found in his survey of United States enterprises — recently supported by Baker *et al*. (1985) — that dividend policy is important and that managers did feel that the decision could affect the value of the enterprise. The Gordon argument, often termed the 'bird in the hand', gives a reason for this in that investors need not be indifferent between income now (dividends) and income in the future (capital gains). The Gordon argument is not without its critics because the additional risk of future income is a function, one presumes, of what the enterprise does with the funds — in other words, the riskiness of the capital projects it invests in (Chapter 7). This is not necessarily a function of time, rather the total risk of the enterprise — systematic and unsystematic risk. This can be tested for, linking the beta of the share to the dividend policy. The studies on this are inconclusive.

However, an interesting point to consider is the issue of duration. With a high-coupon bond versus a low-coupon bond of equal lives, the former is a shorter bond in terms of duration. By analogous reasoning, if we take two equivalent shares, one of which has a higher dividend, then that one will be shorter in terms of duration. We can go further and argue from bond price theorems that the higher-coupon bond is less risky than the low coupon. The argument holds analogously for shares, too. Following this line further, managers can actually reduce the risk of their shares by paying dividends. Dyl and Hoffmeister (1986) present a test of these for the United States and find that a linkage exists.

So on a theoretical basis we have irrelevance and relevance. For the former to hold, given that dividends are an institution, either enterprises and investors are irrational — which might seem surprising given the discussion in Chapter 3 on the EMH — or dividend behaviour is costless to enterprises and households, which given market imperfections it is clearly not. We treat these imperfections in order in section 10.4 of the text and below in section W10.4.

Reference has been made in many chapters, including Chapter 10, to the Chowdhury and Miles (1986) study which utilized published data from financial statements for 650 firms. The study focused on dividends and debt in long-term financial decisions. They utilized the following flow of funds model:

$$d - b - e - f = p - t - i$$

where: d = gross dividends paid

$\quad\quad b$ = the flow of new debt finance with residual maturity exceeding one year — called 'strategic' debt

$\quad\quad e$ = new equity finance (together d, b and e constitute 'strategic' finance)

$\quad\quad f$ = the flow of net trade credit *plus* short-term debt finance with maturity under one year *minus* net acquisitions of liquid assets

$\quad\quad p$ = profits

$\quad\quad t$ = corporation taxes paid

$\quad\quad i$ = fixed investment and stockbuilding.

Their *a priori* reasoning saw the dividend decision as part of a strategic decision set (see Chapter 1), which would have the short-term assets acting as a buffer to the unfolding of micro and macroeconomic factors — interest rate movements, cost changes, tax changes, inflation rates, etc. While the authors recognize the limits of their study, the conclusions are interesting and have been quoted quite often in the text. However, in Tables W10.2 and W10.3 we summarize the impact on dividends (and debt too) for two sets of changes — expenditures and receipts, and tax and interest rates.

Table W10.2   The effects of changes in expenditures and receipts on dividends and strategic debt (pence per additional £1 of expenditure/receipt)

	Effect on dividend payments[a]		Effect on stock of strategic debt[b]	
	Short-run[c]	Long-run[d]	Short-run[c]	Long-run[d]
£1 change in:				
Gross profits	9[e]	12	−16[e]	−70
Investment	$\frac{1}{2}$[e]	1	26[e]	135
Financial assets	−6[e]	−9	12[e]	60
Tax payments	12[e]	23	19[e]	71
Interest payments	—	—	−14	−70

Notes: [a] Sample average £2.1 million.
[b] Sample average £14.9 million.
[c] Contemporaneous effect — within one year.
[d] 75% of the long-run effect occurs by the end of two years for dividend payments and by the end of seven years for the stock of strategic debt.
[e] Estimate statistically significant at the 95% level — long-run effects are calculated so standard errors are not applicable.

Table W10.3   The effects of changes in tax rates and interest rates on dividends

Changes in tax and interest rates	Long-run[a] % change in dividends
Cut in corporation tax rate from 50% to 40% with 5-year gilt at average[b] rate	+2.4
Cut in imputation rate from 33% to 30%	−10.1
Cut in marginal income tax rate from 30% to 29%	+21.0
Company becomes tax exhausted at current[c] tax rates	−7.1
5-year gilt rate up 1 percentage point at average[b] tax rates	−9.2
Interbank rate up 1 percentage point (relative to 5-year gilt)	+3.2
Dividend yield up 1 percentage point (relative to 5-year gilt)	−9.2

Notes: [a] 75% of the long-run effect occurs by the end of two years for dividends.
[b] Average value from 1971 to 1984.
[c] At 1987 values.

Table W10.2 revealed the lags in adjustment. Firms responded to higher profits by increasing dividend payments in both the short and long runs. The effects of changes in tax and interest rates on dividends are illustrated in Table W10.3, indicating the sensitivity of dividends to these changes.

W10.4   Market imperfections

(a) Transaction costs

The enterprise in paying the dividends and in raising the equivalent cash by debt or rights issues incurs transaction costs (see Chapter 8 for details of these). The investor incurs agency costs in monitoring enterprises and in the home-made dividends of MM (selling shares to produce the cash).

(b) Clientele effect

This is an intuitively appealing argument, but difficult to test. Do some investors prefer income and others capital gain? They may do so because of their particular needs, and additional factors such as transaction costs and taxation can add to this. Certainly in the Coats Patons case (pp. 574–80), the clientele effect appears to be present. The text also suggests that there may be tax-induced clienteles, and the apparent smoothing of dividend payments may be a reaction by firms to a perceived clientele.

(c) Taxes

Tax regimes at both corporate and personal levels can produce distortions which induce a particular behaviour. Of course this can be the intention, e.g. to discriminate in favour of retentions to increase them and, hopefully, capital investment. The progressivity of personal income tax adds to this discrimination. Note too that some institutions are treated differently so that gross funds, e.g. pension funds, including those administered by life insurance companies, are exempt from all taxes.

There have been a number of different corporate tax regimes and we can summarize their effects briefly:

1958–65 Largely neutral as between retentions and distributions
1966–73 Favoured retentions
1973– Favoured distributions

The empirical evidence on the effect of the tax regime suggests that, apart from in the very short-term, dividend behaviour has not been affected by a change in regime. However, there are other factors at work, including dividend controls.

(d) Asymmetric information

We make the point in various parts of the book that there is asymmetry of information among shareholders themselves and between shareholders and managers. So dividends can be a market signalling device. The idea originated with MM, who argued that if an enterprise has established a long tradition for paying dividends, then if it changes downwards this may be interpreted as bad news. If they are a signalling device then we say that dividends have information content. In the semi-strong form of the EMH (Chapter 3), we saw that they are indeed a form of publicly available information. But precisely what information is open to question. Certainly the empirical tests are inconclusive, though for the United States the study by Baker *et al.* (1985) reveals that managers are aware of the signalling issue.

W10.5 Dividend procedures

Following the theoretical discussions and the issue of imperfections, business enterprises really have three major policy alternatives:

1. dividends as a residual determined by the investment and other financing plans;
2. retained earnings as a residual so that either financing or investment is changed to accommodate whatever dividend policy is adopted, e.g. dividend stabilization;
3. simultaneous dividend policy, i.e. neither totally residual nor totally independent.

Option 1 is not generally followed, so we are left with 2 and 3. Dividend stability would appear to be an objective of the managers of many enterprises. However, the recession of the early 1980s in particular has caused many enterprises to re-evaluate this. Enterprises have had more latitude than, say, Coats Patons had in 1974. The recession was so deep-seated and obvious that enterprises were able to explain their decisions with stark economic facts and not rely on the vague signals of the 'information content' hypothesis.

W10.6   Alternative policies

The main point here is the reinvestment of dividends and scrip dividends. The former, if optional, allow both clienteles the choice and can be an attractive proposition to get over transaction costs of reinvestment by individuals and of enterprises too. Likewise with scrip dividends. Neither avoids personal tax liability, so they are neutral in this respect.

W10.7   International dimension of dividend policy

This is included to broaden the issue of dividend policy, since dividends can be an important vehicle for multinationals to move funds from some host countries to other host countries or to the parent. There are important risks here that are focused on in the text.

W10.8   Discussion questions

Note: Suggested answers to questions 10.1–10.5 are given in section W10.11 on pp. 580–4.

10.1   Explain the following terms:

1. residual theory of dividends;
2. clientele effect;
3. asymmetric information;
4. signalling properties of dividends;
5. the 'bird-in-the-hand' argument.

10.2   Discuss what is meant by the information content of dividends. How does this concept fit in with the efficient markets hypothesis?

10.3   'The board is aware of the importance of paying dividends.' Discuss this statement in terms of establishing a dividend policy for companies.

10.4   What importance do you consider should be attached to dividend policy as a determinant of share value?

10.5   'The value of a dividend to investors must be balanced against the opportunity cost of the retained earnings lost as a means of equity financing. Thus we see that the dividend decision must be analyzed in relation to the financing decision' (Van Horne). Discuss.

10.6   Discuss the information content of dividends hypothesis in the light of recent empirical tests.

10.7   Discuss the relationship between dividend payments and the investment behaviour of enterprises which have a capital-rationing problem.

10.8 Appraise the available empirical studies on dividend policy. Utilize the Coats Patons case if necessary to illustrate your arguments.

10.9 Analyse the concept of an optimal dividend distribution policy for an enterprise.

10.10 In what circumstances can an enterprise making investment decisions disregard the decision about what dividends to pay?

10.11 'It is unlikely that predictive models can be found to test user information content (of dividend announcements) in an objective and generalizable fashion because of the empirical infeasibility of finding optimal models' (P.A. Taylor). Do you agree?

10.12 Discuss whether the growing institutionalization of shareholding in the United Kingdom impacts a greater clientele effect which enterprises have to consider in their dividend policy.

10.13 Contrast the Miller-Modigliani dividend model under certainty and uncertainty.

10.14 What effects, if any, does the present tax regime have on an enterprise's dividend policy?

10.15 By accepting . . . (a scrip dividend) shareholders must still pay the tax due on dividend income and there would be dilution of share price and possibly dilution of future share earnings. Discuss this statement.

W10.9 Worked problems

Note: Answers to problems 10.1–10.3 are given in section W10.12 on pp. 584–5.

10.1 ZYX plc follows a residual dividend policy and it has the following projections for the next year:

1. internally generated earnings of £4 million;
2. eligible capital investment projects of £8 million;
3. a target debt-equity ratio of 60/40.

Consider how much ZYX should pay out to its shareholders in the form of a cash dividend and how it should handle its financing needs (if any).

10.2 ABC plc has 1,000,000 shar s which currently sell for £10 each, and there are earnings available for distribution of £1 million. The management of the enterprise is contemplating a cash dividend of 50 pence per share.

1. Calculate the current EPS and P/E multiple.
2. If the enterprise decides on a scrip dividend, what effect can we expect this to have on the enterprise and the shareholders?
3. If the enterprise decides on a share purchase at £10.50, how many shares can be repurchased to replicate the cash dividend payment?
4. Assume that the enterprise has investment opportunities of £1 million but still wants to pay the 50 pence dividend. Analyse the effect of the financing on the enterprise and the shareholders.

10.3 Norwood Limited is a medium-sized concern in the engineering industry. It has a good track record of profits and last year it made

£4 million after tax. It attributes some of its success to its investment appraisal methods and it is currently appraising six projects (see table). The enterprise has followed a policy of financing its expansion from within the organization and sees no reason to deviate from this in the present case. However, Norwood has a target rate of return of 14%.

Project	Initial outlay £	Expected return
A	1,000,000	25%
B	500,000	30%
C	100,000	10%
D	400,000	15%
E	1,000,000	16%
F	1,000,000	20%

1. Calculate both the average and marginal rates of return with respect to the retention ratio and insert the cut-off rate of return.
2. Determine the optimal retention ratio.

10.4 Select an ordinary share and track its share price before and after the dividend announcement. Discuss your findings. (*Hint:* Use the industry index or the whole index as a control variable over this period.)

10.5 Assume that, as in the case of Coats Patons, a firm decides to delay a cash dividend in one year. The amount of the dividend in question is £2.10 for the year and the assumed reinvestment rate is 15%, with a discount rate of 11%. Assuming that the dividend is paid as one payment, what impact will there be on the share price of the firm?

10.6 XYZ has earnings of £12 million and it is considering an optimal distribution/retention policy in the light of a number of investment opportunities (see table). If all of these were followed, they would completely exhaust the earnings. The firm has an estimated required rate of return of 20%.

Project	Required investment £m	E(R) %
A	5	25
B	2	20
C	1	15
D	1	21
E	0.5	19
F	2.5	24

Discuss the issues involved

W10.10   Case study: Coats Patons

Cases in the literature on dividend policy are few and far between. Although the events described here took place in 1975, the principles underlying the case are still relevant. The mid-1970s was quite a traumatic period in the economic life of the United Kingdom (and of the corporate sector in particular). If you wanted to place the case in perspective, you could go back and familiarize yourself via the newspapers and periodicals (e.g. *The Economist*) of the period. These should be available in the library in bound form or on microfilm. The firm no longer exists as a separate entity since it is now part of Coats Viyella plc.

> To the financial Cloud-cuckoo-land in which we are living we have, we think, introduced an element of realism in terms both of the shareholders' short and longer term interests.
>
> (Coats Patons, 29.5.75)

Coats Patons Ltd is a multinational with its head office in Glasgow. The principal activities of the company and its subsidiaries are the production and sale of cotton and synthetic threads, wool and synthetic yarns and fabrics, fashion garments, knitwear and children's wear. Additionally, the group makes zip fasteners, die castings and mouldings and also trades as merchants in these products. The company formed in 1961 as a result of an amalgamation between J. and P. Coats Ltd and Patons and Baldwins Ltd. The group has extensive overseas production and trading interests through a series of subsidiary companies and Table W10.4 indicates the geographical sources of sales, profits and net assets.

Table W10.4 Geographical source of profits, turnover and net assets 1971–4

	UK	Europe	N. America	S. America	Africa, Asia and Australia	Total
(a) Profit source (%)						
1971	15.6	25.2	24.3	16.0	18.9	100
1972	18.8	25.6	20.9	16.2	18.5	100
1973	22.9	24.2	15.6	17.5	19.8	100
1974	26.9	36.1	6.4	18.4	12.2	100
(b) Turnover (%)						
1971	40.1[a]	16.5	22.5	6.9	14.0	100
1972	35.6	18.4	23.7	7.5	14.8	100
1973	35.7	18.4	20.0	8.7	17.4	100
1974	37.3	20.7	18.3	9.6	14.1	100
(c) Net assets (%)						
1971	43.3	14.1	20.9	7.6	14.1	100
1972	39.0	14.9	22.7	7.9	15.5	100
1973	39.6	15.1	20.7	8.6	16.0	100
1974	38.9	17.5	19.8	9.4	14.4	100

Note: [a] Including exports.

The company by 1975 had acquired a reputation for an above-average dividend yield (see Tables W10.5 and W10.6) and the shares had been bought for their regular flow of high income, particularly by gross funds. For the period 1969–73 the company made an average return on its net capital employed of 17.54%.

The chairman, Mr C.W. Bell, writing in his annual report in May 1974, stated that he was reasonably confident about the outcome for 1974, despite the difficult trading conditions. He thought the latter would not only persist, but intensify, though he thought that the geographical diversification of the group would be to its continuing advantage. By the half-year stage, however,

Table W10.5   Earnings and dividend yield

	Coats Patons[a]		FT 500-share[b]	
	Earnings yield (%)	Dividend yield (%)	Earnings yield (%)	Dividend yield (%)
1964	15.9	13.5	9.57	5.53
1965	15.7	13.0	7.77	5.44
1966	15.6	13.0	7.93	6.02
1967	15.3	13.0	5.90	4.51
1968	17.6	13.5	4.45	3.24
1969	14.7	13.5	6.0	3.93
1970	12.8	13.5	7.04	4.58
1971	15.8	13.5	5.27	3.43
1972	24.7	14.1	5.75	3.37
1973	39.0	14.8	11.55	5.10
1974	37.5	5.4	33.97	13.17

Notes: [a] Adjusted to be comparable.
        [b] End December.

the company warned of a marked drop in expected profit and gave an interim dividend of 5.4%. On 29 May 1975 Mr Bell announced better-than-expected profis of £47.3 million (down from £54.15 million), despite setbacks in Australia and the USA. He forecast that these falls in profit would be temporary, but more significantly he announced that Coats would not pay a final dividend. Instead, the group offered a 1 for 25 scrip issue with a proposed arrangement to cut down the expense of selling small numbers of shares. This was intended to appeal to the 36,500 small (1,000 units or less) shareholders on the register at that time.

Table W10.6   Earnings per share (adjusted) and ordinary shares in issue

	EPS (pence)	Shares in issue (voting rights 1 for 4 shares)
1971	4.5	264,461
1972	6.5	264,461
1973	9.6	266,040[a]
1974	8.9	266,040
1975	6.9	276,681[b]

Notes: [a] In January 1973, 1,578,660 shares issued as part consideration for the acquisition of the remaining capital not already owned of Needle Industrial Group Ltd.
        [b] Scrip issue, 1 for 25.

Table W10.7   Summary results for 1973–4

	1973 £000s	1974 £000s
Sales	414,524	448,210
Trading profit	67,299	64,183
Depreciation	10,392	10,385
Interest	5,336	9,549
Goodwill	97	124

Table W10.7   Continued

	1973 £000s	1974 £000s
Profits of associates	836	1,590
Investment income	327	348
Surplus on investments sold	347	52
Surplus on assets realized	1,162	760
Profits pre-tax	54,146	47,257
Taxation	24,094	20,095
Net profit	30,052	27,162
Investment grants	335	388
Minorities	3,742	2,930
Attributable	26,645	24,620
Extraordinary losses	—	1,111
Preference dividends	48	48
Ordinary dividends	6,977	2,394
Retained	19,620	21,067

Note: Provision for UK tax at 52% is £5.37 million (£4.6 million in 1973) after DTR of £7.09 million (£6.72 million) and includes deferred tax of £3.77 million, of which £1.27 million represents capital allowances, and £2.49 million stock relief (£4.29 million), of which £154,000 represents capital allowances and £4.13 million stock relief. Over-provision prior years is £230,000 (£407,000) and overspill £300,000 (same). Foreign tax is £14.51 million (£19.87 million). Associate tax is £743,000 (£330,000).

A summary of the results for 1973 and 1974 is contained in Table W10.7. They indicate that the earnings for ordinary shareholders, before an extra-ordinary loss of £1.11 million on sale of subsidiaries, amounted to £24.6 million (£26.6 million in 1973), which was equal to 9.2p per share (10p in 1973). The group had made significant fixed capital investment acquisitions and sundries totalling £22 million, and borrowing had increased by £24 million. The group's cash flow of £34.7 million was more than absorbed by the effects of inflation, which necessitated an additional investment of £37 million. The total cash deficit was £24.6 million, although the chairman was at pains to point out that there was neither a trading nor a cash crisis and the unused borrowing facilities amounted to £40 million. The experience at Coats was, of course, mirrored by the whole industrial and commercial sector in this period, as Table W10.8 indicates.

Table W10.8   Cash surplus/deficit and bank borrowing: industrial and commercial companies

	Cash surplus/(deficit) £m	Bank borrowing £m
1970	−515	1,126
1971	710	732
1972	795	2,988
1973	−800	4,504
1974	−4,063	4,411
1975[a]	−794	418

Note: [a] The large initial allowances together with the stock appreciation concession meant that in 1975 on a sample of major companies analysed by stockbrokers Phillips and Drew over two-fifths would only have paid ACT in that year.

If a dividend had been levied at the 1973 level, the cash deficit of the group would have risen by £7.01 million, including a full charge of £2.47 million ACT which would not be immediately recoverable. The justification that the board made for its unanimous decision not to pay a final dividend was therefore that it would have to borrow to pay the dividend, though some financial commentators argued at the time that to pursue the full logic of inflation accounting would recognize the attractiveness of borrowing. Additionally, it would be presenting the Chancellor with a sizeable amount of revenue as the imputation system denies effective double tax relief when dividends are paid out of profits which have not borne a full corporation tax charge (owing to the bulk of them having been earned abroad). Conserving the cash within the business, the directors argued, would be in the best short- and long-term interests of the shareholders as retentions would be worth more to Coats than to most of its shareholders. This point was developed in the Lex column of the *Financial Times* on 31 May 1975:

> The after-tax return on capital employed last year was 8.7 per cent: because of the ACT problem, £100 in its hands becomes £65 in the hands of the standard rate taxpayer, who has to find an investment yielding about 13½ per cent after tax in order to produce a similar return.

Table W10.9   Coats Paton share price 1974–5

	Net asset value (pence per share)	Pence per share[a] High	Low
1964	45	64	46½
1965	44	56	43
1966	45	59	36½
1967	48	68	40
1968	49	88½	63½
1969	59	85½	47
1970	51½	56½	36½
1971	51½	74	43½
1972	56	79	43½
1973	62½	72	39
1974	68½	57½	22½
1975[b]		58	23½
1975[c]		64½	22

Notes: [a] Adjusted to be comparable.
[b] Prior to the dividend announcement of 29.5.75.
[c] For the full year.

The immediate result of the decision was a fall in the share price of 6½ pence to 48½ pence (see Tables W10.9 and W10.10 for the share price data) within two days. The market capitalization had fallen by £22 million, with many financial institutions and others voicing concern over the decisions. As a result of this groundswell of opposition, Rowe and Pitman, stockbrokers to the group, announced a get-together in the City of the interested institutions and the merchant bank advisers, Morgan Grenfell. This meeting took place on the Tuesday following, amid rumours that the dividend might be paid after all. In the event, after a two-hour meeting attended by 30 institutional representatives, neither side changed its position, though it appears that Coats undertook not to repeat the exercise. However, the 'institutions' were not content with this. The investment protection committee of the Association of Unit Trust Managers decided to recommend that

Table W10.10 Coats Patons share price, the FT Actuaries price index for the textile sector and the FT-500 industrial and commercial index: daily, 23 May–18 July 1975

Date 1975	Coats Patons closing price (pence per share)	Price indices Textile sector	500-share
23.5	57½	144.39	151.59
27.5	56½	145.07	152.11
28.5	55	142.78	149.91
29.5	48½	140.58	148.28
30.5	46½	138.45	147.43
2.6	50	141.10	151.70
3.6	50	141.35	152.21
4.6	48½	144.06	154.93
5.6	47	142.80	155.21
6.6	46½	143.34	156.14
9.6	46	138.61	151.69
10.6	45	134.22	148.08
11.6	45	135.31	145.76
12.6	44	132.09	144.32
13.6	45	136.37	146.66
16.6	45	135.76	147.03
17.6	49	137.66	146.03
18.6	47	134.44	144.88
19.6	46	133.21	144.49
20.6	47	137.52	146.62
23.6	45	131.73	142.47
24.6	45	128.22	139.23
25.6	46	130.37	139.78
26.6	46	125.43	136.36
27.6	45	124.28	134.38
30.6	45	123.15	131.06
1.7	47	132.68	137.41
2.7	49½	137.68	141.96
3.7	47½	131.48	138.21
4.7	48	135.77	142.41
7.7	48½	133.89	140.70
8.7	48½	135.66	142.69
9.7	50	138.74	145.4
10.7	48½	134.03	142.96
11.7	46½	130.61	140.47
14.7	45 XC	130.30	137.63
15.7	45 XC	130.20	139.55
16.7	44½ XC	127.04	138.72
17.7	43 XC	122.08	135.68
18.7	44 XC	122.68	134.82

Note: XC = ex scrip.

members (holding about 5% of the shares) should vote against the adoption of Coats Patons' accounts, and there were rumours that some institutions could also decide to vote against the re-election of directors.

In a further reply to the criticism Coats announced on 17 June that it intended making a total dividend payment for 1975 at a level effectively 12½% above what the shareholders received in 1973. Mr Charles Bell stated that the group would pay an interim dividend of 0.9444p net per share for

1975 brought forward to December. Whilst profit forecasts were difficult and 'the present position is not good', he felt that the cover for the 'normal' dividend was very considerable so he hoped to recommend a final of not less than 1.7673p net per share, which would be equivalent to a total gross payment of 4.1718p per share for 1975.

Concern was still expressed by the institutions, however, particularly the unit trusts, that Coats might not be able to obtain Treasury approval as the 1975 dividends were not the result of a recovery situation. Indeed Morgan Grenfell regarded the Coats case as 'unique' and said that they would be very surprised 'if the Treasury took the view that this was other than a very special situation and if they did not cooperate'.

The forecast of further dividend resumption did little to quell the storm of protests. Mr. F. Beecham, chief investment manager of the Public Trustee Office, in a letter to the *Financial Times* (26 June) protested on behalf of the thousands of private trusts to whom 'The Coats Patons Board's decision to pass its dividend comes as a very real embarrassment as their beneficiaries endeavour to cope with inflation.' He went on to indicate that, under trust law, scrip issues of shares made in these circumstances could not be sold for the benefit of income beneficiaries. This letter appeared to strengthen the resistance of the other institutions, particularly pension funds holding probably 10% of the shares, some through nominees; as gross funds, these were particularly hit by the decision. The insurance companies, however, were less vocal in their opposition, provided the Coats case was a one-off event. Their portfolios have a smaller equity element.

The apparent wrath of institutions caused the author of the Lex column to write that:

> British Leyland crumbled and the institutions — publicly, at least — said nothing. Burmah Oil embarked on its fatal plans for world domination, and the City scarcely murmured ... [yet the] ... figure of £7m — equivalent to about 1 per cent of the money raised by rights issues this year ... is all that we are talking about. (30.6.75)

At the annual general meeting held on 11 July 1975 the directors of Coats were attacked not just for the financial implications of the dividend decision for some shareholders and the effect it had had on the share price, but for the apparent remoteness of the company, which had now resulted in a lack of long-term confidence among shareholders. Additionally, representatives of the institutions, for instance the Church Commissioners, the Central Board of Finance (3 million votes) and the chairman of the Investment Protection Committee of the Association of Unit Trust Managers, called for the appointment of non-executive directors as endorsed by a recent statement from the CBI.

The resolution to make the scrip issue and adopt the report and accounts was carried on a show of hands of the 200 or so shareholders present, but the results of the poll on the scrip issue revealed 17.2m votes in favour and 6.5 million against.

Discuss the case.

W10.11   Suggested answers to discussion questions

10.1 1. *Residual theory of dividends.* Dividends are only paid out if the capital needs of the enterprise (i.e. projects with positive NPVs) are fully met and there are funds left over. As corporate profits are cyclical, but capital investment plans involve long-term commitments, then dividends take up the slack, as it were.

Financial managers cannot follow both a policy of stable dividends and a policy of long-term commitment to capital investment, unless they are willing to borrow in times of need to achieve both. With an objective of shareholder wealth maximization, if the enterprise can invest in profitable projects (i.e. in excess of the cost of capital) and earn a higher return than the shareholders can in their alternative investment opportunities, then it should follow such a policy. Issues arise to strengthen and weaken the approach with market imperfections.

2. *Clientele effect*. This is an appealing and persuasive argument that enterprises attract particular types of shareholder by their nature and actions. In this case, the argument is on dividend clienteles, but the clientele argument could apply to leverage, growth enterprises, fashion shares, etc.

   The argument runs like this. Enterprises establish a track record for giving or not giving dividends. Shareholders recognize this and because of their preferences — receiving income now instead of the future because they need it for consumption, or because of uncertainty ('bird in the hand'), or the tax argument — having attracted these clients, companies find it difficult to suddenly change their policy. The Coats Patons case illustrates this. The empirical evidence on dividend clienteles is generally not supportive — perhaps a surprising result.

3. *Asymmetric information*. In the context of dividends and dividend policy, this applies to the fact that shareholders and managers have incomplete and different information. Managers do not know how shareholders will react to a dividend change; likewise shareholders are not party to the information that is available to managers. The result of asymmetry in information is the information content of dividends, where dividends have signalling properties. This is taken up in 4. below.

4. *Signalling properties of dividends*. With asymmetry of information as in 3. above, dividends can be represented as signals from the managers of the enterprise to the shareholders and financial markets. For the successful transmission of the signal, it has to be encoded and decoded. Evidence for the USA (from a survey) points to the perception of investors, that dividends are a signalling device of future company prospects. With some exceptions, empirical studies indicate that dividend changes do convey some unanticipated information to the market. There is still some controversy because this would deny the EMH. Thus it might be that dividend announcements do not signal new information but only confirm already known or forecasted events.

5. *The 'bird-in-the-hand' argument*. This arises from the existence of uncertainty. If certainty exists and there are no transaction costs, dividends can be capitalized into the share price as the enterprise invests them internally at NPVs of 0 or greater. If shareholders need the cash now, they can engage in a home-made dividend policy of selling some shares to create the flow of income. With uncertainty, a series of other issues arise:

(a) The required rate of return, k_e, rises as dividend pay-out is reduced. Risk-averse investors are not indifferent to the division of earnings into dividends and capital gains in the share price.

(b) It follows that to offset a 1% reduction in dividends requires a more than 1% increase in g (in the Gordon model).

(c) With volatile stock markets, the maintenance of the increase in share price is not guaranteed. Shareholders may prefer to have the cash and invest it or spend it, particularly with the presence of *agency* costs.

10.2 Parts of this question were covered in question 10.1 above. The information content of dividends arises if there is asymmetry of information where investors have incomplete and unequal information on the enterprise compared to managers. Financial managers do not themselves possess equal information on how investors will react to a given policy change. With the existence of an agency problem, shareholders have agency costs of monitoring the actions of the managers, and the dividend announcement is a major piece of information from the enterprise to the market. Enterprises can use the announcement as a signalling device and therefore encode a message. Investors can also view the announcement as a signalling device and attempt to decode the signal. Of course the enterprise may not be signalling, yet investors think it is, and vice versa! Even if both parties accept that signals are being passed and received, there might still not be effective communication as the investors cannot decode the signal.

We made the point in the text that recent survey evidence suggests that on average the respondents saw dividends as a signalling device of future company prospects. Investors are therefore looking for the enterprise to give them 'accurate' information. However, companies appear to be reluctant to cut dividends as a cut can be perceived as bad news, even if there are sound reasons given — as, say, in the Coats Patons case (though we disagree with the validity of the reasons in that case).

In terms of a game theoretic framework the enterprise is either correct or incorrect in *its* decision to reinvest in the enterprise and the market is either correct or incorrect in *its* assessment of the decision of the enterprise. The outcomes are of course *ex post*, but the decisions are taken *ex ante*. If both are correct, the shareholders have endorsed the action of the managers. If the shareholders are correct and the managers are not, shareholders would, one presumes, not endorse the cut in dividends. In the reverse of this, managers will still attempt to go ahead but will find opposition.

In relating the concept of information content to the EMH, the problem arises that, for the weak and semi-strong forms of efficiency, all publicly available information is impounded in the share price. Presumably prior to the announcement there are other signals pointing to the decision the enterprise takes and how shareholders would react. If not, the signals will contain new information which will be impounded immediately. The empirical evidence confirms signalling, but not necessarily of new information: rather it confirms already known or forecast events via previous and concurrent earnings information.

Two methods can be used to test for information content and therefore indirectly, or even directly, the EMH — abnormal trading and the abnormal return approach. Both are discussed in the text and the latter one is more popular. The tests suffer from methodological weaknesses and we refer to the Taylor article which points to the joint hypotheses — the same argument raised in the empirical tests for the EMH in Chapter 3.

10.3 This question is an exact quotation from Airfix Limited some years ago. It is apparent from the empirical evidence that enterprises are conscious of the dividend issue. Some, particularly family enterprises and some small speculative growth enterprises, often do not pay dividends. This is accepted and a clientele can develop for the capital gain. For the others that do pay dividends, particularly if there is stability, managers may have little discretion over their payment, unless there are severe economic constraints, because the cut could signal that problems existed within the enterprise — the signalling approach.

We established in the text that the evidence informed us that managers clearly regard dividends as an important aspect of enterprise policy — despite the dividend irrelevance theoretical arguments. This is very reminiscent of the behavioural approach of Lintner — dividend pay-outs affect share price. The maintenance of share price is important to financial managers as it is a key to the raising of additional finance and to preserving their own security (from a hostile takeover). It would appear that managers are also aware of clientele and signalling effects and because of the asymmetry of information have to be careful in what they do as they are not sure how investors will react. The latter may use dividends to minimize agency and monitoring costs.

So despite the strong theoretical underpinnings of the irrelevance school, the imperfections and so on lead us to recognize the importance of dividends even if we do not fully know why. We can see that enterprises may have little discretion over the payment of dividends, although they may innovate a little by using swap dividends or have dividend reinvestment plans.

10.4 The theoretical controversy to this question is really a polar one, between the relevance and the irrelevance schools. The Gordon valuation model shows how dividends are important, but an increase in d (dividend) will be offset by a decrease in g (the enterprise's growth rate). If the change in d is balanced by an equal but opposite change in g, then a change in dividend policy will not affect share value. Before you go into this further, you may consider the case of the enterprise that does not pay a dividend at all. How is share value determined in that case — asset base, an earnings model, etc.? In other words, bear in mind that the dividend valuation model is only one model of share valuation.

If it is a valid model, then what importance can be attached to it given the two polar views of irrelevance and relevance? The relevance one really is one of uncertainty. Beyond that we are into market imperfections, asymmetry of information, transaction costs, taxes, clienteles, etc., all of which can be relevant, but unfortunately make the dividend controversy a puzzle. The net result is that enterprises think it is important and adjust their policy accordingly, hence the behavioural approach of Lintner for dividend stability.

10.5 If the enterprise follows a *residual* dividend policy, then it only distributes what it cannot use internally, and to hold on to that would produce a misallocation of resources as negative NPV projects would have been accepted. If, however, it does not follow such a policy but

rather one of, say, dividend stability, then either its capital investment is a residual and will vary with the business cycle or it has to
borrow in some periods to make up the needs for funds. But what of
the periods of surplus? If it cannot be distributed — since stability is
the order of the day — it will be reinvested either in short-term assets
or perhaps in hastily thought-of capital projects with implications for
corporate earnings.

If the payment of the dividends requires borrowing to make up the
cash for 'good' projects, then several issues arise, such as:

1. transaction costs of the financing, including time and trouble;
2. taxation of the dividends so that the actual increase in wealth to
   shareholders is reduced;
3. external review of the enterprise's borrowing decision to reduce
   agency costs.

W.10.12   Answers to worked problems

10.1 ZYX has needs of £8 million but available funds of only £4 million. With
a residual dividend policy and assuming these capital needs have
positive NPVs it should presumably pay nothing out. If that were so it
would still have a financing need of £4 million. If its current capital
structure is in optimal balance prior to the retention of £4 million which
is regarded as equity, then it should raise the £4 million in the following
manner:

> Total financing needs = £8 million
> 60% debt = £4.8 million
> 40% equity = £3.2 million

With £4 million internal a case can be made to:

1. distribute £0.8 million and use the £3.2 million as equity for retained
   earnings;
2. borrow £4.8 million in debt.

If it does not wish to maintain an optimal capital structure, or if it was
out of line, then it could retain all of the £4 million. The presumption is
that this residual policy is known and accepted by investors. The actual
debt issued could vary (see Chapter 8), e.g. floating rate notes, short or
long term, etc.

10.2 1. EPS = £1,000,000/1,000,000 = £1 per share
      P/E = 0.50/1 = 0.5 times
   2. If the scrip dividend involves the creation of new shares rather than
      the repurchase of shares, more shares are outstanding. The dividend
      is worth £500,000, so if we take the market price of £10 it will lead to
      the issue of 50,000 new shares. Of course the £1,000,000 can be
      reinvested presumably at an NPV >0. If it can earn the equivalent of
      the present earnings, then there will be no dilution. This is debatable.
      They could earn more or less. Given a downward-sloping demand
      curve for investment, it could be less. The other issue is timing.
      There may be some temporary dilution until the earnings come on
      stream.
         If the scrip was by a repurchase, then EPS would rise. See 3. below.

3. The dividends are £1,000,000 so at a price of £10.50 there would be 95,238 shares repurchased.
4. If it pays the 50p dividend, this will cost £500,000 — half the earnings. It will need to borrow the £500,000 equivalent to the cash dividend. If it does this with debt, this will increase the debt–equity ratio, which may or may not be beneficial depending on the present ratio and how it fits into the desired balance sheet structure. The questions raised in Chapter 8 of short versus long term also arise. What of preference shares? There are the other issues of transaction costs.

10.3 £4 million after-tax profit, a target rate of return of 14%, current investment needs of £4 million, so it can raise all the capital needs internally — a policy it likes to follow. Ranking by expected returns:

Project	£	% Total	Cumulative budget	%$E(R)$	Average R %	Marginal R %
B	500,000	12.5	12.5	30	30	30
A	1,000,000	25	37.5	25	26.67	25
F	1,000,000	25	62.5	20	24.0	20
E	1,000,000	25	87.5	16	21.71	16
D	400,000	10	97.5	15	21.03	15
C	100,000	2.5	100.0	10	20.75	10
	4,000,000					

The average is a weighted one calculated as follows. For the addition of A it is:

$$0.125 \times 30 + 0.25 \times 25 = 3.75 + 6.25$$
$$= 10\%$$

As this is 37.5% of the budget, the weighted average is:

$$10/37.5 \times 100 = 26.67\%$$

Likewise for the addition of F it is:

$$0.125 \times 30 + 0.25 \times 25 + 0.25 \times 20 = 3.75 + 6.25 + 5$$
$$= 15\%$$

As this is 62.5% of the budget, the weighted average is:

$$15/62.5 \times 100 = 24\%$$

For an optimal outcome projects are accepted until the cut-off point is reached or the funds exhausted, whatever comes first. The enterprise we know has sufficient funds to cover all of its investments — with a cut-off rate of 14% it can accept up to project D, i.e. 97.5% of the total budget, leaving C rejected. Therefore the enterprise will distribute £100,000 in cash dividends. The enterprise is following a residual dividend policy.

11 Cost of capital and capital structure

Learning objectives

The aims of this chapter are to:

- explain further the concept of the weighted average cost of capital;
- explain how to calculate the specific cost of capital for bonds, preference shares and ordinary shares;
- demonstrate the difference between book and market values;
- demonstrate the problems that a divisionalized organizational structure can bring;
- explain the concept of the capital structure of the enterprise from both a practical and a theoretical standpoint;
- appreciate that differing costs of capital across countries can give a competitive advantage to those companies that can access 'cheap' funds.

W11.1 Introduction

So far in the text we have talked about the cost of capital as if we knew what it meant. Indeed by using the definite article *the* we were being even more emphatic about it. However, our discussion in the previous two chapters in particular illustrates the range of different borrowing media and therefore the many different costs of capital. In Chapter 11 of the text and in this Workbook we identify the specific costs of raising equity, retained earnings and new shares, debt and preference shares, and the problems of providing a weighting to produce a weighted average cost of capital.

Much of our discussion, however, is focused on the debt-equity financing decision. This is an important one principally because of the tax shield — interest payments are tax deductible. What we find is that in the MM world of perfect markets and no taxes the total market value of the enterprise is independent of the amount of debt in its capital structure, i.e. the financing decision is an unimportant determinant of share value. It is the investment decision that is important. The financing decision is irrelevant because the individual can undo anything that the enterprise does by way of financing. Once we allow for market imperfections — taxes, transactions costs, etc. — then a different picture emerges.

W11.2 The weighted cost of capital

If we require a single value of the cost of capital to be used, in the capital-budgeting decision, then unless the enterprise is entirely equity financed, we need an average of *all* sources. Even with a 100% equity there are differences between the cost of retained earnings, rights issues and other forms of issuing shares. However, the question you should pose yourself is: should an enterprise use a weighted average cost derived by whatever means? Is there not a case for incremental costs based on the source of financing? If an enterprise has a particular project which it is considering, why should it use an average of all its costs? Why not use the actual cost — incremental of debt or equity or whatever? This point was raised extensively in Chapter 9 where we examined the switching from short- to medium- to long-term financing.

One of the major criteria for the switch was yield differentials. However, a word of caution here. We tried in the previous chapters to talk in terms of the interrelationships of variables — to view the enterprise holistically. So it is important to see how an individual borrowing decision impacts on the whole structure of borrowing. To give a case in point — as was seen in the text — if an enterprise decides to raise more debt finance and take advantage of its relative cheapness, it cannot ignore the effect of this on:

1. the existing debt-holders;
2. the shareholders.

The additional debt will add additional financial risk and this will affect the *overall* cost of capital.

What we argue for here is a desired balance sheet structure for the enterprise and an attempt by the enterprise to maintain it. Of course this desired structure will change as macro-economic events, such as inflation, interest rates, etc., unfold and the ability of the firm to cope with those is tested. In addition, even without these external factors, the firm still might not be able to do this as it cannot raise all its additional finance in the exact proportion to the desired capital structure, say 25/75 (debt/equity). However, through time it will attempt to maintain such a structure, so the weights used can reflect this long-run relationship. Whether the desired capital structures should be set in terms of market or book values we discuss later. This is an important issue because debt is expressed in nominal terms and higher inflation reduces the value of the principal and the interest service payments. If interest rates rise to compensate for the inflation (the Fisher effect), then the market value of the debt will fall. If firms can pass on the increased costs in higher prices, equity prices may well stay stable or rise so that the debt-equity ratio will improve, giving the firm more capacity to borrow. The rise in equity prices in the period 1982 to 1987 is an illustration. If equity prices fall sharply, as they did in the mid-1970s and in the October crash of 1987, then gearing levels rise. All of these movements in the gearing ratio are extraneous to the firm itself, yet it cannot ignore them as they impact on its capital structure.

W11.3   Cost of specific sources of capital

(a) Bonds

(i) *The basic bond valuation method*
We begin the discussion of bond valuation by returning to our basic model of financial mathematics in Chapter 4. We may use the principles stated there to value a bond.

There are two elements to the return on almost all bonds: the interest received and the capital repayable at the date of the bond's maturity. At any point in time each of these can be valued separately then added together, based on the current ruling rate of interest. Let us be more concrete and consider the problem posed in Fig. W11.1. Before we calculate the current value we should perhaps clarify the situation in 1974. The bond was issued at a discount of £5 per £100: in other words, purchasers paid £95 then to receive a bond with a face value of £100. Thus the effective rate of interest they received was 13% × (100/95) = 13.68%. (Well, actually it wasn't. There is a further factor of capital growth. But we shall come back to that soon. For now, let us take 13.68% as a working example.) So why not just issue a bond at 13.68%? The answer is, simply, that this would be messy. Though contemporary market interest rates suggested a rate had to be offered of between 13.5% and 14%, it would look odd to issue a bond stating a nominal rate of 13.68% on its face. By issuing a 13% bond at a discount this problem has been resolved. The bond *says* 13%, but the effective rate to the original purchaser was 13.68%.

We wish to value a bond redeemable at the end of 1999. It is now the end of 1987. The bond was originally issued in 1974 at a discount of £5 and a coupon of 13%. Interest is payable annually in arrears. Current market rates for a bond with a similar risk and term are 9%. What would be the current price per £100 nominal value of the bond?

Figure 11.1   Current value calculation.

Now let us come back to 1987. The bond has 12 years left to run. Thus if we buy the bond, we buy the right to receive (all figures per £100 nominal value) £13 each year for the next 12 years, and £100 at the end of that time. We must discount these amounts at 9% to get a 9% yield. So the value of the bond will be:

$$£13a_{\overline{12}|} + £100v^{12} = £13 \times 7.161 + £100 \times 0.356$$
$$= £128.69$$

Intuitively you should be able to see why the price has now risen above par. The bond is paying 13%, but current yields are only 9%. So a higher price will be necessary to make a face value payment of 13% equal to a lower actual real return.

It may be instructive to return to the first day of the bond. (We said, you remember, that the 13.68% was not quite right.) Then the bond-holders paid £95 to receive £13 for 25 years plus £100 at the end of that time. So the yield can be found by solving for i the equation:

$$95 = 13a_{\overline{25}|} + 100\, v^{25}$$

which (after some trial and error) gives a discount rate of 13.715%. You can also verify that, if you discount the RHS by 13%, the answer is indeed £100 — as you would expect for a bond issued at par.

(ii) Bonds in the cost of capital
With these preliminaries in mind, we may return to furthering the discussion. The key element here is the tax deductibility of the debt, or tax shield as it is

often referred to. With the cut in the rate of corporation tax at 35%, the value of this shield is correspondingly reduced. In floating the new debt, the enterprise has to give at least the equivalent coupon or package of coupons and discount/premium to tempt investors. In Chapter 8 we discussed some of the aspects of the issue including the lack of bond ratings in the United Kingdom, and therefore the difficulty of actually assessing the risk. Depending on how much debt is already issued, the enterprise may have to offer a higher yield to investors to compensate for the additional financial risk arising from the extra leverage. This point is taken up in the text and later in this Workbook chapter.

One point made in the text that requires further clarification and development is the option pricing argument. Whilst we still cannot develop it fully, you should at least intuitively understand what is happening as we covered option pricing, albeit briefly, in Chapter W8. Recall that a *call* option is the right to buy and a *put* option the right to sell. In the two situations covered in the text:

1. As the bond-holders have prior claim to the assets as more and more bonds are issued, they stand before the claims of the shareholders over the assets of the enterprise — bought by debt and equity (including retained earnings). The bond-holders, as we said in the text, are not too happy about cash dividends as they would prefer these to be retained to guarantee them their security — asset values can drop and even if secured it is always useful to have additional security. Of course asset values can increase too, in both real and money terms, but the value of the debt is fixed in nominal terms, so the shareholders can simply buy out the debt-holders and take the post-liquidation value of the enterprise in cash or have the ownership of the assets intact. This is equivalent to a call option which the bond-holders have *written* and the shareholders have purchased. Now the ability of shareholders to exercise this will depend on the provisions in the debt contracts.
2. The analogous situation is that, if asset prices fall and the enterprise is going under, the shareholders really have a *put* option on the assets. They can simply walk away and leave the bond-holders to take the risk in liquidation. Provided the ordinary shares are fully paid, there is no further recourse to the shareholders.

This is an interesting dimension to the valuation bonds that you can follow up in more advanced finance courses.

One other point raised in the text is the use of the Hawanini and Vora (1982) method of yield approximation. The example given in Fig. W11.2 will hopefully help to follow it through.

Two points not raised in the text are the use of convertible debt (which was covered in Chapter 8), and the issue of zero-coupon bonds (also known as deep-discounted bonds). The latter are, as the name suggests, bonds that carry little or no interest, but which are issued at a hefty discount to their face value. All the profit on them is capital gain which is only taxable when they are disposed of, or mature.

The CAPM can, as Chapter 7 indicated, be applied to bonds. The problem with this is the thin trading in the United Kingdom and the lack of an accepted market index. For the latter it would be possible to use either the Bank of England index or high-coupon debenture and loan stocks or the FT-Actuaries index. The latter is not restricted to high coupons.

XYZ plc plans to issue a 20-year bond (par value of £1,000) with a $12\frac{3}{4}$ coupon. Flotation costs are 20%.

Using equation 11.3 from the text and reproduced below:

$$k = \frac{I + \left(\dfrac{P - NPD}{n}\right)}{P + 0.6\,(NPD - P)}$$

we would have:

$$\frac{127.50 + \left(\dfrac{1{,}000 - 980}{20}\right)}{1{,}000 + 0.6(980 - 1{,}000)} = \frac{127.50 + 1}{1{,}000 - 12}$$

$$= \frac{128.50}{988}$$

$$= 13\%$$

This is the before-tax cost. With a corporation tax rate of 35% the after-tax cost for XYZ would be 8.45%.

Figure W11.2 Yield approximation.

(b) Preference shares

As there is no tax shield on preference shares, they have waned substantially in importance apart from a big upsurge in 1985 when there was a series of large increases in convertible preference shares (that is, preference shares that have rights attached to them to convert them at some specified future date or dates into another form of security — in particular, equity). Preference shares may increase in importance as the value of the tax shield on debt drops with the lowering of the corporation tax rate. Convertible preference shares in particular could be attractive as they can be issued at a low coupon.

(c) Equity

The cost of equity capital is a thorny issue as it involves the valuing of the retained earnings as well as the costs of new issues. Most new issues are rights issues and involve the issuing of securities to rank *pari-passu* with the existing shares of which we have a trading history, know the dividend yield, etc. Provided the capital-budgeting methods are in place to select projects in excess of the cost of capital then we can accept the rationale for the new issue of capital. Exactly the same rationale can be applied to retained capital; we made this point in Chapter 10 on dividends, since retained funds are really retained dividends. However, we have a circularity here because we need to know the cost of capital to appraise the projects, decide whether they are worthwhile and therefore to decide on the new issue and/or the retention! The only real difference between the two sources is the transaction costs of issuing the ordinary shares and we dealt with those in Chapter 8.

We discuss three methods for share valuation.

(i) Bond yield valuation
This takes the idea of a capital market line developed in Chapter 6 and, from this, positions the shares. However, we have to assume equilibrium for this,

for bonds are not actively traded in the main, we we are not likely to obtain an accurate measure of risk from them to be able to add the risk factor for shares. So it is a nice idea to add a risk premium to bonds, but not too workable.

(ii) Dividend valuation
We have come across this several times in the book, but note the caveat again on the frequency of the payment of the dividend. This can distort the usual Gordon model.

(iii) CAPM
This is by far the easiest method if the shares are quoted, but once more we are assuming something about equilibrium.

The example we give in the text (p. 279) is a simplified one, but it attempts to warn you that you can get conflicting answers, and if we had used an earnings-based model we could have gone further in producing divergent answers.

Returning to the case of new issues, provided we rule out price pressure — and the Marsh (1979) study quoted in Chapter 8 should be taken as an authoritative one — then we are left with the flotation costs. Now as in Chapter 8 we take issue with the case of rights or placings and the undervaluing of these, but the overall impact of these costs across the whole of the equity base of the enterprise is small. It can, therefore, be argued that the costs of retained earnings and new issues are identical.

(d) Depreciation provisions

This is an item that raises a lot of difficulty at times. We do not include depreciation in calculating the WACC, yet it is not costless to the enterprise and at times it can be a significant item. However, you have to be clear in your own mind why these provisions are there. The enterprise, as we discussed in Chapter 1, is to be seen as something permanent. It has to maintain itself, indeed grow, through time as capital wears out. So the concept of depreciation is like a sinking fund to do just that. It is usually historical, based on the asset cost. That is why in the DCF calculations we automatically allow for depreciation by recovering the original capital sum. The enterprise is not obliged to survive and may choose to liquidate, and the provisions themselves may not be adequate to provide for replacement of the capital stock (though there are legal provisions to prevent the reduction of capital). However, that is a different issue. Here we are concerned with cost and we follow the usual practice of arguing that these provisions have an opportunity cost equal to the WACC.

W11.4   The proportions used

In our comments on the WACC, we mentioned that the weights used in its calculation had to come from a desired capital structure, but we had a problem over whether to use book or market weights. We argue for market values with all the difficulties these entail. Of course, financial reporting is based largely on book values, certainly with respect to bonds, retained earnings, etc. It would be nice to be able to use them, as they have greater stability through time, but they are in our view, and that of others, *not* strictly the correct ones to use. It does cause problems to use market values as you have to work out bond values — and this is difficult if there is no active market — and you have to attempt to adjust for the risk of the enterprise, etc. The share price at least should be available from the stock market. However, because of the frequent changes in these values it is impossible to maintain an equilibrium desired capital structure. It would require adjustments daily — retiring bonds, issuing more bonds, issuing shares, etc., and given transactions costs and the capital market constraints we referred to in Chapter 8, it is simply impossible. So the text argues for the establishment of upper and lower bounds where corrective action can be taken.

W11.5   Differing costs of capital internationally

This is a new section to the book since the first edition, and illustrates the fact that differing interest rate structures internationally will encourage the movement of capital and the tapping of funds from markets where funds are cheaper. This strategy has the risk of currency fluctuations, but this risk can be hedged particularly if it is short-term borrowing. The competitive advantage that some countries, e.g. Japan and West Germany, have enjoyed from cheaper funds is discussed and comparative data are given. With the greater integration of financial markets, these differences in the cost of capital will narrow, but investment incentives and differing tax treatments are also relevant here as they impact directly on costs of capital too. We cite an article by McCauley and Zimmer (1989) and urge readers to reference it.

W11.6   Divisional cost of capital

In this section we recognize that enterprises are generally multi-product. They can reduce their risk by diversifying, and really they are like an investor with a portfolio of securities with different risks, etc. The difference is that the assets do not trade separately. To use a simple WACC without taking account of the intra-organization risk differences can lead, as Fig. 11.3 illustrates in the text, to the wrong decision of acceptance *or* rejection. The idea of using the appropriate cost of capital which reflects the risk is very sensible. Like so many things in finance the idea is simple; doing it is more difficult. It is like trying to measure how successful a merged set of companies is — how do you separate them out to do this once they are merged?

What we propose is the standard answer of using surrogates: trying to identify similar single product companies to the project that you are analysing and using their beta. There are lots of assumptions and difficulties here, such as how good the surrogate is, equilibrium in the market, etc. But really that is the best we can do if we want to fine-tune a little.

W11.7   Capital structure

In this short section we try and portray once more a theme of this book — the interdependence of decisions of investment and financing, and the constraints these decisions have on them from both within and outside of the enterprise. Thus as we saw in section W11.4 on proportions, the enterprise cannot maintain its desired structure. But how does it decide on a desired

Table W11.1 The leverage effect: balance sheet data

	Company		
	X	Y	Z
Equity (£1 shares)	200	800	1,000
Debt (10% interest payable) (£)	800	200	–
Total financing (and total investment) (£)	1,000	1,000	1,000
Case A			
Cash flow from trading (£)	200	200	200
Less: Interest on debt (£)	80	20	–
Cash flow for equity (£)	120	180	200
Return on equity (%)	60	22.5	20
Cash flow per share (£)	0.60	0.225	0.20
Cash flow on total investment (%)	20	20	20
Case B: Assuming fall in cash flow on total investment of 20%			
Cash flow from trading (£)	160	160	160
Less: Interest on debt (£)	80	20	–
	80	140	160
Return on equity (%)	40	17.5	16
Cash flow per share (£)	0.40	0.175	0.16
Cash flow on total investment (%)	16	16	16
Fall in cash flow on total investment (%)	20	20	20
Fall in cash flow per share (%)	33.3	22.2	20
Case C: Assuming an increase in cash flow of 20%			
Cash flow from trading (£)	240	240	240
Less: Interest on debt (£)	80	20	0
	160	220	240
Return on equity (%)	80	27.5	24
Cash flow per share (£)	0.80	0.275	0.24
Cash flow on total investment (%)	24	24	24
Increase in cash flow on total investment (%)	20	20	20
Increase in cash flow per share (%)	33.3	22.2	20

position in the first place? With the cost of debt cheaper than equity, why not go for 99.99% ... debt? The cheapness of debt narrows if the company is tax exhausted, so that is one factor alone that is relevant because of the increased financial risk of the enterprise to both bond-holder and shareholder. The debate in the literature centres on how the limits are set — is there an optimal limit to the debt–equity ratio, or is the limit set just prior to bankruptcy?

In reality the gearing levels in the UK are low. In a survey (Bank of England, 1988a) for the period 1970–86, a level of 20% was found for the period of the late 1960s and 1970s, with a rise in equity prices from 1982. The level had fallen to 12% by 1986 — hardly anywhere near the 99.999%! This level is well below that in many other countries, e.g. West Germany and Japan, and in part is a function of the market-based capital market in the UK (as with the USA), where companies are constantly being assessed and researched and where a more short-term view has to be taken of their strategic decisions. In this environment the additional financial risk that comes from debt, the tax exhaustion of some companies and the inability at times to tap debt markets have all led to the low gearing ratio. In the 1980s, when there has been a marked incentive to take on debt, this has been more in the form of bank financing.

The theoretical issues are discussed in this section, and just as in the irrelevance/relevance debate in Chapter 10, we have a traditional–MM debate which, once imperfections are allowed for, reduces to some consensus.

W11.8   Capital structure theory

To illustrate the impact of leverage and handle the theoretical issues we use a numerical example from Dobbins and Pike (1982) which links in with the home-made leverage table (Fig. 11.7) in the text.

We commence with three enterprises X, Y and Z that have the same investment schedule, but different financing strategies. Because they share the same investment plans, they have the same EBIT.

> Enterprise X has a 80/20 debt-equity ratio
> Enterprise Y has a 20/80 debt-equity ratio
> Enterprise Z has a 100% equity financing.

Assuming each share sells for £1 and the interest cost is 10%, Table W11.1 sets out the situation for the three enterprises (case A) and then repeats it for a 20% fall in EBIT (case B) and a 20% rise in EBIT (case C). All of this is for a no-tax regime. The crux of the argument is that, as the interest cost is a fixed one, when the EBIT falls the enterprise with debt has less left over for its shareholders.

For the first case, before the changes in EBIT take place, we can see that X has the highest return on equity (ROE) and Z the lowest. When the cash flows fall, although the fall is the same for all companies — 20% — the effect is differential, 33.3% for X, 22.2% for Y and 20% for Z. The situation is reversed for the case of an increase in EBIT. So the effect of the leverage is more risk for the shareholders — risk of gain *and* loss. This risk is not from the business *per se*, only from the financial risk from the financing package.

The values given in Table W11.1 are book values, so what should the shares in the three companies sell for? If we start with the all-equity-financed enterprise (Z), we can simply use the dividend valuation model on the assumption of a 100% pay-out (it does not matter actually given the issues raised in Chapter 10), but we need a discount rate. If we can assume 15% and assume the £200 continues for ever and does not grow, then:

$$\frac{200}{0.15} = £1,333$$

If we assume now that the debt is valued at par (which we should not assume, but it makes things easier), then in Table W11.2 we can derive the market value of equity for enterprises X and Y as a residual. This is the MM view — the different financing policies do not affect the value of the enterprise.

Table W11.2   Bringing in the market value

	Company		
	X	Y	Z
Market value of debt (£)	800	200	–
Market value of equity (£)	533	1,133	1,333
Value of investment schedule (£)	1,333	1,333	1,333
Cost of equity (k_e)	$\dfrac{120}{533} = 22.5\%$	$\dfrac{180}{1,133} = 15.9\%$	$\dfrac{200}{1,333} = 15\%$

Using Tables W11.1 and W11.2 we can then calculate the k_e for the three enterprises. They use the cash flow from equity divided by the market price, so we have:

120/533 = 22.5% for X
180/1,133 = 15.9% for Y
200/1,333 = 15% for Z

We thus have a rising k_e schedule as per Fig. 11.6(b) and a constant value of the enterprise as in Fig. 11.6(a) in the text. The increase in k_e is the compensation for the additional financial risk borne by the shareholders from the leverage.

To arrive at the WACC, we know that the market value of the enterprise is invariant at £1,333. So too is the WACC at 15%. As Fig. 11.6(b) showed, k_0 does not change. We illustrate this numerically in Table W11.3.

Table W11.3   Weighted average cost of capital

	Debt	Equity	Total
Enterprise X (£)	800	533	1,333
D/E ratio (%)	60	40	100
WACC	60% × 10% + 40% × 22.5% = 15%		
Enterprise Y (£)	200	1,133	1,333
D/E ratio (%)	15	85	
WACC	15% × 10% + 85% × 15.9% = 15%		
Enterprise Z (£)	–	1,333	1,333
D/E ratio (%)	0	100	
WACC	0 + 15% = 15%		

(a) The traditional view

The traditional view as expressed in Fig. 11.4 in the text can be shown numerically with the same three enterprises, but instead of k_0 rising as it did in the previous case of MM, it stays constant at 15%. What we then find is that the market value of the enterprise rises for the levered enterprise — see Table W11.4.

Table W11.4   No change in k_e with increasing leverage

	Company		
	X	Y	Z
Market value of debt (£)	800	200	—
Market value of equity (£):	800		
X: $\dfrac{120}{0.15}$	800		
Y: $\dfrac{180}{0.15}$		1,200	
Z: $\dfrac{200}{0.15}$			1,333
Market value of investment schedule	1,600	1,400	1,333

Of course, in this case the value of the enterprise is rising continuously, but in the text we argue that it would peak and this would be the dual of the k_0, the overall cost of capital. MM argue that this overvaluation of X and Y cannot remain because rationally shareholders must perceive that the three enterprises are identical in their EBITs and only differ in financing, and since enterprises X and Y are riskier than Z by virtue of the leverage, k_0 must rise. If there were to be these overvaluations, shareholders would exploit them by conducting an arbitrage procedure, and this was outlined in the text (pp. 293–4) with the continuation of the same numerical example.

(b) With the introduction of tax

With tax the MM position changes. Table W11.5 shows that there is a gain from tax equivalents to the value of the tax shield. Therefore the market value of the enterprise (P) increases by the value of the tax shield (as per Fig. 11.9). The tax shields are £125.8 and £44.4 for X and Y respectively. If these are capitalized at the same rate as the cash flows for shareholders, they are equivalent to £28.3 and £7.00 respectively. The point made by Myers (1974) is that they should be capitalized at the cost of debt k, which is 10%.

(c) Bankruptcy costs

In the event of a default the bond-holders will attempt to salvage what they can from the enterprise. However, there will be a loss of cash flows through the quick sale of fixed assets, sale of inventories, legal costs, etc. The argument expressed in the text is that these costs have a present value which can offset or partly offset the tax shield. Fig 11.9 illustrates this. Miller (1977) argues that the importance of bankruptcy costs is overstated. His is a general equilibrium model which focuses on the differential tax treatment of shareholders and bond-holders. He argues that this can eliminate the tax shield and therefore the advantage of debt finance. The argument runs like this. Shareholders can eliminate a lot of tax on their return if they take capital gains rather than the income in the form of dividends. So as long as the corporate tax rate which gives rise to the tax shield is greater than the personal tax rate, the enterprise can issue debt until the corporate tax rate equals the marginal tax rate of the marginal bond-holders. With the substantial cut in corporation tax to 35% and the standard rate of 25%, it is clear that this equivalent will not be long in coming. Miller's overall conclusion is that there is an equilibrium capital structure of debt–equity that will exist for the whole corporate sector, but not for a particular enterprise. However, the substitutability argument by Miller can be challenged, just as in Chapter 10 we showed the problem of home-made dividends (see Table W11.5).

Table W11.5   The gain from taxation

		Company	
	X	Y	Z
Net profit (£)	308	308	308
Bond interest (£)	80	20	0
Profit net of interest (£)	228	228	308
Tax at 35% (£)	79.8	100.8	108
Cash flow from trading after tax (£)	148.2	187.2	200
Market value of debt (£)	800	200	–
Market value of equity (£):			
X: $\dfrac{148.2}{0.225}$	658.7		
Y: $\dfrac{187.2}{0.159}$		1,777.4	
Z: $\dfrac{200}{0.15}$			1,333
Market value of enterprises (£)	1,458.7	1,377.4	1,333
Less: Value of enterprise without tax shield (£)	1,333	1,333	1,333
Market value of tax shield (£)	125.7	44.4	0
Capitalized value of tax savings (at cash flow rate) (£)	$\dfrac{28.3}{0.225} = 125.8$	$\dfrac{7.06}{0.159} = 44.4$	= 44.4

W11.9   Discussion questions: cost of capital

Note: Suggested answers to questions 11.1–11.5 are given in section W11.12 on pp. 604–6.

11.1   Suppose that an enterprise finds that its cost of capital changes. Would this affect the attractiveness of investment projects appraised and undertaken three years ago?

11.2   'The concept of the cost of capital does not have any operational relevance.' Discuss this statement in relation to the raising of finance from both specific and mixed sources.

11.3   Outline the arbitrage mechanism in the original Modigliani–Miller model.

11.4   'Debt finance is cheap (as illustrated by EPS) compared to all-equity financing.' Discuss this statement.

11.5   'The weighted average cost of capital can be used as the discount rate for assessing new projects.' Evaluate this statement.

11.6   'As to the differences between our modified model and the traditional one, we feel that they are still large in quantitative terms and still very much worth trying to detect. It is not only a matter of the two views having different implications for corporate financial policy (or even for national tax policy). But since the two positions rest on fundamentally different views about investor behavior and the functioning of the capital markets, the results of tests between them may have an important bearing on issues ranging far beyond the immediate one of the effects of leverage on the cost of capital' (Modigliani and Miller, 1963). Comment.

11.7   Explain the intuitive appeal of the cost of capital idea, and discuss some of the serious difficulties which materialize on a close examination of the concept.

11.8   Explain the main issues relating to corporate debt financing and discuss the contribution of Modigliani and Miller in this area.

11.9   'If it weren't for taxation and the tax system, corporate finance would be a subject of little significance.' Discuss.

11.10   'The concept of the cost of capital is rendered virtually useless as a tool of financial analysis by the restrictive conditions under which its use is valid.' Discuss.

11.11   What problems arise in measuring the cost of capital for a non-traded enterprise or a division of an enterprise?

11.12   'Investment projects should reflect the systematic risk of the project under consideration.' Discuss.

W11.10   Discussion questions: capital structure

Note: Suggested answers to questions 11.1–11.4 are given in section W11.13 on pp. 606–8.

11.1   Why do/should enterprises attempt to maintain a proper balance between debt and equity within their capital structure?

11.2   As an enterprise increases the proportion of debt in its capital structure, why might the cost of debt and equity both increase?

11.3   'The investment projects of an enterprise should be financed entirely by debt.' Discuss.

11.4   Discuss the proposition that, apart from tax considerations, an enterprise's financial structure has no influence whatsoever on its cost of capital.

11.5   Compare and contrast the various approaches researchers and others have developed with respect to the introduction of leverage into the capital structure of the enterprise. Comment also on the empirical findings.

11.6   Is there an optimal capital structure?

11.7   Discuss the current state of knowledge on the question of corporate debt-financing policy in the light of the theoretical and empirical work on the matter.

11.8   What advice would you give to an enterprise seeking guidance on the proportion of debt for which it would aim in its capital structure?

11.9   Use appropriate financial models to analyse critically and check the validity of the 'cost of capital' concept, in the presence of risk and taxation.

11.10   'The optimum balance sheet is a useless concept!' Discuss.

11.11   How can an enterprise determine its debt capacity limit? Should short-term debt be included?

11.12   An enterprise has conducted its regular cash flow analysis which has indicated a 'safe' level of debt. Can that enterprise operate right up to this level?

11.13   Discuss the interrelationships between the risk emanating from the operation of the enterprise and the optimal financial structure.

11.14   'Market value is the relevant criterion for making financing decisions.' Discuss.

11.15   'Leverage involves the financial manager in a trade-off between risk and return.' Discuss.

11.16   Does the use of debt increase the value of the enterprise?

W11.11   Case studies

(a) Shaw Engineering

The Shaw Engineering case study is fairly straightforward. It is in two parts to contrast the conventional methods of calculating the cost of capital and the use of the CAPM. Questions are given at the end of each of the two parts.

Part I
Shaw Engineering Ltd manufactures machine tools and power transmission equipment. Despite the relatively poor performance of the industry, the company has been very successful in its sales and it has achieved a rapid but variable growth rate. Its sales in 1985 were £40 million compared to £9 million ten years earlier.

The firm had become a market leader and had achieved considerable success in selling its products abroad. Indeed by the end of 1985 over 50% of its sales were attributed to overseas customers. They now had modern production facilities which had low manning levels with flexible working costs. The current chairman, Mr S.E. Swinburn, in his 1985 report stated that

The company is sufficiently autonomous and well equipped to respond quickly and positively to future market developments ... but it would need to invest in new plant as well as to further improve its marketing and sales promotion.

Despite this apparent optimism, the chairman had begun to be concerned about some of the current capital-budgeting techniques used by the company. This resulted from his attendance at a one-week course (for chief executives) at the London Business School.

He had returned armed with new insights. He started informed discussions with the finance director and together they decided to raise the issue of introducing new procedures at the next board meeting. In the meantime they started by preparing some documentation on their current practices. These were contained in a draft memorandum (Fig. W11.3).

Present practice

1. DCF methods used with sensitivity analysis performed to produce the data on the expected returns.
2. Cost of capital calculation derives from:
   (a) 15% required rate of return on new ordinary shares and retained earnings, chosen by virtue of what it is felt others in the industry use;
   (b) the actual cost of the funds from other sources — debentures and preference stock.

Problems and issues for discussion

1. Should the short-term source of funds, trade credit, bank loans, etc., be included?
2. Should market, book value or some other weighting scheme be used?
3. Should the cost of 'equity' funds be reworked?
4. To issue another debenture would require 18% coupon for a 20-year maturity.
5. To raise funds from a preferred share issue would require a 15% dividend.
6. To raise funds from a rights issue would result in the share price, currently £1.00, falling to 80 pence. [The shares were quoted on the ISE.]

Figure W11.3   Draft memorandum on capital budgeting and financing procedures

Both men surveyed the past record of the company and were confident that, given their assessment of the future trading environment, they could achieve a percentage growth rate of at least 10% in the firm's earnings (and dividends). They felt that they had been successful in raising funds in the past and that their present capital structure was probably as near optimal as could be achieved. Their future capital expansion plans would require for 1986 the raising of another £2,000,000, of which they estimated that retained earnings for 1986 could yield £400,000.

Questions

1. Estimate the company's marginal cost of capital for the projected future capital outlay. Assume a 50% tax rate.
2. Discuss the fundamental problems and issues raised in the memorandum. Additionally, discuss the implication of allowing for flotation costs of issue and the possibility that the expansion plan might change the risk class of the firm.

Table W11.6   Balance sheet for year ended 31 December 1985

Assets	Liabilities and capital	£
	Creditors and accruals	5,640,000
	Current taxation	110,000
	Bank overdraft (secured)	1,000,000
	Final ordinary dividend	250,000
	Current liabilities	7,000,000
	Debenture stock	
	($8\frac{1}{2}$% due 1988/93)	1,000,000
	Preferred stock	
	(6% with £100 par)	400,000
	Ordinary shares	3,500,000
	Reserves:	
	Share premium	100,000
	Retained earnings	4,000,000
£16,000,000		£16,000,000

Part 2

The finance director, Fred Davison, attempted to perform the calculations to estimate the cost of capital for the company and followed the traditional method of using a weighted scheme. However, both he and the chairman felt that many fundamental problems remained. They were particularly concerned with the cost estimates of new equity funds and the cost of retained earnings. They were dissatisfied with simply using the 15% required rate of return as they felt it did not have sufficient foundation. Fred had been wrestling with the issue and had even looked at his lecture notes from his professional examination days. The problem arose primarily from the valuation model he was seeking, which made the critical assumption that dividends continued indefinitely at a constant rate of growth. He knew that the experience of their own firm and the engineering industry as a whole indicated that dividend pay-out had been erratic. Additionally, government controls had not always allowed them to make increased payments when the firm was enjoying a more profitable time. He discussed this with the chairman, and Stan Swinburn recalled that at the London Business School course he had attended, lectures had been devoted to the CAPM. After consulting the course handouts, Stan confirmed that the model could be used to estimate the firm's equity cost of capital. He produced a draft memorandum of the model for the benefit of Fred Davison (Fig. W11.4)

1. The 'riskiness' of the ordinary shares of a firm has two elements: *systematic* or market risk and *unsystematic* or specific risk. Systematic risk cannot be diversified away, but unsystematic risk can, i.e. the part of the variance of its returns can be diversifiable. Both kinds of risk contribute to the overall variability of a share price.
2. The systematic risk gives rise to the risk premium, and the beta coefficient measures the undiversifiable risk. Beta can be defined as:

$$\beta_i = \frac{\text{Cov}(x_i x_m)}{\sigma^2_m}$$

where x_i = rate of return on the ith security
          x_m = rate of return on the market portfolio
          σ^2_m = variance of the market returns

Figure W11.4   CAPM: Discussion draft

To make use of the formula in Fig. W11.4, not only are data required on Shaw's ordinary shares earnings but also an estimate of the risk-free rate of interest for the period as well as estimates of the returns for the stock market as a whole. The two men met and discussed the memo and eventually produced, for a ten-year period, a set of hypothetical data (Table W11.7).

Table W11.7

	Rate of return on Shaw Engineering shares	Rate of return on market portfolio	Risk-free rate of interest
1976	6.0	8.0	3.0
1977	9.0	11.0	4.0
1978	12.0	14.0	5.0
1979	16.0	12.0	5.0
1980	8.0	14.0	6.0
1981	6.0	10.0	5.0
1982	8.0	8.0	4.0
1983	12.0	16.0	6.0
1984	20.0	18.0	7.0
1985	16.0	20.0	8.0

Questions
1. Compute Shaw's beta coefficient. Evaluate this with respect to the market portfolio.
2. Using the CAPM, what is the cost of equity capital for Shaw Engineering?
3. Discuss the usefulness of the CAPM for calculating the equity cost of capital.

(b) SBS Limited

This case study involves the interesting issue of mergers and the resulting capital structure. Three enterprises in a similar line of business, but with different capital structures, come together. You are required to set up the criteria you think are appropriate for a combined capital structure. In essence, what we would like you to do is to think of the criteria for a 'desired' capital structure.

Three companies were considering a merger. The financial arrangements of the merger involved the purchase by SBS Ltd of the ordinary share capital of Hallam Tools Ltd and Viness Ltd. The three boards of directors had agreed on the general principle of a merger but a detailed proposal would have to be put to the ordinary shareholders.

After a valuation of each of the three businesses made by an independent firm of accountants (on the basis of past profits, future prospects, market values, the worth of net assets), the negotiators from the three boards met and in the course of bargaining they reached a tentative agreement. This gave the following comparative values of the total interests of the present ordinary shareholders of the three companies as percentages of the present equity interests of SBS shareholders.

SBS	100%	
Hallam Tools	56.25%	(i.e. 1,350,000 shares equivalent)
Viness	35.42%	(i.e. 850,000 shares equivalent)

This would involve the issue of a further 2,200,000 shares, bringing the total number of SBS ordinary shares issued to 4,600,000 of £1 each par value.

The proposed merger would involve further capital needs of about £4 million net after surplus short-term assets held by Viness had been utilized and after various rationalizations had taken place. Of the £4 million, about £1

Table W11.8   Capital structures as at December 1986

	Hallam Tools £	Viness £	SBS £
Working capital (current assets − current liabilities)	1,250,000	650,000	3,000,000
Debenture 8% (1991/2)	–	–	2,000,000
Cumulative 8% preference shares	–	–	800,000
Ordinary shares (£1)	1,000,000	500,000	2,400,000
Share premium	330,000	170,000	550,000
Retained earnings	900,000	900,000	2,000,000

Notes:
1. Preference shares: 8% cumulative dividend payable half-yearly. Voting rights (one vote per £1 share) to be exercised only in the event of dividends being six months in arrears. Further issues of shares require the prior consent of the existing preference shareholders and current coupons would be 12%.
2. Debentures: 8% to be repaid on 31 December 1992 but can, on giving three months' notice, be repaid after 31 December 1991. The stock is secured by a first floating charge over the undertaking of SBS Ltd and no further prior or pari passu stock may be created. The stock is quoted with its most recent price being £59.
3. Ordinary shares: £1 per share. The price ranges of the three shares prior to the merger were:

		1984 £	1985 £	1986 £
Hallam	High	1.46	1.57	1.61
	Low	1.40	1.28	1.30
Viness	High	3.35	3.90	4.51
	Low	3.15	3.26	4.00
SBS	High	1.70	1.78	2.30
	Low	1.50	1.35	1.50

The share price of SBS after the announcement of the merged talks was £2.30. The dividend forecast was 18%, which on the current share price of SBS gave a current dividend yield of 7.8%. With the synergy expected from the merger, a growth rate of 8–10% was to be expected in dividends.

million would be for working capital, and an estimated £1 million was available from retained earnings. The current financing of the three separate entities is given in Table W11.8, and the other relevant information is contained in the notes to this table.

Question
Discuss the issues involved in proposing a capital structure for the merged group of companies in accordance with the criteria you feel are appropriate.

W11.12   Suggested answers to discussion questions: cost of capital

11.1 There are various strands to this question:
   (a) If the company has financed the investment project out of short-term capital, then it cannot ignore the fact that its cost of capital has changed. This is the danger of using a short-term instrument to back a long-term commitment. Presumably if the firm can switch to longer-term financing, it can only now do so at a higher rate than previously. This will have the effect of raising the hurdle rate and the attractiveness will diminish.
   (b) If the project has been financed by a 20-year bond, then the coupon rate is fixed and just as the interest rate structure rises, raising the cost of future issues, it can fall too. There is no need to change the cost of capital in this particular project. The higher interest rates may have led to a recession, which makes this project less attractive. This, however, is a result of the rate structure, not the cost of capital *per se*. Existing bond-holders will take capital losses and if the firm suffers in the recession, the bonds could be perceived as even riskier, causing prices to fall and yield to rise further.
   (c) If financing is out of retained earnings or out of a new issue of shares, the matter is a little more complex. When the project was undertaken, presumably it had a positive NPV which was communicated to the market in terms of a higher share price — quite how, as we know, it is difficult to assess! If the project is on track but the required return by shareholders rises, presumably the project cannot deliver. Now of course, as we say above, it could be that the required return falls in the next period, and financial managers can address this by having a policy of dividend stability. Nevertheless, the fact that the project cannot deliver must detract from the firm's image and impact on its ability to raise further finance.
   (d) The issue of higher costs of capital as a result, say, of the cyclical nature of interest rates is an important one for the firm and the economy. The same project with the same gross cash flows can be evaluated differently — acceptable in one time period and not in another. Can this be right? Well, of course, within the cycle of nominal interest rates there could be a trend, say upward, caused by the Fisher effect. The project in money terms could increase because of inflation, and this could permit higher returns to shareholders. If they suffer from money illusion, they will evaluate the project as more attractive. If not, they could not change the evaluation provided the *real* returns were the same.
   We could go on to illustrate other points that arise in the question, but attention could focus on the inherent riskiness of the project. Has it

changed? Does a firm use a weighted cost of capital averaged over, say, several bond issues and other sources, or does it use incremental? The key may lie in how shareholders react. With asymmetry of information, etc., they may just react very negatively to the project and the firm. Really this question is wide open to many different lines of discussion.

11.2 The quotation is provoking in that it asks you to define the terms on which it is answered. Notice *the* cost of capital, so we are talking about something quite specific. In the text this could be the use of WACC, trying to use an overall measure for the firm that reflects its capital structure and presumably one that would preserve the capital structure. Hence the use of mixed sources. If the firm has 20% preferred, 30% debt and 50% equity (retained earnings and capital issues), it can use these same proportions to raise finance if it is happy with its capital structure, and appraise projects using an overall cost of capital — a single hurdle rate. This has a lot of appeal but:

(a) Firms can rarely proceed in this way. They generally raise finance from specific sources — a rights issue, bonds and retained earnings, and the transaction costs and other market factors involved (scale economies) can dictate this. Timing is another consideration.

(b) Firms can accept or reject projects incorrectly as we illustrate in the text. Surely it is better to use a hurdle rate that reflects the interest risk in the project as the CAPM illustrates? Presumably if a firm takes on new projects which are riskier, this will be reflected in their share price. The firm will have to make a higher return to compensate shareholders for the risk. It seems reasonable, then, that the inherent riskiness of the project should be taken account of, though risk-adjusted discount rates have their problems too.

(c) To operationalize the CAPM is difficult, but not impossible as we try to show.

(d) What of market and book values for the capital structure weights?

11.3 To understand the arbitrary mechanism'of the MM model it is important to see the underlying assumptions — no transaction costs, perfect capital markets, etc. Arbitrage as a mechanism is one that brings prices into line so that if there are two identical firms their market value should be the same — the law of one price.

The example we use in the text is in Fig. 11.7. There are three firms with identical cash flows from trading, *but* different financial structures and different market values. The example is also used in the Workbook.

As the firms are identical in all respects (i.e. in the same risk class and earnings the same) except their financial structure, why should this affect market value? Shareholders should be indifferent to capital structures as:

(a) a higher leverage gives higher yield to compensate for the risk (see Fig. 11.6(b));

(b) the firm benefits from the cheaper sources of debt finance, but the two cancel out so there is no effect on market value.

If there is arbitrage an individual can buy and sell, in effect create his or her own leverage and profit from the switching. Presumably, if a sufficient number of arbitrageurs did this, the effect would be to bring price movements in the shares such that equity is brought about. We would expect a numerical example, similar to the one used in the text, to be utilized to show the steps involved to exploit the price differences.

Of course, the original MM model did not allow for tax and there are a lot of practical considerations involved which would reduce the efficiency of the arbitrage process.

11.4 Debt finance is cheaper than equity for two reasons:

(a) it is less risky to an investor so the market prices debt lower (in terms of the capital market line);
(b) the tax shield.

Although debt can be an attractive investment in terms of its reduced risk *vis-à-vis* equity for the firm, it involves a *commitment* it has to service and eventually repay (unless it is a convertible and this option is taken up). This increased leverage or gearing of financial risk is reflected in the risk perceived by shareholders, who will therefore ask for a higher yield to compensate, i.e. the market prices their equity share to reflect the risk. So the cheapness of debt is a two-edged sword — it is purchased at the price of the financial risk.

The modified MM and the traditional viewpoints are very similar in these early stages of leverage — both illustrate an increase in the value of the firm from the use of cheap debt. EPS will increase, but it will be more volatile.

Firms that do not use debt presumably are not acting in the share-holders' best interest. Another factor to reinforce this is that debt-holders do not carry votes, so the issue of debt does not dilute control. So all round it seems an attractive proposition. Where the problem arises is when the firm attempts to increase debt to higher and higher levels. The market steps in to price not only the increased financial risk to shareholders, but the financial risk to bond-holders too. Even if the firm has the desire to increase debt to these levels, which tells us something about the risk attitude of the managers, the market may place con-straints on the firm's ability to borrow.

11.5 This point was raised in questions 11.1 and 11.2 so we need not repeat all the discussion. But to summarize:

(a) Is the WACC based on book or market values? We argue for market values, which is a bit of a problem to work out. (Note the Shaw Engineering case here.)
(b) Rarely can firms raise additional finance in the exact proportion implied in the weights.
(c) There are dangers in using weighted averages, even if market based, where projects have different risks (see Fig. 11.3 in the text). We would therefore recommend the use of the CAPM, though there are operational problems with this.

In short, be careful when using the WACC.

W11.13   Suggested answers to discussion questions: capital structure

11.1 In the question the word 'proper' is used. This requires some explana-tion. It implies some desired or necessary relationship. This could come from within the firm, or be forced on the firm from outside, or a mixture of both. In the chapter we discuss the sort of rules of thumb that the market may use, e.g. debt must not exceed $x\%$ of total financial assets, or interest payments on debt must be covered four or five times by earnings. We make the point, though, that it depends on the nature of the firm. Financial leverage requires either stability of earnings or steadily rising earnings. Otherwise the firm risks loan default. These are market constraints. Whether they are binding constraints on the firm depends on the risk preferences of its managers. Raising debt is attractive as it is cheap and shareholders will, one presumes, demand it given the effects it has on the market value of the firm. It carries a risk of default and loss of employment for the manager. If you believe in a utility function of managers which includes security, then high leverage rates will probably not feature. At least with ordinary shares you can forgo the dividend and not involve default, though you could invite a hostile takeover bid. Still shares may give you more latitude than bonds that have to be paid.

The net result of having these norms and constraints is that internal policy is constrained so that even if the firm wishes to push beyond the norm it might find that it cannot — see below. Whether that constraint is actually at the minimum of the k_0 curve is debatable. It is more likely to be at either side of the minimum k_0 (in the traditional model).

The impetus for debt and maintaining a proper balance is also of interest. In an MM world, without bankruptcy costs, there is no 'proper' balance with those costs as there is with a traditional world — a least-cost solution.

11.2 The short answer is risk.

(a) *Bond-holders* — they stand before preferred and equity holders, but they may not be secured. Even if they are, there is no guarantee that the asset the mortgage is secured on will eventually sell for its appraised value, as in a recession prices may fall below the con-servative basis of 60–70% financing of value that has been done. Other unsecured bond-holders will see more and more of them around seeking claims on assets if there is a default. As leverage can increase EPS, but also increase its volatility, and as coupon pay-ments are a fixed charge that have to be met, then as leverage increases still further, the risk of bankruptcy is a very real one. Of course, this might not arise if market forces prevent the levels increasing to this point.

(b) *Equity* — leverage introduces financial risk and this requires compensation. We would therefore expect k_e to rise as leverage rises.

11.3 Notice in the question the word 'should' — a normative statement. If firms do not follow the debt path, the argument is that they should, though we could involve empirical evidence to see if they do (they do not!). Following MM (adjusted for tax), there is every incentive for a firm to raise all of its external finance by debt. If this were possible, presumably a firm would be neglectful if it did not. We have seen in the USA in particular the heavy use of leveraged buy-outs and the concern expressed that firms have 'too much' debt in their structure. Some recent failures have highlighted this, particularly with the use of junk bonds. However, modifying MM for bankruptcy does bring a limit in the increase in the market value of the firm, though shareholders would wish the firm to expand their leverage still further, then sell out just before bankruptcy.

For the traditional view, there is an incentive pro-debt, but not 99.9%. The issue is to find the optimum as this is the least cost for the overall cost of capital k_0. However, we can make a case out for not using k_0, but the specific costs of capital, to reflect the risk of the proposal, though this will, of course, feed back to an overall k_0.

There is also the question of what kind of debt. This is a side issue in this particular question.

11.4 This could break down to a pre- and post-tax MM discussion. In the original MM (1958) without tax, the financial structure was irrelevant. Whatever a firm did, a shareholder could unravel it through the market, so it did not matter whatsoever. With the introduction of corporate tax (in 1963) the analysis shifts — financial structure is important as increased leverage with the existence of the tax shield leads to an increase in P_T, the market value of the firm up to 99.99% leverage (100% is impossible owing to the legal needs for some shareholders in the firm). So here financial structure is crucial. The introduction of bankruptcy costs modifies this position. If we go further into Miller's argument (see section W11.8(c)), then we need to take account not only of corporate tax, but personal taxes too. We came across similar arguments in Chapter 10 on dividends, and in Chapter 8 on the issue of preference shares.

The traditional view with its U-shaped k_0 curve does not rely on taxes for this. It would accentuate the initial fall in K_0 and probably shift the minimum profit to a higher level of leverage.

So for MM without taxes, financial structure does not matter. For the traditional view without taxes, it does matter. Hence the debate.

12 An assessment and a projection

W12.1 Introduction

The nature of the conclusions we have reached in the main text for Chapter 12 are not the kind that are easily amenable to treatment in a Workbook. Just as we took stock at the final chapter of the text, so you should take stock at this final stage. There have been a great many topics in this book. The links among many of them are clear. Other links are not so clear. The full implications of option pricing models, for example, are still uncertain, for all financial instruments can be treated as options. Similarly the problems of CAPM in terms of tests may be resolved more readily through the arbitrage pricing model.

Although it is always dangerous to separate theory from practice, some pointers are available that require a distinction at this stage. You have learned the theory, which like much of economics relies on assumptions. Yet, also like much of economics, something approaching the theoretical conclusions seems to have been observed in the real world. For those parts of the text that deal with theory then, their working through must be understood, as must the interlinkages between their different parts.

Yet the theory should, we must suppose, lead to practice. To what extent does the theory guide or explain practice? This should be a question for you to ponder, though comments have been made at various parts of the Workbook and text.

In addition there is the matter of institutional development. In the later parts of this book we have laid emphasis on certain features of the changing world of finance. For the UK one such feature has been the deregulation of the City — the so-called Big Bang. Another has been the increasing internationalization of capital markets. In long-term securities this has meant a tendency for UK companies both to seek quotations on foreign stock exchanges for their equity and debt (in the case of the USA, more indirectly through the issue of American depository receipts) and to raise funds through the euromarkets. Foreign companies likewise seek a quotation on the International Stock Exchange. In short-term investment, this tendency to internationalization has become if anything even more pronounced, for the increased technology that has been developed in banking has led to a massive increase in dealing and aritrage opportunities among the world's markets, and risk taking by individuals and companies on the markets and the Chicago and London futures markets has developed. Currently, because of its geographical position, London has retained importance in international securities dealing since, along with New York and Tokyo, it offers 24-hour dealing opportunities. It will probably retain its prominent position in the face of competition from Zurich and Frankfurt, though this is by no means assured.

You are advised, therefore, to keep in touch with current developments in finance, to be aware of the changes taking place and to attempt to reconcile them with the theory the book has developed. Theory has no claim to provide the answers to all the questions raised by finance. It should, we hope, enlighten practice and guide future action.

W12.1   Case study: Bula Mines Limited

We offer one case study in this final chapter, that of Bula Mines. Features of earlier parts of the book are important to an analysis of the case. It is a real-life and comparatively recent case, and the problem to be solved is one that faced a number of people, so *your* approach can be compared with their approaches. The case has two parts. Part B is contained in the teacher's guide that accompanies this book. This case is reprinted with permission from *Cases in Corporate Finance* by E. Dimson and P. Marsh (Wiley, 1988).

Part A
(This case was written by Elroy Dimson as a basis for class discussion, rather than to illustrate either effective or ineffective handling of an administrative situation.)

Bula Limited, a privately owned Irish company, was set up to exploit a deposit of zinc and lead ore in The Republic of Ireland. In 1974, the Irish government arranged to purchase 24% of the equity and were given 25% of the equity free of charge by the owners. An arbitration panel was set up to value the company. The arbitrators had to decide on the price at which the government would acquire its stake in the mine, and were to hand down their decision on 12 November 1976.

The Story
In 1970, a rich deposit of lead/zinc ore was discovered beneath the farmland of one Pat Wright, an elderly Irish farmer. Lacking the resources or expertise to develop this himself, he sold the land (about 120 acres or 300 hectares) to Bula Ltd, a company owned by Tom Roche, managing director of Cement Roadstone, his son-in-law, Michael Wymes, and a colleague, Richard Wood. The terms were £500,000 cash, £300,000 when mining commenced and a 20% stake in Bula Ltd. By July 1974, Bula had negotiated a participation agreement in outline with the Irish government. The government agreed to buy 24% of the equity in Bula, and to accept a further 25% as a gift. The price at that time was not agreed, and was to be the subject of arbitration. Estimates by Bula then valued the company at about £10m, while the government had been advised that the mine was worth much less than this.

Further information released then revealed the following holdings in Bula Ltd:

Roche family	30%
Wymes family	30%
Patrick Wright	20%
Richard Wood	20%

The terms of payment were to be:

Half payable within 3 months of agreement
One quarter payable after 1 further year
One quarter payable after 2 further years.

The freehold of the land belongs to Bula, as did all mining rights and minerals underneath the land. This is unusual and stems from a quirk of the law under which Pat Wright originally purchased the land. This fact means that the value of the mine is higher than normally would be the case, since otherwise, under a Minerals Acquisition Order, the Irish government could lay claim to the minerals and then license the mining company as a producer of the ore. However, the circumstances of the land freehold prevented this.

In October 1974, Bula announced the retention of RTZ Consultants to carry out a feasibility study of the part of the zinc and lead ore body owned by Bula. The ore body itself is in an area called Navan. The other part of the ore body is owned by a company called Tara, which does not own its section of ore freehold. However, Tara was further advanced at that time in its evaluation of the ore body. The split ownership of the Navan ore caused the government much embarrassment. The original idea was to purchase compulsorily both the Bula and Tara sector, and lease them to Tara to operate. However the compulsory purchase order on the Bula section failed as related above, leaving the government no option but to allow separate development.

Technical appraisal continued, and facts began to trickle out. In July 1975, RTZ Consultants delivered their report to Bula. By December 1975, a detailed comparison of the Tara and Bula mines was published [Table W12.1].

Table W12.1   Comparison of the Tara and Bula mines

Information	Tara	Bula
Estimated ore body	63m tonnes	19.6m tonnes
Probable extraction rate per year	2.2m tonnes	1.0m tonnes
Estimated initial production date	Early 1977	Late 1977
Predicted employment: Construction	1,100	600
Production	800	300
State holding of equity	25%	49%
Cost of State holding: First 25%	Nil	Nil
Remainder	Nil	Fixed by arbitration
State representation on board	2 directors[a]	2 directors
State receipts: Company tax on profits[b]	50%	50%
Royalty on profits	4½%	Nil[c]
Other receipts	Annual rent	Nil[c]
Estimated overall proportion of mine profits accruing to state	67%	74%

Notes:
[a] Or 25% of the board membership of Tara.
[b] Capital allowances of 120% of investment expenditure may be written off against taxable profits.
[c] No royalty is payable by Bula because the Bula ore body is privately owned.
[d] Or 62% excluding the stake to be purchased by the government.
Sources: Irish Times, 13.12.1975, and RTZ Consultants report

At about this time, it was revealed that it would be necessary to divert the River Blackwater in order to fully mine the deposits. Costs would be shared by Tara and Bula, and were estimated to be about £2m. However, this proposal started to draw a lot of protests from environmentalists and fishermen, who took the view that the salmon would be disturbed. The companies replied that diversion was necessary to get at almost 12m tonnes of ore.

In order to provide a satisfactory basis, both for Bula's planning effort and for valuing the government's share in the mine, Bula commissioned a detailed feasibility study of its whole mining operation. The study was undertaken by Bechtel, a prestigious international firm of mining consultants.

Technical Data

Comprehensive technical data was provided by Bechtel in their report dated April 1976. The report was essentially a feasibility study of the whole Bula mine undertaking. The ore reserve figure in the Bechtel study was that calculated by RTZ Consultants, using evidence gleaned from 202 drill holes bored on the Bula site: 'The geographical interpretations and the *in-situ* undiluted reserves developed by RTZ Consultants and presented in their July 1975 report were checked and accepted by Bechtel. These have been used to estimate mineral reserves and for the preliminary mine planning.'

This technical information was accepted as the best available by almost everybody involved in valuing the mine. In particular, there was general agreement about the quantity and quality of the ore body [Table W12.2]. Neither were capital costs a subject for controversy: Bechtel's projection that the mine would require an initial investment of approximately £22.6m during calendar years 1977 and 1978 seemed reasonable. Diversion of the river and further underground work would be required before underground mining could commence. This would cost a further £5m at 1977 prices.

Table W12.2 Bula mine's estimated ore reserves

Category of reserves	Quantity (tonnes millions)	Lead reserves %	Zinc reserves %	Combined lead/zinc %
Measured (open pit)	9	1.1	7.2	8.3
Measured (underground)	5	1.9	9.0	10.9
Total measured reserves	14	1.4	7.8	9.2
Additional indicated reserves	6	0.8	4.4	5.2
Total measured and indicated	20	1.2	6.8	8.0

Sources: Irish Times, 8.2.1977, and Irish Independent 12.9.1975.

Some people felt differently about the operating costs, which were projected by Bechtel to be at the rate of £5 a tonne for open pit working, and £8 a tonne once underground operations were phased in during 1986. The objections were raised primarily by financial analysts, who pointed out that Bechtel's cost figures were substantially below the expenses disclosed in the annual accounts of other Irish mining companies [see Table W12.3].

Table W12.3   Operating expenses as a proportion of total income for Bula and comparable companies

	1973 %	1974 %	1975 %	Projected %
Northgate	45	55	80	
International Mogul	46	56	65	
Bula (Bechtel projections):				
Open cast				28
Underground				45

Source: Irish Times, 8.2.1977.

Another point of contention was the likely course of metal prices over the life of the project. A study by R.J. Lee, published in 1976, had shown that the annual average price of zinc in the UK and USA during the period 1900–1974 had changed very little in real terms, though there appeared to be a 25-year cycle in zinc prices. It was therefore asserted by a financial journalist that 'The current price of zinc, $795 per tonne, totally understates the value of the metal. It is the price at the bottom of the zinc demand cycle. If the metal demand/price cycle repeats itself as it has done for the past 25 years then zinc will rise rapidly in price over the next three to five years' (J. O'Neill, *Irish Business*, March 1977). Under this scenario, zinc, and perhaps lead, prices would rise faster than operating costs.

The converse point of view was held by another writer: 'Uncertainty surrounds the likely future movements of metal prices. If these were to increase relative to costs then obviously future cash flows would increase. However, this is thought unlikely to happen. ... Operating costs in Bula are likely to increase relative to the value of metal and so net income is likely to fall' (J. O'Reilly, *Irish Times*, 8 February 1977). Despite the disagreement over the likely course of prices and costs, virtually all published valuations of the Bula project assumed that sales revenues would move in line with the general level of inflation. For example, it was forecast by O'Neill that, at 1977 prices, sales revenues would remain at the level of £19m per year from 1979 to 1995 inclusive, while O'Reilly estimated revenues of £18m per year through till 1996.

Valuing Bula Mines
The task of valuing the mine was undertaken by the London Institute of Arbitration. Advisers were retained by the Irish government and by Bula Limited. The RTZ Consultants and Bechtel reports were made available to both parties. The advisers were asked to submit a written valuation of the mine to the arbitration panel during the course of summer 1976.

Compound Interest

Table 1 The amount to which 1 grows at interest rate i after n periods $(1 + i)^n$

	1%	2%	3%	4%	5%	6%	7%	8%	9%	10%	11%	12%	13%	14%	15%
1	1.0100	1.0200	1.0300	1.0400	1.0500	1.0600	1.0700	1.0800	1.0900	1.1000	1.1100	1.1200	1.1300	1.1400	1.1500
2	1.0201	1.0404	1.0609	1.0816	1.1025	1.1236	1.1449	1.1664	1.1881	1.2100	1.2321	1.2544	1.2769	1.2996	1.3225
3	1.0303	1.0612	1.0927	1.1249	1.1576	1.1910	1.2250	1.2597	1.2950	1.3310	1.3676	1.4049	1.4429	1.4815	1.5209
4	1.0406	1.0824	1.1255	1.1699	1.2155	1.2625	1.3108	1.3605	1.4116	1.4641	1.5181	1.5735	1.6305	1.6890	1.7490
5	1.0510	1.1041	1.1593	1.2167	1.2763	1.3382	1.4026	1.4693	1.5386	1.6105	1.6851	1.7623	1.8424	1.9254	2.0114
6	1.0615	1.1262	1.1941	1.2653	1.3401	1.4185	1.5007	1.5869	1.6771	1.7716	1.8704	1.9738	2.0820	2.1950	2.3131
7	1.0721	1.1487	1.2299	1.3159	1.4071	1.5036	1.6058	1.7138	1.8280	1.9487	2.0762	2.2107	2.3526	2.5023	2.6600
8	1.0829	1.1717	1.2668	1.3686	1.4775	1.5938	1.7182	1.8509	1.9926	2.1436	2.3045	2.4760	2.6584	2.8526	3.0590
9	1.0937	1.1951	1.3048	1.4233	1.5513	1.6895	1.8385	1.9990	2.1719	2.3579	2.5580	2.7731	3.0040	3.2519	3.5179
10	1.1046	1.2190	1.3439	1.4802	1.6289	1.7908	1.9672	2.1589	2.3674	2.5937	2.8394	3.1058	3.3946	3.7072	4.0456
11	1.1157	1.2434	1.3842	1.5395	1.7103	1.8983	2.1049	2.3316	2.5804	2.8531	3.1518	3.4785	3.8359	4.2262	4.6524
12	1.1268	1.2682	1.4258	1.6010	1.7959	2.0122	2.2522	2.5182	2.8127	3.1384	3.4985	3.8960	4.3345	4.8179	5.3503
13	1.1381	1.2936	1.4685	1.6651	1.8856	2.1329	2.4098	2.7196	3.0658	3.4523	3.8833	4.3635	4.8980	5.4924	6.1528
14	1.1495	1.3195	1.5126	1.7317	1.9799	2.2609	2.5785	2.9372	3.3417	3.7975	4.3104	4.8871	5.5348	6.2613	7.0757
15	1.1610	1.3459	1.5580	1.8009	2.0789	2.3966	2.7590	3.1722	3.6425	4.1772	4.7846	5.4736	6.2543	7.1379	8.1371
16	1.1726	1.3728	1.6047	1.8730	2.1829	2.5404	2.9522	3.4259	3.9703	4.5950	5.3109	6.1304	7.0673	8.1372	9.3576
17	1.1843	1.4002	1.6528	1.9479	2.2920	2.6928	3.1588	3.7000	4.3276	5.0545	5.8951	6.8660	7.9861	9.2765	10.7613
18	1.1961	1.4282	1.7024	2.0258	2.4066	2.8543	3.3799	3.9960	4.7171	5.5599	6.5436	7.6900	9.0243	10.5752	12.3755
19	1.2081	1.4568	1.7535	2.1068	2.5270	3.0256	3.6165	4.3157	5.1417	6.1159	7.2633	8.6128	10.1974	12.0557	14.2318
20	1.2202	1.4859	1.8061	2.1911	2.6533	3.2071	3.8697	4.6610	5.6044	6.7275	8.0623	9.6463	11.5231	13.7435	16.3665
21	1.2324	1.5157	1.8603	2.2788	2.7860	3.3996	4.1406	5.0338	6.1088	7.4002	8.9492	10.8038	13.0211	15.6676	18.8215
22	1.2447	1.5460	1.9161	2.3699	2.9253	3.6035	4.4304	5.4365	6.6586	8.1403	9.9336	12.1003	14.7138	17.8610	21.6447
23	1.2572	1.5769	1.9736	2.4647	3.0715	3.8197	4.7405	5.8715	7.2579	8.9543	11.0263	13.5523	16.6266	20.3616	24.8915
24	1.2697	1.6084	2.0328	2.5633	3.2251	4.0489	5.0724	6.3412	7.9111	9.8497	12.2392	15.1786	18.7881	23.2122	28.6252
25	1.2824	1.6406	2.0938	2.6658	3.3864	4.2919	5.4274	6.8485	8.6231	10.8347	13.5855	17.0001	21.2305	26.4619	32.9190
26	1.2953	1.6734	2.1566	2.7725	3.5557	4.5494	5.8074	7.3964	9.3992	11.9182	15.0799	19.0401	23.9905	30.1666	37.8568
27	1.3082	1.7069	2.2213	2.8834	3.7335	4.8223	6.2139	7.9881	10.2451	13.1100	16.7386	21.3249	27.1093	34.3899	43.5353
28	1.3213	1.7410	2.2879	2.9987	3.9201	5.1117	6.6488	8.6271	11.1671	14.4210	18.5799	23.8839	30.6335	39.2045	50.0656
29	1.3345	1.7758	2.3566	3.1187	4.1161	5.4184	7.1143	9.3173	12.1722	15.8631	20.6237	26.7499	34.6158	44.6931	57.5755
30	1.3478	1.8114	2.4273	3.2434	4.3219	5.7435	7.6123	10.0627	13.2677	17.4494	22.8923	29.9599	39.1159	50.9502	66.2118
40	1.4889	2.2080	3.2620	4.8010	7.0400	10.2857	14.9745	21.7245	31.4094	45.2593	65.0009	93.0510	132.7816	188.8835	267.8635
50	1.6446	2.6916	4.3839	7.1067	11.4674	18.4202	29.4570	46.9016	74.3575	117.3909	184.5648	289.0022	450.7359	700.2330	
100	2.7048	7.2446	19.2186	50.5049	131.5013	339.3021	867.7163								

Table I   Continued

	16%	17%	18%	19%	20%	21%	22%	23%	24%	25%	26%	27%	28%	29%	30%
1	1.1600	1.1700	1.1800	1.1900	1.2000	1.2100	1.2200	1.2300	1.2400	1.2500	1.2600	1.2700	1.2800	1.2900	1.3000
2	1.3456	1.3689	1.3924	1.4161	1.4400	1.4641	1.4884	1.5129	1.5376	1.5625	1.5876	1.6129	1.6384	1.6641	1.6900
3	1.5609	1.6016	1.6430	1.6852	1.7280	1.7716	1.8158	1.8609	1.9066	1.9531	2.0004	2.0484	2.0972	2.1467	2.1970
4	1.8106	1.8739	1.9388	2.0053	2.0736	2.1436	2.2153	2.2889	2.3642	2.4414	2.5205	2.6014	2.6844	2.7692	2.8561
5	2.1003	2.1924	2.2878	2.3864	2.4883	2.5937	2.7027	2.8153	2.9316	3.0518	3.1758	3.3038	3.4360	3.5723	3.7129
6	2.4364	2.5652	2.6996	2.8398	2.9860	3.1384	3.2973	3.4628	3.6352	3.8147	4.0015	4.1959	4.3980	4.6083	4.8268
7	2.8262	3.0012	3.1855	3.3793	3.5832	3.7975	4.0227	4.2593	4.5077	4.7684	5.0419	5.3288	5.6295	5.9447	6.2749
8	3.2784	3.5115	3.7589	4.0214	4.2998	4.5950	4.9077	5.2389	5.5895	5.9605	6.3528	6.7675	7.2058	7.6686	8.1573
9	3.8030	4.1084	4.4355	4.7854	5.1598	5.5599	5.9874	6.4439	6.9310	7.4506	8.0045	8.5948	9.2234	9.8925	10.6045
10	4.4114	4.8068	5.2338	5.6947	6.1917	6.7275	7.3046	7.9259	8.5944	9.3132	10.0857	10.9153	11.8059	12.7614	13.7858
11	5.1173	5.6240	6.1759	6.7767	7.4301	8.1403	8.9117	9.7489	10.6571	11.6415	12.7080	13.8625	15.1116	16.4622	17.9216
12	5.9360	6.5801	7.2876	8.0642	8.9161	9.8497	10.8722	11.9912	13.2148	14.5519	16.0120	17.6053	19.3428	21.2362	23.2981
13	6.8858	7.6987	8.5994	9.5964	10.6993	11.9182	13.2641	14.7491	16.3863	18.1899	20.1752	22.3588	24.7588	27.3947	30.2875
14	7.9875	9.0075	10.1472	11.4198	12.8392	14.4210	16.1822	18.1414	20.3191	22.7374	25.4207	28.3957	31.6913	35.3391	39.3738
15	9.2655	10.5387	11.9737	13.5895	15.4070	17.4494	19.7423	22.3140	25.1956	28.4217	32.0301	36.0625	40.5648	45.5875	51.1859
16	10.7480	12.3303	14.1290	16.1715	18.4884	21.1138	24.0856	27.4462	31.2426	35.5271	40.3579	45.7994	51.9230	58.8079	66.5417
17	12.4677	14.4265	16.6722	19.2441	22.1861	25.5477	29.3844	33.7588	38.7408	44.4089	50.8510	58.1652	66.4614	75.8621	86.5042
18	14.4625	16.8790	19.6733	22.9005	26.6233	30.9127	35.8490	41.5233	48.0386	55.5112	64.0722	73.8698	85.0706	97.8622	112.4554
19	16.7765	19.7484	23.2144	27.2516	31.9480	37.4043	43.7358	51.0737	59.5679	69.3899	80.7310	93.8147	108.8904	126.2422	146.1920
20	19.4608	23.1056	27.3930	32.4294	38.3376	45.2593	53.3576	62.8206	73.8641	86.7362	101.7211	119.1446	139.3797	162.8524	190.0496
21	22.5745	27.0336	32.3238	38.5910	46.0051	54.7637	65.0963	77.2694	91.5915	108.4202	128.1685	151.3137	178.4060	210.0796	247.0645
22	26.1864	31.6293	38.1421	45.9233	55.2061	66.2641	79.4175	95.0413	113.5735	135.5253	161.4924	192.1683	228.3596	271.0027	321.1839
23	30.3762	37.0062	45.0076	54.6487	66.2474	80.1795	96.8894	116.9008	140.8312	169.4066	203.4804	244.0538	292.3003	349.5935	417.5391
24	35.2364	43.2973	53.1090	65.0320	79.4968	97.0172	118.2050	143.7880	174.6306	211.7582	256.3853	309.9483	374.1444	450.9756	542.8008
25	40.8742	50.6578	62.6686	77.3881	95.3962	117.3909	144.2101	176.8593	216.5420	264.6978	323.0454	393.6344	478.9049	581.7585	705.6410
26	47.4141	59.2697	73.9490	92.0918	114.4755	142.0429	175.9364	217.5369	268.5121	330.8722	407.0373	499.9157	612.9982	750.4685	917.3333
27	55.0004	69.3455	87.2598	109.5893	137.3706	171.8719	214.6424	267.5704	332.9550	413.5903	512.8670	634.8929	784.6377	968.1044	
28	63.8004	81.1342	102.9666	130.4112	164.8447	207.9651	261.8637	329.1115	412.8642	516.9879	646.2124	806.3140			
29	74.0085	94.9271	121.5005	155.1893	197.8136	251.6377	319.4737	404.8072	511.9516	646.2349	814.2276				
30	85.8499	111.0647	143.3706	184.6753	237.3763	304.4816	389.7579	497.9129	634.8199	807.7936					
40	378.7212	533.8687	750.3783												

Present Value.

Table II The present value of 1 at interest rate i after n periods v^n

	1%	2%	3%	4%	5%	6%	7%	8%	9%	10%	11%	12%	13%	14%	15%
1	0.9901	0.9804	0.9709	0.9615	0.9524	0.9434	0.9346	0.9259	0.9174	0.9091	0.9009	0.8929	0.8850	0.8772	0.8696
2	0.9803	0.9612	0.9426	0.9246	0.9070	0.8900	0.8734	0.8573	0.8417	0.8264	0.8116	0.7972	0.7831	0.7695	0.7561
3	0.9706	0.9423	0.9151	0.8890	0.8638	0.8396	0.8163	0.7938	0.7722	0.7513	0.7312	0.7118	0.6931	0.6750	0.6575
4	0.9610	0.9238	0.8885	0.8548	0.8227	0.7921	0.7629	0.7350	0.7084	0.6830	0.6587	0.6355	0.6133	0.5921	0.5718
5	0.9515	0.9057	0.8626	0.8219	0.7835	0.7473	0.7130	0.6806	0.6499	0.6209	0.5935	0.5674	0.5428	0.5194	0.4972
6	0.9420	0.8880	0.8375	0.7903	0.7462	0.7050	0.6663	0.6302	0.5963	0.5645	0.5346	0.5066	0.4803	0.4556	0.4323
7	0.9327	0.8706	0.8131	0.7599	0.7107	0.6651	0.6227	0.5835	0.5470	0.5132	0.4817	0.4523	0.4251	0.3996	0.3759
8	0.9235	0.8535	0.7894	0.7307	0.6768	0.6274	0.5820	0.5403	0.5019	0.4665	0.4339	0.4039	0.3762	0.3506	0.3269
9	0.9143	0.8368	0.7664	0.7026	0.6446	0.5919	0.5439	0.5002	0.4604	0.4241	0.3909	0.3606	0.3329	0.3075	0.2843
10	0.9053	0.8203	0.7441	0.6756	0.6139	0.5584	0.5083	0.4632	0.4224	0.3855	0.3522	0.3220	0.2946	0.2697	0.2472
11	0.8963	0.8043	0.7224	0.6496	0.5847	0.5268	0.4751	0.4289	0.3875	0.3505	0.3173	0.2875	0.2607	0.2366	0.2149
12	0.8874	0.7885	0.7014	0.6246	0.5568	0.4970	0.4440	0.3971	0.3555	0.3186	0.2858	0.2567	0.2307	0.2076	0.1869
13	0.8787	0.7730	0.6810	0.6006	0.5303	0.4688	0.4150	0.3677	0.3262	0.2897	0.2575	0.2292	0.2042	0.1821	0.1625
14	0.8700	0.7579	0.6611	0.5775	0.5051	0.4423	0.3878	0.3405	0.2992	0.2633	0.2320	0.2046	0.1807	0.1597	0.1413
15	0.8613	0.7430	0.6419	0.5553	0.4810	0.4173	0.3624	0.3152	0.2745	0.2394	0.2090	0.1827	0.1599	0.1401	0.1229
16	0.8528	0.7284	0.6232	0.5339	0.4581	0.3936	0.3387	0.2919	0.2519	0.2176	0.1883	0.1631	0.1415	0.1229	0.1069
17	0.8444	0.7142	0.6050	0.5134	0.4363	0.3714	0.3166	0.2703	0.2311	0.1978	0.1696	0.1456	0.1252	0.1078	0.0929
18	0.8360	0.7002	0.5874	0.4936	0.4155	0.3503	0.2959	0.2502	0.2120	0.1799	0.1528	0.1300	0.1108	0.0946	0.0808
19	0.8277	0.6864	0.5703	0.4746	0.3957	0.3305	0.2765	0.2317	0.1945	0.1635	0.1377	0.1161	0.0981	0.0829	0.0703
20	0.8195	0.6730	0.5537	0.4564	0.3769	0.3118	0.2584	0.2145	0.1784	0.1486	0.1240	0.1037	0.0868	0.0728	0.0611
21	0.8114	0.6598	0.5375	0.4388	0.3589	0.2942	0.2415	0.1987	0.1637	0.1351	0.1117	0.0926	0.0768	0.0638	0.0531
22	0.8034	0.6468	0.5219	0.4220	0.3418	0.2775	0.2257	0.1839	0.1502	0.1228	0.1007	0.0826	0.0680	0.0560	0.0462
23	0.7954	0.6342	0.5067	0.4057	0.3256	0.2618	0.2109	0.1703	0.1378	0.1117	0.0907	0.0738	0.0601	0.0491	0.0402
24	0.7876	0.6217	0.4919	0.3901	0.3101	0.2470	0.1971	0.1577	0.1264	0.1015	0.0817	0.0659	0.0532	0.0431	0.0349
25	0.7798	0.6095	0.4776	0.3751	0.2953	0.2330	0.1842	0.1460	0.1160	0.0923	0.0736	0.0588	0.0471	0.0378	0.0304
26	0.7720	0.5976	0.4637	0.3607	0.2812	0.2198	0.1722	0.1352	0.1064	0.0839	0.0663	0.0525	0.0417	0.0331	0.0264
27	0.7644	0.5859	0.4502	0.3468	0.2678	0.2074	0.1609	0.1252	0.0976	0.0763	0.0597	0.0469	0.0369	0.0291	0.0230
28	0.7568	0.5744	0.4371	0.3335	0.2551	0.1956	0.1504	0.1159	0.0895	0.0693	0.0538	0.0419	0.0326	0.0255	0.0200
29	0.7493	0.5631	0.4243	0.3207	0.2429	0.1846	0.1406	0.1073	0.0822	0.0630	0.0485	0.0374	0.0289	0.0224	0.0174
30	0.7419	0.5521	0.4120	0.3083	0.2314	0.1741	0.1314	0.0994	0.0754	0.0573	0.0437	0.0334	0.0256	0.0196	0.0151
40	0.6717	0.4529	0.3066	0.2083	0.1420	0.0972	0.0668	0.0460	0.0318	0.0221	0.0154	0.0107	0.0075	0.0053	0.0037
50	0.6080	0.3715	0.2281	0.1407	0.0872	0.0543	0.0339	0.0213	0.0134	0.0085	0.0054	0.0035	0.0022	0.0014	0.0009
100	0.3697	0.1380	0.0520	0.0198	0.0076	0.0029	0.0012	0.0005	0.0002	0.0001					

Table II Continued

	16%	17%	18%	19%	20%	21%	22%	23%	24%	25%	26%	27%	28%	29%	30%
1	0.8621	0.8547	0.8475	0.8403	0.8333	0.8264	0.8197	0.8130	0.8065	0.8000	0.7937	0.7874	0.7813	0.7752	0.7692
2	0.7432	0.7305	0.7182	0.7062	0.6944	0.6830	0.6719	0.6610	0.6504	0.6400	0.6299	0.6200	0.6104	0.6009	0.5917
3	0.6407	0.6244	0.6086	0.5934	0.5787	0.5645	0.5507	0.5374	0.5245	0.5120	0.4999	0.4882	0.4768	0.4658	0.4552
4	0.5523	0.5337	0.5158	0.4987	0.4823	0.4665	0.4514	0.4369	0.4230	0.4096	0.3968	0.3844	0.3725	0.3611	0.3501
5	0.4761	0.4561	0.4371	0.4190	0.4019	0.3855	0.3700	0.3552	0.3411	0.3277	0.3149	0.3027	0.2910	0.2799	0.2693
6	0.4104	0.3898	0.3704	0.3521	0.3349	0.3186	0.3033	0.2888	0.2751	0.2621	0.2499	0.2383	0.2274	0.2170	0.2072
7	0.3538	0.3332	0.3139	0.2959	0.2791	0.2633	0.2486	0.2348	0.2218	0.2097	0.1983	0.1877	0.1776	0.1682	0.1594
8	0.3050	0.2848	0.2660	0.2487	0.2326	0.2176	0.2038	0.1909	0.1789	0.1678	0.1574	0.1478	0.1388	0.1304	0.1226
9	0.2630	0.2434	0.2255	0.2090	0.1938	0.1799	0.1670	0.1552	0.1443	0.1342	0.1249	0.1164	0.1084	0.1011	0.0943
10	0.2267	0.2080	0.1911	0.1756	0.1615	0.1486	0.1369	0.1262	0.1164	0.1074	0.0992	0.0916	0.0847	0.0784	0.0725
11	0.1954	0.1778	0.1619	0.1476	0.1346	0.1228	0.1122	0.1026	0.0938	0.0859	0.0787	0.0721	0.0662	0.0607	0.0558
12	0.1685	0.1520	0.1372	0.1240	0.1122	0.1015	0.0920	0.0834	0.0757	0.0687	0.0625	0.0568	0.0517	0.0471	0.0429
13	0.1452	0.1299	0.1163	0.1042	0.0935	0.0839	0.0754	0.0678	0.0610	0.0550	0.0496	0.0447	0.0404	0.0365	0.0330
14	0.1252	0.1110	0.0985	0.0876	0.0779	0.0693	0.0618	0.0551	0.0492	0.0440	0.0393	0.0352	0.0316	0.0283	0.0254
15	0.1079	0.0949	0.0835	0.0736	0.0649	0.0573	0.0507	0.0448	0.0397	0.0352	0.0312	0.0277	0.0247	0.0219	0.0195
16	0.0930	0.0811	0.0708	0.0618	0.0541	0.0474	0.0415	0.0364	0.0320	0.0281	0.0248	0.0218	0.0193	0.0170	0.0150
17	0.0802	0.0693	0.0600	0.0520	0.0451	0.0391	0.0340	0.0296	0.0258	0.0225	0.0197	0.0172	0.0150	0.0132	0.0116
18	0.0691	0.0592	0.0508	0.0437	0.0376	0.0323	0.0279	0.0241	0.0208	0.0180	0.0156	0.0135	0.0118	0.0102	0.0089
19	0.0596	0.0506	0.0431	0.0367	0.0313	0.0267	0.0229	0.0196	0.0168	0.0144	0.0124	0.0107	0.0092	0.0079	0.0068
20	0.0514	0.0433	0.0365	0.0308	0.0261	0.0221	0.0187	0.0159	0.0135	0.0115	0.0098	0.0084	0.0072	0.0061	0.0053
21	0.0443	0.0370	0.0309	0.0259	0.0217	0.0183	0.0154	0.0129	0.0109	0.0092	0.0078	0.0066	0.0056	0.0048	0.0040
22	0.0382	0.0316	0.0262	0.0218	0.0181	0.0151	0.0126	0.0105	0.0088	0.0074	0.0062	0.0052	0.0044	0.0037	0.0031
23	0.0329	0.0270	0.0222	0.0183	0.0151	0.0125	0.0103	0.0086	0.0071	0.0059	0.0049	0.0041	0.0034	0.0029	0.0024
24	0.0284	0.0231	0.0188	0.0154	0.0126	0.0103	0.0085	0.0070	0.0057	0.0047	0.0039	0.0032	0.0027	0.0022	0.0018
25	0.0245	0.0197	0.0160	0.0129	0.0105	0.0085	0.0069	0.0057	0.0046	0.0038	0.0031	0.0025	0.0021	0.0017	0.0014
26	0.0211	0.0169	0.0135	0.0109	0.0087	0.0070	0.0057	0.0046	0.0037	0.0030	0.0025	0.0020	0.0016	0.0013	0.0011
27	0.0182	0.0144	0.0115	0.0091	0.0073	0.0058	0.0047	0.0037	0.0030	0.0024	0.0019	0.0016	0.0013	0.0010	0.0008
28	0.0157	0.0123	0.0097	0.0077	0.0061	0.0048	0.0038	0.0030	0.0024	0.0019	0.0015	0.0012	0.0010	0.0008	0.0006
29	0.0135	0.0105	0.0082	0.0064	0.0051	0.0040	0.0031	0.0025	0.0020	0.0015	0.0012	0.0010	0.0008	0.0006	0.0005
30	0.0116	0.0090	0.0070	0.0054	0.0042	0.0033	0.0026	0.0020	0.0016	0.0012	0.0010	0.0008	0.0006	0.0005	0.0004
40	0.0026	0.0019	0.0013	0.0010	0.0007	0.0005	0.0004	0.0003	0.0002	0.0001	0.0001	0.0001	0.0001		
50	0.0006	0.0004	0.0003	0.0002	0.0001	0.0001									

Present Value of Annuity.

Table III The present value of 1 per period at the end of each of n periods $a_n = (1 - v^n)/i$

	1%	2%	3%	4%	5%	6%	7%	8%	9%	10%	11%	12%	13%	14%	15%
1	0.9901	0.9804	0.9709	0.9615	0.9524	0.9434	0.9346	0.9259	0.9174	0.9091	0.9009	0.8929	0.8850	0.8772	0.8696
2	1.9704	1.9416	1.9135	1.8861	1.8594	1.8334	1.8080	1.7833	1.7591	1.7355	1.7125	1.6901	1.6681	1.6467	1.6257
3	2.9410	2.8839	2.8286	2.7751	2.7232	2.6730	2.6243	2.5771	2.5313	2.4869	2.4437	2.4018	2.3612	2.3216	2.2832
4	3.9020	3.8077	3.7171	3.6299	3.5460	3.4651	3.3872	3.3121	3.2397	3.1699	3.1024	3.0373	2.9745	2.9137	2.8550
5	4.8534	4.7135	4.5797	4.4518	4.3295	4.2124	4.1002	3.9927	3.8897	3.7908	3.6959	3.6048	3.5172	3.4331	3.3522
6	5.7955	5.6014	5.4172	5.2421	5.0757	4.9173	4.7665	4.6229	4.4859	4.3553	4.2305	4.1114	3.9975	3.8887	3.7845
7	6.7282	6.4720	6.2303	6.0021	5.7864	5.5824	5.3893	5.2064	5.0330	4.8684	4.7122	4.5638	4.4226	4.2883	4.1604
8	7.6517	7.3255	7.0197	6.7327	6.4632	6.2098	5.9713	5.7466	5.5348	5.3349	5.1461	4.9676	4.7988	4.6389	4.4873
9	8.5660	8.1622	7.7861	7.4353	7.1078	6.8017	6.5152	6.2469	5.9952	5.7590	5.5370	5.3282	5.1317	4.9464	4.7716
10	9.4713	8.9826	8.5302	8.1109	7.7217	7.3601	7.0236	6.7101	6.4177	6.1446	5.8892	5.6502	5.4262	5.2161	5.0188
11	10.3676	9.7868	9.2526	8.7605	8.3064	7.8869	7.4987	7.1390	6.8052	6.4951	6.2065	5.9377	5.6869	5.4527	5.2337
12	11.2551	10.5753	9.9540	9.3851	8.8633	8.3838	7.9427	7.5361	7.1607	6.8137	6.4924	6.1944	5.9176	5.6603	5.4206
13	12.1337	11.3484	10.6350	9.9856	9.3936	8.8527	8.3577	7.9038	7.4869	7.1034	6.7499	6.4235	6.1218	5.8424	5.5831
14	13.0037	12.1062	11.2961	10.5631	9.8986	9.2950	8.7455	8.2442	7.7862	7.3667	6.9819	6.6282	6.3025	6.0021	5.7245
15	13.8651	12.8493	11.9379	11.1184	10.3797	9.7122	9.1079	8.5595	8.0607	7.6061	7.1909	6.8109	6.4624	6.1422	5.8474
16	14.7179	13.5777	12.5611	11.6523	10.8378	10.1059	9.4466	8.8514	8.3126	7.8237	7.3792	6.9740	6.6039	6.2651	5.9542
17	15.5623	14.2919	13.1661	12.1657	11.2741	10.4773	9.7632	9.1216	8.5436	8.0216	7.5488	7.1196	6.7291	6.3729	6.0472
18	16.3983	14.9920	13.7535	12.6593	11.6896	10.8276	10.0591	9.3719	8.7556	8.2014	7.7016	7.2497	6.8399	6.4674	6.1280
19	17.2260	15.6785	14.3238	13.1339	12.0853	11.1581	10.3356	9.6036	8.9501	8.3649	7.8393	7.3658	6.9380	6.5504	6.1982
20	18.0456	16.3514	14.8775	13.5903	12.4622	11.4699	10.5940	9.8181	9.1285	8.5136	7.9633	7.4694	7.0248	6.6231	6.2593
21	18.8570	17.0112	15.4150	14.0292	12.8212	11.7641	10.8355	10.0168	9.2922	8.6487	8.0751	7.5620	7.1016	6.6870	6.3125
22	19.6604	17.6580	15.9369	14.4511	13.1630	12.0416	11.0612	10.2007	9.4424	8.7715	8.1757	7.6446	7.1695	6.7429	6.3587
23	20.4558	18.2922	16.4436	14.8568	13.4886	12.3034	11.2722	10.3711	9.5802	8.8832	8.2664	7.7184	7.2297	6.7921	6.3988
24	21.2434	18.9139	16.9355	15.2470	13.7986	12.5504	11.4693	10.5288	9.7066	8.9847	8.3481	7.7843	7.2829	6.8351	6.4338
25	22.0232	19.5235	17.4131	15.6221	14.0939	12.7834	11.6536	10.6748	9.8226	9.0770	8.4217	7.8431	7.3300	6.8729	6.4641
26	22.7952	20.1210	17.8768	15.9828	14.3752	13.0032	11.8258	10.8100	9.9290	9.1609	8.4881	7.8957	7.3717	6.9061	6.4906
27	23.5596	20.7069	18.3270	16.3296	14.6430	13.2105	11.9867	10.9352	10.0266	9.2372	8.5478	7.9426	7.4086	6.9352	6.5135
28	24.3164	21.2813	18.7641	16.6631	14.8981	13.4062	12.1371	11.0511	10.1161	9.3066	8.6016	7.9844	7.4412	6.9607	6.5335
29	25.0658	21.8444	19.1885	16.9837	15.1411	13.5907	12.2777	11.1584	10.1983	9.3696	8.6501	8.0218	7.4701	6.9830	6.5509
30	25.8077	22.3965	19.6004	17.2920	15.3725	13.7648	12.4090	11.2578	10.2737	9.4269	8.6938	8.0552	7.4957	7.0027	6.5660
40	32.8347	27.3555	23.1148	19.7928	17.1591	15.0463	13.3317	11.9246	10.7574	9.7791	8.9511	8.2438	7.6344	7.1050	6.6418
50	39.1961	31.4236	25.7298	21.4822	18.2559	15.7619	13.8007	12.2335	10.9617	9.9148	9.0417	8.3045	7.6752	7.1327	6.6605
100	63.0289	43.0984	31.5989	24.5050	19.8479	16.6175	14.2693	12.4943	11.1091	9.9993	9.0906	8.3332	7.6923	7.1428	6.6667

Table III Continued

	16%	17%	18%	19%	20%	21%	22%	23%	24%	25%	26%	27%	28%	29%	30%
1	0.8621	0.8547	0.8475	0.8403	0.8333	0.8264	0.8197	0.8130	0.8065	0.8000	0.7937	0.7874	0.7813	0.7752	0.7692
2	1.6052	1.5852	1.5656	1.5465	1.5278	1.5095	1.4915	1.4740	1.4568	1.4400	1.4235	1.4074	1.3916	1.3761	1.3609
3	2.2459	2.2096	2.1743	2.1399	2.1065	2.0739	2.0422	2.0114	1.9813	1.9520	1.9234	1.8956	1.8684	1.8420	1.8161
4	2.7982	2.7432	2.6901	2.6386	2.5887	2.5404	2.4936	2.4483	2.4043	2.3616	2.3202	2.2800	2.2410	2.2031	2.1662
5	3.2743	3.1993	3.1272	3.0576	2.9906	2.9260	2.8636	2.8035	2.7454	2.6893	2.6351	2.5827	2.5320	2.4830	2.4356
6	3.6847	3.5892	3.4976	3.4098	3.3255	3.2446	3.1669	3.0923	3.0205	2.9514	2.8850	2.8210	2.7594	2.7000	2.6427
7	4.0386	3.9224	3.8115	3.7057	3.6046	3.5079	3.4155	3.3270	3.2423	3.1611	3.0833	3.0087	2.9370	2.8682	2.8021
8	4.3436	4.2072	4.0776	3.9544	3.8372	3.7256	3.6193	3.5179	3.4212	3.3289	3.2407	3.1564	3.0758	2.9986	2.9247
9	4.6065	4.4506	4.3030	4.1633	4.0310	3.9054	3.7863	3.6731	3.5655	3.4631	3.3657	3.2728	3.1842	3.0997	3.0190
10	4.8332	4.6586	4.4941	4.3389	4.1925	4.0541	3.9232	3.7993	3.6819	3.5705	3.4648	3.3644	3.2689	3.1781	3.0915
11	5.0286	4.8364	4.6560	4.4865	4.3271	4.1769	4.0354	3.9018	3.7757	3.6564	3.5435	3.4365	3.3351	3.2388	3.1473
12	5.1971	4.9884	4.7932	4.6105	4.4392	4.2784	4.1274	3.9852	3.8514	3.7251	3.6059	3.4933	3.3868	3.2859	3.1903
13	5.3423	5.1183	4.9095	4.7147	4.5327	4.3624	4.2028	4.0530	3.9124	3.7801	3.6555	3.5381	3.4272	3.3224	3.2233
14	5.4675	5.2293	5.0081	4.8023	4.6106	4.4317	4.2646	4.1082	3.9616	3.8241	3.6949	3.5733	3.4587	3.3507	3.2487
15	5.5755	5.3242	5.0916	4.8759	4.6755	4.4890	4.3152	4.1530	4.0013	3.8593	3.7261	3.6010	3.4834	3.3726	3.2682
16	5.6685	5.4053	5.1624	4.9377	4.7296	4.5364	4.3567	4.1894	4.0333	3.8874	3.7509	3.6228	3.5026	3.3896	3.2832
17	5.7487	5.4746	5.2223	4.9897	4.7746	4.5755	4.3908	4.2190	4.0591	3.9099	3.7705	3.6400	3.5177	3.4028	3.2948
18	5.8178	5.5339	5.2732	5.0333	4.8122	4.6079	4.4187	4.2431	4.0799	3.9279	3.7861	3.6536	3.5294	3.4130	3.3037
19	5.8775	5.5845	5.3162	5.0700	4.8435	4.6346	4.4415	4.2627	4.0967	3.9424	3.7985	3.6642	3.5386	3.4210	3.3105
20	5.9288	5.6278	5.3527	5.1009	4.8696	4.6567	4.4603	4.2786	4.1103	3.9539	3.8083	3.6726	3.5458	3.4271	3.3158
21	5.9731	5.6648	5.3837	5.1268	4.8913	4.6750	4.4756	4.2916	4.1212	3.9631	3.8161	3.6792	3.5514	3.4319	3.3198
22	6.0113	5.6964	5.4099	5.1486	4.9094	4.6900	4.4882	4.3021	4.1300	3.9705	3.8223	3.6844	3.5558	3.4356	3.3230
23	6.0442	5.7234	5.4321	5.1668	4.9245	4.7025	4.4985	4.3106	4.1371	3.9764	3.8273	3.6885	3.5592	3.4384	3.3254
24	6.0726	5.7465	5.4509	5.1822	4.9371	4.7128	4.5070	4.3176	4.1428	3.9811	3.8312	3.6918	3.5619	3.4406	3.3272
25	6.0971	5.7662	5.4669	5.1951	4.9476	4.7213	4.5139	4.3232	4.1474	3.9849	3.8342	3.6943	3.5640	3.4423	3.3286
26	6.1182	5.7831	5.4804	5.2060	4.9563	4.7284	4.5196	4.3278	4.1511	3.9879	3.8367	3.6963	3.5656	3.4437	3.3297
27	6.1364	5.7975	5.4919	5.2151	4.9636	4.7342	4.5243	4.3316	4.1542	3.9903	3.8387	3.6979	3.5669	3.4447	3.3305
28	6.1520	5.8099	5.5016	5.2228	4.9697	4.7390	4.5281	4.3346	4.1566	3.9923	3.8402	3.6991	3.5679	3.4455	3.3312
29	6.1656	5.8204	5.5098	5.2292	4.9747	4.7430	4.5312	4.3371	4.1585	3.9938	3.8414	3.7001	3.5687	3.4461	3.3317
30	6.1772	5.8294	5.5168	5.2347	4.9789	4.7463	4.5338	4.3391	4.1601	3.9950	3.8424	3.7009	3.5693	3.4466	3.3321
40	6.2335	5.8713	5.5482	5.2582	4.9966	4.7596	4.5439	4.3467	4.1659	3.9995	3.8458	3.7034	3.5712	3.4481	3.3332
50	6.2463	5.8801	5.5541	5.2623	4.9995	4.7616	4.5452	4.3477	4.1666	3.9999	3.8461	3.7037	3.5714	3.4483	3.3333
100	6.2500	5.8824	5.5556	5.2632	5.0000	4.7619	4.5455	4.3478	4.1667	4.0000	3.8462	3.7037	3.5714	3.4483	3.3333

Table IV The sum at the end of n periods that results from the accumulation of 1 at the end of each of n periods at interest rate i

$$S_n = [(1 + i)^n - 1]/i$$

	1%	2%	3%	4%	5%	6%	7%	8%	9%	10%	11%	12%	13%	14%	15%
1	1.0000	1.0000	1.0000	1.0000	1.0000	1.0000	1.0000	1.0000	1.0000	1.0000	1.0000	1.0000	1.0000	1.0000	1.0000
2	2.0100	2.0200	2.0300	2.0400	2.0500	2.0600	2.0700	2.0800	2.0900	2.1000	2.1100	2.1200	2.1300	2.1400	2.1500
3	3.0301	3.0604	3.0909	3.1216	3.1525	3.1836	3.2149	3.2464	3.2781	3.3100	3.3421	3.3744	3.4069	3.4396	3.4725
4	4.0604	4.1216	4.1836	4.2465	4.3101	4.3746	4.4399	4.5061	4.5731	4.6410	4.7097	4.7793	4.8498	4.9211	4.9934
5	5.1010	5.2040	5.3091	5.4163	5.5256	5.6371	5.7507	5.8666	5.9847	6.1051	6.2278	6.3528	6.4803	6.6101	6.7424
6	6.1520	6.3081	6.4684	6.6330	6.8019	6.9753	7.1533	7.3359	7.5233	7.7156	7.9129	8.1152	8.3227	8.5355	8.7537
7	7.2135	7.4343	7.6625	7.8983	8.1420	8.3938	8.6540	8.9228	9.2004	9.4872	9.7833	10.0890	10.4047	10.7305	11.0668
8	8.2857	8.5830	8.8923	9.2142	9.5491	9.8975	10.2598	10.6366	11.0285	11.4359	11.8594	12.2997	12.7573	13.2328	13.7268
9	9.3685	9.7546	10.1591	10.5828	11.0266	11.4913	11.9780	12.4876	13.0210	13.5795	14.1640	14.7757	15.4157	16.0853	16.7858
10	10.4622	10.9497	11.4639	12.0061	12.5779	13.1808	13.8164	14.4866	15.1929	15.9374	16.7220	17.5487	18.4197	19.3373	20.3037
11	11.5668	12.1687	12.8078	13.4864	14.206	14.9716	15.7836	16.6455	17.5603	18.5312	19.5614	20.6546	21.8143	23.0445	24.3493
12	12.6825	13.4121	14.1920	15.0258	15.9171	16.8699	17.8885	18.9771	20.1407	21.3843	22.7132	24.1331	25.6502	27.2707	29.0017
13	13.8093	14.6803	15.6178	16.6268	17.7130	18.8821	20.1406	21.4953	22.9534	24.5227	26.2116	28.0291	29.9847	32.0887	34.3519
14	14.9474	15.9739	17.0863	18.2919	19.5986	21.0151	22.5505	24.2149	26.0192	27.9750	30.0949	32.3926	34.8827	37.5811	40.5047
15	16.0969	17.2934	18.5989	20.0236	21.5786	23.2760	25.1290	27.1521	29.3609	31.7725	34.4054	37.2797	40.4175	43.8424	47.5804
16	17.2579	18.6393	20.1569	21.8245	23.6575	25.6725	27.8881	30.3243	33.0034	35.9497	39.1899	42.7533	46.6717	50.9804	55.7175
17	18.4304	20.0121	21.7616	23.6975	25.8404	28.2129	30.8402	33.7502	36.9737	40.5447	44.5008	48.8837	53.7391	59.1176	65.0751
18	19.6147	21.4123	23.4144	25.6454	28.1324	30.9057	33.9990	37.4502	41.3013	45.5992	50.3959	55.7497	61.7251	68.3941	75.8364
19	20.8109	22.8406	25.1169	27.6712	30.5390	33.7600	37.3790	41.4463	46.0185	51.1591	56.9395	63.4397	70.7494	78.9692	88.2118
20	22.0190	24.2974	26.8704	29.7781	33.0660	36.7856	40.9955	45.7620	51.1601	57.2750	64.2028	72.0524	80.9468	91.0249	102.4436
21	23.2392	25.7833	28.6765	31.9692	35.7193	39.9927	44.8652	50.4229	56.7645	64.0025	72.2651	81.6987	92.4699	104.7684	118.8101
22	24.4716	27.2990	30.5368	34.2480	38.5052	43.3923	49.0057	55.4568	62.8733	71.4027	81.2143	92.5026	105.4910	120.4360	137.6316
23	25.7163	28.8450	32.4529	36.6179	41.4305	46.9958	53.4361	60.8933	69.5319	79.5430	91.1479	104.6029	120.2048	138.2970	159.2764
24	26.9735	30.4219	34.4265	39.0826	44.5020	50.8156	58.1767	66.7648	76.7898	88.4973	102.1742	118.1552	136.8315	158.6586	184.1678
25	28.2432	32.0303	36.4593	41.6459	47.7271	54.8645	63.2490	73.1059	84.7009	98.3471	114.4133	133.3339	155.6196	181.8708	212.7930
26	29.5256	33.6709	38.5530	44.3117	51.1135	59.1564	68.6765	79.9544	93.3240	109.1818	127.9988	150.3339	176.8501	208.3327	245.7120
27	30.8209	35.3443	40.7096	47.0842	54.6691	63.7058	74.4838	87.3508	102.7231	121.0999	143.0786	169.3740	200.8406	238.4993	283.5688
28	32.1291	37.0512	42.9309	49.9676	58.4026	68.5281	80.6977	95.3388	112.9682	134.2099	159.8173	190.6989	227.9499	272.8892	327.1041
29	33.4504	38.7922	45.2189	52.9663	62.3227	73.6398	87.3465	103.9659	124.1354	148.6309	178.3972	214.5828	258.5834	312.0937	377.1697
30	34.7849	40.5681	47.5754	56.0849	66.4388	79.0582	94.4608	113.2832	136.3075	164.4940	199.0209	241.3327	293.1992	356.7868	434.7451
40	48.8864	60.4020	75.4013	95.0255	120.7998	154.7620	199.6351	259.0565	337.8824	442.5926	581.8261	767.0914			
50	64.4632	84.5794	112.7969	152.6671	209.3480	290.3359	406.5289	573.7702	815.0836						
100	170.4814	312.2323	607.2877												

Table IV Continued

	16%	17%	18%	19%	20%	21%	22%	23%	24%	25%	26%	27%	28%	29%	30%
1	1.0000	1.0000	1.0000	1.0000	1.0000	1.0000	1.0000	1.0000	1.0000	1.0000	1.0000	1.0000	1.0000	1.0000	1.0000
2	2.1600	2.1700	2.1800	2.1900	2.2000	2.2100	2.2200	2.2300	2.2400	2.2500	2.2600	2.2700	2.2800	2.2900	2.3000
3	3.5056	3.5389	3.5724	3.6061	3.6400	3.6741	3.7084	3.7429	3.7776	3.8125	3.8476	3.8829	3.9184	3.9541	3.9900
4	5.0665	5.1405	5.2154	5.2913	5.3680	5.4457	5.5242	5.6083	5.6842	5.7656	5.8480	5.9313	6.0156	6.1008	6.1870
5	6.8771	7.0144	7.1542	7.2966	7.4416	7.5892	7.7396	7.8926	8.0484	8.2070	8.3684	8.5327	8.6999	8.8700	9.0431
6	8.9775	9.2068	9.4420	9.6830	9.9299	10.1830	10.4423	10.7079	10.9801	11.2588	11.5442	11.8366	12.1359	12.4423	12.7560
7	11.4139	11.7720	12.1415	12.5227	12.9159	13.3214	13.7396	14.1708	14.6153	15.0735	15.5458	16.0324	16.5339	17.0506	17.5828
8	14.2401	14.7733	15.3270	15.9020	16.4991	17.1189	17.7623	18.4300	19.1229	19.8419	20.5876	21.3612	22.1634	22.9953	23.8577
9	17.5185	18.2847	19.0859	19.9234	20.7989	21.7139	22.6700	23.6690	24.7125	25.8023	26.9404	28.1287	29.3692	30.6639	32.0150
10	21.3215	22.3931	23.5213	24.7089	25.9587	27.2738	28.6574	30.1128	31.6434	33.2529	34.9449	36.7235	38.5926	40.5564	42.6195
11	25.7329	27.1999	28.7551	30.4035	32.1504	34.0013	35.9620	38.0388	40.2379	42.5661	45.0306	47.6388	50.3985	53.3178	56.4053
12	30.8502	32.8239	34.9311	37.1802	39.5805	42.1416	44.8737	47.7877	50.8950	54.2077	57.7386	61.5013	65.5100	69.7800	74.3270
13	36.7862	39.4040	42.2187	45.2445	48.4966	51.9913	55.7459	59.7788	64.1097	68.7596	73.7506	79.1066	84.8529	91.0161	97.6250
14	43.6720	47.1027	50.8180	54.8409	59.1959	63.9095	69.0100	74.5280	80.4961	86.9495	93.9258	101.4654	109.6117	118.4108	127.9125
15	51.6595	56.1101	60.9653	66.2607	72.0351	78.3305	85.1922	92.6694	100.8151	109.6868	119.3465	129.8611	141.3029	153.7500	167.2863
16	60.9250	66.6488	72.9390	79.8502	87.4421	95.7799	104.9345	114.9834	126.0108	138.1085	151.3766	165.9236	181.8677	199.3374	218.4722
17	71.6730	78.9792	87.0680	96.0218	105.9306	116.8937	129.0201	142.4295	157.2534	173.6357	191.7345	211.7230	233.7907	258.1453	285.0139
18	84.1407	93.4056	103.7403	115.2659	128.1167	142.4413	158.4045	176.1883	195.9942	218.0446	242.5855	269.8882	300.2521	334.0074	371.5180
19	98.6032	110.2846	123.4135	138.1664	154.7400	173.3540	194.2535	217.7116	244.0328	273.5558	306.6577	343.7580	385.3227	431.8696	483.9734
20	115.3797	130.0329	146.6280	165.4180	186.6880	210.7584	237.9893	268.7853	303.6006	342.9447	387.3887	437.5726	494.2131	558.1118	630.1655
21	134.8405	153.1385	174.0210	197.8474	225.0256	256.0176	291.3469	331.6059	377.4648	429.6809	489.1098	556.7173	633.5927	720.9642	820.2151
22	157.4150	180.1721	206.3448	236.4385	271.0307	310.7813	356.4432	408.8753	469.0563	538.1011	617.2783	708.0309	811.9987	931.0438	
23	183.6014	211.8013	244.4868	282.3618	326.2369	377.0454	435.8607	503.9166	582.6298	673.6264	778.7707	900.1993			
24	213.9776	248.8076	289.4945	337.0105	392.4842	457.2249	532.7501	620.8174	723.4610	843.0329	982.2511				
25	249.2140	292.1049	342.6035	402.0425	471.9811	554.2422	650.9551	764.6054	898.0916						
26	290.0883	342.7627	405.2721	479.4306	567.3773	671.6330	795.1653	941.4647							
27	337.5024	402.0323	479.2211	571.5224	681.8528	813.6759	971.1016								
28	392.5028	471.3778	566.4809	681.1116	819.2233	985.5479									
29	456.3032	552.5121	669.4475	811.5228	984.0680										
30	530.3117	647.4391	790.9480	966.7122											

Bibliography

Aharony, J. and Swary, I. (1980). Quarterly dividends and earnings announcements and stockholders' returns: An empirical analysis. *Journal of Finance*, March, pp. 1–12.

Akerlof, G. (1970). The market for 'LEMONS': Quality, uncertainty and the market mechanism. *Quarterly Journal of Economics*, Autumn, pp. 488–500.

Alexander, S.S. (1961). Price movements in speculative markets: Trends or random walks? *Industrial Management Review*, May.

Allen, D. (1986). Model that is at odds with logic. *Accountancy Age*, 27 November, pp. 34–5.

Altman, E.A. (1968). Financial ratios, discriminant analysis and the prediction of corporate bankruptcy. *Journal of Finance*, September, pp. 589–609.

Altman, E.I. and Subrahmanyan, M.G. (eds) (1985). *Recent Advances in Corporate Finance*. Irwin, Homewood, Illinois.

Anderson, W.M.L. (1965). *Corporate Finance and Fixed Investment: An Econometric Study*. Harvard University, Cambridge, Mass.

Ando, A. and Modigliani, F. (1963). The 'life cycle' hypothesis of saving: Aggregate implications and tests. *American Economic Review*, March, pp. 55–84.

Ang, J. (1975). Dividend policy: Informational content or partial adjustment. *Review of Economics and Statistics*, 1975.

Arnold, T.S. (1984). How to do interest rate swaps. *Harvard Business Review*, September-October, pp. 96–101.

Atrill, P. and McLaney, E. (1987). Stockbrokers' profit forecasts: Are some forecasters more reliable than others? *Investment Analyst*, January, pp. 29–32.

Backus, D. and Purvis, D. (1980). An integrated model of household flow of funds allocation. *Journal of Money, Credit and Banking* **12**, pp. 400–21.

Bain, A.D. (1973). Flow of funds analysis: A survey. *Economic Journal*, December, pp. 1055–93.

Bain, A.D., Day, C.L. and Wearing, A.L. (1975). *Company Financing in the UK: A Flow of Funds Model*. Martin Robertson, London.

Baker, G. (1980). *Compensation and Hierarchies*. Mimeograph from Harvard Business School.

Baker, H., Kent, G.E.F., and Edelman, R.B. (1985). A survey of management views on dividend policy. *Financial Management*, Autumn, pp. 78–84.

Ball, R. and Brown P. (1968). An empirical evaluation of accounting income numbers. *Journal of Accounting Research*, Autumn, pp. 159–78.

Bank of England (1978a). *United Kingdom Flows of Funds Accounts 1963–1976*. London.

Bank of England (1978b) Companies' long-term financial decisions. *Quarterly Bulletin*, May, pp. 261–4.

Bank of England (1980). Dividend payments: Some recent trends, *Quarterly Bulletin*, pp. 33–41.

Bank of England (1982). Venture capital. *Quarterly Bulletin*, December, pp. 511–13.

Bank of England (1983). *Money for Business*, 4th edn. London.

Bank of England (1983). Unlisted securities market. *Quarterly Bulletin*, June, pp. 227–31.

Bank of England (1984). Venture capital in the United Kingdom. *Quarterly Bulletin*, June, pp. 207–11.

Bank of England (1985a). Developments in leasing. *Quarterly Review*, December, pp. 582–85.

Bank of England (1985b). The unlisted securities market. *Quarterly Review*, December, pp. 537–42.

Bank of England (1987). Pre-emption rights. *Quarterly Bulletin*, November pp. 545–9.

Bank of England (1988a) The financial behaviour of industrial and commercial companies, 1970–86. *Quarterly Bulletin*, **28**(1), 75–82.

Bank of England (1988b). Share re-purchase of quoted companies. *Quarterly Bulletin*, August, pp. 382–90.

Bank of England (1990a). Venture capital in the United Kingdom. *Quarterly Bulletin*, February, pp. 78–83.

Bank of England (1990b). New equity issues in the United Kingdom. *Quarterly Bulletin*, May, pp. 243–52.

Banz, R.W. (1981). The relationship between return and market value of common stock. *Journal of Financial Economics*, March, pp. 3–18.

Bass, R.M.V. (1979). *Credit Management*. Business Books. London.

Basu, S. (1977). The relationship between earnings yield, market value and return for NYSE common stocks: Further evidence. *Journal of Financial Economics*, June, pp. 124–56.

Bates, J.A. (1964). *The Financing of Small Business*. Sweet and Maxwell, London.

Baumol, W.J. (1952). The transaction demand for cash: An inventory theoretic approach. *Quarterly Journal of Economics*, November, pp. 545–56.

Baumol, W.J. (1958). On the theory of oligopoly. *Economica*, Vol. XXV, pp. 187–98.

Baumol, W.J. (1982). Contestible markets: An uprising in the theory of industry structure. *American Economic Review*, March, pp. 1–15.

Beaver, W.H. (1968). The information content of annual earnings announcements. *Empirical Research in Accounting: Selected Studies*. Supplement to *Journal of Accounting Research*, pp. 67–92.

Beedles, W.L. (1984). Some notes on the cost of new equity, *Journal of Business Finance and Accounting*, Summer, pp. 245–51.

Beranek, W. (1966). *Working Capital Management*. Wadsworth, Belmont, California.

Berle, A.A. and Means, G.C. (1932). *The Modern Corporation and Private Property* (revised edn, 1967). Harcourt, Brace and World, New York.

Black, F. (1976). The dividend puzzle. *Journal of Portfolio Management* (2), Winter, pp. 5–8.

Black , F., Jensen, M.C. and Scholes, M. (1972). The Capital Pricing Model: Some empirical tests. In M.C. Jensen (ed.), *Studies in the Theory of Capital Markets*. Praeger, New York.

Black, F. and Scholes, M.S. (1973). The pricing of options and corporate liabilities. *Journal of Political Economy*, **3**, pp. 637–54.

Black, F. and Scholes, M.S. (1974). The effects of dividend yield and dividend policy on common stock prices and returns. *Journal of Financial Economics*, May, pp. 1–22.

Boulding, K.E. (1956). General systems theory: The skeleton of a science. *Management Science*, April, pp. 197–208.

Brealey, R.M. and Myers, S.M. (1984). *Principles of Corporate Finance*. McGraw-Hill.

Brennan, M.J. (1970). Taxes, market valuation and corporate financial policy. *National Tax Journal*, December, pp. 417–27.

Brennan, M.J. (1971). A note on dividend irrelevance and the Gordon valuation model. *Journal of Finance*, December, pp. 1115–22.

Brenner, M. (1977). The effect of model misspecification on tests of the efficient market hypothesis. *Journal of Finance*, pp. 57–66.

Bridge, J. and Dodds, J.C. (1975). *Managerial Decision Making*, Croom Helm, London.

Bridge, J. and Dodds, J.C. (1978). *Planning and the Growth of the Firm*, Croom Helm, London.

Brigham, E.F. and Gapenski, L.C. (1987). *Intermediate Financial Management*. Dryden Press, San Diego, California.

Briston, R.J. and Tomkins, C.R. (1970). The impact of the introduction of corporation tax upon the dividend policies of the UK companies, September.

British Bond Ratings (1974). Exposure draft. *Investment Analyst*, December, pp. 17–26.

British Bond Ratings (1976). A reply. *Investment Analyst*, March, pp. 5–16.

Brooke, M.Z. and Remmers, H.L. (1970). *The Strategy of Multinational Enterprise*. Longman, London.

Brooks, J. (1971). *Business Adventures*. Pelican, London.

Buckland, R. and Davis, E.W. (1989). *The Unlisted Securities Market*, Clarendon Press, Oxford.

Carpenter, M.D. and Miller, J.E. (1979). A reliable framework for monitoring accounts receivable. *Financial Management* **8** (4), Winter, pp. 37–40.

Charest, G. (1978). Split information, stock returns, and market efficiency — I. *Journal of Financial Economics* **6**.

Chen, H. and Kensinger, J.W. (1958). *The Ownership Structure: Corporate Financial Decisions*. Mimeograph from the School of Business, Southern Methodist University.

Chowdhury, G. and Miles, D.K. (1987). Companies' long-term financial decisions: dividend and debt: evidence from company accounts data. Bank of England *Quarterly Bulletin*, May, and *Discussion Paper*, No. 28.

Chowdhury, G., Green, C.J. and Miles, D.K. (1986). Companies' short-term financial decisions. *Bank of England Quarterly Bulletin*, pp. 78–80.

Cissell, H. and Cissell, R. (1973). *Mathematics of Finance*, 4th edn. Houghton Mifflin, Boston, Mass.

Clarkham, J. (1989). Corporate governance and the market for companies: aspects of the shareholders role. *Bank of England Discussion Paper*, No. 44.

Clayton, G., Dodds, J.C., Ghosh, D. and Ford, J.L. (1974). An econometric model of the UK financial sector: Some preliminary findings. In Johnson, H.G. and Nobay, A.R. (eds), *Issues in Monetary Economics*. Clarendon Press, Oxford.

Coase, R.H. (1937). The nature of the firm. *Economica*, pp. 386–405.

Cooper, D.J. (1975). Rationality and investment appraisal. *Accounting and Business Research*, Summer, pp. 198–202.

Copeland, M.A. (1952). *Study of Money Flows in the United States*. National Bureau of Economic Research, New York.

Copeland, T.E. and Weston, J.F. (1983). *Financial Theory and Corporate Policy*, 2nd edn. Addison-Wesley, Wokingham, Berks.

Corbett, J. (1987). International perspectives on financing: Evidence from Japan. *Oxford Review of Economic Policy* **3**(4), pp. 30–54.

Cox, J.C., Ingersoll, J. and Ross, S.A. (1981). The relation between forward prices and futures markets. *Journal of Financial Economics*, pp. 321–46.

Cragg, J. and Malkiel, B. (1968). The consensus and accuracy of some predictions of the growth of corporate earnings. *Journal of Finance*, **23**, pp. 67–84.

Cranfield School of Management (1979). *Finance Leasing Research Report*. Cranfield School of Management, Bedford.

Cross Report (1986). *Recent Innovations in International Banking*. Bank for International Settlements, Basel.

Cyert, R.M. and March, J.G. (1963). *The Behavioural Theory of the Firm*. Prentice-Hall, Englewood Cliffs, New Jersey.

Daellenbach, H.G. (1974). Are cash management optimization models worthwhile? *Journal of Financial and Quantitative Analysis*, September, pp. 607–26.

De Angelo, H. and Masulis, W. (1980). Optimal capital structure under corporate and personal taxation. *Journal of Financial Economics*, pp. 3–30.

De Leeuw, F. (1965). A model of financial behaviour. In Duesenberry, J., Fromm, G., Klein, L.R. and Kuch, E. (eds), *Brookings Quarterly Econometric Model of the United States*. Rand McNally, Chicago, pp. 465–530.

Demsetz, H. (1983). The structure of ownership and the theory of the firm. *Journal of Law and Economics*, June, pp. 375–90.

Devereux, M. (1987). Taxation and the cost of capital: The UK experience. *Oxford Review of Economic Policy* **3** (4), pp. xvii–xxxii.

Dobbins, R. and Pike, R. (1982). How much should a firm borrow? *Managerial Finance* **8** (1), pp. 17–22.

Dodds, J.C. (1979). *The Investment Behavior of British Life Offices*. Croom Helm, London.

Dodds, J.C. and Dobbins, R. (1985). Institutional transactions in financial assets. *Managerial Finance* **11** (3/4), pp. 26–60.

Donald, D.W.A. (1970). *Compound Interest and Annuities Certain*. Cambridge University Press, Cambridge.

Donaldson, G. (1984). *Managing Corporate Wealth*. Praeger, New York.

Dryden, M. (1970). Filter tests of UK share prices. *Applied Economics*.

Dundas Hamilton, J. (1986). *Stockbroking Tomorrow*. Macmillan, London.

Dyl, E.A. and Hoffmeister, J.R. (1986). A note on dividend policy and beta. *Journal of Business Finance and Accounting*, Spring, pp. 107–15.

Edwards, J. (1987). Recent developments in the theory of corporate finance. *Oxford Review of Economic Policy*, **3** (4), pp. 1–12.

Elton, E.J., Gruber, M.J. and Rentzler, J. (1983a). Employing financial futures to increase the return on near cash (treasury bill) investments. *Working Paper 301*, September. Graduate School of Business Administration, New York University.

Elton, E.J., Gruber, M.J. and Rentzler, J. (1983b). Intra-day tests of the efficiency of the treasury bill futures market. *Review of Economics and Statistics*.

Fama, E.F. (1980). Agency problems and the theory of the firm. *Journal of Political Economy*, April, pp. 288–307.

Fama, E.F. and Babiak, H. (1968). Dividend policy: an empirical analysis. *Journal of the American Statistical Association*, December, pp. 1132–61.

Fama, E. and Jensen, M. (1983a). Separation of ownership and control. *Journal of Law and Economics*, June, pp. 301–26.

Fama, E. and Jensen, M. (1983b). Agency problems and residual claims, *Journal of Law and Economics*, June, pp. 327–50.

Fama, E.F. and Macbeth, J. (1973). Risk, return and equilibrium: empirical tests. *Journal of Political Economy*, May/June, pp. 607–36.

Fama, E.F. and Miller, M. (1972). *The Theory of Finance*. Holt, Rinehart and Winston, New York.

Fama, E.F., Fisher, L., Jensen, M. and Roll, R. (1969). The adjustment of stock prices to new information. *International Economic Review*, February, pp. 1–21.

Fawthrop, R.A. and Terry, B. (1976). The evaluation of an integrated investment and lease financing decision. *Journal of Business, Finance and Accounting*, Autumn, pp. 79–111.

Feldstein, M.C. (1964). The social time preference discount rate in cost benefit analysis. *Economic Journal*, June, pp. 360–79.

Ferris, P. (1962). *The City*. Pelican, London.

Findlay, M.C. and Williams, E.E. (1980). A positivist evaluation of the new finance. *Financial Management*, Summer, pp. 7–17.

Fisher, I. (1930). *The Theory of Interest*. Holt, Rinehart and Winston, New York.

Fouse, W.L., Jahnke, W.W. and Rozenberg, B. (1974). Is beta phlogiston? *Financial Analysts Journal* **30**, pp. 70–80.

Francis, J.C. and Archer, S.H. (1971). *Portfolio Analysis*, 1st edn. Prentice-Hall, Englewood Cliffs, New Jersey.

Francis, J.C. and Archer, S.H. (1979). *Portfolio Analysis*, 2nd edn. Prentice-Hall, Englewood Cliffs, New Jersey.

Franks, J.R. and Hodges, J.D. (1978). Valuation of financial lease contracts: A note. *Journal of Finance*, May, pp. 657–89.

French, K.R. (1980). Stock Returns and the Weekend Effect. *Journal of Financial Economics*, **8** (1), pp. 55–69.

Friedman, M. (1957). *A Theory of the Consumption Function*. University Press, Princeton, New Jersey.

Friend, I. (1973). Mythodology in finance. *Journal of Finance*, August, pp. 329–52.

Galletly, G. and Ritchie, N. (1986). *The Big Bang*. Northcote House, Plymouth.

Gillespie, R.J. (1984) Workstation technology dominates conference. *Pensions and Investment Age*, 12 November, pp. 25–6.

Gitman, L.J., Moses, E.A. and White, I.T. (1977). An assessment of theory, practice and future trends in cash management. Paper presented at the annual meeting of the Financial Management Association, Seattle, October.

Givoly, D. and Lakonishok, J. (1979). The information content of financial analysts' forecasts of earnings: some evidence on semi-strong inefficiency. *Journal of Economics and Accounting* **1**, pp. 165–85.

Gordon, M.J. (1955). The Payoff Period and the Rate of Profit. *Journal of Business*, **28**, pp. 253–60.

Gordon, M.J. (1959) Dividends, earnings and stock prices. *Review of Economics and Statistics*, May, pp. 99–105.

Graham, B. and Dodd, D.C. (1951). *Security Analysis: Principles and Techniques*. McGraw-Hill, New York.

Grout, P. (1987). Wider share ownership and economic performance. *Oxford Review of Economic Policy* **3** (4), pp. 13–29.

Hackett, J.T. (1985). Concepts and practice of agency theory within the corporation. In E.I. Altman and M.G. Subrahmanyan (eds), *Recent Advances in Corporate Finance*. Irwin, Homewood, Illinois.

Hamilton, A. (1968). *The Financial Revolution*. Penguin, Harmondsworth.

Hartley, W.C.F. and Meltzer, Y.L. (1979). *Cash Management*. Prentice-Hall, Englewood Cliffs, New Jersey.

Haugen, R. and Senbet, L. (1978). The insignificance of bankruptcy costs to the theory of optimal capital structure. *Journal of Finance*, pp. 383–93.

Hawanini, G.A. and Vora, A. (1982). Yield approximations: a historical perspective. *Journal of Finance*, March, pp. 145–56.

Hayes, R.H. and Garvin, D.A. (1982). Managing as if tomorrow mattered. *Harvard Business Review*, May–June, pp. 70–79.

Hemmings, D.B. (1982). An introduction to options. *Managerial Finance* **8** (2), pp. 15–21.

Henderson, P.D. (1968) Investment criteria for public enterprise. In R. Turvey (ed.), *Public Enterprise*. Penguin, Harmondsworth.

Hertz, D.B. (1964). Risk analysis in capital investment. *Harvard Business Review*, February.

Higson, C.J. (1986) *Business Finance*, Butterworths, London.

Hillier, F.S. (1963). The derivation of probabilistic information for the evaluation of risky investments. *Management Science*, April.

Hirshleifer, J. (1968). On the theory of optimal investment decision. *Journal of Political Economics*, August, pp. 329–52.

Hodgman, D.R. (1963). *Commercial Bank Loan and Investment Policy*. University of Illinois Press, Illinois.

Hopewell, M.N. and Kaufman, G.G. (1973). Bond Price Volatility and Term to Maturity: A Generalised Respecification. *American Economic Review*, **63**, pp. 749–53.

Hudson, T.G. and Butterworth, J. (1974). *Management of Trade Credit*. Gower, Aldershot.

Hull, J.C. and Hubbard, G.L. (1980). Lease evaluation in the UK: current theory and practice, *Journal of Business Finance and Accounting*, Winter, pp. 619–37.

Ibbotson, R.G. and Jaffe, J.F. (1975). 'Hot issue' markets, *Journal of Finance*, pp. 1027–42.

Ingham, G. (1984). *Capitalism Divided?* Cambridge University Press, Cambridge.

International Monetary Fund (1986). International capital markets: Developments and prospects. *Occasional Paper 43*. IMF, Washington, DC.

Jackson, P.D. (1984). Financial asset portfolio allocation by industrial and commercial companies. *Discussion Paper Technical Series, No. 8*. Bank of England, February.

Jennings, E.H. (1974). An estimate of convertible bond premiums. *Journal of Finance and Quantitative Analysis*, January, pp. 35–56.

Jensen, M.C. (1968). The performance of mutual funds in the period 1945–1964. *Journal of Finance*, May, pp. 389–416.

Jensen, M.C. (1986). Agency costs of free cash flow, corporate finance and takeover. *American Economic Review*, May.

Jensen, M.C. and Bennington, G. (1970). Random walks and technical theories: some additional evidence. *Journal of Finance*.

Jensen, M.C. and Meckling, W. (1976). Theory of the firm: Managerial behaviour, agency costs and ownership structure. *Journal of Financial Economics*, October, pp. 305–60.

Jensen, M.C. and Smith, C.W. (1985). Stockholder, manager and creditor interests: Applications of agency theory. In E. Altman and M. Subrahmanyam (eds), *Recent Advances in Corporate Finance*. Irwin, Homewood, Illinois.

John, K. and Kalay, A. (1985). Informational content of optimal debt contracts. In E.I.

Altman and M.G. Subrahmanyan (eds), *Recent Advances in Corporate Finance*, Irwin, Homewood, Illinois.

Kay, J.A. (1976). Accountants too could be happy in a golden age: the accountant's rate of profit and the internal rate of return. *Oxford Economic Papers* **3**, November, pp. 447–60.

Kay, W. (1986). *The Big Bang: An Investor's Guide to the Changing City*. Weidenfeld and Nicolson, London.

Keane, S. (1983). *Stock Market Efficiency: Theory, Evidence and Implications*. Philip Allan, Oxford.

Kendall, R. (1953). The analysis of economic time series part I: prices. *Journal of the Royal Statistical Society* **96**, Part I.

Keynes, J.M. (1930). *A Treatise on Money*, Macmillan, London.

Keynes, J.M. (1936). *The General Theory of Employment, Interest and Money*. Macmillan, London.

Kim, E.H. (1978). A mean-variance theory of optimal capital structure and corporate debt capacity. *Journal of Finance*, pp. 45–63.

Kirkman, P. and Nobes, C. (1976). Dividend policy and inflation. *Accountancy*, October, pp. 71–4.

Klammer, T.P. and Walker, M.C. (1984). The continuing increase in the use of sophisticated capital budgeting techniques. *California Management Review*, **27** (1), pp. 137–48.

Knight, F.H. (1921). *Risk, Uncertainty and Profit*. Houghton-Mifflin, Boston, Mass.

Kraus, A. and Litzenberger, R. (1973). A state-preference model of optimal finance leverage. *Journal of Finance*, September, pp. 911–22.

Larcker, D., Gordon, L. and G. Pinches (1980). Testing for market efficiency: A comparison of the cumulative average residual methodology and interaction analysis. *Journal of Financial and Quantitative Analysis*.

Laub, P. (1976). On the informational content of dividends, *Journal of Business*.

Lawson, G.H. and Windle, D.W. (1965). *Tables*. Oliver and Boyd, Harlow.

Lee, C.J. (1986). Information content of financial columns. *Journal of Economics and Business* **38**, pp. 27–39.

Lee, T.A. and Tweedie, D.P. (1981). *The Institutional Investor and Financial Information*. ICAEW, London.

Lessard, D.L. (1986). Finance in global competition: Exploiting financial scope and coping with volatile exchange rates. In Michael E. Porter (ed.), *Competition in Global Industries*. Harvard Business School Press, Boston, Mass.

LIFFE, (n.d.). *The London International Financial Exchange: An Introduction*, 2nd edn.

Lintner, J. (1956). Distribution of incomes of corporations among dividends, retained earnings and taxes. *American Economic Review*, May, pp. 97–113.

Lintner, J. (1962). Dividends, earnings, leverage, stock prices and the supply of capital to corporations. *Review of Economics and Statistics*, August, pp. 243–69.

Lintner, J. (1965a). The valuation of risk assets and the selection of risky investments in stock portfolios and capital budgets. *Review of Economics and Statistics*, February, pp. 13–37.

Lintner, J. (1965b). Security prices, risk and maximal gains from diversification. *Journal of Finance*, December, pp. 587–615.

Lister, R.J. (1981). The cost of retained earnings. A comment on some recent works. *Journal of the Royal Statistical Society* **96**, Part I.

Litzenberger, R. and Ramaswamy, K. (1979). The effect of personal taxes and dividends on Capital Asset Prices: some empirical evidence, *Journal of Financial Economics*, June, pp. 163–95.

Lorie, J.H. and Hamilton, M.T. (1973). *The Stock Market: Theories and Evidence*. Irwin, Homewood, Illinois.

Lowe, E.A. (1972). The finance director's role in the formulation and implementation of strategy. *Journal of Business Finance* **4** (4), p. 61.

Lumby, S. (1984). *Investment Appraisal*, 2nd edn. Van Nostrand, Wokingham.

Macaulay, F.R. (1938) *The Movements of Interest Rates, Bond Yields, and Stock Prices in the United States since 1856*. National Bureau of Economic Research, New York.

McCauley, R. and Zimmer, S. (1989). Explaining international differences in the cost of capital. Federal Reserve *Bank of New York Quarterly Review*, Summer, pp. 7–28.

McIntyre, A.D. and Coulthurst, N.J. (1985). Theory and practice in capital budgeting. *British Accounting Review*, Autumn, pp. 24–70.

Macmillan Committee (1931). *Committee on Finance and Industry Report*, Cmd 3897, HMSO.

MacQueen, J. (1986). Beta is dead: Long live beta! In Stern and Chew (eds), *The Revolution in Corporate Finance*. Blackwell, Oxford.

Markowitz, H.M. (1952). Portfolio selection. *Journal of Finance*, March, pp. 77–91.

Markowitz, H.M. (1959). *Portfolio Selection*, Wiley, New York.

Marris, R.L. (1964). *The Economic Theory of Managerial Capitalism*. Macmillan, London.

Marsh, P. (1977). An analysis of equity rights issues on the London Stock Exchange. Unpublished PhD dissertation, London Business School.

Marsh, P. (1979). Equity rights issues and the efficiency of the UK stock market. *Journal of Finance*, September, pp. 839–62.

Marsh, P. (1980). Valuation of underwriting agreements for UK rights issues. *Journal of Finance*, June, pp. 693–716.

Mayer, C.P. (1986). Corporation tax, finance and the cost of capital. *Review of Economic Studies* **53**, pp. 93–112.

Meeks, G. and Whittington, G. (1975). Giant companies in the United Kingdom, 1948–69. *Economic Journal*, December, pp. 824–43.

Meeks, G. and Whittington, G. (1976). The financing of ousted companies in the UK. Background paper to *Report No. 2, Income from Companies and its Distribution*. Royal Commission on the Distribution of Income and Wealth, HMSO.

Midland Bank (1986). Investment and the tax system in the UK. *Midland Bank Review*, Spring, pp. 5–13.

Miller, M.H. (1977). Debt and taxes. *Journal of Finance*, June, pp. 261–75.

Miller, M.H. (1986). Can management use dividends to influence the value of the firm? In J.M. Stern and D.H. Chew jr (eds), *The Revolution in Corporate Finance*. Blackwell, Oxford.

Miller, M.H. and Modigliani, F. (1961). Dividend policy, growth and the valuation of shares. *Journal of Business*, October, pp. 411–33.

Miller, M.H. and Orr, D. (1966). A model of the demand for money by firms. *Quarterly Journal of Economics*, August, pp. 413–35.

Miller, M.H. and Scholes, M.S. (1978). Dividends and taxes. *Journal of Financial Economics*, December, pp. 35–7.

Modigliani, F. and Brumberg, G. (1955). Utility analysis and the consumption function: An interpretation of cross-section data. In K.K. Kurihara (ed.), *Post-Keynesian Economics*. Allen and Unwin, London.

Modigliani, F. and Miller, M.H. (1958). The cost of capital, corporation finance and the theory of investment. *American Economic Review*, June, pp. 261–97.

Modigliani, F. and Miller, M.H. (1963). Corporate income taxes and the cost of capital: A correction. *American Economic Review*, May, pp. 435–43.

Moir, C. (1987). Big bang: Uneasy calm as the dust settles. *The Observer*, 15 February, p. 31.

Mossin, J. (1968). Equilibrium in a capital asset market. *Econometrica*, October, pp. 769–83.

Moyer, R.C., McGuigan, J.R. and Kretlow, W.J. (1987). *Contemporary Financial Management*, 3rd edn. West Publishing, St Pauls.

Mullins, D. and Homonoff, R. (1976). Applications of inventory cash management models. In S.C. Myers (ed.), *Modern Developments in Financial Management*, Praeger, New York.

Murphy, K.J. (1985). Corporate performance and managerial remunerations: an empirical analysis. *Journal of Accounting and Economics*, April, pp. 11–42.

Myers, S.C. (1974). Interactions of corporate financing and investment decisions: implications for capital budgeting. *Journal of Finance*, March.

Myers, S.C. (1977). Determinants of corporate borrowing. *Journal of Financial Economics*, November, pp. 147–75.

Myers, S.C. (1987). Finance theory and financial strategy. *Midland Corporate Finance Journal*, Spring, pp. 6–13.

Myers, S.C., Dill, D.A. and Bautista, A.J. (1976). Valuation of financial lease contracts. *Journal of Finance*, June, pp. 799–819.

Neuberger, A. and Schwartz, R.A. (1989). *Current Developments in the London Equity Market*, New York University School of Business Working Paper No. 532.

Orgler, Y.E. (1970). *Cash Management*, Wadsworth, Belmont, Calif.

Ott, M. and Santoni, G.J. (1985). Mergers and takeovers: The value of predators' information. Federal Reserve Bank of St Louis, December, pp. 16–28.

Owen, G.W. (1982). The demand for money by companies. *Management Decision*,

Palframan, D. (1989). Why small banks big. *Management Today*, November, pp. 157–63.

Parkin, J.M., Summer, M.P. and Ward, R. (1973). Wage behavior in an open economy, excess demand, generalised expectations and incomes policies in the UK. In K. Brunner and A.H. Meltzer (eds), *Proceedings of the Conference on Wage and Price Controls at Rochester University*.

Peasnell, K. and Ward, C.R. (1985). *British Financial Markets and Institutions*. Prentice-Hall, Englewood Cliffs, New Jersey.

Penrose, E.T. (1959). *The Theory of the Growth of the Firm*, Blackwell, Oxford.

Peters, T.J. and Waterman, R.H. (1982). *In Search of Excellence: Lessons from America's Best Run Companies*, Harper & Row, New York.

Peterson, D. and Rice, M. (1980). A note on ambiguity in portfolio performance measures. *Journal of Finance*, December, pp. 1251–6.

Pettit, R. (1973). Dividend announcements, security performance, and capital market efficiency. *Journal of Finance*, December, pp. 993–1007.

Pettit, R. (1976). The impact of dividend and earnings announcements: A reconciliation. *Journal of Business*, January, pp. 86–96.

Pike, R.H. (1988). An empirical study of the adoption of sophisticated capital budgeting practices and decision-making effectiveness. *Accounting and Business Research*, **18** (72), pp. 341–51.

Plender, J. and Wallace, P. (1985). *The Square Mile: A Guide to the City Revolution*. Hutchinson, London.

Porterfield, J.T.S. (1965). *Investment Decisions and Capital Costs*. Prentice-Hall, Englewood Cliffs, New Jersey.

Quinn, L.R. (1989). How corporations use off-exchange instruments. *Futures*, **18** (3), pp. 44–7.

Radcliffe, Committee (1959). *Report of the Committee on the Working of the Monetary System*, Cmnd. 827, HMSO.

Rayner, A.C. and Little, I.M.D. (1966). *Higgledy Piggledy Growth Again: An Investigation of the Predictability of Company Earnings and Dividends in the UK 1951–61*. Blackwell, Oxford.

Reinganum, M. (1981). Misspecification of capital asset pricing: Empirical anomalies based on earnings yield and market values. *Journal of Financial Economics*, March, pp. 19–46.

Reinhart, U.E. (1973). Break-even analysis for Lockheed's Tri-Star: An application of financial theory. *Journal of Finance*, September, pp. 821–38.

Riding, A.L. (1984). The information content of dividends: Another test. *Journal of Business, Finance and Accounting*, Summer, pp. 163–76.

Ritter, J.R. (1984). The 'hot issue' market of 1980. *Journal of Business*, **57**(5) pp. 215–40.

Ritter, J.R. (1987). The costs of going public. *Journal of Financial Economics*, **xix**.

Ritter, J.R. and Chopra, N. (1989). Portfolio Rebalancing and the Turn-of-the-Year Effect. *Journal of Finance*, **44**(1), pp. 149–66.

Roll, R. (1977). A critique of the asset pricing theory's tests: Part I: On past and potential testability of the theory. *Journal of Financial Economics*, March, pp. 129–76.

Rosenberg, B. and Rudd, A. (1986). The corporate uses of beta. In J.M. Stern and D.H. Chew Jr (eds), *The Revolution in Corporate Finance*. Blackwell, Oxford.

Ross, S.A. (1976). The arbitrage theory and capital asset pricing. *Journal of Economic Theory*, December, pp. 341–60.

Ross, S.A. (1977). The determination of financial structure: The incentive-signalling approach. *Bell Journal of Economics*, Spring, pp. 23–40.

Ross, S. and Wachter, M. (1973). Wage determination, inflation, and the industrial structure, *American Economic Review*, September, pp. 675–92.

Rozeff, M.S. and Kinney, W.R. (1976). Capital market seasonality: the case of stock returns. *Journal of Financial Economics*, **3**(4), pp. 379–402.

Rubinstein, M.E. (1973). A mean-variance synthesis of corporate financial theory. *Journal of Finance*, March, pp. 167–81.

Rubner, A. (1966). *The Ensnared Shareholder*, Penguin, Harmondsworth.

Russell, G.R. (1990). *Initial Public Offers: Report of the Review Committee*. The Stock Exchange, London.

Rutterford, J. (1983). *Introduction to Stock Exchange Investment*. Macmillan, London.

Ryan, R.L. (1982). Capital market theory: a case study in methodological conflict. *Journal of Business, Finance and Accounting*. Winter pp. 443–58.

Samuels, J.M. and Wilkes, F.M. (1986). *Management of Company Finance*, 4th edn. Van Nostrand, Wokingham.

Sarig, O. and Scott, J. (1985). The puzzle of financial leverage clienteles. *Journal of Finance*, December, pp. 1459–68.

Sarnat, M. and Levy, H. (1969). The relationship of rules of thumb to the internal rate of return. *Journal of Finance*, June.

Scapens, R.W. and Sale, J.T. (1981). Performance measurement and formal capital expenditure controls in divisional companies. *Journal of Business, Finance and Accounting*, Autumn, pp. 389–420.

Scott-Quinn, B. (1990). A strategy for the International Stock Exchange. *National Westminster Quarterly Review*, May, pp. 43–58.

Sharp, C. (1981). *The Economics of Time*. Martin Robertson, Oxford.

Sharpe, W.F. (1963). A simplified model for portfolio analysis. *Management Science*, January, pp. 277–93.

Sharpe, W.F. (1964). Capital asset prices: a theory of market equilibrium. *Journal of Finance*, September, pp. 425–42.

Sharpe, W.F. (1985). *Investments*, 3rd edn. Prentice-Hall, Englewood Cliffs, New Jersey.

Shepherd, W.G. (1984). Contestability vs Competition. *American Economic Review*, September, pp. 572–87.

Sheppard, D.K. (1971). *Growth and Role of UK Financial Institutions, 1880–1962*. Methuen, London.

Simon, H.A. (1976). *Administrative Behaviour*, 3rd edn. Free Press, New York.

Simpson, W.G. and Ireland T.C. (1987). Managerial excellence and shareholder returns. *American Association of Individual Investors*, August, pp. 4–8.

Singh, A. and Whittington, G. (1968). *Growth, Profitability and Valuation*, Cambridge University Press, London.

Smith, A. (1968). *The Money Game*, Michael Joseph, London.

Smith, C.W. (1985). The theory of corporate finance: A historical overview. In E.I. Altman and M.G. Subrahmanyan (eds), *Recent Advances in Corporate Finance*. Irwin, Homewood, Illinois.

Smith, C.W. (1986). Investment banking and the capital acquisition process. *Journal of Financial Economics*.

Smith, K.J. (1979). *Funds to Working Capital Management*. McGraw-Hill, New York.

Spence, M. (1973). Job market signalling. *Quarterly Journal of Economics*, **87**, pp. 355–74.

Steele, A. (1986). Note on estimating the internal rate of return from published financial statements. *Journal of Business Finance and Accounting*, Spring, pp. 1–13.

Stern, J. (1986). Mis-accounting for value, in *Six Roundtable Discussions of Corporate Finance with Joel Stern* (ed. D.H. Chew, jr). Quorum Books, New York.

Stewart, T.H. (1987). *How Charts can Make You Money*, Woodhead-Faulkner, Cambridge.

Stock Exchange, The (1986). *The Big Bang*. Public Affairs Department, The Stock Exchange, April.

Stone, B.K. (1971). The uses of forecast and smoothing in control-limit models for cash management. *Financial Management*, Spring, pp. 72–84.

Stone, R. and Roe, A. (1971). The financial interdependence of the economy 1957–66. No. 11 in Cambridge Department of Applied Economics, *The Programme For Growth*. Chapman and Hall, London.

Sykes, A. (1976). The lease-buy decision: A survey of current practice in 202 companies. *Management Survey Report No. 29*. British Institute of Management, London.

Taylor, P. (1979). The information content of dividends hypothesis: Back to the drawing board? *Journal of Business Finance and Accounting*, **6**(4), pp. 495–526.

Taylor, P.J. (1982). Leasing in theory and practice. *Managerial Finance* **8** (2), pp. 6–14.

Thomas, W.A. (1989). *The Securities Market*, Philip Allan, London.

Titman, S. (1981). The effect of capital structure on a firm's liquidation decision. Unpublished PhD thesis, Carnegie-Mellon University.

Todhunter, R. (1947). *Text-book on Compound Interest and Annuities Certain*, 4th edn. Institute of Actuaries, London.

Topping, S.L. (1987). Commercial paper markets: An international survey. *Bank of England Quarterly Bulletin*, February, pp. 46–53.

Treasury, H.M. (1985). *Economic Progress Report*, September/October.

Treynor, J. (1965). How to rate management of investment funds. *Harvard Business Review*, Jan.–Feb., pp. 63–75.

Treynor, J.L. and Black, F. (1976). Corporate investment decisions. In S.C. Myers (ed.), *Modern Developments in Financial Management*. Praeger, New York.

Vickers, Sir G. (1967). *Towards a Sociology of Management*. Chapman and Hall, London.

Warner, J. (1977). Bankruptcy costs: Some evidence. *Journal of Finance*, pp. 337–47.

Watts, R. (1973). The information content of dividends. *Journal of Business*, April, pp. 191–211.

Watts, R. (1976a). Comments on 'The Informaton Content of Dividends'. *Journal of Business*, January, pp. 81–5.

Watts, R. (1976b). Comments on 'The Impact of Dividend and Earning Announcements: A Reconciliation'. *Journal of Business*, January pp. 97–106.

Weston, J.F. (1989). Divestitures, mistakes and learning. *Journal of Applied Corporate Finance*, Summer, pp. 68–76.

Whitley, R. (1986). The rise of modern finance theory. *Accounting, Organizations and Society*.

Williamson, O.E. (1964). *The Economics of Discretionary Behaviour: Managerial Objectives in a Theory of the Firm*. Prentice-Hall, Englewood Cliffs, New Jersey.

Williamson, O.E. (1970). *Corporate Control and Business Behaviour: An Inquiry into the Effect of Organizational Form on Enterprise Behaviour*. Prentice-Hall, Englewood Cliffs, New Jersey.

Williamson, O.E. (1975). *Markets and Hierarchies*. Free Press, New York.

Williamson, O.E. (1983). Organization form, residual claimants, and corporate control. *Journal of Law and Economics*, June, pp. 351–66.

Wilson Committee (1980). *Committee to Review the Functioning of Financial Institutions Report*. Cmnd. 7837, HMSO.

Wilson, R. (1968). The theory of syndicates. *Econometrica*, **36**(1), pp. 119–32.

Wolff, C.C.P. (1986). Pre-emptive rights versus alternative methods of raising equity on the London Stock Exchange. *Investment Analyst*, April, pp. 3–15.

Wood, A. (1975). *A Theory of Profits*. Cambridge University Press, Cambridge.

Yoshikawa, T. (1988). *Summary of Surveys of Management Accounting Practices in UK and Japan*. Unpublished, University of Edinburgh.

Zenoff, D.B. (1967). Remittance policies of US subsidiaries in Europe. *Banker*, May, pp. 418–27.

Zysman, J. (1983). *Governments, Markets and Growth: Financial Systems and the Politics of Industrial Change*. Cornell University Press, Itheca.

Index